About the Author

Stanislas Yassukovich was born in Paris of a White Russian émigré father and a French mother. Settling in the United States at the outset of World War II, he was brought up on the North Shore of Long Island, N.Y., attending Green Vale School there, Deerfield Academy in Massachusetts, and Harvard College. After service in the U.S Marine Corps, he joined White, Weld & Co., New York investment bankers and was posted to its London office. Yassukovich subsequently formed and managed European Banking Company, became a Deputy Chairman of The Stock Exchange, London, Chairman of the Securities & Futures Authority, and, finally, Chairman of Merrill Lynch Europe, Middle East & Africa. After service as a non-executive director on various boards, he retired to the South of France. He was made a Commander of the Order of the British Empire, and is a Fellow of the Royal Society of Arts. He is married to the former Diana Townsend, and has three children: Tatyana, Michael and Nicholas.

Dedication

To my wife Dinnie who will not read this as she has heard it all before.

Stanislas M. Yassukovich

Two Lives: A Social and Financial Memoir

AUSTIN MACAULEY
PUBLISHERS LTD.

A CIP catalogue record for this title is available from the British Library.

ISBN 9781785548710 (Paperback)
ISBN 9781785548727 (Hardback)
ISBN 9781785548734 (E-Book)

www.austinmacauley.com

First Published (2016)
Austin Macauley Publishers Ltd.
25 Canada Square
Canary Wharf
London
E14 5LQ

Acknowledgments

As this is an anecdotal memoir, and not a strictly historical account, I have not researched it intensively. For context, and some degree of chronological order, I have relied on three works: Chris O'Malley's Bonds without Borders; David Kynaston's The City of London – Volume IV 'A Club No More', and David Landes's Bankers and Pashas. I have quoted them in every case. Of course, I have used public sources of general history where appropriate.

Many readers mentioned will say "but, it was not exactly like that" or "but, I didn't really say that" or "you didn't say that". Everything in this memoir is as I remember it – not necessarily exactly how it happened. I have rendered conversation in dialect form to create atmosphere. I have not sought to quote any one verbatim. Some conversations are imaginary, but illustrative of the anecdote concerned. We all know that our memory of what happened is never pristine, and sometimes highly selective. If there is interest in this memoir, it is because it is how one participant in the events described, remembers them, and the impact they made on his life. For those interested in a proper, detailed account of the period covered, I recommend David Kynaston's definitive work on the City, and Chris O'Malley's official history of the Eurobond market.

Many have helped me remember names. John Stancliffe, Lisa von Clemm, Michael Dobbs-Higginson, Brewster Righter, Richard Freeman, Graham Ross-Russell, Dinnie Yassukovich, Ariane Wellin, Tatyana Yassukovich, Ogden White, Jr. Charley Lee, David McGovern and Frank Shields – plus a few others whose names I have forgotten. James Volney Righter did valuable research to discover details of the Bramwells of Boston. Sir David Walker asked the archivist at Barclays Bank to research the history of Ronald Parvin. I thank all warmly. Christopher Morgan gave valuable early editing assistance. Joe McChristian and my son Michael helped assemble the photographs, and Barbara Leotoing gave me technical help. My thanks to them all.

I am particularly grateful to George Montgomery III, who was willing to share with me materiel he has researched for his history of the White family.

But my most grateful thanks go to the large number of friends and colleagues, who over a period of many years, kept encouraging me to undertake this work. I sincerely hope they will not be disappointed.

INTRODUCTION

"The waving wheat can sure smell sweet,
Deep in the heart of Texas"

−Popular Song−

I begin this anecdotal account of two lives − my father's and mine − with the song phrase quoted above for no good reason. My father had no connection whatsoever with Texas, at least as far as I can recollect. There is a photograph of him in the cockpit of a fighter plane, an air force officer perched above him, which might have been taken at a Texas air base on the sort of VIP visit investment bankers are often subject to. But I am almost sure it was taken at Grumman Aircraft's headquarters at Bethpage, Long Island. If my father ever visited Texas, he did not report the event to his family. I was only in Texas twice in my life; as a member of a City of London delegation sponsored by the so-called Invisibles Committee and later to call on a company whose identity I forget. The Invisibles Committee mission − to promote the export of financial services provided by City houses − was the first to a non-sovereign state, although, of course, Texas is a state in the United States with a proud, if brief, history as an independent country. The visit was made to coinside with the opening of a route by Caledonian Airlines and it quickly became a sort of Scottish love-in. almost every welcoming speech by the local dignitaries cited the number of Scots involved in the defence of the Alamo − the number grew with each speech. A British consul, Roy Fox, had made a great hit with the local magnates, on the golf course, and generally promoting British business interests. At one banquet at the Petroleum Club in Houston, located on the top floor of an impressive sky scraper, we were seated at an immense horseshoe shaped table. All eyes were on the speaker but I noticed a gigantic cockroach slowly making its way towards the top table. So did Roy Fox's capable assistant. He slowly brought his napkin from his lap, and, as the beast passed his place, he scooped it up in a deft and elegant gesture.

During this period, I was often part of Invisibles Committee delegations as a representative of the "Eurotrash" population of the City which had brought the Eurocurrency and Eurobond markets to London where they were beginning to form the core of the City's international activity. It was my task to explain these markets to audiences in the regions visited. I could do it in my sleep, and often did. I sometimes think that the beginning of the slow decline of the City as the world's premier financial centre dates from those awkward exercises in self-promotion. Much later, I was to initiate and chair a project backed by the City of London Corporation designed to analyse and document the basis of the City's competitive advantage. This was a great mistake, I now recognise, and I had been so warned by a Government minister – Lord Young, and the City has been on a downhill slide ever since.

But none of this explains my use of a quote from a popular song about Texas. The point is there is no point. I am a devotee of shaggy dog stories. I have tried to live my life as a sort of shaggy dog story and this series of flash backs and nostalgic souvenirs is designed to be structurally consistent. There is something about Texas which suggests sweep in an historical sense; the stuff of sagas, as they say. Of course, the reader needs assurance that he or she is not embarking on a saga – far from it. But the writer needs inspiration and if this is provided by Texas, why not? Having denied a good reason for the reference, I hope I have provided the bad reasons.

My father, Dimitri Mikhailovich Yassukovich, was born in St. Petersburg in 1898 and came to the United States as a White Russian émigré in 1918. Unable to follow the family tradition of a military career as a result of the Bolshevik Revolution, but multi-lingual like all Russians of his class, he found work in Wall Street and eventually joined White, Weld & Co. Having opened that firm's London office in 1933, and been responsible for the Credit Suisse relationship established in the late 1950s, he was effectively the founder of what became Credit Suisse First Boston, a leading international investment bank and was so acknowledged by the late Michael von Clemm at an anniversary gathering of CSFB. His career was entirely internationally oriented and focussed on cross-border portfolio investment and capital market activity. I joined White, Weld, after service in the U.S. Marines, in 1961 and was posted to London just as Euromarkets activity was getting underway, although these markets were derived from those which had existed pre-war and even in the nineteenth century. There is little that is truly new in the financial world. I began something of a retirement in 1998.

This souvenir spans the 100-year period between my father's birth and my semi-retirement. Memoirs of pre-Revolutionary Russia are a rouble a dozen, I appreciate, but my father's early youth is not without interest because of the events which placed him in a more advantageous position than so many of his fellow émigrés who ended up driving taxis in Paris or attending rich wives in Palm Beach. There were many occasions when I dreamt wistfully of being the son of such a union. But the century in question also covers the rise of global capital markets, as they are now called, and the evolution of the institutions and individuals who now handle capital flows which, even in the context of today's world gross national product and trade, are without precedent in terms of volume and velocity. When speaking at conferences, I was often introduced as a "father of the Eurobond market". I used to respond by saying that, if all the "fathers of the Eurobond market" were laid end to end, younger investment bankers would be greatly relieved. Success has many fathers: only failure is an orphan. If I was a father, then my father was a grandfather, as he established the presence of White, Weld & Co. in Europe – a recognized building block of what has become the international capital market we know today.

I do not intend an accurate and documented account. There is the problem of memory. Mine has never been good and it has yet to improve with age. My father told us stories of his youth in scraps over many years. He never wanted to set down a formal record. My father maintained his story lacked interest. I can only hope he was wrong. I have certainly never kept a diary. All I have to supplement a patchy memory are my appointment diaries. But I intend to make full use of the investment banker's natural affinity for embroidery in the absence of a precise grasp of the facts. If some of the events I will describe below did not actually happen, they could well have happened, given the context at the time. Even the Securities Exchange Commission has not been able to curb the practitioner's tendency to fill in gaps with a bit of imagination, at least in verbal presentations, despite their enforcement of tedious accuracy in documents. Once, when White, Weld was co-managing a convertible Eurobond issue for Banker's Trust, then a wholesale commercial bank at the heart of the Wall Street establishment – now a Deutsche Bank subsidiary, I was on the road show led by Frank Manheim, a partner in Lehman Brothers who were running the books, i.e. lead managing. Frank was an investment banker of the old New York school. Even more to my liking, he was a fox hunter and, at one point, a joint Master of the Galway Blazers, an Irish pack which has specialised in cosmopolitan Masters, such as John Houston. Like all investment bankers of the old school, he was mostly style on the outside but total integrity and common sense on the inside. We were calling on one of the big three Swiss Banks. Frank was making his pitch and quoted expected earnings per share for Banker's Trust for the next quarter at a certain figure. The granite faced Swiss on the other side of an empty desk seized a pause in Frank's flow to hold up a hand, reach into a drawer, pull out a Lehman Bros. research report, and point out that the Lehman banking analyst was using a different and lower figure. Frank did not flinch.

"A misprint," he snapped. The Swiss banker's eyebrows rose slightly over the top of his steel rim glasses and the presentation carried on.

"That's a bit of a problem, a misprint in your research report," I said in the corridor outside.

"No misprint at all," said Frank, "I couldn't remember the number so I made it up."

I was impressed.

"My boy," continued Frank, in a friendly manner, "never let 'em know you don't know."

This was sound advice but difficult to follow. This is not to claim that I possess some overwhelming integrity or honesty which makes white lying impossible for me. It is more that I could not bear to look foolish when caught out. So I have followed a principle as an investment banker of always admitting ignorance but claiming to know someone who could supply the facts and in most cases, I did know someone. It is at this point that I should admit that I am not a banker, or even an investment banker, at all. I have practised as a banker for many years, with some limited success, but that is a very different thing. I know I am not a banker because I have known so many real bankers: Herman Abs, Sigmund Warburg, Jacob Rothschild, André Meyer, Jacob Wallenberg, John Young, John Schiff, Bill Salomon, Robert Lutz, Robert Genillard, David Rockefeller, George Moore, Al Gordon, Pierre Haas, Enrico Braggiotti, Wilfrid Guth, Rainer Gut, Willie Purvis, Bill McDonough, Abdullah Amar Saudi, Danny Davison, Henry Hoare – to drop just a handful of names from across the spectrum. To know a real banker is to know that one is not, particularly if the art of banking – or investment banking, to distinguish from your local bank manager – is a subject of fascination to one, and one has read books about international finance as others read detective stories.

How, then, have I pulled it off, so to speak? I will admit, immodestly, to being a fine actor. In fact, a career on the stage would have been my preference and I now live the theatrical life vicariously through my actress daughter, and have even taken up acting myself, much to her amusement. One or two other God given attributes have helped me play at banking: I am a speed reader and read not even by paragraph, but by page. And I have always been able to speak extemporaneously in front of any kind of audience. In a conference dominated world, this has been a help in carrying off my life role. But it is the style question which has characterised my interpretation of the part of a banker. Even my severest critics would agree, I believe, that I have always managed to create something of an "haute banque" style in the operations I have been responsible for. I leave aside the question of substance, for the moment. Gert Whitman, one of Sigmund Warburg's earliest partners in London – whom my father had known in New York in the 'twenties as a Lee Higginson partner called "Tookie" Weismann – was a stickler for style. He once caught his junior partner Bernard Kelley using a pen with green ink to sign at a closing. "You may be Irish, but that is totally un-*haute banque*," he said. There was no question that the House of Warburg was the last proponent of *haute banque* style in the City of London, blending as it did the quality of high Jewish banking in pre-war Germany with London merchant banking traditions. Of course there was also substance, now largely gone, together with the style.

9

When I went recently to call on Marcel Ospel, then running Warburg's for Swiss Bank Corporation, he was wearing a blazer in the City on a Friday.

Of course, an actor rarely manages to chronicle the theatre, since he or she tends, when writing memoirs of any kind, to be preoccupied with personal issues. "When I opened that autumn in *Orestes Furioso* at the Lyceum – to rave reviews, my marriage was already in difficulty", tends to be the style of theatrical souvenirs. I hope that in these pages I will be able to stick to the main theme, which is international finance in the latter part of the twentieth century, whilst evoking the particular atmosphere in which my father lived in the early part of the century. Many friends have suggested I should write a history of White, Weld & Co. given the role that firm played in the creation of the Eurobond market in particular. This I have not attempted to do. Originally established in New York in the 1890s by Harvard classmates, the firm enjoyed a special relationship with J. P. Morgan, made a particular mark in natural gas pipeline financing, became prominent internationally for its Eurobond business, partially spun off its international arm, became CSFB, and was ultimately acquired by Merrill Lynch. White, Weld did generate a particular style and a variety of special talents, particularly in its international activities, and as such was distinguished from the general run of so-called "white shoe" houses such as Kidder, Peabody or Smith Barney. It was never a "bulge bracket" house: that coterie of originating investment banks that were listed out of alphabetical order in advertisements announcing a capital market transaction. It did make the short list of investment banks that were joined in an anti-trust action known as "The United States vs. Morgan Stanley et all" in which Judge Harold Medina issued a celebrated judgement, chastising the Government for wasting taxpayers' money in bringing the action, and containing one of the most brilliant descriptions of investment banking as practiced in Wall Street. White, Weld figures heavily in these souvenirs. In addition to having provided my father with a career and station in the new world, friends of great loyalty and the chance to spend half the year in the western Europe he loved, the firm also employed me when I was technically unemployable and put me in the right place at the right time. White, Weld stamped on me, and on so many others who went on to have more brilliant careers, some indefinable but indelible quality approach to the business.

The capital market side of international investment banking has undergone a massive transformation as a result of the evolution of information and communications technology. Markets that were hand-crafted are now operated through assembly line techniques. Whether this change will stifle the innovative nature of these financial activities remains an open question. Design changes in automobiles accelerated post the model T, but it could be argued that there were fewer revolutionary changes. In the Euromarkets community, we prided ourselves as pioneers. In fact virtually all of our innovations were adaptations of instruments or techniques already established in the U.S. financial marketplace. An exception might be the floating rate note which crossed the Atlantic in a westerly direction. All financial innovation is newsworthy at first and then mundane. The specialists engaged are stars at the outset – and paid as such – and then become assembly line operatives. I did not make myself popular with the top hatted brigade in the City by pointing out that trained chimps could probably operate the discount market. I risk the same opprobrium from the lads in red braces by suggesting that today's international securities market doesn't require very high grade human intervention and therefore doesn't receive it. Perhaps the vogue for quantitative derivative instruments requires unusual numeracy in practitioners – but that seems to be accompanied by a total lack of common sense. The corporate finance, or mergers and acquisitions departments of the major investment banks claim to offer a more bespoke service, but in fact the market is shared between very few credible players and conflicts of interest ensure that each gets a slice without much need for anything in the way of flare. The seniors who pitch are rarely those who execute, and merely memorising the Takeover Code does not a corporate financier make.

Change is something that happens when you are not looking. As long as I was an active practitioner and engaged in trying to mature and evolve the markets, I remained persuaded of their underlying integrity and quality, and this sentiment extended to the people and firms involved. As soon as I retired from active participation and began to view the business as a user – in my capacity as a non-executive director of companies – rather than as a provider, I became convinced it had all gone to hell. Nevertheless, I cannot deny that a career in international investment banking has permitted me to live in a manner to which I became accustomed at an early age, due to the ceaseless efforts of my father to introduce me to what is sometimes referred to as "the very best". My mother worried about this paternal policy, fearing a consequent weakening of moral fibre. On the other hand, after early fecklessness which I shall take pleasure in recalling, I was motivated to apply myself to my field of endeavour to finance a quality of leisure moments unobtainable in any other honest manner. As will be revealed, these moments were much engaged with horses. Fine horses are quality assets which lose their value instantly upon purchase and use, rather like tins of caviar. I cannot blame my father for having infected me with a love of horses, although he did teach my sister and me how to ride. Later he viewed my fox hunting and polo playing with bemused approbation, although he was less taken by my very modest forays into racing. Horses, and particularly hunting, were for me of huge therapeutic value in combating stress – perhaps an overstressed modern malady – and therefore played a significant, if indirect, role in my business life.

The environmental forces, as opposed to hereditary ones, which shape our lives are made of people: nannies, teachers, friends and employers. My father had an enormous influence on me despite the fact that he spent very little time with me, by modern standards. In terms of that modern measurement, man hours, he spent less time with me than anyone involved in my upbringing. Yet, I can think of few moments in my professional life, or in general, when I have not imagined how he would react to a situation and to my choice of action. I believe I remember every piece of advice he ever gave me, even though I have so often been delinquent in applying his wisdom. Much of it would be regarded today as frivolous or pertaining to a world long gone. But my values, such as they are, are his, however inadequately they have been applied. If these souvenirs contain an element of tribute, it is both intended and insufficient.

CHAPTER I

Jasonia!

A "Zawotanic" or clan war cry, also a designation of arms in Polish/Lithuanian heraldry

Genealogy is a subject which interests few in general but a far larger number in the particular, or as it pertains to their own pedigrees. In no country is the interest in personal genealogy greater than in that haven of egalitarianism, the United States of America. Americans outbuy the British for such works as *Burke's Landed Gentry*, in bogus Lordships of the Manner, and all other paraphernalia designed to demonstrate the importance of breeding. Their own "blue book", the *Social Register*, is a model of anti-egalitarianism, despite a growing incursion into its pages by new money, and, in American terms, that real social horror: politicians. Originally, divorce meant exclusion but if this policy had been maintained, the publication would have starved to death years ago. In an age of pre-marital co-habitation, the book cross-references females with their married names under a section entitled "Married Maidens". Holiday residences are listed under "Dilatory Domiciles". Those of us who remain listed, and many are delisting as the publication's exclusivity inevitably declines, see it as a handy telephone directory and a reminder of who married whom. The ladies' previous husbands are all listed in brackets. The gentlemen are spared their marital history in print. In no country in the world is social rank as important as in America, founded on the principle that all men are created equal. The Founding Fathers made no mention of women but then, neither did Jean Jacques Rousseau. Despite American pre-occupation with sexism, the most prestigious American societies, all focussed on heredity, are segregated. "The Daughters of the American Revolution", "Colonial Dames of America", and "Daughters of the Cincinnati", on the one hand, "Colonial Lords of Manors", "Sons of the Revolution", on the other. "Mayflower Descendants" are presumably co-ed. Ladies' societies predominate.

I make no apology for my interest in my own pedigree. I am anti-egalitarian. I consider egalitarianism to be at the heart of political tyranny. The

13

concept that all men are equal defies the evidence of one's own eyes and was invented by those wishing to secure ascendancy over others. It is also inconceivable that breeding should have obvious consequences for animals but none for humans and to so claim is an example of human arrogance. Political and philosophical egalitarianism has also undermined the real truth: that all men are equally important, which is a very different thing from being equal. Nature is full of elements which are of equal value, but are obviously not equal. All this being said, there is no doubt that preoccupation with a personal pedigree is generally regarded as elitist and even snobbish, although this last criticism, I would contest since I believe snobbism is about a desire to hobnob only with those of a higher social standing.

My family is of Lithuanian-Polish origin and like many of similar ilk would love to claim descent from a brother or kin of Rurik the Dane – sometimes known as Rurik the Red, or the Rus, hence Russia. This is the Viking Chieftain who colonised greater Russia. But there is no evidence to support such a claim. More likely is a descent from one of his soldiers. The family name is actually Jasiukowicz. When my father transliterated the name from Cyrillic to Roman letters on arrival in America, he used the spelling he thought would ensure more accurate pronunciation. In fact the choice had been made for him, since when my grandfather arrived in Washington at the head of the Russian military mission; a standard transliteration was applied by the Embassy. Of course, my non-Russified cousins still spell the name correctly as they always rendered it in Roman letters. A great number of immigrants in America, often of Jewish origin, whose names end in "owicz" or "ewicz" – which means descendant from, or clan of – suffer their names being mispronounced with a soft "w" rather than hard "v" sound and an end sound to rhyme with "blitz" rather "bitch". I am sure we would have survived. But I would not have had the pleasure of hearing George Plimpton, rendering once at the Porcellian Club in Cambridge, Massachusetts, open with the phrase: "I often have an itch to kick Stani Yassukovich". Speaking of the "Porc", as the oldest gentleman's club in America is nicknamed, the great family of Bohemian magnates Lobkowicz had two or three of the family settled in America who were members, and they coped with persistent mispronunciation of their famous name with no ill effects.

My forebears would have been knights, in the service of various magnates. An ancestor Jan, or Ivan, obtained the Dyrwaniszi estate in Vilno Province in 1604 from Zygmunt III, the first of three Vasa dynasty of Sweden members to be elected Kings of Poland, after the last of the Jagiellon kings. Zygmund's mother was Catherine Jagiellon and his father John II, King of Sweden. After being elected King of Poland in 1587, Zygmund also became King of Sweden in 1592. Jan Jasiukowicz and his ancestors bore arms of the "herby" Jasienczyk, also known as Jasiona, and, sometimes, Klucz: Azure, a Key or pale wise, upwards and turned to the Dexter, and for crest five ostrich feathers Argent issuing from a Coronet Or. This requires some explanation. The Polish system of heraldry is entirely different from the rest of Western Europe. The same coat of arms is shared by several families, usually unrelated. Such groups of families are called "herby" and their arms have names of their own, thought to date back to ancient war cries used by clans or other family groups. Their arms are designated "proclamation-arms" by heraldic specialists. A vaguely similar structure might be Scottish clans and their tartans. My own herby Jasienczyk includes the Michafowski family – Austrian counts and French Imperial barons, who obviously blew with the prevailing wind, and the Polish branch of the Tartar princely family Shirinski. The clan war cry "Jasiona" strikes me as unlikely to provoke fear in the hearts of the enemy, even if shouted very loudly. The Polish nobility, known as the *szlachta*, were in theory all equal and untitled, the exception being the few great families of magnates, such as the Potocki or Zamoyski, who bore the title Prince. Foreign titles such as Count or Baron were granted by foreign rulers and were rare until Russian monarchs of German origin, such as Catherine II, started sprinkling them about. The same is true of Russia itself where only one genuine Russian title existed: Prince or *Kniaz* and the rest of the nobility were untitled, until foreign influences, mostly Germanic, infiltrated. Crests on all Polish/Lithuanian arms carry the same coronet, placed on a helm. This posed a problem for an Austrian friend of mine, Max Turnauer, until recently Ambassador of the Sovereign Order of the Knights of St. John and Jerusalem to Prague. Max's sense of hierarchical distinctions within the nobility is so *recherché* that he separates those with covered crowns – kings, princes and some dukes – from those with mere coronets which are, of course, open on top and used by the aristocratic masses. We were once at one of his very grand shooting parties down in Dorset where we sat down twenty-five or so for dinner. Copperplate written place cards named my wife and me as Prince and Princess Yassukovich. I gently informed our host that we were not of the covered crown variety. Undaunted, Max had us down the next evening as Count and Countess – wrong again, of course, but by then I was reluctant to lower the tone of the guest list any further and spent the balance of the weekend as an imposter.

Most are aware of the recent history of Poland, a sad story of frequent territorial rape made easy by the country's lack of natural boundary defences. Less well-known is the fact that the thousand-year history of Poland includes a period of more than two hundred years as the Commonwealth, the largest state in Europe at the time, incorporating Lithuania , Byelorussia, the Ukraine, large parts of modern Germany, and for that matter, large parts of modern Russia – a total of almost one million square kilometres. The Commonwealth in 1600 had a population of 10 million, twice that of England and two thirds that of France. Only 40 per cent were true Poles, the rest belonging to two main ethnic groups, Lithuanian and Ruthene. But scattered about the empire, as it truly was, could be found an astonishing variety of nationalities:

Germans, of course, in the port of Gdansk, English and Scots in Elbing, Hungarians and Italians in Krakow and Wilno, Armenians, Tartars in the Ukraine and, in every city, Jews. No city was without a ghetto and together, the Jews made up close to ten per cent of the population. They were tolerated but entirely separate, speaking Hebrew, Yiddish and even Tartar in some areas.

But a distinctive social structure separated Poland from the rest of Western Europe, had led, in a way to the creation of the Commonwealth and, some could say was the source of the nation's political vulnerability. This was the *szlachta*, or nobility. Like the Jews, it also comprised some ten per cent of the population, but its members were all powerful and entirely enfranchised. In theory, their nobility and their exclusive right to the vote as members in permanence of the Seym, or parliament, were drawn from their obligation to bear arms in defence of the realm. This obligation became unenforceable, but the *szlachta* continued to defend their rights to the point of mania against attempts by the magnates to devise a more oligarchic form of government and against attempts by successive elected monarchs to gain greater freedom of action. Poland – and so the Commonwealth – was an elective monarchy, a system which could be described as the worst of both worlds. Missing was the stability which stems from the continuity and legitimacy of hereditary monarchy. Missing also was the accountability associated with an elective office subject to confirmation or change at regular intervals. Poland was a Royal Republic, a political concept as effective as a lame thoroughbred or a cold mince pie. The rediscovery of Rome and things Roman by the European intelligentsia during the Renaissance convinced educated Poles that theirs was a system blessed by the great traditions of antiquity. As Adam Zamoyski points out in his definitive work *The Polish Way*, to be a member of the *szlachta* was like being a Roman citizen; they were the "pupulus Romanus" while the rest of the population were the "plebs", who counted for nothing and had no rights at all.

By the mid-sixteenth century, the *szlachta* were extraordinarily cosmopolitan and dynamic to some extent in that successful merchants and even Jews and peasants were able to gain admission through services to the King or sponsorship by magnates. Within this top ten per cent of the population were to be found Lithuanian and Ruthene boyars – such as my family – Prussian and Baltic nobles, Tartars, Moldavians, Bohemians, Magyars, Armenians and Italians. Their economic status varied enormously. At the top were the fabulously rich magnates, maintaining courts and life styles that made some western monarchies look shabby. At the bottom were impoverished nobles in menial service to fellow nobles or living like peasants. The rich were certainly not portfolio investors, or even given to aggressive land accumulation – which took place only through inter-marriage – but they spent their fortunes on jewels and other physical manifestations of wealth: horses galore with jewel encrusted and embroidered saddle clothes and fancy tack and

16

equipages. We, their modern descendants, would consider it of unspeakable vulgarity – whilst hankering after the horse side, I must admit. The poor *szlachta* spent their lives hanging on to their noble prerogatives for dear life. One of these was the right to attend the election Seym, the occasional convocation at which a new king was elected. In-between, a more complex bicameral system existed involving deputies elected by the szlachta divided into constituencies. Tens of thousands of nobles would gather for the election Seym, held in a large field lined with tents and other stands where factions organised support for their candidates. The horse was a key symbol of nobility, even more than in the West. Polish military strength has always been cavalry. Impoverished nobles would turn up with spurs strapped to bare feet, boots being beyond their means.

My family's first benefactor Zygmunt III, first of the Vasa dynasty, was not a great success. He sought to overturn the policy of religious tolerance seeking to establish a Catholic ascendancy, tried to undermine the Seym, and had to apologise. He took a leave of absence to claim his Swedish inheritance when his father John III died, was unpopular in Sweden, left his uncle as Regent, and was ultimately deposed by the Swedish Parliament, who determined that his son Wladislas could only succeed to the Swedish throne if he turned Protestant. Back in Poland, Zygmund started a war which almost led to the loss of Livonia, constantly breached the Polish constitution by carrying out secret diplomatic initiatives and marrying a Hapsburg, and generally made himself unpopular with the *szlachta*. After trying to totally undermine the Seym, he faced open rebellion and was only just saved by the fact that the two Grand Hetmen, commanders of the Polish and Lithuanian armies, Chodkiewicz and Zolkiewski, stood by him. The rebels were not punished, so widely supported was their cause. Zygmunt died in 1632 and a Seym took half an hour to elect his eldest son Wladislas IV whose reign saw the Commonwealth's prestige reach a summit. The fact that every other European nation of importance was engaged in the Thirty Years War, the newly enthroned Romanov dynasty was busy consolidating power in Russia, and the Sublime Porte was not threatening Europe, gave the Commonwealth unique political leverage. Wladislas was urged to become Holy Roman Emperor, on the death of Ferdinand II, received representations from sixteen foreign courts seeking to place eligible princesses when his wife died and, in 1641, William of Brandenburg, the Great Elector, knelt in homage to Wladislas to receive the tenure of the Duchy of Prussia. Fifteen years later, the Commonwealth was dead as a political force in Europe. Fortunately my family appears to have enjoyed the favour of this great King who, in 1643, confirmed land grants to Pyotr Jasiukowicz, son of Jan, and appointed him to a court position – Cupbearer.

With all its grandeur and glory, the Commonwealth of the Kingdom of Poland and the Grand Duchy of Lithuania, or the Two Nations, as it was called for short, incorporated fatal flaws. One of the most obvious was that, leaving aside myriad minorities, there were three principal tribes, not two. The Ruthenes, mostly Orthodox, had mingled with the Lithuanians in the sense that their noble classes had merged, yet they were jealous of their separate identity and this served to drive a wedge between Lithuania and Catholic Poland. Added to the main ingredients in this cocktail were Tatars, Moldavians, Muscovites, Germans, Jews and sundry other European migrants. The Commonwealth had a frontier, like the American West, in the Ukraine, and the scramble for its rich farm land amongst all these competing interests served to blow off steam but caused tensions with the indigenous Ukrainian magnates. These were truly impressive. The Ostrogski family owned a hundred towns and 1,300 villages. The Wisziowiecki owned 38,000 homesteads with 230,000 tenants. Commonwealth hegemony in the Ukraine was further complicated by Catholic and Orthodox rivalry. The Orthodox interest, led by Prince Ostrogski, allied itself with the Protestants. The Catholic effort was Jesuit led. Adding colour to the chaotic panorama were the Cossacks, a breakaway Tatar group – "Cossack" means "free soldier" in Turkish – whose nomadic and military life style was to make them permanent sources of instability, especially when the whole region became part of the Russian Empire. Wladyslaw tried to enlist them in an ill-fated Crusade project. After strong opposition from the Sejm, the initiative got nowhere but triggered an uprising in the Ukraine by a joint Tatar/Cossack force which ultimately led to an alliance between the Commonwealth and Muscovy.

In all the turmoil of the 17th century, my family clearly kept their nose clean and increased their land holdings in Lithuania. Jan Jasiukowicz's great grandson Andrei acquired an estate in Oszmiany Province called Zeliadz, near the town of Swieciany – Swieciany today – one of the oldest Lithuanian towns. His great granddaughter, who married a gentleman called Czechowicz, possessed another estate near Sweciany called Kapadlo, but by then Lithuania existed no more except as one of what my father always called the "Baltic Provinces" of the Russian Empire. Andrei was prolific and sired seven sons. The sons had varied careers indicating integration into civil society, even a tendency to adopt bourgeois professions – evolving from the pure soldier/landowner tradition of the *szlachta*. One, Anton, had a purely military career. But Mikhail became a surveyor and an arbiter of land boundary disputes. My direct ancestor Ignatii became a lawyer and served as chairman of the investigatory council of the civil court at Kovno. Kovno was an important commercial town in the Middle Ages but had suffered slow decline as a result of the increasing russification of Lithuania – which was formally annexed by Russia in 1795, during Ignatii's lifetime. Its main activity was as an entrepôt for trade between the Commonwealth and Prussia. Ignatii married a Russian, one Bona Bielopetrovna. Perhaps this influenced their son's decision to serve in the Imperial Russian Army. Ignatii's brother Mikhail, the land surveyor, died young and Ignatii served as guardian and trustee of his nephews' estate –

Byalozorovo, also in the Kovno area. These nephews, Ignatii and Wilhelm, appear to have been twins.

Ignatii had four sons and two daughters. The eldest, my great grandfather Stanislas became a general in the Guard's Sapper regiment of the Imperial Russian Army. The Guards were army strength in the Imperial Russian military, as opposed to a brigade, as in the British army, and contained several cavalry and foot regiments as well as artillery and sappers. But it was his younger brother Ignatii who was to become by far the most successful of my branch of the family. If it hadn't been for the unfortunate intervention of the Russian Revolution and two world wars, my sister and I would have been disgustingly rich. This Ignatii Jasiukowicz might be described as the Carnegie of Eastern Europe. He founded the Southern Russian Dneprovsky Metallurgical Society – SRDMS – which was to become the leading blue chip on the St Petersburg Stock Exchange. He built a huge company town in Kamenskoy – now Dneprodzerzhinsk – on the Dnieper River. Housing for employees, two churches – Roman Catholic and Russian Orthodox, municipal buildings, concert halls – even a yacht club, all rose from the original riverside village through his entrepreneurial energy.... Initial capital for the enterprise had been supplied by the Cockrill steel interests of Belgium, originally founded by the Scottish ironmaster John Cockrill. SRDMS became the largest manufacturer of steel and metallurgical products in Eastern Europe and the core of a huge monopoly, created by Ignatii Jasiukowicz, called Prodamet. In 1910, with a combined capital of 300 million roubles and 100,000 employees, Prodamet, with Jasiukowicz as chairman, had united 90% of the metallurgical plants of the Russian Empire and concentrated 85% of Russian sales of ferrous metals, exporting worldwide. A biography of Ignatii Jasiukowicz, by a Professor Slonevski has recently appeared. I cannot resist the temptation to quote from it, undermining any vestige of family modesty. The translation is by Marina Bradbeer, wife of Professor Paul Bradbeer: "To Jasiukowicz's list of virtues one should add his extraordinary honesty and fidelity to his word. For him *verbum Nobile* was not an empty sound. He shunned the temptation of speculative profit. On one occasion, a certain society wished to initiate a play on the stock exchange to increase the value of its shares. To this end they wanted to use Jasiukowicz's reputation as an excellent administrator. But Jasiukowicz was furious at this manoeuvre. He wrote a letter publically declining the position he had been offered, though many people would have considered it an attractive post whereby they could make money without any effort."

Jasuikowicz's prosperity and prestige as one of the leading industrialist in the Russian Empire provided an opportunity to redress a deficiency in his side of the family. As younger sons of younger sons a few generations back, we were the landless, cadet branch of the family. Jasiukowicz decided to purchase a country estate. He first looked to Lithuania where most of his relations were. The estates which had come down through the senior branches were all in Lithuania – except one, which was in modern day Latvia. But, as a Pole, Jasiukowicz was not allowed to hold property in Lithuania. This requires some explanation. Unfortunately, I am unable to provide it. How can a Russian subject, from an old Lithuanian family, chairman of one of Russia's largest industrial complexes, with an elder brother a general in the Tsar's Sapper Guard Regiment, not be allowed to acquire an estate in Lithuania? All one can say is that the Russian Empire was riddled with anachronisms; to be a subject of the Tsar did not mean one was a citizen of Russia. One can site the case of the British Empire where a subject of the King Emperor in India was not necessarily a citizen of England. In the northwest corner of the Russian Empire, history played the critical role in determining the relationship between the residents or citizens of the nations and the government in St. Petersburg. The three most important components were the Kingdom of Poland, the Tsar as King, and the Grand Duchies of Finland and Lithuania, where, naturally, the Tsar was Grand Duke. Finland was by far the most autonomous of these, with its own parliament, university, Lutheran religion and distinctive language. The Finnish gentry might serve in the Russian Army. The national hero of eventual Finnish independence, Marshal Mannerheim, had attended the Corps of Pages in St. Petersburg. But Finland was a different case in almost every respect. The Grand Duchy of Lithuania, on the other hand, was quite fully integrated – with the same local government institutions as metropolitan Russia. My great aunt Evgenia Krassovskaya was married to the Marshal of Nobility in Vilnius – the rough equivalent of a Lord Lieutenant. Primarily Orthodox Lithuania had never rebelled after its incorporation into Russia in the late 18th century. Poland was another story altogether. Fiercely nationalistic, constantly restive under the Russian yoke, Poland had rebelled at least three times since its partition, the last and most violent in 1848. Poland's integration into the Russian Empire had been in fits and starts; periods of relatively benign rule alternating with periods of brutal occupation and attempts to obliterate Polish language and custom. The Polish nobility, the *schlachta*, were only incorporated into the Table of Ranks in the nineteenth century, and after some thinning out of nobles deemed potentially troublesome and rebellious. The Table of Ranks, instituted by Peter the Great, was the key to the hierarchical structure of pre-revolutionary Russia. The military and civil service – the only occupations open to nobles – were ranked equivalently, i.e. a colonel had as civilian counterparty a state counsellor. Once one reached the rank of colonel, or its civil service equivalent, one was entitled to a patent of nobility. This was Peter's idea of introducing a meritocracy, unusual in 17th century Europe. Certainly a few achieved this social mobility, but by and large, birth still determined position in the Table.

Barred from acquiring an estate in Lithuania, Ignatii settled on the estate and village of Chodow, in the Kutno District, in the vicinity of Poznan. Some 535 hectares, the estate had belonged to the Jastrzhembovsky family in the 18th century and had been acquired by a German family von Treskow who expanded the manor house in 1857 in an Italianate style and then sold it to Jasiukowicz in 1897. It was to become a refuge for my grandmother after the Bolshevik Revolution. Ignatii's son Stanislas lived there until WWII when the Germans captured it. It was subsequently seized by the Communists – my cousin Hanna Schlenkier. Stanislas's daughter, may well regain it after a lengthy legal process.

But Stanislas Jasiukowicz, my name sake, deserves some attention, as he became a celebrated martyr of the Soviet rape of Poland after the Allies had ceded Eastern Europe to Stalin at Yalta. Educated at the University of Munich, a leading political figure in the interwar years, he moved to Warsaw after Chodow was confiscated by the Germans. Active in the conspiratorial activities of the Polish National Party, which he had chaired before the war, he was arrested and jailed in 1942. Released in 1943, Stanislas Jasiukowicz was named deputy to the Vice Premier and delegate to the Polish Government in Exile in London – but unable to leave Poland. During the Warsaw Rising, he worked closely with General Bor-Komorowski on relief for the civilian population. When the Rising was crushed by the Germans – the Soviet Army sitting quietly on the sidelines to allow this. Jasiukowicz moved to Krakow with leaders of the Delegate's Council to the London Government. The "liberating" Soviets disbanded the Home Army, which had been the resistance to German occupation. Thousands of its members were disarmed and shipped to Russia where most were never heard of again. Nevertheless, Polish Resistance heroes tried to co-operate with the Soviets and, in March 1945, General Okulicki, who had succeeded Bor-Komorowski in command of the Home Army, together with Delegate Jankowski, were invited to a conference with Soviet General Ivanov, under written guaranties of safety. Jasiukowicz and several other members of the Delegate's Council were also invited.

Okulicki and Jankowski, together with Puzak, Chairman of the National Unity Council, were the first to travel. Everyone was under the impression that they were going to discuss measures to assure final victory and the formation of a postwar civilian government. On arrival in Pruskow, the three were immediately deported to Moscow and thrown in the Lubianka. Initial discussions with Ivanov had established that, after a meeting with Marshall Zukov at Pruskow, the delegates would all travel to London for discussions with the Government in Exile. When the twelve strong delegation, headed by Stanislas Jasiukowicz, arrived in Pruskow, presumably unaware of the fate of Okulicki, Jankowski and Puzak, they were told Zukow would now meet them at his own HQ near Poznan, and an aeroplane was waiting to take them there. With a lack of suspicion which boggles the mind, on 29th March, they boarded the plane, were flown straight to Moscow and incarcerated in the Lubianka. A major show trial was prepared and Western objections, voiced even by Churchill, were ignored. Stalin told the Moscow correspondent of *The Times*: "... These Poles have never been invited by the Soviet authorities for discussions. They have been arrested as saboteurs with the well-known saboteur Okulicki at their head. The arrest was carried out in consultation with the Polish Government in Lublin." All of this was a lie. The captives were tortured and told to confess to avoid death sentences. Okulicki was sentenced to ten years, Jankowski to eight and Jasiukowicz to five. The rest received shorter sentences or were released. Jasiukowicz's fate was unknown until 1990, during Perestroika, when an attaché at the Russian Embassy in Paris called Jasiukowicz's daughter, who was living in France, to say documents had now been released indicating that Jasiukowicz had died in prison shortly after sentencing. The Kutno branch of Solidarity placed a marble plaque to his memory in the family chapel on the Chodow estate.

CHAPTER II

"Is he in the Engineers?"

-From Pushkin's "The Queen of Spades" (translation T. Keane)-

Having tested the reader's patience with so much family history, I move now to the direct line, starting with my great grandfather General Stanislas Ignatievich Yassukovich, born in 1839. As he is really the first fully Russified of the family, having made the Imperial Army his career, I will revert to the transliteration of the name from Cyrillic characters to Roman which was used henceforth on my side of the family. My father's decision to adopt this on arrival in America in early 1918 did result in some confusion. In the Cyrillic alphabet, one letter, together with a so-called hard sign, indicates the sound "cha", as opposed to "sha". Equally, one letter indicates the sound "ya" – so my name in Russian is two letters shorter. The first syllable is straight forward but the last is often transliterated as "tch", as, for example, in Tchaikovsky. So my father first wrote the name as Yassukovitch and it appears as such on my birth certificate. But then, for reasons unknown, he dropped the "t". I followed suit – naturally. This has cost me hours of explanation when required to show original documents for identification.

Great grandfather Stanislas was a military engineer, as was his son Mikhail, my grandfather, and my father would no doubt have entered the Guard's Sappers, if history had permitted. He would have had to go from the Corps of Pages to the Engineer's Academy. It was the custom in the Corps of Cadets to allow the youngsters to wear their uniform cap at the same angle as worn traditionally in their father's regiment, the assumption being that that is where they were headed. I have a class photograph of my father's Corps and several caps can be seen worn at rakish angles, to one side or the other. Apparently these indicated Cavalry regiments. My father's cap is rather boringly sitting squarely on his head. My father considered the Sappers the "family regiment". His knowledge of Imperial Army uniforms was extraordinary for one who had left Russia so young. But then he had been in uniform since the age of eight, and in Russia uniforms abounded and civilian clothes were hardly ever worn by the military. This is evidenced in the many old photographs of country house parties and other non-military occasions where most of the men are in uniform.

The hero, or anti-hero, in Pushkin's short story *The Queen of Spades* is a young officer of Engineers called Hermann, a Russified German. Pushkin is making a German joke of this character. German jokes in Russia were a bit like Belgian jokes in France, or Polish jokes in America. A presumed national characteristic is being parodied. Germans were seen as honest, diligent and hardworking, but somewhat humourless. Laughing at them did not stop the Russian land owning class from employing them as agents and managers – precisely because of these character traits. In the story, Hermann is in constant attendance at card parties in the rooms of Narumov of the Horse Guards – but he never touches a card. He is chided about this by the other, hard gambling officers and replies "I am not in a position to sacrifice the necessary in the hopes of winning the superfluous". This is supposed by Pushkin to be a fine example of German stuffiness. I often quoted this when I was being approached to become a "name" at Lloyd's. Tchaikovsky wrote a celebrated opera based on the Pushkin story. Although, my father was an average opera fan, he made a particular thing of attending every production of *The Queen of Spades* he could get to. But his interest was less than musical; he was checking on the costumier's accuracy with Hermann's uniform – no piping on pockets, metal buttons. Afterwards, when asked: "Didn't you love that performance?" he would reply "No! Hermann's uniform was the wrong colour, there was the wrong number of buttons and the epaulets were entirely wrong!" So much for the Metropolitan Opera. The Sappers were sometimes referred to as *Le Génie de la Garde*", as pre- revolution Russians loved using as many French expressions as possible. This led to an entirely mistaken idea that engineers were brighter than, say, cavalry or artillery officers. In fact *génie* is merely the French word for engineer and does not indicate genius.

The first interesting fact of my great grandfather's military career is his religion. The first line in the biography of Yassukovich, Stanislav Faddei Mikhail Ludwig from the Russian State Military Archive is "born 11.8.1839 from the nobility of the Saint Petersburg province, *Roman Catholic*." Not being of the established state religion does not seem to have hindered him. One could remark that at that time a Roman Catholic could not be commissioned in the British Army. Unusually, he did not attend the Cadet Corps but entered the army through the Nikolaevsky Engineering School as an acting officer and then a military engineer ensign, continuing beyond the normal term for a postgraduate course in the Theoretical Department. He became 2nd Lieutenant in 1859 and was graduated with honours in 1860 for assignment to the staff of His Imperial Highness the Inspector General of Engineers – obviously one of the Grand Dukes, but the record doesn't show which. From there he was appointed to the Krondstadt Engineers Brigade. In 1863, still a Lieutenant, he began to accumulate an extraordinary collection of decorations: the Order of

St. Stanislav 3rd grade, then 2nd grade in 1872, and 1st grade in 1892; The Order of St Anna 3rd grade in 1869, 2nd grade in 1881, and 1st grade in 1896. He got the St. Vladimir 4th grade in 1884 but seems to have gone no further in this order. But he managed to get an Officer's Cross in the French Legion of Honour in 1883 and in the same year, the Japanese Order of the Rising Sun 4th Grade. One wonders how he coped with all this heavy metal hanging around his neck at court balls. He must have been on good terms with this Inspector General of Engineers as he seems to have had a series of rather cushy assignments by Imperial order, including in 1886 a three-month tour of England, France, Belgium, Switzerland and Norway to visit metal works with regard to the preparation of materials used in fortifications. In 1890, again by Imperial order, he was in Western Europe to learn in situ about the best panel bridge systems in France, Belgium and Germany. His "boon doggling" continues when in 1892, "on His Imperial Majesty's pleasure" he is sent to Germany to inspect sewage works for the sanitation of barracks and France to inspect light panel bridges for railways of the Eifel system used by the French government. Naturally, he doesn't miss out on the Paris Universal Exhibition in 1889 where, by Imperial order, he visits the sections relating to construction technology. Of course, his military record does not mention what else he visits in Paris. His main domestic accomplishment seems to have been in connection with the Zakaspijskaya military railway where he was active in various senior capacities. He was also a busy committee man, serving on and chairing endless bodies dealing with military communications, fortress armament, military railways and bridges – and as an expert in investigations following rail accidents. He was appointed General Lieutenant in 1898 for "distinction in service". This is a curious honorary title. In the ordinary course, he had made Captain in 1869, Lt. Colonel in 1873, Colonel in 1877 and Major General in 1887. At career's end, he managed another visit to the Paris Exhibition of 1900, to visit construction works and retired that year on permanent sick leave with "uniform and pension", as his military record states. One can surmise that this sickness stemmed from overindulgence on his many foreign trips and, indeed, in the photograph I have, he looks distinctly well fed.

Stanislas had married a Varvara de Billo – or possibly Billot – a French lady living in St. Petersburg. I know little of her. But the St. Petersburg of the time was highly cosmopolitan with a large French colony, some still there in exile from the French Revolution. French tutors and governesses were fashionable. Perhaps Barbara was one. They had two children: Mikhail, of which more below, and Evgenia, who was to marry the Marshal of the Nobility in Vilnius district, one Krassovsky. In retirement, Stanislas lived in one of the many *datchas*, or villas, on Vassilevskii Island, one of the several islands in the Neva, in the Viborg Quarter of St. Petersburg. He sat on some corporate boards: Russian-Foreign Merchant Bank, Kronstadt/Orienbaum Steamship Company, Imperial Russian Technology Company and Kronstadt Water Society.

I wonder about his financial situation. My father spoke very little about his grandfather except once to suggest he had been something of a gambler. Apparently he was a frequent visitor to Monte Carlo but considered it an inappropriate venue for a family holiday. So he bought a villa in Lausanne – in Pully, on the Lac Leman, not far from where the Hotel Beau Rivage is now situated. Here he would leave the family before moving on to the green baize tables in Monaco. But it seems to me unlikely he would not have exploited the fact that his younger brother Ignatii was a leading industrialist at the head of one of the St. Petersburg stock exchange's blue chip companies. As an engineer himself, Stanislas must have been well placed to play this particular stock. From what we know of Ignatii's ethical nature, inside information would not have been made available – but still, it was a growth stock. Perhaps Stanislas lost it all in Monte.

My grandfather Mikhail Stanislavovitch Yassukovich was born on 27th August 1870 and he is described in his military record as "son of Major General, native of Petrograd region, Orthodox faith". This tells us the record was compiled during the 1914 war when St. Petersburg had changed its name to Petrograd, the former seeming too Germanic. But it also shows grandfather had changed his religion. This could not have been for career reasons. The Imperial Russian establishment was loaded with Roman Catholics, Lutherans, Moslems and even Buddhists. Great grandfather certainly didn't suffer career wise from being left-footed. It can only be that Mikhail adopted the faith of his wife Maria Dimitrievna Erassi von Dilenius. This name has been tampered with, one might say. What on earth is the "von" doing in there? But that is how my father rendered it in his correspondence. She could not have been less German. The Dilinius is genuine as it's in Mikhail's military record. She had a far more exotic background – from the Phanariot Greeks of the Ottoman Empire. When Constantinople fell to the Turks in 1453, Mehmet II initially deported the remaining Christians, surprisingly leaving the Jewish population, but soon after the city was repopulated from the newly conquered territories and Greeks settled in the Phanar section, clustered around the Patriarch, who the Sultan recognised as the spiritual and secular head of his Orthodox subjects. The Phanar sector was probably so named after the Greek word Fanari, a nautical term meaning lantern or lamp, but used to designate a lighthouse. The great lighthouse of Constantinople was not far. The Phanariots claimed descent from the Byzantine nobility, supplemented by the Moldavian, Wallachian and Albanian nobility. They emerged as an educated elite dominating the administration of the Turkish Empire's Greek and Balkan domains and populating the Sublime Porte's diplomatic corps, keeping Hellenism alive – which ultimately fuelled Greek independence. Celebrated Phanoriotes were the Cantasuzene, Paliologue and Ypsilanti families. As the Russian Empire clashed increasingly with the Turks, the Phanariotes slowly dispersed into Romania and Southern Russia. My grandmother's family would have been amongst these. She was educated at the Smolny Institute, the leading school for daughters of the nobility. And it was an education which made the typical education accorded Western ladies seem primitive. Smolny girls studied all the sciences: chemistry, physics, mathematics and biology; philosophy, politics, geography, divinity were all basic subjects – as were the classics... They were taught in and had to be fluent in Russian, French, German and English, with Italian and Spanish as optional extras. Naturally the liberal arts, literature, music, drawing, sculpting were all in the curriculum. When my French mother corresponded with her mother-in-law in the 1930s, she was astounded at the fluency and literary quality of her French language.

I never knew my grandmother and my father hardly spoke of her; I have no idea what their relations might have been. But I am convinced she was no fun at all. Strict, stern and unbending is how I see her in my imagination. She was an heiress of a Moscow based fortune, although she is described as being of St Petersburg in my grandfather's record. Their marriage was strained by the fact that they lived in some style on her money. My father did recount one story illustrating this. As an engineer, my grandfather was into every modern gadget and appliance. Theirs was an early electrified house. They had a telephone – No. 2066. There were internal water closets on every floor. He owned an early motorcar. Apparently the WCs malfunctioned occasionally, and the butler would so inform his master as he descended the stairs in full dress uniform for a court function, his wife still dressing. Eagerly the general would attack the domestic appliance to diagnose and repair the problem. But oily water would splash on the gold braid of his sleeves and Madame would remind him that replacing stained, expensive gold braid would inevitably be for her account.

Grandfather's military career was peppered with academic assignments, as had been his father's. But he was educated in the 1ˢᵗ Cadet Corps, where he would have started at the age of eight. There were cadet corps in every major town, but the one in the capital was the most prestigious and enjoyed the patronage of the Tsar. In August 1888, grandfather formally entered the service as a "Junker, rank of private" in the Nikolaevsky Engineering Academy. His status indicates that, although non-commissioned and of the lowest military rank, he is of the noble class. It seems rather like the distinction that used to be made at Oxford and Cambridge between those who were paying fees and those who were not – although in Russia, military education was State funded. The Nikolaevsky was located in what is still called the Engineer's Place, or the Old Michael Palace, built by Paul 1 between 1797 and 1800 in the Spasskaya Quarter north of the Neva. He remained, rising to Corporal in 1889, Sergeant Major in 1890, and graduating as 2ⁿᵈ Lieutenant and assigned to 10ᵗʰ Sapper Battalion in August 1891. But in September of that year he was transferred to the Imperial Guard's Sapper Battalion for trial service and transferred permanently in December 1892. The main advantages of moving from a line regiment to the Guards were St. Petersburg location and a smarter uniform. He is back at the Nikolaevsky for graduate studies in 1894 and in 1896 is appointed second in command of the Guard's Sappers as a Captain, appointed to the Kronstadt Fortress Engineering Service in '97, then assistant to the head of works on the buildings of the St. Petersburg Hospital, medical school and prison. This sounds like a high ranking janitor's role. In 1900 he is appointed tutor in electro technology at the Nikolaevsy and in 1902 full professor in electro technology and applied mechanics, having been awarded the St; Stanislav 3rd Grade in the previous year. Following in the tradition of his father, he attends endless congresses and conferences "on the pleasure of His Imperial Highness the Inspector General of Engineers" dealing with water supply systems, communications, even one dealing with the effect of lightening on reinforced concrete structures. He spends a good deal of 1905 and 1906 on vacation, including abroad. In fact his record strikes one as being peppered with long periods of idleness and conference attendance, which is the same thing, in my opinion – having yawned through countless World Bank/IMF meetings and Davos forums. Grandfather still managed to be promoted to 2nd Grade of the Order of St; Stanislav in 1909, 2nd Grade of the order of St. Anna in 1913, and 4th Grade of the St. Vladimir in 1915. He was Colonel in 1906 and Major General in 1916.

An anecdote my father enjoyed telling deals with grandfather's duty in Moscow supervising the installation of permanent military radio stations. This was in September 1914, a month after the outset of war. He was billeted in an apartment directly over the HQ of Engineers in Moscow and so could stroll down to work each morning. His day uniform included narrow trousers with a strap under the sole of the boot. Seeking greater comfort, grandfather had a boot maker fix dress spurs to a pair of patent leather bed room slippers. When standing they looked exactly like well- polished boots. However, on a visit by the Inspector General – a Grand Duke, grandfather was invited to sit down and the trouser leg inevitably rode up a bit, revealing the substitution. His Imperial Highness is reputed to have said: "Mikhail Stanislavitch, your inventiveness as an engineer has no limit – I will have a word with my own boot maker". The war does not appear to have exposed my grandfather to very great dangers. In fact, in July of 1915, he was granted "Imperial Favour for extremely diligent and zealous service and work necessitated by the current circumstances of the war", quoting from his military record, and in October 1916 he was appointed Head of the Physics Department of the Nikolaevsky Engineering Academy. His next assignment was to be of great significance to the family and could be cited as responsible for the fact that I am sitting where I am. But some background is necessary to imagine the reason behind it, as grandfather's military record ceases in 1917.

Reading between the lines of my father's scarce comments on his father, I conclude that the General, as he was always called by his second wife, was a feckless playboy, notwithstanding his brilliant career. He was a spendthrift, living on his wife's money and, ultimately to be supported by his hard working son. In restaurants and nightclubs, his signature order was: "champagne et *faite suivre!*" – keep them coming! But his most momentous characteristic was that he was libidinous to an extreme. No likely female escaped his amorous advances: maids, governesses, friends and relatives of his wife – he was indefatigable, a Russian Don Giovanni. When, in 1929, my mother was taken to meet her new father-in-law in the New York apartment he then occupied, he promptly made a pass at her – under the nose of his second wife. Of course, his long suffering first wife put up with this behaviour during their marriage of over 20 years. Divorce was unknown in such circles. But then he did the unthinkable. He ran off with a Moscow heiress half his age and abandoned his wife and three children. This would have occurred during the war, probably in about 1916, or perhaps early 1917, as he was promoted to Major General in December 1916. But the powers that were in the Imperial Army must have been scandalised. One must bear in the mind that the Army was struggling to survive a desperate battle with Germany on the Eastern Front, political turmoil in the capital and sagging morale. In the Duma, power was in the hands of the Mensheviks, moderate socialists, but the Bolshevik contingent was gaining in confidence; the government was still reeling from the assassination of Rasputin; St. Petersburg society suspected pro German influences at Court; the Tsar had assumed overall military command from his cousin Grand Duke Nicholas Nickolayevitch, a great mistake, as he was miles away as the situation in the capital deteriorated; the Imperial Family were reclusive, nursing the Tsarina's understandable, but hysterical obsession with the Tsarevitch's illness – haemophilia; the German High Command had given Lenin access to Russian prisoners of war, to foster revolutionary attitudes – they were subsequently to sneak him into Russia in a sealed train; Bolsheviks were infiltrating factories, promoting strikes – it was, to put it simply, a total mess. Not a good moment for a scandal involving a general officer. In February 1917, riots broke out in St. Petersburg and troops, even of prestigious Guard regiments, began to mutiny. On March 15th, the Tsar abdicated and first named his son as successor, but then changed his mind, thinking of his son's illness, and named the Grand Duke Michael as his successor. In fact the Russian monarchy is appointive, not hereditary – the Tsar appoints his successor, usually his eldest son but not always. But this change of mind has caused confusion ever since. Technically, the Tsar became his son's subject after his first decision, and only the Grand Duke Michael, whom he had appointed regent, could make a new succession decision. The Grand Duke declined. A Provisional Government was appointed by the Duma, under Prince Lvov, a senior civil servant and former minister who served briefly, and was succeeded by an ambitious lawyer from the minor nobility, Alexander Kerensky. He would incur my father's undying enmity, by arresting the Tsar and the Imperial Family at the Winter Palace. The Provisional Government expressed a strong determination to continue the war effort to the immediate relief of the Allies, who had been horrified by the unfolding events in St. Petersburg, fearing a collapse on the eastern front could allow the transfer of significant German forces to the western front.

Now comes the "nail in the shoe", the small, apparently inconsequential event that altered my family history. The context: on April 15th, 1917, President Wilson asked Congress to declare war on Germany. Fed up with attacks on U.S. shipping and other provocations, America decided to join the allies, despite strong isolationist and anti-war sentiments in the nation, particularly in the mid-west which was rather pro-German. The U.S. was the first government to recognise the Provisional Government in Russia. A delegation – the Root Commission – was sent to Petrograd. With America now in the war, it was necessary to convince Washington to help shore up the highly fragile Eastern Front. This might save the deteriorating political situation at home. I can see a group of General Staff officers in conference, their medals and orders glistening, their gilded shoulder boards on hunched shoulders. Who to send as head of a Military Mission to Washington? Silence and head scratching. Suddenly a bright spark speaks up: "Why not send Yassukovich? His behaviour has scandalised Petrograd society. Let's get him out of circulation – we have enough of a morale problem as it is".

Another pipes up: "Not as stupid an idea as it sounds! Sorry, Alexei Petrovich!" – To the first who spoke. "Who was that little heiress he ran off with?"

There follows a brief gossip session. Lunch is due to be served; a waiter has brought zakouski and vodka to the sideboard.

"Decided! Yassukovich goes to Washington," says the senior officer presiding; "Agreed!" they all shout, the odour of the zakouski having made them forget what a stupid idea it was. Of course, there might have been a serious reason – but on the face of it an officer with diplomatic experience would have been preferable to a military engineer. There would have been plenty who had served as military attachés at foreign embassies. I have no date for the appointment. Kerensky was War Minister under the first Provisional Government, but it might have been a Foreign Ministry decision. Pavel Milyukov was Foreign Minister in March, but a further crisis prompted a reshuffle and Mikhail Tereshchenko became Foreign Minister in April, the month America joined the war. One has to imagine the Military Commission to Washington was an important appointment – gaining U.S. military support was critical. It's hard to believe the choice was as frivolous as I describe. The appointment would have been made in time for grandfather, relaxed as ever, to take the Trans-Siberian RR to Vladivastok and then continue by ship to San Francisco, arriving there end July 1917. He travelled with all necessary household goods, including sheets and towels, believing, no doubt, that Americans lived in tepees. With him was his second wife, the "little Moscow heiress" Antonia Netchvalodova, my beloved step grandmother – of which more later.

The Allies great concern was that the Eastern Front would collapse, a concern now also shared by the U.S. Little was known about the Provisional Government, but it contained strong anti-war voices. On arrival in San Francisco, a press conference was arranged for the General. He would have never heard of such a barbarous custom. Apparently he made a particularly stuffy reply to a questioner, and a jolly journalist slapped him on the back and said "Well, General, you're in the U.S. of A now!" In Imperial Russia, if you touched a General Officer, you were taken around the corner and shot. My grandfather's worst suspicions about America were confirmed. But the news wire story of his mission was carried between 30 July and 2nd August by a large number of regional papers, including such as the Marble Rock Journal, of Marble Rock, Iowa, the Webster City Tribune of Webster City, Iowa, the Lowell Sun, of Lowell, Mass., etc., etc. What desperation for news must have haunted small town editors! But it was front page for the Washington Post, under the headline "Russian Asks for Troops". The gist was the same everywhere: "The presence of American troops on the Russian front would be fatal to Germany" according to General Michael Yassukovich, Chief of the Russian Military Committee who was here today..." Clearly the general was working his way east. The Fort Wayne Sentinal reported the General was accompanied by four staff officers. The Reno Evening Gazette reported that "General Yassukovich, chief of the Russian Military Commission who are here today, said 'If America will send men to Russia, she will furnish an army that will add to a Russian army of a million men that may...'"

How pathetic and hopeless was my poor grandfather's mission. But it saved his life, as he would have been shot after the Bolshevik revolution in October; and indirectly, enabled my father to make a new life in America. Boris Bahkmeteff had been appointed Ambassador to Washington by the Provisional Government. He arrived in June, replacing a namesake Grigory Bahkmeteff, who was unrelated. Boris Bahkmeteff was a distinguished civil engineer who went on to lecture in hydraulics at Columbia University, gaining a full professorship there and authoring learned scientific works. He continued to be recognised as Ambassador until 1922, as the U.S. certainly did not recognise the Bolshevik government that took power in the October Revolution. General Yassukovich moved to New York City. Hugely qualified, he refused to find work, as a general in the Imperial Russian Army did not work, in his considered opinion. Finally there was no money and he accepted an engineering post with a railway company. He became the darling of New York society ladies and I have a photograph of him riding in Central Park, in uniform, accompanied by a bowler hatted and veiled lady riding side saddle. He died in a Greenwich, Connecticut nursing home in 1941. His obituary in the *New York Times* on October 25th of that year, under the sub headline "Czarist Fought the Austrians – Headed Military Commission", says he held a command on the Austrian front, which I do not find in his military record. But it also mentions he was responsible for the construction of the Moscow Radio

station. This would have been when the incident of the spurred bedroom slippers took place. Madame la Generale, as she was officially known, or "Tonia"
to the family, was active in the Russian Orthodox Church in Exile and, when
widowed became Head of the International Section of the New York Public
Library, where I often visited her in the 1950s. She had also been educated at
the Smolny Institute.

CHAPTER III

*"They bore within their breasts the grief
That fame can never heal–
The deep unutterable woe
Which none save exiles feel"*

-William Edmonstoune Aytoun-

My grandfather had three children: Irina, born 4th February 1896, Marie born 20th December in the same year, and Dimitri born 16th June 1898. My father Dimitri Mikhailovich Yassukovich, to give him his full name on this introduction, never celebrated his birthday. Apart from the complicating factor that Russia never adopted the Julian calendar, and so there is a gap in dates, the Russian tradition was to celebrate the name day, rather than the birthday. Mind you, he never celebrated his name day either (24th September). He was certainly christened in the Russian Orthodox Church and, as we will learn, asked for a Russian Orthodox funeral, but he was not a religious man, despite attendance, when he could, at the Easter Mass at the Russian Church in Paris – to hear the music. His two elder sisters were almost twins, born 11 months apart, and were very close. I have the impression they were not so close to their younger brother. Photographs taken in the same year show the sisters together, arms linked. But there is separate photo of little Dimitri, dressed as a girl, and sitting sadly on a stool in the nursery. There is no photo of the three together. They were all born in a house at Shpalernaia 6, just behind the French Quai on the south bank of the Neva, so named as the French embassy was at one end. From there one joined the English Quai, similarly named. The house was a typical St. Petersburg town house with a courtyard inside large enough for a carriage and four to enter and turn. I saw the house from the outside on my first visit to Leningrad with a small group of friends on a Thompson week end tour. We had equipped ourselves with a recently reprinted Baedeker Guide to Russia published, with unfortunate timing, in 1914. These guides were incredibly detailed, down to the exact rooms and wall locations of paintings in the Hermitage. We had a nice little in tourist girl guide on our small bus. As she sang out "On your left, the headquarters of the First Soldiers Soviet!" We read and shouted from our Baedeker: "The Sheremetieff

Palace!" At first she was annoyed. But one evening at tour's end, she asked if she could borrow the Baedeker for the night. Next day she turned up with dark circles under her eyes and said, "I didn't sleep all night! They only give the history of our City up to Peter the Great, then the October Revolution – nothing in between. It was fascinating!" I offered to send her a copy but she said no – it would be confiscated. It was all very pre-Perestroika. Viewing a cell at the Fortress of Peter & Paul, we were told it was the one where Gorky had been incarcerated by the cruel Tsarist regime. It was almost exactly the time when Sholzanitsin had escaped to the West and was writing about the Gulags. *Plus ça change...* That night in a café, a group of youths were staring at us and whispering. Finally one came over and asked if we could send him an album of The Rolling Stones. I did. I wonder if it reached him. An old friend of my father's had told him his old house number was unchanged. It was and I crossed the Alexandrovsky Bridge from the Leningrad Hotel, found the house and started to snap away. It had been turned into flats, of course, and the big doors to the courtyard were closed. My photography attracted some attention so, after a time, I doubled back to discover at the hotel that I had omitted to put any film in the camera. I had to go back in the afternoon and attract some more attention. My father appreciated the snapshots.

My father's early upbringing was traditionally nursery confined and he had little contact with his parents. He had an English nanny, and like all children of his class, spoke French to his parents, English to his sisters and Russian to the servants. He was to learn German first at the Reformierte Schule, a Lutheran children's school in St. Petersburg, where many Orthodox parents sent their sons to perfect their German. They were already in a military style uniform.... At around ten years old, it was enrolment in the 1st Cadet Corps. I have a small photograph of him standing alone, almost at attention, but with his head turned slightly to the side. He is in a broad square, wet with recent rain, in his cadet uniform, in front of an imposing building which may be the HQ of the 1st Cadet Corps. It is one of the saddest photos I know. The only story he told us about his days as a cadet was concerning the dress uniform, donned at least once a week for parade. This included skin tight, white buckskin trews. The only way to get into them was to wet them first and let them dry on you, when they became rather stiff. My father would claim that he spent his whole career as a cadet with a head cold. Sniffles or no, his grades were excellent. I have his final report card which he had translated in America for admission to his short period at Columbia University. "This diploma is issued by the 1st Military Cadet School to Cadet of the Vllth Class Dimitri Mikhailovich Yassukovich, son of Major-General, who has successfully completed the full course... etc. etc." Grades on a 12 point system: Gods Law (Divinity!) 12; Russian, written 9, oral 10; French 12, German 12, Algebra 8, Geometry 10, Trigonometry 10 Analytical Geometry and Application Algebra 9, Analysis of infinitely smalls 9 (what can this be?), Physics 9, Natural History 11, Cosmography 9, Geography 10, History 10, Chemistry 9, freehand drawing 12. Average mark 10.06. It is interesting to compare this curriculum to a modern one at any Western prep school. The diploma is dated May 25, 1917. It is signed by the Director, Lt. General Grigorieff and the Inspector of Classes Major General Luneburg. This last name is an indicator of how prominent the Baltic nobility were in the Imperial Army. They were even more prominent in the Diplomatic Corp, and at Court; the Lord Chamberlain of the Imperial Court was Count Freidrichs. This was politically unsettling, to say the least, when World War I broke out.

The St. Petersburg my father grew up in was an intensely cosmopolitan capital. Peter the Great not only built the city on marshland, filled in with the bones of the slave workers, it was said; but he was the legator of a multinational tradition which persisted until the Bolsheviks carried out what today would be called ethnic cleansing. Determined to drag his people kicking and screaming into the 17th century, Peter embarked on a celebrated tour of Western capitals to observe the modern arts and sciences lacking in primitive Russia. He travelled incognito but the identity of the tall, brawling, barrack room bully was soon known to most. A famous painting shows Peter in a wheelbarrow being pushed through the box hedges in the garden of his hapless landlord in Greenwich, outside London. But he was not just on a learning curve; he was also on a recruiting drive. Dutch, English and Scotts were targeted particularly for their skills in ship building, trade, commerce and iron working. My father's best friend in his boyhood was named Yuri Havemann – known subsequently as Jury in America. Yuri was descended from a Dutch naval architect who remained to join the Russian establishment. A friend of ours, Peter de Brandt, has the same origin. His family became barons. Later, the French arrived in strength after their revolution. Most of the purveyors of luxury goods in St. Petersburg were French. A colleague at European Banking Co., Jean-Pierre Marchand, told me his grandparents had owned a large department store in St Petersburg. Of course, as the empire grew, so did the community of various nationals. My father showed me the list of his two dozen classmates at the Cadet Corps. He pointed out that only slightly over half had true Russian names; the rest were Polish, or from the Baltic Provinces – Lithuania, Latvia and Estonia, also East Prussia, Serbian, Georgian, and Finnish. Neighbouring, but independent Orthodox Kingdoms such as Bulgaria and Rumania, populated St. Petersburg with their noble families, for example the Tchatchavadses from Georgia and the Cantasuzene from Rumania. Serbian families were either subjects of the Austro-Hungarian Empire, or of the Russian – such as the Miloradovitch. Obviously Russia supported Serbian nationalism against the Catholic Austrians – one of the causes of World War I. Peter introduced a further element into Russian society after finally defeating King Charles XII of Sweden in the Great Northern War 1700-1720. This war, where the advantage swung back and forth in an almost regular pattern, had geopolitical causes of such complexity, that an account certainly does not belong here. Peter was so impressed by the quality of Swedish manhood that he refused to repatriate the officer prisoners at war's end – against established convention, married them off to Russian wives and persuaded/bribed them to become Russified. A number of Swedish families became members of the Russian nobility – to name a few: Armfelt, Fersen, Enckell, Holtoer, Cronhjelm, Grabbe, etc., etc.

After graduating from the 1ˢᵗ Corps of Cadets in May 1917, my father would have normally gone on to the Corps of Pages; in fact he had been appointed and become a Page Candidate in 1915 – a candidate only, because final admission was still dependent on an entrance exam. His certificate of appointment gives me a clue as to when his father had run off with Antonina Netchvalodova. It is addressed to my grandmother Maria Dimitrievna. This seems odd. Why it was not addressed to the father? Because it was known he had eloped with the young Moscow heiress? A word about the Corps of Pages is in order.

Founded by the Emperor Paul 1ˢᵗ, the Corps of Pages is best described as a sort of combination of Eton and Sandhurst. Essentially a school to prepare the officer corps, its graduates also entered the civil service. Appointment was by birth in that you had to be a son or a grandson of a General or an Admiral, or the civil service equivalent: Collegiate Counsellor. My father qualified because his grandfather was a Major General. At the time of his appointment as a Page Candidate, his father was only a Colonel. The scholastic curriculum was of the highest standard but the schools distinguishing feature was that its pupils served as pages at Court, on a rote basis. During the winter months the school was quartered in the Vorontsov Palace. In summer, when the Court moved to Tzsarkoe Selo, the school moved too. Page duties were standard page duties: standing at attention outside key doorways, holding trains of court dresses, etc., etc. Glorified footmen, one might say. Tradition claimed Pages drew lots to see who would stand outside the Tsar's bedroom on Easter morning, as the custom was HIM would kiss three times the first person he saw – prince or peasant – and proclaim the Easter greeting "Christ is Risen!". The story is rubbish as surely the first person he would see would be his valet. There were celebrated graduates of the Corps, such as Pushkin and Rimsky-Korsakov and, basically, the whole of the Establishment passed through its portals. The school insignia was a Maltese cross. The history behind this is interesting: When Napoleon rampaged through Europe, the Knights of St. John of Jerusalem in Malta faced destruction and dissolution. A Grandmaster was dead and a rump of Knights in Rome, despairing of finding a Catholic sovereign in Europe to succeed, due to the depredations of the Corsican upstart, invited Paul 1ˢᵗ – an Orthodox – to become Grandmaster of the Order. Paul was delighted and accepted – he loved regalia. He promptly abused his position by appointing all the then members of the newly formed Corps of Pages as knights of the Order. In fact he founded a Chapel for the Order attached to the Vorontsov Palace, where Roman Catholics could worship, get married, etc. And so the Maltese cross became the Pages' insignia; I have my father's – a version candidates were allowed to wear.

Marvin Lyons, recently deceased, was a distinguished Canadian scholar, and the leading expert on the pre-revolutionary imperial military. At the heart of his historical work was a biographical dictionary of the Corps of Pages, as yet unpublished. He was also the most knowledgeable on the diaspora of the Russian nobility and stayed in touch with many of its most distinguished families. Ours hardly fits that bill, but he became a friend of my father's because the latter helped him acquire an impressive collection of memorabilia from the Corps of Pages – a collection of such worth it has prompted the museum mafia of St Petersburg to stoop to some skullduggery to get their hands on it. Lyons set up a foundation to work on the acquisition of the Vorontsov Palace in order to house the collection in the most appropriate home. He kindly made me one of the 25 trustees, all former Pages or Page Candidates, or sons thereof. Unfortunately, we have as much chance of succeeding as of restoring the Russian throne, and the collection will probably go the Hoover Institute in California.

In 1917, my father began his final year at the Corps of Cadets when the situation in Russia was deteriorating rapidly. After a brief period of patriotic jubilation following the declaration of war in August 1914 – a war widely supported at first, and some early victories in Gallacia, things turned sour militarily and politically. With the best of intentions, Nicholas II made a fatal mistake when he assumed overall command of the army in the summer of 1915. Morale had started to erode in 1916 after a series of defeats, mistakes by recently called up commanders and supply shortages. Mutinies broke out and desertions increased. Nicholas proved a poor Commander –in – Chief. He had to leave the Tsarina Alexandra to rule; she was increasingly unpopular being of German origin, obsessed with the Tsarevitch's ill health, and seen as under the thumb of the charlatan Rasputin. She sacked and named new Prime Ministers with bewildering frequency and angered the Duma. The economy, the fastest growing in pre-war Europe, began to suffer from serious war strain, strikes broke out, shortages appeared and the liberal leaning deputies in the Duma, now a majority, pleaded with him to form a new constitutional government as he had done after the 1905 revolution. Nicholas considered this unacceptable in wartime. He began to lose widespread support, even of the nobility, and the popular mood, which had been universally sympathetic to the Imperial Family only three years previously, shifted ominously.

The 22nd of February – old style – 7th March in our calendar, was International Women's Day. I wonder if contemporary feminists realise how old their movement is. A series of meetings and rallies in Petrograd – renamed when war broke out – quickly turned into violent demonstrations. The Tsar ordered the army to quell these. Informed by Mikhail Rodzianko, President of the

Duma, of the gravity of the situation, his response was dilatory, perhaps because the Tsarina had told him everyone was over-reacting. But the Petrograd garrison mutinied – even the Volynsky Life Guards, and Cossack units refused to control the crowds. The Tsar worsened the situation by proroguing the Duma, leaving an authority vacuum. Deputies set up a Temporary Committee and the Socialist members re-established the Petrograd Soviet, first created in 1905 to represent workers and soldiers. The Tsar was advised to abdicate by senior generals and ministers and he did so on 2nd March, not only on his own behalf, but also on behalf of the haemophiliac Tsarevitch Alexei, naming his brother Grand Duke Michael Alexandrovitch as successor. This was actually unconstitutional, as a regency should have first been declared under the Grand Duke. In fact this was the Tsar's initial decision, but he changed his mind. The Grand Duke effectively declined, saying he would only accept a decision of the Constituent Assembly which should define the form of a permanent government. Of course, they never got around to that before the Bolshevik coup d'etat in October. So Grand Duke Michael was never Tsar and the throne is in fact vacant and the various claims of so-called pretenders from the Romanov family in later years are moot.

When my father graduated from the Corps of Cadets in June, 1917, a provisional government under Prince Lvov was in place. Efforts were being made to continue the war effort. But the provisional government was forced to share power with the Petrograd Soviet, supported by the Socialists – the Mensheviks. The war effort was stalling due to a breakdown in discipline and morale in the army. Ordinarily, my father would have entered the Corps of Pages, having passed the entrance exam and already become a Page Candidate in 1915. But these were not ordinary times. The Corps of Pages was disbanded in 1917 and everyone, including new entrants, was assigned to various military colleges. My father was assigned to the College of Military Engineering, a natural choice in view of his antecedents. My father spoke little of this turbulent period. The famous Order Number 1 was issued March 1st, 1917. This was to lead to the final disintegration of the Imperial Russian Army. Point 4 stated that "the orders of the Military Commission of the Duma – part of the Provisional Government – shall be executed only in such cases as do not conflict with the orders and resolution of the Soviet of Workers' and Soldiers' Deputies". Lenin had arrived in Petrograd from exile in Zurich in April, supposedly smuggled in on a sealed train organised by Germany. He had been allowed to visit Russian prisoner of war camps inside Germany. Lenin sought to seize control of the Bolshevik Party with anti-war propaganda and during July, further unrest and violent demonstrations, including soldiers and sailors, prompted the Provisional Government to arrest prominent Bolsheviks. Lenin fled to Finland and Prince Lvov was replaced by Alexander Kerensky.

Kerensky promulgated a series of liberal measures, including full freedom of speech, the end of capital punishment, etc., but his greatest sin, in my father's eyes, was to arrest the Imperial Family. They had been in protective custody at Tsarkoe Selo, the summer residence since February. They were induced back to the Winter Palace and the Tsar, Tsarina, Tsarevitch, and the four Grand Duchesses were all arrested and sent into exile in near Siberia, together with the children's English tutor, other staff and a few courtiers-in-waiting. The entire Imperial Family was subsequently assassinated on Lenin's orders, having refused to leave Russia. Nicholas II has recently been made a Martyr of the Russian Orthodox Church. Whatever his weaknesses and shortcomings, he refused to save himself and died for his country. Kerensky ended in exile in the United States in the 1920s and was befriended by New York State Senator Joseph Simpson. Having moved on to California, he stayed at the Simpson's New York town house when visiting. I took out – you won't catch me using the expression "dated" – the Simpson's much younger, after thought daughter, Sally. One evening I was introduced to Kerensky. "I know who your grandfather was," he said to me, looking severe and professorial. When I got home I told my father.

"You didn't shake his hand?!" he exclaimed. Well, of course, I had to say I did. "Go and wash your hands!" was his reply; the incident was never mentioned again.

Kerensky's regime fared no better than Lvov's. A brief counter offensive on the eastern front petered out, anti-war sentiment grew, promises of land, jobs and food couldn't be met, and the anti- Bolshevik parties squabbled. A strange episode involving a putative counter coup by Commander-in- Chief Kornilov – possibly engineered by Kerensky himself – destroyed the Provisional Government's credibility. Lenin returned and the Bolsheviks plotted to seize power by increasing its position in the Worker's and Soldier's Soviets in all the major cities of the Empire. On 1st September the All-Russian Central Executive Committee of Soviets received demands from 126 local soviets urging it to take power. The revolution started in Tallinn, the capital of Estonia and spread to Petrograd two days later on 25th October, 5th November in the new style Gregorian colander, when Bolshevik operatives seized control of Government buildings. In fact it was rather bloodless. Contrary to subsequent Soviet propaganda, when some Reds went to seize the Winter Palace, they found it virtually empty and got lost in its extensive passages. The Military Engineers Academy, where my father was in attendance, was entrusted with the defence of the Central Telephone Exchange and my father was captured and spent two weeks in a dungeon in Kronstadt. He was released and reassigned to a new Red Army division. But he exploited his Polish/Lithuanian background and managed to join a newly formed regiment of Polish Lancers in Minsk. Here began his brief military service on the eastern front, which was not far from collapse. But he was out of Petrograd when wide spread arrests of all opposing elements began and his father was in Washington, his mission to raise American support for the eastern front now rendered redundant. The Bolsheviks were arresting and often shooting senior officer remnants of the Imperial Army which, as nobles, they did not trust to officer the new Red Army. So it was that my grandfather's indiscretion, if one can describe so mildly the abandonment of his wife and children, probably saved his life.

My father's service on the eastern front was to last only weeks but he did once give us a colourful description of the Lancer regiment's tactics against German machine guns. Apparently these swung horizontally in a limited arc but not vertically. The technique consisted of a charging in a zigzag pattern, then leaping over the machine gun position, wheeling about and sticking the machine gun crew in the back with the lance. Some horses were slower than others, my father added, laconically. We never learned, my sister and me, of exactly what was happening at this time to the rest of the family – apart from grandfather who was in the U.S. with his second wife Tonia. My father was strangely silent about this. I think the break-up of the family had affected him as profoundly as the Revolution, and he was reluctant to talk about it. My aunt Marie Magdalena Mikhailevna arrived at Chodow, a family estate in Poland, in 1918. She married Vladimir Junosza-Stepowski, a Polish nobleman, in 1930. They had one daughter, Danuta, born in 1931, my only and much beloved cousin. I have no cousins from my mother's side. My other aunt Irina had married Georgi Aleksandrovitch Koliubakhin, of the Vitebsk Province nobility. His father was a Lt. General and Georgi was accepted in the accelerated course of the Corps of Pages in 1916, a programme initiated at the beginning of the war. When the Corps was disbanded in 1917, he was assigned to Engineer troops. He served in the Volunteer White Army during the civil war, was captured and shot. We don't know the date, or exactly what happened to Irina and her little girl, born in 1916 or 1917. My father's understanding was that after her husband was executed, she was sent to Siberia, with her child. I have a photograph showing her with a little girl of four or five. This could be around 1921. My father made great efforts to trace her during the '20s and '30s but with no success. But my poor grandmother did not manage to leave Russia until 1920, ill and stretcher bound in a goods train.

Lenin and the Bolsheviks had seized power on the back of anti-war sentiment and offer to end it. In December 15, 1917, an armistice was agreed with the Central Powers (Germany, Austria, Turkey and Bulgaria). Negotiations for a peace treaty began at Brest-Litvosk, but initial German demands were rejected by the new Soviet government. In February, 1918, Germany repudiated the armistice and seized the Baltic Provinces, Belarus and Ukraine. When a treaty was finally signed on March 3rd 1918, Bolshevik Russia had to accept even worse terms than originally offered by the Central Powers.

This most critical of years in my father's early life remain shrouded in uncertainty. During 1917, the Emperor had abdicated, the Imperial Family was arrested, the monarchy was effectively abolished, the Russian-German front collapsed, my father's military career prospects were ended, his father abandoned the family and eloped with a much younger lady – it is difficult to imagine a more momentous year in the life of a 19-year-old. In later life, he did mention casually his brief incarceration in Kronstadt Fortress, that most popular keep for political prisoners since Peter the Great. He never referred to the ironic fact that his grandfather had been responsible for its renewed fortifications as a military engineer. He also spoke with pride of his service in the Polish Lancer regiment – his only actual war experience. But he recalled, or refused to recall, no detail of his day-to-day experiences. My only evidence comes from a letter he wrote to his friend Marvin Lyons in February of 1976, when they were in active correspondence concerning the salvation of Corps des Pages archives. "Yes, I would have entered the Corps under normal circumstances", he wrote. "When disbanded in 1917, all were assigned to various military colleges, myself to the Engineers, to which was entrusted the defence of the Centrale Téléphonique in October – Russian calendar – 1917. Upon the Bolshevik takeover, I spent two weeks in a dungeon in Kronstadt. When liberated and assigned to a Red Army division, I took advantage of my Polish origin to join a newly-formed Polish Lancers Regiment in Minsk. When the Russian-German front collapsed, I roamed around for a while and made my way to Norway in October 1918. My saga, as you can see, is much less dramatic than that of most of my countrymen". That's it. With his world disintegrating around him, my father either suffered a curious memory lapse, or the events were so traumatic that he refused to discuss them later. I was able to fill in some gaps from my step-grandmother Tonia, née Netchvalodova, who we dearly loved. Of course, she was already in America in 1917. But in the same letter to Marvin Lyons, my father makes an apparently inaccurate statement. He explains his emigration to the U.S. was "made possible by my father Major General M.S. Yassukovich, being head of the Russian Military mission in Washington". But he suggests the mission arrived in late 1916, whereas press reports suggest it was in July 1917. Tonia also told me that my father's exit from Bolshevik Russia had been facilitated by an old family coachman/chauffeur who had taught him to drive an automobile, one of the first in St. Petersburg. Apparently this family retainer had Bolshevik sympathies and found himself in the visa/passport section of the revolutionary government, but, out of affection for the young man, provided my father with a forged passport. We always understood he first reached Stockholm where he contracted the Asian flu which was devastating war torn Europe and killed more people than the War. This he did speak of, but being young and fit him survived. At the time it was not understood that the influenza virus existed in several varieties. It is only recently that DNA research has discovered that the epidemic of 1918/19 was brought to Europe by U.S. troops from Fort Leavenworth, Kansas where poorly diagnosed cases had been reported just prior to departure of units to the European war theatre. It is now assumed, that the virus had originated in Mexico. In any case, either my father forgot that he went first to Stockholm, or he did actually go to Oslo, as he told Marvin Lyons. At any rate, we will never know what his "roaming around" consisted of. Years later, my niece Alixe Reed married a journalist, Rob Glenn, who was interested in spoken history. He tried to get my father to talk into a tape recorder about those early days. My father refused. "Every émigré who could hold a pen has written memoirs," he claimed – "mine would be boring!"

"But what about the grandchildren, and great grandchildren?" protested Rob. No luck – my father wouldn't play.

CHAPTER IV

"Till all success be nobleness
And every gain divine"

-Katherine Lee Bates from the lyric of "America the Beautiful"-

When my father arrived in America, my grandfather had already moved to an apartment in New York. His mission was, of course, redundant. America did not recognise the Bolshevik government until the mid '20s and a brutal civil war was beginning in which British and U.S. troops intervened in support of the White Army, but to no avail. The Russian Embassy in Washington, under Ambassador Boris Bahkmeteff was still accredited, and I have a copy of a document issued by the New York Consulate authorising a trip to Canada for my father. Bahkmeteff soon accepted an appointment to a professorship in hydraulic engineering at Columbia University. There were sufficient embassy funds available to allow my father to study for six months at Columbia and I assume Bahkmeteff was instrumental in arranging this. My father had arrived penniless, and my grandfather was living off those same remaining funds. Naturally, his second wife's considerable fortune was lost in the revolution. My father recalled going to the Opera with his father and stepmother and being surprised to find himself in the stalls. He had never been in anything but a box at the theatre or opera. He also had to become accustomed to carry money. Soon the money ran out and, at first, grandfather would not consider seeking gainful employment, despite his excellent qualifications. "A General of the Imperial Russian Army does not work," he stated. Like many Russian émigrés, he and Tonia became popular in New York society and he was often to be seen riding in Central Park, in field uniform, accompanied by a fashionable dowager.

His brief attendance at Columbia terminated by lack of funds, my father was in no doubt that he had to work to eat and he was keen to move out from under the influence of his feckless father. He often used to say that those members of the Russian diaspora who were under 30 at the revolution generally managed to adapt to life in the West and mostly succeeded, whilst the older ones could not and ended up driving taxis in Paris or marrying rich

American ladies. Actually, this was not so true of the artistic members of the Russian Establishment, such as Diagallef, Nijinsky and countless other artists, musicians, etc. Several émigrés made careers in Hollywood advising on the spate of films set in pre-Revolutionary Russia. But the traditional view has prevailed. I once shared a conference platform with Lady Thatcher, then ex-Prime Minister. At the reception after, I was standing near as she extolled the success of the Overseas Chinese, exiled by communism. "Not like the White Russians!" she drawled, "They all ended up as Paris taxi drivers."

I could not resist chiming in and said, "Very true, by and large, Lady Thatcher."

Quick as a flash she took my arm and said, "Oh, but I don't mean *your* father, Stani!" There is a bonus to having an unpronounceable surname: big wigs call you by your Christian name, implying closer acquaintance than actual. Talk about milking a compliment. As if in response to a comment made well after his death, and determined to exploit the much vaunted land of opportunity where circumstances had landed him, my father went in search of work – rather than a rich girl to marry. Still, he faced some difficulty as his military education in Russia was not a convincing qualification for an American civilian employer. But he had languages – not so common even amongst the best educated Americans. He spoke faultless English, French, German, Russian and Polish. He ventured down to Wall Street and secured a modest position with a firm called Prince & Whitely. This house, already established by the time of the Spanish American War, described itself in a 1901 edition of Poor's Manual – a precursor of Standard & Poor's, the rating agency – as "Bankers and Brokers, Exchange Court Building, No 52 Broadway, New York … All Classes of Railway Stocks also Grain, Provisions, Petroleum, and Cotton, Bought and Sold on Commission. Special Attention Given to Investments". This last bit to indicate that Prince & Whitely was not just a commodities house. They were also the first NYSE member firm to establish a private telegraph wire and office in Washington and were known for having given its own traders and clients several minutes' advantage before the market shock following the assassination of President Garfield in 1881. But their interest in young Yassukovich was that they not only had important foreign trade and overseas correspondents, they were also specialist in international arbitrage.

The evolution of international financial markets tracks with remarkable fidelity the evolution of communications technology. Telegraph, telephone, telex, fax and now, the internet have each ushered in a new era. With the laying of trans-Atlantic cable in the late 19th century, international finance took a great leap forward. Even today, that first innovation lives on with the expression "cable" to mean the U.S. \$/£ exchange rate, still in use in the modern foreign exchange market. The pound sterling is the only currency for which the UD dollar is quoted against rather than the other way around, a tradition briefly at risk when the pound sank almost to parity in the '70s. In the early 20th century an increasing number of common shares of transnational companies were quoted on several exchanges. South African gold mining shares – known in the market as "kaffirs" – were quoted in Johannesburg, Paris, and London, Berlin and popular in New York. A number of American mining shares were quoted on the Paris Bourse and many American common and preferred shares were quoted in London – known as "Yankees". This produced opportunities for time arbitrage: the purchase/short sale of shares in one centre for resale or short covering in another, the time lapse involved in telegraph communication allowing for price movements which could be substantial. An alleyway off Throgmorton Street in the City of London, close by Capel Court, the Bank of England and the Stock Exchange, was called Shorter's Court; arbitrage jobbers congregated there and fired off cables via fleet footed lads who ran back and forth from the Cable Office. Just as Capel Court was named after Sir William Capel, a Lord Mayor of London in the 16th century, I suspect Shorter's Court was named after a Mr Shorter, and had nothing to do with the business of selling short. But I have no idea who he was. In the 1920s and '30s, a popular arbitrage stock was the Victor Talking Machine Company, a predecessor of RCA and a number of other offshoots. Its logo was the famous dog listening to a megaphone speaker –"His Master's Voice". Roughly half the company was owned in the UK and the other half in the U.S. Shares were quoted in both London and New York. On occasion, a volume several times the company's market capitalisation was turned over in the arbitrage market. Arbitrage houses, such as Prince & Whitely in New York, maintained joint accounts with jobbers in London and brokers in the other major centres. Gains and losses were split down the middle; the relationships were so strong that they acted as a single agency, one partner effectively committing the other's capital in large positions with no time for consultation. *Dictum Meum Pactum* in spades.

Of course New York/London traffic posed no language problems. In those days, east coast Americans spoke English with only a slight twang and wrote it like the English. But the ability to draft cables quickly and accurately in French and German was in short supply as there were few linguists on Wall Street. So began my father's first gainful employment and his education in the international securities market. He never really looked back. He was soon joined at Prince & Whitely by other compatriots, including his childhood friend Juri Havemann, and a member of the distinguished Stroganov family. This émigré hated it when, on being introduced, he was immediately queried about *Boeuf Stroganov*, a dish invented by a French chef to the family in the 19th century. "I cannot stand that dish!" he would exclaim, "the ruination of good beef." Personally, I love it – and make quite a decent example. Apparently, it was a while before this new career provided my father with total independence. He still lived with his father and stepmother and would see his weekly salary dissipated in the night club excursions which the General was fond of. This was Prohibition and the era of "speakeasy" drinking establishments. The champagne which was my grandfather's favourite tipple was smuggled from Canada. I was told that a favourite establishment of his was the Copacabana nightclub. When I entered nightclubbing age in the 1950's, I mostly frequented El Morocco and the Stork Club – the Copacabana was associated with the Mafia by then. Finally, my father was able to secure his own lodgings. These consisted of one room so small, he could open the cupboard and bathroom doors, and the drawers of the dresser without getting out of bed. His most important budget item was laundry as he had such an active social life that keeping his stiff fronted dress shirts and collars clean, starched and shiny was his overriding concern. It was white tie and tails most evenings. Years later, Mondays at the Metropolitan Opera afforded his only full dress occasion and, with a dearth of satisfactory laundries in New York, my father airmailed his dress shirts and wing collars to Claridge's in London to be dealt with and returned.

The "Roaring '20's", when Prohibition caused alcohol consumption to soar, has been chronicled more than any decade in American history. It was a prime example of America's love affair with extremes. The belated entry of the U.S. into WWI had a far greater impact on the national psyche than the comparatively few casualties would suggest. Compared to British, French and German losses, America escaped lightly – of course, with a much shorter engagement. This was well illustrated in 1964 at Henley Regatta when the entire Harvard crew of 1914 was able to climb into a boat and row a lap of honour to commemorate the fiftieth anniversary of their earlier appearance. At stroke was former Massachusetts Governor and Senator Leveret Saltonstall. I would guess that very few, if any members of the Oxford and Cambridge crews of 1914 survived the Great War. Still, returning veterans of the Expeditionary Force under General Pershing felt that they were owed a major celebration. The national mood was now one of new confidence. The prominent role played by President Wilson in the Paris Peace conference, when he seemed able to impose American values on both the allies and the vanquished – with questionable consequences – the war-induced boom in manufacturing and agriculture, the increase in telephone and motorcar ownership, the new motion picture industry – all combined to give Americans a huge lift, and to reinforce the "sky's the limit!" philosophy which the westward expansion of the 19th century had established. This new mood is beautifully captured in F. Scott Fitzgerald's short story *May Day,* where two demobbed soldiers are bingeing in Manhattan, and end up drunk in a skyscraper lift. "Which floor?" asks the lift boy. "Top floor!" says the first soldier. "No! Higher" says the other. "Yes! Higher! Higher!" they both chorus.

John Kenneth Galbraith has written the definitive account of the economic excess which led to the Great Crash of '29, although history assigns a far greater significance to this event than justified, as a cause of the great depression of the 1930s, which was much more the result of misguided monetary policy in Europe. We shall soon see proof of this as roughly the same misguided policies are being pursued in Europe today – with similar consequences to follow. I know little of the detail of my father's career at Prince & Whitely during this exciting decade. It was the period when, in the investment world, the traditional asset mix giving preference to fixed income securities over equities was dramatically reversed. The focus was domestic – on U.S. blue chips and various investment trusts floated to capture the appetite for equity. But the taste for foreign securities was also rising, and Prince & Whitely capitalised on this. As well as the main commodities, the firm also dealt in foreign exchange. Higher yielding bonds issued through New York by emerging Latin American and Eastern European countries began to come into prominence, as the U.S. dollar was just beginning to rival the £ sterling as a reserve currency. This was the origin of the Foreign Dollar Bond market – of which much more later in this memoire. The foreign arbitrage desk at Prince & Whitely, manned by some Russian émigrés with an old "coffee grinder" calculating machine, was a main supplier of foreign stocks and shares to the banks and investment houses of the Street.

I knew more about my father's social life than his business activity during this period – not from him, but from various family friends he had met at the time. In particular, one or two happily married ladies, I knew as friends of the family, told me quite candidly that they had been madly in love with my father. Photographs of him of the period show someone with the exotic, Rudolf Valentino look fashionable at the time. He certainly "got around", as they say. It is interesting to note how working hours in Wall Street and other financial centres have evolved. They were very civilised in those days – even more so in the City of London, where as late as 1961, when I arrived in the City, Rothschild's only started work at ten o'clock. The new technology of today, which has produced explosive growth in financial market velocity, seems to have lengthened working hours whereas logic would suggest they should be shortened. Not only did my hardworking father enjoy considerable leisure by current standards, but he found himself part of a new crowd much lionised by society. The Great War had produced a large exodus of glamorous, well-educated and potentially eligible young men from Europe to the land of opportunity. I say "potentially eligible" as they were mostly well born paupers. They came not only from the former Russian Empire, but from Germany, Austro-Hungary, France and so on. Europe lay in ruins. Political turmoil was rife – except perhaps in England. But the restless English veteran still had the Empire to emigrate to: Australia/New Zealand, the Rhodesia's, etc. The Continental émigré found cosmopolitan New York and the American dream more to his taste. A rich and highly cultured German Jewish bachelor called Fleischman had acquired a substantial mansion on Fifth Avenue, and kept a large household, including a French chef. He befriended and entertained European émigrés with great enthusiasm and probably provided financial assistance to more than one. Nowadays, of course, one would immediately assume a homosexual inclination and motive. But, the world was far less preoccupied with sexual orientation than now, and the thoroughly heterosexual young men that crowded Fleischman's dinners and receptions were entirely unconcerned. My father met a great many friends there, including the Clemm twins. Their family name was actually Clemm von Hohenloe, and they were kinsmen of the princely German family of Reuss. The twins changed their name to von Clemm for convenience sake, and their son and nephew became my closest friend, colleague and collaborator, the late and much lamented Michael von Clemm.

Amongst the young ladies my father escorted – and apparently became quite serious about, was Dolly, only daughter of Duveen, the great art dealer. He had settled in a Fifth Avenue mansion and was busy flogging Great Masters to the oligarchs of the day, such as Samuel Kress, the retail magnate. Duveen sold the Italian works in partnership with Bernard Berenson who, from his famous Villa Il Tatti in Florence, supplied him with often rather dubious authentications. Of course, my father was not to know that – no one suspected at the time. Many years later, I met the famous Dolly. She had married a distinguished orthopaedic surgeon called Bobby Burns and lived in a Mayfair town house. She was very kind to my wife and me when we were a newly married couple living in London and invited us to her grand dinner parties. At these she enjoyed mixing both ends of the political spectrum and one was likely to see both Peregrine Worsthorne and Harold Wilson in active banter over the port – Dolly having sent the other ladies upstairs but remained herself to animate the conversation. In the drawing room was a portrait of Dolly as a young girl by Augustus John. She had been a striking, dark, raven haired beauty – a classical Rebeccah. But time and easy living had not been kind to Dolly physically, and I noticed a similar pattern with other American ladies, also understanding they had been within range of being my mother, as they were inclined to boast about my father having been a favoured escort back in the 'twenties. Dry martini cocktails and cigarettes are not recommended for the preservation of soft, girlish voices.

My father was much in demand as a spare man, and this role led, in a way, to my existence. It is certainly the moment to introduce my mother, who I hold entirely blameless for the principle fault in my upbringing: an attachment to luxury and the best of everything. Denise Jeanne Marguerite Henri was born June 21st, 1904 in Paris and fibbed about her age in later life – but by only four years, insignificant in percentage terms when she passed fifty. She always claimed to be eleven years younger than my father, but in fact, as my sister discovered, glancing at her passport when travelling together, the gap was six years. We should have guessed by a story she told. In the First World War, the Germans were at the gates of Paris, and children were evacuated – my mother to a small chateau in Brittany belonging to cousins. She remembered the thrill of running around barefoot on the lawn with her cousin. The lad had an English nanny from Cornwall, and when they went to Mass

48

one Sunday, the priest gave his homily in Breton and the nanny was amazed she could understand it – as she had been brought up speaking Cornish. My mother died at the age of 100 and a half, having fallen doing her morning exercises. My maternal grandfather was a reluctant banker, much preferring the literary life. But, of a Norman family of little means, he had to settle down working for his cousin as a partner in a Paris private bank called Dupont & Furlaud – Dupont being the cousin and rather forceful mentor. I have the extraordinary collection of leather bound, first editions of all the great French writers of the romantic period, illustrated with coloured engravings and lithographs, which my grandfather collected – some seven hundred volumes. I have yet to make a start on the entire works of Honoré de Balzac in forty-seven volumes. Dupont & Furlaud had as a speciality: the introduction of American mining shares on the Paris Bourse. I have already mentioned the appetite of the French for mining shares, but one should also recall the French were amongst the earliest foreign investors in American assets, buying tracts of land in New England in the 18th century. In the early 19th century, August Belmont represented the French Rothschilds in America. He went on to found the Wall Street firm of Dillon, Read. There was a successful investment company called Franco-Wyoming partly owned by French investors, in which Dupont & Furlaud had an interest. As a result of this transatlantic business, Dupont & Furlaud had a host of American correspondents in New York and other major centres. One of these was a Mr Gerald A Bramwell of 235 Commonwealth Avenue, Boston and my grandfather decided to send his youngest daughter Denise to stay with the Bramwells, learn English and all about America – a country he admired greatly, knew well through business, but had never visited. It seems he felt no need to send her to England to learn the language. I have failed to discover the exact nature of the relationship with the Bramwells. Mrs Bramwell was called Faithful and they had a daughter called Eileen and a son called Gerald Ames, at St. Mark's School in the late '20s. There was an American mining engineer called J. Herbert Bramwell, much involved in the development of coal mines in West Virginia, founding a town in his name which still exists. He died in Paris in the late 1890s. He had brothers; one married a Miss Moffat and the other, Percy Bramwell, was a well-known man about town at the turn of the century. It is possible the connection was through mining finance. My mother kept in touch with Eileen Bramwell, but she died long ago. The Bramwells invited Harvard undergraduates to entertain their young guest, but these were keen to improve their French and so my mother was rather short of English conversation. When they were all to go to New York City to attend a ball at the Plaza Hotel ballroom – which I knew well in later years. It was felt a French speaking escort was needed. Someone suggested a multi-lingual Russian émigré called Dimitri Yassukovich. He arrived a bit late. The family went on to Lake Placid, a fashionable winter sports resort, for the weekend. My father followed. Shortly after, Denise returned to Paris. Three months later, my father turned up there, took Denise out to dinner and proposed. This would have been only his third encounter with his bride-to-be. My grandfather fired off a series of cables to U.S. correspondents seeking references. Russian émigrés were not thought to be universally genuine, and were frequently fortune hunters. Reports were apparently favourable and they were married on 22nd July 1929 at St. Phillippe du Roule, near the Parc Monceau. My father's best man was Patrick Hennessy, playboy heir to the Cognac fortune, who was much in New York in the '20s.

Established with his bride in New York in a small apartment on Third Avenue, my father was offered a partnership in Prince & Whitely, but he needed to raise $25,000 – no small amount in those days. He had made many well-heeled American friends, but he was reluctant to ask them. He also had a feeling that an equity bubble might be close to bursting. Amongst his friends were two Yale graduates from prominent families in Grenwich, Connecticut: Joseph Verner Reed and John D. Barrett. Both were to play prominent roles in our family life. Joseph Reed was the scion of a Colorado mining and real estate fortune. His grandfather had been a typical prospector of the Golden West, making important silver discoveries but also having the good sense to acquire significant land holdings in the area in which the City of Denver was to rise from the Colorado plain. The Reeds also became investment bankers in Denver and promoted mining shares nationally and abroad. There is no evidence they ever dealt with Dupont & Furlaud in Paris, but the coincidence is striking. Joseph V. Reed's father had lived a life of leisure, largely travelling in Europe and his son was born in France. On coming down from Yale – where contemporaries included Cole Porter, Monty Wooley and Rudy Vallee – Joseph Reed enjoyed a substantial fortune but had no interest in business or finance. His passion, and clear vocation, was the arts – theatre in particular. He became a Broadway angel, partnering with Kenneth McGowan in a production company McGowan & Reed, producing such hits of the time as *Springtime for Henry*, casting Helen Hayes in various roles and discovering Katherine Hepburn. Reed went on to found the American Shakespeare Festival Theatre in Stratford, Connecticut, was cultural attaché to Ambassador Amery Houghton in Paris, founded the Hobe Sound Company which developed Jupiter Island, Florida, was a great collector of art of all classes, and wrote several books, including a classic: *The Curtain Falls,* about his theatre experiences. A polymath of exquisite taste, culture and kindness, he married Permilia Pryor, whose family owned the Winchester Arms Company. They had four sons and a daughter. The eldest son married my sister and all the brothers were schoolmates and close friends of mine all my life. John D "Jack" Barrett was another example of the highly cultured and cosmopolitan Americans who populated the East Coast. He and my father travelled extensively together in Europe. Jack Barrett ran the Bollingen Press, the publishing arm of the Mellon Foundation, which published all the works of Karl Jung. Jack was my father's best friend and my godfather. The Reeds and the Barretts immediately took to my mother when she arrived as the bride of their good friend Dimitri. They were all Francophiles and French speaking and there is no question that the warmth of their welcome and the lifelong friend-ships that ensued were the major factors in the acclimatisation and American-isation of my mother. On the other hand they were exceptional, and this left my mother with a somewhat misleading impression of the country in which she lived for the rest of her life. I used to suggest to her that the friends and acquaintances with which kind fate had surrounded her, emanating as they did from the great cities and their fashionable suburbs and resorts – the elite, in fact, were not necessarily typical of the country as a whole.

CHAPTER V

The client always comes first

-An old principle, now thoroughly outdated, which used to underpin the practice of investment banking-

Sometime after his arrival in New York, my father had joined Squadron A, a fashionable National Guard cavalry regiment with an armoury on the Upper East Side. My father's military upbringing left a permanent mark which persisted through his life. In those days he missed being in uniform, and this gave him a weekly opportunity to wear one. Squadron A claims to have invented indoor polo, which was played, three a side with a soft, mini soccer ball, on the parade and exercise arena in the armoury. I doubt the claim. In summer there were manoeuvres in upstate New York, and my father recalled the painful business of leading a mule with a dismantled machine gun packed on its back, the water cooled barrel of which would bang against the accompanying rider's knee. In addition to satisfying my father's military nostalgia, he made many friends at Squadron A. One of these was Alexander "Alec" White, son of Alexander M. White and nephew of Harold T. White. Their meeting was to have significant consequences. It not only shaped my father's future life and career – and mine, for that matter, but it created an association which was to become a major factor in the revival of an international money and capital market in the years following the Second World War. I say "revival" advisedly, and to gainsay those who claim the Euromarkets, as they came to be known, as a great innovation – an original invention, the brain child of its earliest pioneers, such as Sigmund Warburg, Bob Genillard, Andre Coussement, Armin Mattle, Hans Jorg Rudloff, Michael von Clemm, etc. – and even myself. The wheels which drove this great phenomenon were clad in tyres which in the automotive world would be called "retreads". Almost every instrument, every market practice, every financing concept, every syndication system, every practitioner behaviour and tradition, had existed before – as far back as ancient times, or been imported and adapted from techniques already developed in the American financial markets. As I approach the main theme of my memoir, it is important, if disappointing to the reader, to point out I will not be describing a financial revolution.

The New York stock market finally collapsed in late October, 1929. Much has been written about the Great Crash of '29 and I don't propose to add anything. As well as the carnage inflicted on private fortunes and market participants – although the number of those who threw themselves from upper stories in Wall Street has been exaggerated, a great many financial houses failed. Amongst those "hammered" was the venerable house of Prince & Whitely. The expression stems from the fact that, when a stock exchange official announced to the floor the name of a suspended firm, he banged a hammer down on the podium. I never learned the precise nature of the defalcation, but almost everyone in the Street was seriously overextended by then, not to mention the investing public. In the following days, my father was at a Squadron A drill and he mentioned casually to Alec White his relief that he had failed to find the capital to take up the partnership offered by Prince & Whitely and was therefore unscathed by their failure. "But you are out of a job!" Alec might well have said.

"As is my whole team," replied DY.

Alec White had a much laid-back style and often uttered important messages as if he was remarking on the weather.

"Well, we've been thinking about starting up a foreign department. Why don't you bring the whole bunch over to us?"

And so it was that my father and his four or five colleagues on the international arbitrage desk of Prince & Whitely picked up their "coffee grinder" calculator and went over to White, Weld & Co. at 14 Wall Street. They saw no reason to leave the calculator to the receivers.

My father's new home from home was a venerable house founded originally in May, 1895 by one George Barclay Moffat, then a general partner of the firm of Spencer Trask & Co., and his brother-in-law Alexander M. White of the Harvard Class of '92, who had first worked as a clerk at Spencer, Trask. The new firm was called Moffat & White and the two partners, with a cashier, an office boy and a stenographer occupied two rooms on the first floor of 30 Pine Street. The firm began by specialising in the shares of the various subsidiaries of the Bell Telephone Company. So for the time, they were in the high technology end of the market. In 1897, the firm moved to 1 Nassau Street, the old Manhattan Trust building and by 1905 business growth required a move to larger offices on the 12th floor of the Hanover National Bank building at 5 Nassau Street. In 1912, the firm moved again to 14 Wall Street where my father and his team eventually joined them in 1929. It is a tragedy that a proper history of White, Weld, leading up to the time it was acquired by Merrill Lynch in 1978, was never written. I can think of two reasons. The firm was almost obsessively conservative, never advertised – except the traditional "tombstone" announcements of capital transactions completed – and generally maintained a low profile. The moment to write such a history would have been when White, Weld gained particular prominence with the rise of the Euromarkets in the 1960s. However, for reasons that will be revealed further on, that period saw a widening split between the head office in New York and the fast growing international franchise run from Europe. So even a history strictly for internal consumption would have had to touch on awkward and contentious issues. By the time the semi-forced sale to Merrill Lynch occurred – on devastatingly unfavourable terms, the moment had passed. In 1915, the firm prepared a brochure summarising its history and setting out, in some detail, its organisation. The terminology is interesting as it has changed significantly. Then the firm had only a few departments: "Order and Trading", "Cashiers", "Statistical" – which would now be "Research", and "Office". The partners in charge of each are listed, but next to "Buying Department", it simply says "The Firm" i.e. everyone was responsible for finding and soliciting new business. The expression "cage" appears frequently: "Purchase and Sales Cage", "Security Cage", Bookkeeper's Cage", etc. I still remember areas in the New York and Boston offices, in the 1950s, fenced off by ceiling to floor wire mesh walls. In 1915, White, Weld already had branches in Boston, Chicago, Buffalo and Cleveland. The partnership evolved in the early 20th century. From 1902 until 1908, Harold T. White, brother of the founding partner Alexander M. was a partner, but he left in 1908 to found a firm called W. A. & A. M. White. I know nothing of its history. In 1905, Francis Minot Weld, class of 1897 at Harvard, joined the firm of Moffat & White. The Welds were a very old Boston family with a history in shipping. This first Weld in the firm had been with Blodget & Co. In 1906, Harold B. Clark, Harvard '01, became a partner, having been a salesman since graduation from Harvard. In May, 1910, the co-founder George Moffat retired as a general partner, becoming a special partner with liability limited, and the firm changed its name to White, Weld & Co. In 1912, four more partners were added: William Rutter, W. J. K. Vanston, Philip Cabot and Henry Thompson. One can assume they were all Harvard men. The 1915 brochure of the fairly newly renamed White, Weld & Co. offers insights on the business in its detailed description of organisation. The day-to-day commission business is fairly self-evident with references to listed, unlisted, options and so forth. But what is meant by "Outside Securities" or "Half stocks" is less clear. The "outside securities" might be foreign, or listed on regional exchanges. The section on The Buying Department lists "Competitive Buying" – most fixed income issues were underwritten and sold through competitive auction. "Buying through a Company's Fiscal Agent", "Buying Where Business comes to us through our Prestige or Banking Connections". The use of the word "prestige" here is the only example of self-promotion in the brochure. "Buying where we Become a Partner in the Business Offered by Other Houses" We would call this Syndicate. In fact the business of Wall Street changed little in these halcyon years before the Crash and the Glass-Steagal provisions of the early '30s. Although the commercial banks were just that, many participated in securities underwriting. But their core business was deposit taking and commercial lending. Many NYSE firms were bankers as well, as they kept client funds on deposit, accommodated overseas correspondents and carried out some banking functions such as letters of credit and commercial paper – but their core business was securities: underwriting/distributing, trading, buying and selling on commission. The "trust-busting" administration of PresidentTheodore Roosevelt and a series of legislative reforms had dampened down the hectic merger mania of the railroad and industrial consolidations of the late 19th century.

But the Roaring 'twenties had seen a huge expansion in equity investment, as already noted, and the White, Weld that my father joined in 1929 was largely an equity house. This is not to say that bonds as an asset class had been totally relegated. Most trustees of estates, endowments, etc. were restricted to bonds. In F. Scott Fitzgerald's iconic classic of the period *The Great Gatsby*, the narrator Nick Carraway is a Wall Street bond salesman.

Wall Street had begun to come under regulatory pressure in the early part of the 20th century as a result of market scandals and increased volatility, beginning to affect a larger number of citizens as prosperity created a larger share owning class. The huge concentration of financial power represented by Wall Street began to trouble Congress. A committee chaired by a Senator Pujo decided to investigate what was known as the "Money Trust" – the word "Trust" having become synonymous with evil monopoly after President Theodore Roosevelt's reforms. Anti-Trust legislation was initiated at this time and is still very much with us. The Pujo Committee identified three banks and their leaders as the nucleus of this concentration of power: J. P. Morgan of Morgan, James Stillman of National City Bank, and George F. Baker of First National Bank. In one of those exercises in statistical extrapolation so beloved of politicians, the committee totted up the sum total of assets deemed to be under the control, or quasi-control, of these three titans. First they added the value of the direct shareholdings of the three in their banks and closely affiliated industrial interests, such as railroads. Then they added the aggregate value of the assets of the 70 odd industrial companies on which the three or their sons served as non-executive directors. This all came to the tidy sum of U.S. $ twenty-two billion. Add three zeros and you have an approximate current value. Of interest to Pujo were the "auxiliaries" or "secondary powers" which comprised the Money Trust. "Radiating from these principal groups", said the Pujo Committee report, "and closely affiliated with them are smaller but important banking houses such as Kissel, Kinnicut & Co., White, Weld & Co. and Harvey Fisk & Sons, who receive large and lucrative patronage from the dominating groups, and are used by the latter as jobbers and distributors of securities, the issuing of which they control but which for reasons of their own they prefer not to have issued or distributed under their own names. Lee, Higginson & Co., besides being partners with the inner group, are also frequently utilised in this service because of their facilities as distributors of se-

55

curities." So there you have it. This was the first anti-trust attack on Wall Street by Washington. A second was to follow in the 1950s in a celebrated action called "The United States vs. Morgan Stanley et al", heard by a Justice Medina, who after more than a year, threw the case out and castigated the U.S. Attorney General for wasting the Court's time. Both Pujo, and the Attorney General in the later case, were contending that the U.S. capital and money markets were a vast monopolistic conspiracy based on interlocking affiliations and massive "mutual back scratching", reciprocal conventions and practices. Pujo provides evidence for what I always understood to be a special relationship between White, Weld and the House of Morgan – a relationship which continued with Morgan, Stanley after the Wall Street reforms of 1933/4 had split commercial and investment banking. Many years later, in the 1960s when Morgan, Stanley still had no European presence, their very charming senior partner John Young thought nothing of making White, Weld's Zurich office his own when visiting that city. He would pop in, greet everyone affably, sit at an empty desk and start making his calls. This annoyed my then ultimate boss and senior partner in Europe, Bob Genillard. He complained to my father, who was a friend of John Young, and Bob's boss. DY replied that White, Weld had made so much money over the years as a favoured distributor and syndicate member in Morgan Stanley issues, that accommodating John Young in our office was the least we could do in gratitude.

Of course, White, Weld did not depend entirely on the patronage of J. P. Morgan to build its franchise and after the Great War, continued to develop all lines of business in equities – with no particular sector emphasis – bonds, corporate and municipal, but not in commodities, which many similar houses did. I don't know to what extent White, Weld suffered from the great market crash. Unlike contemporary investment banks, they did not maintain large positions and it is noted in the brochure that they did not deal on margin. One of the causes of the '29 meltdown had been that brokers were offering 75% margin facilities. Since the market fell by more than 30% in October, the underwater population was greater than those able to float. The firm must have been in fairly good shape to contemplate expanding into foreign business. For an old line, very "clubby" house to welcome a group of total foreigners – none of which had been to Harvard, was fairly earth-shaking. It must have been soon after his arrival that my father began to be called "DY". I suppose "Dimitri" was just too exotic. This appellation stuck with him throughout his career and was so widely used in the Street that he sometimes received correspondence addressed to "Mr Deewhy". My father's first task would have been to create a capability of dealing in foreign securities. No doubt he immediately contacted Prince & Whitely's overseas correspondents. One such, joint account partner would have been the London jobbing firm of Medwin & Lowy. When I arrived in London in 1961, one of my many introductions was to the then senior partner Joe Lowy who received me in his "box" in Throgmorton Street and explained why the dual capacity system then in force on

The Stock Exchange, London was far superior to the broker/specialist system on the NYSE. Medwin & Lowy were big in "Yankees" and it was Mr Lowy who regaled me with tales of the arbitrage coups the joint account of White, Weld and Medwin & Lowy had pulled off from Shorter's Court back in the '30s. Before the shock waves of the Great Crash, overseas interest in American investments had been on the rise, particularly in Europe. In Latin America, where the U.S. $ was already king, investment exposure to the U.S. for the rich had always been the norm. In Europe, a short-lived postwar boom began to be replaced by industrial unrest, political instability and a failure of monetary management. Speculative bubbles are nothing new. John Law's great Louisiana scam in France laid a foundation stone for the French Revolution. The South Sea bubble is legendary. In modern times there had been Hatry in the '20s in London and, of course, Ivar Kruger, the Swedish Match king, in the late '20s/'30s might be said to have been the Madoff of his time. He built an empire issuing paper of various classes in the European centres whilst cooking the books of his holding company. He travelled to New York seeking a Wall Street sponsor when his star in Europe was highest and called first at J. P. Morgan's offices, corner Broad & Wall Streets. The young partners crowded around, excited by this new prestigious potential client. After discussing a number of ways they could introduce him to the American capital markets, they remarked that, of course, merely as a formality, he would have to be received by the "Old Man". This was senior partner J. P. Morgan Jr., son of the celebrated J. P. After a decent interval, Kruger emerged from J. P. Jr's office and was courteously walked to the lift by the "Old Man". "What a charming man!" said J. P. after the lift doors closed. "Of course, we will do no business with him. He is obviously a crook." Crestfallen, the young partners wondered how to salvage something from the situation and decided to build some reciprocity by introducing Kruger to Lee, Higginson & Co., then based just down Broad Street in the palatial Lee, Higginson Bank building. As Pujo had noted back in 1913, Morgan and Lee, Higginson were not only geographically close, they were often linked in large transactions. Lee, Higginson was delighted at this new gift from their munificent neighbour and proceeded to place Kruger & Toll securities with their American accounts. There was no end to the services they would provide this new client. They even contacted Chiang-Kai-Shek, head of the Kuomingtang Nationalist Government in China to request a monopoly in matches for the whole of China for Kruger – which he happily granted. But, in early 1930, Kruger & Toll collapsed and Ivar committed suicide in Paris. Lee, Higginson and its partners were ruined.

The Crash of '29 wiped out more than half the member firms of the NYSE and banks began to fall like ninepins, a disaster which soon spread to the large population of regional banks and which persisted throughout the early'30s. But White, Weld not only survived but began to develop a substantial foreign business. The fledging foreign department based on DY and his team soon received a major collaborator and a partnership was born within the firm which would lead to greatness. A young Belgian called Jean Cattier joined in December of 1930. Cattier hailed from a Belgian family much connected with the Wallonia oligarchy which dominated Belgian finance and industry, the Janssens, Boels, etc. Through the Société Générale de Belgique and the Banque Générale de Belgique, steel and other heavy industries had grown to an importance well beyond the small size and relatively modest geopolitical standing of the host country. Of course it was the Congo which made the difference and it's Union Miniere, then the world's largest supplier of uranium, was the jewel in the crown. Jean's brother Pierre had been a much injured motor racing car driver. He and his wife also became great friends of my parents. As a child, I was impressed by Pierre's extraordinary consumption of cigarettes. He was the archetypal chain smoker, lighting one off the other with no interruption. His son John also came to White, Weld and was to become one of the principal architects of White, Weld International and a much valued collaborator and friend of mine. It should be noted here that nepotism was not only rife in those days but actually valued and encouraged. So it was that the nephew of one leading foreign partner and the son of another, were to help execute the potential of the foundations laid by their uncle and father. After WWII, the firm had a very busy office in Hong Kong, managed by G. T. Yuan, who had been a private banker in Shanghai before the war and the local correspondent of White, Weld. One day one of DY's partners in New York pointed out that everyone in the Honk Kong office was related to G. T., even down to the office boy and messengers. Wasn't this a bit unusual? My father explained that this was Chinese custom and as a result the office did not need to incur the expense of bonding the employees because none would dishonour the family be stealing even a pencil.

Jean Cattier, the new addition to the foreign department was three years younger than my father, born and educated in Belgium and having served internships in banking in Vienna, Amsterdam, Budapest, Brussels and London, Jean arrived in the U.S. in 1926. He worked first for Blythe, Witter and then became the U.S. representative for the Belgian investment bankers Raymond Buurmans. Jean had a splendid career at White, Weld and in many other affiliations. He became a partner in 1931, just before my father, and Chairman of the Executive Committee from 1955 until 1965. He and DY were a unique double act, as well as being intimate friends. Their backgrounds, personalities, skills and other attributes were entirely different but totally complimentary. Jean was a bond man and believed that safe and satisfactory returns on a private portfolio could best be achieved by a judicious investment and trading in foreign dollar bonds, the fixed interest asset class of choice for international clients. DY was an equity man and believed that long-term investment in the common shares of the leading American blue chip companies was the best route to investment success. Warren Buffet agrees. Jean Cattier achieved a higher level in the partnership than my father. This caused no jealousy or bitterness at all. Jean had two advantages: he was omnipresent in New York

58

whereas my father spent more and more time – eventually almost half the year, in Europe. But Jean had a wisdom and strategic insight much valued by his partners. In modern parlance, DY was essentially a relationship banker. Jean Cattier was an organisational and inside banker, whose unique perceptions of industry trends made him the right man to steer the whole firm at critical times. My father was the first to endorse that view. Together they forged the foreign department of White, Weld which was to become a key player in the resurgence of an international capital market, based largely in London.

CHAPTER VI

It's A New World

-Song by Harold Arlen & Ira Gerswin, written for the film *A Star is Born-*

Wall Street obviously suffered a major decline in general activity after the Great Crash as all lines of business, particularly the issuance of new securities, began to dry up. But firms had greater control of costs in those days. They were almost all partnerships and the partners were almost all comfortably off. There was no nonsense of bonuses having to be paid regardless of results. Partnership distributions ceased or were sharply curtailed but the partners did not starve. One small example of 1930s life style is the fact that Tommy Hitchcock became a 10 goal polo player – and a national celebrity, as polo had a national following – whilst working at Lehman Brothers. One has only to watch the Hollywood films of the early '30s to see that the lifestyle of the moneyed classes was not seriously reduced. President Herbert Hoover tried to mitigate the oncoming recession by major public works projects such as the Hoover Dam, and the disastrous Smoot Hawley Tariff Act. Protectionism was the knee jerk reaction to deteriorating economic conditions at the time, as economic science had not yet discovered that this policy was akin to throwing petrol on the fire. But the real conflagration was in Europe. At war's end, everyone was keen to get back on to the gold standard, then the Valhalla of international monetary stability. Great Britain went back in 1925. For Germany the return to a gold standard was a disaster. Hugely excessive reparations demanded by France, required Germany to ship all its gold, and then to print money, leading to the runaway inflation of the Weimar era, with well-known political consequences. The Gold standard was a recipe for deflation. The theory was that fluctuations in national external account balances would be adjusted by transfers of bullion by the central banks. A country in surplus would have increased its money supply, thus labour and material costs would have inflated to reduce its competitive advantage, and the reverse would happen for a country in deficit on its external account, as money in circulation would reduce, lowering costs through deflation. Unfortunately economic cycles are not so neat and are less than predictable Exchange rates were effectively frozen and national monetary management rendered impossible. Curiously, the European Currency Union of the present day is producing a similar effect, proving the adage that the political class has an aversion to learning from experience. In 1931, Austria's largest bank Creditanstalt, failed, producing a Europe-wide banking crisis. If the Crash of '29 and the subsequent U.S. protectionism had cocked the trigger for a global recession, this was the trigger pulled.

Foreign investment in U.S. securities had rocketed in the booming 1920s. But after the Crash and the subsequent depression, which really deepened in 1931, European portfolio inflows virtually collapsed. Strangely, direct investment increased slightly. But it is difficult to understand what inspired the partners of White, Weld to develop a foreign business. But then it is difficult to understand why Alec White hired DY and his team immediately after October 1929. With the addition of Jean Cattier in December 1930, one might assume simplistically that the cost of the foreign department had doubled. However, undeterred by this reversal of fortune for the whole of the securities industry, White, Weld decided to open offices abroad. External shocks seem to have been like adrenalin to White, Weld partners. Market crashes in '29? – open a foreign department. Washington unleashes a major assault on Wall Street in 1933? – open offices abroad. And, it was certainly, not just a major assault, but a revolution. The Securities Act of 1933 imposed national regulation on the issuance, underwriting and distribution of securities, requiring that new issues be registered with a newly formed Securities & Exchange Commission. Previously this activity had only been regulated at state level – the so-called "blue sky" laws. Unfortunately, these were left in place, adding to the administrative burden of national regulation. Franklin Delano Roosevelt, the "New Deal" President, seeking to appoint the first Chairman of the SEC, is reputed to have asked advisors: "Who's the biggest crook on Wall Street?" The answer came back: "That's easy: Joe Kennedy." "Good", said FDR, "He's our man!" The old theory that poachers make the best game keepers was well-established in Washington. The Banking Act of 1933, in addition to new authorities for the Federal Reserve System to supervise deposit banks, contained four provisions which came to be known as Glass-Steagall. These were not enshrined in separate legislation, as has been often assumed. They essentially required that commercial banks cease and desist from underwriting, trading and distributing securities, effectively limiting their involvement in the securities business to custody and clearance functions. This was revolution on Wall Street. The major banks all hived off their investment banking businesses to new partnerships in which they were forbidden to have any direct interest, although blood remained thicker than water. The most celebrated of these divorces was the creation of Morgan, Stanley & Co. – out of J. P. Morgan. A further Securities Act of 1934 regulated trading on exchanges and secondary markets. Nothing would ever be the same again – except that it would, in a slightly different form, some eighty odd years later.

DY moved to Paris in 1933, produced a daughter – my sister Ariane, and opened an office for White, Weld in the Champs Elysées. My mother's first sojourn in New York, in an apartment under the Third Avenue "L", had been brief, and her return to her native city was to be for her a golden period in her life. They settled into a bijou apartment in the Rue Octave Feiullet, near the Avenue Henri Martin, within easy walking distance of the Bois de Boulogne. They had a cook, butler, house maids, a ladies maid for my mother and a Swiss nurse for the children – all this on my father's relatively modest salary. But his salary was in U.S. $. Life in France was relatively cheap. In fact a good many Americans, their resources seriously depleted by the Crash, went to live in France. At the end of the '20s, France enjoyed the most favourable economic health in Europe. In 1927, France was the largest holder of gold in the world and reserves grew from 18 billion francs to 80 billion in 1930. There was no unemployment – the work force had been seriously depleted by the war. The French saved in gold – not in shares. They were unaffected by the Crash of '29. All seemed set fair. Interest rates were kept high to sustain a strong franc. But when the depression hit, it hit hard. The government of President Flandin had to ease up on a restrictive monetary policy. The Banque de France began to lose reserves. He was replaced by Pierre Laval who tried deflation, but then had to accept a deficit. It is said that when the saintly fall, they fall the furthest. Having been a paragon of monetary and fiscal purity, France was in crisis, its fall from economic grace sudden and profound. Unemployment soared. The government tried to reduce wages and provoked trade union outrage. Riots toppled the Laval Government and the Popular Front, an alliance of Socialists and Radicals, with communist support, led by Leon Blum, was elected. From now on, until the outbreak of war in 1939, France teetered on the edge. Official devaluation occurred in 1936, but the franc remained persistently weak A power struggle between far left and far right led to strikes, riots, government crises and a general sense of impending doom.

All of this seems to have passed my mother by, and I often chided her about it later on. For her life in Paris in the '30s was an extremely comfortable round of delights. The social whirl intensified, costume balls abounded, smart nightclubs and revues attracted talent from all over. Social life was one great explosion of *après nous le deluge.* For my parents there were weekends of golf at Mortefontaine, holidays at Le Touquet and Deauville, motor trips on empty roads, a Cote d'Azur un-blighted by development, skiing at Chamonix, and grandparents to dandle the children on their knees. My sister Ariane, born in April 1933, was so named because a current bestseller was a pot boiling novel called *Ariane, Jeune Fille Russe.* I marvel at the frivolity of this. I was born in February of 1935 and named, more seriously, after my great grandfather. We both saw the light of day at a fashionable natal clinic called the Chateau du Belvedère, which still exists in Boulogne-Billancourt. The good sisters who attended the cosseted mothers were shocked that my father never turned up. He was not comfortable with babies, or children for that matter, and had the handy excuse that visiting hours coincided with the busiest time in the office – when the NY market opened at three o'clock Paris time. Instead an old family friend called Bernard d'Escayrac would call as he worked at the Renault factory nearby and would stop on his way home to his apartment in Paris. My mother noticed the nuns looking from Bernard to the children, first my sister and then me, trying to spot a suspicious resemblance. Bernard was to remain a faithful family friend and, having no children of his own, was like an uncle to us both. He ended up running the operations of the perfume house Guerlain for the Americas. We children also lived a charmed life. We would be taken to the Bois de Boulogne where we played with a little Pattino girl, whose parents were neighbours. She ended up eloping with Jimmy Goldsmith and died in childbirth. An early memory is falling on a rock, opening a gash in my head and watching as the blood slowly suffused my nurse's broad white collar, as she carried me home. I also recall sitting on my grandfather's knees as he showed me picture books. Apparently my favourite was *1914*, which contained photographs of the monarchs and prime ministers who had, inadvertently or not, taken us into the Great War. There were also costume parties for children and I have photos of my sister in a Russian peasant girl dress and myself in the breast plate and helmet of a Polish Lancer.

Meanwhile, my father began to do a land office business in the White, Weld office in the Champs Elysées. The office was located rather conveniently for lunch just down from The Travellers, a highly cosmopolitan gentlemen's club established in the former Hôtel Paiva, a mock gothic extravaganza built by a sugar daddy for one of the "Grandes horizontales", as the courtesans were known at the turn of the century. My father liked to populate the overseas offices with customer's men, as they were then known – registered representatives became the eventual *nomenclature*, hailing from society circles. Men about town of good families forced to seek gainful occupation, they were French, Swiss, Belgian and Armenian, such as Gordon Turgel – who was to play a part in our lives. There was a de Montgolfier from Switzerland and a delightful, alcoholic Irishman called Johnny Haines. They were frivolous but productive. One morning, enjoying a moment of idleness, they were crowded around a bay window, ogling the elegant ladies traipsing down the Champs Elysées. One particularly well-dressed and petite lady caught their attention and they began making mock hand signals, beckoning her. At first they were delighted, if surprised, to see the lady turning towards the office building door. But this sentiment turned to consternation as they realised that the lady was Denise Yassukovich – the boss's wife. Such embarrassing frivolity apart, White, Weld, Paris found itself very much in the right place to exploit a growing flight of capital. After beginning the postwar decade with a strong economy, low unemployment, a balanced budget, high national and private gold reserves and a good deal of hope, France faltered and then began to stumble in the general malaise that followed the Creditanstalt collapse in Vienna in 1931. This, more than the Wall Street crash, was the trigger for the Great Depression. As is so often the case, almost all the macro-economic decisions taken were the wrong ones. France's political structure turned out to be more fragile than originally thought. Extremes of left and right emerged. Governments, based on loose coalitions, began to fall, deficits rose, gold reserves evaporated and confidence waned. Conditions in neighbouring countries were unhelpful. Inflation destroyed the Weimar Republic in Germany and the National Socialists began their march to power. Civil war broke out in Spain. All European currencies seemed at risk – even the pound sterling. The United States and the US dollar were the obvious safe havens. Although a great deal of Jewish money from Germany went to Switzerland, so great was the general disillusionment with Europe's future, that even that traditional haven suffered – simply by being in Europe.

There were not that many American financial institutions with offices in Paris – either investment or deposit banks. J. P. Morgan, which had been in Paris as Morgan, Hardges since the 19th century was one. An investment house called Fenner & Beane was also there. Many years later, when I was Chairman of Merrill, Lynch Europe, Middle East & Africa, I was visiting our private client office in Paris, managed by the long serving Merrill Lynch executive Jerry Villalba. He told me I was to meet the firm's oldest client and indeed a very distinguished and elderly gentleman, who turned out to have a son I knew at Dillon Read in London, told me his story. He was of Venezuelan origin, Jewish and a long-time resident of Paris before the war. Fearful of what was happening everywhere, but particularly in Germany, he had opened an account and put much of his life savings with the Paris office of Fenner & Beane. He managed to escape back to South America at the outbreak of war. After the war, he travelled to New York to "visit his money", as he described it. To his horror, he could find no Fenner & Beane in the NY telephone directory. He was distraught and told his tale of woe to a friend. "Try Merrill, Lynch," said the friend with a reassuring smile. Of course, Merrill had merged to become Merrill Lynch, Pierce, and Fenner & Beane. There was his account, safe and sound and having increased substantially in value. In today's world of money laundering safeguards and client due diligence red tape, one wonders if the same could occur today. White, Weld, together with its compatriot institutions, was literally deluged with new clients seeking the safety of a U.S. financial domicile. One day, a rather jolly Englishman walked into the White, Weld office in Paris and sent his card in to my father. He was Ronald Parvin, the General Manager of the Barclay's Bank branch in Biarritz, that popular watering spot for the rich and famous near Bordeaux. Ronnie – as we always knew him – was a typical example of the best of British clearing banking as it was then. Barclay's had a traditional presence in France and an upmarket customer base. Ronnie had served in Brighton, Paris, Le Touquet, Marseille and Nice. He was a crack golfer and had even been seconded to a

King's Bank unit in Germany. Cox's & King's was the British Army Officer's bank of choice. He had married a French lady. My father listened to a fascinating tale from him, one that illustrates the great unease of the times. A Spanish lady from Bilbao had walked in to Ronnie Parvin's office at Barclay's Biarritz carrying a large satchel, the contents of which she dumped on Ronnie's desk. There glimmered a huge pile of jewellery, gold ingots, share and bond certificates, cash and various items regarded as stores of wealth. The lady was terrified by the threat of civil war and its aftermath and wanted Mr Parvin to turn everything into liquid assets and invest the lot under a power of attorney she was prepared to sign on the spot. After valuation, it all came to close to a million pounds sterling. Clearing banks did not handle investments in those days – except to provide custody. In the UK, they were accustomed to appoint brokers on rotation and assign their customers to the broker of the moment for investment advice and transaction, a practice which rather stunned me when I arrived in London in 1961. Ronnie did not fancy his own country as a safe haven. Although, Britain had recovered from the worst of unemployment and the General Strike of 1926, the depression triggered by the banking crisis of 1931/32 had hit the country hard. Devaluation after leaving the gold standard and further industrial unrest was sapping confidence – hence Ronnie's visit to White, Weld in Paris. The account stayed with the firm throughout the war. When Ronnie Parvin retired, the Spanish lady passed the mandate to him personally. One of my most vivid impressions of the White, Weld office at One Union Court, when I arrived in 1961, were the regular visits of Ronnie to our then manager John Rasch. I was often invited to join the two for pink gins, followed by a four course lunch, with two wines at the Savoy Grill, always with a toast to the Spanish lady in Bilbao – my presence perhaps a tribute to DY, the originator of the account. Lunch was followed by a brief investment review and an occasional purchase or sale. We did not "churn"! When Ronnie Parvin died, John Rasch inherited the mandate even in retirement. When the lady died, she left the bulk of her fortune to the Royal Life Boat Association. Her husband's fortune was based on a Bilbao fishing fleet – often in British waters, and often subject to rescue.

My father had opened a London office for White, Weld in 1934 – originally as a joint venture with Old Broad Street Securities, a small merchant bank seeking a U.S. tie. The first office was in the Gerling Global Assurance Building in Cornhill. I have a vague recollection that the drunken Irishman Johnny Haines might have gone over from Paris as manager. Together with France, Britain had avoided imposing exchange controls following the financial chaos which struck after the Creditanstalt failure. Churchill, as Chancellor, had made the momentous decision of leaving the Gold Standard, the foundation, it seemed at the time, of world monetary stability and economic well-being. Devaluation had provided economic relief in the short-term but also prompted capital flight and eliminated the City as a provider of long-term finance in sterling to international borrowers. London remained a leading international financial centre and the "bill on London" – bills of exchange and letters of credit accepted, i.e. guaranteed by City merchant banks – remained the leading instrument for financing international trade. But "Yankees" were still a highly popular part of equity portfolios, together with "kaffirs". White, Weld now had the joint account with a jobbing firm specialised in overseas equities, Medwin & Lowy, which my father had managed for Prince & Whitely. DY began establishing agency relationships with banks, brokers and institutions with a traditional investment exposure to the United States. Not least among these were the investment trusts and insurance companies clustered in Charlotte Square in Edinburg. A good example was, and is, Scottish Widows. Scottish institutions had been pioneer investors in western real estate during the nineteenth century: cattle ranches in Texas and Montana, pineapple groves in Florida, forestry in Oregon. Scottish American Mortgage had been a provider of commercial mortgages to the U.S. for generations. Their interest in American equities was instinctive.

In late 1938, my father decided to move to London. The Paris office was well-established and doing well. I imagine he felt London needed personal attention, and as a partner in the firm, he was better placed to develop relationships there. My mother was not at all pleased. She recalled visiting houses, finding they all smelt of cabbage, the staff quarters were lamentable, the streets and, therefore the interiors, were awash with coal dust. Furthermore, the food was inedible, the ladies badly dressed, the social customs barbaric – ladies left the dining room for the gentlemen to smoke cigars and drink port, and the cook and butler intimidating. For my mother, it was leaving heaven to enter hell. I don't think she ever recovered from her aversion to London and English life. For my father, it was the opposite. He was in seventh heaven. He was of an intensely anglophile Russian generation. In the 18th century, Russia had become Francophile. French tutors, refugees from the French Revolution, found work on country estates. Children of the nobility were bought up speaking French which became the language of society. French and all things French dominated Russian culture. In the late 19th century and early 20th, a change occurred. Suddenly English nannies, race horse trainers, dogs, gardens, customs in general became "in". The Tsar corresponded with the Tsarina in English. The English Club in St. Petersburg was the club of choice. And so my father was a lifelong admirer of all things English. Already in the late '20s he had patronized the Saville Row tailors Anderson & Sheppard and they "made" for him, as tailors say, for the rest of his life, and for me, and for my son Nicholas. He had his shoes made by Lobb in St. James's and this led to an awkward moment for my mother. One of my father's classmates at the Corps of Cadets had been Prince Dmitri of Russia, a grandson of Nicholas I, who had escaped the Bolsheviks with his aunt the Dowager Empress on a Royal Navy frigate sailing from the Crimea. He and my father hooked up again at the Travellers in Paris and renewed a childhood friendship. Prince Dmitri also had his shoes made by Lobb and his feet, and therefore his last, were the same as my father's. Dmitri lent him a pair whilst he was waiting for his own and my mother spotted them in a cupboard, saw Prince Dmitri's name inside, and suddenly thought she was married to a member of the Imperial family in hiding. Such romantic notions were not uncommon at the time.

Our mother finally found a house which smelt a bit less of cabbage, in Norfolk Crescent, in between Oxford and Cambridge Squares. This was then the unfashionable side of Hyde Park, but handy for Paddington Station and the West Country – not that my parents ever ventured there. We had a butler called Smith, tall enough to lift our tricycles, with my sister and me already aboard, over the railings and into the crescent garden. More significantly for us a nanny was engaged – Miss Peterson from Peterborough. Nanny terrorised our mother, rather than her wards. She caught mother calling me "Stani", the widely acknowledged diminutive for my Christian name. "Madam!" exclaimed Nanny... "His name is Stanislas and he should be called so by all." Mother was rather taken aback, but complied. Nanny had worked for the Lithaby family. Years later, I met John Lithaby, a senior partner of Panmure Gordon in the City. We discussed whether some bond existed between children raised by the same nanny. I thought perhaps; he thought not. I suspect he considered Nanny had let the side down by going to work for a foreign family. In those days nannies were known by the surname of their employing family. Poor Nanny – she took us to Hyde Park, every day, in one of those big double carriages, lacquered in black, fashionable at the time. The nannies met to gossip discreetly about their employers. She had to introduce herself as "Nanny Yassukovich". I imagine another nanny saying "Bless you!" assuming Nanny had sneezed. Through the nanny mafia my parents met Sir John and Lady Child. He was an officer in the Scots Guards, and she was Canadian. Mother and Lady Child became fast friends, even sharing the same fortune teller, and this helped mother to acclimatise. Ariane and I played with the Child children in the Park, and Dirdre, sister of the actor Jeremy Child, and I have kept in touch ever since. I suppose through that connection, Nancy Mitford came to dinner one night. Apparently when the men went up to the drawing room after finishing their port, they found Nancy standing on her head, her long skirt, tastefully gripped between the ankles. She was showing the ladies a latest well-being technique. Before dinner, my sister and I were always paraded and introduced to the guests, Ariane dropping curtsies and I kissing ladies' hands. Then, it was back to the nursery. In Nancy Mitford's classic novel *The Blessing*, about a dysfunctional Anglo-French marriage, a children's party in Paris is described; among the guests are a brother and sister named Oriane and Stanislas. I wonder if the author didn't make a note of our names that evening in 1939, getting one letter wrong. One day, again I suspect through Lady Child, mother was persuaded to volunteer me to present a purse to Queen Mary at a charity garden party at St. James's Palace for the National Council for Maternity and Child Welfare. Nanny rehearsed me for weeks. Sadly, at my first quasi theatrical gig, I froze. The *Daily Mirror* of July

6th 1939 splashed it across the back page, under a 25 point headline: "HE DIDN'T KNOW WHEN TO STOP" There I am, dressed in a short-sleeved, Peter Pan collared silk shirt, grey flannel shorts, white knee stockings – one sagging slightly, and buckled, patent leather shoes. I am bowing low in front of Queen Mary who is sitting holding a parasol. I have one arm folded neatly against my middle in front but the other is stuck straight out behind, fingers splayed. It was, of course, supposed to be tucked against my back. I had bowed, handed over the purse, and then bowed again. But I forgot what to do next and remained bowed. A subsidiary photo shows a lady-in-waiting gently leading me away. The occurrence drew a rare smile from Queen Mary. Nanny did not know whether to be mortified or secretly pleased by the publicity. I have the clipping where she has just written "Stanislas" under the main photo.

I have little recollection – I was only 4 ½ – or evidence of the business of White, Weld's London office in the late 1930s. The arbitrage activity in Shorter's Court continued a pace and the joint account with Medwin & Lowy was still in place. Although the devaluation of the pound sterling in 1933 had ended London's pre-eminence as an exporter of capital through foreign bonds denominated in sterling, London was still a financial hub and a centre for foreign securities activity. I do remember my father telling me that, with their joint venture partner Old Broad Street Securities, WW had undertaken a financing transaction for the Société de Bains de Mer in Monaco, the controlling entity of the Monte Carlo casino. He found this amusing since his grandfather was known to have dropped a fortune there. London in the mid to late 1930s began to receive an influx of German Jewish bankers, bringing with them the cosmopolitan financial culture which had always characterized German private banking. Many became friends of DY. Oscar Joseph of Leopold Joseph & Sons, "Bli" Bleichroeder at Samuel Montagu, Francis Hoch, at Singer & Friedlander – all were on my list to contact when I came to London in 1961. But I was given a warning anecdote about Mr. Hoch. Although Britain had no exchange controls in the '30s, Germany had, after the financial turmoil of the collapse of the Weimar Republic. Singer & Friedlander had engaged in a transaction in violation of German exchange controls and been heavily fined, an incident published in the British press. My father met Francis Hoch in a City street and commiserated. "My dear Dimitri," said Francis, with a smile, "we made three times the fine on the deal." My father was shocked. How might he react, one wonders, to the practice today of banks budgeting for regulatory fines as a cost of doing business. Other friends made then became my early contacts in London. George Loveday of Read, Hurst Brown, whose son Mark became a senior partner of Cazenove, Victor Brooks and Nils Taube of KitKat & Aitken, the latter a Russian baron, David Scholey's father Dudley, then a partner of Guinness Mahon, whose name my father always pronounced with a soft "sch" – David became a great friend, and the leading light at S G Warburg. During this period, my father opened an office in Amsterdam and found a charming and extremely competent manager

68

in Manfred Rothbart, who was to make a considerable contribution to the firm after the war by introducing to his boss a young Cambridge graduate named John Stancliffe. DY had found an experienced Englishman named John Rasch to manage in London. He also recruited as an administrative manager and all around office "mother" – one Joyce Goodrich, whose loyalty and help in all matters in any way connected with the firm, DY and his family, knew no bounds.

And so, as war loomed in 1939, White, Weld had a strong presence in London and on the Continent, probably more entrenched than rival American houses whose business was essentially to serve the large American population in Europe. White, Weld's European client base was almost entirely European and it enjoyed correspondent relationships with a large number of banks, brokers and institutions which were to form the basis of its postwar overseas franchise. In the first week of September, 1939, mother, Ariane and I were on holiday in Vichy, France – without Nanny and only mother's maid. Our father was hard at work in London. He rarely accompanied on family holidays, being allergic to children. I can remember standing on a balcony outside our hotel suite and listening to a sound lorry, with big bell shaped loudspeakers on the roof, blaring out news of the invasion of Poland and the impending declarations of war. Panic ensued. DY rushed to make arrangements to ship us instantly to New York. There was no time to get back to London and collect Nanny and our things. Mother was still a French citizen, although we, the children, had been registered at birth at the U.S. consulate in Paris and had American passports. Father managed to get a visa for Mother, but not for her maid. She was French, in any case, and was happy to go home to Normandy. Passage was booked on a French line steamship leaving for New York from Cherbourg, and Gordon Turgel, a charming Armenian from the Paris office, was asked to escort us. DY was to stay behind to close the European offices. He closed Paris and Amsterdam, but decided not to close London, leaving John Rasch and Miss Goodrich in charge. He took this decision on his own and neglected to inform his partners in New York. Such was the informality and trust which characterized partnership arrangements in Wall Street at the time – which no one ever enquired. I am sure he told Jean Cattier, but he would not have dreamt of breaching DY's confidence. The decision was to have very useful consequences many years later. I have memories of the passage over. My sister Ariane pulled me back from a porthole which I had half climbed out of whilst Mother was in the bathroom; the first of several occasions when she saved my life. Gordon Turgel took us to the bar one day and said, "Don't say a word to your mother, but I am going to introduce you to something very American.... Barman! Two Coca-Colas! – and a whiskey for me." Of course, Mother found out and was furious. She was not a happy lady on that crossing. Although, she had enjoyed her brief sojourn in New York after her marriage in 1929, she was now leaving her parents and sister behind to an uncertain fate in a Europe at war. She had no doubt DY would be fine and would soon join. I assume she was grateful that she had married a partner of a New York investment bank and was now headed for safety.

CHAPTER VII

The Gentle Calling of High Finance

-Chapter heading from David Landes' *Bankers & Pashas*-

The time has come to introduce the heroine of my narrative. I have decided on a heroine, rather than a hero, because she was at first a thing of beauty. She then went on to mother a large brood of offspring – some not so beautiful. I must first use her maiden name, of course. Jane Austin does not introduce a Mrs Darcy nor Shakespeare a Juliet Montagu. But even here, there is a dilemma. My heroine was to become known as the Eurobond; but she was born simply a foreign loan, before her début as a foreign dollar bond. But a lavish debutant party she had, so my heroine will be introduced as the Foreign Dollar Bond, until she undergoes a transformation as dramatic and life-changing as marriage. I make no excuse for the lengthy discourse on her family background which now follows. She is just as entitled to a genealogical introduction as my family – if not more so. The Eurobond was to become the core of White, Weld & Co.'s successful international franchise in the second half of the 20th century, and White, Weld was at the heart of the life and career of my father and me.

The practice of a borrower, usually the sovereign, contracting a loan in his own jurisdiction to have it subscribed by a lender, or lenders in another is as old as time. This is because if the borrower needed to borrow, he had probably run out of sources in his own realm and had to look to foreign, often itinerant lenders, such as Templars, Jews, merchants, or other mercenary elements. There is an old adage, almost entirely neglected throughout history, which cautions: never lend to the prince unless you are prepared and able to collect by force, because, if he defaults, you will never win a judgment in the prince's own court. Earliest cross border loan arrangements were always recorded in some manner, but they were bi-lateral contractual agreements and were not usually transferable. The princes facing bankruptcy and having recourse to foreign borrowing in the Middle Ages were usually illiterate and relied on monks to record their transactions. As history relates, in a good many cases these contracts were not worth the parchment they were recorded on –

to paraphrase Sam Goldwyn's famous malapropism. In ancient times we find the first examples of cross border finance and the first examples of default.

The first financial instrument in wide use internationally was the bill of exchange. Used exclusively by merchants trading across borders, this was simply an acknowledgement of a debt and a promise to pay at some future time in another place and in another currency. It laid the foundation stone for all future methods of international payment and, therefore, of international trade, or as we now grandly call it: global trade. But this was the quintessential short-term financial instrument. Its critical characteristic, as with its successor instrument, the letter of credit, was that it was self-liquidating and absolutely had to be issued in connection with a genuine underlying transaction of purchase and sale of goods. This principle held good for centuries until it was ultimately degraded by greedy bankers. It was the bill of exchange which created the first members of a trade – banking is not a profession – now generally called banking. Today we have any number of variations of this trade: investment bankers, commercial bankers, private bankers, deposit bankers, mortgage bankers. I could go on by listing: foolish bankers, dishonest bankers and phony bankers. But the first bankers were merchants and, therefore, ultimately: merchant bankers. The primacy of the merchant title carried on until fairly recently. As late as the mid-nineteenth century, bankers on the Court of the Bank of England were still listed as "merchants". Merchants slipped into being bankers because they were forced to handle money to trade internationally. The bill of exchange had a dual function. It ensured that the seller in one place got his money from a buyer in another place and that the buyer got his goods. Without such a facility, commerce would have not developed beyond face-to-face transactions. But since a time lapse between payment and delivery was unavoidable, finance was needed and this involved interest, forbidden by the Catholic Church. The bill disguised the interest in two ways: through the exchange involved in a multi-currency trade and the discount to face value involved in the bill's ultimate collection. It is widely assumed that the dominant position of Jews in finance is because their religion does not forbid the charging of interest. This is an oversimplification. If it was sinful to charge interest as a lender it was also sinful to pay interest as a borrower. In fact, Jews and Arabs in the Levant were simply in the best position to exploit the explosion of trade in spices between the East and a Europe without fridges to conserve food. Spices were to the Middle East then what oil became in modern times. Arab banking is as old as Jewish banking. I used to point that out to bemused colleagues when I was on the board of Arab Banking Corp International. In Europe and in the U.S., most of the old established merchant and investment banks were merchants to start, mostly in soft commodities: Lazard and Lehman in cotton are classic examples. Barings dealt in coffee from Java and iron from Russia. Even the early Rothschilds dealt in staples like quill pens and umbrellas. But, beginning as early as the 17th century, standards began to slip. The age old principle that paper was issued only for self- iquidating transactions began to be flexibly interpreted. The age of "accommodation" had begun. "Banker's bills", "finance bills", "open credits" – a plethora of devices to obtain money on commodities and transactions that never were, began to emerge. Apologists would say that additional liquidity was created. Money was effectively being printed, thus financing the expansion of commerce and investment. The problem, as always, was – where were the brakes? If I was a trained economist, I could produce an algebraic formula which correlated the expansion of transactional volume and the population of participants, with a decline in financial standards. Put another way, the more people at a party, the more likely it is to get out of hand. That was certainly the case when I was a teenager. An early example of problems due to bankers' excesses was in 1763 when Amsterdam and Hamburg "were shaken by an unprecedented crisis whose severity was due largely to the collapse of a wide and complicated network of systematic accommodation", according to financial historian David Landes. He goes on to say: "The most treacherous aspect of accommodation and overtrading was that those very houses that would not dream of conniving at these methods, found themselves inexorably drawn into the all-embracing web of paper credit. After a certain point, it was impossible to say where bad bills left off and good bills began." Substitute "derivatives" for "bills" and you have a neat description of the Lehman Bros. crisis. We have a similar example of a breakdown in basic banking principles today in so-called "covenant light lending".

Merchant banking in its purest form was about financing trade. Even after, merchant banks in Europe diversified into investment and private banking, trade finance remained a core business. This is illustrated by what was the most exclusive club in the City when I arrived in 1961. The Accepting Houses Committee was comprised of the main merchant banks and admission was next to impossible for new comers. Sigmund Warburg had to buy an existing member, Seligman Brothers, to gain admission for his newly founded S. G. Warburg. The core business of the accepting houses, as they were still called, was just that: the acceptance, i.e. the endorsement, of commercial bills. This form of guarantee constituted an off-balance sheet item, in effect, and the volume of acceptances outstanding was significant in relation to the rather modest capital shown in merchant bank balance sheets. As a result, these privileged houses were permitted to keep "hidden reserves", their extent known only to the Bank of England. Modern proponents of full disclosure in all matters financial are, of course, horrified. But one might point out that full disclosure did nothing to contain the last financial crisis, which brought banks world-wide to the brink of collapse, after the Lehman debacle. The beauty of it was that most people though these hidden reserves were far greater than they were in reality, and accepting houses had almost unlimited access to the money market. When they finally had to be disclosed, under pressure from the auditing profession, there was general astonishment. The honourable title of "merchant bank" began to be abused in the 1980s by ignorant practitioners in Wall Street who described the practice of taking equity stakes in companies to provoke a merger or restructuring, as "merchant banking". Ironically, equally ignorant practitioners in the City described the same activity as "investment banking". Of course it was nothing of the sort in either case. Fortunately, the emergence of private equity funds restored a healthy differentiation in financial functions. However, the orgy of post Big Bang consolidations in the financial services industry finally confined the art of merchant banking to the history books. Only two great names survive: Lazard and Rothschild, but they are the exceptions which prove the rule.

Germane to my story, however is the evolution of merchant banking towards investment banking, which one can trace to the end of the 18th century. For the best definition of investment banking I have ever come across, I turn again to David Landes and his seminal opus *Bankers and Pashas.* "Investment banking is essentially the provision of funds for long term use. This may take the form of contracting for an issue of government bonds, or the flotation of industrial stock, or loans on mortgages. The important thing is that, in contrast to commercial banking, which aims at financing specific business transactions of limited maturity, investment banking is intended to make possible the creation or utilisation of durable capital. It implies, therefore, the immobilisation of funds of either the banker or the ultimate investor over a considerable period of time." This may seem a lengthy definition, but on close examination one finds a summary description, of everything we used to do at White, Weld & Co., as did also our Wall Street competitors. The first part is an obvious description of the new issue business. The reference to "utilisation of durable capital" is the agency broking business, because this ensures the liquidity of outstanding securities and hence facilitates new capital formation. The "immobilisation of funds of either the banker or the ultimate investor" refers to the capital tied up in underwriting and market making and the investment portfolios of clients. The evolution of the classical merchant banking business model towards investment banking is also the story of families, generally of some minority group forced to emigrate and settle in an accommodating jurisdiction. Inter-marriage within groups helped to form cohesive dynasties and formed an eventual basis for the syndication of large transactions. In Germany, the great Jewish banking families were the Oppenheims of Cologne, the Bambergers of Mainz, the Habers of Karslruhe, the Heines and Warburgs of Hamburg, the Mendelsohns of Berlin, and, of course, the huge Frankfurt contingent: the Rothschilds, Sterns, Speyers, Erlangers, Goldschmidts, Shusters and Seligmans. The Calvinists, chased from pillar to post in the Thirty Years War, scattered to Geneva, Basel, Genoa, and London – finally congregating in Paris in the early 18th century. They formed a great Franco-Swiss banking community with families whose names still resound: Necker, André, Haller, Vernes, Greffulhe, Hottinguer, Mallet, Cottin, Odier, Schlumberger, etc. Another example of an ethnic banking fraternity would be the Greeks. They were refugees from Turkish domination and after the Greek revolt of 1821, they dispersed to Egypt, Italy, France and England. Families like the Zarifi, Zafiropoulo, Rodocanachi, Ralli and Vlasto established franchises specialising in Mediterranean commerce. Sadly, many of these names are forgotten. After retirement as a general partner of White, Weld, my father took on various consulting assignments. One was for Bankers Trust of New York who had just acquired a small merchant bank in London called Rodocanachi. The head of international for bankers was Dick Bliss, whose father Arthur Bliss was a former Chairman of the Bank of New York. Sadly, the son lacked the father's distinction. Bliss, accompanied by his consultant DY, set off for the traditional courtesy call on the Governor of the Bank of England. After the usual exchange of pleasantries, the Governor walked his visitors back to the lift. "Oh, and by the way," he said, almost as an aside, "I hope you won't change the name. It may be a small bank, but it's very old name and we value that in the City."

"Nonsense!" said Dick Bliss to my father, when they were back on the street, "of course we'll change the name."

"I wouldn't," said DY.

"But he didn't give us an instruction; it was just an idle comment," protested Bliss. "Dick, that's the way the Bank works. It's called 'the Governor's eyebrows'. They drop gentle, discreet hints. You ignore them at your peril," explained DY.

Of course, Bliss went ahead and changed the name, first to Rodo International and then to Bankers Trust International, and the Bank found several ways of expressing their displeasure. A co- CEO of BTI was Dimitri de Gunsburg, of an old and distinguished banking family – he should have known better, but probably was not consulted.

I believe Chris O'Malley, author of a complete history of the Eurobond market: *Bonds without Borders,* is correct in tracing the origin of securitized foreign lending to the early 17th century and to Amsterdam. He correctly identifies the Dutch East India Company, chartered in 1602, as the first company to issue shares to a wide audience of investors. The wealthy Dutch discovered that investing in securities was a portable and flexible money management technique. With a small domestic capital market, they were amongst the first private investors to develop a taste for foreign loans, which yielded a couple of hundred basis points over domestic government loans. The facility for many investors to participate in a single loan was due to securitization – the representation of a financial contract between parties by a negotiable instrument of title. By the end of the 17th century, Amsterdam, the trading hub of the age, became a centre for the issuance and subscription of foreign loans. This represents the first coming of age of foreign loans. It is a pre-dep party for my heroine. And the first major lead manager, top of the 18th century League Table of lead managers, was undoubtedly Hope & Co. of Amsterdam, as described by O'Malley. Originally a Scottish family, the Hopes came to Amsterdam via Rotterdam as merchants and bankers and, after the Seven

Years War ended in 1763, floated loans for Sweden, Russia, Poland, Portugal and Bavaria. These were almost always linked to trading concessions in various commodities: diamonds from Brazil, wheat and timber from Russia. Hope & Co. remained bankers to Russia until the revolution, competing with Mendelsohn of Berlin. But here again, this great name was the victim of a piece of pure vandalism by one of our 21st century mega banks, Fortis, originally a farmers' co-operative. In the consolidation wave that began in the 1960s, Hope had merged with Mees & Zoonen, another great Dutch name. Then Mees & Hope was acquired by ABN, then merged with Pierson, also a great name, when Fortis acquired ABN AMRO. Finally, after further wasteful expenditure of shareholders' funds on acquisition goodwill, the private banking business of the new banking monstrosity was named ABN AMRO Mees-Pierson, and the great name of Hope & Co. was consigned to the dustbin of financial history. The perpetrator of this cultural crime was an American ex-Citibanker, hired to save Fortis from the consequences of its over expansion. Poetic justice partially prevailed, as Fortis, plagued by a series of strategic mistakes, limped to virtual bankruptcy in the post Lehman crisis, to be rescued by Dutch and Belgian taxpayers.

Amsterdam maintained a quasi-monopoly of the issuance of foreign loans well into the 18th century, although as the volume and diversity of activity expanded, Paris and London began to build market share. The players were the merchant banks who were now diversifying their trade related business into investment banking. But international financial activity was still almost entirely trade related and the volume of foreign loans ebbed and flowed with contractions and expansions of foreign trade which, in turn, depended on cycles of war and peace. The French Revolution and the Napoleonic wars which followed, led to an almost total hiatus. But one very notable and remarkable exception is described by O'Malley, quoting from the archives of Baring's of London. The Louisiana Purchase was the first territorial expansion of the newly formed United States of America. Napoleon, who had the colony from Spain, was an eager seller as he needed the money and saw Louisiana as a strategic liability in a future war with England. The U.S. had insufficient reserves to finance the purchase and Hope & Co. joined with Barings in London to arrange for the U.S. to issue $15 million worth of 6% bonds to the French Government, who then sold them on to Hope and Barings at 87 ½, who placed them all successfully at par. The underwriters were so confident of success they advanced funds to the French ahead of the issue. The bonds bore coupons allowing for semi-annual interest payments in three centres: Amsterdam, London and Paris. This was certainly the first time the U.S. tapped the foreign bond market; it was probably the earliest example of co-management, and the format, $100 bond denominations with semi-annual coupons payable in different locations, was to become hence forth, with very little variation, the format for widely distributed foreign bonds. And it was the first "foreign dollar bond". That generous difference between the underwriters purchase price and the sale price to investors – which became known as the "gross spread", carried on in the 19th century, but did not survive the communications revolution of modern times, sadly for the investment banking trade. It hovered at 2 ½ % for long maturities for a while in the four decades after WWII, but then began to erode and is down to a few, infinitesimal pips today. But this first great bond deal took over two years to be completed. Today's billion dollar deals are done in hours.

At the end of the Napoleonic wars the foreign market sprang back to life with a series of what might be called re-construction loans. The first major deal was for the loser, France in 1817, through the established co-management team of Hope & Co. and Barings. But, as is often the case in major wars, the winners were in worse financial straits, particularly the "Holy Alliance" of Prussia, Russia and Austria. Prussia was the first in the market through Nathan Rothschild in London. The issue of £5 million was sterling denominated and in bearer bonds. Some government borrowers at the time still preferred registered form. There was a sinking fund to ensure amortisation and coupons payable in several centres. Yielding well over British "consols", British investors flocked to subscribe, but a conscious effort was made by Rothschild to distribute though out Europe, using the Rothschild network as a selling group. A further issue was made four years later in 1822. The historian Niall Ferguson considers these the first Eurobonds in his book *The Origins of Value OUP*, presumably because of the international distribution. Previous foreign bonds had been largely, but not exclusively, distributed in the country of the subscribing bank. The bearer bond format, coupons payable in several centres, a sinking fund and cross border distribution is indeed the overall structure which prevailed from then on in the sovereign foreign bond market. A Russian loan was floated at this time, through London, in sterling, with a coupon payable in roubles at a fixed rate in St. Petersburg. Multi-currency interest payment options were to become a regular feature. London began to emerge as a major centre for the flotation of foreign loans. The wealth of the English merchant class and a relatively low supply of domestic bonds were helpful, but the presence of the house of Rothschild, and, of course, Barings, were key factors. Lord Byron, in a famous poem, wrote "Who keeps the world in pain or pleasure… Jew Rothschild and his fellow Christian Baring". This was not the last time that international business was to be attracted to the City, not by some Government policy, but by the presence of certain banking firms.

According to O'Malley, between 1822 and 1825, British merchant banks issued 20 foreign bonds totalling £40 million of which 12 were for new Latin American Republics. Many were syndicated, including amongst Continental houses, again setting a pattern which was to prevail, especially for the larger loans. Apparently, again citing O'Malley, Nathan Rothschild wrote to his colleagues in 1865 "I think you will not only require your friend Baring, but likewise some joint-stock banks to unite with you, and however disagreeable it may be to have such partners, if it is the means of making the affair go down, you ought not to mind it" I have not found a better quote for illustrating the *hauteur* and general disdain with which merchant banks regarded clearing banks, even up to my early days in the City in the 1960s. Trading in these bonds was active. This is illustrated by the fact that the London Stock Exchange established a "Foreign Funds" market, eventually absorbed in the main market in 1830. This is recorded in Ronald C. Michie's "*The Global Securities Market*" and represents a supreme historical irony. When the Eurobond market began to take off in London the late 20th century, the London Stock Exchange – or to give it its formal, and presumptuous name: The Stock Exchange, London – studiously ignored this new exotic breed of security. There were two main reasons: it was "foreign" and the houses involved were "foreign" – mostly – horrors! – American. Even Warburg's, becoming a major player in this new market, was "foreign", ignoring the fact that every established merchant bank had foreign origins. But the other reason was that Stock Exchange rules required that a portion of every new issue of listed securities be allocated to the jobbers by the broker to the issue. The jobbers had not the slightest idea what to do with foreign currency bonds. Indeed, due to exchange controls and the "dollar premium", bonds in foreign currency were unsaleable to domestic investors. The result was that the broker simply dumped his allocation in the market. Of course, at this time liquidity was ensured entirely through an over-the-counter market, and the stock exchange listing was a formality, but an important one, to give the bonds investment grade status, suitable for institutional investors. London could have easily altered its rules to accommodate this new market – but it didn't, and the bonds were all listed in Luxembourg.

Latin America became a major source of foreign loan business for London in the 19th century – perhaps the British Empire's final victory over its traditional enemy, the Spanish Empire. As this market developed a role emerged for so-called foreign loan contractors. These were individuals whose business it was to unearth potential borrowers, in those days, primarily sovereign governments, their municipalities and agencies, and introduce them to issuing houses – for a commission, of course. These men became known as "five percenters", presumably their standard commission. Few merchant banks maintained agents of their own abroad, and certainly not in every potential borrower country. This changed when certain countries, such as Egypt, became such persistent borrowers as to justify a permanent presence there by foreign bankers. When I first came to London, I met a partner of Rothschild's who, before the war, had spent three months of every year travelling around Latin America. A possibly apocryphal story is that one of these loan contractors turned up in the City with a mandate from a certain, but unfamiliar, Central American state, to raise a loan of £2 million. He toured around the usual suspects and got one merchant bank to commit to underwriting the loan. History is unclear as to which. The issue was about to be launched when it was discovered that the country in question was entirely nonexistent, an invention of the loan contractor, who had been hawking a forged mandate. Apparently few bankers had an up-to-date world map in their office, and in any case, weren't these funny little Latin American countries being created overnight from the remnants of the Spanish Empire? British commercial interests in Latin America, railways in Brazil and Argentina, in particular were notable at the time. Paris, as a financial centre for foreign loans was more focused on the Levant. New York was not a contender until much later. Sterling as the reserve currency in the 19th century, made the City the natural domicile for international financial transactions of all types. This persisted until the Great War. A rather nostalgic reminder of this is an announcement that appeared in the British press on October 1st, 2014, some one hundred years after the commencement of that cataclysmic event: "CITY OF PERNAMBUCO (RECIFE) 5% GUARANTEED LOAN OF 1910 'ASSENTED PLAN A' (The "BONDS"). On behalf of the issuer, Lloyds Bank plc hereby gives notice to holders of the outstanding Bonds of the issuer's election to redeem the outstanding bonds at par on 1st November 2014. Interest will cease to accrue, etc., etc." I wonder how many tore this bond, and the remaining coupons, out of the frames hanging in the downstairs cloakroom and rushed to Lloyds Bank at 33-33 Perrymont Road, Haywards Heath, West Sussex to collect the principal and interest due after 114 years.

Until the mid-19th century, foreign bonds were the exclusive financing domain of sovereign entities. The introduction of the railways and the vast amounts needed to finance their construction, are another important staging point in the history of the foreign loan market. Domestic capital markets in the U.S. and the UK in particular had insufficient depth to accommodate the vast borrowing needed to fund railway construction. Although railway finance began as a domestic endeavour, it soon became cross-border and railway issues joined the burgeoning foreign loan market. The launch of the telegraph in the early 1830s began to link capital markets and exchanges and facilitated cross border subscription and trading of foreign loans. Before that it had been Reuter's pigeons and the semaphore. A nice example of the use of international communications for an insider dealing scam is to be found in Alexander Dumas' *the Count of Monte Christo* when the hero ruins his enemy, now a banker, by arranging a false semaphore message on the Carlist rebellion in Spain, causing the price of Spanish bonds in Paris to collapse. Whereas access to the foreign loan market had previously been dominated by sovereigns financing war and its aftermath, as well as other typical excesses in general expenditure, real industrial development projects began to diversify the investor's choice in the fixed income market. This historical development is an interesting harbinger to the introduction of American blue chip borrowers to the Eurobond market following U.S. capital controls in the late 1960s. The mid-19th century, might be described as a heyday of the foreign bond market.

Issues by public and private borrowers, denominated in several currencies, payable in several countries, issued by banks in several centres, subscribed by investors internationally, traded on several exchanges – all this, measured in monetary volume, and relative to gross domestic products of the developed economies, puts the great Eurobond volumes of the late 20th century in some perspective; The main centres were now London and Paris. In Paris, one could say that the house of Erlanger & Cie was playing a similar lead role to that played by Hope & Co. in Amsterdam in the early 18th century. They specialised in the southern United States before, during and after the Civil War. It has often been assumed that, because Britain sympathised with the Confederacy, as the main source of cotton for its northern mills, London was also the centre for Confederate finance. This is not entirely true. In fact, London merchant banks were reluctant to arrange loans for the South. It was Erlanger in Paris who pulled off a major investment banking coup in 1863 by arranging an issue of £3 million or FFr 75 million – an exchange rate which would delight a contemporary tourist – with a fixed coupon of 7% and the unusual feature of an exchange option against cotton at a fixed price of 6 pence per pound. The issue was distributed in London, Liverpool, Paris, Amsterdam and Frankfurt, and even Gladstone, Chancellor of the Exchequer was said to have subscribed, according to O'Malley. These became known as "cotton bonds" and some regard them as the earliest Eurobonds. The gross spread was comfortable. Erlanger subscribed at 77, took a 5% commission and reoffered at 90. You wouldn't have wanted to own them after Gettysburg. Interesting is the inclusion of Liverpool in the selling syndicate. As the port of entry for cotton, Liverpool is where the planters and other Southern gentlemen banked. In *Gone with the Wind,* after the War, Scarlett O'Hara goes to Rhett Butler, desperate for a loan to save her beloved Tara from the carpetbaggers. "But my money's in Liverpool", he pleads. I like to think Rhett banked at Rathbones, the old established Liverpool house, now a successful London wealth manager. The author Margaret Mitchell had done her homework.

The aftermath of the Civil War produced another fascinating chapter in our heroine's early history. David Landes gained access to the archives of de Neuflize, Schlumberger in Paris, Fruhling & Goschen in London, and Arnhold & Bleichröder in Frankfurt. He has written a fascinating story of Egyptian Finance in the 1860s and '70s in *Bankers and Pashas.* By 1860, the United States supplied 5/6th of the cotton for the great mills of Manchester and Rouen. When the Civil War broke out and the Southern ports were blockaded, disaster struck. It was not overnight. Shortages never are. In the first half of 1861 cotton was around 7 ½ pence per pound. By October it was 12 pence. During the summer of 1862, the price soared and by August was 26 ½ pence per pound. The only alternative suppliers of cotton in any volume at this time were India and Egypt, but Indian cotton was short fibred and generally unsuited to European textile machinery. Egyptian cotton on the other hand, called Jumel, was the closest to the top quality, American Sea Island staple. However, production was way below the volumes from the Punjab and Bengal. This changed in the 1830s due to a supreme effort by Mohammed Ali, founder of the Khedivial dynasty and father of modern Egypt. But Mohammed Ali overdid it, adopting a system of cultivation which destroyed the incentive of the *fellahin* to produce Jumel. Agricultural reform was only realised two reigns later under Said, but Mohammed Ali had been a great westerniser in other respects, importing European specialists, particularly French, to direct the modernisation of the state. French and English interests both competed and collaborated for stakes in the new El Dorado. Countries become fashionable almost overnight in commercial and financial circles. During their period in the limelight they almost inevitably exploit their position to excess, usually by over borrowing. Then they fade slowly and, soon everyone has forgotten why they were famous. A similar phenomenon is to be seen with show business celebrities. Of course, with Egypt, it was the cotton boom after American supplies dried up during the Civil War which was to make it the country of the future, for a while. But, even before this, in the 1830s through to the 1860s, Egypt was enjoying a geo-political renaissance, due in large part to the establishment of an Alexandria-Suez link, major infrastructure investment under Said, and an expansion of trade with Europe. It was during the reign of Ismaïl Pasha, Viceroy of India, the first great Khedive, Ismaïl the Profligate, as he became known, that it first went right – and then went wrong. Ismaïl succeeded in 1863, and in the thirteen years following Egypt's national debt rose from £3.3 million to £93 million. By 1876, Egypt was bankrupt.

The orgy of borrowing which characterised Ismaïl's reign, began with a French entrepreneur called Edouard Dervieu who dabbled in steamship operations and had established a trading concern in Alexandria. Through a friendship with Alfred André, of a great banking family, Dervieu established a representative relationship with André's banking house in Paris, Adolphe Marcuard & Cie, and a leading member of that exclusive tribe *La Haute Banque Protestante*. At first Dervieu funnelled trade finance business to his friends in Paris – good old, classical, self-liquidating commercial bills. Even as this volume grew, the glamour now associated with Egypt ensured their roll over by lenders in Paris and other European centres. The rot first set it under Ismaïl's predecessor the Viceroy Saïd. In 1858, pressed by commitments he had made to the newly formed Suez Company, and apparently at the suggestion of Ferinand de Lesseps, Saïd began to issue bearer bonds of short maturity. In this way, he escaped the vigilance of his usual creditors and also circumvented the need for his suzerain, the Sultan in Constantinople, to approve a formal loan. From then on it was downhill. The interesting aspect of this historical diversion is that the borrowing frenzy that ensued ushered in a cut throat competition between investment bankers which had not existed before. Dervieu and his friends at Marcuard, which was renamed Marcuard, André & Cie in 1862, soon had competition from Oppenheim, Neveu & Cie, Fruhling & Gos-

hen, and eventually even joint stock banks in Paris, such as Société Finan-cière and Credit Mobilier. All maintained representation in Alexandria, paid court to the Khedive, contrived to push commercial contracts his way, bribed his officials, spread rumours about their competitors and lied to their head of-fices. Accommodation was the principle competitive tool, and David Landes records the endless correspondence between the agents and their increasingly nervous head offices. "Just one more additional facility and I am certain of the mandate – all will be repaid!" "I hear our competitor is about to offer a short-term loan of XX millions. You must allow me to increase our limit, or we shall lose the next major loan issue." Every argument and every trick in the book was used to cajole head offices into accommodating the Khedive, well beyond any level of prudence, in order to secure mandates for loans which would be effectively subscribed at 85 and reoffered to the investing public at par. In my old-fashioned up bringing as an investment banker, I was taught never to offer short-term finance which could only be repaid by a bond issue which had not yet been awarded, and might, in any case, go to a com-petitor. But this kind of tactic to secure business began to proliferate towards the end of my career. Once, when I was at Merrill Lynch, I was trying to se-cure an M&A mandate from a major U.S. conglomerate interesting in dispos-ing of a large and well-known affiliate. The head of the money market divi-sion told me to offer a commercial paper facility without limit to the client as an inducement. "Without limit!?" I queried.
"Well, you know..." he replied, "The market will set the limit."
A clever reply, but it was not my idea of investment banking.

The sad case of Egypt, where almost everyone lost money, did not cause much of a dent in the growing appetite for foreign bonds. We know that greed and fear are the real drivers of securities markets, rather than supply and de-mand, as the economists used to teach. Foreign bonds always offered a yield comfortably in excess of the home markets' government bonds, for good reas-on, given the incidence of default. Bonds were still the dominant asset class. Despite the speculative flurries in railway or other "hot" stocks, no trustee or *paterfamilias* would dream of investing the family fortune in other than fixed interest securities, i.e. bonds. In those palmy days of low or nil inflation, wealth was measured in income, not capital. Anthony Trollope's Victorian heroines had dowries of so much a year. "A thousand a year – and in the funds!" exclaims Lady Bracknell, about a prospective son-in-law in Wilde's *Importance of Being Ernest"* – the "funds" being gilt-edged British Govern-ment bonds. Foreign bonds had other advantages in addition to superior yield. They were almost always in bearer form. Denominations varied according to the currency of issue, but it was usually possible to stuff a pile into one's suit-case if it became necessary to flee, whether from creditors or foreign in-vaders. The interest coupons attached could be presented for payment in any of several centres – usually Amsterdam, London, Paris and Frankfurt. Rapid industrialisation, the communications revolution of the telegraph, the growth of stock exchanges, and general peace in the second half of the century – all served to increase international capital flows exponentially. Corporate issuers, mostly connected with infrastructure development, began to crowd the market. According to Ranald Michie, by 1914 corporate bonds and stocks had overtaken government debt and about 60% of all securities in existence were private sector issues. Foreign bonds were beautifully engraved. This was to give defaulted bonds value as collector's items and decorators' features in the 20th century. Industrial bonds contained motifs of the activity of the issuer: trains chugging through idyllic scenery, modern looking factories with perfect smoke trails issuing from tall chimneys, water works, dams, etc. Government and municipal bonds were often even more elaborately engraved with royal and imperial coats of arms, views of famous landmarks, and lightly draped maidens holding torches of liberty or crowns of vine leaves. My heroine, the foreign bond, was truly a thing of great beauty at that time. Capital flows tracked the great strategic alliances. When President Faure of France was received by Nicholas II of Russia in 1897, the band of the Guards played the *Marseillaise*, to the astonishment of the monarchists assembled in St. Petersburg. A lasting friendship between the two nations was declared. Russia's alliance with France formed the Triple Alliance with England, which was to confront the Central Powers, Germany and Austro-Hungary, in the Great War. It also opened a new market for Russian bond issues. Russia had been a foreign borrower since earliest times, through Hope & Co. in Amsterdam and Barings in London. Bankers to the Russian Empire were Mendelssohn of Berlin and the de Gunsburgs. This family was granted a patent of nobility and the title baron by a sovereign German Prince. When they settled in St. Petersburg, their title was recognised by the Tsar and they became virtually the only Jewish members of the Russian nobility. A Baroness de Gunsburg, of Dutch origin, became a friend of my mother in New York, and her son Dimitri a lifelong friend of mine – he of Bankers Trust International. Despite the strong German element in the Romanov Dynasty, Germany became a less suitable market for Russian bonds after the French alliance. But in the late 19th and early 20th Centuries, Russian bonds were offered in France and gobbled up in great volume by the *rentier* class there. Sadly, they were worthless after 1917 and many a French attic held piles of *les Fonds Russes,* which became an iconic symbol of the impoverishment of the French bourgeoisie after *la Guerre de '14.*

Until the outbreak of World War I, the pound sterling was the principle reserve currency, although the bulk of national reserves were held in gold, and certainly the currency of choice for international trade and financial transactions. This was the era of the "bill on London". O'Malley estimates that more than 60% of global trade was financed, invoiced and settled in sterling. This made London the unquestioned leader in the issuance of foreign bonds. Activity began to decline with rising tensions in Europe, but still Latin American borrowers – such as the City of Pernambuco mentioned earlier, semiautonomous Balkan states, municipal and infrastructure borrowers from Austro-Hungary and the eastern Mediterranean, were still in evidence. With the outbreak of war, it all closed down. Savings had to be quickly repatriated to finance the war. The U.S. repurchased vast amounts of its securities held by European investors, and England, France and Russia floated loans in New York. J. P. Morgan became principle banker to France, raising more than half a billion dollars. Russian loans were the most difficult to place. The Jewish houses of Wall Street: Kuhn Loeb, Solomon Brothers, Goldman Sachs, etc. boycotted Russian paper in protest at the pogroms carried out in the reign of Nicholas I.

The belligerent nations closed their stock exchanges and abandoned the Gold standard. Only the New York Stock Exchange remained open and only the U.S. Dollar remained convertible into gold. In the few relatively short years of the First World War, the United States, the U.S. Dollar and New York replaced Great Britain, the Pound Sterling and London as the main sources of international capital. By 1920, O'Malley cites the U.S. as the world's largest creditor nation. Despite the equity boom of the 1920s, New York was able to replace London as the foreign bond capital of the world. Latin American borrowers like Chile and Peru raised loans. The newly independent countries emerging from the break-up of the Austro-Hungarian Empire, such as the Kingdom of Serbs, Croats and Slovenes – the future Yugoslavia – issued foreign dollar bonds. O'Malley cites interesting examples: The First Bohemian Glass Works 7.5% issued 1927 due 1957, City of Warsaw 7% 30 year bonds issued 1928. All were to default during World War Two. I was to come across an amusing relic of this first mini boom in foreign dollar bond business. I was on my first visit to Brazil in 1961, accompanying a senior White, Weld partner, Buck Remmel. We had a lead on some potential Brazilian borrowing. We experienced the usual frustration of endless waits in the outer offices of various ministers. These were always crowded with people having no apparently urgent business but happy to lounge about talking to each other as, ever quarter of an hour or so, a waiter passed through offering little cups of coffee – the *cafezhino*. Buck and I were calling on a major insurance company, sipping our *cafezhino*, when our host said, "Oh, we have one of your people on our staff here – at least he's ex-White, Weld – I'll have him called up." We were nonplussed. An elderly American gentleman appeared.

"Yes, I was with White, Weld and I was sent out here in '38," he explained. "There was a big potential project to cut a tunnel through one of the hills here in Rio. I was supposed to secure the mandate. I met with ministers, with mayors, and with contractors. I got promises. Nothing happened. I cabled New York; 'keep at it', they said. I waited and visited some more. The war in Europe broke out. I cabled again; 'stay a bit longer', they replied. I fell in love with a girl, married her, and decided to stay. I cabled my resignation. The tunnel never happened." I suggested to Buck he had better send a wire to Mrs Remmel, assuring her we would come home. I cannot resist a further diversion. I was fond of Buck Remmel. He was not a typical White, Weld partner, not being a Harvard man. But he treated me like a real investment banker, although I was hardly more than a trainee. I was in the research department at that time and was looking at a Moody's sheet on Horn & Hardart, an early pioneer of fast food chains, one might say. Theirs was an unusual concept: the restaurant wall was lined with little glass front boxes with a coin slot and a price displayed. Inside one saw the prepared dish: a slice of apple pie, a wedge of cottage pie, a burger, a piece of cheese, etc. One put in the appropriate coins and the little glass door opened. One popped one's choice on one's tray and sat at a table. I decided this interesting, modestly priced purveyor of meals needed further funding. I went to Buck Remmel and, to my astonishment, he agreed.

"Let's call on them," he said.

"Me too?" I asked, amazed I could join a partner in a client call. Off we went to Trenton, New Jersey, or some such unlikely locale where Horn & Hardart's modest HQ was situated. It was the first time I had witnessed the classical investment banker's pitch – called schmoozing, by the cynics. The Chief Financial Officer was impressed.

"No one from Wall Street has ever called on us before!" As we talked on, it became clear they had no particular interest in expanding and no need for finance.

"Well, we think your stock is undervalued," was Buck's final comment. "We'll do a research note on it."

I don't remember seeing it. I think Horn & Hardart disappeared some years later, with the rise of the real fast food chains. For an investment banker, the first ever pitch is like the first girlfriend – unforgettable.

By the end of the all too brief inter-war years, and despite the traumas of market crashes and depression, the foreign dollar bond – my heroine, now in the full bloom of early womanhood, was well-established as a fixed income security of choice, especially for the more cosmopolitan investor. Some institutional holders existed, particularly international insurers. A major White, Weld client, before and after the War, was C. V. Starr, an insurance company founded in Shanghai by an American, Cornelius Van der Starr. They were to evolve into AIG of New York, eventually headed by the controversial "Hank" Greenberg, and much implicated in the Lehman failure crisis of the recent years. But individual investors predominated. The international, private clientele of White, Weld, managed by DY and Jean Cattier, would have held foreign dollar bonds in a balanced portfolio. The bearer nature of foreign dollar bonds, indeed foreign bonds in all currencies since the early 19th century, gave rise to the perception that this was an instrument for tax evasion. When, after the war, the market revived and eventual transmogrified as the Eurobond market, an iconic figure known as the "Belgian Dentist" was invented by some pundit reporting on the apparently new activity. He, or she, was represented as the typical Eurobond investor. Prosperous, as are all dentists, living in Belgium where taxes are particularly unpopular, this mythical investor has an account at a Luxembourg bank, with a safe deposit box, and every quarter, or half year, takes the train from Brussels to Luxembourg, takes a bond or bonds from the box, clips coupon or coupons, cashes them in. All this assumes a paying agent in Luxembourg, rarely the case. Our dentist takes the train home to the spouse and kiddies, and the tax man knows nothing. Like all such figures, the Belgian Dentist was a product of an overactive imagination by some commentator. The only dentist I know of who was an entirely genuine historical figure was the *Chef de Cabinet* of the European Union Commissioner Edith Cresson, and he was from Lille, on the Franco-Belgian border. Appointed by President François Mitterrand, both an ex-Prime Minister and ex-mistress, Madame Cresson was a member of the Commission presided by Jacques Santerre – known as Jacques Sancerre, which was sacked in its entirety by the European Parliament, who cannot sack commissioners individually. Madame Cresson's appointment of her dentist as her chief of staff, who drew his stipend without having to give up his practice, was cited as an example of the corruption of that body of European *fonctionaires.* The distinguished financial journalist Christopher Fildes quotes me as remarking "One might give ones ex-mistress a diamond bracelet, but one does not appoint her a European Commissioner." The tradition that Eurobonds were a tax dodger's favourite portfolio asset lingered on for years. Investors were known as "coupon clippers", and were seen as the main private client base of the Swiss banking fraternity. Swiss banks have now taken a serious, if not entirely fatal, knock as a result of their entrance into information sharing agreements with first Germany and ultimately the U.S. Treasury. But it is worth remembering that the Swiss private client tradition has little to do with taxes, since income and estate tax are a relatively new invention. Swiss bank secrecy had everything to do with protection against sequestration and goes back to the time of the French Revolution. The largest single capital flight to Switzerland was prompted by German Jews in the 1930s who were not so much fleeing taxes as outright sequestration of their money. The other great selling point for Switzerland as a domicile for private fortunes is the absence of probate. The Swiss client can, by simple instruction to his banker, leave his Swiss based fortune to his mistress, or a stray dogs' home, without fear of challenge by his formal heirs. The other advantage of bearer bonds with coupons attached was that it is more difficult to apply withholding taxes, that increasingly popular device for taxing cross border investment. This has largely disappeared with a proliferation of double tax agreements, where tax withheld can be reclaimed, but with a good deal of paperwork.

There is no question that the emergence of the foreign dollar bond market in New York before the Second World War, and its revival afterwards – up to the imposition of the U.S. Interest Equalization Tax in July 1963 – was the bedrock from which the Eurobond market was to rise to such prominence. My heroine had come of age as a Foreign Dollar Bond. The format for such bonds was already well-established as has been described above. But the methodology of issuance, underwriting and distribution was pure Wall Street, and was to prevail in the ensuing Eurobond market – despite a clumsy attempt to apply a British construction to the first Eurobond for the Italian issuer Autostrade, by Warburgs in London. Every Eurobond issue, whether through American or European investment bankers, was to follow the Wall Street pattern. The underwriting and selling syndicate hierarchy consisted of the manager, and increasingly co-manager(s), the underwriters, ranked according to the percentage of their commitment in a "special" or "bulge" bracket, then major bracket and then minor bracket. Then a selling group was constituted which included the underwriters but spread to a larger number of houses who took no underwriting commitment, but engaged to distribute on a "best efforts" basis for a commission. The gross spread had settled in the post War period to 2 ½% for long maturities, usually 15 years. This was divided: ½% for management, ½ per cent for underwriting and 1 ½% for the selling commission. So a lone lead manager earned ½% on the total amount, plus ½ % on the amount underwritten and 1 ½% on the amount distributed. An underwriter who distributed the whole of its underwriting thus earned 2% on that amount. For short maturities, usually 5 years, the gross spread was 2%, divided in similar proportions throughout the syndicate. Where there were co-managers, the lead manager was designated as the "book-runner" and had a larger share of the management commission. In recent times as the size and complexity of capital market issues has increased dramatically (and gross spreads shrunk); and syndicates somewhat regionalised, with the addition of "global coordinators", the oxymoronic phrase "co-book-runners" has crept in, leading one to imagine co-Grand National jockeys and co-Formula One drivers. In had been the practice in Wall Street to announce the completion of capital market transactions with block advertisements in the financial press, showing the details of the issue and then the underwriting syndicate in hierarchical formation: lead manager, co-manager, special bracket, major bracket and minor bracket, alphabetically in each section. The selling group was not publicised. These were known as "tombstones". The practice was carried on in the Eurobond market and produced a comfortable new source of revenue for the *Financial Times* and other publications – even the *Economist*. It was the duty of juniors like me to proofread these tombstones and there was hell to pay if one failed to spot a misprint. I became quite good at this. There was no rhyme or reason to the placement of commas and full stops in the names of the investment banking houses. One just had to get it right. Those of us quite handy at proofreading were known as "comma catchers".

And so my heroine is now poised on the threshold of perhaps the most dynamic phase of her life. She is the product of a turbulent and dramatic family history, as I have tried to show. Her early years were perhaps more glamorous than those she will now face as her career expands. Her suitors will be less elegant, and increasingly mechanistic in the exploitation of her charms. But the role she will have played in the two lives the subject of this memoir remains central – which is why I pay her so much attention. Sadly, lavish engraving of bond certificates became too expensive, like the silk brocades of Bianchini Ferrier of Lyon for the *haute couturiers* of Paris, and so Eurobonds which have defaulted are no longer worth framing and hanging in the cloakroom. My heroine lost beauty but gained fame.

CHAPTER VIII

"I'll Take Manhattan, the Bronx and Staten Island too"

-1929 Song by Rogers and Hart-

Everyone knows New York is a big-headed city. In fact, few great cities are as pleased with themselves as New York. A famous cartoon cover from the *New Yorker* magazine shows a blown up profile of Manhattan, with a fore shortened background of the rest of the American continent, all the way to California, looking like a near suburb of the city.

When we landed at the tip of Manhattan on our French Line steamship – it might have been the *Normandie*, Mother was in a better mood. She had regained the memory of happy days as a newlywed in a small apartment on Third Avenue, where the "L" trains thundered overhead. We had had a safe passage, as it was the "phony war" and German submarine action had not started yet. We children had been entertained by Gordon Turgel during the trip and he now accompanied us all to our temporary quarters at the Carlisle Hotel, a service apartment belonging to Benny Clarke, one of DY's senior partners, son of one of White, Weld's founders. Father was not expected for several weeks. He was presumed to be closing down all of the firm's offices – but, of course, he was not closing London. But there was also the house in Norfolk Crescent and all the things to pack up and prepare for shipment. He soon wired that he could not secure a visa for Nanny, so a nurse/governess was engaged. DY's partners, and their wives, went out of their way to ensure our comfort and security. White, Weld was like a family. It seems it was the order of the day that this poor foreign and junior partner, and his poor, foreign wife must be given every assistance. Alec White's wife Posie was in town to take Mother shopping. Other wives competed to take her to lunch. Partners looked in on their way home from downtown to make sure we were all right. All this made an impression on Mother that she never forgot. The Carlisle Hotel, on the corner of 76th Street and Madison Avenue, is an imposing and luxurious establishment. We lived in comfort. One day our new governess took us to Central Park. We were in our best London outfits: tweed overcoats with velvet collars, leggings and little round hats. There were toy sail boats on a pond in the park and I reached too far trying to grab one. In a trice, I was in the drink. I would like to recall that, in the tradition of all drowning persons, my whole life passed before me, short as it was – but I don't. In any case, our governess was gossiping with another and it was Ariane who pulled me out. The second time she saved my life. Returning to the Carlisle, I soaking and my sister damp, we caused amusement in the lift, as a puddle began to form at my feet. The governess was sacked on the spot. The Carlisle has a special place in my memory. Years later, when I was about 12, we were back at the Carlisle for a winter, having closed our house on Long Island. I was allowed to go down and roam about the lobby from time to time. One day I entered the lift to find Mary Pickford and her then husband, the cowboy star Buddy Rogers already there. They had a suite above us. A floor or two down, a gentleman got in. A few floors further and the lift stopped, clearly between floors. I immediately noticed that our most recently arrived passenger was beginning a claustrophobic panic attack. Buddy Rogers picked up the emergency phone – lifts were automatic by then, listened for a moment, put it back on the hook and said, with a little smile, "It's busy." The gentleman's panic attack worsened – he was in a muck sweat by now.

"I'm joking!" said Rogers "they'll be here in a few minutes – they know we're stuck". Both Rogers and Mary Pickford had also noticed our fellow passenger's serious malaise, and Miss Pickford began an impromptu entertainment. She sang "Isn't it a lovely day to be caught in the lift", she danced, she busked, she and Rogers did a quick comedy sketch based on an Abbot & Costello routine – they were making a successful effort to relax the poor man. I was enthralled. Far too soon, the lift doors opened and some steps were handed down by hotel staff so we could climb out. The poor man was almost in tears of gratitude. We had enjoyed ten minutes of superb entertainment by two world famous film stars. I am sure he never forgot it – nor did I.

DY finally arrived to report that all was arranged in London. The house was to be sold. It took some time. It was hit in the Blitz and only finally sold when the area was redeveloped after the war. I immediately enquired whether my favourite toy had been packed. This consisted of a London Bobby which came apart in the middle, probably originally containing sweets. I was assured it was safe. In fact, the contents of the house had ended up in two separate ships for the Atlantic crossing – only made some months later, when the German submarines were at their devastating work. One ship went down. Everything that should have been shipped together had not been. The lamps had survived, the lamp shades gone down. Pairs of chairs and other articles had also been divided – and, worst of all, one half of my Bobby had gone on one ship and the other half on the other. I was devastated. Our Carlisle sojourn came to an end, a house was rented in Westbury, Long Island and Father began to commute – as he was to do the rest of his working life. The choice of the North Shore of Long Island was prompted by the fact that most of his partners had houses there: the Alec Whites in Oyster Bay, the David Welds in St. James, Tom Choate in Syosset, Jean Cattier and Buss Hovey in Locust

Valley. We eventually settled in Locust Valley. This part of the world played a critical part in my formative years, and, I dare say, my father's life and career as well. In English law, an important but subtle difference exists between residence and domicile. It dominates aspects of the tax code. Residence is easy – it's where you are now living. Domicile is where you were and where you intend to return to. – Even if it's just to be laid to rest. It's a difficult legal concept because how do you prove an intention? Only by carrying it out. But if I am asked the question: where am I domiciled, my inclination is to say Locust Valley, Long Island, N. Y., regardless of strict legalities, or even facts. That is the measure of the mark left on me by my years growing up on the North Shore of Long Island.

A big sand bar, running from Manhattan due east to Montauk Point, Long Island was a flat, and relatively featureless place mostly given over to potato farming and clam and oyster gathering. In the late 19th century it was discovered by the financial, legal and industrial gentry of New York City who purchased and laid out great estates, very much along English lines. Equestrian activities and sailing predominated. The Meadow Brook was one of America's oldest packs of foxhounds, Westbury was the polo capital in the '20s and '30s, and Long Island Sound was the scene of great regattas. The great "old money" families of the East were still represented when we settled there, although their great estates were breaking up under cost and staff pressures brought on by the depression and then the war. The Whitney, Winthrop, Vanderbilt, Gerry, Pratt, Bostwick, Bancroft, Davis, Pidot, Mackay, Babcock, Phipps, Mills, Hitchcock, Cravath, Auchincloss, Doubleday, Pell, Flagg, Milburn, Morgan, Guest, Post, Davison, Duryea, Knott, Lamont, Pierrepoint, von Stade, Wilmerding, Clark, Grace, Jennings, Gibson, Tiffany families, to name just a handful, comprised the "estate people", as the local tradesmen referred to them (even when their estates were truncated, or no more). Perhaps the most famous "estate person" was President Theodore Roosevelt from Oyster Bay, "Even oysters down in Oyster Bay do it" lyricized Cole Porter in *Let's Do It*. The North Shore – we looked down on the South Shore – was not just a "WASP" ghetto. Otto Khan of Kuhn, Loeb was a large land owner. John Schiff, also a partner of Kuhn, Loeb, became a member of the Piping Rock Club, the country club of choice and a bastion of Episcopalian society. The Episcopalian church St. John's of Lattingtown, with an interior imported from England by J. P. Morgan, whose Glen Cove estate abutted, was known as "Piping Rock at prayer". Schiff served on the membership committee at Piping Rock and is reputed to have black balled a Jewish candidate, saying "one Jew in this club is enough". I strongly suspect this story as being apocryphal. The estate owners commuted to Wall Street, often by sea plane, but eventually formed a syndicate to finance and build the Long Island Railroad, famous for its ability to lose money. There was a club car, which my father would board at Locust Valley station. This had comfortable wicker chairs, backgammon tables and a black steward to serve drinks.

I had reached the age when I was beginning to take notice of my father. Ours was very much a nursery upbringing and our parents were somewhat distant figures, although we never suspected them of not being loving. For a short while, I thought all parents were always in evening clothes as ours were so clad when they came to say good night. The boat trip over had brought my sister and me closer to our mother. Our parental relations had been somewhat strained by their efforts to ensure we were fully bilingual. Our mother tongue was French and when we came to London, aged five and four, we were made to speak English, of course. It was Nanny's main mission. My sister Ariane recalls rushing to say goodbye to Father in Norfolk Crescent as he left one morning for the City. "Au revoir, Papa!" she exclaimed, arms outstretched.

"Speak English!" he rejoined, coldly and slammed the door.

I am prepared to accept most of this anecdote, except the slammed door. Smith, the butler, would have been standing there to hand Father his bowler hat and umbrella, and no door would have been slammed. Nevertheless our father was somewhat cold and lacking in affection towards us. It was his way, and I suspect a product of his own upbringing. He was formal. Our parents said "vous" to each other, at least in front of us and company. We said "vous" to them and they said "tu" to us. Nowadays, everybody says "tu" to every-body. But it is received wisdom, or should be, that a daughter's relationship with her father is more important that the son/mother relationship. My sister suffered from our father's coldness. I did not, perhaps because I was aware that he favoured me – another cause of legitimate complaint by my sister. But, as has been demonstrated by her propensity to save me from drowning, and other disasters during my feckless youth, she held no grudge against me. My father was certainly my principle mentor and the person I most admired. He was elegance personified: perfectly dressed, but not with sartorial affectation, a military carriage, graceful gestures, and a quiet and well-modulated voice. He was always impeccably groomed. His clothes were by Anderson & Shep-pard, his linen and ties by Hawes & Curtis, his shoes by Lobb, and his hats by Lock. He was a bit of a chain smoker and carried a two tone gold, flat cigar-ette case by Faberge given to his father by his regiment, the Guard's Sappers to celebrate his 15th year. My father had had the inscription rubbed out in case it was found by the Bolsheviks when he was leaving Russia. But he had his father's, his and my names engraved later, and I carried it at very posh events. He really did smoke a great deal, waking in the night to light up. He stopped suddenly after a heart attack in his 50s. It happened on one of the Queens crossing the Atlantic. He was on the dance floor when he suddenly felt unwell. So he sat down, lit a cigarette and downed a glass of champagne. The next think he knew he awoke in his cabin. The ship's doctor was sitting next to him. "I delighted you've come to," said the worthy medic. "You can-not imagine the forms I have to fill out when a passenger dies on board". He pointed to DY's cigarette case. "No more of that, I'm afraid". Father continued to carry the case for some years, to offer cigarettes to others – but he never smoked another himself.

The business of White, Weld's Foreign Department, as it was still known throughout World War II, was essentially servicing a large clientele of European émigrés fleeing war in Europe, trading and broking foreign securities, especially foreign bonds, and maintaining correspondent relationships with those overseas houses and institutions still able to deal in New York, such as Latin American banks and South African brokers. The European contingent now in New York was substantial. Many were clients that White, Weld had acquired through Paris, London and Amsterdam. A wave of fortunate Frenchmen, who had managed to get themselves and their money out before the collapse of France, now turned up in New York. Some had come via Morocco, as the iconic film *Casablanca* so vividly depicts. Amongst these clients, some became family friends. One such was Edouard LeRoux, a Norman peasant who had made his fortune speculating on the Paris *Bourse* before the First World War, or *Avant quatorze,* as the French of a certain generation always said. It was a source of fascination to me that someone could have made a stock exchange killing in such ancient times. LeRoux had married Thérèse Fabre, heiress to a shipping fortune. They had two children, Francine and Gerard. Francine became a great friend of my sister and married a partner of Dillon Read. The LeRoux had purchased a large estate in Glen Cove, very near a property rented by the exiled King Zog of Albania. We used to be taken there to play with the young LeRoux and it was a sort of wonderland of toys and gadgets for the delectation of children. A very mechanical gardener had transformed a large sled by attaching treads and a lawn mower engine, and we would roar around the soft winter snow, to the concern of Madame LeRoux, whilst DY and Edouard LeRoux discussed investment strategies over sherry. M. LeRoux spoke not a word of English which in no way impeded his life style in America, as he surrounded himself with bilingual servants. Another friend/client was Morisot, an artist no way related to his namesake Berthe. He painted portraits of Ariane. The French colony in New York frequented a bistort called *Le Veau d'Or*, mid-town between Madison and Lexington Avenues, where the speciality was *cervelle au beurre noir.* No doubt brains are banned now. Years later when I was at secondary school, Mother took me to lunch there and Morisot was at the bar. I had my back to the bar and Mother waved at him in a friendly way. He ignored her. My mother couldn't understand it. It turned out he thought she was lunching with a toy boy and was trying to be discreet. The last woman in the world to be entertaining a toy boy would have been my mother. White, Weld was also building a South American clientele. By now our father spoke Spanish, as well as English, Russian, French, German and Polish. He never got around to Italian. A good many refugees from war in Europe had gone to South America. In fact Uruguay had taken steps to compete with Switzerland as a haven for flight capital. It seems extraordinary now, but quite a few people in Europe feared Switzerland would be unable to resist the Nazi onslaught. In fact Germany spared the Swiss, because they didn't think it worthwhile to devote the military effort it would have taken to overcome the extensive defences installed in the Swiss valleys, and a great many Nazis had savings salted away in Swiss banks – just in case. White, Weld had an agent in Uruguay and a facility for domiciling accounts there. Amongst DY's friends from "south of the border" was an amusing Guatem-alan called Julio Herrera. He owned a good deal of his native country. My father had given him some sort of position in the firm, presumably because he introduced a large Latino clientele. Julio was a great joker and my sister and I found him hugely entertaining. My mother did not, and I'm not sure what DY's partners thought. He used to turn up in Wall Street wearing a full head monkey mask. Once he sent a message to my mother that DY was not taking his usual train home to Locust Valley but wanted to meet her at Le *Veau d'Or* for dinner. Mother accordingly motored into town to find Julio at the restaur-ant, assuring her that DY was to join them any moment and plying her with Dry Martini cocktails in the meantime. In fact Father arrived home, to be told by the butler that Madam had gone to town. By now, Mother was legless at the restaurant and had to be driven home by Julio, who thought it was all hys-terically funny. Mother had a serious sense of humour failure and wouldn't speak to Julio for some time. The Hererras had two children Lito and Philip who were at grade school with us. Lito went back to have his estates in Guatemala confiscated by revolution.

1940 and 1941 were years of great normality in America. No one really expected the U.S. would join the war in Europe. Public opinion was strongly against, particularly in the Middle-West where a strong German immigrant community was openly pro-Nazi. No one suspected that President Roosevelt was actively plotting with Churchill, behind the back of Congress, to provide assistance to the British war effort. FDR had sent his former Chairman of the SEC Joseph Kennedy as Ambassador to the Court of St. James – a very pecu-liar appointment. Kennedy, an Irishman after all, was violently anti-British, much to the embarrassment of his children who mixed happily with English society. The Ambassador bombarded Washington with predictions of Eng-land's imminent demise and urged the State Department to form an alliance with Nazi Germany, whose renaissance of its economy, he much admired. He was joined in this view by no less a celebrity than Charles Lindburgh, the great aviator. My father, who was as strongly pro-British as Kennedy was anti, was shocked at the extent of pro-German sentiment in all classes of soci-ety in New York – with the obvious exception of the Jewish fraternity. But life in general, and certainly on the North Shore of Long Island, carried on as be-fore. There was polo at Meadowbrook in Westbury, hounds still hunted three times a week, there was the annual steeple chase meeting at Piping Rock, and the autumn event at the Horse Show grounds. New York society columnists reported the comings and goings of debutantes at the Stork Club and LaRue, the fashionable night clubs of the period. Elderly dowagers were shocked at this departure from the discretion which had been the mark of "good society". They considered that only birth, marriage and death should be recorded in the press. The expression "café society" was born at this time. East Coast society wintered in Palm Beach, and summered sailing off the resorts of the Maine coast, Bar Harbour, Prout's Neck, and Northhaven. In-between seasons, were spent shooting quail in Georgia, salmon fishing in Alaska and deep sea fishing off Cuba. The Stock Market had finally rallied after an economic resurgence following the depression, the dust bowl crisis and even, FDR's substantial increase in taxation. Franklin Delano Roosevelt was considered an out and out socialist by the moneyed classes. But it is remarkable how great wealth survived the depredations of his fiscal policies, which were unashamedly redistributive. This is due to the fact that great wealth in America was largely invested in equities, rather than land, as in England – and equities revived, and, with blips here and there, never looked back.

By 1941, the Yassukovich family had settled in a house called "Bittersweet" off Piping Rock Road, Locust Valley – in fact within the grounds of the Club, on a hill overlooking the 18th fairway. After the first rental in Westbury, we had rented a house belonging to John Litt, also on Piping Rock Road. In a barn, Mr Litt had a wooden horse, surrounded by chicken wire, to practice his polo strokes. I used a similar, very quiet beast, in Gloucestershire, when I took up polo. There was a very woolly white dog called Blanco. In the winter, the swimming pool had logs tied around the edge to prevent frost cracking the fabric. The ice was more than thick enough for my sister and me to learn to skate. In fact, Father was very keen on ice dancing and practised with a lady friend on the pool, a windup gramophone playing waltzes nearby. There was great excitement when Bittersweet was located and purchased. The house, a typical stucco and timbered, smallish mansion had been built by a Mr. Cravath, of a famous Wall Street law firm, for his mistress. The Cravath residence was directly opposite, at the far end of the Club, next to the Horse Show grounds, and presumably this intensely respectable lawyer could gaze across the golf course to his paramour whilst breakfasting opposite Mrs. Cravath. He had added a critical feature to the house: a large, high ceilinged drawing room with French windows giving on to a terrace, built specifically to accommodate some pickled wood panelling he had acquired from the ruins of a French chateau. Our parents' collection of English and French period furniture could have been chosen specifically for this house, it went so well. Both parents were besotted by period furniture and questions of interior décor in general. In fact, the only subject my sister and I ever heard them fight over was to do with décor. And bitter, and sometimes almost violent, these altercations could be. My mother favoured the French style, particularly Louis XV. My father much preferred Hepplewhite, Sheridan and the other English greats. So far so good, as compromise was easy, since late 18th and early 19th English furniture goes very well with the less ornate style of Louis Quinze, whilst swearing terribly with Louis Quatorze. But the devil is in the detail in interior decoration. My mother, like so many French, considered that French taste and culture, was, and would always be, at the very centre of civilisation. She had been brought up to believe that Russians were only recently civilised savages from the steppes, having just shaken off the brutal hooliganism of Ghengis Khan and his barbaric horde. "Gratez un Russe, et vous trouvez un Tartare!" was an expression known to every French school child – scratch a Russian and you find a Tartar. As a result Father's opinions on matters decorative were often greeted by a certain disdain. In fact, the expression of our mother's which was to become as familiar as the call of the lark was: "Mais, Dimitri – vous êtes fou!" Nevertheless, the mixture of French and English which was the style of all of our parent's interiors over the years, always excited admiration. Furthermore, my sister and I absorbed a great deal on the subject and I am absolutely convinced that we could each have pursued highly successful careers as interior decorators.

It became time for my sister and me to start school, and Green Vale School, founded 1928 as a primary school for the "estate people", was the obvious choice. We would cross the large neighbouring property which belonged to the Craigmyles, and wait, on the other side of Piping Rock Road, for the school bus, sitting on a post and rail fence – which is still there today. Bobby Craigmyle became a great friend. The family had a farm as a holiday place, in deepest Connecticut and I would be invited to stay. Mrs. Graigmyle told my mother that she was overcome by my large brown eyes when she came to tuck us in at night. I remember that because it was the first and last time such a comment was ever made about me. Green Vale School was divided into "blues" and "golds", the school colours – siblings usually separated. My sister was a "blue" and I was a "gold". To this day when I meet a Green Vale Old Boy, or Old Girl, I offer to guess their colour. Of course, I have a 50% chance of being right, but for some strange reason; I never fail to guess correctly. Our arrival at school marked our first realisation that we were different. We had not mixed with American children before. Of course, we had a very different sounding name. There were one or two English wartime evacuees with American cousins, but they had familiar sounding names. But the main difference was in the way we lived at home. We spoke French at home as our parent's concern to maintain our bilingual heritage now expressed itself in a fear we would forget our mother tongue. But our home life style was very different. It was not just that we had a Swiss butler, French cook and various maids; servants were kept in most of our school mate's homes. We also had a French governess, and when we visited our school mates, we were amazed that they were able to walk freely into their kitchens, open the fridge and pull out Coca Colas. This beverage was banned at Bittersweet and we were certainly not allowed in the kitchen except by special permission. As a result, we tended not to suggest home visits to our friends. My sister Ariane showed an early propensity for social ease and interpersonal skills, as they have come to be known. I don't think she suffered very long from a sensation of being "different". I did, however, and I tried to compensate for my insecurity by becoming a shameless show-off. My disruptive attitude in class was to persist though out my primary school days, and this unfortunate character trait has plagued me, if in a somewhat milder form, all my life. During one of the war years, heating fuel became scarce and it was decided we should close the house and spend a year in town at the Westbury Hotel. My sister and I amused ourselves out of school hours, somewhat like the character in *Eloise at the Plaza*, in various forms of mischief, including summoning the lifts and then hiding around the corner. Ariane was placed at Brearley School and me at Allan Stevenson, both fashionable institutions. Ariane did brilliantly, adapting instantly; I was a disaster. My disruptive behaviour worsened and resulted in my being ejected from the classroom, time after time. Mother was summoned for emergency meetings with the Headmaster. One day, back in his study after yet another eviction, he told me: "the next time you're thrown out of class – you're out of the school". Needless to say, the next day I got the boot again for talking back to the teacher. Out in the hallway, I heard the heavy steps of the Headmaster slowly climbing the stairs. I was in a panic. I opened the classroom door: "Please, please, please, Sir! Can I come in, please, sir! I promise to be good!" The teacher was so taken aback by this uncharacteristic outburst, that he let me back in.

Back at Green Vale, the following year – probably 1944, I was determined to improve and ended up winning a prize for English composition. I looked forward to prize day and dreamt of the marvellous book that might be mine. I was called up and handed a copy of *Walden* by Henry David Thoreau, perhaps the most boring book in the whole lexicon of American literature. It is still unread. We made lifelong friends at Green Vale. I played American football, baseball and lacrosse. We had a French Canadian sports master named "Frenchie" Julien and so were the only grade school playing that great Canadian game, a men's game in America, whereas it's the ladies who play it in England. We did mass calisthenics to the marches of John Phillips Sousa, tobogganed down a modest hill in winter and had a field sports day in spring, where I won the high jump. Our social life was indelibly marked for me by the Friday evening dancing classes held at Piping Rock Club under the tutelage of the socially well-connected Willie de Rham, partnered by a rather swish lady, clearly his mistress, and a demure, older lady at the piano. Here we were to learn to waltz, foxtrot, samba and tango – and another strange skipping sort of ballroom exercise – the polka. The girls were attired in organdie frocks and the boys in blue blazers. Here I became aware of the strange American custom of a precise linkage of generations during formative years, i.e. eleven-year-old boys danced with eleven-year-old girls, twelve year olds together, etc. This was to lead to the disastrous custom of girls marrying men of the same age, which I suggest is the biggest reason for the high divorce rate in America. It is obvious that a twelve-year-old girl is significantly more mature than a twelve-year-old boy. At dancing class, they were always taller as well, it seemed. This led to the inelegant sight of couples struggling around the floor, the boy with his face at the level of budding breasts – leading to early libidinous thoughts, the stronger girl obviously leading and talking her head off, as she had been told by her mother, quite rightly, that her partner would be too shy to maintain a conversation. Willie de Rham also held dancing classes in New York City, and he made it clear that he considered us backward country hicks, compared to the advanced and suave members of his City class. One Friday evening he turned up with a couple from his town class who danced an exhibition number for us rustics. They made the worst impression on us. We boys considered him smarmy and pretentious, with his slicked down hair and to tight blazer. The girls thought his partner a stuck up tart, although, of course, they would have been unaware of such a term. I loved these occasions, however wasted – as we all ended up doing the "nightclub shuffle" in later life.

DY commuted daily by the Long Island RR, in the comfort of the club car. In summer he wore a straw boater with a ribbon in the colours of the Racquet Club of New York and in the winter a Homburg hat, considering a bowler too "Londonish". We were conscious of Mother's concerns over her family in Paris, and the war in Europe had some exposure at Green Vale, due to the presence of British evacuees. One was a young Oliver Fox-Pitt, father of William, the Olympic Thee Day Event gold medallist. Oliver was to become a valued colleague at White, Weld in London, before leaving to start his own boutique. He remembered his wartime days on Long Island, and his annoyance when, out with the Meadowbrook Hounds, he was put on a pony and a lead. In England, aged five, he had already been out on his pony with no lead. But, in general, most of America languished in a false sense of peace. "Thank God, it's not our war this time" was a wide spread sentiment. When the Japanese attacked Pearl Harbour on December 7th 1941, America was at war. In the history of the world, full of colossal strategic errors, this one still stands out as the greatest. Admiral Yamamoto, on being congratulated, is reputed to have said: "All we have done is awaken a sleeping giant". As part of the awakening, White, Weld partners began to go to war. As most were keen sailors, Alec White led a contingent to the U.S. Navy. Jean Cattier was commissioned in the U.S. Army and pursued a distinguished career in intelligence. He had first left to join the Belgian forces in 1940, but after their collapse returned to join the U.S. Army. In the summer before we settled at Bittersweet in 1941, we rented the Cattier house which was close by. There was a lovely pond with a row boat and one day, when I was rowing our then governess, sitting opposite, I could not help noticing she was without knickers. Of such items are childhood memories made. It was decided that DY would not join the colours, although he might have just been of eligible age. But someone had to stay behind to keep the foreign flame burning, and now so many WW clients were from occupied allies: France, Belgium, Holland, Denmark and Norway. Of course, many of our school friends had fathers who went off to

98

war. Our lives hardly changed. There was talk of shortages and some black market activity at the local petrol station, owned by a Mr. Smith. He used to fill the tank with a wink, which became a nervous tick after the war. The comic books were filled with cartoons of yellow men of outrageously villainous appearance, being dispatched by GIs all resembling Greek gods. I spent a good deal of these years roaming in the woods with two whippets – my father favoured this breed of dog because he felt they went well with 18th century furniture. He liked to point out that Frederick the Great had whippets at Sans Souci. One summer I contracted a massive case of poison ivy, which was rampant on the Island. From scratching it soon turned to boils and I spent weeks in bed listening to soup operas on the radio.

The foreign department of White, Weld, without Jean Cattier, simmered gently. Perhaps at the close of the War, a new recruit appeared – I say perhaps, as I think he was a find of Jean Cattier's, who was back at work in 1945. This was a young New Yorker called Harold Mandelsohn who was to become not only the general manager of the foreign department of White, Weld, but its rock of Gibralter. Despite having no European background, he became extremely knowledgeable on foreign dollar bonds and foreign securities in general. Harold was a primary support to the two foreign partners DY and Jean Cattier, and a critical aid to the overseas offices when they were re-established. He fed those prices, notice of new issues, company information, and gossip from the Street, ideas and moral support. There were no Reuters or Bloomberg screens in those days. The daily telex from Harold was the lifeblood of the Hong Kong, London, Amsterdam, and Zurich branches. He was totally reliable. If Harold said it was this way, it was this way; if he said it was that way –that's how it was. Foreign clients, whether private or corporate, doted on him. Often they would specifically ask to see him. Harold was warm and personable. DY could be rather cold and formal. Harold was principal mentor to the intake of new personnel in the Foreign Department – including myself. When Harold Mandelsohn was made a partner of White, Weld & Co., the event was a front page story in the *Wall Street Journal*. This requires some explanation. Well into the 1960s, Wall Street houses were divided by religion and, to some extent, class. There were the great Jewish firms, whose partners comprised *Our Crowd*, as described by Stephen Birmingham in his book of that name. Kuhn, Loeb & Co., Lehman Brothers, Salomon Brothers, Lazard Frères, Goldman Sachs, Seligman Brothers, Wertheim, Bache & Co. Some of these began early to take on Christian partners. There was Joe Thomas, Senior Partner at Lehman, as well as Marcel Palmarro, from Monaco. He was a friend of DY's and lived at Centre Island, near Oyster Bay. He was Honorary Consul for the Principality in New York, parked his car where he liked and used to comment that he was the only subject of Monaco who was neither a croupier nor a policeman. Actually, he was eventually to be joined in his occupation by Enrico Braggiotti, also from Monte Carlo and head of International at Banca Commerciale Italiano. Salomon had Christian partners early on and Seligman Brothers, a great investment banking firm in the 19th century, was eventually taken over by Protestants and became purely an asset management house. Then there were the WASP houses, sometimes referred to as "white shoe" firms – this from the "preppy" fashion of wearing scuffed, white buckskin shoes – I was never without at my prep school. Prominent amongst these were Morgan, Stanley & Co., Kidder, Peabody & Co., White, Weld & Co., Clark, Dodge & Co., Harriman, Ripley & Co., Drexel & Co., First Boston Corporation, Smith, Barney & Co., Dillon, Read & Co., Glore, Forgan, & Co. Stone & Webster Securities Company., Blythe & Co. Harris, Hall & Co. Eastman, Dillon & Co. All of these were included in the "Wall Street Seventeen" – the defendants in the celebrated (and failed) anti-trust case brought by the United States Government against "Henry Morgan, and Harold Stanley, trading as Morgan, Stanley & Co., et al." As it happens, White, Weld was listed at number four in the list. The only Jewish houses included were Kuhn, Loeb and Lehman. Somehow, Salomon, Lazard, Bache and Goldman Sachs escaped. Merrill, Lynch, Pierce, Fenner & Bean also failed to make the defendant's list, but that is entirely understandable as that firm was not engaged in investment banking until much later, when it acquired White, Weld – a disaster to be recounted later in this narrative. Merrill, Lynch was distinguished in several ways. It was not seen as "white shoe" as being essentially Roman Catholic, the firm was a pure agency broker, with a vast network of offices and registered representatives, the "customer's men" of yore. It was the firm that "brought Wall Street to Main Street" and it served a middle to low income client base. If America's success as a capitalist nation is largely due to the fact that a large proportion of its population has a direct, ownership stake in its vast corporate sector, Merrill Lynch can take a good deal of the credit. And so Harold Mandelsohn was the first Jew to be made a partner of a WASP, "white shoe" firm. It was not until 1979 that Morgan Stanley admitted a Jewish partner – Lawrence Barnard. Now all the walls have fallen, of course, but in a perverse way, perhaps, these religious divides acted as a basis for corporate loyalty and *esprit de corps.*

In the postwar period, White, Weld began to recruit the coterie of talent which was to be the basis of its eventual greatness in the euro-market. But just servicing a foreign clientele in New York was not enough; an international presence had to be rebuilt. At war's end, my father had begun traveling to Caracas, Venezuela, where he had become friendly with one Reinaldo Herrera y Uslar, Marques de Torre Casa – to give him his full name. A Spanish aristocrat, born in Caracas, having inherited vast sugar estates, Herrera also owned most of the land in between Caracas and the Country Club, which was the direction in which the city was developing in the boom years after the war. Reinaldito, his son, became a friend of my sister's and married the celebrated Carolina who built a great fashion empire. Oil had been discovered in the Lake Maracaibo basin as early as 1914, with Shell as the first major concessionaire. In 1944, a number of new concessions were awarded and a surge in production took place with one million barrels a day reached in Lake Maracaibo by 1945. American imports of oil rose sharply with the postwar economic recovery, prompting increased sales of motor cars. It took some years before the Arab members of OPEC would begin to dominate U.S. oil imports. DY became greatly taken by the Venezuelan potential and one day announced to the family, gathered for Sunday lunch that he was seriously considering moving lock, stock and barrel to Caracas, Venezuela, where he would make his fortune and that of his partners at White, Weld. "Mais, Dimitri, vous êtes fou!" exclaimed our mother, using one of our most familiar household expressions. Of course, we didn't move to Caracas, but DY became virtually a commuter. On one occasion, he was the only passenger on a PanAm flight leaving Caracas, just before a *coup d'etat* closed the airport. He was interviewed on the evening news and my sister and I were amused by his laid back replies to a frustrated journalist, looking for a sensational account. Coups were the traditional stanza endings of Latin American history and for many years constituted a gentlemanly pursuit. The incoming dictator treated his outgoing victim with respect, and did his best to provide him with a comfortable exile. In the almost certain knowledge that his own regime would end with a coup, he wished to set a precedent for his successor. In Venezuela there were coups in 1945 and again in 1948 – probably the one DY escaped on his lonely PanAm flight). Marco Perez Jiménez, a military man who had participated in the '48 coup, gained power in a vaguely legitimate election in1952. His dictatorship of some seven years ushered in a period of rapid development and prosperity still remembered to this day, when one often hears from the lips of elderly Venezuelans the phrase "in the good old days of Perez Iménez". Yes – he was eventually convicted of having embezzled $200 million, a miserly sum by today's dictatorial standards, but during his reign, massive infrastructure development, significant inward investment by U.S. and other foreign companies and wide spread improvement in living standards, changed the face of the nation. The Perez Jimenéz boom, financially fuelled by increased oil production, attracted an influx of top American companies such as Socony, Phillips, Goodyear, General Electric, Sears, Gulf, Celanese, IBM, and Europeans, such as Phillips Lamp, and even Rolls-Royce... In 1947, an investment firm called La Financiera Venezolana S.A., had been a co-founder of the Caracas Stock Exchange. Its principal shareholders were some Wall Street houses: White, Weld, First Boston, Kuhn Loeb and Kidder, Peabody. A veteran English banker called John Stone, previously with The Bank of London and South America, known as BOLSA, was general manager. But only White, Weld, through DY, had shown an interest in exploiting this presence. Perhaps the others though the place was just too unstable. Then the New York Stock Exchange introduced a rule that member firms with foreign affiliates had to own either less than 5%, or more than 95%, and DY persuaded his partners to buy out the others. DY liked "unstable". John Stone, the general manager, was a typical Britisher gone native. He was in the habit of sitting in his non air-conditioned office with his trouser legs rolled up and his feet in a bucket of ice water beneath his desk, a huge slab of highly polished Venezuelan hardwood. An elderly Frenchman called André Brunet, who had been WW's nominated member of the Caracas Stock Exchange since the outset, was virtually the only other permanent fixture. The business potential was an investment banker's dream. The incoming blue chip American companies were keen to finance their investment in Bolivars. The major oil companies, operating at Maracaibo, had pension funds for their growing number of employees invested in Bolivar denominated assets – but they were not too keen on Venezuelan government bonds. White, Weld's new Venezuelan entity negotiated issues of Bolivar denominated notes by the blue chip U.S. companies and sold them to the oil company pension funds. Another, more bread and butter business, was the origination of "*Avals*". These were $ denominated short-term notes, issued by contractors exploiting the oil lease boom, guaranteed by local banks and insurance companies – hence "*Aval*", which means acceptance, or guarantee, and reinsured at Lloyds of London, which were placed in New York and Europe. When the Perez Jiménez bubble burst, Lloyds lost billions, but White, Weld had withdrawn from the business in time.

To staff this new foreign presence, White, Weld created a team that was to become the nucleus of the firms re-establishment in Europe, and its consequent Euromarkets prominence. At the time, a Dutchman called John Loudon was in charge of Shell's burgeoning activity in the Maracaibo basin. He became the top man at Royal Dutch Shell. My father used to tell him that the one thing White, Weld and Shell had in common was that their international teams had both been formed and trained in Venezuela. Two Loudon sons became friends of mine; John was at Lazard's and then Rothschild, and George at AMRO, and a colleague at European Banking Company. DY's most significant recruitment – with the Venezuela operation in mind – was a young Swiss called Robert Genillard. How young is not really known, as he fibbed about his age in the interview, fearing he would be seen as two young. Like all good Swiss, he spoke perfect French, German, Italian, English and Spanish. His people were hoteliers and his father owned and managed hotels in Villars and in Italy. His mother was English – and thereby hangs a tail. Bob was not partial to the English and it took me some time to realise why. His English grandparents had been holidaying with their daughter at a Swiss resort hotel. The daughter fell in love with the son of the owner/manager, announced her intention of marrying him – and did so. Her county family were so incensed at what they consider an unsuitable alliance that they boycotted the daughter for life, refusing even to attend at her deathbed. Not surprisingly, the child of that alliance considered that his mother had been the victim of an outrageous piece of English snobbery. Bob Genillard had everything it takes to become a leading international banker of his generation: looks, presence, self-confidence, profound intelligence, judgment, foresight, overwhelming ambition for his firm and himself, and an ability to lead and inspire his colleagues. Bob was also someone who knew his mind. When the Zurich office of White, Weld was opened under his management, he and his Aruba, Dutch Antilles-born wife Nina wanted to put their children in the French school. The authorities came to him and said that as a Swiss, even though Vaudois i.e. French speaking, he could not put his children in the French school which was only for foreigners. Bob said he didn't want his children to be taught in Switzerdeutsch, which some regard as a disease of the throat, and he would leave them where they were. The authorities came back and said the children would be removed by force. Bob replied that he could not stop them, but he would have the *Time Magazine* Zurich based correspondent, plus a photographer, present to record the event. "Perhaps we can come to some arrangement, Herr Doktor Genillard," replied the authorities. The children stayed. A daughter, Ariane, – named, dare I suggest, after my sister? Became a distinguished correspondent for the *Financial Times* in Frankfort – clearly not disadvantaged in the German language by her attendance at the French school in Zurich.

Another Swiss to join the Caracas office was Serge Sarasin, of a prominent Swiss banking and medical family. Serge was a relation of a great family friend, Rosemarie, eventually to be Comtesse d'Escayrac-Lauture, wife of Bernard, who the nuns at the Chateau du Belvedère, where Ariane and I had been born, had regarded with suspicion as the regular visitor to our mother. Serge had been educated at McGill University in Toronto and impressed us children by the speed with which he navigated the Long Island roads on his visits to the parents. Serge courted for years and eventually married a beautiful model girl from the Deep South, whose hands appeared in every jewellery ad, and who eventually became a great Geneva hostess. They both greatly admired DY and named a son Dimitri. John Cattier, nephew of Jean Cattier, after Yale and service in the U.S. Army, soon joined the team. John was to become the administrative brains behind White, Weld International, Bob Genillard's closest collaborator, and one of the founders of Euro Clear. John was the ultimate cerebral banker – not an originator or even a relationship banker, but a defining source of interpretation and judgment with regard to transactions or functional activity being proposed by his colleagues. A tribute to the value of nepotism – dare I say it. Another recruit of Jean Cattier's was a Belgian from Louvain: Jacques Appelmans married to an American lady and a dedicated family man. Not for Jacques the frantic late night sessions, or last minute voyages. Jacques was a strict nine-to-five man with little time for business entertainment or other extra-curricular activities. But his contribution was considerable, even though one was never sure of exactly what he did. The answer, I suspect, was all the important things which others were neglecting in their haste to do their own thing. What I do recall is that it was Jacques who was the initial scout and organiser once DY had secured permission to open in Zurich, circa 1954. Jacques rented a house near Lausanne where I was doing time, so to speak, in a summer course at the University. I went to help him compiling client records, as private clients from the Caracas operation were being transferred to WW's new Swiss entity. It was my first exposure to the typical international private client's portfolio, containing – yes, you guessed it: foreign dollar bonds.

Another of DY's momentous recruitments was John Stancliffe, and this through the intermediation of Manfred Rothbart. Manfred was a Dutch Jew of immense culture and charm who had made the Amsterdam office of White, Weld a great success. He owned a bijou residence outside Amsterdam, but his cousin Herbert owned an estate in the Chilterns in England, where he had resided for some time. Amongst his friends was the Stancliffe family, who even resided in a house on his estate during the war to keep their children from harm's way. But it was Manfred who learned that DY was looking for someone to add to the never closed, and now revived, London office. He arranged for young Stancliffe to meet my parents who were staying with Herbert at Chenkenden Court. Just down from Cambridge, where he had been a varsity "oar", Stancliffe was looking for a job but had apparently no particular bias towards finance or the City. It took DY about an hour to persuade John, using the pitch I was to use thereafter when I was team building: it matters not what field of economic activity interests you: energy, manufacture, retail, communications, media, shipping – whatever; as an investment banker you will get more than a taste of them all. John did his formative stint in Caracas from 1957. Once settled in the London office, John was to suffer a bit from one of DY's more bizarre recruits: an Irish American called Jack Gallagher, who apparently reminded DY of the Johnny Haines in the prewar Paris office. Jack Gallagher certainly shared his Irish predecessors drinking habits. He was immensely social and popular in the City despite his somewhat curious appearance, with red hair curling over his collar. Although born and brought up in New York, where he was reputed to have courted a Rockefeller daughter, Jack had gone so native in London that P. G. Wodehouse might have considered him over the top. He spent hours on the phone, particularly towards the weekend, organising his social life – to the despair of John Stancliffe. He did cultivate widespread City contacts, which must have produced some commission business, but he was a bit of a disaster. Still, he was responsible for my being assigned to London – as will be recounted later in this story. He refused to fly and so travelled to New York to report, by ship. One day, having ostensibly gone to visit Head Office, he simply disappeared from the face of the earth. A warm body was needed urgently to help Stancliffe and the now ageing, but still nominal general manager in London – John Rasch.

The "good old days of Perez Jiménez", harbouring White, Weld's first major postwar international venture, only lasted a short while, but the personnel and client base that resulted was to be a corner stone of the firms European franchise. In April of 1959, La Financiera Venezolana S.A., Investment Bankers and Brokers a subsidiary of White, Weld & Co., New York, investment bankers since 1896, so described on the firm's brochures, gave a reception for DY and Alec White – a "last hurrah", perhaps. All the Venezuelan establishment figures in the guest list, with their corporate or diplomatic affiliations shown. Reinaldo Herrera Uslar's is listed as "landed fortune". One Robert Bottome, "broker" was to be a major source of clients. Also present were the Vollmers, Venezuela's wealthiest family – a sugar fortune. Several representatives of the Mendoza Group were also in attendance. What is clear is that in less than ten years, White, Weld had built an astonishing number of connections in what was then Latin America's premier emerging economy. Its present state makes one weep.

CHAPTER IX

"That slender riotous island"

-F. Scott Fitzgerald describing Long Island in *The Great Gatsby*-

I have never been certain how to best explain the expression "formative years". It is both imprecise in its meaning and broad in its scope. It is generally supposed to encompass the years between one reaching conscious age, another imprecise phrase, and full manhood or womanhood. But the formative process, I would argue, is in fits and starts and does not begin and end so neatly as, say, at five and eighteen, or at three and twenty-one. Nowadays, social commentators are obsessed with teenagers, a category of recent invention. One finds no teenagers in the family novels of Balzac and Trollope, perhaps because they were then regarded as basically uninteresting. I suppose Trollope's *The Duke's Family,* is an exception that proves the rule. I consider teenagers to be still uninteresting – and annoying to boot; but their trials and tribulations, addictive habits and sex lives are the stuff of endless contemporary comment, fictional treatment and general concern. Teenage also now seems to start as early as eleven or twelve and one finds people behaving like teenagers in their late twenties. As I am now about to treat a period I regard as my "formative years", I must find some *apologia* and the only one that strikes me is that, for better or worse, the years I spent on the North Shore of Long Island between 1941 and 1957 marked me indelibly, like a tattoo one may regret having contracted in a moment of weakness, but which one sees every day. You might think this obvious, but I would disagree. I know many who either don't remember, or don't wish to remember, their formative years and certainly don't consider them important in later life. But for me, every aspect of my later life has been impregnated with impressions, memories and feelings of those dozen or so years I spent growing up domiciled on that "riotous island", and this with both negative and positive consequences – mostly negative, I fear. What passes for my education is also encompassed by this period – in three institutions of learning: Greenvale School, Deerfield Academy and Harvard College – although I acquired a good deal of my general knowledge from my parents and their friends.

My sister and I lived more of a home life at Bittersweet than our contemporaries for two reasons: our European heritage which tends to stress family life, and the fact that we enjoyed the company of older people – in particular parental friends and partners/colleagues of DY. I think our school mates at Greenvale were rather more minded to seek out and enjoy the company of their contemporaries. Our favourite week end visitor was Jury Havemann, DY's oldest Russian friend and now well-established at White, Weld, where he never made partner, through lack of ambition, I suspect. He had been married briefly to an American lady named Barbara, who moved to California. Mother went to stay with her to recover after contracting malaria – there were stagnant pools of water on sandy Long Island. Barbara had the English actor and leading member of the Beverley Hills Cricket Club, Reginald Owen, as a friend, and I believe he made a serious pass at Mother. But Jury had only one son who lived with his mother, so he was at least an uncle to us and played with us each weekend, to our father's amusement. In winter he helped us build igloos in the snow, which collapsed just before cocktail time; in the summer he played threesome tennis with us, running back and forth in a great sweat. With guests at dinner, we dined early in the servant's dining room, and Jury joined us, already changed, Martini in hand. He would start by opening his cigarette case and offering one to Ariane; "Of course, you don't smoke – do you mind if I do?" first to Ariane, who would shake her head, and then to the Governess, who would glower. Jury would tell us endless "shaggy dog" stories, which usually began "A man walks into a bar". In one case it was "A horse walks into a bar, sits on a stool and orders a Dry Martini. There is only one other customer watching. The barman shakes the Martini and puts it in front of the horse. The horse points at it with a hoof and says 'you forgot the olive'. The barman fetches the olive, the horse downs the Martini, pays, and walks out. The other customer exclaims 'that's incredible!!' 'What's incredible?' replies the barman 'Anyone can forget an olive.'" Jury was very fond of dry Martinis. In summer he would pour out the dregs of the shaker on to a patch of pachasandra before mixing his second. The patch seemed to thrive and Jury explained it loved the gin. Of course it was the melted ice it loved. At tea, my mother, before pouring, would ask Jury, "Perhaps you would prefer a whiskey and soda?" Jury would consider this question as if it was being asked for the first time. We always knew the answer. It was Jury who explained to me later in life why you cannot get a decent Martini in London and for the same reason you cannot get a decent gin and tonic in New York. It's the difference in proof of the gin – too weak in London and too strong in New York. Another in the list of valuable lessons I learned from my father's friends.

One Russian visitor was rather painful. Valentina, a fashionable dress designer of Russian origin – my father would comment: "place and date uncertain" – was often escorted by my godfather Jack Barrett. On arrival,

Valentina, covered in costume jewellery, would rush to Ariane and me: "Ah! The beau-ti-ful chil-dren!! Ariashka! Stashka!" and smother us with hugs and kisses, the sharp edges of her costume jewellery digging into our flesh. It was like being enclosed in an iron maiden. Valentina had a career designing for Hollywood, and one sees "Gowns by Valentina" in the credits of black and white films of the period. She was married to George Schley, but he normally escorted Greta Garbo at this time, and they were thought by some to be a "ménage à trois", particularly as Garbo was bisexual. In later years, Valentina would consider my godfather at her beck and call – 'phoning him when he was staying with us in Senlis, saying "Come Jacques! We go to Gritti Palace in Venice – drink champagne!' When he thought me old enough to understand, DY explained to me that Jack Barrett was "neutral" by which he meant, neither one way nor the other. Sexuality was not then the subject of endless fascination and politicking as it is now, and we were aware, but hardly concerned. "Gay" was a word used to describe parties and nights out. Still in the Russian vein, one day a piano tuner was summoned from the city, and it was announced that a Russian friend was to bring Sergei Rachmaninoff to lunch and, who knows? – He might agree to play. My father rather thought not, as the great man was on a coast to coast concert tour. Rachmaninoff was a friend of my grandmother's, who moved in artistic circles in St. Petersburg. It also transpired that Rachmaninoff had left Petrograd for Stockholm on the same boat as my father in 1918, but they had not connected. He played, he lunched and he left, patting Ariane on the head and urging her to persevere with her piano studies. She didn't.

We were always aware of who wore the trousers in the couples who came to stay. Bernard d'Escayrac and Rosemarie Sarasin were together, but unmarried for some time, as she waited for a divorce. We always referred to them as "the Rosemaries". Eventually, they bought a house in Oyster Bay. Their neighbours were the Brewster Righters, whose son, also Brewster, became one of my closest friends. Mr. Righter impressed our father, who adored eccentricity, by coming to dinner one night in a perfectly cut dinner jacket and a pair of white tennis shoes. I went to visit at their house and young Bruce decided to teach me to drive. We were 12. He put me behind the wheel and I drove straight into the back of the garage. Rosemarie was madly social and Bernard used to put "MD" behind his name, explaining he was *"docteur en mondanités"*. Once a Princess of France was a guest of the Englehards in New York and Rosemarie went into overdrive organising a dinner for the young to meet *"Son Altesse Royale"*, and reminding everyone she was to be addressed as "Madame" even though unmarried. I was home on Christmas break from Harvard, and Rosemarie phoned my mother to stress how honoured I was to be included in the dinner and so on and so forth. Of course, I had already met *Son Altesse Royale* at El Morocco with mutual friends and on my arrival at the dinner, the Princess came up to me and said "*Stani! Bon soir, comment va tu?*" to the disgust and consternation of Rosemarie. It was already the custom of young people in France to say "*tu*" to each other on first acquaintance. Bernard had become head of Guerlain, the perfumers, for the Americas, and had a smart office on Park Avenue. I made a point on calling in at the start of the Christmas Deb party season in New York. He would always say how kind and thoughtful it was of me to call on an old fogey at the height of the party season. He would then press a bell and say to his secretary: "A *flacon* of *L'Heure Bleu* for my young friend – it is the most appropriate for *les jeunes filles*!" Naturally, I was a hit with my girl for the evening, and equally naturally, Bernard was fully aware of my hidden agenda – but he played the game and I loved him for it. He gave me bits of advice: "*Mon petit Stanislas,*" as he always called me, "*souviens toi que dans la vie tout s'arrange – mal – mais tous s'arrange*". "Always remember that in life everything gets fixed – badly – but it gets fixed." He also enjoined me only to marry a pretty girl, rich or poor – but never an ugly girl, no matter how rich. This, because ugly girls were bitter all their lives. I doubted that. Funnily enough, Rosemarie was hardly pretty, nor rich. The Guerlain brothers, Jean-Pierre and Jean-Jacques who ran the family business, were great friends and DY was advisor to them, not just for portfolio investment but on some strategic issues as well. Jean-Pierre's wife Christiane, heiress to a dairy products fortune, was the greatest lady shot in France, champion at *Tir au Pigeons* in Monte Carlo – a rather nasty sport involving released pigeons- and well-known on the Scottish moors. She was beautiful and elegant. The Jean-Pierres were childless and they were particularly kind to Ariane and me. Christiane was on the best of terms with all the *haute couturiers* of the period. When I was about 15 and in Paris, Christiane took me to a couple of fashion shows. At Dior, she decided to take me back stage where I was suddenly confronted with several drop-dead gorgeous model girls in various stages of undress, as they changed for the next parade. Christiane looked at me and asked if I was having a heart attack. One must remember that access to female nudity for boys in America was much more restricted that today – no TV and no 'top-shelf' magazines. In fact, I really was interested in fashion, not just for the charge my adolescent hormones had just experienced. My mother had her evening gowns made by Jean Desses, or Balanciaga, her suits by Coco Channel and her day dresses by Pierre Balmain. I followed fashion and even thought of becoming a designer. I believed I had ideas. On the evening after the show, still shaking, I was at dinner with the Jean-Pierre Guerlains and seated next to Balmain who had just returned from Bangkok, having designed the entire trousseau of the new Queen of Thailand – from undies to umbrellas. I hesitatingly communicated my possible interest in becoming a dress designer.

"I suppose you would design the kind of dresses you like to see women wearing?" said the great man.

"Of course!" I replied.

"My dear young man (*Mon cher jeune homme*) – choose another profession. You seem under the impression that women dress for men. Nothing could be further from the truth. They dress for other women. I have only just met you, but I must tell you that I don't think your feminine side is sufficiently developed to have an instinct about what women wear and why." End of dream.

The parents' dinner parties were always an occasion for Ariane and me as well. We would have supped and donned dressing gowns before their dinner was announced, and, having done the round of curtsying and hand kissing, we would repair to the top of the stairs, just out of sight. Francis the butler would announce dinner in the French manner, *Madame est servie,* and the guests would troop down the short stairs to the dining room, chattering away, with only a few regulars like Jury stealing a glance and a smile at us above. As soon as the dining room door closed, we would rush to the drawing room, drain the cocktail glasses (it was bad form to take a pre-dinner drink to the table in those days) and scoff the remaining canapés. We knew fairly well how much time we had before Francis would have finished serving the first course and would return to clear the drawing room. We only got caught if some lady sent him to retrieve a purse. Our state of inebriation after finishing off all the drinks would depend on how abstemious the guests were, and how full the glasses. The household was run on very Continental lines. Mother always had breakfast in bed, and did so every day of her life, even when she had no staff and had to get it herself. At Bittersweet, she had a vast bedroom, French windows looking out on the lawn, a huge Emperor sized, and satin-covered bed and, exceptionally, entirely French furniture. It must have been the bedroom of Mr. Cravath's mistress. During breakfast, Cook would be standing at the end of the bed, pad in hand, to discuss the day's menus. If we were admitted, we would sprawl on the bed, the size of a boxing ring, as it seemed to us, and wait for the menu meeting to terminate. Sometimes we would hazard an interjection: "Please, can we have butterscotch pudding?" Heading the staff, which included a couple of maids, was Francis, the Swiss butler, whose name was Siegenthaler, but he was called by his Christian name in the French fashion rather than by his surname, English style. He much preferred valeting my father to his other duties and was rather disrespectful to his mistress, referring to her sarcastically as *Madame votre sainte mère* when speaking to the children. Then, of course, there was a succession of governesses who came and went for reasons that, today, would have kept an industrial tribunal busy with unfair dismissal cases for months. One turned out to be a Quaker. She took us to the Quaker Meeting House in Locust Valley, one of the oldest in the country. We were fascinated, but when our mother found out, the lady was sacked. Another fell ill and when Mother proposed to call a doctor, she declined, admitting she was Christian Science – immediate dismissal. The longest serving and the most brutal was a Madame Beaugrand, who enjoyed twisting one's wrist in punishment for transgressions, which were numerous. Father's bedroom was across a small passage from Mother's, with the bathroom at one end, and must have been a dressing room, as there was hardly room to swing a cat, which we could no longer have, as it scratched the furniture. He had a small mahogany bed stand against the wall, also a fireplace and his desk against the only window. We could not help noticing the disparity in our parent's accommodation. They never shared a bedroom, which we didn't find that odd and were rather surprised when we came across the sleeping arrangements of our friend's parents. On the other hand, it is worth remarking that our parents never divorced, whereas we had precious few friends whose parents were *not* divorced. They used to brag about double presents at Christmas and in a rare and unique fit of identity crisis, Ariane told her friends that Mother was actually stepmother. She wanted to fit in. When Mother discovered this, she was furious. I understood completely.

Ariane had adapted to our school life far better than I. She was hugely popular with both girls and boys, poised, soft-spoken, with a carriage and a manner which distinguished her amongst her peers. She relished being different (except for that one lapse about a stepmother) and would soon learn to exploit it socially. On the other hand, I still suffered from being different and compensated by showing off and generally making a nuisance of myself. At one stage – I might have been 12 or 13 – I decided to become a man of the people, or rather, a boy of the people, thinking this might lead to integration. After all, the "people" were mostly of immigrant stock. I adopted a quiff hairstyle, popular at the time, and tried to imitate the *patois* of the local lads. The trouble was there were few boys of the people for me to associate with, other than sons of the neighbour's gardeners. At one point I took to caddying at Piping Rock, not strictly allowed for member's sons – but the caddy master turned a blind eye. The caddies, mostly Italian lads from Glenn Cove, where a Little Italy existed, were bemused by my presence and told me graphic stories of their female conquests. As a sexual education it was perhaps a touch raw, but I listened with polite interest. I never cashed in the vouchers I received from the members, who must have wondered why their accounts were not charged. But I began then to play golf at the right age. But my period of pretended slumming came to an end when I discovered the new social fashion of our time and place: sophistication. It was Ariane who pointed out to me the significance of this new pose. A young man named Morton Smith appeared in our midst and the cry went up, "He's so sophisticated!" This was an almost exact equivalent of today's expression "cool", still much overused by pre-teen and teen. But there is a huge difference. "Cool" today seems to signify unkempt, ill-mannered, slouched, incomprehensible in speech and generally anti-social. Perhaps there is some connection in that in both cases it is an essentially languid pose which is affected. Sophisticated meant well groomed, hair well cut, shaved, neatly dressed, well-spoken – although we all assumed an accent still known as "Locust Valley lockjaw", well-mannered but, above all, worldly. The sophisticate danced beautifully, produced just the right corsage, knew the right places to go, the right people, the right conversational gambits, the right sports, the right books, and in everything sought to appear as grown up as possible – certainly older than his years. Of course, this was to lead to some excess in smoking and drinking as well. And it was drink that was the curse of our sophisticated generation, to paraphrase Wilde – rather than drugs, the "cool" vice. I found it easy to adopt this new fashionable pose, largely because of my European upbringing. My sister was born sophisticated. A delicate liver prevented my tumbling into alcoholism, even if I tested the limit somewhat. I have no idea what happened to Morton Smith, but I fear the worst.

The American scholastic year provides an exceptionally long summer holiday. Schools at all levels used to break up in the first week of June and autumn term began soon after Labour Day, the first Monday in September. So it was in summer that we "lived". Many of our friends went off to summer camps where they played at being red Indians in the woods. Mother considered this an aberration by her peers as she looked forward to spending more time with us. This meant lunches in the outdoor dining porch, when my sister would kick me under the table, and nights for us spent on a screened porch just off Mother's room, to escape the heat. In the twin beds we could whisper to each other about the iniquities of our current governess – normally we had separate rooms. Ariane was sent to summer camp once, at her request, I think. She came down with the measles and had to be evacuated by DY, together with Nelje Doubleday, Nelson's sister. Incidentally, I had a mad crush on Nelje. I seemed to be more attracted to Ariane's female classmates than my own. I was also besotted with Kira Hawkins, whose mother was Russian and a frequent conversation partner of DY's. Her brother Ashton ended up as legal counsel to the Metropolitan Museum of Art. But then, I also broke all convention by developing a passion for Linda Lowry, whose brother David was a beau of Ariane's. My secret love was discovered when I got off the Greenvale School bus to attend a party of 7th graders, where Linda would be. But I was an 8th grader, and I received a serious ticking off from my classmate Lela Leslie, who would have accused me of paedophilia, if she had been familiar with the word. At about this time, whilst Ariane was at summer camp, the parents and I set off by train for Wyoming to stay at a dude ranch, Bear Paw – near Jackson Hole, then truly a one saloon town, now a huge ski resort. We stopped off in Chicago and stayed with DY's partner Brick Meers, whose Chicago office was one of White, Weld's most productive. In Lake Forrest, the Meers gave us a steak which I have never forgotten. Bear Paw Ranch had been recommended by the Joseph Verner Reeds, and marched with the huge Rockefeller property, now Grand Teton National Park. DY was amused that none of the locals seemed to appreciate the French origin of the name of this section of the Rockies – Big Tit. I became an apprentice wrangler and returned the following summer on my own as a full-fledged wrangler. My day began at five o'clock when I rode out to collect the horses which had been released the night before, with bells on a few. They were usually grazing within a few miles of the corral. I would listen for the sound of a bell and then, having come across them, would round them up and drive them back to the corral, emitting the traditional "yippee yea's" and striking my chaps with my coiled rope. It was important to remember to open the coral door before leaving. I forgot once and the horses ended up grazing the lawn in front of the breakfasting guests. Then I breakfasted and prepared to saddle up for morning ride. This involved going into the corral, roping the correct horse, leading it out, and tacking it up. I practised roping for hours on a fence post (lassoing, as it is known in Europe). I could still do it today. I also learned to rope calves, chasing them at the gallop, dismounting, chucking them down by grabbing the offside legs and binding the four legs with a small rope held between the teeth.

Summer was also trips to Europe, always by ship, accompanied by heavy Vuitton luggage. I was induced to go by parents seeking to separate me from inappropriate associations, eventually a female relationship – a subject of particular parental disapproval. Ariane preferred to stay at home, with friends. She never had inappropriate associations – except perhaps one, but he produced mirth rather that concern. He was a funny Frenchman, brought home only once and, after he was found to have cleaned his shoes with a white linen towel in the downstairs cloakroom, he was no longer considered a threat. All her friends, of both sexes, always passed muster – not quite in my case. I much enjoyed these European visits and felt close to my roots. For DY it was essentially work. His partners used to pull his leg. For them Europe was a playground. "Tell us, DY, how you get away with being on holiday all summer?" they would josh. He did do endless rounds of business visits but for the time off he did take, DY loved motoring and would stick to the white, or smallest, roads on the Michelin maps. One saw rural France in all its glories and the Michelin guide assured my culinary education. Once, we met up with Jean Cattier and his new bride at the famous restaurant *Chez Point* in Vienne, near Lyon. Three starred and owned by the most famous chef of his time, this was a gastronomic monument. Jean Cattier's first wife was a show girl called Ruth. It was hard to think of Jean as a stage-door Johnny, but he certainly had the eye. Ruth was beautiful but unsophisticated, to put it mildly. At one point (pun intended), during the *maître d'hôtel's* discourse on the fare, she leaned over to my mother and whispered, "Gee! What I wouldn't give for a hamburger and a coke!" Without blinking the *maître d'hôtel* enquired how she would like her burger cooked and soon the *sommelier* brought an ice bucket with a bottle of Coca-Cola wrapped in a linen towel. That was a proper luxury restaurant. If you tried that today in a starred Michelin restaurant, you would get a haughty look and the miscreant would probably be asked to leave. Point had been the mentor of Henri Soulé, the restaurateur who came with the French pavilion to the 1940 World Fair at Flushing Meadow in New York. Soulé stayed behind and opened *Le Pavilion* in Manhattan, which became the venue of choice for the elite of the city. DY, one of the first businessmen to travel frequently to Europe immediately after the war, would bring him items unobtainable in the U.S., such as *paté de fois gras,* thus earning him seating at the best tables. There were usually so many celebrities scattered about, one had difficulty concentrating on the food, which was so good enthusiasts travelled from Paris to dine there. Back on the Continent, our parents frequented a Cote d'Azure resort called *Le Val d'Isquière,* not far from St Tropez. I suffered a severe liver attack from overindulgence in the sauces at the restaurant there, and my mother fed me a charcoal preparation which helped. I began to associate Europe with the glamorous life I craved, without really knowing it, and I was indulged in this by my father – to the dismay of my mother, who had realised early on that I was fundamentally lazy and feared, quite correctly, that I might be corrupted by an addiction to the "best" of everything. In addition to the top hotels and restaurants we frequented, my father took me to all the best shops and suppliers he patronised. I had my first dinner jacket made by Carracenni in Rome and he then took me to Anderson & Sheppard in Saville Row, where my tail coat and morning coat was made. My first black tie was not a success. When I showed up at a party in New York, my friend George Fowlkes said, "It fits like a glove – too bad it doesn't fit like a dinner jacket." Whether it was The Antique Porcelain Company in London or Louis Vuitton in Paris – where DY would ask for Monsieur Vuitton, who would come out from the back to serve him – I came to know every supplier of the "best". Sadly, Mr. Weinberg's shop is no more and Vuitton is now a vulgar supplier to the Asian market. My father's theory was that the only way to motivate me was to accustom me to a life style that would force me to work hard, as he certainly did not intend to leave me an inheritance. To this day, I am not sure who was right.

Secondary school time arrived and what are known as "prep schools" had to be chosen for Ariane and me. Here is a fine example of Anglo/American linguistic confusion. What are prep schools in America are public schools in England, i.e. private secondary schools. Public schools in America are State schools. What are known as prep schools in England, are pre-prep schools in America. I once listened in fascination to a conversation between my wife and my mother about dressing the children. It went on for half an hour, labouring under a fundamental misunderstanding. When my wife talked about a vest, she meant an undershirt. But my mother took it to mean a waistcoat, known as a vest in America. I thought is so amusing I didn't intervene. My sister was sent to Westover, one of a clutch of fashionable girls' public schools, in the English meaning, which includes Farmington – or Miss. Porter's School, to give it its proper name, Foxcroft – very horsey – and Garrison Forest. There was a certain muchness about them, except that each instilled a distinctive handwriting and I was able to tell which girlfriend was writing me at boarding school by looking at the envelope. My father claimed that all Farmington girls had the same walk. Some consider that there is a Benenden walk in England – a "jolly hockysticks" pace of sorts. Westover was a great success and Ariane still goes to reunions. For me the choice was dictated by Permelia Reed, a very determined lady indeed. The Reeds were intimate friends, stemming from the warm reception they had given both father and mother on their arrivals in America – as already mentioned. Every Fourth of July we went over to Greenwich, Connecticut, to their vast spread Denbigh Farm for Independence Day fireworks and endless entertainments. The driveway was lined with brown paper bags filled with sand with a lit candle stuck inside. The children's toys and gadgets were unimaginably varied and plentiful. There was a resident tennis pro. The four boys became great friends and Ariane married the eldest – Adrian. Permelia Reed was a strong and wilful lady but, as with Lady Thatcher, dare I say it – her heart was always in the right place. The Reed boys went to Deerfield Academy and so Stani must go to Deerfield Academy. "There is to be no discussion about it, Dimitri!" I still hear her saying. It was an inspired choice, as Deerfield was a truly unique establishment.

Located in an historic colonial village in north western Massachusetts – on the autumn foliage tourist route, Deerfield was famous for its Headmaster, Dr. Frank Boyden, the only private secondary school head master to make the cover of *Time Magazine*. Dr. Boyden had founded the school as a young man down from Amhurst College, and was well into his '70s when I arrived. A little man physically, and somewhat wizened, he had a commanding presence as he stood at daily assembly, the boys all seated cross-legged on the floor, whilst a master called Mr. Sullivan, called the roll at breakneck speed. Dr. Boyden was always dressed in a series of identical blue serge double-breasted suits with a white shirt and maroon four-in-hand tie, eschewing the "preppy" look of tweed jacket, grey flannel bags, regimental tie and scuffed, white buckskin shoes favoured by the masters, and universally adopted by the students. Every aspect of the school bore his mark and no departure from his model escaped his notice. Technically, the school was Congregational, after the sect of the colonial church in the village, which had not a vestige of any religious motto or artefact inside. But most of the boys were Episcopalian, with a smattering of Presbyterians, but only a handful of Catholics. We few were bussed to neighbouring Greenfield for Mass on Sunday. There may have been a Jewish boy or two, but not practicing. East Coast origins predominated, but we had rather more boys from the Midwest than our peer group, and we had an heir to the King Ranch in Texas and a son of David Selznick from Hollywood. Notables have continued to attend, as the present King of Jordan is an old boy, as is his brother. The school was big on games, playing other New England schools like Andover, Exeter and Choate in soccer, American football, ice hockey, baseball and lacrosse at three levels up to varsity. Dr. Boyden, known as the "Head", and vulgarly as the "Quid", would drive a horse and buggy around the playing fields observing the games, and knock out "grounders" to the infielders at baseball practice. The Masters were drawn heavily from Amhurst and Dartmouth. A Mr. Crow, spare and snobbish, from Chicago, supervised the debating team and talked politics to us. He told me my debating style was too vicious, and also that he knew something about me so terrible he could not disclose it. I still don't know what it was. A Mr. McGlynn, birdlike and Scottish, taught English composition and literature, and was my favourite. If my grammar offends you, he is to blame – or my editor, if I am lucky enough to have one. A Mr. Poland, gaunt and humourless, taught maths and physics – at which I was hopeless. A Mr. Merriam, small and powerful, was a sports master and accused me of cowardice because I avoided contact at lacrosse. I explained that, as I played at crease, it was my responsibility to avoid being wiped out by a burly defence man, particularly classmate Mike "Bull" Durham, who was one of my best friends. A Mr. Oates, alcoholic and shaky, was music master and conducted the chorus. He had written the school song and was proud to count amongst his old boys the musical comedy star Gordon MacCrae and the light opera tenor Robert Rounsville. His favourite soloist in our class was Kim Townsend, who was the best at everything he did, whether academic or sporting, but still managed to be popular. I immediately fell in with a rather bolshie crowd, got caught smoking, neglected homework and generally behaved badly. On a parental visit, my mother was horrified to be told by Dr. Boyden that I was the most difficult boy he had ever encountered. "But, Mummy!" I expostulated, "He says that to all the mothers! Think about it – he has been headmaster for over fifty years. It is statistically impossible that I should be the most difficult boy he has ever had!" I was very pleased with this entirely logical argument, but my mother did not buy it, never forgot the Head's comment, and continued to tax me with it, even when I was Chairman of Merrill Lynch Europe, Middle East and Africa and thoroughly grown up. The Head finally appointed me a cheerleader. We had the duty of marshalling the crowd at football games and so it was a position of responsibility. It improved my behaviour sufficiently to avoid expulsion and to gain admittance to college. A number of boys from Greenwich, including Sam Reed and John Barrett, nephew of my godfather, were kind to me. We played invented games in the dormitory corridors, tried to age apple cider to an alcoholic level short of the jug exploding and looked forward to our spring breaks in Hobe Sound, Florida – the Reed fiefdom. There is no question that Deerfield was an exceptional educational and moral experience for me, just first in ranking to my years in the U.S. Marine Corps. I retain many vivid memories, but two above all. At the beginning of autumn term, when the foliage was at its most glorious, the Head would say at assembly: "Look up at the hills, boys, look up at the hills!" Akin to looking at green grass on the rifle range to clear the vision, a look at nature is a psychological purifier. At the end of term he would say, "Let's finish up strong, boys!" knowing all too well the human tendency to relax before a task is fully completed.

My *vie mondaine*, as Rosemarie d'Escayrac would have said, kicked off during my first years at Deerfield. It had not taken me long to realise that I could piggy-back on my sister Ariane's social success. We are only 22 month apart in age, and I just qualified for some of her parties. Generously, she often arranged for me to tag along. I began to be widely known as "Ariane's brother", even receiving invitations addressed as such, and, to this day, there are many friends on Jupiter Island who are uncertain of my real name but know me perfectly well under that title. Ariane had a pre-deb party at Bittersweet which was one of Lester Lanin's first gigs on Long Island and he came himself with a small group. Of course, I was in eager attendance and it was the beginning of a long love affair with the music of Lester Lanin, which was based almost entirely on the American Song Book. Lanin, and Meyer Davis, were to the debutante season what the combined band of the Brigade of Guards is to the Trooping of the Colour. In later years, Lester Lanin became a favourite of the Queen Mother, whose knowledge of American musical comedy stemmed from her friendship with Adele and Fred Astaire, who she had met in the 1930s as Duchess of York. The American debutante season is a phenomenon with early roots in the English custom of presentation at Court for young ladies of quality. In the absence of a Sovereign, the American debs were presented to a pair of New York society matrons at a Cotillion, first of the Christmas season of New York balls. In a typical example of American overstatement, the poor girls were required to be escorted by two white tie and tailed young swains, one either side, as they floated up to the platform for the curtsey. From those debs who had not been able to collar two victims during the summer break, one received pleading letters at school during autumn term. It was thus I learned to recognise the handwriting of different schools. To require young ladies of good society to shamelessly solicit escorts in this way seemed to me just short of putting them on the street in fishnet tights, a split skirt and a string handbag for twirling. Perhaps in the old days it was all arranged by diktat from the parents. Once I became fully engaged in this social charavari, I would be in white tie and tails four nights a week during the Christmas season in town. At four in the morning, a hamburger joint on Madison Avenue, called "Hamburger Heaven", would contain one or two taxi drivers and a dozen or more bright young things in taffeta evening gowns and white ties and tails, downing burgers after some nightclubbing exercise. It was the custom to repair, after the ball, to the night clubs of the moment which were LaRue, the Stork Club and El Morocco. These offered discounts to the fashionable young, and placed them at prominent tables, as added decoration – to offset the tired businessmen and their questionable ladies. At the time, Cholly Knickerbocker, alias of a popular gossip columnist, reported on the social life of what was becoming known as café society. Proper society shunned this publicity – at least the older generation did. Ariane was under strict instructions not to set foot in LaRue, or any other such venue, under any circumstances. Our parents had a small flat in town on 63rd Street, for the convenience of Ariane's New York engagements, once her deb season got under way. It so happens it was just opposite LaRue, but Ariane did not imagine that the parents would be spying through the window at 2:30 in the morning – so one night she decided to chance it. They were not so invasive as to be on watch, but the next morning there appeared in Cholly Knickerbocker's column an item: "Seen last night on Bindy Banker's arm at LaRue, Ariane Yassukovich, lovely deb daughter of Wall Streeter Dimitri Yassukovich". A busy body rang Mother to alert her, and there was the proverbial to pay. Before these palmy days, when I had just turned sixteen, friends and I used to frequent the jazz clubs, off Broadway – particularly Eddie Congdon's, where the lighting was dim and the bartender short-sighted. The drinking age in New York State was then 18, but this was not so strictly enforced in those days. Now young people are expected to die for their country at the age of 18, but they cannot be served a beer until they are 21. At Eddie Congdon's we listened to great jazz and downed whiskey sours one after another, perhaps thinking the citrus content was providing vitamin C. But it was the summer party season which set me on a course of early decadence. In summer, I also found a way of anticipating my legal drinking years. With Rene Ponvert and Bobby Craigmyle, we sailed a Lightning class centre board sloop out of Seawanaka Yacht Club on Centre Island, Oyster Bay. One day we got ourselves leeward of a huge yacht belonging to Mrs Merryweather Post, of the breakfast cereal fortune. We paddled frantically, drifting slowly towards the great gin palace, the deck of which was at the height of our mast, white uniformed officers glaring at us from the railing. We just managed to get back into the wind and round. At Seawanaka, we had quickly discovered that the bartenders at the weekly Saturday night dinner dances were lax in their enforcement of the drinking age. At 16 it was possible to get a driving permit in New York, valid only for daylight hours. This restriction was universally ignored. It is hard to believe today, but the Nassau County police were remarkably solicitous to "estate people". Bobby Craigmyle had such a permit, so we went to the Saturday night parties at Seawanaka, white dinner jacketed – *de riguer* at the time – and gorged ourselves on whiskey sours, inevitably worse for wear on the way home, with Ponvert occasionally sick on his white dinner jacket. My mobility contributed to my fecklessness. At 14, I had been given a Velosolex, a French bicycle with a small motor that rested on and drove the front wheel. At 15, I was given a Vespa scooter. I was, in fact, spoilt rotten. On my scooter, with my friend Sandy Schwartz riding pillion, we rushed about – to the Piping Rock Beach on the Sound, and then back to the main club house to devoir club sandwiches in the billiard room, with a beer, if there was a friendly older person to order it. Once 16, and now with permit, I drove my mother's car. After that it was downhill all the way.

It was the moment in American literary history when F. Scott Fitzgerald was rediscovered, largely due to a story written by a Hollywood script writer and novelist, Bud Schulberg, who had been assigned to accompany Fitzgerald to Dartmouth College to prepare a script for a college life movie, a popular theme at the time. Fitzgerald's last days in Hollywood have been much chronicled. Hopelessly alcoholic, almost entirely forgotten by the public and the *literati*, desperately caging the odd script assignment, one of America's greatest writers cut a pathetic figure. An English gossip columnist in Hollywood, Sheila Graham, tried to succour him, to little avail, and he died in 1941. In his story, Schulberg described the drunken and disastrous journey to Dartmouth he made with Fitzgerald, in a way that captured the public's imagination. *Gatsby* and other works were reprinted, sales of Fitzgerald's books soared, critics pretended they had always valued him, and nostalgia for the Roaring Twenties took hold, with even the Charleston reintroduced at dances. No one succumbed to this new and somewhat faddish revival more completely than Ariane's brother. I began to eat, sleep and dream Fitzgerald – but perhaps more to the point, to drink Fitzgerald. I began to dress like him, with button down collared shirt, knit tie with horizontal stripe, loose tweed jacket, etc. I reckoned I was living in Gatsby land, after all. I started looking about for a Zelda. I imagined us frolicking in the fountains outside the Plaza Hotel, after a night on the town. Unfortunately, none of my girlfriends seemed slightly mad like Zelda. One day, I came across a girl on a bicycle at the bottom of our drive. She was dressed in grey flannel Bermuda shorts and a button down collared shirt. She was not really beautiful, more pert, with the boyish look of the "flappers" of the 'twenties: I could just imagine her with the shingled hairstyle of the time, dancing the Charleston. She was Sally Simpson and she told me her mother had rented the house just near us, at the end of our drive. Her history was odd. Her father, who died when she was a baby, was State Senator Joseph Simpson – the same who had entertained Alexander Kerensky, exiled Head of the Second Provisional Government in Petrograd in 1918, reviled by my father for having been responsible for the arrest of the Imperial Family. Sally was obviously a very late, and no doubt accidental, child, as her mother was now almost senile, deaf as a post, spending most of her time playing gin rummy with her friend Mr. Rothschild, who might, or might not, have been of the great banking family. A French governess, called always Mademoiselle – I never knew her name – had been responsible for the upbringing of Sally, and was still in attendance, despite the fact her ward was now 16. There was an elder sister, but she was married and had moved far away. Mademoiselle welcomed my arrival as the favourite, and quickly, permanent escort of her charge, because we could converse in French, and she entertained the hope that I would have a positive, reforming influence. Poor deluded lady! «*Monsieur! Que vat'on faire pour améliorer la conduite de la petite?*» Sir! What will we do to improve the behaviour of the little one. I was alarmed by the reference to "we" and considered the use of the term "*la petite*" faintly ridiculous. Sally drank like a fish, smoked like a wet log, drove like a maniac, thought only of parties and was generally out of control. Mademoiselle, who genuinely loved her ward, was deeply frustrated and could not complain to her mistress Mrs. Simpson, who seemed to care less about Sally's welfare. Once when, together with Mike Durham, we were playing bicycle polo on the lawn of another rented house, Sally had a fall – being worse for wear as usual – and cut her leg quite badly. We trooped in to the drawing room, me carrying Sally with my shirt wrapped around her bleeding leg. Mrs

Simpson was playing gin rummy with Mr. Rothschild. Mike shouted at her in his best, for the deaf, voice, "Just off to the hospital, Mrs. Simpson. Sally's cut her leg and may need a couple of stitches."

Mrs. Simpson, quietly discarding a card, never looked up and just said, "Alright – try and be back for tea." She continued playing and we set off, Sally having refreshed her drink, which she carried to the car. As Sally and I began to spend all our spare time together, getting up to no good, the dreaded phrase "they're going steady" began to be heard abroad and my parents became alarmed. Sally's reputation had preceded her. It was clearly time to cart the boy off to Europe.

My godfather Jack Barrett arranged and agreed to accompany my father and myself on a trip to Samothrace, an island in the north Aegean Sea, where an ancient sanctuary was being excavated. Uncle Jack worked for the Mellon Foundation, and became head of the publishing side, which among other works, published the entire oeuvre of Karl Jung. Paul Mellon's first wife was allergic to horses, a disaster akin to a lady allergic to flowers marrying a horticulturist. Having no need to skimp, Mr. Mellon sent her to Zurich to consult Jung, who cured her, inspiring Paul to become a patient himself – perhaps to treat symptoms of guilt over his extreme wealth. Uncle Jack used to visit Jung in Ascona every year, but as his publisher, not his patient. The Foundation was financing the archaeological works at Samothrace which were under the supervision of Professor Stein of New York University. It was a tricky dig; there had been several earthquakes in ancient times and the sanctuary had tumbled into a ravine, and rebuilt after each quake. Separating each era was challenging work. Of course, the site was famous for the Winged Victory, now at the Louvre in Paris. We took a sort of ferry which sailed once a week from Alexandropoulos, and were billeted in an old school house with sepia portraits of heroes of the Greek Revolution on the walls. There was no electricity or running water on the Island and each morning we swam in a sea so clear one could see underwater life for what seemed miles. Turning on one's back one, one gazed at a colour fiesta of blue sea, yellow sand and purple mountains, which would have seemed grossly overdone in a painting. On arrival, we had joined the crew at dinner under the olive trees, consisting of roast goat, rice, tomatoes and retzina, the local wine which tastes like kerosene. Assembled were several NY University students, a museum curator, one or two older experts, and a representative of the Greek Ministry of Culture – there to ensure nothing was pinched.

"Anything happening out there?" enquired one. We announced that North Korea had invaded South Korea, the UN had resolved to intervene, and President Truman had ordered the U.S. Military to lead a UN force. In other words, it was war.

"Really?" replied our interlocutor. Then, turning to all, "I think I found something really interesting in the far left trench today; it may just be linked to the collapse of that north wall in the 345 quake we've been looking into."

120

It was clear that everyone was only interested in the Fourth century BC and had not the slightest interest in the 20th AD. I played at being an archaeologist, being stationed at the head of a trench where the workmen passed bits of pottery up to me. I had a several paper bags. I placed the blue bits in one, the coral bits in another, the grey bits in a third, etc., etc. I decided instantly to study archaeology. One day it was announced we were to pay a courtesy visit to the mayor of the only town on the Island. We were all mounted on donkeys and wound our way through the hills to the village where a table had been dressed in the middle of the square, and Greek coffee, strawberry jam and ice cold water were served. I sat next to the mayor, who asked me in broad American, "Where are you from?"

"A little place called Locust Valley, near New York – you've probably never heard of it," I replied. The mayor laughed.

"I sure have! I owned the movie theatre in Glen Cove for 20 years!"

Of course that was where I had seen my first motion picture – *Jane Eyre* with Orson Welles and Joan Fontaine. We used to go to Saturday matinées with Greenvale mates, and try to put an arm around one of the girls in the dark. The Mayor had sold up, returned to his native village and been elected by acclamation. During our stay, what was thought to an arm of the Winged Victory was found. Great excitement ensued, and an immediate diplomatic tussle on how to join up the limb and the lady. Obviously the Greeks favoured the Louvre shipping the Winged Victory to Athens, and the French the reverse. I'm not sure the issue was ever resolved. After Samothrace we went to Istanbul, where Uncle Jack annoyed the immigration officials by writing Constantinople on his entry form. We visited Saint Sophia, where the Mellon Foundation was also financing the restoration of the acres of mosaic. There was scaffolding everywhere and technicians were working with dentist's tools, carefully cleaning every individual, tooth-sized, stone in the mosaics, which had been thickly painted over several times by the Ottoman invaders. The trick was to get to the original colour without damaging the stone.

On our return, there were still a few weeks before the start of school, now Deerfield, and I took up with Sally again. We rampaged about, drinking heavily and playing at Scott and Zelda. Mademoiselle was distraught, and my parents were increasingly concerned. Even friends were disapproving. Our relationship had reached the heavy petting stage. I was worried myself. I knew I was on a slippery slope, but I couldn't stop. I was addicted. I told myself that, if it was to end tragically, the romantic drama of the whole experience would be enhanced. I believe I was playing a role – a further indication that I probably should have gone on the stage. We said tearful goodbyes after a Labour Day dance – always the last event of the season. Normally summer romances ended with sincere, but usually unfilled, promises to write. We didn't bother – we knew we would be back together at Christmas holidays – a bad omen. At Christmas it was the winter deb season and I was of age to be a full participant. By now the parents had a larger apartment in midtown Manhattan. I

121

was committed to escort other girls to various balls, but I always contrived to get together with Sally, even though she had other escorts as well. The barbaric, but highly convenient American custom of "cutting in" ensures one is never stuck. This is wonderful, if exhausting, for the popular girl, as she can change partners every two minutes. It is less so for the wall flower. Irving Berlin puts it nicely: "Must you dance, every dance, with that same fortunate man?

You have danced with him since the music began;
Won't you change partners, and dance with me …"

Sallywas no wall flower, but I suspect her popularity was due to curiosity about the real nature of her relationship with me. The Simpsons owned a large and very gloomy town house on 92nd Street, between Park and Lexington, at the limit of fashionable Manhattan. There Sally lived with her deaf mother and Mademoiselle, with occasional visits by her sister, and some staff. That Christmas, she decided to throw a party and invitations were broadcast widely. Unfortunately, the word was also broadcast widely and there were more uninvited that invited. There was chaos, with people who had not gained admission shouting in the street outside. I think the police arrived at one stage. There was no supervision, although the sister and her husband were staying. The sister was disgusted and the brother-in-law amused. By midnight the drink had run out and an exodus occurred. It was on this fateful night that I met Kerensky, he was staying and had spent the evening in a distant library with Mrs. Simpson, who, of course, was hardly bothered by the noise. He came down when almost all had left and Sally's brother-in-law was surveying the mess. "It looks just like the Russian Revolution, Professor!" he exclaimed, jocularly. Kerensky scowled. I was then introduced and the handshake took place. Kerensky, still scowling, acknowledged an acquaintance with my grandfather, the General, and that was it. The party was talked about for months after. Sally thought it was all just wonderful. Our relationship intensified. We spent hours in front of the fire in the great drawing room, listening to Handel's *Water Music*, over and over again – occasionally interspersed with Vivaldi's winter from *The Four Seasons*. We lunched every day at a favourite bar/restaurant, where a model whaling ship floated in a big glass aquarium. Every fifteen minutes, a storm blew up in the aquarium; the "sea" became heavier and heavier, the sky darkened, the wind began to blow and the ship rocked almost to the point of capsizing. Then it would all calm down in the same order. I found this terribly symbolic. At deb balls, we now contrived to slip away early, and went back to 92nd Street, careful not to wake Mademoiselle, which was not difficult as the house was large. Our relationship had now reached a level which can only be described as most unsuitable to our age and station. It must be stressed that, at that time, in the far distant 1950s, premarital sex was a "no, no" in our circles. In the very few cases when it was suspected, it became known quickly. I can recall only one case: Pete Bostwick and Lilly Knott. They married, and have lived happily ever after. Quite apart from the defiance of convention, I knew perfectly well that I was too young for such intensity. I had not the emotional maturity, despite the fact that everyone always commented on how mature and grown up I seemed. I was supposed to be "sophisticated" and "suave". But I was truly affected by all this, in a way difficult to explain. I can only surmise, as I say – that I was just too young. However, I learned how to dress back into my white tie and tails in the dark – and eventually even in the back seat of a motorcar – hardly a lesson of career value. At dawn, I would walk home, down the shining pavements of Park Avenue, the steam rising from the manholes and early taxi cabs bouncing on the uneven street. I would let myself in, very quietly. I can't believe my mother didn't suspect what was up. I only recall her distaste at finding lipstick on my white silk evening scarf. One day, she decided to take me to a Park Avenue psychiatrist. I don't think Mother had ever gone to a "shrink", but she was partial to medical specialists in general. In his palatial office, Mother explained, with much Latin verve and emotion, that I was deeply troubled, in a most unsuitable relationship, neglecting my school work, clearly heading for disaster, and so on and so forth. I sat there, dressed as usual in my Anderson & Sheppard dark grey suit and waistcoat, neat shirt with a collar pin supporting a paisley silk tie, a calm and slightly bemused expression, fingering a silver cigarette case – clearly too polite to light one. After a while, the Doctor said, "I'll have a word with the lad, madam – my secretary will take care of you outside." After the door had closed, the "shrink" leaned over the desk to me and said, "I think your mother needs help." Noting my surprise, he continued, "Let's have a smoke and chat a while." We did. He had been to Andover, and so we talked about Deerfield /Andover rivalries at sports. After a short while, Mother was invited in and I waited outside. On the way home, I could tell she was annoyed. Eventually, I wormed out of her that the Doctor had just described me as a typical teenager and told her not to worry. I don't think he billed her.

After school broke up in June, it was time for the country deb party season – and what parties they were. I think them worth describing because, although they are still given, and probably even more lavishly, I doubt they are imbued with the same style. They belong in this memoir, because even now, I can sometimes close my eyes and hear them. Certain songs bring them back. These are to me as the *madeleines* were to Proust. The parties were sometimes dinner dances, sometimes after dinner balls, with supper laid on. Huge tents were erected on great lawns, satin or silk lined, with tunnels leading to annexes, where there were bars serving anything and everything. Champagne fountains recycled vintages – although rumour had it that less well-heeled hosts substituted ginger ale after one o'clock when no one knew the difference. The flower arrangements competed in number and sumptuousness. At one famous "do", given by a Chicago retail fortune heir with a large estate, artificial swans made entirely of fresh gardenias, and gondolas, floated on an artificial lake. Supper buffets supplied scrambled eggs and bacon, griddle cakes and sausages. And the music played on and on. Lester Lanin primarily, and Meyer Davis, were the favourites and their style was unmistakable. It consisted of bouncy, fox trot tempo arrangements of the American Song Book classics, interspersed with a few waltzes, sambas and, of course, the Charleston. The music was almost continuous, individual players slipping quietly on and off the band stand in one's or two's for their break. Each number was linked to the next with a one or two bar "riff" played by the piano and guitar, the rhythm remaining unbroken, so that one danced on to "dum dum, dum dum – ta da – dum dum, dum dum", and then straight into the next tune. Somehow the orchestra changed music sheets during this moment. If it was a change from a fox trot to a waltz, for example, then the riff would be several bars long to change the metre appropriately. The result was one could dance, sit out, cut in, go to the bar, slip away to the bushes, or to the car park, without missing a beat, so to speak. For very popular girls it was exhausting and they had to plead with a partner for a break. The overall effect was somewhat orgiastic, perhaps, but in a totally innocent way, as the venue and its décor exuded elegance, even if the opulence would have shocked the puritanical ancestors of many of the early American families represented. My mother couldn't understand why I had to go to them all, since it was always the same format, the same music and the same people. But that was the point: it was one long, uninterrupted party for several weeks in June. I could hear the music in my head from the moment of waking late, and through the day, until the next party that night.

Less innocent, and certainly a great deal more dangerous than even a real orgy would have been, was the amount of alcohol consumed by 18 year olds driving themselves to and back from the parties. Serious accidents were frequent. Parents lived in a certain fear, and many insisted on taxis and had chauffeurs to ferry their young. Everyone knew someone who had been killed or maimed as a result of drunken driving. At one celebrated party, the poor deb had been so intimidated by the sheer scale of the extravaganza arranged to present her to people she knew already, that she refused to leave her room. Not all the hundreds present noticed her absence. Her father decided to give a more modest repeat a few weeks later, in the hopes she might be induced to dance at her own party. Due to some recent motor crashes involving drunken debs delights, drivers had been arranged and their services were offered at the door to departing guests. I was with my friend Sandy Schwartz, and driving Mother's Chevrolet, as usual. Waving side the proffered chauffeur as beneath our dignity, we set out, both fell asleep and crashed into a parked car somewhere on the outskirts of Glen Cove. Our vehicle being unserviceable, and with no sign of the other car's owner, we set out on foot. I got home at dawn, and the next morning, with the maternal car missing from the drive, the worst was feared. I was guilty of leaving the scene of an accident, had ruined my mother's car and my sin was compounded in my father's eyes by the fact that the son of the worthy family whose car I had struck, was serving in Korea. My father compared my outrageous behaviour to that of a spoilt French aristocrat riding roughshod over the peasants' crops after a night of drunken carousing. It might have been the following year when the parents were away and I was staying with the Whites in Oyster Bay, together with my friend and partner in Fitzgeraldian antics Joseph Verner Reed, Jr. We had attended a party for one of C. V. Whitney's daughters, on his estate Green tree, where the first version of the film *Sabrina Fair*, with Audrey Hepburn, William Holden and Humphrey Bogard, was shot. The dancing was in the indoor tennis court where a scene to the tune of *Isn't it Romantic* takes place in the motion picture. Our behaviour was far from romantic. We were amongst the last to leave and Joseph decided it would be fun to see if the pool furniture would float. The pool was just below the Whitney's bedroom and, perhaps for that reason, we chucked the furniture into the water. It didn't float. Off we went, got hopelessly lost, and near Beaver Dam, Mill Neck, as I was to describe it later – "a tree suddenly jumped from the side of the road and hit us". The noise was such that a lady making coffee in her kitchen at the end of a longish driveway came down in her dressing gown to see what had happened. She found Joseph brushing shattered windscreen out of his hair and dancing in the road, singing *Mountain Greenery,* and me still behind the wheel, adjusting my bow tie. Neither of us suffered any injury, but the car was a total wreck and was parked for weeks outside of Smith's Garage in Locust Valley, where all of DY's cronies boarding the LI RR club car could see it and snicker. I must immediately report, without waiting for the right chronological moment, that Joseph Reed went on to have a most distinguished career. ADC to Eugene Black, President of the World Bank, then to David Rockefeller, Chairman of Chase Manhattan Bank, Chief of Protocol in the Administration of the first President Bush, U.S. Ambassador to the Kingdom of Morocco, Deputy Secretary General of the United Nations, etc. I have a photo of him in white tie, covered with medals and orders, looking like a preppy version of Emperor Haile Selassie.

The parental rage which followed each of these events defies description. But my affair with Sally Simpson continued to cause concern – not least to myself. We were not always at the same parties, but all too frequently. Sally had become possessive and jealous – out of character. The parents contrived to organise diversions. They were in Europe for a good part of most of these summers. One year I was sent as an intern to the Boston office of White, Weld. I sat at a desk in front of a man called Townsend Horner who was engaged in an acrimonious divorce. I learned more about divorce law than about investment banking. I contrived to sneak back to Long Island every weekend, staying with Sally in the house her mother rented. She continued to play gin rummy with Mr. Rothschild, and Mademoiselle continued to weep on my shoulder about *la petite* – now 17, and less maidenly than ever. The next year I was enrolled in a summer course at the University of Lausanne. I was billeted in a *pension* run by a Mademoiselle Davidof a distinguished family of academics. A lovely old house called *Beaumont* on the Avenue de Beaumont had once been a substantial property on the heights of Lausanne. The ladies of the David family had served as *institutrices* with prominent Scandinavian families and now ran an establishment at their somewhat reduced property, for young people studying in Lausanne. Mlle David expressed surprise at my presence, since I seemed fluent in French. I had not the nerve to tell her I was there due to parental disapproval of a love affair, and explained my mother had complained of my having a Belgian accent when I spoke the word for kitchen as *"cweesine"*. She pretended acceptance of this. Jacques Appelmans, from White, Weld and his family had rented a house nearby, and he was preparing documentation and the transfer of clients to what was to be White, Weld & Co. A. G., a new Swiss entity to be established in Zurich. I spent as much time as I could assisting him, my family connection justifying the breach in client confidentially that technically my work entailed. This consisted of fitting cards, on which was written the full name of a security, date of purchase, any subsequent sales, etc., into a metal plate with little slots and the client's name on top. Thus the client's portfolio, and movements were recorded and filed in a cabinet fitted to take the plates. The hugely primitive nature of this is truly mind stretching in the light of current technology, where a click or two with the computer mouse shows absolutely everything one needs to know about the client, his or her portfolio, its positions, with full performance statistics and accompanying graphs. Having experienced both systems, it is as though I had helped paint the animals in the caves at Lescaux, and now watched a nature film on television. Jacques and his family were kind to me and made me feel at home. Of course, he knew of my situation. I fell in love with Lausanne, then still with the University located centrally in the old town. Unfortunately, I did not find a girl to fall in love with on this occasion and so, on my return, it was back to my old ways and my inappropriate girlfriend.

CHAPTER X

"Dum vivimus vivamus! Each day a new"

-Anon, traditional-

The chapter recounting my Harvard career will be short, but not interrupted – as was my short Harvard career. That I was there at all was due to a now disappeared practice of the Ivy League colleges, which was to source the bulk of its intake from the leading private secondary schools – mostly located in the Northeast. Although they all officially deny it, they now operate an admissions system of carefully graduated quotas based on ethnicity, religion, colour, geographic origin, class and sexual orientation. This does not necessarily cause them to discriminate against the leading prep schools –American terminology – because these increasingly operate the same system. Nevertheless, graduates of these schools have a very narrow quota window at such as Harvard, Yale and Princeton. The idea is to ensure maximum compliance with current political correctness, as it pertains to social diversity. I doubt any sociologist would deny that this policy has been a contributing factor in the decline of the WASP ascendency as national leaders in the fields of business and finance. I exclude politics, because with the obvious exceptions of the Roosevelts in the Presidency, Senators Saltanstall, Lodge and Bush, Governors Rockefeller (2) and Weld, American political life has not been WASP dominated. Diplomacy is another matter, and, until very recently, a good many career diplomats were WASP. But I would argue that the virtual disappearance of the WASP population from the ownership and direction of Wall Street is the most striking, and must be largely attributed to the fact that it is no longer so concentrated in a relatively few establishments of secondary education and higher learning.

But in 1953, the right school pretty well assured admission to an Ivy League institution – just as the right public school in Britain opened wide the Oxbridge gates. As a highly unsatisfactory student at Deerfield, I still managed to pass my College Entrance Exam, and having applied to Princeton and Harvard – was admitted to both. Despite the fact that my hero Fitzgerald was a Princetonian, I chose Harvard. In freshman year, one is quartered in historic

Harvard Yard, and I roomed with close friends Brewster Righter and Michael Durham. We spent a good deal of time drinking, talking and burning the furniture when we were cold in winter. I quickly realised I was like a child in a sweet shop. The stacks at Widener Library are not only a bibliophile paradise, one can wonder at random, and come across Radcliffe girls doing the same. Radcliffe College was more than a sister establishment. Its curriculum was identical to that at Harvard, and every course, lecture, seminar or tutorial had a smattering of its student body. But the ladies enjoyed their own campus, privacy and institutional loyalty. A Radcliffe degree was an exact equivalent of a Harvard degree. Unfortunately this came to be less than universally recognised, and so eventually the two institutions merged in to one co-educational college. As an undergraduate, one was at Harvard College, but the University comprises a large number of distinguished graduate colleges in every known academic discipline, and their lectures are open to all registered students at the University. One could spend the day dropping in on lectures in every branch of the arts and sciences. In fact there were over 50 graduate degree programmes at Harvard. As for culture, one was also overwhelmed. One of my favourite pastimes was dropping in to Memorial Hall to listen to E. Power Biggs, then a world-class organist, rehearsing Bach. The problem is that I began to sample as many counters in this sweet shop as I my stomach could cope with, to the neglect of the courses I was signed up for. Another time waster was my habit of auditing those lectures where an attractive bevy of Radcliffe girls could be found. A very popular first-year course was naval history taught by the distinguished naval historian Samuel Elliot Morrison. Popular courses had nicknames and this one was called "Boats". I was soon in arrears on attendance and papers due for the courses I was enrolled in, and placed on probation.

In freshman year, one might be elected to the Hasty Pudding Club, a popular watering hole with a long history. In sophomore year one was eligible to be elected to a so-called final club. These establishments were of varying character and seniority, and only a minority of college students belonged – or even knew of them, as they recruited mostly from legacies, i.e. sons of graduate members. A fairly noncontroversial listing according to precedence would be Porcellian, AD, Delphic, Fly, Spee, Owl and one or two others I can't recall. I was elected to the Porcellian Club. I will not say very much about the Porcellian Club because... well, one just doesn't. An anecdote is in the public domain, however. When President Theodore Roosevelt, a Porcellian, was on a state visit to Kaiser Wilhelm, they were out riding together when an aide galloped up bearing a telegram for the President. Excusing himself to his host, the President tore open the envelope, read the telegram and exclaimed, "Oh, bully!"
"Good news?" enquired His Imperial Majesty.
"Absolutely," replied Teddy, "my daughter is engaged."
"I take it you approve of the young man?" continued the Emperor.

"Of course! He's a Porcellian!" was the reply.

Kaiser Wilhelm was nonplussed and later commissioned an ADC to enquire as to the meaning of this. The young officer, having done some quick research, came back and reported, "It seems to be an organisation that worships pigs." The young man in question was Nicholas Longworth. The club is as famous for people who were not elected. J. P. Morgan, Jr. was not, but was elected to the Delphic. Having the means to do so, he arranged that the gas lamps at the club house should remain lit all night, to give the appearance of great social activity. Ever since, the Delphic has been known as the Gas Club. More than one historian speculates that Franklin Delano Roosevelt harboured bitterness towards the Establishment, because he failed to be elected to Porcellian, despite his cousin Teddy, and despite having been to Groton, perhaps the most famous of the Episcopalian prep schools. The American author John Dos Passos wrote a short story called *The Graven Image* about a Porcellian Club member applying for a position in Washington to a nonmember Harvard classmate, now an under Secretary of State. He senses a degree of bitterness in his interlocutor and spends the interview convincing his class mate that he has had a far more successful career; that, after all, here he is, a Porcellian, a supplicant for a job – so what has it done for him? Finally, our hero thinks he has mollified his interviewer and that the position is his, but ruins it by remarking on leaving, "Of course, you never would have made it in a thousand years." The graven image of the title is a reference to the charm of a running boar we wear on a watch chain. It was prominent in the photographs of our member Richard Whitney, the disgraced President of the New York Stock Exchange, as he was carted off to start his jail term.

The social activity of my class and club mates varied and was rather formal by current standards. For example I never went to class or out in the street without a jacket and tie and usually wore a suit. We made friends with and often went out together with a group of like-minded Radcliffe girls, which included Lisa Hunnewell, who was to marry Michael von Clemm, also a Porcellian. Once we all decided to go tea dancing at the Ritz Hotel in Boston, an entertainment which still existed at the time. Within this select group of Radcliffe girls was a very nice and popular girl called Gail Jones. She was differentiated not only by the fact that she was black, but also because she was the daughter of the great jazz singer Lena Horne. Off we went, all togged up, for our afternoon of nostalgic dancing to the small, live orchestra which officiated, as one munched one's cucumber sandwiches in between turns on the floor. We were noticed as we came in, because we were well-dressed. But when I got up to dance with Gail, the room suddenly fell silent, except for the band, and I could see everyone was staring. I could feel Gail tense slightly, but we danced on, sat down, drank our tea and no one in our party said anything about it. It was 1954, and it was Boston – not Savannah. Once we challenged some Radcliffe girls to a game of field hockey, not played by men in America. We determined to go easy on the delicate things, avoiding unnecessary contact and roughness. We were soundly beaten and came off the field black and blue, some of us limping for days after. Michael Durham and I played lacrosse in our freshman year, and at a match against the Deerfield varsity team, I scored twice and was able to cock a snoop at Mr. Merriam, who had accused me of cowardice. In sophomore year, we took up fencing, together with Bruce Righter, the foil for me, epée for Durham and sabre for Righter. We had a Hungarian fencing master who told me I could be another d'Orliola if I worked at it. I didn't. I didn't work at anything.

My affair with La Simpson was beginning to cool, much to my relief and her annoyance. Sally had gone to Garrison Forest and she is mentioned, not in entirely positive terms, in Topsy Pell's wonderful book *We Used to Own the Bronx*. Topsy, who was at Greenvale, was niece to my friend John Jay Mortimer, also a Porcellian, even though she was older, because Mrs. Mortimer, of Tuxedo Park, had a clutch of children that spanned two normal generations, John Jay being the youngest. Topsy's book tells the story of her rebellion against her family and WASP background, executed most dramatically, by her joining the Black Panthers, the militant African American group. Topsy was also at Garrison Forest and had some kind of fight with Sally. Sally went on to a small ladies college in Western Massachusetts and we would meet in various clandestine venues in Cambridge. Then the makings of a tragedy, starting out as a comedy, appeared in an invitation to audition for a part in the Hasty Pudding Show, an iconic annual event. Always a musical, with female parts played in drag by men à la Shakespeare, the event claimed a history of the famous. In their year, Lerner and Lowe, of *My Fair Lady* fame, had written the show. The class of 1957 production *On the Rocks,* was a 1920s spoof, in the manner of Sandy Wilson's *The Boyfriend.* Of course, the era appealed to me. Joe Raposo, who was rooming with Jeffrey Selznick's son Daniel, brother of my Deerfield school mate, wrote the score. Many years later, I was watching one of Frank Sinatra's several "last" performances on television, when he suddenly said, "Here's a song Joe Raposo wrote for me." Well, I thought, Joe Raposo wrote a song for me. I was given the part of the butler in *On the Rocks*. The action took place at a country house party, and Joe added the song *What Is So Remarkable about Love?* Especially for me. I also sang a duet *I've Got a Place in Devon* with Fred Schwartz, the heir to the toy fortune F.A.O. Schwartz, playing my lady friend in drag. Joe Raposo, who was of Portuguese ancestry, went on to have a brilliant career, writing all the music for the TV children's serial *Sesame Street*, several films and musicals. His number *Sing*, recorded by The Carpenters, made the charts. We were well into our run when a dean of the College, F. Skiddy von Stade, came with his wife, looked down the cast list, spotted my name and whispered to his wife, "That man's on probation!" One was not permitted to engage in any extra-curricular activity, sporting or cultural, whilst on probation. Expulsion was immediate. Mine followed shortly, but I was allowed to finish the run. Friends considered my sentence excessive and there was talk of appeal. But there was no appeal. In any case, F. Skiddy von Stade was of a Long Island family, totally establishment, probably a friend of at least one White, Weld partner, and there was no way he was going to allow himself to be seen making any concession to a spoilt brat from a privileged background. F. Skiddy's daughter Fredericka has had a stellar career as an opera singer. Years later we went to see her in one of her early triumphs at Glyndebourne, singing Cherubino in *The Marriage of Figaro*. We were with Peter Hoguet, a long time beau of Ariane's, who had known her since childhood. I could not help thinking of the role her father had played in my life. To say my father took my rustication badly is a gross understatement. He was humiliated. He went to Alec White and offered his resignation. White, Weld was a Harvard house if it was anything. My father's action was based on the belief that if an officer's son disgraced the regiment, the officer resigned.

"Don't be ridiculous, DY!" said Alec, who was Harvard to his fingertips and had raised the money to found the Business School. "Your partner, and my brother Ogden, never graduated. Stani can probably be re-admitted after a year – it is not a disaster." He then added something which profoundly shocked my father. "And after all, DY – Stani did make Porcellian!" DY considered, with total justification, that the many hours I had spent at 1324 Massachusetts Avenue, the stately home of the PC, had not made a positive contribution to my Harvard career. He could not know it, but he was wrong, but for reasons I couldn't explain.

Worse was to come. It was arranged I should go to Lausanne and pass a year as a stagière, or intern, at the Banque Galland & Cie, correspondents of White, Weld, and managed by an old friend of DY's Edouard Adam. The original Galland had been honorary British Consul in Lausanne in the 19th century and the establishment was as typical a private bank as one can find in the Cantons of Switzerland. I was to apply for re-admission from there, once I could attach convincing references, extolling my behaviour and repentance for past fecklessness. During my year in Lausanne, I met my future wife and so the period deserves a separate treatment, which will be forthcoming. But Harvard was not yet finished for me, as I was re-admitted after a year, but not yet a reformed character. I was still on probation of course, and soon fell again to grazing the many academic and social pastures which constitute Harvard University. It was a time when the drip-dry suit had been introduced, the research laboratories of the DuPont Company, having devised the material for this useful product. I purchased for myself an elegant gabardine suit, highly appropriate for summer wear – it was late spring. After a leisurely, and liquid, luncheon with friends, I decided to test the drip-dry claim made for this garment, ambled over to the Elliot House Bridge and executed a perfect dive into the Charles River, having checked for any passing skulls or other craft. After an elegant crawl to the shore, I was met by University proctors, and to put it simply – my number was up. It was strictly against regulations to jump from any bridge into the Charles River, and this was a prima facie violation of my probation. I was out for the final count. The suit dried on me quite quickly. My father was in Europe. He issued a non-negotiable ultimatum. I was to enlist in either the French Foreign Legion or the United States Marine Corps. There is some doubt as to whether I would have been eligible for the first option, as born in France of a French mother, I am considered French, and Legionnaires must be foreign – except for officers, of course. My father considered the Marines the only proper military unit of the Armed Forces of the U.S., as the Army and the Air Force salute uncovered. The sight of an Air Force officer, with a plastic cover on his cap and carrying an umbrella, used to drive my father to distraction. In any case, I reasoned the Legion was probably no longer quite as depicted in the film *Beau Geste*. I went down to Times Square, where recruiting booths of all the services are to be found. Choosing the right one, I was received by a beribboned Master Sergeant, with many service stripes on his sleeve, who processed my enlistment as a private in the USMC.

CHAPTER XI

"I look upon Switzerland as an inferior sort of Scotland"

Lady Holland, in a letter to Lord Holland

Before beginning an account of my career as a U.S. Marine, I must return to my long-suffering father, as, after all, his life and career continued. My father bore the shame and dismay of his son's transgressions with remarkable fortitude – a tribute to his strength of character. He was not so discouraged as to shirk from fulfilling his own mission, and he received considerable support from his partners and friends. I have the letters he received from my godfather Jack Barrett, and his friend Joseph Verner Reed Sr. They offer him consolation and reflections on the follies of youth. They must have been difficult to write because none could remind their friend of his own early indiscretions, since he appeared to have had a blameless, if traumatic, youth. But DY's partners were no doubt relieved that he did not miss a beat in the further development and enhancement of White, Weld's international franchise, and his closest partner Jean Cattier was soon back full-time, after a period serving in John J. McCloy's occupation commission in Germany. White, Weld was now located at 40 Wall Street and the foreign department was growing. A significant addition was a young Frenchman called François Champion. François, a native of Provence, had served as a 16-year-old in the French Resistance, clearing the way for the Allied sweep through the south of France, blowing bridges and harassing the retreating Germans. Contact and liaison work with American GIs made him bilingual. After the war, many ambitious young Frenchmen made their way to New York to seek their fortunes. François made the unusual decision to head for the heartland and found employment with a municipal bond house in Kansas City. Municipal bonds are tax exempt, fixed income securities issued by states, municipalities and other non-federal entities. François learned his trade calling on farmers in a beat up station wagon, and selling them "munies". After a while, he ventured east to the big city and was hired by Lehman Brothers. I am unsure how DY was able to poach him, but François became a key player in the international team. He was the most natural and skilled private banker I have ever met. His bed side manner was impeccable, consisting of charm, knowledgeable advice communicated in simple terms, and above all, an unswerving optimism. Through currency crises, stock market crashes, geo-political upheavals, or family troubles, François would smooth the furrowed brow of the most hysterical of investment clients. Little old ladies doted on him, and cynical investment managers would call him to have their spirits lifted by his soothing tones. There was more than a touch of Pangloss in his approach, but his blind faith in the U.S. blue chip equity as the Valhalla of investment strategies always provided long term justification for his bullishness. He was always kind to me during my troubled youth and highly supportive of me as a White, Weld colleague and partner.

As the Perez Jiménez boom in Venezuela receded into political chaos, it was clear a new international initiative was needed to exploit the talents, experience and contacts of the Genillard-led team which had now been assembled. DY had always had his eye on Switzerland, and the need for a new domicile for client capital fleeing Caracas, provided urgency. Switzerland has become largely identified with bank secrecy linked mainly to tax evasion. But its haven status predates the introduction of direct taxation of income and fortunes by several centuries. Even today, much of its client base hails from jurisdictions were no or very little direct tax is imposed on individuals. Swiss bank secrecy was always, and still is, designed to protect private clients against sequestration, exchange controls and devaluations, and other threats to the preservation and mobility of their capital. The Swiss banking tradition has always favoured capital preservation over performance and, as a result, Swiss banks have tended to scrape the bottom of the league table rankings of investment total returns. In the end it's a question of taste: the roller coaster ride of high returns, or the steady jog of a balanced portfolio buggy pulled by a reliable horse. With the passion for performance, particularly since the development of the alternative sector, volatility has become more entrenched. Of course, the choice between the beta gorged "hedgie" from Jermyn Street, or the dour, steel rim spectacled, gentleman from the Bahnhofstrasse, is one between extremes; there are a great many variations in between. Tax information exchange agreements have made a large dent in the European clientele of the Swiss private banks, and their venture into the institutional field has not been entirely convincing. But there is no decline in political instability in the world and much new wealth now comes from areas where fortunes may be made quickly, but are also subject to unpredictable interference, if not lodged safely.

Perhaps because of the surfeit of domestic alternatives, there were few U.S. investment houses with a Swiss presence in the '50s. Merrill, Lynch, Pierce, Fenner & Beane was in Geneva, as was Bache & Co. – both providing American brokerage services to the private banks and international community there. First National City Bank was also present in Geneva. No one was in Zurich, save one remarkable exception. American Express Company had been in Zurich since the 19th century, and, even more remarkably, were members of the Zurich Stock Exchange. The reasons why are lost in the mists of time. I once asked James Robinson III, who ran American Express and then joined White, Weld. He said he would find out, but never did. In any case the canton of Zurich was steadfast in refusing the establishment of any foreign financial institution within its jurisdiction. This was not Zurich's only peculiarity. For many years a militant, ladies organisation called the *Frauenverein* was self-appointed guardian of the City's morals. Their lobbying succeeded in banning nightclubs and forcing early closing on alcohol serving establishments. The result was that Zurich was called by some the wickedest city in Europe, as every variety of vice flourished behind closed doors, nurtured by the sweetness of the forbidden. My father felt it timely to challenge, not the *Frauenverien,* I must stress, but the ban on foreign financial houses. He had become friendly with Dr. Hugo Frey, partner of the venerable Zurich law firm of Niederer, Kraft & Frey. This last also felt it was time Zurich joined the world, and suggested to DY that the key was to secure the sponsorship of one of the 'Big Three'. These titans of the Swiss banking establishment were: Credit Suisse, Union Bank of Switzerland, and Swiss Banking Corporation. Dr. Frey's analysis – and he had given much thought to the subject – was that Credit Suisse, who had opened a branch in New York in 1940, an unusual step at the time, was the most likely to be sympathetic. Its CEO was a Dr. Kurz, and I am unsure of the arguments put forward by DY, but Kurz agreed to sponsor an application, which presumably meant convincing his "Big Three" colleagues of the merits of this revolutionary step. All seniorbankers were also Colonels in the Swiss Army, or so it seemed, and perhaps the matter was discussed at a bivouac during annual manoeuvers, but the upshot was that White, Weld & Co. A. G., a "financial establishment of a banking character" was incorporated as a wholly owned subsidiary of White, Weld & Co., New York. The designation was a special Swiss category of authorisation, meaning less than that of a full, deposit taking bank. An office was secured in the Claridenstrasse, a short street just beyond the Baur-au-Lac Hotel, named after a mountain one can view across the lake. Thus was established the presence which was to grow into the heart and soul of White, Weld International, and to father Credit Suisse White Weld, Credit Suisse First Boston, and ultimately the investment banking arm of Credit Suisse itself. Neither DY, nor Dr. Kurz, nor, I am willing to bet, Bob Genillard, its first general manager and ultimately WW's senior international partner, nor DY's partners in New York, imagined at the time, how big an oak tree this acorn was to become. Perhaps I wrong Bob – he was a visionary.

White, Weld's opening in Zurich followed on closely from the re-opening of the foreign dollar bond market in New York. Naturally, my heroine had spent the war in a fitful slumber; a sleeping beauty waiting to be awakened by some investment bankers. The post war economic circumstances of Britain, and the Bretton Woods Agreement, put paid to any notion that London might resume its role as a centre of international bond issuance. The dollar was now to be the dominant reserve and investment currency, and New York the issuing house to the world. The market re-opened with an issue on behalf of the World Bank in 1947, and O'Malley, in *Bonds without Borders*, calculates that some $14 billion in foreign dollar bond issues was raised between 1946 and 1963 – when my heroine reached marriageable age and became the Eurobond. As O'Malley points out the issuers were largely governments, government agencies and municipalities. The Commonwealth of Australia made 13 trips to this market. There were 4 issues for the Kingdom of Belgium, 3 for New Zealand, 2 for the Kingdom of Denmark, 3 for the Japanese Development Bank, 4 for the European Coal and Steel Community and various entities of the French and Italian Governments floated issues. There were issues for the Cities of Oslo and Amsterdam – this last a small issue lead managed by White, Weld. The most active lead managers were Morgan, Stanley, Kuhn Loeb, Lazard Frères, Harriman Ripley, and First Boston. Morgan Stanley topped the league table as Australia was its client and the firm had a grip on French entities. All of these issues were registered with the SEC, in compliance with the 1933 Securities Act, and all were underwritten and distributed in the classical Wall Street format of lead manager, special bracket and ordinary underwriters, further supported by a large selling group. But the critical trend during this period was the emerging distribution pattern. With resurging economies, seeded by the Marshall Plan and a growth in world trade, U.S. dollar liquidity was increasing significantly in Europe. The U.S. deliberately encouraged an out flow of dollars in the first postwar decade, and as U.S. corporates stepped up direct investments, the U.S. began to run a payments deficit as of 1950. This new off shore $ liquidity brought my heroine's sister, the Eurodollar deposit, on to the world stage. But I will save a description of her debut until I reach London, for that is where her coming out party was held. Foreign dollar bonds issued in New York were increasingly subscribed by newly prosperous and $ minded investors resident in Europe. O'Malley reckons that by the late 1950s more than 75% of New York issues were taken up by discretionary accounts managed by Swiss, Dutch or Benelux banks. To reflect this, SEC registered issues, such as those of the European Coal and Steel Community, were being listed in Paris, Brussels and Luxembourg. But this was of purely symbolic value. Liquidity in these issues was provided by an over-the-counter, secondary market maintained by a few houses of which White, Weld became a leader. In Zurich, a new recruit was to become a legend in his time. Walter Koller joined to run the bond book during the European time zone. White, Weld, New York, was already a major market-maker in foreign dollar bonds. A complicated devise allowed these to be traded over-the-counter, even though they were listed on the New York Stock Exchange. I believe this consisted of putting some token amount of a trade through the bond section of the NYSE. Bonds were not dealt in by specialists on the floor like equities. The chief foreign dollar bond trader at WW New York was Joe Collandro, a gum chewing Brooklynite, with a nervous tick.

The firm published an annual directory called "Foreign Dollar Bonds" in which was listed every outstanding issue with full particulars plus price and servicing history. A section called the "Grave Yard" showed all bonds in default. The editor was an eccentric and brilliant researcher called John Fountain. John was an absentminded professor type whose daily appearance always produced a surprise, as some article of clothing was either missing or on backwards. Once, after he had arrived several days in succession without having shaved, he was asked if he was growing a beard. "We'll see," he said, "I'm going to test the new Wilkinson blade." The famous sword maker had decided to compete with Gillette and its shares had soared. John was a practical and thorough researcher. There was not a thing about foreign dollar bonds that John Fountain didn't know.

White, Weld & Co. A. G. was a subsidiary of New York, not a branch. Client accounts were domiciled in Zurich and the company had a contractual arrangement with its parent allowing it to take orders for execution in New York. This was thought to be important to avoid its transactions in securities being subject to Swiss stamp tax. When Walter Koller made a trade in the morning in a foreign dollar bond, the contract was issued to the counterparty by White, Weld in New York – not by WW A. G. Joe Collandro had passed him the "book" the night before, and Walter passed it back for the New York opening, so both traded the same book and provided liquidity to the market in two time zones. But it was considered that no trades were being made in the Swiss jurisdiction, as confirmation emanated from abroad. The Swiss stamp tax was deeply imbedded in the fiscal system. Even when it became clear that it was preventing Switzerland from becoming a centre for international securities trading, the Swiss refused to rescind it – a decision which would have required a federal referendum, in any case – with little prospect of succeeding as the Swiss are not partial to bankers at the popular level. When I arrived in the Zurich office in 1961, Walter had acquired an assistant, a young German named Oswald Grübel. Ozzie, as he came to be known by all, spoke not a word. When he did he was usually chastised by Walter. He was allowed to take the call and quote some prices, but when it came to a possible trade, he had to hand the phone to Walter. I have never met a more cowed and retiring individual. He had a brilliant career and ended up as Chairman of Union Bank of Switzerland. There is a moral here: silence and a retiring nature at the outset may bring a greater career result than the brash, noisy, know-it-all pose adopted by modern apprentice bankers, particularly MBAs, in Wall Street and the City. Walter Koller became perhaps the greatest of a coterie of secondary market traders that pioneered the trillion $ a minute global fixed income securities market which exists today. Together with other legendary figures such as Julius Strauss, Tom Beacham, Stanley Ross, Walter Imthurn, Armin Mattle, Rolf Hallberg and Dick Weguelin, these were the sergeant majors of the army that was to capture the European capital markets. Whilst the primary market originators swanked about like staff officers at HQ, taking credit for each victory, as new issues began to proliferate, none of it could have happened without the secondary market to provide liquidity. The contribution to this process from Europe's established stock exchanges, including London, was less than negligible. Walter Koller also pioneered the education and qualification programme for bond dealers, under the aegis of the International Bond Dealers Association, the IADB – the markets first trade association. Always in Montreux, lasting a week, and terminating in qualification exams, this event provided an opportunity for networking, and the friendships formed between dealers were one of the elements that maintained ethical conduct in the market.

Walter had a unique trading style. We all use "link words" to gain time as one thinks of how best to express a thought. Unfortunately the ubiquitous "you know", has become a link word cemented into the language of English youth. For Walter Koller, the link word was "eventually" as in: "Kingdom of Norway 5s? Well, 98 ¼ to 99... but... eventually... I can make you 98 ½ to 7/8ths in size? "If the counterparty heard the word "eventually", he could be pretty sure Walter was going to narrow the spread. One of Walter's favourite counterparties was Julius Strauss at Strauss, Turnbull in London, the only London Stock Exchange member firm which could tell a foreign dollar bond from its elbow. Julius had worked out a way of playing the role of jobber when he was a broker, in happy violation of the dual capacity system. "That old fox", Walter used to say as he seized the 'phone from Ozzie. Their struggles to pick each other up, i.e. to gain an unexpected price advantage, were a delight to listen to. Sometimes it became a bit acrimonious, but they really formed a mutual admiration society. Another early member of the Claridenstrasse office was Jacques Schmidt who handled equity business. The daily telex from Harold Mandelsohn in New York was the lifeblood of the office, in the absence of a Reuters or a Bloomberg. It contained the latest financial news, price movements of note, share recommendations from research and, most importantly, new issues. When a foreign dollar bond went into registration, it was maximum alert and all hands to the phones and telex's. White, Weld's presence in Zurich, its central role in the secondary market, and its long established correspondent relationships with banks, brokers, fund managers and institutions throughout Europe, gave it unique distribution power in foreign dollar bonds. This was recognised by lead managers, particularly Morgan, Stanley, one of the most active originators. None of the principle led managers: Morgan Stanley, Kuhn Loeb, Harriman Ripley, First Boston Corporation, Lazard Frères had a securities distribution presence in Europe. Kuhn Loeb ultimately had a one man representation in London; Lazard Bros in London and Lazard, Paris were domestic houses in each of those centres. Underwriters were not under any particular obligation to "indent" to the amount of their underwriting, which left bonds for the wider selling group. Underwriting groups were not formed entirely for the distribution power of its members but also with reciprocity and overall syndicate relationships in mind. This element of mutual back scratching was one of the arguments used by the Government in Washington in trying to prove an anti-trust conspiracy in the Street, in the "Morgan Stanley *et al"* case. Issues were negotiated then. The terms were established at the end of the registration period by negotiation with the issuer having regard to market conditions but also to the level of interest indicated by the underwriting and selling group. Issues were priced to sell and an immediate discount to issue price in the secondary market, unless caused by a sudden change in market conditions, was to be avoided. The skill of the lead manager "running the books" consisted in judging the genuineness of indications of interest from the group, and then making allocations accordingly. A practice of over allocation became common – known as the "green shoe", after an equity issue for a shoe manufacturer of that name, when the technique was first used. This was effectively a short position, allowing the manager to mop up loose securities subscribed by so-called "stags" seeking a quick profit if the issue went to an immediate premium. Issuing houses regarded this as market stabilization. We had great difficulty explaining this to Michael Howard, the minister in the Thatcher government steering the first Investment Act through Parliament, as part of "Big Bang". I was on a City committee that met almost through the night with the Minister. We were seeking exemption for this practice, unknown then in the domestic market, from the new regulations aimed at market malpractice. "How can I explain to my colleagues in the House of Commons that this is anything other than sheer market manipulation?" the poor man pleaded. It was, indeed, a difficult case to make. Michael Howard, as a barrister, was accustomed to arguing difficult cases. He saw our point – one might call it a greater good argument – and gained the exemption in the bill. The emerging Eurobond new issue market in London would have suffered if he hadn't.

Because of its superior placing power, White, Weld was able to receive hugely generous allocations, way above its nominal underwriting commitment. But despite sometimes placing close to half the issue, membership of the special bracket eluded the firm. These were the underwriters who appeared out of alphabetical order in the "tomb stone" announcement of the issue and normally had a higher underwriting – but not necessarily selling – allocation. This was because the syndicate "mafia" in Wall Street abhorred change and considered any departure from tradition as a slippery slope. Special bracket status, eventually termed bulge bracket, depended on the record of origination. White, Weld was not a very frequent lead manager in those days. Syndicate managers were all powerful and enjoyed clubby relationships with each other. They even had their own annual publication, *The Bawl Street Journal*, a spoof edition of *The Wall Street Journal,* in the same format, and full of satirical articles, ads and cartoons. Most were "in" jokes, incomprehensible to any but Wall Street insiders. Charlie Lee was White, Weld's syndicate manager, and pressure from Genillard & Co. in Europe to reflect the firm's placing power in a higher position in foreign dollar bond underwriting syndicates, fell on stony ground. That was not how the system worked. Charlie had married one of Ogden White's daughters, was White, Weld to his fingertips, and greatly admired in the Street. It was during this period that John Young's occasional visits to the Zurich office – which he made his own – provoked a complaint from Bob Genillard. And it was to the privileged allocations WW received from Morgan Stanley that DY referred to in justification of its senior partner's apparent abuse of hospitality. It would seem that already then, there was not a great deal of recognition in New York of the potential value of the franchise that Genillard was building in Europe, under the overall supervision of DY and Jean Cattier. These two were not the type to bang the table and brag and Genillard did not spend much time in New York lobbying. Back at head office Harold Mandelson acted as the leader or first violin of the foreign department orchestra, which was growing in range and skills under its three principle conductors.

It would be going too far to suggest that the very gradual drifting apart of the two sides of White, Weld began at this date. But, on reflection, I believe some very early signs were emerging. In the first place, the firm's international talent was now all abroad. One might call it a brain drain. Genillard, John Cattier, Appelmans, Champion, Stancliffe, and Sarasin – all were now posted abroad. DY spent half the year in Europe. Jean Cattier, a growing strategic influence within the partnership, could be somewhat aloof, as all very brainy people are inclined to be. This left only Harold Mandelson as a day-to-day representative of the international business in New York. White, Weld's domestic franchise was not standing still. The 1950s and '60s saw considerable development in energy infrastructure in the U.S. – particularly in natural gas pipelines. The great gas reserves in Texas and Oklahoma were harnessed for transmission to the eastern conglomerations. A partner of White, Weld & Co., Francis Kernan, made this patch his speciality, and he secured pipeline financing mandates for some of the principle projects from companies like El Paso and Transcontinental. White, Weld became a leader in this area, together with Stone & Webster Securities, the financial arm of a major engineering firm. This house was, of course, well placed, encompassing the two key disciplines in one organisation. It is surprising that Stone & Webster was the only American example of this combination. In Europe, engineer/contractors had become financiers, particularly in the railway boom. Examples are Henderson in Britain and Edouard Dervieu in France and Egypt. Pipeline finance is the purest example of project finance. As in shipping, the carrier is the securing asset, the off take the source of re-payment and the input is easily obtained. Kernan was a great friend of Senator Prescott Bush, the senior senator from Connecticut. He introduced the senator's eldest son George, just down from Yale, to an entrepreneur called Hugh Lidke. Lidke had just acquired a very old, but rather run-down company called Pennzoil, which had been established when the first American discoveries of oil were made in Pennsylvania. Pennzoil was a manufacturer of lubricating oil for the automobile industry, but Lidke decided to move the company to Texas and enter the exploration and production business there. Lidke gave young Bush a job, which was to lead too his fortune, his state governorship and his presidency. White, Weld was improving its position in equity issuance as well. The late '50s saw major secondary offerings of blue chip companies, such as Ford and DuPont, as the founding families grew, and sought diversification of their fortunes. Issuing companies influenced the lead manager's selection and ranking of underwriters, so a relationship needed to be developed with the issuer as well as with the lead manager. I recall riding in a taxi downtown with DY and Alec White and hearing the latter announce with pride that a major position had been secured for White, Weld in a large Ford secondary offering – a transaction which had excited competitive frenzy in the Street. I had grown up exposed to the thrill of the chase for mandates, the quarry which raises the blood lust of investment bankers, and is only bested by a gallop behind hounds in full cry after the elusive fox. I recall DY coming home from the office when I was quite young, bearing a small tin of frozen orange juice concentrate. White Weld had secured the lead management position for an initial public offering of shares in the Minute Maid Company. My mother thought the product absolutely disgusting. I also knew early on the frustration of failing to secure a position one felt the firm deserved due to its placing power. I was to experience it very directly in the early days of the Eurobond market.

White, Weld was also strong in the utility market with a much admired research team concentrated on one of the most popular asset classes in U.S. portfolios. In addition to a steady stream of common, preferred share, and debt offerings, the utility sector was a source of fee income for investment bankers, due to the regulatory system established early in its history. Permitted levels of customer charges were established by reference to the rate of return on capital invested, adjusted for inflation. The congressional committees and regulators responsible for regulating utility charges relied on submissions from the industry, supported by testimony from investment bankers, on the minimum rates of return allowing utilities to finance capital investment. A trip to Washington, testimony authoritatively delivered, supported by charts, etc., earned the investment banker a tidy fee, paid by the utility. It was not the most popular of gigs, as Washington was a dull town in those days, and the practice of maintaining a mistress in a Watergate apartment was the exclusive preserve of politicians.

As White, Weld Zurich was building the foundation from which the great edifice of White, Weld Europe was to rise, I was spending my enforced sabbatical year at Banque Galland & Cie in Lausanne. After my first expulsion from Harvard, I had travelled with my mother on a French Line steamer to Europe, to be met by a stony faced father who, almost wordlessly, took me to Lausanne and the office of Edouard Adam, the kindly Neuchatelois who managed the bank. DY was slightly put off when, on enquiring what a suitable living allowance should be, as I was to be unsalaried, Adam cited the high cost of a whiskey and soda at the Palace Hotel. Galland had an estate agency department which handled sales and rentals for clients, as well as tax efficient investments in land, particularly vineyards. A Serbian gentleman originally called Popov was in charge. He had been a member of the junior Jugoslav tennis team on a tournament trip to Switzerland, had defected, and been adopted by a rich widow called Madame Mercier, whose name he then took. I met him only once because he quickly fell in with tuberculosis and had to take leave. M. Adam placed me in charge of the department, despite my youth and total lack of business experience. Unconcerned that I might inadvertently sell a rental or rent a sale, Adam assured me I would be assigned a secretary who would help me with my written French, which, as with most French speakers not educated in French, was rocky. This kind lady, much amused to be assisting a 19-year-old university reject, did exactly that and more. I was assigned M. Mercier's commodious office with a huge map of Lausanne and its environs on the wall behind my desk. I was also given a camera with which to photograph properties, and which I used taking artistic photographs of swans on the Lac Leman.

For my accommodation I turned to the Pension de Beaumont, where I had been billeted during my summer course at the University. Mlle David explained that they were now essentially taking in young ladies, but in view of my previous custom she would make an exception for me – as, in fact, she was already doing for another *Monsieur,* because he was the son of a distinguished Swiss diplomat. He turned out to be a friend of mine called Daniel Wagnière, whose father was Swiss Observer at the United Nations, and a friend of my parents. In fact his American mother was a relative of the Whites of White, Weld. Daniel was cramming for his Swiss university entrance exams, and being dyslexic, needed acute concentration space. Why a pension filled with beautiful and nubile Swedish, Brazilian, Canadian and other assorted young ladies was deemed an appropriate venue for his purpose, I forgot to enquire at the time. He passed into the University of Zurich, gained a doctorate in agronomy and ended up as President of Sandoz America, retiring as deputy CEO of the parent company in Basle, just before it merged to form Novartis. I arrived, carrying my Vuitton suitcase, at the garden gate in the Avenue de Beaumont, opposite the Hôpital Nestlé. *Les jeunes filles* were engaged in playing a boisterous game of ping-pong doubles on a table set in the pleasantly run-down garden. One of them made an instant impression. She was dressed in tight fitting tartan trousers, a black, short sleeved, woollen jersey, and a red scarf around the neck and ballet shoes. She wore an ivory bracelet and had a short haircut with a fringe. Her style, movement and neck line were reminiscent of Audrey Hepburn. She was called Diana Veronica Obré Townsend and she hailed from Lowdale Farm, Mazoe Road, Salisbury, Southern Rhodesia, where her Anglo-Irish family had farmed since 1898. She had been sent to Switzerland to learn French and, as I used to josh later on, how to wear shoes. Mlle David had been most impressed by her mother's stories of Africa, recounted at tea when she was delivering her daughter. One was a famous – or infamous – story about a one-eyed farm manager who, when taking a break from supervising a gang, would take out his glass eye, place it on top of a stake, and tell the work force not to slack off as he would still be watching them. Mrs. Townsend was able to render the key phrase in "kitchen kaffir", the semi-dialect with which Europeans and Africans communicated at the time. Such a story would not go down in Switzerland today, as it has become the most politically correct nation in Europe – with the possible exception of Norway. But Mlle David found it funny, though she would have been horrified, even then, had she been accused of condescension towards the native population of Africa. Needless to say, I was bowled over, or out – one might say, by this lovely girl and began a courtship which was facilitated by the fact that Dinnie, as she was nicknamed, attended daily a school just opposite the Banque Galland in the Avenue du Théâtre. This was the Ecole Vinet which had a course for *les jeunes etrangères.* "Finishing" young ladies, whether boarding or day, is one of Switzerland's oldest industries – together with coo-coo clocks, as Harry Lime would have put it. In Switzerland, as on much of the Continent at the time, everyone broke for lunch. This produced four traffic jams a day. I had been given a WW Beetle to beetle around in – a sign my father had a soft side. It had Zurich plates and when I made a slight traffic error, other drivers would shout insults: *"salle Zurichois!"* There is little love lost between Swiss cantons – especially across the language divide. In this vehicle I drove Dinnie back and forth to her school and me to my office. I took her to the motion pictures. A great favourite was an ex-GI actor called Eddie Constantine. With a pockmarked face and atrocious American accent, he played a bourbon swilling private eye in such rough and tumble films as *Ca Va Barder!* – Almost impossible to translate: "it's going to be big brawl!" – is close. We dined and danced at the Place Hotel, and I bored the poor girl stiff with tales of my misspent youth. We went riding and I fell off. We toured the countryside. We had an old-fashioned, unconsummated romance, and, although I was nothing like the young men she had grown up with, and she was nothing like the girls I was used to, we fell in love, bound together by being total opposites – for life, as it turned out. When we parted, each to return to our respective continents, we thought it was for good. But that is another chapter.

My work at the Banque Galland's estate agency was not challenging and with the help of my permanently amused secretary, I soon got the hang of it. I visited houses, photographed and wrote up the brochure, always careful to mention *vue imprenable,* a statement of the obvious as every house had a view of the lake. I went to fix or take down *A Vendre* signs in the vineyards and, even at eight-thirty in the morning, would be asked to split a bottle of white wine with the *vigneron* – an offer it was discourteous to refuse. But this consisted of splitting the whole bottle with one glass, exchanging shot by shot –

an infallible method of getting thoroughly soused. I would turn up at Mlle David's luncheon table the worse for wear, to the amusement of the girls. Mlle David had a niece called Mme Goss who espoused every left wing cause and opinion, was violently anti-American, but treated me with surprising affection, whilst castigating me as the worst example of a spoilt rich kid she had ever encountered. One day she told us she had invited a friend from Geneva to lunch. "Don't be drunk!" she said to me. A nice, mild-mannered and scholarly looking gentleman turned up and we talked about birds in America. He was an expert on Audubon.

"What does he do – teach at the university?" I asked Mme Goss, when he left.

"He did," she replied, "but he's now President of the Swiss Communist Party"

"Good Lord! How many party members does he have?" I was fascinated.

"Seventeen, at last count," replied Mme Goss.

There was a lovely granny living on the top floor of the spacious house who was called "Mamps". She had a permanent twinkle in her eye and followed with great relish the growing attachment between Dinnie and myself, whereas her daughter Mme David viewed it with some alarm, wondering no doubt whether she should drop a line to Mrs. Townsend back in Rhodesia. Once someone produced a bull whip and Mamps watched me cracking it from her top floor window. She used the expression about scratching a Russian and finding a Tartar, which I heard then for the first time. There were also the three children of Mme Goss. The eldest Laurent was a passionate jazz aficionado, Thomas studied dance and ended as premier dancer with the Helsinki Ballet and a daughter now lives at Beaumont and is writing its history. In those days, we were 18 at table.

Life in my spacious office at 8 Avenue du Théâtre was full of pleasant surprises. One day an English lady arrived at reception on the ground floor with her darling daughter in tow. Ann, for that was her name, was here to be "finished", and might there be an English speaking officer in the bank who could open an account and see to her financial needs during her *séjour*? Of course, came the gracious reply and the two visitors were promptly escorted upstairs to my office. My loyal secretary no doubt suppressed a snigger as she announced the pair. "That boy is going to look after my daughter!" queried Mrs. D'Arcy-Smith in mock horror, for that was her name. I suggested that since Ann was here to learn French, might it not be sensible for her to be dealt with by a more mature French speaker? But Mrs D'Arcy-Smith softened as she looked around my enormous office, perhaps surmising I must be someone important, despite my youth, and thus unlikely to make an attempt on her daughter's virtue. The upshot was that Ann became a lifelong friend of my wife and me. She married John Dexter, whose family had a Milan based insurance agency representing most UK insurers in Italy, and whose younger brother is Ted Dexter, oft-capped English cricketer and athlete *extraordinaire.*

Ann has almost forgotten her French but is totally fluent in Italian, having lived in Milan and at Lake Como most of her adult life.

It is said that, for an investment banker, the first transaction is as memorable as the first love affair. Since I would prefer my first love affair to be as unmemorable as possible, I will recall with pleasure my first deal. It came through an intermediary who arrived in my office and said he was mandated by a lady to sell her huge forestry estate of some tens of thousands of hectares in the Jura, straddling the Franco-Swiss border. This was not our usual fare, but I thought I could lose little by following up. The lady was anxious to remain as much in the background as possible, but the intermediary was prepared to provide me with all the *bona fides* and references required. He did so, together with a great deal of technical detail on the history of the forest, tree varieties, growth patterns, harvesting, annual yields, etc., etc. I told him I would get back. Should I consult the Boss or not? Perhaps, not quite yet. I had read somewhere recently that pension funds favoured forests as an asset class providing long-term, inflation protected returns. I asked my knowledgeable secretary to put a call through to Nestlé's headquarters in Vevey. In those days, you found a real person on the switchboard, rather than a recorded message with a dozen options. I asked the real voice if she could put me through to whoever was in charge of the *fonds de retraite.* I had little knowledge of the institutional investment management scene, which I thought was just mutual funds, and assumed all companies managed their pension funds in-house. As it happens Nestlé did. A pleasant man came on the line and I told my story. To my amazement he expressed interest. A meeting was set up at a café near the forest at 9:00 o'clock in the morning. The Nestlé man arrived with his forestry expert. The intermediary was hung over and drank several Fernet-Brancas, an herbal liquor recommended for that condition. We toured the property, driving through rides cut in the forest, and crossing the frontier into France and back again several times. The forestry expert talked forest to several woodcutters and sundry keepers. We looked at the trees and made appropriate noises of appreciation. Repairing back to the café the intermediary switched to white wine. A price discussion began; Nestlé opened the bidding, the intermediary countered, Nestlé adjusted, the intermediary stuck and stuck fast. Even by his fifth glass of white wine, he was immovable. End of meeting. On the way out, the Nestlé man took me aside and said, "Contact the principal directly. Monsieur Intermediary is just protecting his commission, which I suspect is too high. Our offer is reasonable." I went back to the bank and asked to see M. Adam. I told him the story. He took down some directory and found the name of the lady owner of the property. He asked his secretary to call the lady. I sat in front of his desk as he gave her an exact account of my meeting. She then clearly assumed control of the conversation because M. Adam was reduced to occasional interjections: "*bien entendu ... naturelment... tout a fait d'accord...mon avis aussi...*« Finally came à final flourish: «*Je suis ravi que cette affaire puisse se terminer si agréablement et je me ferait le plaisir de communiquer vos remerciements et vos meilleurs vœux au jeune homme qui s'en est occupé avec distinction».* I am delighted this affair has been concluded so pleasantly and it will be my pleasure to communicate your thanks and best wishes to the young man who handled it with distinction. My boss put down the phone and came around his desk to seize my hand. All I had to do was ring the man at Nestlé and tell him their offer was accepted. I then handed it over to our legal department. I learned later the intermediary had complained and threatened to sue for *détournement de mondat* – meaning interference in his mandate from the client. Our lawyer said he hadn't a hope. I have forgotten the numbers now; they were large and the bank earned a fat commission, and the lady placed the proceeds on deposit with Galland. I had done my first deal. I have never forgotten that.

My year in Switzerland was coming to an end, and my carefully drafted applications for re-admission to Harvard, supported by warm references from M. Adam, had been successful. I have already revealed the result of my further Harvard sojourn. DY was spending more and more time in Europe as White, Weld's international business continued to grow. He began to seriously consider establishing a European residence. Bittersweet, our home on Piping Rock Road, had been sold. My mother was not happy. She felt she was losing the home in which the children had grown up and her Americanization had been completed. Had I not been so preoccupied with my own messy life, I would have been equally distressed. A major chapter was brought to a close and the future plot was anything but predictable. Ariane had married Adrian Reed, a West Point graduate, eldest of the children of my parents' close friends Joseph and Permelia Reed. Ariane was now an Army wife stationed in Hokaido, Japan. My father felt there was no need to keep the Long Island property; there was an apartment on East 79th Street and Lexington in New York and about to be a house on Jupiter Island, Hobe Sound, Florida. In late summer, I motored from Zurich to the South of France with the parents. We stopped in Aix-en-Provence where my father admired the branch of the Banque de France in the Cours Mirabeau, the "main drag" of Aix. "How I would have loved to be the manager of the Banque de France in Aix and live in the apartment on the "bel étage" of this 18th century *hôtel particulier!"* he mused. My mother looked a bit sour. She feared the worse. She had no desire to acquire a house in France, despite being French – or perhaps because she was? Undeterred, DY popped into a local estate agent who offered to show him the Chateau de Vauvnargues, and historic and dilapidated pile just outside town – available for a song. Once there, we entered the cavernous great hall and Mother uttered her familiar phrase *"Mais Dimitri, vous êtes foux!"* A cursory inspection revealed that an amount equivalent to the then national debt of France would be required to restore the place. Pablo Picasso bought it a few years later, and a daughter lives there now. I would love to know how many bathrooms have since been installed. But DY was not to be frustrated for long and found a more convenient way of satiating his appetite for *les vi-*

elles pierres, that is to say, a period house in France, in the historic town of Senlis, near Chantilly, an easy commute to a Paris office of White, Weld.

Senlis was the first capital of France as Hugues Capet was elected king there in 987, and the Capetian dynasty ruled France until Charles X in 1825 – with a slight interruption under the Corsican upstart. Its cathedral, lovely church of St. Pierre, cobbled medieval streets, ruins of its ancient royal chateau and surrounding forests, give the town a unique charm and have attracted residents of all nationalities and vocations. My parents had first rented a house in Senlis belonging to Comte and Comtesse de Gramont, kinsman to the Duc de Gramont whose estate and chateau at Mortefontaines dominated the environs of the town. The "old Duke" as he was inevitably referred to by anyone born before 1914, was a great host and his house parties were celebrated for their elegance and the variety of the guests. Once Marcel Proust had been invited – he of interminable prose. It was the custom of guests to sign the guest book on arrival. As Proust approached the book, pen quivering in his hand, the Old Duke was heard to say "Your name only, please, M. Proust – your name only!" The DYs soon acquired a taste for the area and made several friends there, including: "Bunny" Carter, head of J. P. Morgan in Paris – *la Banque Morgan,* as it is known to the French, Denise de Leusse, whose daughter Pauline married young David Carter, also at Morgan, Philippe Julian, artist/author/decorator, Thérèse de Caraman-Chimay, who, at the age of 75, rode out in the early morning for the race horse trainers in Chantilly, "Chip" Bohlen, U.S. Ambassador to France, who spoke Russian with my father, Henri and Jacqeline de Pontalba, who had married because their nearby, respective chateaux marched together, Thomas Kernan of Condé Nast, editor of *Maison & Jardins* and President of Vogue Patterns, and sundry others – but, in particular, Burrell and Dolly Hoffman, an architect/decorator couple. It was they who signalled the availability of a part 16th/part 18th century townhouse, called *l'Hôtel de Cornouailles*, or alternatively, *l'Hôtel de St. Anne,* or even by some, *l'Hôtel de la Marine,* located in the Rue du Chat Harêt – Street of the Feral Cat, just opposite the ruins of the Royal Palace and a few hundred metres from the Cathedral. Anyone without a limited budget should have been wary of a house with three names, but my father was enchanted by this. was an American architect who had studied at the *Beaux Arts* in Paris and was particularly adept at restoring period houses in France, installing American creature comforts without in any way violating the architectural purity of the property. His wife Dolly was that rare style of decorator who could mix museum pieces with articles picked up in the flea market, leaving a finished product which bore no trace at all of the professional decorator, but which reflected the unmistakable good taste of the owner – even if the owner had no taste to begin with. Of course, Dolly only had to provide practical assistance to my parents, as their taste was hers as well. The Hoffmans had lovingly restored a house in the same street. Burrell did a remarkable job restoring our house which formed an L shape around an interior courtyard, with one part 16th century with a corkscrew, stone staircase, and the other part pure 18th century. There was a walled garden on the other side. There was a beautifully proportioned, high ceiling drawing room in the older wing, perfect for hanging tapestries against the stone walls and for high backed Louis XIII chairs placed near the great stone fire place. An 18th century room in the other wing made a perfect dining room – something which didn't actually exist in French houses at that time. Dolly Hoffmann found some old panelling being thrown an away by a local builder and had it restored and adapted. Above was my mother's very master bed room, in the style to which she had become accustomed. As usual, my father had a tiny room across a passage, resembling a monk's cell, with burlap on the walls and a huge volume of *Lives of the Saints* on a book stand. But DY had his own bathroom for the first time. Senlis is extremely scenic whilst avoiding a Disneyesque twee-ness. I use the present tense, because, as a result of an initiative by DY and others, a citizens' committee for the preservation of the town was formed at this point, and Senlis has been protected from development, despite Charles de Gaulle Airport being only 30 km away. The presence of three large forests, Ermenonville, d'Halat and Chantilly, all state protected preserves, have also ensured the safety of Senlis. The town is a favourite site for shooting historical films. I once witnessed a TV series being shot with an all Japanese cast, impeccably costumed in *Three Musqueteers* style. Once we were asked if the courtyard could be used for a scene for yet another remake of *The Man in the Iron Mask.* The scene, which lasts all of two minutes in the final cut, consisted of a closed carriage and horses driving in through our *porte cochère* and someone holding a brief conversation with Cardinal Mazarin inside. The shoot was to take all day. Ralph Richardson was playing the Cardinal. As they were setting up, Sir Ralph approached my father and said, "This is going to take all bloody day! I don't suppose you would be kind enough to let me take a nap somewhere?"

"Of course," replied DY and showed him to his monk's cell.

"Just the ticket!" said the great thespian, then examining the room, "Are you in holy orders, by chance?" DY explained he was an investment banker.

"Praying for the market to go up, are you?" said Sir Ralph, with a wink. My parents spent from May to October in the house in Senlis, until it was finally sold in 1984, when my father became very ill. My wife and the children used to go for a holiday every summer and I would commute to the Paris office. For the children it was like being in the theatre. We all changed for dinner, of course, DY and me in black tie and the boys in neat ties and blue blazers. DY wanted to dress them in sailor suits, as in St. Petersburg – but Dinnie put her foot down. Our Scots nanny Helen sat at table keeping an eagle eye. The children learned to be served and to help themselves of sometimes complicated dishes without dropping anything. Their enjoyment was enhanced by the fact that we had an extraordinary cook called Madelaine who knew how to prepare meals in the traditional, home fashion – not the phony, restaurant style *haute cuisine*, popularised by celebrity chefs and served at home by the unknowing newly rich. I still have mother's menu cards: *Oeufs Galli-Marie; Canard aux cerises; petits pois; salade/fromage; Gourmandises pralinée* or another: *Fonds d'Artichauds farcies; Fauxfilet Roti, haricots verts; pommes duchesse; Fromage; Glace au Rhum* or, even: *Koulibiak; Gigot d'Agneau; tomates grilles; flagelots; Fromage; "Peches Melba.* I could go on, but I salivate whilst writing. My father was a keen golfer and we played often together at the Mortefontaine Golf Club, where he had been a member since his Paris days in the '30s. The very pretty 18 hole course had been developed from the Old Duke's private, nine hole course and was laid out in an area surprisingly reminiscent of a Scotland, with thick heather rough and northern pines. I once joined a foursome with Van Galbraith, of rubber duck in the bath leading to floating rate note fame, Ambassador "Chip" Bohlen and DY. The Ambassador teed off and drove a good 300 yards, eliciting from Van Galbraith the comment: "You sure put your big, fat ambassadorial ass into that one!" My father took an instant dislike to Galbraith from that moment on, and always referred to him as "that vulgar man". Ambassador Bohlen took no offence. He wouldn't – he was a Porcellian. Van often stayed with David and Pauline Carter in Senlis. At the time Van was running Morgan & Cie which had been set up in Paris as a joint venture between J. P. Morgan and Morgan, Stanley to take the Euromarkets by storm. It didn't. Van ended up as American Ambassador to France himself. Shall we say there was a distinct generation gap – greater than the actual years, between someone like Van Galbraith, and my father.

The house in Senlis, and the time he spent there, represented the summit of my father's cultural and social life. For him it was a dream come true. The combination of Franco and Anglophile sentiments which had been the hallmark of his class in Imperial Russia, could now achieve fulfilment with his six months residence in France, punctuated by frequent trips across the Channel. He loved life in France, its history, its culture, its food and its social conventions. He started work on a history of the *Hôtel de Cornouailles* almost immediately. Here is to be found the explanation of the alter name *Hôtel de la Marine.* It's lengthy, complicated and not definitive, but the guess is that an official charged with supplying masts to the navy was amongst the owning families; or, the presence in a four cornice of a carved sailing vessel, marked the marriage of one François de Ladmiral to a daughter of the house. More amusing for me is the history of one of the families. An Etienne Le Bel, acquired the house in 1595. He was socially mobile, as we would say today, acquiring positions and titles to match, so that a great granddaughter could go by the resounding name of Louise-Victoire Marie Madelaine Le Bel de la Boissière de Séry. This young lady became maid of honour to the Princess Palatine, wife of the homosexual Duc d'Orleans, brother of Louis XIV and mother of the young Duc, who became regent at the start of the reign of the young Louis XV. Although warned by the Princess against any hanky-panky with her son, who was of the very opposite inclination of his father, Mlle de

Séry was duly seduced and impregnated by the randy young Duc d'Orleans. In fact she had a second child, the first dying in child birth. This survivor was known as the Chevalier d'Orleans. Mlle de Séry became *maitresse attitrée* to her lover, presiding at his rowdy dinners at the Palais Royal, gaining the title of Comtesse d'Argenton and even the right to be called simply "Madame", normally reserved for wives of princes of the blood. Unfortunately, the lady provoked the ire of Madame de Maintenon, last mistress, and morganatic wife, of Louis XIV. The Sun King's reign was setting and he was under the thumb of that lady, the only one who could stand his bad breath. The Duc d'Orleans was ordered to chuck his much loved mistress, who was consoled with a nice chateau and two million *Louis d'or*. She was still quite young and married a young scamp called the Chevalier d'Oppède, younger son of the Marquis d'Oppède, Ambassador to Spain, and nephew of the Bishop of Beauvais. He beat her and was killed in a duel with a fellow officer in 1710. Now it so happens we live in Oppède, opposite the fortress village where the ancestor of that hapless toy boy was responsible for the brutal suppression of a heresy in the Luberon valley in the 16th century. One of the favourite, small world, or full circle, stories in my collection. These and other bits of history, such as one concerning Anne, daughter of Tsar Jaroslav of Kiev, when Russia was still Kieven Rus or Muscovy, who married Henri Ier of France, and founded the church/abbey of St Vincent in Senlis. Ann of Kiev was the granddaughter of Tsar, later Saint, Vladimir of Kiev, who brought Christianity to Russia, having married a Byzantine princess. For my father, this combination of Viking and Byzantine heritage, the Kieven Tsars being direct descendants of the Viking Rurik the Rus, was an irresistible attraction. He loved the Isle de France, where villages are called en-France, a reminder that the original Kingdom of France was surrounded by the larger Duchies of Burgundy and Normandy and the older Kingdom of Britainy, the Counties of Lorraine, Aquitaine and of Provence, and was indeed pint-sized, and a kingdom only because of papal anointment. The village of Roissy-en-France was to become Charles de Gaulle Airport. You can still see the great tree that stood in the village green. DY was less interested in the passage of Joan of Arc in Senlis in 1429, as he thought she had "lost the plot" militarily at Crepy. My father had the charming habit of talking about historical events as if he had just read about them in the morning paper.

DY's partners in New York had ceased by now to pull his leg about his long summers in Europe; the growing success of the firm's implantation in Zurich, and the soon to be significant presence in London, put paid to any notion that Europe was just a playground. His being able to witness at close hand the development of his brainchild, added to the pleasure of the Senlis residence for DY. My father was a delegator before the concept became the subject of long lectures at MBA courses. In fact DY was much advantaged by having had no formal business training whatsoever, as his management skills – not his strong point – were based on common sense. And common sense told him that Bob Genillard had just the attributes required to carry on building the White, Weld franchise in Europe. After all, Bob had turned La Financiera Venezolana into Venezuela's premier investment bank whilst still in his 20s. So, whilst retaining oversight and providing moral support. DY delegated the running of White, Weld in Europe to Genillard, and Harold Mandelson was the mainstay of the foreign department in New York, with Jean Cattier far more present in NY than DY. This is a good point to put into some perspective the contributions of the main architects of White, Weld International. DY was essentially a relationship banker. He was not a "mover and shaker". But even his detractors, few as they are, would agree he gave an unmistakeable style and gravitas to White, Weld's image and prestige in the marketplace. Jean Cattier, as I have already indicated, was a strategist, a financial and economic thinker, and an invaluable source of support to the whole project and those engaged in it. He also had widespread, senior contacts in Europe. Genillard was a "doer", an executor of agreed strategies, a superb tactician, farsighted, and an inspiration to his team. He was also in no doubt whatsoever about himself and his talent. This inclined him to a self- congratulatory attitude somewhat at odds with the Anglo-Saxon tradition of understatement. A few years ago a splendid dinner was organised by a WW old boy, David Reid-Scott, to mark the anniversary of the end of Credit Suisse White Weld – the final chapter of the White, Weld Europe story. Bob was on his feet with an oration which contained a perhaps excessive series of references to his good self. "Siggy Warburg used to call me at home!" was a particularly striking example. Well, it is absolutely true that in the early days of the Eurobond market, Warburgs often found itself lead managing an issue which it was incapable of placing. Warburgs had very limited placing power. And Sigmund would often send out a distress call to White, Weld, and he had certainly armed himself with Bob Genillard's home phone number, and we certainly bailed Warburgs out of some heavy positions. But least some of the younger White, Weld alumni begin to think that the firm might have best been named "Genillard & Cie", John Stancliffe rose to his feet and reminded everyone that the originators of White, Weld in Europe had been Jean Cattier and DY, and the nephew of one and son of the other were here present! Loud applause – embarrassed grins from Johnny Cattier and me.

CHAPTER XII

"...to the shores of Tripoli"

-Extract from the U. S. Marine Corps Hymn-

I quote only this fragment – the full line is: *"From the Halls of Montezuma to the Shores of Tripoli; We will Fight our Country's Battles on the Land and on the Sea"* – because I spent but little time in Mexico in my life, but I did spend time "on the shores of Tripoli", when I served as Deputy Chairman of ABC International Bank, a principle shareholder being the Central Bank of Libya. The cleaning up of the Barbary pirates in the first days of America's existence as an independent nation, represented its first strategic service to Europe. I would site another as being the heroic actions of the 6ᵗʰ Marine Regiment at Belleau Wood, in the closing days of World War One, which led to the entire regiment being awarded the French *Medaille Militaire*, the *fouragère* of which is still worn by the 6ᵗʰ Marines, now part of the 2ⁿᵈ Marine Division. U.S. Marines tend to be a bit of a bore about the Corp's history, largely because it is drilled into us at boot camp. You will have already detected I am proud to have served as a U.S. Marine. The American Marines trace their history to the Continental Marines which was the colonial branch of the Royal Marines, serving in the American colonies. The Royal Marine emblem is the Globe and Laurel and the U.S. version is the Globe and Anchor. In each case, the globe symbolises the reach of the mission – the seas worldwide. Originally, Marines were sharpshooters in the rigging firing on the enemy crew in naval engagements. They also provided security on ships at sea, and that duty remains. The Royal Marines are a smaller force and emphasise commando operations. The U.S. Marines are currently three divisions, have their own air strike capability, plus armour and artillery. The Corps was the only foreign purchaser of the vertical take-off aircraft developed by the British. U.S. Marines are focussed on amphibious operations. The Corps belongs to the Navy Department, and, since the Commandant sits on the Joint Chiefs of Staff Committee, the Navy effectively has two members whilst the Army and Air force have only one each. The Chairman of the Joint Chiefs is occasionally the Marine Corps Commandant. The Captain General of the Royal Marines, currently HRH the Duke of Edinburgh, pays an annual visit to the Commandant at the U.S. Marines ceremonial HQ at Quantico, Virginia. American Embassies are traditionally guarded by Marines – the only country in the world that maintains this custom. Since their rules of engagement prevent them from acting in any but the most extreme emergencies, one wonders what the point is. The Marines have always been a volunteer force exclusively, even in wartime. They have served in more places than any other branch of the armed forces, save the Navy. They have been mounted in China and the Philippines, giving rise to the expression "Horse Marines". They occupied and ran the Republic of Haiti for three years in the early part of the 20th century. The First Marine Division, headquartered at Camp Pendleton in California, fought in Korea and distinguished itself at the Chosin Reservoir, in a battle as famous for we Marines, as the engagement at the Imjin River is for the Gloucester Regiment of the British Army.

I have already described the circumstances which led to my second expulsion from Harvard College. The DuPont Company, inventors of the drip-dry material I was so generously testing, with no regard to my own safety, never expressed the slightest interest in my result – no doubt considering their own laboratory tests sufficient to the purpose. The Harvard authorities took an understandable position, given my appalling record to date, and considered my adventurist instincts might be better served elsewhere. Until my dive into the pristine waters of the Charles River, I had continued my erratic sampling of the intellectual cornucopia which is Harvard and Cambridge, Massachusetts. I did even submit a paper to a course in French Literature, given in French, by a visiting professor from the Sorbonne. My theses, lifted to a degree from a work entitled *Les Femmes dans l'Histoire de France,* was that all important historical events in France had been driven, by women, if from behind the scenes, and that French culture and literature were also dominated by women – the best books being about the female of the species. I cited the obvious historical examples: Eleonora d'Aquitaine, Catherine de Medici, Josephine Beauharnais, Empress Eugenie – not forgetting the mistress of President Edgar Faure, in whose arms he died of heart seizure. In culture and literature, I ranged from the mistress of Molière to the mother of Marcel Proust, extolling also my favourite works *Chansons de Bilitis* and *Aphrodite* by Pierre Louys, both concerned with nubile girls. The professor was not impressed. He gave me a pass for originality, but considered my work frivolous and disrespectful, even insulting to the dignity of France. Leaving aside the dignity of France, his review was an excellent summation of my Harvard career.

My parents were in Europe when the moment came to execute my choice, the alternative of the French Foreign Legion having been quickly dismissed. I loved the film *Beau Geste*, but already then one of the great regrets of my life was fixed in my mind. Real life is not like Hollywood. I went down to Times Square and enlisted in the U. S. Marine Corps. I spent my time in the Marines with my name misspelt, as the recruiting master sergeant took it from my birth certificate where it still had the "t" at the end. I went to stay with my sister in Greenwich, Connecticut for the few days before I was due to report. On leaving, I left my signet ring in her safe keeping, considering the Marines would have no interest in the fact that I was armigerous. On the train from Penn Station, heading for Parris Island, South Carolina, I saw one contingent that was to be part of my recruit platoon. They were New York slum kids, straight out of central casting. They had all recently been given the choice between reform school or enlistment in the Marines, by some Magistrate before whom they were appearing, charged with an affray of some kind. Only one exhibited some bitterness, explaining to me at length that it had been the rival gang which was armed with bicycle chains, and he had not even opened his flick knife, so the charge of armed assault was a "stitch up", all because the arresting officer's advances to his sister had been spurned. It all seemed like a script conference for *Westside Story*. There was much discussion about our destination, and speculation that recent events might have softened the notorious brutality of boot camp drill instructors. Indeed, three drill instructors, having inadvertently drowned some of their recruits, had recently been court-martialled, presumably for will full destruction of government property. A celebrated former Commandant of the Marine Corps, General "Chesty" Puller had appeared in their defence. Puller was famous for, amongst other incidents, walking down a line of U.S. Army Lorries in Korea, and smashing out their headlights with the butt of his 45 calibre pistol, because the column was in the way of his faster moving unit. General Puller's testimony was essentially that the training of Marines was what it was to save their lives in combat, all the better to fulfil their mission "on the land and on the sea" and that disciplining drill instructors for a slight accident whilst they were doing their job was a political gesture designed to mollify ignorant public opinion, and the members of the court-martial should all be ashamed of themselves. I am not sure the General was entirely helpful. The DIs were found guilty and each lost a stripe and gained a reprimand in their record. We would soon see what effect, if any, the public interest in the case had had on training methods at Parris Island.

On arrival at the nearest station to Parris Island, which is connected to the mainland by a causeway, we were billeted in nearby barracks for our first night, under the command of a Drill Instructor wearing the traditional campaign hat, a broad rimmed brown felt cover, recognisable to the general public as it is the hat worn by Smokey the Bear, a cartoon character who guards against forest fires in the national parks. I now gained one of my most lasting impressions. Our original group from New York City had now been joined by a bunch of farm boys who had arrived on another train from the Middle West. They consisted largely of hefty, milk fed, high school football heroes, who had joined the Marines to impress their girlfriends. Our temporary DI, of course, gave us our first taste of the abusive, foul-mouthed language with which we were to be addressed for the next few months. During that first night, it became apparent to me that not one of my new mates had ever spent a night away from home. The slum kids had always gone home from their gang warfare, and the football heroes had always had Mum and apple pie, on a daily basis. I, on the other hand, had been to boarding school. I became a lifelong adherent of boarding school. These tough new recruits were absolutely shattered by their first experience of life in a barracks. The next day we were bussed to the main camp to begin the process of induction, uniform and rifle issue, wrapping of civilian clothes for posting home, medical and dental inspection, series of injections against unnamed conditions, and heads shaved, this last traumatic for the NY slum kids, whose long greasy locks were their symbols of virility. Our newly formed platoon, No. 116, of E Company, 1st Battalion, Marine Corps Recruit Depot, included two mavericks amongst the slum kids and farm boys. One was a Negro from the south – there were very few black Marines in those days – and the other was a "college boy", meaning me. We had three heavily decorated Korean veteran Drill Instructors: T/Sergeant Wills, a red-necked southerner, S/Sergeant McKenzie, a lean and benign Scot, and Sergeant Lacoursière, a brutal and sadistic French Canadian. Their first task was to weed out a number they deemed, on first inspection, unlikely to "make it". By coincidence or not, they were all three Puerto Ricans from the NYC contingent. We were billeted in Quonset Huts, those tin constructions much in use in World War Two. The tin roof curves straight down to the ground. The hapless three were marched up against the tin, and ordered to keep marching until their knees were sufficiently bloodied – which took at least twenty minutes of banging. To complete their treatment, they were told their shaving was inadequate, covered in shaving foam and shaved with a straight razor by a DI, until the foam was sufficiently red. They were then marched off to sick bay with a recommendation they be given medical discharges. Since we never saw them again, I assume they were. We were a platoon of some seventy odd, larger than a classic Marine rifle platoon which is three squads of thirteen. We here divided by height into four squads and I was given, command of the first – I know not why, but perhaps because I was a college boy and the DI's bet on how long I would last in a squad much taller and tougher. I was expected to adopt the style of command favoured by the DI's. I did so quite quickly, leaving out the usual preambles to every command, which were variations on: "OK... you mother f.....g, s...t eating, c...k sucking, maggots..." It was my first exposure, in volume, to an American slang insult, widely used in the barracks, accusing the recipient of sexual relations with his mother. I don't believe Americans are more given to incest than other nations, but somehow this swearword is quite deeply entrenched in American culture. In any case, my squad accepted my command without a murmur, even out of the hearing of a DI. Quite soon Sgt. Lacoursière discovered, after intensive interrogation, that I knew the family of Douglas Dillon, then recently U.S. Ambassador to France. His daughter Joan had married Jimmy Mosely, a Porcellian, in a lavish ceremony in Paris. They divorced, and Joan married first Prince Charles of Luxembourg, who died in a car crash, and then the Duc de Mouchy. The Prince had adopted a folksy style when Joan brought him to her parents' house on Jupiter Island, and he liked to introduce himself, saying: "Hi! I'm Charlie Luxembourg." As Duchesse de Mouchy, Joan ended up running the family *grand cru* Chateau Haut Brion, acquired by the Dillons three generations ago, having been founded by an Irish wine merchant in Bordeaux named O'Brian. But I digress. Sergeant Lacoursière had done embassy duty in Paris under Ambassador Dillon, and he had had a whale of a time. Even if his French had distinct Canadian tones, it was sufficient to allow him to "pull" the girls, apparently in great numbers. Ha also greatly admired the Ambassador, although he could not have had much contact with him. The result was that I was called "Frenchman", not even mother f...g Frenchman, and made to stand in front of the platoon most evenings and sing the "Marseillaise", in the loudest voice possible. "Did I say f...g at ease?" Lacoursière would scream at the platoon, during my performance. Standing at attention in our skivvies in the evening, sometimes for an hour, was a test of self-control. One was devoured by mosquitoes. If one was foolish enough to slap one, one had to run for an entrenching tool, dig a grave one foot deep and bury the mosquito. The most challenging part was finding it, and at dusk, one would still see a recruit or two on his hands and knees searching. But there is no doubt my course was eased due to this coincidence of mutual acquaintance, and, once again, I was made aware of the old maxim: it's not what you know; it's who you know. The relationship between various DI's and certain recruits was a fascinating window on social mores and intra-American cultural relations. We had one Negro recruit from somewhere down South. Our equally southern, senior DI Sergeant Wills, could have played a dirt farmer in a Tennessee Williams play. He was red-necked personified. On the one hand, he abused, insulted and picked on our black recruit unmercifully; on the other hand, I saw him protecting him and, even, giving him special help on the rifle range at one point. He even intervened on the man's behalf when another DI sought to discipline him. I overheard Sgt. Wills say to another DI, "Sure he's a f...g nigger, but he's my f...g nigger" – the "n" word being still very much in use in those days. It seems the southern bond was stronger than the racial divide. I have seen that in Africa since. Sgt. McKenzie, whose transition from the Scottish highlands to the U.S. Marines was never explained, was the mildest of our three DIs and very weak on profanity, perhaps due to his Presbyterian antecedents. His favourite command on the drill ground was "Don't stick your head out like a turtle!"

Marine Corps recruit training is based on one overriding and simple principle – best expressed early on by one of my DI's "If you don't duck right away when someone shouts 'duck!' you get your f...g head blown off". Every aspect of training is aimed at instilling instant and unquestioning response to an order. I recall an exchange with a DI that illustrates the degree to which this concept is espoused. At Parris Island we moved everywhere, and between every point, at the double. I hardly recall walking anywhere. Once I was summoned by a DI to carry a message. Standing at attention before him and then pivoting to run off, he immediately said, "Back so soon? What took you so long?" I had one foot off the ground. My total acceptance of this principle, after those few months of training, still drives my wife to distraction all these years later. She is obliged to preface every request with "Not now!", as I am inclined to drop whatever I am doing to execute her instruction immediately. Nowhere was this element of training more present than on the drill ground, when the slightest delay in a movement sent the guilty party running around the platoon carrying his M 1 rifle above his head on arms outstretched. The drill instructor had but to shout "f...g satellite!" for the punishment to begin. Sometimes we continued drilling with several satellites. Sergeant Jones in the TV series *Dad's Army* would have been a permanent satellite. The punishment was not as painful or humiliating as being made to run around the platoon holding hands with another recruit during physical training. I found this daily event the most difficult. I was useless at pushups and the long run at the end of an hour of muscle cracking exercises had me wishing for a quick death. We wore so-called "Micky Mouse" suits for this aspect of training, made of garish red and gold coloured jersey. I found them unmilitary. I sustained myself running by mentally dreaming of a frosted bottle of Coke, rattling out of a machine after depositing a quarter. In the 50 C degree heat, the only thing cold was the milk in the mess hall. I hate milk and couldn't drink it as a child. I drank it on Parris Island.

There came a moment when I was made "recruit of the day", for the whole depot! The duty involved was to have one's photograph taken with the commanding General and then act as a sort of under ADC during the day. I reported in summer undress uniform with white Marine cap to HQ. We had women Marines already, of course, but in strictly support and administrative roles. Rumours as to the nature of their own boot camp, mostly of a vulgar nature, circulated freely. They were known as BAMS, meaning "broad assed Marines". There were two as secretaries in the General's outer office. One beckoned me forward to inspect my uniform and began to remove, with tiny nail clippers, what were known as "Irish pennants". These were infinitesimal threads that emerged from seams or edging of one's uniform. I stood at rigid attention in front of the BAM Corporal. An aura of femininity overwhelmed me, and I began to shake uncontrollably. I had not been anywhere near a person of the opposite sex for months. "Relax, Private!" she said. She had called me "Private"! We were told daily we were maggots, not Marines yet. It was a moment of supreme satisfaction. I was given a red armband saying "Recruit of the Day" and photographed with the commanding General. On a tour of the depot, I sat in front next to the driver with the General and his Lieutenant ADC behind. We came across a platoon being drilled. The DI spotted the General's car from the corner of his eye, brought his platoon to a halt, put them at ease and ordered them to take a drink. There was a moment of confusion and it quickly became clear that their canteens were empty. "Take that

DI's name!" barked the General. His ADC got out and walked over slowly. The DI snapped to attention, saluted and stayed like a statue. He'd obviously not been given at ease. I could almost see the beads of sweat sprouting under his campaign hat as the Lieutenant jotted down his name. It was the first time I had felt pity for a DI.

Every recruit platoon had a standard bearer, usually the smallest who marched in front carrying a lance from which flew a triangular pennant on which was sewn the platoon number. If we had been cavalry, it would have been a pennon, as pennant is naval. But we belonged to the Navy – so it was a pennant. Years later, one of my fellow directors, on the board of South West Water, was aware of this distinction when we were discussing a change of name for the company to reflect our diversification into waste management. We became Pennon Group. Attached to a recruit platoon pennant might be several ribbons of different colours denoting "best of depot" in one of the disciplines of our training. These were hard fought for and the DI's in the Sergeant's mess bet heavily on outcomes. The competitive frenzy reached absurd heights over rifle range results. Marines attach great importance to marksmanship due to their heritage as sharpshooters in the rigging of warships. Two full weeks were spent on the rifle range and we moved to different barracks at the far end of the island. It was at this time that I was involved in an event which has weighed on my conscience ever since, and which no doubt figures in my long list of transgressions in St. Peter's big book. Part of the first week was spent "clicking in" – lining up on mock targets and learning to slowly squeeze, not jerk the trigger. When we began actual firing, it was soon evident that one of our number was a hopeless, and irredeemably, bad shot. It was not that he wore glasses. He simply had no hand/eye co-ordination. Clearly he was going to make a dent in our platoon average. One evening I was summoned to the DI's room and ordered to steal the hapless recruit's eye glasses whilst he was in the shower. I did so, put them under my pillow and reported back.

"F...g idiot! Bring 'em here, you mother f...g Frenchman!" I did so.

Next day on parade: DI to recruit, "Where are your mother f...g glasses, maggot?"

"Sir! Lost them, Sir!"

Of course they were government-issue, which always replaced, with the appropriate prescription, private glasses on arrival at the depot. Loss of government property – two weeks in the Brig; and the Brig on Parris Island made normal recruit platoon life seem like a holiday in a beach resort. Our eventual, good results on the rifle range, I suppose, justified this outrageous piece of contrived persecution and false imprisonment – at least in the mind of the DI's. Weeks later, I came across the victim, now released and assigned to another platoon. He was on mess duty. As I slid my tray past him and he spooned on the mashed potatoes, he looked at me and said, "You took 'em?"

with no apparent malice. I nodded and past on. He already knew one follows orders without question.

We swam. I was one of only a half dozen who didn't have to be taught. We did unarmed combat and learned how to kill a man with one's bare hands – a blow from the heel of the hand under the nose, driving the nose bone into the brain, is a useful method. We went on forced marches, and were told never to darn socks, as the darn causes blisters. You throw them away and get new ones. This problem is solved in the Russian Army in a more economic fashion. Their soldiers wrap a long piece of material on the foot in a special manner which ensures it stays in place under the boot. We went to our respective churches. My platoon was half Catholic, half Protestant. I never heard of a Synagogue, there was certainly no Mosque, and Church Call was only on Sunday. We saw one movie towards the end of our boot camp stay, on a big screen at the end of the parade ground. It starred a young Joan Collins, with Richard Burton, and involved four people shipwrecked on a desert island, two white men, one black man and a girl, who is actually a nun, unbeknownst to the others. It seemed a strange choice. We learned everything there is to know about the M 1 rifle, introduced at the end of WWI , in service throughout the next WW, and in Korea. Of course we were quickly acquainted with Marine jargon and traditions. Everything is as if on shipboard. The floor is the "deck", the "walls", "bulwarks", the ceiling, "overhead", and so forth. Leaving a land base is still "going ashore". Sailors are "swabbies" and it is generally assumed that they are all queer. However, medics are called "corpsmen" and they are supplied by the Navy. A wounded Marine quickly learns respect for Naval personnel.

Finally came passing out with much ceremony, in a review in which our DI's carried NCO's swords and we were white capped and in summer dress, stiff khaki drill with three pleats down the shirt back, and ties, but no tunic as it was still over 40 C. I still have my tie clip, but it is called a "neck scarf clasp" on a uniform list. I went home on my first shore leave to find my parents back from their summer in Europe, in their maisonette apartment on 79th Street, where I was allocated a maid's room. I decided to put on "dress blues" for dinner as my father would be in black tie, of course. I had only worn them once for our photographs, taken as we left Parris Island. My father looked me up and down. He seemed satisfied. My mother thought me dangerously thin. DY explained that in Imperial Russia, it was once in uniform, always in uniform, even on leave and in the countryside. He regretted that the American tradition was different and uniform is generally worn only when travelling to and from a military or naval establishment. This is why uniforms are generally in evidence only at railway stations and airports. But America is not a militarist country. Russia was, and still is. I spent my leave in civilian clothes, of course. I had been assigned to the 2nd Marine Division at Camp Lejeune in North Carolina, where I was based throughout my term. We first spent weeks in general infantry training, which was hard but under more benign command than at boot camp. We were now treated as Marines. When unit assignment came, I found myself in Communications Company, Headquarters Battalion. I had absolutely no knowledge of electronics, but it seemed it had been decided I was not to be an infantry man, or "grunt", as they were termed, but engaged in a more cerebral service. The Raytheon Corporation had just supplied the Marine Corps with so-called radio relay technology which permitted uninterrupted two-way voice and data transmission without the need for tedious "over and out", walkie-talkie procedure. In fact a telephone style conversation, with both talking at once, was made possible. This great breakthrough in communications technology was assured by a field team consisting of two half-ton trucks crammed with equipment, each towing a trailer with two diesel power units and carrying collapsible antennae, raised and fixed with guy ropes. So new was this bit of high-tech gear that a civilian Raytheon representative was still posted with our unit. Today, the entire capacity and functionality of our radio-relay field unit is carried as a backpack by one Marine. On manoeuvres we were located some distance back from the line, when we would raise the antennae, start up the power units, twiddle the dials, set the allocated frequencies, and monitor. I always had a copy of *War and Peace* with me, one of the few books you can finish, and then start at the beginning again with no loss of literary satisfaction. We were a unit of four and we took turns staying awake at night, which meant sleeping in the truck between the banks of units, rather than in sleeping bags outside. The space was just too short to stretch out fully. On joint exercises with Army Airborne from Fort Bragg, I eavesdropped out of boredom and listened to a young army officer talking to his girlfriend, in a quite unauthorised use of the system, pleading with her to retract her recent "Dear John" letter. His arguments were so lame and badly presented that I had to fight the temptation to intervene, which the technology allowed me to do. Finally, I was so fed up, I did – but as official operator, telling him politely his use of the system was a breach of security. He rang off immediately, but I sensed the girl was still on so I ventured, "I'm afraid your friend is hopeless."

She replied, "You're too right! Goodnight."

Time was heavy on our hands in Radio Relay Platoon, Communications Company. On Viegues, just off Puerto Rico, which belongs to the Navy, ship to shore bombardment and amphibious exercises have denuded what must have been a lovely tropical island. We were stationed on a hilltop with only our tents to provide shade. Consuming the local rum was our main pastime. It was of four figure proof, or seemed such. We finally noticed that it was flaking the bottom of our tin canteen cups. One of my team was the son of the Manager of the Racquet & Tennis Club in New York, where I was a member. But this gentleman had been in the hotel business and had extensive contacts. When we went on shore leave to San Juan, Puerto Rico, he was able to "comp" us at the best luxury hotel. "Comping" is the practice in the hotel trade of exchanging favours by providing reciprocal, complimentary accommodation to colleagues and their families. We were give an all- expenses paid suite, and swanked about in the bar and nightclub, never leaving the hotel. When the St. Lawrence Seaway was opened, we shipped out to join a flotilla, including the Royal Yacht *Britannia*, engaging in extensive celebrations. Units of the 2nd Marine Division were to stage mock amphibious landings in various Great Lakes cities, complete with Navy Seals surfacing to place explosives on the beach, then landing craft disgorging Marines with fearful battle cries and blank ammunition, followed by support units including radio-relay. A Hollywood film director would have considered the show well below B movie standards. On shore leave we were entertained by the local USO, where well-meaning matrons were to organise clean and healthy leisure events. The mission of the United Services Organisation, set up in World War Two, was essentially to keep troops out of brothels. In Minneapolis, we went to a baseball game with "dates" assigned by the USO. After standing smartly at attention and saluting during the National Anthem. I began the small talk with my very nice looking, obviously Scandinavian, girlfriend for the evening. "What do you do for a job?" was my imaginative opening.

"Oh – I'm secretary to the manager of the Minneapolis branch of a New York investment banking firm called White, Weld. Have you heard of them?" We were off and running and talked White, Weld gossip, hardly watching the game. We sealed our brief interlude with a chaste kiss.

What might have been a serious engagement was the intervention in Lebanon. That much abused country was in crisis following the Suez affair, the subsequent further rise of Nasser in Egypt, the revolution in Iraq and sundry other typical Middle East pressures, which continue to abound today. After some Marines were killed trying to secure the airport, it was decided to stage an amphibious landing on a beach nearby. An expeditionary force had been assembled from the 2nd Marine Division and shipped out from Morehead City, North Carolina, our port of embarkation from Camp Lejeune, to join ships from the 6th Fleet in the Med. We hit the beaches in traditional manner to be greeted by sunbathing girls in bikinis and small boys selling Coca-Colas and copies of the Paris Herald Tribune. After securing our radio-relay and communications system, our CO had some documents to deliver to the U.S. Embassy downtown and took me with him. I suggested we stop off for a drink at the Hotel d'Angleterre – the best in town. He was entirely agreeable and we were served cocktails, in our battle dress, on the terrace, by a waiter who never batted an eyelash. We paid in U.S. $, of course. A few years ago, at a Middle East Association lunch in London, I found myself seated next to the Lebanese Ambassador to the Court of St. James, who asked me about my visits to his country. I replied my first was when I invaded it in 1958. "I'll never forget that!"

161

He said, "I was ten years old at the time and a few of us went down to watch. We thought we were watching a Hollywood movie. We kept expecting to see John Wayne!"

We stayed a month back in the hills behind Beirut. I didn't see the Hotel d'Angleterre again for many years, but used it a good deal when I was covering that part of the world as a banker, as the concierge there, a Swiss, had connections with every *confrère* in the Gulf area hotels, most of whom were relations. It was a useful place to start the trip.

I was eventually given a second MOS, which stands for military occupation speciality, as a French interpreter. One day I was summoned by my CO and told I was to be assigned to a visiting dignitary. He turned out to be a Haitian playboy, the son of a general close to "Papa" Doc, the dictator. Although only 22, he held the rank of colonel in the Haitian Marines. He arrived on base in white slacks and a Hawaiian shirt, driving an Italian sports car. It was immediately apparent that I would have a challenging assignment, as he spoke Creole French – or something like it, and I had to strain to understand him. "*Mon Colonel!*" I began, after throwing my sharpest salute, "*Je crois bien que le Colonel devrait peutêtre se mettre en uniform pour être reçu par le Général.*" I think the Colonel should change into uniform to meet the General. He was not happy about this, as he already had a date in town after his official reception. Nevertheless, when I had delivered him to the VIP suite in the officers' quarters, he soon reappeared wearing a uniform which looked like something out of *The Merry Widow*, as worn by Count Danilo. As I accompanied him on his tour around the base, I began to fall in with his Creole French to some extent, and he began to practise his pigeon English, which consisted largely of profanities. Fortunately, I was not required to accompany him ashore, where his activities frequently required the intervention of the Shore Patrol *Vis* a *Vis* the local police, as he seemed to think his position guaranteed him unfettered access to all females. We normal Marines behaved with considerable restraint, in this respect. I had run into my old friend, and partner in teenage antics on Long Island, Sandy Schwartz, also serving in the 2nd Marine Division. He had been rusticated from Dartmouth College, enlisted a year before me, and was now a sergeant. Together we rented a cottage on Wrightsville Beach, a favourite weekend resort for the prominent citizens of Wilmington, the nearest important town to Camp Lejeune. Wooden houses on stilts, to survive the frequent hurricanes, were lined along a wide and sandy beach. There we spent overnight shore leaves, attempting to recreate a more civilised life style, shaking cocktails, reading, meeting and entertaining young ladies from the Wilmington families who frequented the resort. It was all relatively demure. In general, I had kept my nose clean during my Marine Corps service, and was becoming what is so often described as a reformed character. My only brush with disciplinary action was amusingly indirect. On a long leave, I stayed with my parents on Jupiter Island, Hobe Sound, Florida. Nathanial Reed, my brother-in-law Adrian's brother, was the most engaged in field sports of the four Reed brothers. He is also an eminent conservationist and served as Assistant Secretary of the Interior in the Reagan Administration. Nathanial had organized a white winged dove shoot in the Florida interior. This migratory game bird feeds in sorghum fields, has a rapid, twitching flight and is not so easy to shoot – despite appearing in large numbers. In the shooting party were a number of prominent citizens: company chairmen, bankers, lawyers and an admiral. My father and I were invited. No sooner were we in position than several police cars roared up, sirens wailing. Nathaniel, a very well-known personage in the Florida establishment, was aghast. We were accused of shooting over a baited field, an offence to Florida game laws, and names were taken. Clearly some sort of grudge against the "rich people on Jupiter Island" was involved. As I was a serving Marine, a report was automatically filed with the Judge Advocate General, and sent down my division's chain of command. On return, I was summoned by my CO. As I reported, he was just finishing reading the JAG report. He put me at ease, looked at me quizzically, and said, "What the hell is a lance corporal doing hunting with an admiral!?" I began to explain the circumstances.

"Who are all these people?" He was still reading the list of names contained in the report. I explained they were friends of my father's.

"Well I don't suppose the admiral is standing in front of his CO, so you're excused, corporal – don't go getting into trouble with admirals the next time you're on shore leave." He smiled and tossed the report into his wastepaper basket. I had not seen my CO smile before.

On another earlier leave, I had been in New York for a few days and an old friend and fellow Porcellian, John Jay Mortimer, suggested we attend a costume ball at the Tuxedo Club. Tuxedo Park had been developed in the late 19th century by Pierre Lorillard, the tobacco magnate, who had purchased and imported an entire Polish village to provide staff for the club and the residents. Descendants were still in evidence and some were markers at the real tennis court at the club, where I had often played. John Jay and I first repaired to a leading costumier in town and I picked out the uniform of a general in the Austro-Hungarian Imperial Army – a lovely white tunic festooned with gold braid, sky blue trousers with a red stripe, patent leather boots with dress spurs, and an appropriate row of medals. These clinked satisfactorily as I danced with former girlfriends. It was a pleasant evening for a Marine private.

I had settled in to life in the Marines after a while and thought seriously about "shipping over", our term for re-enlistment. So far my only route to a commission had been the possibility of being accepted in the NAVCAD programme, which trained Naval and Marine pilots, at Pensacola, Florida, and provided a commission if one could complete the programme. I sat an entrance exam, but my maths was, and is, hopeless. I also made a poor impression at the interview panel. When asked what my favourite aspect of Marine life was, I replied, "drill."

"Not particularly relevant to flying, is it? Seems like infantry is your bag," commented an interviewer. So that was that. But I thought I might eventually qualify for a commission, normally very difficult without a college degree in the U.S. Armed Services, through the intelligence section – which I might be assigned to with my interpreter MOS. The U.S. was not yet engaged in Vietnam, but I feel sure that, if I had re-enlisted, I would have served in liaison duties with the French speaking Vietnamese military. But the more I thought about it, the more doubts began to form in my mind. I felt that I was might be cut out for the military through my heritage and natural inclinations. But it was increasingly evident to me that the United States did not assign the same social importance to the military as did other countries, such as the United Kingdom, and of course, Imperial Russia. I remembered my father's rather scathing comment about limited uniform wear in public. This suggested a certain lack of pride in the profession. The absence of militarism is, of course, entirely consistent with America's historical traditions; in particular the early reliance on citizen soldiers, and even the requirement that military and naval academies achieve geographic balance through senatorial appointment, thus avoiding an elite officer corps from one region. Presumably this was one of the traditions of British life which the early colonists wished to throw off. In the circles I had grown up in, despite the distinguished wartime military careers of so many, it was generally regarded that someone who chose the military as a profession couldn't "make it on the outside". Perhaps I shouldn't have been so conformist. I had been following a correspondence course provided by the New York Institute of Finance, largely to while away the hours, but also as a kind of hedge. I was therefore in a position to sit, by correspondence, the exam for qualification as a New York Stock Exchange Registered Representative, which I duly passed. And so the moment came for my demobilisation. I was awarded my good conduct medal and, as I reported for the final time, wearing its ribbon and standing sharply at attention, he said, "At ease, corporal – now, are you absolutely sure you don't want to ship over? Immediate promotion? Pay rise?"

I replied, "No, thank you, Sir!"

"It's pretty tough out there – what are you planning to do?"

"Wall Street, Sir!"

The captain shook his head in disbelief, then shook my hand, and I was dismissed. Turning sharply on my heel, in best Marine style, I marched out. It was not to be my last contact with the Corps. Soon after arriving in London, several months later, and still technically a reservist, I decided to report to the senior Marine officer, as one is meant to do – although most don't bother. I found a Lt. Colonel, attached to the U.S. Naval Command, just across from the embassy in Grosvenor Square. "Damn it all," he said, "what the hell are you playing at? I now have to file a report, and someone's going to notice I'm overdue for reassignment!" I apologised and he softened a bit, admitting some other incident was bound to provoke a transfer. He telephoned me a month later to say he was reassigned to HQ at Quantico.

There is no question in my mind that my relatively brief service in the U.S. Marine Corps transformed me from a feckless youth to a responsible and motivated adult. Much as my wife complains about my exaggerated reactions to her mildest requests, I would have not acquired a sense of duty in any other manner. It may be facile to so conclude, perhaps, as the passage of years might have done the trick. But I suspect I would have done myself and those around me a good deal of damage, before some other life changing event, or lapse of time, might have put me on the right path. My service fell in between Korea and Vietnam and so I saw no actual hostilities. But my training left a certain mantle on my shoulders which I have retained ever since. For this reason, I mourn the end of mandatory military service in America, Great Britain and many other European countries. I believe the problems of delinquency and persistent youth unemployment are exacerbated by the absence of this critical phase of discipline and training. I know the professional military are not in general agreement, as they viewed selective service as a drain on precious time and resources, best spent, in their estimation, on the standing forces. There is also the problem that professional standards are diluted by the presence of temporary officers and ranks in peacetime. It is a debate with no chance of conclusion, as a resumption of mandatory military service is politically impossible. As for myself, to the Marine Corps, its heritage, its ideals – and my time serving, I will remain *semper fidelis.*

CHAPTER XIII

"Better fifty years of Europe than a cycle of Cathay"

-From Tennyson's *Lochsley Hall*-

On my demobilisation, I returned to no fatted calf, or even a discussion as to my future, for my parents were in Europe, as was increasingly usual. It would seem it had been generally assumed, presumably even by the partners of White, Weld, that I would be joining the firm. That I should be consulted oc-curred to no one, perhaps because it was understood that I was unemployable in any self-respecting occupation, being without a college degree, and my only career opening lay in the practice of good old-fashioned nepotism. Some rest and recreation had been planned. I first went to my sister's to collect my signet ring, now rather loose, and then spent a few days at the parents' apart-ment on 79th Street, looking up old friends, being feted by some, and treated by others as if I had never been away. I enjoyed that form of reception best. I was to join my parents in London for Ascot week. I had no idea on leaving that I was undertaking a fundamental change of residence and, that barring short periods and even shorter, if frequent visits, I would never reside in the United States again. My father was hardly a racing man but he enjoyed the Royal Ascot meeting because he loved ritual and tradition. Aliens obtained badges to the Royal Enclosure through their Embassy, against an assurance one was not divorced. This was, of course, before the Royal Enclosure be-came the zoo it is today. But I cannot imagine the no divorce rule, then en-forced for British subjects, held for foreigners, as the American contingent in the Royal Enclosure would then have been minimal. Certainly exceptions would have been made for prominent owners such as Jock Whitney – who be-came U.S. Ambassador himself. My father's insistence on attending the whole of Ascot week had become part of the tradition of the London office of White, Weld. John Rasch, who had kept the office going during the war whilst fire watching at night, was still nominally the manager. The business of the office during hostilities had been ensuring liquidity for U.S. and other foreign securities to the extent possible within the confines of an extremely complex series of exchange controls. A significant amount of foreign assets were dom-iciled in London, even when the risk of Nazi invasion was at its height before the Battle of Britain, much of it owned by investors in occupied countries, or non-belligerents such as from Latin America. An example is the enormous assets connected to the Belgian Congo, including in particular Union Minière, then the largest producer of uranium. Banque Belge, a U.K. subsidiary of Générale de Banque, the financial arm of the Belgian Soiciété Générale, was custodian of assets with a value far in excess of its own capital, and its parent, in occupied Belgium, offered no guaranty. This wartime experience is an example of the extraordinary reputation the City of London still held internationally.

The executive manager of the White, Weld office was the eccentric Jack Gallagher, who thought nothing of spending Ascot week racing himself, under the nose of his boss. Jack's excuse was the well-worn concept that socialising with clients during their leisure hours was not malingering but engaging in "relationship building". And it is true that a good part of the City could be found at Ascot during the Royal Meeting. Doing the work back at the office was the long-suffering John Stancliffe. In retrospect, I cannot help but wonder how John tolerated what must have been DY's most questionable recruitment. It can only have been through loyalty to my father. My parents and I were guests of DY's old flame, the Hon. Dolly Burns, who with her distinguished orthopaedic surgeon husband Bobby, entertained a very large house party at their very large house, nearby Ascot Race Course. Dolly's father, Lord Duveen had domiciled his large fortune abroad. It had been acquired dealing in Old Masters – often of doubtful attribution, and no one questioned, in those days, the fact that a peer of the realm did not see fit to repatriate a fortune gained abroad. Dolly was thus able to maintain houses in London, Jamaica and the South of France, despite the exigencies of exchange control. The regime at Dolly's Royal Ascot house parties was rigid. Prompt morning departure for the racecourse, tea on return followed by bridge and additional guests for dinner. The guest list was eclectic: some English but a marked cosmopolitan element in which we counted, naturally. Nubar Gulbenkian arrived in a chauffeur driven, much adapted, London black cab, adorned with woven, yellow bamboo panels... Nubar was the son of the famous "Mr. Five Percent", an Armenian who had negotiated the first Persian oil concession and amassed a vast art collection, which was first to be housed in a Swiss museum. Surprisingly, the Swiss refused Gulbenkian the tax arrangement he sought, and the result is the Gulbenkian Museum in Lisbon. Nubar was a large, black bearded gentleman, associated with the stock exchange firm Vickers da Costa. He had adopted most British customs but was out hunting one day wearing an orchid buttonhole. "We do not wear orchids out hunting," commented a hunt member.

"Of course you don't – you are English!" snapped Nubar, "But I am Armenian."

One not so English custom, was his tendency to opportune any young thing he could get his hands on. A fellow house guest at Dolly's was an American lady with her debutante daughter. One day, the daughter was anxious to go shopping in town, and Nubar, indicating he had business as well, said he would gladly miss a day's racing to give her a lift. We were never sure what happened exactly, but the American mother left in a huff before dinner, with daughter, threatening a visit to the police. Apparently Nubar's attentions to the young lady in the back of his London cab had overtaken the usual bounds. "Silly woman!" said Dolly. "She's upset my table." Dolly was fastidious about *placement*. Nubar appeared at dinner, entirely unfazed. Although, the house was very large, Dolly's hospitality filled it to the brim, and I was billeted in Bobby's dressing room on a small bed. This small but perfectly comfortable room was right next door to the master bedroom and, upon waking, I could hear Dolly "selling" me to some hostess giving a dinner before some debutante ball, to which she had already cadged an invitation for me. Her sales pitch described me as a paragon of cosmopolitan youth, assigning physical and mental attributes to me so outlandishly exaggerated that I realised I would face a crisis of expectation, unless I could find an excuse for not going. I couldn't, of course, and so experienced my first English deb dance. I considered myself at the time to be something of an expert on debutante balls, having attended more than my fair share. I cannot remember the name of the unfortunate young lady who was the object of the event in question but, on a scale of one to ten, I rated it about two. The décor was nonexistent, the music lamentable, the champagne undrinkable, the ladies dresses unflattering and the young men boorishly behaved. Apart from all that, everyone seemed to find the proceedings tedious, both sexes assuming a pose of ennui seemingly fashionable in social circles at the time. I ended up stuck with my dinner partner whom I had foolishly asked to dance as soon as we arrived. She must have offended her peers, who perhaps considered her contaminated by consorting with an American, as no one came to my rescue. I believe she was a Heathfield girl. She had no conversation whatever. I made a vow to myself to never attend an English ball again.

After a quick Continental tour, I was to start my career at White, Weld in the Zurich office at 35 Claridenstrasse. Staffing the small office were the presiding partner Bob Genillard, Jacques Appelmans, who I believe was also already a partner, François Champion, the famous Walter Koller, Jacques Schmidt and, cowering in the shadow of Koller, a silent Ozzie Grubel. Johnny Cattier, Jean's nephew, and Serge Sarasin were still in New York. But here at the Swiss subsidiary – White, Weld & Co. A. G. was the small team that was to grow into the great Euromarkets powerhouse of the next fifty years or so. I was assigned appropriately menial tasks, mostly to do with client records and portfolio movements. Many clients were familiar from my time in Jacques Appelman's Vaudois villa, assembling their portfolio cards on metal files. It is difficult for today's bankers to imagine that in the pre-digital age, bank data, including accounts and statements, was collated and recorded mechanically, and almost by hand. Prevailing systems were mostly supplied by NCR, the old National Cash Register Company, founded in the 1890s, which only introduced magnetic tape technology in 1957 and transistor based main frame computers in 1962. The personal computer was still years away – but then so were "fat finger" mistakes. The principle source of noise in those otherwise quiet days in the Claridenstrasse was Walter Koller trading foreign dollar bonds, complaining about that "old fox" Julius Strauss in London. "Ach, Julius! I get a better price from Tommy Beecham; well… maybe… eventually… I bid you 99 5/8ths?" Always the "eventually" link word and always the intensity, as if each trade was the most important. Tom Beecham was the trader at Wood Gundy, the only substantial player amongst the Canadian houses in London. The other major secondary market traders at that time were Kidder, Peabody, soon to be joined by the great Stanley Ross, who had started as Julius's right hand at Strauss, Turnbull, Deutche Bank – Manheim branch, Banca Commerciale Italiano, Stockholm's Enskilda Bank with Rolf Hallberg, a future Eurobond statesman, Kredietbank, Luxembourg, which was to produce a great originator in André Coussement, Samuel Montagu, where George Gazon was the trader. It is interesting to note that in those early days, only a handful of the active traders were in London and only three, Julius Strauss, Stanley Ross, and Paul Sherwood, were with a London Stock Exchange firm, and only one, George Gazon was with a merchant bank. None of the other London issuing houses: Warburgs, Hambros, Lazard, Rothschild, Schroeders, M. Samuel, Kleinwort Benson, etc. had any secondary market presence – even years later when the Eurobond market was in full flower. But then the main foreign dollar bond issuing houses in New York, such as Morgan, Stanley, Kuhn Loeb, First Boston, Harriman Ripley, and Lazard Frères eschewed involvement in secondary market trading, and it was left to minor, over-the-counter specialists, such as Weedon & Co. to provide liquidity. This class distinction between primary market and secondary market operators was to last another generation.

My time in Zurich provided my first exposure to White, Weld; to investment banking, capital markets, portfolio management, investment asset classes, investment client preferences and habits, the European banking community, Swiss financial services markets and policies, and how to dress, talk and eat like an international investment banker. My subsequent City education was to supplement, but change few of these early lessons. Genillard, Appelmans, Champion and I repaired for lunch most days to the Grill at the Baur au Lac Hotel, a few hundred metres from the office and reached by a stroll across a canal and the hotel garden. It seemed rather an extravagance for an in house lunch, and I wondered at the time whether DY checked the office expenses. The food and service were exemplary. In those days everything was served from chafing dishes on a side table, keeping the habitual second helping hot. A great speciality was steak tartare, seasoned to order in front of one. Lunches of this kind are certainly no longer best practice in the banking world. But for the second time in my life, I listened on these occasions. It was all shop talk and I absorbed a great deal of the basic knowledge I was to use in my later career, listening to my senior colleagues those few weeks in Zurich. Back from lunch, we would find Koller on the phone to Joe Collandro at WW in New York, as charge of the book would pass to him at opening in New York. Walter would be giving Collandro a complete briefing on markets in Europe, interest rate trends, significant trades, the latest on issues in progress and other relevant news. Koller could continue to trade, of course, and Collandro's counterparties in New York would include other Wall Street houses filling orders from Europe as, by now, the largest demand for foreign dollar bonds was emanating from an increasingly prosperous European clientele. Koller and Collandro knew John Fountain's Foreign Dollar Bond manual by heart and had its editor at their disposal for amendments and explanations. They were able to engineer profitable arbitrages. One of Koller's favourites was the Peru 3%, from the mortuary section of the manual – misnamed, as this listed bonds still outstanding, but in default, and so not yet dead. Like many defaulted and restructured exchange issues of the inter World War years, the Peru 3% loan had a "money sinking fund", that is to say the obligor provided a fixed sum of money each year to retire a part of the issue, rather than being required to purchase a fixed number of bonds. The lower the market price, the more bonds could be retired and the shorter the theoretical average life became. As the sinking fund due date approached, Koller, would start buying, giving the impression he was acting for the fiscal agent, when he had probably already filled the sinking fund order at lower prices. As the price rose, he would start selling short. When the market realised the annual sinking fund amount had already been disbursed, the price would fall, and Koller would cover his short. The bonds traded in the 40 to 50 price range. Most traders had only the vaguest notion of how many Peru 3% were still outstanding. John Fountain knew exactly.

I had virtually no social life in Zurich, and the *frauundverien* ensured the absence of any even vaguely louche establishments, so my evenings were tedious. There was a nine hole golf course at the Hotel Dolder Grand where François Champion and I played occasionally. This second of the Zurich hotels in importance hosted the entire family and suite of President Tubman of Liberia during the summer when they occupied a good half of the hotel and the national flag flew from the roof. Liberia, founded by American former slaves during the administration of U.S. President Monroe – hence the capital Monrovia, was virtually owned by the Firestone Company when tires were still made of real rubber. One assumes President Tubman was visiting his medical advisors rather than the national treasury, no doubt deposited in his name in a Swiss Bank for safety's sake. In the absence of frivolous pursuits, I spent time briefing myself on the political and economic situation. I had entirely lost touch with economic news whilst in the Marines. Sandy Schwartz and I spent time reading endless newspapers at our cottage in Wrightsville Beach during shore leaves. Sandy was already evincing a strong interest in journalism which was to lead to a distinguished career in the publishing and editing of various regional papers in America. But our focus was on human interest stories rather than economics and business. I was not to know it then, but my career was commencing in a decade which was to see unprecedented growth in the western economies, the emergence of new economic powers, such as Japan, and the start of a major expansion in world trade, with consequent implications for monetary activity. The decade also saw the gradual collapse of the global monetary arrangements which had been concluded in an obscure New Hampshire town called Bretton Woods. In the tradition that victors always suffer the severest postwar malaise, rather than the vanquished, which soon prosper from reconstruction, Great Britain was left with huge war debts, and faced the gradual dismemberment of its empire, the source of its 19th century prosperity. This presaged the potential decline into domestic obscurity of the City of London – latterly the world's premier financial centre.

But salvation was at hand, and this seems the right moment to introduce the mother of my heroine. Although, she, the Eurobond market, was still in gestation as the Foreign Dollar Bond market, what might be described as her maternal vessel, was already in existence since the late 1950s. This was the Eurodollar market, perhaps more broadly described as the Eurocurrency market. A simple, pocket description of a Eurocurrency is a national currency which is deposited, lent and traded in jurisdictions other than that of the country of issue. The phenomenon was to spread beyond the U.S. dollar to the pound sterling and the deutschmark. The founder of the Eurodollar market is unquestionably Sir George Bolton, then Chairman of Bank of London and South America, known as BOLSA, and, more significantly, a member of the Court of Directors of the Bank of England. As David Kynaston points out in his master history *The City of London* - volume IV, Bolton not only saw a way of transforming his bank from a regional to an international force, but also began to believe "that Eurodollars might give the City an international future in a world after sterling". The driving geo-political and economic force was the increasing accumulation of U.S. dollars in the hands of newly prosperous European interests, and the reluctance to place these dollars in U.S. based banks, particularly on the part of Soviet and East European banks, for fear of cold war inspired U.S. sanctions. But another powerful element was the American Regulation Q, which imposed a penal levy on one month deposits placed with U.S. Banks. The prefix "euro" was not a thought-out, piece of geographic nomenclature, but was inspired by the telex answer back of the Soviet Bank for Foreign Trade's Paris subsidiary, one of the principle depositors in the Eurodollar market. The most significant aspect of this new market was that it was centred in the City, within British exchange control, rather than in Frankfurt, Paris or Zurich, all in countries with no exchange control. Kynaston quotes the French financial commentator Paul Turot as citing London's "excellent technical organisation" and "its abundance of specialised personnel" as reasons for the siting of this new financial market in London.

This is very true, but the liberal attitude of the monetary authorities, HM's Treasury and the Bank of England, successfully lobbied by Sir George Bolton, was critical. A major justification of this attitude was, perversely, the existence of exchange control. Because the pound sterling was protected against capital outflows, or unmanageable monetary expansion/volatility, the existence of foreign currency activity in the City posed no threat to monetary stability. Having no exchange control, German monetary authorities feared, and continued to fear, as the Euromarkets spawned an investment bond progeny, that the use of the deutschmark as a currency for commercial lending or capital market activity, beyond the strict control of the Bundesbank, posed unacceptable risks to its monetary management. BOLSA, London branches and subsidiaries of foreign banks and a few merchant banks were the major early players in this market. Hambros was active as their large roster of shipping clients operated in U.S. Dollars. Schroeder's was "dollar friendly" as they were the only merchant bank with an important New York business – J. Henry Schroeder Banking Corporation. Kleinwort Benson and Brown Shipley were the other merchant bank participants. The clearing banks were frozen out of the market by the requirement that they hold 8% of any deposit, in whatever currency, with the Bank of England. What is most remarkable, and difficult to explain, is the fact that the merchant banks, major participants in the Eurocurrency market, and all major issuing houses in the domestic capital market, failed to spot the potential for a capital market expression of the Eurodollar market, namely the Eurobond market, until relatively late in the day. On the other hand, S. G. Warburg, a non-participant in the Eurodollar market, became a Eurobond pioneer. Hambros did follow soon after, due to a blue chip Scandinavian client base. It did not take long to find borrowing clients to maximise returns on Eurodollar deposits. U.S. Corporations were investing heavily in Europe and happy to borrow Eurodollars from London banks. Trade finance, through L/Cs discounted in London, was increasingly provided in U.S. dollars. The first syndicated loan in Eurodollars was on behalf of IBM World Trade. The deposit market was an interbank telephone market, and a benchmark rate was soon agreed. Term loans were made on a floating rate basis at a margin over the benchmark with a six months rate review. This is exactly how term loans by banks in the U.S. have been made for years, against various base rates indicating the cost of the lending banks' wholesale deposits; early evidence that, when it comes to the structure of financial operations, we "euro trash" didn't invent a thing. Despite his ludicrous claim, Minor Zombanakis, a leading originator and syndicator of medium term, Eurodollar bank loans, did not invent the London interbank offered rate, later known as LIBOR, which was already informally in existence in the late 1950s. One possible explanation for the failure of most London merchant banks to spot the capital market opportunity suggested by the growth of the Eurodollar market is that they were wedded to the domestic debenture market structure: a stock exchange listing, with a mandatory allocation to jobbers, underwritten by subscribing institutions, nominative, and an asset based security structure. Foreign Dollar Bonds, the precursors of Eurobonds, were listed, but liquidity was provided by a dealer to dealer market, they were underwritten by distributing investment banks, and they were in bearer form, secured exclusively by negative pledge clauses. For the average London merchant banker, they were an alien and strange beast. To Sigmund Warburg, a former partner of Kuhn, Loeb in New York, and from a German banking tradition, they were entirely familiar.

My initiation into White, Weld via the Zurich subsidiary was now completed and a further, but highly portentous, career interval was planned by my father, at the invitation of an old friend, Louis Franck. Louis was an imposing man, with a loud, brash and overwhelming manner which either impressed one, or put one off, depending on one's degree of sensitivity. The son of a Brussels art dealer, Louis had entered banking and risen to the top of Samuel Montagu, a merchant bank originally founded by one Montagu Samuel in the 1860s in Liverpool as a bullion dealer, handling gold coming in from the American and Australian gold rushes. But another, unrelated Samuel family already had an eponymous bank in the City, and so the Liverpool Samuel simply reversed the name when the business was moved to London. Louis had no doubt first known DY through the Belgian connections of Jean Cattier, and the family friendship had been further strengthened when Evelyn, Louis's beautiful wife, and their two children Eric and Martine were evacuated to Long Island during the war. They were near neighbours of ours in Locust Valley and we children played together often. Eric was at Harvard with me, and found himself unsuited to a career in banking, much to his father's dismay. He married a Zurich girl, Inez Schwartzenbach, and became an art dealer and gallery owner. Dabbling as an angel in the theatre, he was a co-producer of the musical *Hair*. Martine, whose girlhood was made somewhat difficult by her bluff and overbearing father, married the celebrated photographer Henri Cartier Bresson, became a noted photographer in her own right, and was a cofounder of the Magnum Photo Agency in Paris. Cartier Bresson was amused at having a father in law younger than he, and Martine was very kind to our photo journalist son Michael, inviting him to lunch and an afternoon spent chatting to Henri in their Paris apartment. Michael never forgot a throw-away line of Cartier Bresson's. They were talking about black and white vs colour photography, and Henri said, "As Matisse used to say to me 'light kills colour'." Of course they were near contemporaries, but to young Michael, it was like Leonard Bernstein quoting a conversation with Debussy. Eric had also been rusticated by Harvard and, when Dinnie and I were together in the Pension Beaumont in Lausanne, he was working in Winterthur and kindly invited us for the weekend to the Franck residence in Gstaad, the Chalet Arno, whilst his parents were away. Dinnie was embarrassed to find a maid unpacking her very modest suitcase with a few very modest clothes, and I was taken aback to see the original of Van Gogh's *Le Bébé Goriot* hanging in the downstairs cloakroom. Louis had inherited a not inconsiderable collection of impressionists from his dealer father. Many years later, I invited Martine Cartier Bresson to cut the ribbon for a little street in Bonnieux, where we were living, which had been renamed the Rue Julien Levy, in honour of a celebrated gallery owner in New York – the first to handle photographs as works of art. A Harvard dropout, Levy had been mentored by Stieglitz, and, in Paris, befriended by Man Ray, Marcel Duchamp and Bernice Abbot. He managed to rescue part of the collection of plates of the early French photographer Atget, and his gallery in New York introduced Cartier Bresson and other photographers to American collectors and became a centre of the surrealist movement, handling works by most of its members. Levy had retired to a holiday house he owned in Bonnieux. Martine gave a charming speech about her deceased husband's close friend and presented to the Mayor a photo taken by herself of Cartier Bresson pointing a Leica double lens camera at Levy, in the courtyard of his house. The Mayor subsequently lost it – or more likely, trousered it.

Louis Franck had suggested to DY that I would benefit from a *stage*, or internship, as we now call it, at Samuel Montagu. Naturally, I was not consulted. Quite rightly, my father did not think me worthy of consultation on career moves, considering I was jolly lucky to have any at all. In those good old days of nepotism and correspondent relationships, internships were popular with private banks. The theory was that if the son of a partner in a correspondent bank, or of a commercial customer, had an enjoyable time in London, he would be inclined to steer business to his former hosts for the rest of his business life. Hambros used this marketing tool extensively with sons of their Norwegian shipping clients. My internship package, unremunerated of course, was of an extraordinary and atypical generosity. I was housed in Eric's own spacious basement flat in Eaton Square, below his parents' flat, which was spread across two town houses. A Spanish valet, Manuel, was assigned to look after my needs, and, after serving me breakfast would help pick out my outfit for the day. Martine was also away, studying in Paris, and her Morris Mini-Minor, was put at my disposal – without her being consulted, I learned much later. Clearly my introduction to working life in London was of a nature supportive of my father's theory of motivating me by introducing me to the best, but a serious violation of my mother's counter theory that the good life would prolong my feckless inclinations. I can only revert to an Americanism by saying that I was "blown away", by Samuel Montagu. The house had style, heaps of style. It was truly *haute banque*, but with a Continental flavour, distinguishing it from a Warburg which was somewhat more austere and North German. But Montagu was also a money machine; a founder of the London Gold Fixing and major precious metals dealer. In the war, Louis Franck had risen to the rank of Colonel in British Intelligence with the mission to track down and, where possible, seek Allied control of the world's gold bullion supplies. His acquired knowledge served Montagu well in the post war years, when gold remained a significant asset class, even though price controlled by the U.S. It has been suggested that Louis Franck inspired Ian Fleming's character *Goldfinger*. Louis frequently had a conversation with DY about White, Weld's overheads, excessive in his view. "All those branches!" he would say, "Just cost centres, they don't make serious money." It wasn't just White, Weld; Louis thought the business model of all the Wall Street houses deeply flawed, the exception being Lazard Frères, where his close friend, and supplier of stock market tips, André Meyer, presided.

Housed in an elegant town house in Old Broad Street, almost opposite the City of London Club, the working areas were efficient and understated. The executive floors, containing the Partner's Room, the dining and meeting rooms had been decorated by Janssen, the celebrated Paris interior decorator. In the Partner's Room, sat, at elegant Empire style table desks, Louis and his partners: David Montagu, scion of the founding family, later the 2nd Lord Swathling; Evarard "Evvy" Hambro, who had avoided the family bank; John Nash, an Australian, who was later to hand me a huge piece of business; "Bli" Bleichroeder, of a famous German banking family, who handled investments, and one or two others I forget. Sitting in a corner, and generally neglected, was a very Jewish looking gentleman, referred to as "Mr Sydney", I think, whose role was never explained or referred to. I believe, however, that he was a family member who looked after some Jewish charities and trusts established by the Montagu family. On arrival, I was invited to join the partners at lunch. There was always at least one other, outside guest. All gathered for sherry in the Partner's Room. I noticed that they all had the same shirt. It transpired that Louis had ordered bolts of a lightly pinstriped, cream coloured silk in Hong Kong, had them made up as shirts for each partner, to be worn with a stiff collar, of course, and made it clear that he expected them to be worn as a sort of partner's uniform. Luncheon was perfection, and not over copious. A joint of cold ham and salads were on a sideboard as an alternative choice to the hot meal. Only a white wine was served; a very light Swiss Valais from a vineyard Louis had purchased for his, and the bank's, exclusive use. Swiss wines are generally never exported, as supply matches domestic demand. Scattered around the walls were some of Franck père's masterpieces. Amongst the stewards serving was Manuel, who after valeting me in Eaton Square, was on duty at the bank. A programme had been worked out for me, together with a few other *stagières*, of various nationalities, and I was to move gently from department to department, observing and learning the workings of a London merchant bank. One of my fellow interns was to become a lifelong friend. David Mann was the son of Francis Mann, a German Jewish émigré who became senior partner of Herbert Smith. Francis Mann was the leading expert of his generation on international law and jurisdictional conflict. His most celebrated case, which took years to resolve, centred on obligations, contracted in different jurisdictions, by various interests of the Spanish tycoon and former tobacco smuggler Juan March, who was reputed to have hired a submarine during the Spanish Civil War, to transport his gold bullion to the vaults of the Bank of England. David and I spent many a mo-

ment of intellectual and humorous discussions, and worked together on transactions, as he stayed on at Montagu when I was at White, Weld. I began on
the money desk under Brian Hawkins which was located behind a counter in
the entrance lobby. Counters for wholesale banks have a different significance
than the one with a window where you used to cash a cheque at your clearing
bank. They were the first piece of banker's furniture, initially a simple bench
– *banco* in Italian, hence the appellation "bank". But they are still referred to
in indicating a *nostro* transaction as in letters of credit "presented over our
counters". Very few banks involved in financing trade through L/Cs have
counters, but the expression still has meaning. The money desk managed the
bank's liquidity, through the discount market, which before the advent of the
"repo" market, was the principle vehicle for ensuring liquidity in the banking
system. The money desk itself made money by "gapping" i.e. borrowing
short-term and lending slightly longer term, exploiting the yield curve. When
I started up European Banking Company in the early '70s, an inverse yield
curve had been in existence for long enough for a young trader on our money
desk to express surprise when I told him it was an historical anomaly, and the
norm was for short term interest rates to be lower than long term rates. It was
whilst sitting by Hawkins that I first became acquainted with the daily, morning visit of a "bill broker" – the vulgar term for a partner in a Discount House,
wearing a silk top hat. The custom was to start the brief conversation with reference to any subject other than money, finance, the City, etc. Cricket, racing,
hunting, shooting and, in extremis, politics were *de rigeur.* Finally, the query
"Need any money today?" was casually dropped, and a transaction did, or did
not ensue. On average, the small talk took five minutes and the deal took one.
At the end of the morning, Hawkins would work out if he was long or short
on the book, and sometimes scrambled to either place an unexpected arrival
of cash, or to borrow a shortfall.

But my most exiting stay, which was to have a career long influence on
me, was in the Foreign Exchange Department, directed by another German
Jewish emigré called Julius Weinberg. Julius not only ran, he conducted the
Forex department – much as von Karajan conducted the Berlin Philharmonic.
Seated at a large oval table with a dozen or so dealer positions, each consisting of a panel of some twenty little lights which flashed when the direct line
was opened, and stayed lit whilst it was in use, Julius missed nothing and
could spot a sour note in the chaotic chords of a busy day. The direct lines
were to counterparties: clearing banks, foreign banks in London, forex
brokers, other merchant banks, commodity brokers, etc. Woe to the dealer
who neglected a flashing light for longer than Julius considered proper.
"Light! Light!" he would shout, "Vy are you sleeping?" accompanied by
sharp rapping of his pen on the table. Julius seemed indeed to be maintaining
a tempo. There were several phones at each position and a dealer had to
juggle them to keep more than one line open. There would be pauses, like a
legato in a symphony, and thus momentarily idle dealers. Julius expected ini-

tiative and proactivity. "Call! Call! Can't you see cable is moofing?" Or to another: "Dumkopf! The light vas fleshing and has stopped! You haf a trade missed!" The dealers were mostly young lads from the East End of London, sons of Cockney barrow boys, no doubt. They were sharp, quick-witted, numerate and natural traders, brought up listening to bargains being closed in seconds. If Julius had a thorn in his side it was to be found across a sliding window which separated his forex dealing room from the bullion room, where three or four dealers traded gold, silver, platinum and palladium. In charge was an elegant Englishman, who clearly made less of an impression on me than Julius because, although I spent a week in the bullion dealing room, I cannot remember his name. Nor can I remember the reason for the antagonism that existed between the two. Perhaps it was rivalry between profit centres. Several times in a day, the window would slide back and a bullion dealer would enquire: "What's cross?" The cross rate in foreign exchange is the rate between two foreign currencies; in this case it would have been $/Swiss, or "swissie" as the Swiss franc is known. The reply from Julius was usually accompanied by a sarcastic remark of sorts, which was then responded to with equal disdain. Of course, most mornings, the senior bullion dealer was in attendance at the fixing, which took place at Rothschild's in New Court. The London Gold Fixing had been created in 1919, with Samuel Montagu as one of the founding members. Activity in the bullion dealing room was much more sedate. Of course, gold was still held at $35 an ounce by the U.S., and so traded narrowly around that benchmark. The only serious rival to the London Gold Market was Zurich, but the Bank of England had given its home market a boost in 1959, by removing the restriction on forward dealing, an exchange control measure which had given the Swiss a competitive advantage. Still gold was pretty quiet in those days. Back in Julius's dealing room, however, I recall one incident in particular. One morning, a young lad slammed down the phone with a yelp of triumph. "Vas ist?" barked Julius. The hapless youth, still euphoric, explained that his counterparty had mixed up the spot and forward rate, and our presumed hero had "hit him for the limit", as he put it – i.e. bought or sold an amount for the maximum of the counterparty exposure limit, on the basis of his mistaken quote. Julius went ballistic.

"Mein Got!" he shouted, rising to his feet. I had never seen him on his feet before. He was quite small.

"You call him back! You cancel the trade! You apologise! If ever you pick up someone who makes a mistake, you are dismissed! Do you hear? Dismissed! That goes for all of you. I sack you and you go home to your *mutter* and never in the City again work! The reputation of this *haus* is more valuable than any deal!"

The row had caused the dealers in the bullion room to slide open the window, and this time I saw the head dealer there nodding sternly in agreement with Julius's chastisement. There it was. Reputation was paramount. One did not apply the concept of *caveat emptor* unreservedly to professional counterparties. In dealer to dealer markets, if one made an obvious mistake in a quote, it was pointed out. There was a purely practical reason for this, enshrined in the Judeo/Christian tradition: *Do unto others as you would have them do unto you.* Every dealer knew he was bound to make a mistake one day. Of course, there is an old tradition of trying to outsmart one's counterparty by guessing whether they are a buyer or a seller. An old Stock Exchange story has a broker approaching a jobber, wearing a long black tie, a mournful expression and with a document, looking very much like a probate form, sticking out of his pocket.

"What can you make me in Shell?" queries the broker. Of course the jobber reads him as a seller, settling an estate, and quotes accordingly.

The broker says, "I buy five hundred."

"But I thought you were settling an estate!" says the bested jobber.

"I am," comes the reply, "but my client died a bear."

Walter Koller was adept at reading which way his friend, the "old fox" Julius Strauss, might be, when they were trading foreign dollar bonds. But he would have never taken advantage if Strauss said "98" when he meant "99". I never forgot the admonition Weinberg pronounced that day in the forex dealing room at Samuel Montagu. Of course, I have recorded its spirit, not the exact words. But it was Julius Weinberg and his principles that were truly *haute banque* – rather than the Partner's Room decorated by Janssen. It was with great sadness that I saw those principles melt away in the City after the reforms known as Big Bang.

We interns were fortunate to have as our mentor, and supervisor of sorts, Jeremy Graftey-Smith, whose uncle had been Governor of the Reserve Bank of Southern Rhodesia, a detail of particular interest to me. Jeremy, known universally as "Jinx", was a born entertainer and could have made a career in show business. Indeed the band at a fashionable night club called The Blue Angel, often asked him to join in to render his impression of Louis Armstrong singing *When the Saints Come Marching In*. Jinx was a proficient mimic and he could do the partners of Montagu from Louis Franck, through Evvy Hambro and on down the list. Unfortunately, one or two would walk in whilst Jinx was in full flight with his back to the door. Louis never did, or it would have been curtains for Jinx. One day Jinx invited me to a dinner party at the mews house near Eaton Square he shared with Jeremy Cotton, son of Cotton of Cotton & Clore, the best known property developers of the time. The two bachelors clearly drew a selection of eligible young ladies to their parties, and I found myself seated next to an unusually, but entirely appropriately, named brunette, whose place card read Vivienne Gorgeous. As we small talked, I asked her where she was from.

"Southern Rhodesia," she said sweetly, expecting me to look blank.

Instead, I replied, "I once knew a girl from Southern Rhodesia – a few years back, in Switzerland. She must be married with a family by now."

"What was her name?" asked my gorgeous neighbour.

"She was Dinnie Townsend," I replied.

Vivienne smiled. "Not married at all. She is here in London, working for J. Walter Thompson in Berkeley Square – she's an old friend."

Then, anticipating my question, "But I don't have her number with me. I'll call you at Montagu tomorrow and give it to you."

Not only gorgeous but tactful, my new friend was to ring Dinnie to say she had met this funny man who claimed to know her, and could she give him her phone number? Fortunately the answer was positive, and after some struggle to find a free night in Dinnie's social calendar, I went to fetch her at the flat in the Fulham Road she was sharing with South African school friends, the Murray sisters. On arrival, there was no immediate sign of Dinnie, and "Yoee", for Yolanda, of all things, sat me down in an armchair with a collapsed seat so that my knees were under my chin. She proceeded to interrogate me: who was I? – How did I know Dinnie? – What were my intentions? The grilling continued until finally Dinnie appeared barefooted. She couldn't remember how tall I was and so what heels to wear. I took her to Charko's for dinner, and then to The Black Sheep nightclub in Shepard's Market, which Jack Gallagher had introduced me to. Yoee Murray was to make another dramatic appearance in our family life many years later. Our eldest son Michael, beginning his career as a photojournalist and staying on Dinnie's family farm in Rhodesia, had borrowed an old pick-up truck from his uncle to drive down to Botswana to photograph elephants in the Okavango delta. Once well ensconced in the bush, he was struck down by some virus and carried, virtually insensible, to a native village. When his semi-coma did not seem to abate, and his condition became alarming, the village chieftain ordered him taken to the nearest white owned ranch, some 50 miles away. He was unconscious by now, but when he awoke next day, he found a white lady leaning over him.

"What's your name?" she asked.

"Michael Yassukovich," he groaned.

"Oh, I know your mother!" said the lady. It was Yoee Murray. Michael was not pleased. He thought he was on an exotic adventure trip, far from parental connections. But this was only one of the connections emanating from that fateful dinner party when I was to be reunited with my future wife, despite having been separated by continents, and every aspect of background and family history. Vivienne Gorgeous went on to marry Andrew Waugh, son of Alec and nephew of Evelyn. Andrew, a career naval officer, had been ADC to Admiral Sir Peveril William Paulet, Governor of Southern Rhodesia. One of the William Paulet daughters, Judy, married Michael Colman, and we all became great friends. Many years later, I found myself on the board of a Canadian oil exploration company. After the great North Sea oil boom, someone had discovered oil onshore in Hampshire, and this triggered a frenzy of seismic activity in England and Scotland. I was dozing through a presentation at a board meeting in Vancouver, when the chief exploration office flashed a photo of an estate in Hampshire on his power point presentation, and said:

"We're having a hell of a time trying to get consent out of this landowner who is some kind of mustard tycoon and is worried about his pheasants."

I woke up and said:

"He is Sir Michael Colman, Chairman of Reckitt & Colman. He has the finest natural pheasant shoot in England, and that's one of his prime coverts. He's a friend of mine, and I think I can fix it."

General murmurs of satisfaction – and the presentation continued:

"Now here is another prospective location." A photograph of a wooded area flashed on the screen. "But we're having an even worse problem here. Everybody keeps talking about some guy called Winnie the Pooh!" All eyes turned to me:

"I can't help you there, I'm afraid. Winnie the Pooh is a fictional bear in a children's book and he and his friends lived in that wood, which is sacred ground."

"Jesus Christ!" said the seismic engineer, in disgust.

"Not quite," I replied, "but almost, to at least three generations of children."

When I got home, I rang Michael, with the plans for the seismic shot, discovered it would cause little disturbance, and promised the company would pick up the expenses of one season's shooting. He agreed, they came and found not a trace of oil. They never got near the New Forest.

During my time at Samuel Montagu, I stayed in close touch with the White, Weld London office. The venerable John Rasch was still the nominal manager, but Jack Gallagher was supposed to be the prime mover, backed up by John Stancliffe, newly returned from Caracas. Alan Towner was chief dealer. The office mother figure, organiser of my DY's London life, and all things to do with any White, Weld partner passing through, was the invaluable Miss Joyce Goodrich. My father, who greatly admired her, insisted on addressing her by her surname – as one might the cook. We also had our own Sergeant. In those days the Corps of Commissionaires, retired private soldiers and NCOs, provided the City with messengers, doorkeepers, security guards and general dog's bodies. They were in blue uniform with leather cross belt and pouch, and wore their service ribbons with pride. They were bonded and trudged around the City carrying securities and other documents, worth millions. They all held the rank of Sergeant and were so addressed. Our Sergeant spent a morning showing me how to cross the City, from any direction, on a rainy day, without getting wet. His various routes seemed almost to go through people's private offices; they certainly crossed lobbies and vestibules. The City was only just beginning major development, and interconnected buildings, little alleyways and courts proliferated. But scaffolding was going up everywhere, and one's bowler hat served as a potential crash helmet, as a scaffold joint thudding down on the pavement in front of one was not unusual. Jack took pains to lunch me, dine me and introduce me to his many friends. His appearance and manner was odd, to say the least. Jack had gone native with a vengeance, dressed to the nines in a very English fashion and spoke with an exaggerated Bertie Wooster drawl. His conversation was peppered with accounts of mini disasters which would befall him during his busy day, causing him to return exhausted to his Cheney Walk flat, and to exclaim to his valet "A whisky and soda... quickly, James!" Somehow his pretentiousness amused, rather than disturbed, his City contacts, and business flowed from many.

In those very early '60s, the City of London, was still very much just that – the City of London, and I began a lifelong love affair, as one might with an ageing but still glamorous diva. Recovering from postwar traumas and privations, its social structure was relatively unchanged from the prewar years. The interdependent disciplines which made up its unique business model, remained firmly anchored in their own traditions and collective ethos. The Stock Exchange, and the other exchange markets: Lloyds, Metal, Commodities, Baltic, etc., were self-governing, employed highly selective admission policies – only vaguely based on merit, and were unforgiving when it came to transgressions and abuses of their rules. The merchant banks, clearing banks, foreign banks, discount houses, exchange and money brokers, investment managers, solicitors, accountants, public relations agents, financial printers, doctors providing shots and vaccinations for overseas travel, oyster and wine bars, men's hairdressers, mounted City police, window box gardeners, and even the pigeons, who commuted like everyone else, being largely absent at weekends, constituted a civilised collective unrivalled for atmosphere and unfussy, honest efficiency. Spiritual glue for this fabric was the Wren churches: named for obscure saints, some designated "within" or "without", indicating whether they had been raised inside or outside the old City walls. Many were dedicated to a branch of the Armed Services, or the Merchant Marine, or other special interests. Of course, their congregations were nonresident, and apart from lunchtime services, rectors communicated very indirectly with parishioners. But this phenomenon gave rise to a unique organisation. A priest name Chad Varah, Rector of the Lord Mayor's Church just behind the Mansion House, noticed his parishioners opened up with personal problems more easily on the telephone from home in the evening. He founded The Samaritans, an organisation initially staffed by volunteers manning phones in the basement, which took calls from potential suicides and tried to talk them out of it. City wags claimed the volume of distress calls rose sharply with any major stock market move, regardless whether up or down, as either the longs or shorts were suicidal – but I don't believe this. The Corporation of London was the nation's only nonpolitical local authority, and the Lord Mayor, serving an annual term of office, was strictly neutral on any political issue, even one affecting directly the interests of the City. Observance of this tradition has begun to lapse. It was not generally known abroad that when the Queen visits the city in state, her coach stops at the City boundary, and she asks the Lord Mayor's permission to enter – a holdover from the time when the Sovereign depended on the City to finance wars and the court's expenses. One of the negative results of the internationalisation of the City Financial has been a weakened connection with the Corporation and its Guilds. Many contemporary practitioners are ignorant of their existence. At the heart of the unique and complex organism which was the City Financial, was the Bank of England, referred to then simply as "the Bank". As the monetary authority, the Bank's supervisory remit extended, in strictest terms, to the deposit banks, exchange and money markets, through the discount office, and to the Stock Exchange with respect to Gilts. But its moral authority was felt, and understood, in every area of financial activity. Its influence was applied with subtlety, but was always decisive. Known as the "Governor's eyebrows", it was a quiet word, dropped casually, perhaps accompanied by a change in facial expression, which indicated displeasure or disapproval. But however expressed, its views were ignored at one's peril. The Bank's ushers were dressed in mauve tail coats and seemed to be all ex-Sergeant Majors from the Household Division. In those days the Bank Picket still marched down to guard the Bank at night. The Picket had been established to guard the Bank after it had been attacked during the anti-Catholic Gordon Riots in 1780. The Officer commanding was entitled to dine in the bank with a guest and an allowance of one bottle of claret and half a bottle of port. Once, the arrival of the Picket set off an alarm. An ignorant usher opened the door to find a bearded Guardsman. He assumed he had an imposter before him, not knowing, or having forgotten, that the only bearded Guardsman is the Pioneer Sergeant, who carries an axe on parade. Often, when one walked past the back doors of the Bank, if one was properly dressed and bowler hatted, the usher on duty went to attention and saluted, assuming an ex-officer was passing. One raised one's bowler in response.

In retrospect, a striking characteristic of the City, as I first knew it, was an absence of self-promotion. There existed no Committee for Invisible Exports, no trade missions to foreign capitals, no public relations campaigns, no branding and other marketing gimmicks. The City was still generally confident that it was, quite simply, the most proficient, honest and multi- faceted centre for the conduct of domestic and foreign financial business. This quiet confidence was all the more remarkable in the face of a growing national economic and monetary crisis, emanating from the latent costs of victory in the last war. And the City's traditional international pre-eminence was now fatally undermined by the decline of sterling as a reserve currency. Of course the sterling area, the former empire, now Commonwealth, was still in existence – but its days were numbered. One sterling crisis after another was to follow in the next decade and a half. Britain was hardly in a position to export capital; exchange control was to remain in force for some time, having been removed in Germany – just as rations had remained into the '50s, whilst France gorged with food. Very few people realised then that salvation was at hand. The Eurocurrency market was in its infancy, an activity the *Financial Times*, the

City's newspaper of record, was to studiously ignore for some time. Even Sigmund Warburg was engrossed in seeking to establish his new merchant bank as a traditional domestic player, having acquired Seligman Brothers to gain admission to the Accepting Houses Committee. Warburg's rose to national prominence controversially, adopting a shockingly aggressive stance as a merger and acquisition advisor in the so-called aluminium wars. But the firm was not at all involved in Eurodollar deposit taking and lending. My father was certainly not aware that the City was on the cusp of a great revival in fortune, but he retained an unshakable faith in the UK's powers of recovery. He believed its underlying political stability would survive any economic and financial crisis. He liked to quote the old adage that, at the end of the day, there would be only five kings left in the world: the four in a pack of cards and the king, or queen, of England. DY was an unreconstructed monarchist. So what was the driving force behind the City's confidence? One might opine it was blind faith in its ability to adapt to changing circumstances, even if these seemed overwhelmingly adverse. One might also cite the example of the nation as a whole in the last war, when it had coped with near invasion, vicious bombing, shortages of everything, and general disruption of ordinary life, with characteristic *sang froid*. The City was to suffer another product of post war *angst*: the emergence of social scientists, critical of Britain's traditional social structure, seen by them as hopelessly class ridden, and therefore out of date. As David Kynaston points out in Volume IV of his epic history *The City of London*, the City was under sociological scrutiny from the late '50s, and various commentators gained recognition by disclosing the astounding fact that the City was populated by heavy concentrations of men from the same short list of public schools, universities and clubs. They might also have informed an unsuspecting public that fishing villages on the south coast contained a heavy concentration of fisherman, and miners proliferated in mining areas – in both cases the occupations often passing from father to son. But the "Establishment" had now been discovered with a vengeance, and the concentration and connections of "top decision makers" were put forward as objects of national shame. Natural English reticence discouraged the propagation of counter arguments. It might have been pointed out that it was the "clubiness" of the City which guaranteed a high level of ethical behaviour, without the need for voluminous regulation, as the value of individual and collective reputation is always held highest in a family of like-minded individuals, sharing similar backgrounds.

My stint at Samuel Montagu was now over and I was to take up my predestined place at White, Weld & Co., New York, now at 20 Broad Street, a building adjacent to the New York Stock Exchange. Never has an internship made a greater mark on a professional and personal life. I had rediscovered my future wife, in the face of overwhelming odds, and been able to rekindle a courtship. I had become acquainted with the financial centre where, although I did not know it yet, my career would evolve, and I had been left with a concept of banking style I was to seek to emulate in future. Without doubt, I would have been better off striving to emulate the moneymaking proclivities of the partners of Samuel Montagu, as opposed to their style. After my luxurious accommodation in Eaton Square, I was back in the maid's room in my parent's penthouse apartment at 136 East 79th Street and commuting down town. Various friends of my parents amused themselves giving me frivolous advice. Hector Munn, heir to the Totalizer fortune, urged me to find work up-town as this was much more convenient for lunch at the Racquet & Tennis Club, where I was a member. At the office, I was placed at a desk in the Research Department, under Frank Rittger, who was also responsible for the private client investment advisory service. Frank was astute, professorial, an equity man through and through and much attached to the growth sector. He sought to test my investment knowledge.

"Which do you think is the most conservative investment – U.S. Steel at five times earnings per share, or IBM at fifteen times?"

I guessed a trick question. He thought I would go for U.S. Steel – a widow's stock, generous dividend, and so on.

"IBM," I replied.

"That's the right answer, but you gave it for the wrong reason. I never ask trick questions. It's the right answer because IBM is growing at 10% a year and has every likelihood to continue doing so, whereas U.S. Steel's earnings are flat and likely to remain so for the foreseeable future, so buying its shares is a gamble it will change course, whereas IBM is likely to remain what it is – a growth stock."

End of lesson. Behind me in my desk row was Philip Greer, a Deerfield classmate. He was extremely helpful and taught me the basics of investment analysis. Of course, I had read Graham & Dodd, the bible of security analysis. But a good deal of it went over my head. In those days our only calculating tool was the slide rule, or "slip stick", as it was known. I had seen one used by our maths master at Deerfield, Mr. Poland, as he worked part-time for an engineering firm and laboured over various blueprints whilst we sweated over his classroom assignments. But Philip showed me how to use it. I had a nagging feeling that his highly solicitous attitude had something to do with the fact that my father was a partner. Philip did not stay long with White, Weld, but went on to have a brilliant career in the investment world. He ultimately became chairman of Trustees for Deerfield Academy and I wrote to congratulate him, but was not favoured with a reply. In those days, the senior investment policy partner was Benny Clark, son of one of the firms founding partners, a charming and erudite man. He lived at Bedford Hills, and whilst others were perusing the *Wall Street Journal* on his commuter train, Benny was reading Proust – in French, of course. He had an equally intelligent and charming daughter, but not graced with the sort of looks and personality deemed standard in debutante circles. I was assigned as her escort for her own deb party at the Colony Club ballroom, and some of my colleagues considered I had been given onerous duty. But, in fact, I had the best time, as her conversation was way above the level of the average deb. She married a French count with a bijou château in Normandy. Benny Clark wrote a daily investment letter, sent to private and institutional clients giving his view, and therefore the firm's, on the current investment climate and the significance of various political and economic events. Included were one or two investment suggestions: shares deemed undervalued, and sometimes deemed overvalued, although the firm did not encourage shorting. "The risk is theoretically infinite if you're short, but you can only lose what you've invested if you're long" Benny would say. One day I was summoned to the presence and asked to research a recommendation for the ordinary shares of a company called Homestake Mining which extracted gold in Colorado. There was increasing speculation that the U.S. would abandon its price freeze of gold at $35 per ounce. As American corporates began investing heavily in new capacity in Europe to exploit the economic recovery there, reserves were leaking. The balance of payments position was deteriorating rapidly. Worldwide, things were also moving and the fixed exchange rate system was under strain as trade patterns shifted; the Breton Woods construction was beginning to look shaky.

"You've just been working for the great gold bug Louis Franck in London. You're just the man to determine the impact on the earnings per share of Homestake, if the gold price moves up," said Benny Clark.

"To what level?" I asked.

"Ah! That's for you to decide."

I had my first research assignment and a recommendation was going out to the firm's clients, based on my calculations. I was excited and frightened. Philip Greer took an immediate interest in my assignment and offered to help. I was relieved. We decided to go for two scenarios: $40 and $45. We considered a greater move was unlikely as there would be profit taking on the large bull position which had been building. It was simple enough to calculate gross revenue increases based on current production levels; it was more difficult to estimate any immediate cost impact from the likely increase in production a price rise would provoke. And, of course, what would be the impact on the price/earnings ratio? That would depend on the company's ability to expand production. I took our finished report to Benny and he drafted the section of the daily letter dealing with Homestake. He had already opined on the macro-economic forces at work. I waited for a reaction next day, certain some boffin amongst our readership would spot a mistake. In fact there was only one critic who came up with a tenuous argument about depreciation, which only slightly altered our earnings per share calculation.

A good deal of my leisure time was spent at the Racquet Club where I played real tennis. The real tennis professional was a Basque named Pierre Etchebaster, who entered the Guinness Book of Records as the oldest winner of a professional world title in any sport, beating off repeated challenges by an English professional called Johnson, until well into his 70s. Pierre spent his summers coaching lawn tennis at the Piping Rock Club and he had given my sister and me our first lessons, much favoured by our mother as he was French speaking. Like many Basques, Pierre had begun playing *pelota*, but had landed a job as a marker at the *Jeu de Paumes* in the Rue Launceston in Paris. He emigrated to the U.S. and never looked back. Real tennis is called court tennis in America and at my time there were only seven courts in the country: two at the Racket Club in New York, one each at the Tennis & Racquet in Boston, the Tuxedo Park Club, Jock Whitney's Greentree estate on Long Island, Aiken, South Carolina and in Chicago. It is the original game, created by monks in the courtyards of their monasteries and named after their habit of saying *tenez!* – "Here you are" – as they struck the first ball across the net. Modern real tennis courts resemble the monastery courtyard, with galleries called *dedans* and abutting corners. The ball is played off the gallery roof and the walls, as well as across the net as in the derivative game of lawn tennis. As the locales of courts in America suggest, the game was played by the leisure classes, and a tennis enthusiast called Sam van Allen was concerned it would die, as young men couldn't afford to join the clubs where the courts were. So he made arrangements allowing guest facilities for Harvard men at the Boston Tennis & Racquet, and for Yale and Princeton men at the New York Racquet and Tuxedo clubs. I was on a Harvard team which toured England and we played at Hampton Court, the most famous court of all, where one treads the same floor as Henry VIII, at Queens Club in London, in Oxford and at Hayling Island. In New York, the two leading players were the Bostwick brothers, Pete and Jimmy, whose father had been a celebrated polo player and amateur jockey. I never came close to taking a game off either. Neither would have been able to beat the professional Pierre Etchebaster in a tournament match, but he would let them win from time to time, out of courtesy.

One day, I was in the reading room at the Racquet Club, browsing the magazines, when I spotted the previous week's copy of *The Tattler*, amongst a host of other British publications. I did what is known in film jargon as "a double take". On the cover was a photograph of Dinnie Townsend, lounging elegantly on a rather over gilded *chaise longue*, in Mallet's, the antique dealers. Her sandals were on the floor next to her. Nowadays, one would have picked up the phone and rung one's lady love immediately to find out what it was all about. I had to wait. Prophetically, one of the inside articles announced at the bottom of the cover, was entitled "how to put your daughter on the stage". Our daughter eventually went on the stage without any help from us. I was preparing to settle down to a New York based career and despaired of seeing Dinnie again. She had returned to Rhodesia to spend some time with her mother who was unwell. My parents had sold our family home "Bittersweet" in Locust Valley, as they spent increasing time in summer in Europe, where they had their newly restored house in Senlis, and wintered now in a house they had built on Jupiter Island, Hobe Sound, Florida. In between there was the apartment at 136 East 79th Street, a building which coincidentally had been designed by the same Burrell Hoffman who had assisted in the restoration of the house in Senlis. I was in residence there, often on my own, and I could still week end on Long Island as I was a member of Piping Rock and had plenty of friends there.

In the office, I gravitated eventually to the foreign department where I worked as general dog's body to Harold Mandelsohn, who delighted in familiarising me with the business of the overseas offices in Zurich, London, Amsterdam and Hong Kong, and their particular needs in terms of daily servicing. Each had a slightly different business model. Zurich was central to the international bond business. London and Amsterdam were more equity orientated. Hong Kong was a trader's paradise. The Chinese clients viewed equity exchanges as a more respectable type of casino and generated huge commission income by churning their personal accounts. Not for them the staid, long-term investment policies espoused by Messrs Clark and Rittger. Harold prepared a daily overnight telex general to all the offices with prices, new issue information, financial news, corporate earnings' reports and so forth – all vital for offices devoid of the tape, Bloomberg and only a primitive Reuter's service. Then, as Europe awakened, flashes would be sent almost minute by minute. Telex transmission was priced according to speed; the overnight long "wire", as it was still called, was sent at the slow speed as the channel was shared. Flashes, and execution advices, short and in telegraphic style, went at top speed. Returning on another machine were the orders. Harold soon put me on the telex, and eventually even allowed me some editorial licence, so that I would flash bits of news I picked up in the office which I thought might be of interest to Zurich or London. Sometimes, if my typing was to slow, and there was some urgent flash, Harold would say "sorry", lean over my shoulder, and rattle it out at breakneck speed. Maximum excitement occurred when a foreign dollar bond issue was announced. Harold would get tipped off by friends at Morgan Stanley, even just before the SEC filing release, if, say, a Commonwealth of Australia issue was imminent. Amount, term and indicated coupon would be flashed to Zurich and it was all hands to the phones. Final terms were set at the end of the selling period at that time. The big three Swiss banks were already selling group members then, and would be indenting their demand directly to the book running, lead manager. But Credit Suisse, in particular, expected to be somewhat short-changed on allocation and often subscribed additional bonds through White, Weld to satisfy their in-house demand, particularly in a "hot" issue. And most private banks were not selling group members and would be served directly by White, Weld Zurich. In New York, the firm expected and usually received privileged allocation in these issues, particularly from Morgan Stanley. But Harold worked hand in glove with his partner Charlie Lee, Head of Syndicate at White, Weld, in negotiating allocations. Syndicate relationships were critical in the Street, in those days, and underwriting and selling allocations depended on these. The reciprocity practised amongst originating houses sailed a bit close to the wind, in the aftermath of Medina and the anti-trust accusations, but it was not really anti-competitive. It extended to the institutional client community in that if one of them helped out a house with a difficult issue, they would be rewarded with a more generous allocation of a "hot" issue. If an underwriter was unable to place its minimum allocation, the securities had to be held until the end of a restricted period, usually ninety days, where no one involved in the primary offering could sell. Afterwards, the position would be worked off in the secondary market. A practice then considered unethical was to "stuff" unsold securities from an underwriting into discretionary client accounts – which is not to say it never happened. Even when the Eurobond market began to gather steam, it was a while before the big three Swiss banks: Credit Suisse, Swiss Bank Corporation and Union Bank of Switzerland consented to join underwriting syndicates, as they feared they would be suspected by their private clients of placing unsold positions in their discretionary accounts. The major New York based originating investment banks during these few years of the postwar foreign dollar bond market: Morgan Stanley, Kuhn Loeb, Lazard Frères, Harriman Ripley, First Boston and Dillon Read, had no distribution facility in the Europe market where, increasingly, the bulk of these issues were being subscribed, and subsequently traded. White, Weld's unique position in this regard laid the foundation for its eventual premier role in the creation of the Eurobond market.

I had no reason to believe my sojourn at White, Weld in New York would be anything less than permanent. The foreign department was the obvious place for me. The team was led by Jean Cattier, as he was the senior international partner most often in residence, my father now spending a good half of the year in Europe. In addition to Harold Mandelsohn, the effective department manager, and now a partner, there was my father's oldest friend Jury Haveman, who maintained various correspondent relationships, Ray Crearin, the master originator of short-term paper and unusual transactions, John Fountain, the supreme researcher and editor of the publication *Foreign Dollar Bonds*, Yves-André Istell, a sort of banker's banker – I never knew what he did exactly, Georges Gudefin, a Belgian jack of all trades, and sundry others, representing different nationalities and disciplines. But then the bony fingered hand of fate intervened. Jack Gallagher, nominal manager of the London branch simply disappeared. Amongst Jack's many eccentricities was an absolute refusal to fly, and so his semi-annual trips to report to head office were accomplished by leisurely, first-class sea journeys on a Cunard liner. On this occasion he was thought to have boarded at Southampton, but he never arrived in New York. Clearly he hadn't fallen overboard. He was known to have a brother in the city, but no one knew how to reach him. His valet in Cheyney Walk could shed no light on the matter. No doubt John Stancliffe contacted Susan Douglas, a nice jolly girl who had conceived a most unlikely passion for Jack. Susan was the daughter of Lord and Lady Cecil Douglas. Lord Cecil was an impecunious younger brother of the Marquess of Queensbury, and had served as an advisor to a film based on the life of Oscar Wilde, his kinsman Lord Alfred Douglas having been more than germane to that saga. Lady Cecil was much engaged in organising deb parties and other events. They were all charming. Susan was devastated but totally ignorant of the fate of her recent paramour. No one was able to determine where Jack was, whether he was coming back, and why he had disappeared. There was no question of defalcation or other financial irregularity. DY was greatly embarrassed. As a recruiter, he had scored great successes, with the likes of Genillard and Stancliffe. But no one had ever understood what he saw in Jack Gallagher, except perhaps the ghost of the drunken Irishman who had worked for him in the '30s in Paris, and been so effective with rich old ladies anxious to get their fortunes safely away to America. Of course, John Stancliffe was more than qualified to assume the direction of the London Branch. But he needed some back up, a "bag carrier", and the suggestion was made that Stani might be the answer. My father was naturally loath to support this directly, claiming obvious conflict, but Harold Mandelsohn endorsed the idea enthusiastically and Alec White, the senior partner, was heard to say – in his laconic fashion "It's a natural". And so my life changed again, as a result of a really inconsequential personnel disaster – most were glad to see the back of poor Jack - but I now embarked on a career in a financial centre, the fortunes of which were to change the world of international finance. Pure chance had put me in the right place at the right time.

It so happened that an old friend and fellow Porcellian, John Jay Mortimer was off to London as well, whether for gainful employment or just on a whim, I forget. John Jay had been working for First National City Bank in a garment district branch. He found this unlikely assignment amusing as he liked to say that the Mortimer fortune originated from the supply of uniforms to both sides in the Civil War. I don't doubt the commerce, but I doubt the neutrality. Mrs Mortimer was the doyenne of Tuxedo society and had a series of children spanning a generation and a half, with the result that John Jay was the same age as his niece Topsy Pell. A sister had been seduced, and then her fortune embezzled by the son of one of my maternal grandfather's partners, a Furlaud, of DuPont & Furlaud, the private banking house in Paris. This rather curious connection between my family and the Mortimer's was only recently confirmed to me by Dick Mortimer, John Jay's next older brother. We agreed to share a flat just off Knightsbridge, opposite the Horse Guards barracks. Soon, John Jay found he was able to score repeatedly with English young ladies, and often asked me to delay my return to the flat until the small hours, requiring some initiative on my part as to how to while away these hours. But first a shock was to greet me on my arrival at Heathrow to take up my new assignment. As I travelled into town in a taxi, I saw that many of the advertising billboards were plastered with huge photographs of a couple advertising, on behalf of the Milk Marketing Board, the benefits of milk consumption under the slogan "Drinka Pint of Milk!" The girl holding a glass of this desirable beverage was none other than Dinnie Townsend. Next to her was a male model looking healthy and smug. The advertisement was posted nationwide and was disconcerting, to say the least. The explanation was simplicity itself. Dinnie was back in London with the same menial job at J. Walter Thompson, where she earned a pound or two a week. Amongst her duties was the hand delivery of proofs and documents to contract photographers assigned to various campaigns. Olaf Nissen, a prominent fashion photographer of the time, had a studio in Chelsea Cloisters and one day Dinnie rang his bell with a delivery. He took a look at her and pulled her inside, saying he had an assignment which required a healthy looking model, and all the usual ones looked like death warmed over. He spent the afternoon shooting her and the client liked the result. Nissen suggested she turn professional but Dinnie demurred strongly. On arrival in England she had been befriended and taken up socially by a public relations agent named David Wynn-Morgan. Through him she met some of the celebrated models of the time he handled professionally, and she became easily convinced that such a career was not for a Rhodesian farm girl of simple tastes and no limelight ambitions.

My arrival in the London office, then just recently moved to No. One Union Court in the Barclay's D.C & O building, just off Old Broad Street, was greeted with relief by John Stancliffe, largely because it signalled that Jack Gallagher had now been written off. The main business of the office was institutional brokerage in U.S. equities, still widely held in both England and Scotland. Of course the pound sterling was in an increasingly precarious position, necessitating the continuance of the exchange control measures established in wartime. The main inconvenience to the public was the restriction on the amount of foreign exchange which could be taken on holiday abroad. For capital movements, and in particular overseas investment, the complex wartime controls had been simplified and there now existed the so-called dollar premium pool. In essence, to purchase foreign securities one had to acquire the exchange through this pool, the premium involved fluctuating with supply and demand, which was in turn influenced by the speculative view on the risk of a devaluation of sterling. On sale of a foreign security, one could recover all or part of the premium or even make a gain on its sale. But it meant one took a double price risk on buying foreign equities, and, of course, buying a foreign currency bond was out of the question as the premium destroyed the yield. White, Weld was one of the few houses making a market in dollar premium. Another was Guinness Mahon, where the dealer was John Galvanoni, a favourite counterparty of our dealer Alan Towner. Dollar premium trading was an important revenue source for the London branch of White, Weld, and as the Bank of England kept a close watch on this market, our standing with the Bank was to be helpful in the future development of White, Weld in London. Despite the barrier to foreign investment which the dollar premium represented, there was a continuing appetite for U.S. stocks amongst institutions and the *cognoscenti*. We did a good business with London Stock

Exchange members, such as Read, Hurst Brown; KitKat & Aitken; Fielding, Newson Smith; Strauss Turnbull; Rowe & Pittman; Grieveson, Grant; Hoare, Govett; Laing & Cruikshank; Panmure, Gordon and several others. Among our active merchant bank clients were Robert Fleming; Singer & Friedlander; Ansbacher; Helbert Wagg; Guinness Mahon; Samuel Montagu and Leopold Joseph. Interestingly, we did little business with Rothschild, Lazard, Hambros, Warburgs, and Morgan Grenfell as they had much stronger connections with our competitors in New York. Amongst the clearing banks we were closest to Barclays where Timothy Bevan was an old friend of DY's. I quickly paid courtesy calls on a list DY had given me: Victor Brooks, and Nils Taube at KitKat & Aitken, George Loveday at Read Hurst Brown, Joe Lowy at Medwin & Lowy, Francis Hock and Marcel Pougatch at Singer & Friedlander, Oscar Joseph at Leopold Joseph. Nils Taube came from family of Baltic barons, part of the Imperial Russian nobility. DY had known his relations. Nils was to become one of the great investment gurus of our age. Knowing three generations of Lovedays has given me the opportunity to say "I knew your grandfather" to a current City luminary. On my first trip to Rhodesia, a mining engineer friend of my mother in law came to lunch. "Do you know my son George who is in the City?" he asked. He was Arthur Loveday, who also turned out to be a friend of the Pennoyer's who lived in Locust Valley. Mrs. Pennoyer was a daughter of J. P. Morgan. Now when I see Mark Loveday latterly senior partner of Cazenove, I can remind him I knew his grandfather. We served institutional clients such as Pearl Assurance, National Provincial and, in Scotland, Scottish Widows and Scottish American Mortgage Company. The investment manager at National Provincial, Jim Titford, was keen and knowledgeable on American electric utility shares and actually "day traded" them. I can see John Stancliffe running back and forth between his phone on his desk and the telex machine where New York was flashing prices, and the client was buying and selling on moving quotations. Early on I was sent to Charlotte Square, the investment centre of Edinburgh, as a sort of baptism of fire. The Scottish institutions were amongst the earliest investors in America in the 19th century, in agricultural and ranching land, mortgages and securities in general. I was shown in to the dingy office of one investment manager, a dour, highly Presbyterian gentleman, who seated me in a freezing draft and said, "There is somebody in Wall Street who empties his wastepaper basket into an envelope and sends it to me. Might he be at your firm?" He clearly had little regard for the research output of Wall Street houses. I got my revenge of sorts. Sometime later, we engaged a charming young man called John Eric, Viscount Strathallan, known as "Jeric", and heir to the Earl of Perth. Jeric's mother was sister to Reginald Finck, a Porcellian and Marine Corps officer killed in World War II, and his first cousin Virginia married Thor Thors, son of the then Icelandic Ambassador to Washington, and also a Porcellian. Thor had a long and distinguished career at First National City Bank. I suggested Jeric be assigned Charlotte Square. After a while, John Stancliffe received a call from a friend up there who remarked that only an American firm would have the "chutzpa" to send the heir to a Catholic Scottish peer to solicit business in the heartland of Presbyterianism which is Charlotte Square. But the crowd there were so amused by the inappropriateness of the assignment that they gave Jeric lots of orders. The Scottish institutions provided me with insights into the mentality of the "buy side" of the investment business which no investment banker can be without.

I was as happy as any young man starting a career can be. I wallowed in the general atmosphere of the City and often just walked about absorbing it all. In those days the City was still at work Saturday morning. One of the pieces of frivolous advice my father had given me related to dress. It was alright, DY opined, to be seen in a soft collar on Friday, Saturday morning or Monday, as one was assumed to in the country at weekends. Likewise, the only day a buttonhole was acceptable was on Monday as it would have been plucked from a country garden. Although the expression was no longer in use, weekends were traditionally referred to as a "Saturday to Monday", indicating that government offices, banks, the Stock Exchange, etc. were open Saturday morning, throughout the 19th and early 20th century. Even in my early time in the City, Monday was a slow starting day – but then houses like Rothschild did not begin business until 10:00 AM every day of the week. Years later, when I became Chairman of Merrill Lynch in London, I was informed I would be expected to host breakfast meetings as early at 7:30 in the morning. *O tempora, o mores.* When I was not lunching with my boss John at the Grill & Cheese in Throgmorton Avenue, I would pop into Sweetings, then in lower Old Broad Street, for a smoked salmon sandwich, Gorgonzola cheese with digestive biscuits and a glass of champagne, for the highly affordable price of seven shillings and six pence. Sometimes I would lunch more copiously with my flatmate John Jay Mortimer and his friend John, a partner in one of the discount houses, whose working day ended at lunch. Then of course, there were the substantial lunches at the Savoy Grill, or sometimes, the Great Eastern Hotel, with John Rasch and Ronnie Parvin, who was still looking after the famous Spanish lady from Bilbao. John Stancliffe wisely avoided these sessions, although he certainly appreciated the business resulting and gave Ronnie Parvin serious advice at the office after lunch. We had relatively little London based competition for American business then. On arrival, I called on Hubert Simon, who ran a small office for Carl M. Loeb Rhodes in the City, as he was the senior representative of the New York Stock Exchange in London and he had to validate some aspect of my credentials as a Registered Representative, as we were then known. His daughter Rosemary Brown lived at Oakwood Court in Holland Park, where my family eventually resided, and she and her husband Peter kindly took us in, with the children, when one of the boys set our flat on fire. A very "white shoe" Wall Street firm called Dominick & Dominick had an office run by Dick Hill, who preceded me as an American in the City and stayed quite as long as I did. Kuhn Loeb had no office but maintained a representative, Tony Lund, with an office within Warburg's, indicating the closeness of the two firms. Tony succeeded me at European Banking Company, many years later. The few American banks in London at the time: Hanover Bank, First National City Bank, J. P. Morgan, tended to have long serving Englishmen in charge. Bob Breyfogle had been the manager of FNCB as long as anyone could remember.

I was not yet fully aware of the forces which were already at work in London, and, in a negative sense, on the continent, with respect to the burgeoning market in Eurocurrency deposit taking and lending, because White, Weld was not a deposit taking financial institution. Whereas the Bank of England, and therefore HM Treasury, was gently encouraging this activity, Germany, France, Switzerland and Italy all took steps to prohibit it, mostly by simply banning the payment of interest by their banks on foreign deposits. The reason for this was simple: exchange control. None of the continental centres had this protection against the dangers to domestic monetary policy management which an uncontrolled influx of foreign deposits would pose. In London, on the contrary, Eurodollar activity posed no threat, as it was isolated from the domestic monetary mass by the presence of exchange control. And so the stage was set for a great leap forward as soon as this business could become securitised and a provider of longer term capital. In the meantime, White, Weld in London generated a niche business we called "church pounds" – another example of the ironic benefits of exchange control, normally considered a fatal handicap for a financial centre. Because the dollar premium was a negative indicator of confidence in sterling, the Bank welcomed any permitted transactions which could increase the pool and act as a brake on an excessive premium. The premium usually hovered around the 10% level, but reached 15% in 1965. Certain remittances from abroad, such as reparations payments, were allowed to enter via the pool, which is to say the remitting entity effectively bought sterling at a comfortable discount. One category of permitted remittances was funds from religious organisations being directed to their sterling area churches and missions, located in the former British colonies – but also in Ireland, as this independent country was still in the sterling area. This was a fact much appreciated by British tourists, who could not only take their money to Ireland, but their dogs as well, as quarantine regulations were also jointly administered. Ray Craerin in New York, that great originator of special deals, had developed a relationship with the Seventh Day Adventists, who maintained a substantial presence in Africa. By passing their remittances through the dollar premium pool, they funded their operations at a comfortable discount from the price they would have paid for sterling at the official rate. The transactions involved a passage through the gilt edge market, but this was a functional technicality and the Bank was happy that we acted directly through the premium pool, in which we were a major market maker in any case. We did a land office business for the Seventh Day Adventists, but also for some other churches, and, notably, the Vatican. DY had established a relationship with a Monsignor Gorastazo, a

Basque priest in charge of finances. When my father first called on him, escorted to his Vatican office by a Swiss Guard, he found the Monsignor, with his feet on his desk, reading a copy of *The Wall Street Journal.* The Vatican fed, through church pounds, what seemed an inexhaustible appetite for money in Ireland, and we were instructed to transfer funds to a modest priest in Dublin, who we hoped was not spending them at Cheltenham Race Course, where the entire Irish money supply was said to circulate during the Spring Festival. Often we were able to effect a "cross" between a church pound client and a UK based investor selling U.S. securities and hence generating dollar premium. One day Fielding, Newson Smith rang us – it might have been our good friend Donald Pearce – to say they had an order to liquidate a very large position in Singer Sewing Machines, which needed to be done with care, having regard to price movements in both the shares and in the premium. Over a period of several months, we were able to move the position and deal in volume in church pounds for our religious clients. Later on I began to suspect who Fielding's client might have been, although I never mentioned it to Donald Pearce, who has remained a great friend. Until lately, we used to trade annual lunch dates at Boodle's, his club, and White's, mine. It seemed clear at the time that the block of shares must be a family holding as the large Singer family, had established itself throughout Europe. A famous Miss Singer became Princesse de Polignac, a great Paris hostess at the turn of the century. DY had a great friend called Morty Singer, who had married Madelaine Forbes, and we used to stay with them in Biarritz. Their son Forbes Singer has remained a friend. But I consider the likely candidate was a Mrs. Gar Barker, who I met out hunting, and whose son Fred was Master of the VWH, the pack I mostly hunted with. Mrs. Barker was a Singer heiress, her family was much into horses and fareatmed in Gloucestershire, and we all know horses are the biggest consumers of capital after cable companies and badly managed banks. But I could be wrong.

About this time, I got married. Dinnie had moved flats and jobs. The Murray sisters had married or moved away and Dinnie was now sharing a flat near Knightsbridge, opposite the present Berkeley Hotel, with a Canadian girl called Maggie, who worked for a theatrical agent and was prone to use the politically incorrect expression "queer as a tree full of owls" to describe her clients, and another Rhodesian named Bar who married Simon Grandage, an accountant and eventual colleague of mine. Dinnie now sold ties at Barker's department store, as a senior J. Walter Thompson executive had arrived from New York, toured the offices in Berkeley Square, and said, "What on earth are all these pretty, but useless girls doing here?" I saw more and more of her and gradually weaned her from the smart country house parties given by Yorkshire land owners and other magnates, to which she claimed she had reluctantly become accustomed, to supplement the meagre diet she could afford on her pittance salary and tiny allowance from her father in Rhodesia. Raife Obré Crofton Townsend, an Anglo-Irish gentleman of the old school, a highly successful farmer, polo player and occasional visitor to Irish packs of hounds, had three pet hates: "town types", bankers and Roman Catholics. When he received a letter from his eldest and much loved daughter saying that she was engaged to marry a Roman Catholic banker living in London, he must have had a momentary thought about what transgressions in his life had caused the Good Lord to visit this dreadful sentence upon him. But he rallied rapidly and made plans to come to London for the wedding, considering it would afford him the opportunity of visiting his tailor. He took me to lunch at the Connaught Grill. Once again, the old adage "it's who you know" came to the fore. I mentioned that Daniel Wagnière was an old friend. Now Daniel, who Dinnie had met at Beaumont in Switzerland, was studying agronomy and had required a year of practical experience which Dinnie had arranged for him to spend at Lowdale Farm. My prospective father-in-law had fallen for him in a big way, even tolerating his farming advice, based on one year's study in Zurich. "A man of parts" was how Raife now described him. It was clear that if I was a friend of Daniel Wagnière, I must be all right despite my rather exotic background. I had confirmation of this over the lamb cutlets, when he suddenly said, "I think Dinnie is looking a bit peaked – why don't you take her to Brighton for the week end?" The wedding was still a week away. It turned out Raife wanted to go to the show jumping at Hickstead and felt a bit embarrassed about abandoning his daughter – but I took it as a vote of confidence. We were married at Chelsea Town Hall. My father came, but neither mother could be there for various reasons. A small reception was held at the Basil Street Hotel, where Raife always stayed, a hostel popular with colonials and ladies visiting the Chelsea Flower Show. As an afterthought, Patsy, my new mother-in-law, had sent the youngest daughter Linda, subsequently always known as "Mattie", as an unaccompanied minor, and she walked in, aged ten, with her ticket still in a plastic holder around her neck, entirely self-possessed. The two fathers were deep in conversation at the reception and I longed to know what these two, from opposite poles of the universe, could have to talk about. Mattie was to travel to Scotland afterwards, to stay with the family of Angus Graham, Duke of Montrose, who farmed in Rhodesia and was a family friend. After the reception, I went back to the office to pen a line to my boss John Stancliffe, who was away, to tell him I had married, and to tidy up some work. We dined at Alexander's Restaurant, off the King's Road. It belonged to Alexander Plunkett-Greene, who was married to Mary Quant, a fashion tycoon of the period. We didn't start our honeymoon for a couple of months. In fact, I began to have pangs of conscience and so went to visit a Father Russell at St. Mary's, Cadogan, near Sloane Square. Father Russell had been in the Irish Guards and then worked at Japhets in the City, before being ordained. I explained about my registry office marriage. "We have been a naughty boy," he said, with humour. "But we can fix that – I take it the lady is C of E, but if you send her round, I'll give her the minimum of instruction about marrying an RC – and, of course, don't you forget Confession?" Dinnie duly went to see him. He offered her a gin and tonic, whipped out a silver cigarette case, talked about horses, and extracted a promise the children would be christened and confirmed as Catholics – which was kept. And so we were married for a second time, although, for me it was, strictly speaking, the first.

CHAPTER XIV

"May you live in interesting times"

-A well-known, but entirely fictitious, Chinese curse-

The early 1960s saw a great deal of movement on the geo-political and economic front, increasingly interrelated, as the process of globalisation gathered
pace. One might say it was the confluence of more than one river. The Cold
War was far from over, and President Kennedy, who had raised unreasonable
expectations, was to face the Bay of Pigs and the Cuban missile crisis. He
was yet to make his speech in Berlin where, for some, he called himself a
jelly donut, and for others he expressed empathy with the citizenry post the
blockade. At home, he faced a balance of payments problem, although, compared to today's external financial position and indebtedness, the United
States enjoyed great comparative strength, whilst Britain struggled with
budgetary and trade deficits, and the political traumas of Imperial decline.
White, Weld was not spared the pain of change and events unfolded which
were to cause my father great pain, and to have significant consequences for
the firm's future international franchise. For my father it almost seemed a be-
trayal, as it represented the unravelling of what he considered his greatest
achievement – White, Weld & Co. A.G. of Zurich, and it came from within.
Key to all this was the relationship between White, Weld and Shearman &
Sterling, the great Wall Street law firm. White, Weld was its second largest
client, after First National City Bank. The senior partner of S & S, Fred Eaton
had been Alec White's roommate at Harvard. The two firms were almost
joined at the hip. White, Weld had a lawyer as a partner in the person of Tom
Choate, a Harvard man and a Porcellian. But as is so often the case when one
expects an in house lawyer to save on legal fees, he, or she, simply discovers
more situations where outside legal advice is recommended, and so legal fees
go up. Without any warning, as far as I know, Shearman & Sterling told
White, Weld that the firm was in double jeopardy as a result of its ownership
of the subsidiary in Zurich. Even though it had been strict policy to provide
no account domiciliation facilities to U.S. persons, and its clientele was entirely Latin American, European or Asian, the lawyers argued that the firm
might have to testify to this effect in a U.S. court of law, and it would be

forced to plead the Fifth Amendment against self-incrimination, because to make any comment would be a violation of Swiss law on bank secrecy. Never in the annals of U.S. legal advice has a more ridiculous argument been put forward. In the first place, there was no reason to believe that the IRS would take criminal action against White, Weld; if the issue had been raised, private and confidential negotiation would have satisfied the IRS that the firm did not hold accounts for U.S. persons in Zurich. In the second place, a negative statement, even made publically, such as "We have no U.S. clients in Zurich" would not have been a violation of Swiss law as no clients would have been identified. Even more suspect was the fact that Shearman & Sterling did not give similar advice to their client First National City Bank, which maintained a subsidiary in Geneva. I hate conspiracy theorists, but to this day I cannot rid myself of the suspicion that someone in New York was jealous of the strong presence being built in Europe by Genillard on the foundations laid by DY and Jean Cattier. But I tell myself this would have been totally out of charac-ter. The partners of the firm were almost excessively decent. But the thought of Alec White pleading the Fifth Amendment in a court sent shivers down the collective spine, and there was no choice but to comply with this irresponsible and damaging advice. In any case, what Shearman & Sterling advised, White, Weld always did. I remember the day when DY gathered us together in the London office, having come from Zurich, and told us what had to happen. It was the closest I ever came to seeing tears in his eyes. But the phoenix was already on the rise from the ashes. Bob Genillard and I have somewhat differ-ent recollections of the next, highly fortuitous steps which were taken. Ac-cording to mine, DY, no doubt with Bob, went to see Mr. Lutz, then managing Credit Suisse, and offered to sell WW A.G. to Credit Suisse on three condi-tions. That the bank would sponsor the establishment of a branch in Zurich for White, Weld N.Y. – it must be remembered there were still no U.S. houses represented there; that Credit Suisse would pass all U.S. commission business emanating from the former subsidiary to the new Zurich branch; and finally – and most important of all, that Credit Suisse would agree to sell the business back to White, Weld, should U.S. regulations evolve and permit such. There was to be no written agreement or reference to this undertaking, which was to be deemed a verbal "gentlemen's agreement". Bob does not recall DY having been involved in this interchange – perhaps he was to upset. Several years later, after a good deal of water, both sweet and bitter, had passed under the dam, Bob Genillard was able to return to Credit Suisse and remind Mr. Lutz's successor of the verbal agreement, which was immediately acknowledged, and the business which had been renamed Clariden Finanz, and then, Clariden Bank, passed back to the control of White, Weld's European arm. It helped that the successor in question was Rainer Gut, who had worked for André Meyer at Lazard in New York and returned to take the helm at Credit Suisse, an appointment which raised eyebrows in the Zurich establishment as Gut was Catholic and Zurich was quite definitely Calvinist. Genillard and Gut got on famously, and this whole incident led eventually to one of the most important and productive strategic alliances in the European financial community: Credit Suisse White Weld.

The change in the status of White, Weld's presence in Zurich had further consequences, leading to a move which was to confirm London's position as the epicentre of the emerging Euromarkets. With Zurich now a branch, the construction which had allowed White, Weld's secondary market bond operations to escape Swiss stamp tax, became somewhat doubtful. The branch would no longer be engaging New York on an arm's length basis, as the subsidiary did, but directly. The conclusion was painful but obvious. The secondary market operation, under the great Walter Koller, had to move. Bob Genillard had his eye on Paris. He had a natural affinity for Paris and had just purchased an apartment there, whereas he was not so comfortable in London. He was not alone in thinking Paris might become the financial centre of Europe. All the major Wall Street legal firms, including Shearman & Sterling, had chosen Paris to open offices, serving the American corporates that were aggressively setting up in Europe. Only one, Cleary Gotleib, chose Brussels. There was no exchange control in France. France seemed financially and culturally open-minded, ready to embrace their partners in the new European Coal & Steel Community, surely the precursor to a new European construction of economic unity – so they all thought. Two of the most famous powers in international finance, J. P. Morgan and Morgan Stanley had created a joint venture, Morgan & Cie, to exploit the opening of Europe wide money and capital markets, and had based it in Paris. This might have been partially to avoid conflict with their cousins Morgan Grenfell in London. Merrill Lynch established its European headquarters initially in Paris. There was a powerful consensus ready to bet on Paris, rather than London, which was still bound by exchange controls, with a currency under pressure, a general economic malaise and an attitude exemplified by the famous newspaper headline "Fog in Channel – Continent Isolated". John Stancliffe and I watched the development of Bob's Paris bias with some alarm. After all, no one denied the Eurocurrency deposit market was well and truly in London. And surely the English language was already what all foreign dollar bond dealers spoke. Our London solicitor from Linklaters & Paine, Mark Sheldon, had introduced to us a young man particularly versed in the taxation of branches and subsidiaries of overseas financial houses based in the City. We asked him to set up a meeting with a senior Inland Revenue officer, then based at Somerset House. At the meeting we explained the business of secondary market trading in international bonds. He was unfamiliar with dealer to dealer markets in securities, as, like most, he thought all securities transactions took place on official exchanges. But he readily understood that the dollar premium precluded the participation of domestic investors in this market. "So you are intermediating transactions between nonresident counterparties?"

"Exactly," said John Stancliffe;

"This would seem to be akin to the business London based agents carried on between nonresident commercial enterprises in the old Empire, for example a South African firm selling to India, arranged through a London office."

"Exactly that!" said our young consultant.

"Well, there is a provision in the tax code, dating back to Imperial times, treating such transactions," said our Inland Revenue man.

"Meaning?" we almost shouted in unison.

"If the counterparties are nonresident, the earnings of the intermediary in London are nontaxable."

"So, if this trading activity is moved to the London Branch of White, Weld, the branch will continue to be taxed on an expenses, rather than a revenue, basis?"

"Precisely," was the answer.

Trying to contain our excitement, we made the minimum of small talk and took our leave. On the way out, the Inland Revenue official turned to our consultant and said:

"How is your father – enjoying his retirement?"

"Oh, yes – particularly the golf."

"How I envy him. Please give him my best regards."

Once outside, one of us asked the consultant:

"What was that all about?"

"Oh, my father used to be his boss," came the casual reply.

When we conveyed this news to Bob Genillard, we knew the match was ours. Bob could never resist a legitimate tax advantage. Koller & Co., with the still silent Ozzie Gruble in tow, moved to London. After that, London became the obvious place to trade international bonds. I should have tracked the fate of the IRS official. The eventual revenue produced by international bond trading in London, from all the subsidiary services and affiliated taxable activity, more than justified his original decision. I hope he got a "gong" on retirement. I do not mean to infer that the move of White, Weld's bond trading operations to London was epoch making, or the greatest determinate of the City's future as the Euromarket's capital. No doubt, if we had moved to Paris, the new markets would have still settled in London, with its unique combination of language, support facilities, human capital and welcoming authorities. Bob Genillard would have eventually seen the light and concentrated our Euro business there as well. In fact, Paris never posed a threat to London, at any time during the Euromarket's development. Morgan & Cie's initial success faded, and as a joint venture, it interfered strategically with the plans of each partner. Its managing director Van Galbreath ended up in London at Bankers Trust International – formerly Rodochanachi. It was in London that Van took his famous bath, when, watching his rubber duck bobbing up and down, he conceived the idea of the floating rate note – the Eurobond market's great *Eureka!* moment. Still, I feel we were at the outset of a powerful trend and, slowly but surely, all the players, American, French, German, Swiss,

200

Dutch, Scandinavian, Japanese and sundry others, concentrated their Euromarkets operations in the City.

White, Weld still re-opened in Paris, with François Champion in charge, and our presence there added a significant new element to the European franchise. An Algerian colonial family called Tiné had extensive land holdings there and also a bank called Banque Algerienne de Dépôts et de Titres. Jean Claude Tiné asked his friend Pierre Haas, the senior international partner at Banque de Paris ET des Pays Bas – Paribas, as it became universally known – which institution he might link up with to establish a presence in Paris. Haas was a friend of Genillard, had a close association with Warburg's, and had worked on deals in which Warburg's and White, Weld were prime movers. He liked what he saw of White, Weld and suggested it would be an ideal partner. Bob agreed, taking an immediate shine to Jean Claude, and Banque Française de Dépôts et de Titres was established as a joint venture with offices, together with the White, Weld branch, in the Rue de Teheran, off the Boulevard Haussmann. Ownership of an authorised bank gave us a new dimension, and ability to participate in and originate a wider range of transactions. Our business habits took Jean Claude Tiné aback and he never totally adopted them. When Bob explained there was a morning meeting at nine o'clock, Jean Claude said, "You are joking – I am having my breakfast in bed at that hour." Jean Claude's brother Jean Marie was Chairman of the European division of an American transport conglomerate, Trailer Inc. The two had widespread contacts in France. Jean Claude usually ended his day playing gin rummy with Jimmy Goldsmith at the Travellers Club. The re-opening of Paris was a consolation for DY, still smarting from the WW Zurich affair. But he was about to become a Limited Partner, having reached retirement age. He continued to look after selected clients, in particular the Guerlain family, and he enjoyed going frequently from our house in Senlis to the Rue de Teheran, where he was treated with great courtesy as a patriarchal, almost legendary figure, and much admired by the younger members of the team. In the beautifully restored *hôtel paticulier* in the Rue du Chat Haret at Senlis, my parents entertained in great style, a facility tactfully but extensively exploited for key clients. They made many friends in the area.

Major change was brewing in the City of London. It was now crystal clear that foreign dollar bonds issued in New York were being distributed and traded almost entirely in Europe. No one was in a better position to know this than Julius Strauss, and David Kynaston credits him with inventing the term "Eurobond" as early as 1962. I have no reason to doubt this. After all, if a U.S. dollar circulating exclusively in Europe was called a "Eurodollar", why wouldn't a U.S. issued dollar bond circulating principally in Europe be called a "Eurobond"? But Julius was not the only one to recognise the illogic of Wall Street houses collecting fat underwriting fees on new issues distributed and traded almost entirely outside of their jurisdiction. Sigmund Warburg also realised the writing was on the wall for the foreign dollar bond market in its then current form. He saw the U.S. balance of payments deteriorating steadily, although he would not have anticipated the bombshell dropped by the Kennedy Administration, in the form of the Interest Equalisation Tax, which slammed the door shut on New York as an exporter of capital and the epicentre of world finance. There were stirrings even before this epoch ending event. The Eurodollar deposit market indicated both the liquidity and currency preference of European investors. Sigmund Warburg was unusual amongst London merchant bankers in many ways, but also due to his extensive Wall Street experience – he had been a Kuhn Loeb partner before the war; His partner in London, Gert Whitman, ex-Lee Higginson, also knew the workings of the Street. They both could see that the present position was untenable. David Kynaston reports that in early 1962, well before the IET, Warburgs were considering a London based dollar loan for the European Coal & Steel Community, previously a frequent borrower in the New York foreign dollar bond market. The deal didn't come off for various reasons, but Kynaston suggests one reason may have been that the ECSC was a Kuhn Loeb client. They had handled previous issues. Sigmund Warburg was still a partner of Kuhn Loeb, and was to remain so until 1964. There were toes not to be stepped on. Controversially, I maintain the first Eurobond issue, was not the Autostrade deal, which the Warburg PR machine has so successfully established, but a $20 million placement of 3 year 5% Notes for the Kingdom of Belgium, by Samuel Montagu in May of 1962. Short term bonds were always termed Notes, and 5 year maturities were later to be current in the Eurobond market. True – the notes were not listed, and this disqualifies the deal as the first, for Chris O'Malley. But listing was to become a mere formality for Eurobonds; the dealer to dealer secondary market was the source of liquidity. The Belgian Notes were bearer and entirely negotiable. Georges Gazon at Montagu certainly provided a market, but there would have been minimal turnover due to the short maturity. I believe the Belgian deal was the first true Eurobond issue. In that year, Hambro's was said to be in discussion with the Kingdom of Norway. But Warburg's was quick off the mark with the now famous Autostrade deal. Again, I question some of the now, almost sacred, history of this transaction, recounted in detail by David Kynaston – mostly from Warburg sources. I believe the deal was planned for SEC registration through Kuhn Loeb, but someone got wind of controls in a planning stage in Washington, and Sigmund and Gert Whitman persuaded their Kuhn Loeb partners to switch the deal to London, exploiting the precedent set by the Belgian loan. And indeed, the momentous Interest Equalization Tax struck an unsuspecting market on 28th July 1963. It imposed a 15% tax on the purchase by Americans of foreign securities from foreigners. As Kynaston reports, the Chairman of Morgan Guaranty, Henry Alexander, told his colleagues "this is a day that you will remember forever. It will change the face of American banking and force all the business off to London". How right he was. It is said everyone remembers where they were when some momentous event takes place, such as the assassination of President Kennedy. I remember where I was when a financially momentous, but far less tragic, event took place. I was on a brief visit to head office, and I was standing in the Foreign Department with Harold Mandelsohn when the news of the IET came on the broad news tape. Harold rushed to the telex to flash Zurich, and he turned to me and said, "Boy, are you guys going to make hay now!" This was the first time I had heard someone at White, Weld, refer to the European operations as "you guys". Harold realised immediately that the foreign dollar bond market was going to well and truly move to Europe now, where it belonged, and that our European franchise, so painstakingly built up, was going to come into its own.

Kynaston describes in detail the hoops Warburg had to jump through in order to make the Autostrade issue as London based as possible. There were the issuing restrictions and fees of the Stock Exchange, but where no bonds were likely to be traded; British Stamp Duty had to be avoided by having the actual place of issue off shore; British withholding tax of 42 ½% would apply on any coupons cashed in the U.K., so overseas paying agents had to be named. In fact, it is remarkable how many barriers to this activity existed in London at the time. Strauss, Turnbull and Messel were brokers to the issue. Messel had not the slightest idea where such bonds could be placed, but Julius Strauss certainly did, and he was on the phone to Walter Koller as soon as the issue was released. All of these London based problems were soon to be circumvented, but the Stock Exchange saw no reason to amend their rules, or exempt such issues, and so the listing business went to Luxemburg, and the future competitive position of London merchant banks as Eurobond issuing houses, was diminished. The Stock Exchange's position was both unintelligent and ironic, as in the 17th century, when foreign loans began to be arranged in London, the Stock Exchange had created a special facility to facilitate their trading. Warburg's itself seemed curiously disinterested in the business of distributing and trading the issues they had sponsored. Their first syndication was also a bit strange. The co-managers were Deutsche Bank, Banque de Bruxelles and Rotterdamsche Bank. Deutsche bank was a major market maker in foreign dollar bonds through their branch in Manheim. Banque de Bruxelles had retail distribution serving the iconic "Belgian Dentist", presumed to be the typical bearer bond buyer. But Rotterdamsche Bank must have been there through friendship, as the Dutch were equity minded and didn't buy bonds in quantity. But Warburg's had not seen fit to include an Italian bank in the co-management group, even though Banca Commerciale d'Italia was a major secondary market player. Not particularly in the wake of the Autostrade issue – although Sigmund and Gert Whitman were well aware of our firm's placing power – we began to form a close relationship with Warburg's. Gert Whitman, who had been an advisor to Bundesbank Governor Schacht in the '30's, served on a committee created by the postwar occupation authority headed by John J. McCloy. The committee was charged with the planning the reconstruction of the German banking sector. On this same committee was White, Weld partner Jean Cattier, and the two got on very well. Whitman introduced Jean to Sigmund, and Jean introduced Bob Genillard to Sigmund. The relationship grew closer and closer, as the Eurobond market began to take off – leading to Bob's famous comment "Sigmund used to call me at home". I worked on one of the first deals the two houses did together: a private placement of medium-term notes for Siemens A.G. There were two Italian lads working at Warburg's, known as the "Italian twins", although they were not related. They persisted in turning up a few minutes late for meetings. Warburg's was a stickler for absolute accuracy and timeliness. It was said that, when Sigmund went to a meeting outside the house, he would always arrive early and have his chauffeur drive around the block, so that he could enter the premises at precisely the hour arranged. Gert Whitman used to tick the Italian twins off, in front of the client, which I didn't think was very *haute banque*. But it was at the signing of this deal that Gert caught his partner Bernard Kelley with green ink in his pen.

In spite of our history of placement and trading of foreign dollar bonds – now officially Eurobonds, we faced a challenge to find our legitimate place in the new European syndicates. These would now follow the traditional U.S. structure: lead manager(s), co-managers, major bracket underwriters, minor bracket underwriters, selling group. The commission structure – or "gross spread", was unchanged: 2 ½% for long maturities, 2% for medium. For long bonds, it was ½ % management, ½% underwriting and 1 1/2% selling. Soon after Autostade, Hambros launched a $10 million issue for Norges Kommunalbank, guaranteed by the Kingdom of Norway. White Weld was conspicuous by its absence from the syndicate, yet we were the prime market makers in Norway's outstanding external bonds. We acted for the Ministry of Finance in satisfying their sinking fund obligations. It could be construed that we set the price for Norway in the market. Bob Genillard was not best pleased to say the least, and I think he felt the London office was not doing its job with respect to City relationships. When, a few months later, we learned Hambros was preparing a $25 million issue for the Kingdom of Norway itself, Bob sent me to call on Hambros in Bishopsgate. I was received by a supercilious, patronising, and relatively junior officer called Rupert Hutton. He looked at me as if I had crawled out from under a flat rock. I opened:

"We understand you have an issue in preparation for Norway, and we feel we belong in your underwriting syndicate."

"We already have a broker to the issue – Strauss Turnbull."

"An excellent choice, but I'm talking about the underwriting and selling syndicate. We are the principal market maker in Norwegian bonds."

"We do not include brokers in our underwriting syndicates."

I paused, gritted my teeth and tried to remain calm.

"White, Weld is an old established Wall Street investment banking firm which has been underwriting, distributing and trading foreign dollar bonds for years. Ask Morgan Stanley, if you don't believe me."

"We already have Strauss Turnbull – we don't need you."

"We would be in a position to place a significant portion of the issue. We act for the Kingdom's existing sinking fund."

"Sorry – we don't need you."

Interview over. I left in a rage. For the first time in my life, I entertained a quite un Christian sentiment – a desire for revenge. In fact, I vowed to myself I would get my revenge – and I did. At the time, I felt humiliated, and dreaded having to tell Bob I had failed. Maybe, my direct boss John Stancliffe would have done better. He was, at least, an Englishman. Bob took it well. He was farsighted and confident we would eventually leave Hambros in the dust, and we did. When league tables of new issue managers began to appear in later years – the bank was way below us. All this did not prevent my becoming a great friend of Rupert Hambro, who succeeded me as Chairman of the Association of International Bond Dealers – AIBD, and, together with his wife Robin, we remain friends and neighbours in both Florida and France. Robin Hutton eventually became Director General of the Takeover Panel. Fortunately, this was before I became a member of the Panel, and I was to have no further dealings with him.

A breakthrough was on the horizon, and it came in mid-1964. I'm not sure how we secured the mandate but it would have been through a charming gentleman called Ollie Kailla, an ex-diplomat, and then head of international at Konsallis Osake Bank in Helsinki. Ollie had been Finnish Ambassador to Belgium and our extensive Belgian connections might have been a link. The issue proposed would also be a precedent setter. Heretofore, the market had been the exclusive preserve of public sector issuers – Sovereign governments, municipalities and other governmental entities. Our Finnish borrower was to be a commercial concern called Kesko Oy, a logistics company, and the $12.5 million, ten year bonds were to be guaranteed by KOP, one of Finland's two internationally known commercial banks. It was also a first for me, as I was assigned to do the donkey work on the preparation, syndication and launch of the issue, from our London office. Just as one remembers one's first love, and one's first experience in any number of things, my first Eurobond issue is seared in my memory. Needless to say, Shearman & Stearling was to do the legal work, and we were to stick religiously to SEC style documentation and all the trappings. I even think New York wanted to send over one of the head office new issue people to ensure compliance, but Bob Genillard resisted. We were to establish our own credentials in Europe and our own ability to maintain White, Weld standards. Three Paris based Shearman & Sterling lawyers were to enter our lives and became almost part of the family: Edward Tuck, Tom Nangle and, later, David McGovern. When I arrived in Helsinki, I was taken in hand by Ollie Kailla of KOP, and soon found myself with him in a sauna, together with the drafts of the prospectus we were working on. I am able to observe that documents become brittle and difficult to handle in a sauna. We traded stories and he told me that when the country and the Diet had been threatened in the last war, Finland having been invaded by both Germany and the Soviets, the legislature's last act, before fleeing into the northern forests, had been to pass a bill freezing foreign exchange reserves held in foreign banks, so that they could be utilised exclusively for the servicing of Finland's foreign debts. I used this story often when selling Finnish bonds. It was an illustration of the adage that, when it comes to assessing foreign risk, a sovereign borrower's *willingness* to pay is more important that its ability to pay. Finland, even under the shadow of the Soviet bear, more than deserved its AAA rating. I told Ollie that my family had owned a summer home on the Karelian coast, then part of the Grand Duchy of Finland, and that my grandmother had told the story of leaving her fur coat at a railway station, where passengers to and from St. Petersburg, stopped for tea. As she no doubt owned a great many fur coats, she thought nothing of it. But the following year, stopping at the same station, the station master approached her and said, "*Madame la Général,* here is the fur coat you left behind last year." My grandmother considered that could never happen in Russia, and that the Finns were an outstandingly honest people. Back in London, we had no difficulty establishing a relationship with overnight, financial printers. This facility was to prove yet another plus for London as no other centre on the Continent was able to print financial documents in English for proofing overnight. Financial printers in Wall Street actually provided bedrooms for investment bankers and lawyers, so that they could review proofs immediately. I prepared the telexes inviting syndicate members. We didn't yet have a permanent telex operator, and I was not confident I could prepare a single tape and then broadcast it to the eight or ten underwriters. So I sent an individual telex to each. I worked late into the night and can still hear the clatter of the single telex machine in our Union Court office. I believe the selling group telexes were sent from Zurich. We did not invite Hambros into the underwriting. Of course, Konsallis Osake Pankii was co-manager as well as guarantor. The issue was a success. A "blue" was issued by New York, and we were all very proud. This was a flyer on blue paper that would be circulated internally for any new issue managed by the firm, giving details of the deal and citing those involved. Eventually, when our new issue volume grew in Europe, a "green" would be issued.

Kesko Oy gave us renewed confidence and the other houses had to take notice. Warburg's had included us in an issue they led for Austria with Hambros, Rothschild and Creditanstalt, as had Banque de Bruxelles in an issue for IRI of Italy. But we still had to break into relationships long established, some going back to the 19th century. It might have been Stancliffe, or it might have been Genillard, who decided to assign me Norway. This was in the tradition of the selection of parliamentary candidates in the U.K., where a newcomer is assigned a hopeless constituency to cut his/her teeth on, where the opposing party is well entrenched, in a first electoral attempt. Norway belonged to Hambros Bank. Even children's school books mentioned Hambros as a typical foreign bank. Ship owners sent their sons to train at Hambros. The man in the street knew Hambros. Furthermore, the Kingdom's New York relationships were carved in stone – with Kuhn Loeb and Harriman Ripley. We had a relationship with Christian Brinck, the Official at the Ministry of Finance who was in charge of foreign borrowing, because of our sinking fund services. And I had an introduction from my father to Trigvie Lie, who had been the first Secretary General of the United Nations at Lake Success, and a White, Weld client. He was one of the most famous people in Norway. When I contacted him, he asked me to meet him for a drink in the lobby of the Grand Hotel at five o'clock. As we drank, we talked of this and that, of his happy memories of his time at the UN, of New York, of how much he admired DY, of what I was up to, and so on. As we talked, people passed by, and greeted him, or just waved. The whole of Oslo used to pass through the lobby of the Grand, on their way to the bar, which only opened at five. Finally, Mr. Lie got up and said, "Well that's it – you're fixed up now," and said goodbye. I had expected some further introductions, but from that moment on, everyone I met said "Oh, you know Mr Lie? We saw you with him at the Grand Hotel". I was made. In those pre-North Sea oil days, Norway's fortune lay in shipping and hydro power. It's only multi-national company was Norsk Hydro. The World Bank had financed much of the country's hydroelectric industry after the war, but further development was due to be financed by foreign borrowing. I called on Andresen's Bank, meeting first Nicolai Andresen, who introduced me to his chief international office called Hellum-Jensson. The Andresen family had owned the nation's leading Tobacco Company, manufacturing a cigarette brand called "Teddy", with a picture of Teddy Roosevelt on the packet. Hellem-Jensson's hyphenated name was unusual in Norway, and I never knew him by any other name. He expressed some bitterness about the attitude of Hambros Bank towards the Norwegian Banks, which they either ignored or treated in a patronising way. I told him I thought it odd that no Norwegian banks should be included in Hambros syndicates for Norwegian loans. Hellum-Jenssen replied that it was because of Norwegian exchange control, which did not permit the banks to hold foreign currency securities.

"But surely your underwriting position could be guaranteed by the lead manager so that you could not be left holding any bonds," I said.

"Mr Brinck would never agree," replied Hellum-Jenssen. "He does everything by the book."

"But maybe he could be persuaded that it looks odd that no Norwegian bank has any position or role in the Kingdom's borrowing on the international market – for the prestige of the country's banks."

"You are welcome to try – I'm sure Hambro's has never bothered."

"If White, Weld tries to persuade him, will you help us get a mandate?" I hazarded.

"Absolutely," said Hellum-Jenssen, "and I have just a candidate in mind."

A company named Opplandskraft had in hand a major hydroelectric project damming a valley south of Lillehammer, not yet the fashionable ski resort it was to become. Hellum-Jenssen drove me to Lillehammer, and on the way he recounted his wartime experiences in the resistance, and also how ordinary people had worn a paperclip in their button hole or on their dress on the King's birthday; The Nazi occupiers forbade any sign of sympathy or loyalty to the King, in exile in London, but they couldn't easily ban paperclips. At Opplandskraft's HQ, we were given a warm welcome and a detailed presentation of the project, with slides and graphs and many references to the importance of hydroelectric power to Norway. The project was to be a principle source of power for the City of Oslo. But there was no reference whatsoever to financing. At the end of the presentation, there was an awkward pause, and then Hellem-Jenssen began explaining who I was, of course mentioning that I was a friend of Trigvic Lie, and then launched into a totally over-the-top presentation of White, Weld, intimating that anyone who didn't know the firm was an ignorant countryman, that we had invented the international bond market, that it could not exist without us, and that, furthermore, Hambros Bank relied secretly on us to place all their bonds. I squirmed with embarrassment as Hellum-Jenssen became more and more excited, and began assigning the most extraordinary attributes to White, Weld, almost suggesting that God himself would not think of any other house, had he need of any investment banking services. Finally, he finished and there was another awkward pause. I had identified the finance director amongst those present, and I concentrated on explaining how we maintained liquidity to protect the borrower's standing so that a further trip to the market could be made on the best terms. I explained how sinking funds work and tried to sound technical, but not too technical. I then told them about our European offices, knowing full well that Hambros had only a single representative in Zurich. On the way back, I asked him how he thought it had all gone, fearing the reply. There had been some side conversations in Norwegian as we were all saying goodbye.

"Very well!" said Hellum-Jenssen, "You must prepare a sample offer."

"Do you think they have been in touch with Hambros?" I asked.

"Of course – everyone in Norway always goes first to Hambros. But they liked what you told them. They will wait for your sample offer."

He made no reference to the extraordinary pitch he had made on behalf of a firm of which he had only just met a junior representative. I can't remember what it said on my business card in those days. It might have just been "Registered Representative". I don't think I was Assistant Manager in London yet. Helleum-Jenssen always talked about "sample offers", a term I was not familiar with. But I reasoned it could not be an offer on fixed terms – we were still decades away from the "bought deal". One gave the prospective borrower an indicated coupon level and a price range, citing current market conditions and the quotations of comparable issues. Final terms were negotiated and fixed at the end of the selling period. From Hellum-Jensson's office, I called

Stancliffe and briefed him; he suggested I call Bob directly to discuss terms and conditions. Bob asked if I had seen Chrisitan Brinck at the Ministry of Finance yet. His approval to all Norwegian foreign bond issues, and to all the conditions and management arrangements was necessary – as the Ministry was the effective guarantor. Hellum-Jenssen had told me the Opplandskraft people had already been in touch with the Ministry, but I was reluctant to meet with Brinck, until we actually had the mandate. Bob thought otherwise, and reminded me I had an obligation to my new friend Hellum-Jenssen to make a plea for the inclusion of Norwegian banks in the syndicate. Christian Brinck was a gentleman of the old school. He liked to refer to his small country estate. He had been solicited by many an investment banker in his time and was on familiar terms with the Hambro family, the Wallenbergs of Sweden, John Schiff at Kuhn, Loeb, Al Gordon at Kidder Peabody, at least one senior partner of Harriman Ripley, and, inevitably, Sigmund Warburg. Brinck was a practiced name dropper, and I must have been the most junior person ever to be received by him. Naturally, he opened the conversation by saying "You are a friend of Trygvie Lie?" His manner was courtly and only very slightly condescending. Norway is one of the few kingdoms without an official nobility, as it was a vassal of Denmark until its nineteenth century independence. King Olaf was a grandson of Queen Victoria. If there had been a Norwegian nobility, I'm sure Mr. Brinck would have been a member.

I told my story and Brinck raised a quizzical eyebrow.

"Surely Hambros is dealing with the matter?"

"I think not," I replied. "Opplandskraft has indicated they are prepared to receive a proposal from us."

"Well – that's interesting. If the borrower wishes to deal away from Hambros, we will have no objection. We hold White, Weld in high regard. They have always dealt with our sinking fund purchases in a most efficient manner. You will send me a copy of your proposal, of course."

I resisted the temptation to seize Brinck by the hand and shake it vigorously. I may not be quoting him verbatim, but I certainly remember his using the phrase about "dealing away from Hambros". I had greater difficulty with the proposal to include Norwegian banks in the syndicate. I stressed the question of appearances. Surely their support and participation as local sponsors, if not investors, in an external borrowing was important. I stated it was increasingly the norm, ignoring the fact that it had certainly not been, in the case of Montagu's Kingdom of Belgium, or Warburg's Autostrade loan. But I cited the example of Kansallis Osake Pankii in Kesko Oy, and the inclusion of Creditanstalt as a co-manager in Warburg's recent Republic of Austria issue. "Ah – Creditanstalt! There is a name with a history" mused Brinck. He was thinking of its collapse in 1933 and the great depression. Finally I wrung a somewhat positive, if reluctant answer from this careful official. "If the banks are prepared to give us satisfactory assurances that they will hold no foreign currency securities and remain compliant with exchange control, and White Weld is prepared to guaranty the placement of their underwriting obligation, with foreign investors, we will give the matter positive consideration." He made it clear, indirectly, that we did not have the deal yet.

I wish I could remember the terms and conditions of the Opplandskraft issue. After some negotiation, very much assisted by Hellum-Jenssen, we were awarded the mandate, and the issue was successfully underwritten and distributed. I think my memory of the huge satisfaction I felt at my first origination, has obscured my recollection of the details of the deal. When the "blue" came out in New York, there it was at the bottom of the page: "This business was brought in by Stani Yassukovich". At the closing dinner in a private room at the Savoy, Bob Genillard made a pun – the only time I ever heard him lapse into such an Anglicism, although Bob speaks perfect English – rather better than the English, sometimes. At the Savoy, they thoughtfully supply the presiding host with a little gavel and a small wooden plaque on which to bang it. As Bob rose to speak, he picked up the gavel and said, "Ah, I see I have a Lillehammer here." We always had closing dinners in those days. Speeches were made and gifts were presented – usually silver salvers with the description of the issue engraved. It was all part of a ritual imported from Wall Street, and only slightly adapted. Even the "tombstone", reduced and encased in lucid acrylic, was distributed to all concerned, as a memento, and investment bankers displayed them on their bookcases, like campaign medals. The tombstone was pure Wall Street. It was a formal announcement, looking very much like a death notice, published in the financial press, showing the details of the issue and the underwriters below, ranked accordingly, with legal language in small print specifying that the announcement was for the record only and did not constitute an offer to sell securities. It is interesting, that although the Eurobond market operated entirely out of its jurisdiction, the ghost of the American Securities and Exchange Commission seemed to lurk in the background, as a reminder of the latent extra-territoriality of U.S. regulation which so irks Europeans. Tombstones became a not insignificant source of revenue for the financial press. Absolute accuracy with the names of the underwriters was essential, and I often had the task of reviewing the proof. For example, it was important to remember that Barings had an extra comma in their name: Baring Brothers & Co., Limited. I like to think that the expression "comma catcher" to describe a meticulous proofreader, stems from this – but it doesn't, and refers to lawyers usually. But Opplandskraft was not to be my only larcenous triumph in Norway – larcenous because I was convinced I was stealing the business from Hambros. A hydro company called Sira Kvina had begun in 1963 near Tonstadt, exploiting the Sira and Kvina waterways. Eventually some seven power plants were to be built along these. Again Hellum-Jensson of Andressens Bank introduced me. We were given an extensive tour of the project and Hellum-Jenssen eschewed his highly gilded descriptions of the virtues and skills of White, Weld, as the success of the Opplandskraft issue spoke for itself. The usual "sample offer" was made and there was hardly any question of our being awarded the deal. Christian Brinck's eyebrows rose again, and he must have thought the world as he knew was turning upside down, as two issues in a row were done away from Hambros. My Norwegian experience taught me the inestimable value of co-operating closely with local banks in soliciting business, something the London merchant banks often neglected to do. As I was to notice increasingly as my house developed a competitive stance across a range of business, London merchant banks took the position that the business always came to them. Going out and beating the bushes for business was considered rather vulgar.

Meanwhile, the Eurobond market was developing and diversifying in terms of currency and issue type. Chris O'Malley tracks the history of the Euro Deutsch Mark bond market. This is significant because it signalled that Frankfort was to pose the only significant threat to the rise of the City of London as the world's premier market for international capital transactions. The DM had been liberated from exchange control back in 1958 and foreign bond issues following the strict German structure had been floated, the first being for Anglo-American, the South African conglomerate, in that same year. But Germany announced their own, reverse, version of IET in 1964, to alleviate a burgeoning external surplus – the opposite of the U.S. problem. Foreign investors were to suffer a 25% withholding tax on interest payments made on domestic Deutsche Mark Bonds, but – all importantly, with the bonds of international issuers exempted. There had already been increasing foreign demand for the domestic issues launched by international issuers, and so, just as foreign dollar bonds, subscribed almost entirely by non U.S. investors, had become Eurodollar bonds, so the EuroDM bond market was born. These issues then took the same form in terms of issuance, underwriting and distribution as dollar denominated Eurobonds. Deutsche Bank was the leading issuing house, with Dresdner Bank, WestDeutsche Landesbank and Commerzbank as runners-up. Deutsche Bank had opened this market with an issue for Argentina, an odd choice. This was before the rating agencies invaded the Eurobond market. Argentina had a history of defaulting on its external debt. Scandinavian and Japanese borrowers were prominent EuroDM bond issuers. Deutsche Bank was to become a brooding, almost sinister, presence in the Eurobond market. It aggressively espoused the notion that the Deutsche Mark was clearly the most appropriate currency of denomination of international bonds. That this could hardly be the case for both borrower and lender did not occur to the worthy successors of the great Dr. Herman Abs. A further diversification of great importance occurred when M. Samuel brought out a convertible issue for the Japanese iconic company Cannon Camera, as early as 1963. This was to be followed by Takeda Chemical, the first issue for Van Galbtreath's Morgan & Cie in Paris. The arrival of Japanese multinationals as convertible bond issuers further eroded the monopoly of public sector borrowers, introduced the private sector to the new market, and attracted equity minded investors to supplement their fixed interest brethren in the rapidly expanding international investor market. The Japanese saw Euro-convertibles as a way of making rights issues at a premium, and familiarising new international investors with their companies. They did not suffer the neurotic pre-occupation of British institutions with the question of dilution. Fortunately for us, we had a secret weapon for our attack on the Japanese market, in no less a personage that our senior partner Ogden White, Alec's brother. Tall and elegant, combining great charm with gravitas and judgment, Ogden was very warmly received in Japan; having the name of the firm was particularly prestigious for that very hierarchically minded people. However Ogden's greatest skill was his uncanny ability to match the Japanese name to the Japanese person – faultlessly and regardless of the time lapse between sightings. We all know that the Oriental peoples think that Westerners all look alike. We must also admit that we are not very skilled at distinguishing one Japanese from another. Ogden White would spy a Japanese banker approaching down the corridor at a World Bank/IMF meeting, and cry "Hello! Watanabe-san! I have not seen you since that amusing evening in Tokyo when the Geisha told me where the Dow would be in a month's time" – or words to that effect. And Ogden would be spot on. No other Western banker I have met could pull off that trick. After some softening up visits from Ogden, it fell to me to try and line up some investment banking clients in Japan. Here there was no other option but close co-operation with the Japanese securities houses. The business was essentially in their gift. Nomura, Daiwa, Yamaichi and Nikko each had links with a different *zaibatzu*, the clan like associations linking commercial/industrial companies, commercial banks and securities houses. Each firm was very skilled in playing off one overseas investment bank seeking business, against the others. Each was equally skilled in making one think one was the favoured partner for this potential issue, or another, or perhaps a third, in case the first two fell through. Evening entertainment was the motivating force. Restaurants, bars and nightclubs in Tokyo were outrageously expensive and even the most senior and best paid executives could only frequent them on expense account. Therefore, overseas visitors were awaited with eager anticipation, and would had hardly have time to unpack before they were whisked away for an evening programme of dinner, nightclub and then a tour of various bars, each a little more louche than the last. Aida-san, head of International at Nomura, who always called me Yass'vich-san, was very well-known in these establishments and was greeted warmly by the flock of ladies in attendance. These were the soul of discretion and not even water boarding would have succeeded in prying from them information on which rival investment bankers Aida-san had been entertaining the previous evening. Contrary to popular myth, there was no hanky-panky with these ladies. They were almost excessively attentive; lighting one's cigarettes, pouring one's drinks and anticipating one's slightest and most minor needs – a sort of combination of nanny and big sister. Their conversation was at a high level and they could give you a comparative analysis of the price/earnings ratios of Japanese companies and their U.S. peer group. They were always keen to see snap shots of one's family – which I never carried, I suspect to remind their guest that he had one. I must say that these ladies were among the best turned out, best made up and most charming conversationalists, I have known –whether in kimono or western dress. But at these protracted evenings, business was discussed only in generalities. A friend at Warburg's once told me that on his first visit to Tokyo, he and his team had been subject to the usual round of entertainment and, during the evening, had proposed the terms and conditions of the issue being solicited. Their hosts had agreed enthusiastically with everything, and they returned to their hotel thinking they had a done deal. But the next day, they were told the coupon and price were both to high, the maturity to short – in fact, all the terms had to be revised.

"But you agreed with everything last night!" my friend protested.

"Ah! Last night you our guests – very rude not to agree with guests."

I was told this useful story before my first trip to Japan.

New York had engaged a good-looking and well-educated Canadian called Douglas MacMillan, who was sent to us in London and immediately assigned as my sidekick for our Japanese campaign. He was to become a neighbour in Gloucestershire, a polo teammate, hunting companion and great family friend. Douglas – or Dooglas, as his French wife was later to call him – was very popular with the Japanese – his deportment and courtesy being above the standard they expected from the "straight eyes", as we Westerners are called. Tokyo restaurants are in two categories – those for the comfort of foreigners, having a well where one can dangle one's legs under the table, and the genuine kind with no well, forcing one to sit cross-legged throughout the multi-course meal. There must be an anatomical difference in leg/hip construction between the Japanese and the rest of us. I found the cross-legged position agonising and one rose from dinner, supported by the geisha who had ministered during the meal, almost unable to walk for a few minutes as the legs returned to normal. Visits to the prospective issuer were highly formalistic and never varied. The seating arrangement was identical in every office in the land. A sofa, two armchairs facing and an armchair at each end; the guests were on the sofa, senior guest at the right, senior host on right hand armchair, accompanying Japanese investment banker on his right facing the sofa, less senior host next to him. A silent note taker sat at the end opposite the senior host. As one made one's pitch, the senior host closed his eyes. An occasional nod, and even a grunt, indicated he had not fallen asleep. He considered he was extending a courtesy by closing his eyes to better appreciate one's weighty words. Although he listened in English, he replied in Japanese and the junior host translated. It was all choreographed like a classic ballet which never varies. In fact the negotiation took place behind the scenes between the sponsoring Japanese securities house and the issuer, and the foreign investment banker was presented with a quasi *faite accompli.* We managed to join the rush of Japanese convertibles, managing issues for Olympus Optical, and then for Sumitomo Chemical. After the first we all got Olympus cameras as presents; after the second, we formed a relationship with Sumitomo Bank which was to lead to a joint venture investment bank in London – Sumitomo White Weld. Douglas MacMillan was appointed joint managing director.

On one visit to Tokyo, a partner back in New York made a suggestion to Douglas and me, displaying a weak geographic sense.

"Since you're out there – why don't you drop in to Australia and see what's cooking on the new business front?" was his clever idea.

"He must be joking!" said Douglas, reading the cable. "How are we supposed to get there?"

As strange as it seems today, there were no direct commercial flights from Japan to any Australian city at that time. We managed to get seats on a cargo flight which had seating for about five passengers and island hopped its way to Sidney. It might have been quicker to fly back to London and then to Sidney. Fortunately my friend Ellsworth Donnell at Bankers Trust had given me an introduction to a lady in Sidney, should I ever venture that far. Ellsworth's wife Susan wrote a best seller about Pocahontas, an ancestor of hers, and is now married to Sir Eldon Griffiths, a former MP. After a hair- raising journey of some 18 hours we arrived in Sydney, and I telephoned the lady who imme-diately invited us to lunch at the rotating restaurant atop the newly built tele-phone tower. Below us was a forest of cranes as Sydney was undergoing a construction boom. Half the cranes were red and half were blue.

"See those blue cranes?" asked our hostess, as we gobbled our oysters "They're my husband's." She then invited us to Sunday lunch at her weekend cottage at Palm Beach on the coast north of Sydney. Over our delicious shrimps, we watched a regatta in progress. The boats were all on a final downwind leg.

"See that blue spinnaker?" said the lady. We guessed.

"Yes, that's my husband's yawl." We never met the husband. I never had much luck in Australia. Sometime later, Emory Katzenbach, then managing partner in New York, told us in London that the firm had an important advis-ory assignment from Continental Illinois Bank in Chicago – probably brought in by Brick Meers, the hugely productive Chicago resident partner. Al Miosi, head of International at Continental Illinois wanted White, Weld's advice on whether, and importantly, where, the bank should open a branch or subsidiary in Australia, which was enjoying one of its regular mining booms. Foreign banks were swarming in like flies in the autumn. We were told the Bank had a preliminary preference for Perth. We had a new colleague in London called Ashley Down, whose father had been chairman of the Brisbane Stock Ex-change. Naturally, it was decided Ashley and I should rush Down Under, re-search the question and write a report. I first went to see Jim Wolfensohn, then at Schroeders, who I reckoned was the senior Australian in the City; "Grossly overbanked" was his succinct opinion about the financial sector in his native country. Then I went to see Kit McMahon, another distinguished Australian, at the Bank of England. "Grossly overbanked" was his comment. I wondered whether we couldn't write the report without leaving the office.

But it was not to be. We set out on a hectic 48-hour visit – flying out via Abu Dhabi and back via Hawaii, San Francisco and New York, where we stopped to write our report. As we travelled, Ashley gave me his low-down on Australia's social structure. It seemed there were three categories, or classes – but that was not an appropriate nomenclature in egalitarian Australia. The first consisted of families with "rusty ankles" i.e. descendants of transported prisoners. Then there were the descendants of prison guards and finally those who arrived after the country was no longer a prison colony. Of course the "rusty ankled" were the aristocracy; the prison guard descendant the lowest of the low, and the recent arrivals – well, some OK, some not. We stayed two days at head office to write our report which concluded 1) Australia was grossly overbanked and Continental Illinois would be too late to build any reasonable franchise and 2) if the bank insisted on opening there, Perth was the least favourable location as, although the mining engineers might be clustered there, the finance directors were all in Sydney. Miosi was furious and threatened to withhold our fee. What should have been clear from the outset became even clearer. Management had decided to open in Australia and wanted an independent opinion to support its recommendation to the board. It was my first lesson in advisory assignments. Management uses investment bankers to validate decisions it has already taken, and to bamboozle ignorant nonexecutive directors into nodding through its often disastrous strategic proposals. I had a more pleasant time on a subsequent visit to Australia. Through Bob Genillard's relationship with Allusuiusse, we were mandated to advice on financing the Gove Bay alumina project. The local manager in Melbourne, from the Ticino, had toured the many vineyards owned by Italian immigrants, and gave us a dinner in which some dozen, rare and nonexported wines were served. We flew over the project area – but I remember the wines.

As White, Weld Europe began to take its rightful place in the new and rapidly expanding Eurobond market, our London office began to take on both importance and people. In fact, I believe the firm's legacy is the quality of its team building and White, Weld's Old Boys have gone on to great things. Oliver Fox-Pitt joined us early on, having worked in Canada, a training ground for other City luminaries, such as Peter Stormont-Darling of Warburgs. Oliver worked our institutional client base and went on to found his own firm, Fox-Pitt, Kelton, specialising in the banking and insurance sector. Oliver's wife Marietta came from a very horsey family; her father had been a celebrated amateur jockey before the war. We were staying at her mother's great house in Kent when a Pony Club ball was being held. It was so cold that Dinnie decided to crawl under the overcoats, all piled up on the bed in a ground floor room. Towards the end of the evening, she had disappeared and was found fast asleep only when the departing guests began to take their overcoats. Their son William has become an Olympic Gold medal winner at three day eventing, and Marietta has been a prominent figure in the equestrian world for many years. Steven Rose wrote a letter to John Stancliffe asking for a job which I still remember, as in it he cited his main attributes as having "a clean collar and desire to work hard". After a great career in our London office, Steven joined Paine Webber, after the Merrill Lynch takeover of White, Weld in New York, but eventually set up his own firm specializing in Brazil. I have already mentioned Jeric Strathallan, now Earl of Perth. When Philip Sears came to us through one of the University Appointment Boards, I wrote the letter offering him a position. Our practice was to have the letter typed with a blank space for the starting salary which the writer would fill in by hand. I inadvertently added an extra zero. Philip wrote back a very appreciative letter of acceptance, but had the good grace to mention that he assumed I had erred in writing the figure, and so he accepted the starting salary – minus the extra zero. Phillip eventually was sent to Japan as our permanent representative. After White Weld he was a prime mover in Phoenix Securities, a boutique founded by John Craven which arranged many of the City marriages after Big Bang – and also advised on the many subsequent divorces. John Craven, now Sir John, had been one of Sigmund Warburg's brightest young hopefuls, and as was his habit with the most talented of his employees, Sigmund worked him ruthlessly – presumably to see how much pressure he could stand. John was a Canadian who had grown up and gone to school in South Africa. John telephoned me one day and said he had taken all he could stand, the final straw being the destruction of his marriage. As John described it, returning unexpectedly from one of his frequent business development trips to Canada, he had found "two heads on the pillow" in the master bedroom. I'm sure John meant the experience of being cuckolded to be illustrative of the pressures he had been put under, and his malaise at Warburg's was of a general nature. In any case, he asked me might there be room for him at White, Weld? Of course we jumped at the chance, although Bob Genillard expressed some understandable concern about the possible impact on our very important relationship with Warburg's. We assigned John the Far East; He became one of our most successful originators; a major factor in the development of the franchise of our successor firm Credit Suisse White Weld, and then Credit Suisse First Boston; founder of Phoenix Securities; Chairman of Morgan Grenfell and member of their parent Deutsche Bank's Vorstandt; Chairman of Lonmin, the spun out mining division of Lonrho, and, finally, a Knight Batchelor of the Realm. We have stayed great friends and worked together over the years on this and that.

I don't suppose we can claim credit in Europe for recruiting David Mulford, as I think he was found by New York. But we gave him his springboard. David was a Midwesterner who had won a White House Fellowship, an innovation of the Kennedy administration. Fellows were assigned to various departments of government, sat in on high level meetings and gained privileged exposure to the workings of state. Perhaps David first caught a dose of "Potomac Fever" at this time. David had spent time in Africa and written a book, *The Politics of Independence* about Northern Rhodesia's relatively peaceful but complex march to full freedom as Zambia, under Kenneth Kaunda. Someone in New York had the bright idea that we could use him in Europe and so he arrived in London, keen as mustard and a rapid learner of all our business. David was soon to find himself in the right place at the right time. When circumstances forced major U.S. corporates on to the Eurobond market to finance their overseas development, we sent David back to New York to solicit mandates. He was hugely successful but encountered some in house opposition. The Street was still very relationship minded and poaching of clients was considered "not done". George Montgomery, from a famous San Francisco banking family, was now a partner of White, Weld and had married Alec White's daughter Eleanor. He expressed concerns when David began soliciting the clients of other houses. Of course, David would do so – White, Weld was one of the few in the Street that had the European record, skills and distribution power to float Euro issues for U.S. corporates. And David was skilled in presenting our credentials. In retrospect, the raised eyebrows of the New York partners over his success, was an early sign of the unease that was developing in New York over the success of Genillard and his European partners. But another big break for David was to come. After the big oil price rise in the early '70's, everyone turned their attention to the massive liquidity accumulating in the oil exporting countries. Word got around that the Saudi Arabian Monetary Authority was going to award advisory mandates to help them invest their newfound wealth. A private client salesman in our Park Avenue office mentioned casually that his father was a good friend of the King of Saudi Arabia;

"Your old man knows the king?!" asked one of his bosses.

"Sure, he's the senior eye surgeon at the Lenox Hill. He's operated twice on the King. They keep in touch."

"Good grief – and you're Jewish!"

"Eyes don't have a religion."

"Can your father talk to the King and ask how we can present for an assignment?"

"No problem."

And so it was that White, Weld, together with Baring Brothers in London, were given advisory contracts by SAMA. We sent out David Mulford, and Barings sent out Leonard Ingrahams, with his violin. Leonard formed a string quartet in Jeddah, and David's wife set up an interior decorating business. When SAMA moved to Rhiad, Leonard could take his string quartet, but poor Mrs. Mulford had of course been required to have a Saudi "front man" for her business, as ladies were not permitted such activity. She also had a driver. When she went to move her business, her front man said, "Sorry – it's actually my business and I'm not moving to Rhiad." Life in Jeddah had its moments of tension. One day David discovered that their kitchen boy was running an illicit booze business from the back door. While David was at SAMA, the whole world passed through his office, particularly all the bankers, from David Rockefeller on down. Our David was soon back in Washington, "Potomac Fever", being a recurring condition – like malaria. He was made Undersecretary of the Treasury under Nick Brady. If there were perfect justice in this world "Brady Bonds" would be called "Mulford Bonds", as that innovative plan to deal with sovereign defaults in the late '80s, had David's fingerprints all over it. David flitted back and forth between CSFB and the public sector and became U.S. Ambassador to India under the second President Bush. An unsung accomplishment of that Administration was a major nuclear energy treaty with India. Another great White Weld recruit was David Reid-Scott, who succeeded Mulford as our man with SAMA. David became a star at CSWW, and then CSFB, before going "boutiqueing", a popular career move when the City became the preserve of boring conglomerates.

Even short biographical sketches of the roll call of White, Weld recruits would fill a book. There was John Bult, and early recruit of DY's, a supreme private banker. Ellie Saouf, a Lebanese of charm and professional skill, graced the Paris operation. We "cornered" the writing implements market, employing at one stage Bruno Bich, son of Baron Bich, the ball point king, and Count Anton-Wolfgang von Faber-Castell, who now runs the family business, which has diversified into children's toys. When Baron Bich competed for the America's Cup, we had to release Bruno for duty at Newport. As White Weld was very much a sailing firm, this posed no problem. I think we gained an early reputation for collecting talented people of varied backgrounds. One day I had a call from Johnny Loudon, then at Rothschild. "I've got a young Brazilian here who might interest you. We have no place for him here, but he speaks every main European language and he owns a dinner jacket – just right for White, Weld." Of course I saw him and we hired him. It turned out he had been a child film actor and had featured prominently in David Lean's *Lawrence of Arabia.* He was Michel de Carvalhjo, and he continued with great success through to CSWW and CSFB. He married Freddy Heineken's daughter. Another great and lamented colleague was Dick Bristow who was at Hill, Samuel when we got a call to co-manage a ground breaking sterling convertible for Beecham, of which Kenneth Keith, architect of the merger of his West End house Phillip Hill with M.Samuel, was Chairman. The pound sterling was not a much used currency for Eurobond issues, to say the least, being a semi-permanent resident of a currency hospital. But a convertible was an equity play and the currency risk was effectively hedged, as equity markets rise when the currency falls. One year, back in the '80s, the best performing stock market was Mexico, as the peso had gone down the drain. It was a complicated issue, and long sessions, lasting into the wee hours, were held at Hill Samuel. A lawyer from Simmons & Simmons worked with a bottle of whiskey in front of him. But it was a success, although there were no imitators. After the cheering and the shouting was over, I had a call from Dick who said he had "itchy feet" at Hill Samuel, and might we be interested? Of course, we were, and he joined us forthwith. Dick was a superb technician, and a keen defender of the purity of a properly drafted negative pledge clause. Such a clause constituted the main security of a typical Euro-bond. With it, the issuer undertook to contract no borrowing having seniority over the present bond, in liquidation. Whenever a new issue was under discussion, Dick's attention would focus on the negative pledge clause. Did the borrower accept one unreservedly? Might its lawyers try to weaken it, by for instance allowing a bond holder's meeting to abandon it? He might have been known in the market as Dick "Negative Pledge Clause" Bristow, but for all sorts of reasons, he was held in great esteem by his colleagues, and the clients, who soon came to see that his rather severe manner in negotiations was ultimately to their benefit – like the doctor who proscribes a tough regime. Dick stayed on, through CSWW and then CSFB.

I suppose the minnow we netted which was to become the biggest fish of all, was Michael von Clemm, whose father and uncle, the "Clemm Twins", as they were known in the '20s in New York, had been friends of DY. His father had married a lady from Philadelphia, whose father ran the international subsidiary of First National Bank in the '30s. Michael grew up in Oyster Bay on Long Island, near my home in Locust Valley, and attended Friend's Academy, a rival of Green Vale. I played in a football match for Green Vale against Friend's Academy, and distinguished myself in the half back position by running the ball most of the length of the pitch – but in the wrong direction. In 1941, Michael suffered a traumatic experience when the FBI arrived to arrest and incarcerate his father, who was managing director of a German owned firm manufacturing artificial precious stones for industry. All resident German nationals were so dealt with after Pearl Harbour, when America found itself at war. But it was a blow for a six-year-old boy who thought of himself as entirely American. Michael went on to Exeter and then to Harvard where, joining the Porcellian Club with me, we became increasingly close friends. Despite our similar backgrounds and shared attitudes and interests, we had entirely different scholastic careers. Mine was completely hopeless, and his was brilliant. He took his degree in anthropology in three years and then went on to take a Doctorate at Corpus Christie, Oxford. Michael's was a rare example of a very early marriage, not very common in our circles. The bride was Lisa Hunnewell, a Radcliffe classmate, in the sense that Radcliffe girls shared our Harvard curriculum and so were almost merged. Hers was a prominent Boston family, founders of the town of Wellesley, where they owned a large estate, abutting the famous girl's college. It was a fashionable wedding; the ushers were mostly Porcellian, of course, and Michael insisted we wear spats with our striped trousers and morning coats. We spent some time scouring Boston before finding them. A prominent Episcopalian Bishop was to preside. When he asked Mrs Hunnewell when Lisa had been christened, that charming but somewhat vague lady could not exactly recall, and so the Bishop insisted on a fresh christening, just before the wedding. I stood as Godfather, an odd choice as I was the only Roman Catholic amongst the ushers – but an honour I have always cherished. Whilst taking his D Phil. at Oxford, Michael met the

young chief of the Chaga tribe, who grow coffee at the foot of Mt. Kilamanjaro – with great success, as he was driving a Rolls-Royce. He suggested Michael spend time with the tribe and write his thesis, based on his observations.
So Michael and Lisa set out for Tanganyka, as it was then, accompanied by
David Verney, an Oxford friend. When David's passport was being examined
at Dar Es Salam, the immigration official looked up and said, "How can one
so young be so honourable?" As the son of Lord Willoughby de Broke, David, was of course "The Hon." Michael von Clemm's degrees suggested an
academic career but he joined what was close to being a family firm – First
National City Bank, his grandfather Green having run what was called,
grandly, the International Banking Corporation, a subsidiary of what was then
the First National Bank of New York. He was ultimately sent to the London
Branch in Moorgate, whose senior officer was Bob Breyfogle, who had been
there as long as anyone could remember. We renewed our warm friendship.
The two eldest daughters of each family, our Tatyana, and their Stephanie,
were born within weeks of each other and have been fast friends ever since.
As babies, we took them at weekends to Michael's Aunt Claire in Childrey, in
the Old Berks country. One day she threw her Coutts bank statement to me as
we were sitting in front of the fire, and asked for my opinion on the attached
statement from a broker on her investments. It was my first exposure to what
I considered an extraordinary practice of the clearing and private banks to appoint Stock Exchange members, by rotation, to review their clients' investments.

"Have you ever met these brokers?" I asked, perusing a list of incongru-
ous holdings in various equities.

"Certainly not!" replied Aunt Claire, clearly shocked at the notion.

"How do they know what your investment objectives are?"

"They are obvious – I just want to make money."

"What's this funny company?" I asked, citing an unfamiliar name.

"Oh, that's a very good share. They own the longest bar in Singapore."

I wondered if this was a typical example of the investment habits of the
English gentry.

Michael's career at FNCB was brief, but marked by an innovation we
cooked up together. We noticed, in our endless chats about the emerging Euromarkets, that a missing element was a money market instrument allowing
holders of short term liquidity an alternative to simple bank deposits. In the
U.S. there were negotiable certificates of deposit, in addition, of course, to
Treasury Notes and commercial paper. Why not a Eurodollar negotiable certificate of deposit? FNCB had pioneered negotiable CDs in the U.S. and Michael thought his employers would jump at the chance to claim another first
in Europe. The obstacles were formidable. As David Kynaston points out,
there had not been issued a negotiable instrument of this type, construed under English law, since 1896. And it had to be under English law to distinguish
the instrument from the domestic U.S. dollar market, and place it firmly with-

in the Euromarkets. There was also the problem of whether an obligation of a London branch would bind the head office in all circumstances. A famous case involved deposits at First National Bank in Petrograd. When Russian émigrés tried to claim their funds in New York, the Bolsheviks having sequestered all foreign banks after the October revolution, there had been hesitation and concern, leading to a change in New York State banking law. Henceforth, head office would not honour branch depositors' claims if the branch in question had been closed due to *force majeur*. We reckoned the risk of HM Government nationalising FNCB in London was negligible. FNCB' s London solicitors Coward Chance tackled the problems with vigour. But Michael had to persuade FNCB, which turned out to be challenging. In London, Breyfogle dithered, and New York was indecisive. It was a further example of parental jealousy of their children's success, a phenomenon I was already beginning to sniff at White, Weld. Von Clemm took to waylaying senior officers from New York in the corridors of Claridge's Hotel. It was a revelation to watch Michael pursuing a business objective. He was an unstoppable force. All I had to do was to persuade my firm to be the first market maker, as the negotiable feature was hardly of value if there was no market. All that took was a word with John Stancliffe and a brief call to Bob Genillard in Zurich. Both were enthusiastic. After a good deal of mid night oil had been burned, the first issue took place in May, 1966. I have the date not from memory, but from David Kynaston – and the fact that FNCB's London dollar CD Number 0003, for $1.00, is framed on my wall. 0001 went to Breyfogle and 0002 to Michael. At a press conference at the Great Eastern Hotel, Bob Genillard was asked what sort of volume of London dollar CDs he might expect to see in the coming years. Bob, swallowing hard, ventured "A few hundred million?" It was soon in the billions. At first, these bearer certificates were traipsed around the City by messenger, until First Chicago had the sound idea of establishing a clearing centre at their London Branch. When a new branch manager arrived from Chicago, he was shocked to find the CDs in the vault were uninsured for face value, and he asked the Bank of England to take them into custody. First Chicago's London advisor Christopher Morgan had to engage armed guards and hire a bomb proof van to transfer them. At White, Weld, we found and hired a young man named David Potter out of the discount market to head the trading, and he became one of our stars, continuing on through to CSFB, eventually running Samuel Montagu for Midland Bank, and subsequently Guinness Mahon. One day, Mike Allsop, senior partner at the discount house Allen, Harvey & Ross came to see me and asked if we wouldn't welcome a "modest bill broker" to join us in the secondary market. I was delighted. They were soon followed by Cater, Allen. They made a smart move, as £ sterling CDs were soon introduced, a perfect market for the discount houses, whose traditional role in the domestic money market was soon to end. Foreign banks crowded the CD issue market, and we introduced the first Japanese bank: our good friends Sumitomo Bank. A further flurry of issuers followed, and –although I don't remember this – David Kynaston reports that

the Industrial Bank of Japan went to Rothschild for their issue when they discovered they were fifth in the queue for White, Weld's services.

Michael von Clemm began to weary of FNCB's rather ponderous and
beurocratic style, and he accepted an associate professorship at the Harvard
Business School to lecture in a new course in international finance. Michael
was a natural academic and lecturer, and even as an undergraduate, he had
been nicknamed "Professor". The proximity of Lisa's family home in Wellesley, and of a very familiar watering hole at 1324 Massachusetts Avenue, were
added inducements. But the experience had an unhappy ending. Amongst his
students was an African American gentleman who was clearly insufficiently
motivated, as his attendance at lectures was irregular and his case work
sloppy. Associate Professor von Clemm summoned him to his office;
    "I must warn you that, unless you shape up, you're going to have a prob-
lem passing the exam."
    "I won't have any problem," countered the student.
    "So, does that mean you are going to get cracking and catch up? Nothing
would please me more."
    "It means I won't have a problem because you're going to pass me."
    "I won't pass you unless your work improves."
    "Yes, you will – because I know where your family lives."
Von Clemm reported the incident and handed in his resignation. I doubt
the matter was even investigated. The University was rapidly moving towards
prioritizing diversity over academic potential in its admission policy. Michael
was now at loose ends and I suggested he join White, Weld, but he was hesitant. He told me he had not fully decided to enter the financial services industry. I think he still hankered after academia, and he had his D.Phil. in social anthropology, with a published thesis on the coffee growing Chaga tribe
of Kilamanjaro. I sought ways to tempt him and suggested he join as a consultant, with a fixed term if he insisted, to work on the project of launching
Eurodollar commercial paper – an idea that had come into my head whilst I
was talking to him. The excitement of the Eurodollar CD was still fresh, and
he agreed. I don't think Lisa was loath to move back to London either. My
goddaughter, now sadly widowed, loves London, whilst remaining charm-
ingly Bostonian. She reminds me of a character from a Henry James novel.
And so, we bagged our greatest recruit. As it happens, Schroeder's had
already had a similar inspiration and we discovered they were hard at work.
We were in a race against time to be first out of the stalls. I can't remember
who won the race but I suspect it was Schroeder's, as I would have remembered if it was us. But with the emergence of CDs and commercial paper,
supplemented later by medium-term notes, and, ultimately, Euroequities, the
Euromarkets classified as a full fledge money and capital market – with all
the trimmings and the diversity of participants – all in less than two decades.
It meant the City of London was now the undisputed centre, and as globalisa-

tion of all economic activity immersed the planet, the City's time zone advantage gave it close to world domination in financial services.

Michael von Clemm liked what he saw of the new emerging markets and their competitive challenges; and he liked what he saw of White, Weld – so he decided to take permanent employment. Bob Genillard had a frisson of doubt in view of Michael's sometimes overwhelming personality, but he had witnessed Michael at work on the CD project, and was convinced of his potential contribution. Soon after, I was sitting in my new office in the P & O building, where we had moved after a brief interlude at Winchester House near Morgan Grenfell. The arrival of Koller & Co. from Zurich had expanded our space requirements considerably. A CV crossed my desk, I'm not sure how, but we were starting to attract job applicants as our star rose in the Euro- firmament. The first thing I noticed was that Michael Dobbs-Higginson was born in Southern Rhodesia. "He's got the job," I said to myself, displaying an outrageous prejudice in favour of my wife's compatriots. But the CV went on to show that Dobbs-Higginson had studied as an apprentice monk in the famous Buddhist monastery at Nara in Japan, and therefore was fluent in Japanese. Following this extraordinary experience, he had worked as a Mercedes motorcar salesman in Tokyo. This was for me a sales assignment akin in terms of challenge to selling Wisconsin-made brie cheese in Paris. I scribbled "we must hire this man" at the top of the page and sent it next door to Michael von Clemm. Michael Dobbs-Higginson was to have a brilliant career at White, Weld, then at CSWW and at CSFB. He and von Clemm were a double act of great originating power. Their imaginative exuberance, working the IMF/World Bank meetings, was to strike terror in the hearts of the competition, particularly when I was no longer there to exercise some dignified restraint. The Pacific region became his patch, and we were all three reunited at Merrill Lynch, when I became Chairman Europe, Middle East & Africa based in London, Dobbs Higginson was Chairman Asia Pacific based in Hong Kong, and von Clemm was roving Chairman of something or other based in New York. By then we had matured, and probably grown a bit dull.

A great aim for a Eurobond issuing house was to develop a relationship with a multiple issuer – that is to say a borrower who made repeated trips to the market. We were fortunate twice: with Ente Nazionale Idrocarburi ENI, the Italian state oil company and with Hydro Quebec of Montreal, Canada's biggest hydroelectric power company. I struggled, propped on an elbow in bed, taking corrections in the ENI draft prospectus from Ed Tuck at Shearman & Sterling who would call me late at night from Rome. I struggled further to get the printers in the City to place ENI's logo, the seven legged dragon, in the right size on the cover. We did several successful issues. ENI was very much a relationship developed by Bob Genillard, who was entirely fluent in Italian, his family having owned a hotel in Italy. Our other serial borrower was a relationship brought by Miles Price, a member of the Price Brothers forestry product empire in Quebec. Miles was a brilliant salesman who was eventually made manager of White, Weld's Montreal branch. His appointment and subsequent career proved the old adage that the tendency to make the best salesman the office manager produces the loss of a good salesman and the gain of a bad manager. We had already done a Eurobond issue for the City Of Montreal, and when the Mayor came to London for the signing he went about promoting the forthcoming Olympic Games, which, of course, eventually brought the City to near bankruptcy. Miles certainly introduced Hydro Quebec the company in charge of the James Bay project, Canada's biggest hydro development, which today provides power to the entire northeast corner of the United States. Ed Lemieux was the finance director and the project was largely financed in the Eurobond market. The issue pattern in those days involved the final pricing negotiation taking place when the subscription period had ended. The size of the "book" was usually kept secret from the issuer. We would stress that it was the quality rather than the quantity of subscriptions which counted and referred to the "water in the book" when an issue was heavily oversubscribed. These were amounts being indicated by underwriting and selling group members, over and above what they had received in actual investor subscriptions, designed to pump up their eventual allocation, or just make a quick turn when the issue went to a premium in the after-market. The pricing meeting was a bit of a duel between the lead manager anxious to secure generous pricing and the issuer seeking to squeeze the terms in his favour. I was often leading against Ed Lemieux and would strike off with a cautious review of market conditions, pointing out the risks or overpricing. Once I was about to start my spiel when Ed, with an elaborate gesture, took out a handkerchief and placed it in front of him.

"What's the trouble, Ed, have you got a cold?" I enquired.

"No – I'm just getting ready to cry."

Ed Lemieux was a ruthless negotiator. It wasn't always easy to justify realistic pricing when an issue was known to be greatly oversubscribed, and Ed had extensive contacts amongst the underwriters and would always know. I think I shared with him the old story about an obscure Balkan kingdom which had floated an international bond in the good old days. The lead manager sent a cable saying "Congratulations – your issue twice oversubscribed". The Minister of Finance replied promptly "Thank you – you may allot in full". Students of financial history, which I claim to be, will appreciate that all of the drama and excitement we felt as the Eurobond market galloped to full maturity was based on a somewhat false impression that we were inventing something. Most technical and relationship aspects of the market had existed before, particularly in the 19th century. Perhaps a difference was the presence of so-called loan contractors active in those days. My father would refer to the few remaining independent, free-lance intermediaries who sought to bring transactions to investment banks as "five percenters", the presumption being that such was their fee for introducing business. A famous loan contractor active in the City in Victorian times had shopped around a deal for a small Latin

American republic. He managed to get a contract signed with a merchant bank who agreed to handle the issue, when someone bothered to look up the name of the country in an almanac, and found it was nonexistent. But regardless of whether our pride as innovators was justified or not, we at White Weld were firing on all cylinders in the "swinging sixties". Once installed in the P & O Building, largely occupied by the headquarters of the great shipping firm, we had one or two bomb scares as the IRA persisted in mistaking us for the Post Office. The building was badly built and suffered numerous breakdowns. I remarked in the lift one day "If this building were a ship, it would sink", in the hearing of the P & O chairman, whose office complained to John Stancliffe of my discourtesy.

"Rhodies", or "Zimbos" as former colonials from that now tragic country like to call themselves, have figured in my life in a major way. Of course, my wife Dinnie more than heads the list. But one of her compatriots was responsible for getting the *Financial Times* to finally take some notice of the Eurobond market. Tony Hawkins, now a Professor Emeritus of Economics at the University of Zimbabwe, had been a stringer for the "Pink 'Un", and took a one-year sabbatical in London. Wandering into the FT office, he asked if there were any odd jobs he could do whilst in London. "Well there's a strange new animal called a 'Eurobond' knocking about – probably a flash in the pan, but, still, you might look into it to see if it merits a piece."

"Anyone I should see?" asked Hawkins.

"There's Sigmund Warburg, if he'll receive you. Julius Strauss at Strauss Turnbull and Stani Yassukovich at White, Weld."

When I realised I had a "Rhodie" in my office, I gave him most of the morning. He knew my brother-in-law, Mick Townsend. After a long explanation, tour of the dealing room, etc. Hawkins was convinced his was hearing about a significant City development, having no doubt heard the same from Julius Strauss – I don't know if he saw Sigmund. He went back and told the FT that they should start covering this market. Finally, the FT began printing a short list of Eurobond prices, with a small legend at the bottom saying: "quotes provided by White, Weld & Co.". This caused a problem for our auditor Brandon Gough at Coopers & Lybrand, who took exception to the fact that he was having to rely on our own published prices to validate asset values in our year-end accounts. Normal practice was to rely on Stock Exchange prices for all securities. It took a long time for people to understand the Eurobond secondary market. Another Rhodie I knew well was Andrew Tuckey at Barings. His parents had been friends of my in-laws in Rhodesia and his father had played polo with my father-in-law. Dinnie remembers sitting on the side of the field with Andrew, and watching the cloud of dust move up and down the pitch, with the occasional, brief emergence of a player, which was polo in Rhodesia. When the EBIC shareholders of European Banking Company asked me to sell the bank, I gave the mandate to Andrew. Later he was forced to fall on his sword when the rogue trader Nick Leeson bankrupted

Barings, as he had been head of international, and so the buck stopped with him. I knew Rupert Pennant-Rea when he was editor of *The Economist*, and was as surprised as anyone when a Chancellor of the Exchequer appointed him Deputy Governor of the Bank of England. Despite his no doubt conservative upbringing in Southern Rhodesia, he hit the headlines, having been caught in *flagrente dilecto* with his PA, on the carpet in the Governor's office. He later came to see me to ask if I could recommend him for any nonexecutive board positions that might be going. At the time, I had a rather large portfolio of these, and I think he thought I might have one or two to spare. He had no trouble being appointed head of the Post Office, pre-privatisation, and also became Chairman of Henderson Administration, where I had been a board member for some years. At one point, I was the only man in the City with both a Rhodesian wife and a Rhodesian PA. Her father was Laurence Waugh, the leading stockbroker in Salisbury. One day, a friend rang me and said that a protégé of Harley Drayton, called "Tiny" Rowland was coming to London and looking for connections with both British and international banking houses. Might I be interested in meeting him? I didn't bother to ask why Harley Drayton, a prominent financier and fund manager, was not talking him around the City, as it suddenly occurred to me I could do a good turn to my PA. In those days trunk telephone calls to Salisbury were not cheap, and she couldn't afford to talk to her father very often. I told her to put through a call to her father, have a nice family chat and then pass him to me. Rowland had made a fortune in Rhodesia with the sole Mercedes Benz dealership, mining and tobacco farming. Waugh would know all about him. When he came on the line, I asked him. "He's a crook", was his immediate and brief response. I thanked him, asked him to pass a greeting to my in laws, and rang off. That was that. It is extraordinary that a small country like Zimbabwe has produced so many celebrated personalities, when the European population was never more than 250,000 at its height and the overall population five million, at a guess. Two world-class golfers Nick Price, and Mick McNulty, a winning Davis Cup team, and before it was politicised, a cricket side that more than held its own. Once, when England was playing a Test match in Harare, before going on to a Test in South Africa, they started with a warm up match against a regional eleven. I brought an *Evening Standard* back to Dinnie to show her the back page where a headline screamed: "England beaten by – wait for it – Mashonaland". The winning team of amateurs was without its best spin bowler, who was loading ostriches at his farm, and couldn't play that day.

CHAPTER XV

"The Yanks are coming, the Yanks are coming"

-Refrain from the World War I hit song "Over There"-

For fans of my heroine the Eurobond, the 1960s might be called "the roaring '60s". The first half of the decade produced extraordinary events and subsequent innovations; the second half has not quite as dramatic a history, but nevertheless significant developments occurred. Some of these carried over into the early '70s, as the market broadened and matured. But as volumes soared, new wrinkles were less noticeable and by the 1980s, activity was becoming so established and mundane, that financial journalists struggled for sensational copy. In the '90s, the market became automated, de personalised and, frankly, boring. Although the City was now fully established as the unchallenged centre of international money and capital market activity, the fading of the indigenous houses was a sad and noticeable trend. That other Wall Street tradition, the league table ranking lead managers of syndicated issues, had been imported by the Euromarkets, and in 1968, the top three were Deutsche Bank, White, Weld and Warburg's. The only other British merchant bank in the top ten was Rothschild. Hambros was nowhere. Together with Schroeder's, they had been one of the pioneers of the Eurodollar deposit market. Hill Samuel, the leading domestic issuing house was not present. The big three Swiss Banks were not yet active as lead managers, and Deutsche Bank's leading position was due to a flurry of Euro-DM issues which it dominated. The other active lead managers were mainly Wall Street houses. We were seeing the beginning of the "Americanization" of the City. The more aware domestic community was alarmed. As David Kynaston reports, Rowe & Pittman had tried to get the Stock Exchange to allow Eurobond trading, on a discretionary basis, in 1965. They identified the two obstacles to the Stock Exchange members' participation in this exciting new market. One was the requirement that 15% of a new issue be allocated to the market through the jobbers, who hadn't a clue what to do with the bonds, and the other was minimum commission requirements which were uncompetitive with the secondary market's spreads. The Stock Exchange Council set up a committee under the chairmanship of our friend George Loveday to hear evidence from members.

All the submissions mentioned White, Weld. Julian Martin-Smith and Jamie Ogilvie of Rowe & Pittman said that if their suggestion was accepted they could "hope to compete with White, Weld & Co., if permitted to charge ¼ % or less…" Jock Hunter of Messels said "at present the Stock Exchange could not compete with outside Houses, especially White, Weld & Co." Edgar Astaire of his eponymous firm "felt steps should be taken which would allow the London Broker to become more competitive with the outside Houses such as White, Weld & Co. Alfred Caplin of jobbers R. Layton & Co. wrote "White, Weld & Co. had extensive connections overseas and bid on a net basis. Thus it was quite impossible for jobbers to compete unless they were prepared to make a book", I don't think I could find a greater testimonial to the position my firm had achieved in a few short years, than these comments, independently made by leading City houses. Sadly, I don't think my father ever knew of this extraordinary tribute. White, Weld's presence in London had been largely his creation. The Council agreed to reduce commissions for this business, but refused to drop or amend Rule 88, which required 15% of a new issue to be passed to the market. And so the Stock Exchange effectively resigned its chance to become the listing exchange of choice for Eurobond issues – handing the business to Luxembourg. When I became Deputy Chairman of the Council, after Big Bang, I was surprised how many Council members told me they thought it was the stupidest thing the Stock Exchange had ever done. Actually, it was about to do another stupid thing in refusing to allow European houses to join without a physical presence in London, even though the market had left the floor and gone electronic. This, and other experiences, has led me to ascertain a curious similarity between the City and France, my country of birth and now residence. Both are largely populated with people of individual intelligence, but often collective stupidity.

American commercial banks poured into the City, and many located in Moorgate, which became known as "Yankee Alley". The incomparable Christopher Fildes, the market's favourite financial journalist, wrote a monthly column for *Euromoney* magazine. It purported to be a letter addressed to "Dear Mum" from her son Herbie, manager of the London Branch of the Last National Bank of Boot Hill. Herbie recounted his adventures, trials and tribulations in establishing his bank in this strange and wonderful place which was the City. He struggled to understand its customs and peculiarities, and often had to rely on the "little girl who runs the telex machine" to guide him. Of course, Herbie's letters to his mother back in Boot Hill contained references providing a subtle and insightful comment on City affairs which only his ghost writer could have drafted. *Euromoney* magazine was the brain child of Patrick Sergeant, now Sir Patrick, a financial journalist on the *Daily Mail*. Patrick was one of the very few financial journalists who understood the significance of the Euromarkets phenomena, and he persuaded Lord Rothermere, Chairman of Daily Mail & General Trust to back the launch of a monthly magazine dedicated to this new market. Its first appearance caused great excitement. We felt as the early silent film stars in Hollywood must have felt when the magazine *Silver Screen* first appeared. We had arrived. We had our own magazine. Doubtless the practitioner's addiction to tombstone advertisements publicising their new issues would not have escaped Patrick's attention, and he would have quickly appreciated how many half and full pages he would sell as new issue volume exploded. Editorial content was of high quality, market statistics voluminous, and an appearance on the cover was as prestigious a recognition as one could get. *Euromoney* also caught the conference craze at an early stage. These were seen as networking opportunities and attendance was provided to employees as a perk. They were sponsored by service providers, and countries seeking financial exposure, were very popular and well attended. I declare an interest – I was a frequent speaker and panellist. Patrick's success with this publication, made some of us "Eurotrash' as we were soon to be known, even more conscious of the lack of coverage of our markets by U.K. the media in general. *The Financial Times, The Times, The Economist and The Investors Chronicle* devoted precious little column inches to our market. The fact that domestic investors were absent due to exchange control was a factor, of course. The FT and *The Economist* still picked up tombstone adverts. The fact that foreign houses came to dominate the market didn't help. The FT was, and is, curiously inward looking. When it gave a big dinner at a Livery Company hall to celebrate its 100th anniversary, we were all given a programme/menu with a cover page of the first issue reprinted. I noticed it contained more foreign news items than the contemporary front page. I also noticed that Sir Sigmund Warburg had been placed next to Lucia van der Post, daughter of the writer/philosopher. She edited a FT Saturday supplement entitled "How to spend it". I would have given anything to overhear their conversation.

Somewhat by design, and also due to the history of it European presence, White, Weld was differentiating itself from its Wall Street peer group. It was no secret that Bob saw a bigger potential for our European franchise, than that envisaged by New York. I had managed to persuade Bob and John that we should apply for authorised bank status in London. Our growing money market business seemed to me to justify this and I felt our general standing in the London market, and access to a wider range of City activities, would be enhanced. Perhaps, I was still smarting at Robin Hutton's demeaning comment, now some time ago: "We don't put brokers in our underwriting syndicates" The process was in the hands of James Keogh, a popular Irishman who ran the Discount Office. He and I had enjoyed an amusing incident together. Todd Goodwin in our New York office rang me to say that a friend of his was recovering from an unhappy love affair and wanted to come and work in London. She was a Hungarian lady called Emoeka Kiss and she was well-known in the Street as she had been running the money market desk at the Ford Foundation. I did point out that, at that stage, the only ladies employed in the City were PAs – still called secretaries – and tea ladies. "Let's innovate," said

Todd. Emoeka soon turned up. She was smart and beautiful and she knew money markets inside out.

But John Stancliffe said, "No! If we put her on the desk, our dealers will be constantly trying to impress her, they'll be busting their limits and discipline will break down." I couldn't fault his reasoning, because the situation would be so unusual as to be unpredictable. I called Jim Keogh, told him the story and asked if he had any ideas.

"Stani," he began, "I have two comments to make: First of all, it's too early in the morning for jokes. Secondly, I'm a senior official at the Bank, and you shouldn't be engaging in this kind of leg pull."

"It's not a joke, Jim. She *is* real, her name *is* Kiss, which is actually quite a common name in Hungary, and you can check her out with a friend at the Fed in New York."

"I might just do that," said Jim, somewhat more cordial.

The upshot was, she did get a job with a discount house, but she soon met a Hampshire landowner called , a cousin of an old friend of ours called Sarah Jocelyn, and settled down as the wife of a country squire.

Our application for authorised bank status benefitted hugely from our file at the Bank. We had been the only U.S. house to remain open during the war, DY having fortuitously omitted to inform his partners of this apparent oversight. John Rasch and Joyce Goodrich had been in charge. Too old to serve under arms, John had been a fire watcher. He had also helped administer the complicated exchange controls in place at the time, by facilitating dealings in foreign bonds and shares which still took place in wartime. The City had remained the custodian of significant assets on behalf of foreign nonbelligerents, such as Latin Americans. Our record as a premium dollar dealer was also a big plus. Our application was approved, and the Bank followed its usual practice of "suggesting" we engage a retired clearing banker as a consultant, to assist us with any compliance issues arising from Authorised Bank status. Eric Woolgar, a charming and very retired ex Lloyd's Bank officer, was recommended. He was useful in the launch of London dollar CDs, and attended the press conference with Michael von Clemm and Bob Genillard. White, Weld & Co. Limited came into existence as part of a wider programme of reform and restructuring of our European operations, engineered by Bob Genillard, who was rightly restive under the indirect umbrella of the SEC, whose regulatory regime was increasingly incompatible with our range of business. He wanted the freedom to establish subsidiaries, like the new bank in London and BFDT in Paris. We were now five partners in Europe, Bob, Johnny Cattier, John Stancliffe, Francois Champion and me. Bob also wanted a structure which could provide an equity interest to our senior officers who could not necessarily hope to become partners of the firm in New York. A solution lay in the increasingly close relationship between Bob and Rainer Gut at Credit Suisse in Zurich. Gut had become tired of André Meyer's very dictatorial style at Lazard in New York. Apparently the last straw had been an incident when Rainer was on holiday, fishing on a lake in Vermont, and Meyer had sent a seaplane to pick him up and bring him back to work on some deal. Guth was an investment banker at heart and he longed to break out of the traditional Big Three bias against lead management of new issues. He considered Credit Suisse's huge placing power should be used to support an originating role. Taking an interest in White Weld Europe could be a start. At the same time a relationship had been formed with Daniel K. Ludwig, who had begun in shipping on the Great Lakes, then built a fleet of converted Liberty ships and diversified into industry, hotels, salt mining and forestry. When he came into our lives at White Weld, he was engaged in a vast forestry and agricultural project in Brazil, to produce pulp and rice, a project which ultimately failed. But by 1969, he was already planning major divestitures and had established a foundation in Zurich for cancer research. His man of business was an Americanised Swiss called John Notter. So American did he seem that the people at Credit Suisse were surprised when, during negotiations, he suddenly broke into pure Schweitzerdeutsch. It was thought that Daniel Ludwig, through his new Zurich foundation, might be an investor in a new White, Weld Europe construction. Discussions were protracted, with Credit Suisse as a more than interested participant. The "call" which had been agreed with respect to Clariden Finanz, now Clariden Bank, might be exercised under an arrangement which liberated us from direct U.S. control. The relationship cooled a bit when Daniel Ludwig asked to be proposed for membership of The Links in New York, knowing that Ogden White was a member. This was very embarrassing. Ogden knew there was no chance whatsoever of Daniel Ludwig being elected to the Links, one of New York's most exclusive clubs. In the end, the conclusion of all this was the creation of a new holding company, in the Canton of Zug, called WW Trust, in which Credit Suisse took a major stake, the new Ludwig Foundation a small stake, the balance being retained by White, Weld & Co. in New York. All of the European operations, including White, Weld & Co. Limited, were folded into the new holding. The deal with Credit Suisse represented a watershed. Despite its undeniable logic, the deal made me uncomfortable. It must be remembered that I had grown up with White, Weld and its partners, who had been family friends as long as I could remember. Bob Genillard had not. I could not entirely shake off an end of era feeling. Sometime previously, Johnny Cattier had come to London, taken me to lunch, and asked me how I might feel about going back to head office in New York. I sensed the thinking was that White, Weld Europe was under-represented in New York, now that DY was a limited partner, Jean Cattier about to become one, and in any case, rather above it all. What better candidate than DY's son who had strong social contacts with the domestic partners and knew and understood the European project? I have now to admit that I didn't give it serious consideration – for three reasons. I knew I was now sitting where it was all happening. The Euromarkets were taking off. I was in the right place at the right time. And then I was developing a taste for the English life style. We were buying a place in the country. Finally, I knew Dinnie would not be comfortable as an American corporate wife. Suburban life on Long Island would simply not be her "thing". Thinking about it now, I realise I wouldn't have made a difference. The transatlantic estrangement was already underway. I would either have gone native and failed to represent the interests of Europe, or I would have been seen as a spy of Genillard & Co. But now the die was cast. We were essentially on our own. Our competitive position didn't suffer even a hiccup, and we continued to go from strength to strength. Most in the market were not even aware of the change in our corporate structure.

Meanwhile, the Eurobond market received a major shot in the arm. In some ways, it was even more momentous than the IET as it changed the borrower profile. Faced with a continuous capital outflow, President Johnson announced in January 1968 a new programme designed to achieve a fundamental improvement in the deteriorating U.S. balance of payments. All such programmes always promise decisive results. As Chris O'Malley reports "New mandatory restrictions were placed on U.S. companies' direct overseas investments above set quotas and the former Voluntary Restraint Programme was abandoned". The effect was dramatic; U.S. companies had to finance abroad. According to O'Malley, during the six years this programme would be in place, U.S. issuers accounted for a third of total new issue volume. The principle beneficiaries should have been the Wall Street houses with the strongest relationship with the top blue-chip companies. But due to the great salesmanship of David Mulford, White Weld garnered a host of mandates from other firm's major clients – to the discomfort of George McGovern and Charlie Lee. A glance at the league tables of the late '60's reveal Mulford's greatest selling point, of course. We were always in the top three and sometimes number one. Success breeds success. Actually, White, Weld opened this new market with a straight issue of $20 million for American Cyanamid, which might have been a client of La Financiera Venezolana, but was not an investment banking client in New York. A majority of issues which followed were convertibles, attractive to European investors in American blue ship equities.

In the late '60s, the market began to institutionalise – to an extent. It had been a source of complaint to the great and the good, who purported to oversee the world's financial system, that the Eurobond market was unregulated. This was not strictly true. Every participant was an authorised and regulated entity in its own jurisdiction. But clearly, the market needed some organisation which could represent it *viz a viz* would be regulators, and the world at large. No one felt this more than the secondary market makers, who constituted the beating heart of the market. Led by our own Walter Koller, they decided to organise. Stanley Ross, now at Kidder Peabody, Walter Imthurn, Koller's ex Number 2, now at Weeden, Dick Weguelin at Euro trade, Paul Sherwood at Strauss Turnbull, Georges Gazon at Montagu, Armin Mattle at Bond trade, Tom Beecham at Wood Gundy – these were not just market makers in the ordinary sense, they were the makers of the Eurobond market. Without them, even the great Sigmund Warburg would have been powerless to turn his London merchant bank into a great international issuing house. Chris O'Malley reports that it was Walter Imthurn, who proposed the idea, having worked in Canada and known the Montreal Bond Club. I have no reason to doubt him – Imthurn was an ideas man. In any case, after many jolly meetings, the Association of International Bond Dealers – AIBD, was formed, with a proper constitution, rules and committees – all the trappings. At its first meeting Rolf Hallberg of Stockholm's Enskilda Bank was elected Chairman. After a highly successful term of office, I was to succeed him as the second Chairman. O'Malley reports that delegates at the first Annual Meeting were welcomed with "Mademoiselle Courtine, Gentlemen", as she was the only lady in the hall. Bob Genillard gave an excellent speech in which he foresaw great things for the market, and encouraged the leading nations to merge their own domestic markets into it. In the 21st century, that has almost happened – but not quite. The other piece of critical market organisation dealt with clearing and settlement, which was in disarray, unable to cope with the huge expansion in volume and velocity. Bearer certificates were still dealt with by hand. An AIBD committee chaired by Koller drafted reforms, assisted by Johnny Cattier. He had arranged for the American Cyanamid issue to be closed at Morgan Guaranty in Brussels, as opposed to the usual Luxemburg venue. Cattier then persuaded Morgan Guaranty to establish a regular clearing facility there and Euro clear was born. It worked like a charm as a Morgan subsidiary, until the market participants decided Morgan was making too much money out of Euro clear, and lobbied the bank to turn it into a mutual. Competing facilities then appeared, efficiencies declined, costs rose and everybody would have been better off leaving Euro clear with Morgan Guaranty.

When the famous floating rate notes for ENEL appeared, the market received a nice bout of publicity. But it came from a very unhappy competitor – no less a personage than the famous Minos Zombanakis. In a market full of superstars, Minos stood out. Tall, energetic, highly personable, and an extraordinary salesman, he also benefited from a first-class publicity agent – himself. Minos liked to describe himself as "just a Cretan peasant", but he could have been Governor of the Central Bank of Greece several times over. After an early life in the U.S., he secured a position with Manufactures Hanover Trust as the representative for the Middle East, based in Rome. Minos likes to claim that he invented the Eurodollar Syndicated medium-term bank loan with an adjustable rate of interest. I hate to debunk Minos's various claims because he is a friend of mine. We might have been even closer. One day Dinnie, our daughter Tatyana and I were dining with my parents at Claridge's. It was the time when my father was serving as consultant to Bankers Trust, which accommodated him and my mother rather generously. I spotted Minos and his family at another table and we exchanged waves. A little later a waiter handed me a note. It was from Minos suggesting his son, sitting at his table, and my daughter would make an ideal couple. As has been the case with many most of my life, Minos was clearly wildly overestimating my net worth and, therefore, the size of a potential dowry. Like so many Euromarkets "innovations", the syndicated medium-term credit had been a feature of American finance for years. So had the adjustable rate, which allowed banks to borrow short and lend long without taking an interest rate risk. They could further enhance yield by "gapping" i.e. borrowing very short-term to fund the loan, the only risk being that the yield curve would inverse and the six month rate, usually the term of an adjustable rate, would be set lower than their funding rate. The basis for the rate fixing was usually the Fed's discount rate, or perhaps Treasury bills. The Euro version used a reference rate based on se-lected banks' borrowing cost in the interbank market, eventually known as the London Interbank Offered Rate –LIBOR. Minos claims to have invented this too. But the first syndicated, medium-term Eurodollar bank loan was for IBM World Trade in the late 1950s and the floating rate was fixed on a base rate of interbank borrowing cost. Minos's vehicle for his rise to fame in the syndic-ated loan market was Manufacturers Hanover Limited which the parent set up in 1968. His main sidekick there was Tony Constance, a faithful and skilled executor of Minos's originations. Minos tells the story of how he went from central bank to central bank in the Continental capitals, explaining his "innov-ation" to uncomprehending officials, until he finally settled on the City of London to locate his new merchant bank. Since the Euro-medium-term loan market had been functioning there for years, his odyssey – in the best Greek tradition, seems to have been somewhat pointless.

"Manny Hanny"'s first big deal was for IMI, the Italian state agency In-stituto Mobiliare Italiano. Zombanakis had fabulous connections in Italy. But neither he, nor anyone else, had anticipated that Van Galbreath, who after an early sojourn at Morgan & Cie in Paris, now running Bankers Trust Interna-tional, the former Rodocanachi, would be lounging in his bathtub, watching the rubber duck bob up and down, as he jiggled his toes in the water. Now Van would have been already aware that rubber ducks float, and bob up and down on unsettled water, and also that medium-term bank loans are based on a floating rate of interest. But Euromarkets legend has him leaping from his bath, crying *"Eureka!"* Perhaps his lapse into the Greek tongue was a subcon-scious swipe at Minos Zombanakis. In any case the Floating Rate Note was born. And this was perhaps the only true Euromarkets innovation because, al-though floating rate bank loans were common in the United States, there was no such thing as a negotiable bond with a floating rate of interest on that side of the Atlantic. Its advantages were obvious. Bank participants in medi-um-term loans hold an illiquid asset. Transfers of loan participations were theoretically possible, but cumbersome, as loan agreements contain covenants binding both borrower and lender, whereas only the borrower has obligations in a negotiable bond. At the same time, non-bank investors have no way of participating in the medium-term loan market, so the FRN, having all the characteristics of a bank loan, but being instantly negotiable, serves both categories of capital suppliers. Van took his idea to Warburg's, and, of course, Sigmund loved it. He called Guido Carli, Governor of the Bank of Italy, who also liked it, and proposed ENEL, the Italian electricity authority as the borrower. It was to be a seven-year maturity and $125m – a large amount for a bond issue at the time. There was some discussion as to who should appear as lead manager. Warburg's insisted it should be their good selves as they had brought the borrower. Poor old Van was consoled with the position of book runner, a function never before separated from the lead manager role. The question of a third co-manager required no discussion; it was to be White, Weld – to ensure a secondary market, which was critical to the concept. There was a bit of head scratching in our house, as Koller had never traded a floating rate instrument. No one had. But Allan Towner traded six months CDs, so there was a form of cross-over. David Scholey of Warburg's, Van Galbreath and I toured the potential underwriters in the city, but our first stop, in the tradition of the City at the time, was the Bank of England. Although the Bank had no particular jurisdiction over this type of foreign currency transaction, the fact that it was a first, and likely to be controversial, meant it was just as well to have the Bank's blessing – which they gave, but after some profound questioning about just how such an issue would be placed and traded. Meanwhile, Minos Zombanakis went ballistic. He saw his market niche under serious threat. He flew to Rome, stormed into Carli's sumptuous office and pointed out the higher front end fees as, of course, the Eurobond fee structure would apply, and the fact that subscribers could sell their notes without the consent of the borrower. He had already offered ENEL a syndicated loan on competitive conditions. A compromise was arranged to save Minos's face, but it was not to the benefit of his bank, as it was Warburg's who syndicated an accompanying medium-term bank loan for $300m for the same borrower – at terms dictated by Minos. The FRN, as an alternative Eurobond format, had its moment in the sun with Banker's Trust International leading issues for U.S. corporates Pepsico and Insilco, but then closed for a while, after an issue for Argentina bombed. And Minos's fears were unfounded. As Chris O'Malley points out, in 1971 the volume of classical syndicated medium-term loans totalled between $8 and 9.2 billion whilst the Eurobond market raised only $3.6 billion. The FRN market hardly made a dent in the syndicated loan market. In fact, if Minos hadn't been so attached to his mastery of his part of the market, he could have put his bank in an even stronger position. By persuading his shareholder in New York to seek a partner for Manufacturers Hanover Limited in London, Minos could have found a place in the Eurobond market as well. "Manny Hanny", London, as we all called it, would not have been constrained by Glass Steagal, which prevented U.S. commercial banks from dealing in securities, just as Morgan & Cie in Paris was free from this restriction. Unfairly, Minos is remembered more for having lost a deal, than for his record and undoubted prowess as an originator and syndicater of medium Eurocurrency bank loans.

Meanwhile, the Eurobond market continued its heady growth, both in terms of volume and variety. Press coverage increased and we now had the *Institutional Investor* competing with *Euromoney* in its dedication to covering the market and publishing tombstones. There were gossip sheets publishers, such as Ian Kerr, an ex-Kidder Peabody investment banker who became the market's William Hickey, and Bill Low's provocative weekly *International Insider.* A sign of approaching maturity was the emergence of some exotica, and an early attempt at a Euro-equity issue. A buccaneering entrepreneur called Bernie Cornfeld appeared in Europe and caused great excitement. He began by selling mutual funds to GIs in Germany and then built a Europe-wide sales organisation staffed by motivated and well remunerated salesmen. One of his sales techniques sticks in my mind and is quite clever. Leaving after a failed sales call on a prospect, the salesman was trained to turn around, with his hand on the door knob, and say: "Just one more thing – could you tell me where I went wrong?" Apparently in at least half the cases, the resumed conversation resulted in a sale. Cornfield's holding company was called Investors Overseas Services – IOS, and many saw it as a precursor to a pan European savings market. Cornfeld employed a sort of front man, a member of the Ford family, as his respectable face, because, to be frank, he himself looked like a con artist out of central casting. IOS decided to go public with a share offering underwritten, syndicated and distributed exactly like a Eurobond issue. During its meteoric rise, one of IOS's main supporters had been Hambros, as David Kynaston reminds me. But, although most of the usual suspects joined the underwriting syndicate, Hambros did not, nor did Warburg's or Rothschild. Neither Genillard, Stancliffe nor I had liked the smell of the whole affair, and we turned down an offer of a co-management position. I can't remember who the lead manager was. But we ended up making a serious amount of money out of the issue because, not being restricted as an underwriter, we were able to trade the issue immediately and were, in fact, the principle market maker during the hectic post issue dealings. It was one of Allan Towner's greatest moments as a trader. We didn't consider that market making in the shares implied any endorsement of Bernie Cornfeld or IOS, but rather assisted the naïve investors who had subscribed to the issue. Poor Bernie ended up bankrupt.

Another buccaneer, but at the opposite end of the quality spectrum from Bernie Cornfeld, was Jim Slater, who caused great excitement in the City as an early, bottom fishing, private equity operator. He built an empire called Slater, Walker, his partner being the politician Peter Walker, which specialised in identifying undervalued situations, buying in and extracting hidden value. The City divided to some extent; some saw him as a maverick speculator and others as a breath of fresh air. The much admired *Daily Mail* financial editor

Patrick Sergeant was a strong supporter, although he cooled over some of Slater's later ventures. By the time Slater, Walker came into our lives, the firm had become a full scale merchant bank, engineering and advising on mergers and acquisitions. We were approached to lead manage a trip to the Eurobond market. John Stancliffe and I went to call on the great man. At Slater, Walker we were shown into a common waiting room which had all the appearances of a dentist's office, with well-thumbed magazines on coffee tables. But even more astonishing were the small groups of other visitors, waiting in corners and eying each other suspiciously. I whispered to John, "I can't believe this is a house specialising in M & A! Where's the confidentiality?"

"Must be a new style of doing business," said John.

I was trained to believe it was a sin to allow one client to view another, which is why in a proper investment or merchant bank, clients are immediately whisked in to a room, safe from the gaze of some other, possibly competitor client. If there is an opposite of *haute banque*, I suppose it was Slater, Walker. Nevertheless, Jim Slater made an excellent impression. He had done his homework and we didn't have to make the usual explanations as to how our market worked. Nor did he try and impress us by overstating his company's prospects – we were preparing a $20M convertible issue. We had little difficulty forming the syndicate; Barings, Rothschild and Schroeders came in. I tried very hard to convince Deutsche Bank to join as co-manager to ensure Continental sponsorship. But their syndicate manager was an unshakeable nonbeliever in the Slater, Walker story, and considered the whole thing far too speculative for Deutsche Bank's pristine standards. The issue was heavily oversubscribed. Soon after, I had a call from Jimmy Goldsmith inviting me to lunch with him at the Savoy Grill, then the venue of choice for the business elite. He was intrigued by the Slater, Walker issue and wanted to know all about it. Goldsmith had parlayed the acquisition of a small grocery company into a food conglomerate called Cavenham and wondered if this quoted company might contemplate a similar issue. In the end it didn't come off, but I had a pleasant lunch. Of course, I didn't mention that I had played as a child in the Bois de Boulogne with his first wife Isabel Patino, who died tragically in childbirth – but I thought about it a good deal.

White, Weld in Europe was riding high in those early '70s. We were always in the top three of the league tables, and sometimes number one. Our trading activities were highly profitable. Paris and Zurich were doing excellent business and BFDT, the Paris bank added variety. The relationship with Credit Suisse strengthened, and was to be the firm's ultimate fallback position. White, Weld, New York was not such a happy story. In the 1960s, Wall Street began to experience change, which accelerated through the decade and culminated in the end of fixed commissions on the New York Stock Exchange in 1975 – sometimes referred to as the Street's own "Big Bang". There were a number of trends at play, and none served the interests of medium-sized investment banking houses like White, Weld & Co. The biggest change was in the profile of customers for exchange business. In the late '50s, at least three-quarters of the customer base were private individuals, with the balance institutions. By 1970, the proportions had almost exactly reversed. As average trade sizes increased, the fixed commission structure came under pressure from all sides. Another issue was capital. A generation of younger partners were not so happy to leave a large proportion of any year's profit in the firm. They were getting married younger, wanted to buy houses, taxes had eroded their inheritances; in short, they needed the money. This put the traditional partnership structure under pressure and houses began to incorporate – White, Weld only two years after I joined the partnership. Outside interests, as diverse as Sears Roebuck and Prudential Assurance, bought into Wall Street firms. Mergers increased, producing benefits of scale but culture conflicts and key personnel turnover. There was a generation change at White, Weld. Alec and Ogden became limited partners. Benny Clark was less active. Jean Cattier became Chairman of European-American Bank, the first joint venture of the EBIC group, a collection of seven leading European banks who had joined in an informal association. Emory Katzenbach became Chief Executive, but events seemed to be moving faster than the firm was able to adjust. Neither Alec White's son Sandy nor his son-in-law George Montgomery, our star recruit from San Francisco's Montgomery Street, showed any inclination to take over the reins. Morale in New York was not helped by the fact that Europe was making more money than head office. The tail was wagging the dog. Some expressed the view that Bob Genillard, our European miracle maker, should come to New York and sort things out. This was not to be. I remember one day, Bob walking into my office on one of his London visits, in a bit of a rage.

"Look at this!" he said waving a slip of paper at me. "Can you believe it?"

It was a tax demand from the State of Ohio for something like $16.31.

"I suspect it's your share of the firm's state tax liability," I guessed.

We were still a partnership. In those days, firms had to be registered to offer securities in any State of the Union – the so-called "blue sky" laws, and so became liable for state income tax on profits earned in the state concerned. It strikes me that Bob, a Swiss citizen, would not have been overjoyed at the prospect of becoming subject to U.S. taxation, as he would be if he took up residence there. But more substantial than that, I believe, was an entirely correct assumption on his part that, to turn the firm around, he would have had to knock heads together, fire some long serving employees, and become an absolute monarch. It would have had to be messy and Bob was not the sort of person who could adopt an adversarial attitude to a firm that had given him an opportunity of a lifetime. And so the firm, which had also given DY the opportunity of a lifetime, began a sad decline.

CHAPTER XVI

"I had a farm in Africa"

-The first line in Isaak Dinneson's (Baroness Blixen) novel "Out of Africa"-

I have never drawn a firm line between my professional career and my private life. Having written that, I must immediately correct the terminology. I once referred to banking as a profession in a meeting attended by a senior City solicitor. "Banking is not a profession – it's a trade," he drawled, stretching the "a" in "trade" to emphasise his disdain. The distinction is that unlike lawyers, accountants, vicars, doctors and veterinary surgeons, bankers do not need professional qualifications, and are no better for it, some might say. As for the "career" part, I never considered I had a career as I did not experience the usual steps. I never had to apply for a job but was given one, when I was unemployable, due to my father. Chance placed me in the City of London, just when its revival as an international financial centre was gathering speed. I was "poached" twice, and in hindsight, each move was a mistake, from a traditional career point of view. For me the office was fun, and it had the additional feature of financing the fun I had outside the office. My father's theory that giving me expensive tastes would install in me a work ethic turned out to have merit. At work, I was able to play a role I thoroughly enjoyed, and be surrounded by interesting, talented people, and at play it was exactly the same thing.

In my marriage, chance played the key role, considering the odds against my meeting Dinnie again, after we had parted to return to our respective continents. Marriage as an institution is in decline, but as a subject of sociological analysis, it is in ascendency. As a source of consulting and legal fees, resulting from its fragility, it has never been stronger. I would venture to suggest that this paradox is due to the fact that only a few of us still regard marriage as a sacrament. Most pundits who opine on marriage, and that includes almost everyone, stress compatibility as an essential ingredient to a happy marriage, and infer that compatibility is synonymous with similarity. "They do everything together because they have exactly the same tastes" is a common observation with reference to a successful marriage.

. Our experience is the opposite. It would be difficult to find two people who are as different as my wife and me. Even putting aside the fact that we have entirely different social, geographic and ethnic origins, a search for some element – be it taste, inclination, opinion, habit, or whatever, where we are the same, would be fruitless. Perhaps a love of animals – horses, dogs, cats and wild ones would be the exception that proves the rule. Dinnie is a day person, I am a night person. She likes cold, I like hot. She likes the simple life. Rogers and Hart's *The Lady is a Tramp* could have been written for her as she frequently "gets too hungry for dinner at eight". I am in to formality. I won't catalogue all the ways in which we are different, as they are too numerous. I didn't pay much attention in physics class, but I seem to recall that electrically charged particles, one negatively charged, and the other positive, attract each other. I will leave the reader to decide which, between Dinnie and me, is the negatively charged and which the positive. But the fact remains that my wife and I have remained happily bound together by our differences.

My obsession with genealogy prompts me to describe the origins of Diana Veronica Obré Townsend, my wife's full name. Her parents were afraid she would be called "Di" at school and so nicknamed her Dinnie, which in Ireland is the diminutive for Dennis. Her Townsend family are descended from one of the regicide and dictator Oliver Cromwell's senior captains, one Bryan Townsend. Cromwell rewarded his partners in crime with large chunks of Ireland, in effect creating the Anglo-Irish ascendency. Two years ago, Ireland decided to promote tourism by declaring the "Year of the Homecoming", and the charming Mrs Salter-Townsend, current *chatelaine* of Castle Townsend, the family pile near Skibereen, decided to exploit the subsidy available and convoked a family reunion. Some thirty or so gathered from various locations – America, Canada, and even Singapore. At the opening reception, we few alien spouses huddled in a corner, whilst the Townsends rejoiced and congratulated themselves – on being Townsends. I did not distinguish myself. John Townsend, the family genealogist and archivist, who created the family website, had kindly supplied us all with an abbreviated family tree, tracing the lines up from those present. Running my eye up Dinnie's line, I noticed that her great, great grandfather Thomas had married one Martha Uniacke in 1799. Now the Uniacke's are a far more ancient, and, dare I say it, distinguished family than the Townsends. Anglo-Norman knights who arrived with William the Conqueror, they settled in the southwest of Ireland and owned vast lands, up to and including Cork. Catholic and fiercely royalist, they fought a vicious but hopeless action against the advancing Cromwellian forces and lost most of their land. In the 19th century, a Uniacke converted to Protestantism in order to be admitted to Trinity College, Dublin, became a highly successful solicitor, and to his credit, worked to restore the family fortune. The trouble is, I did dare to say all this in front of several Townsends, earning a rebuke from Dinnie "Why can't you learn to keep your boring old history stories to yourself?" Still, Thomas was so happy to have married "up", that he gave his three sons the middle name Uniacke. One of these, William Uniacke Townsend was Dinnie's great grandfather. Our actress daughter Tatyana likes to mention that she is related to George Bernard Shaw, whenever she is in a GBS play. A Charlotte Townsend married Shaw, and as a widow, became a close correspondent and mother figure to T. E Lawrence, when he came home psychologically damaged after the Arab Revolt. The Obré in Dinnie's name is from her grandmother Ethel Obré, descended from Captain Francis Obré, a French Hugenot who emigrated to the North of Ireland after the revocation of the Edict of Nantes in the late 17th century. He was a signatory of a letter of welcome to William of Orange, when that dubious claimant invaded Ireland. By now, the reader will have noticed that I am of the Jacobite persuasion. On the side of my much loved, mother in law Patricia née Brooks, Dinnie is descended from William Mallet, one of the Conqueror' knights, who ended up with a good deal of Devon. The Mallet-Veale family of Passaford, near Okehampton were badly hit by a 19th century agricultural depression and dispersed their large family though out the empire, one ending up in Cape Town. A Mallet-Veale daughter married Judge Brooks of Salisbury, Southern Rhodesia, Dinnie's maternal grandfather. Freddy Brooks was a great sportsman and his name, F. T. Brooks, is still on the main gate to the Harare sports ground.

When Dinnie and I married, I was in a flat in Sloane Avenue, previously rented by Margaret Truman, and looked after by a Mrs. Lake, who promptly gave notice on learning of my marriage, but stayed long enough to show Dinnie how to make a chocolate mousse. We soon moved to Dawson Place off Notting Hill Gate, not yet fashionable, but never rivalled by subsequent locations, in Dinnie's estimation. Tatyana was born at Nuffield House, Guy's Hospital and delivered by Mr. Lewis, in a dinner jacket, according to family legend, promoted by Tatyana herself. Mr. Lewis was a Bishop's boy, the brother school of Herschel, Dinnie's school in the Cape. A leading gynaecologist, he also captained the Guy's rugby team, when the hospital rugby league in London played to a very high standard. Sadly many of the Australians, New Zealanders and South Africans, who attended London's teaching hospitals, now go to America, and hospital rugby has suffered. Our eldest son Michael started arriving near midnight and we had no live in nanny at the time. So I found a black cab and told the driver to take Dinnie to Nuffield House at Guy's, mentioning that she was in labour.

"Not to worry, Guv," said the elderly cab driver. "If it comes on the way, I can handle it." Entirely confident of his claim, I returned to bed and was woken a few hours later by Dinnie on the phone to say it was a boy. In those days the ladies were confined for a few days and Dinnie's accommodation at Nuffield House was very comfortable. The baby's crib was conveniently placed alongside the mother's bed, for ease of feeding and proud gazing. I kept a bottle of whiskey in a cupboard and would drop in after work for an evening drink and visit, to please the nurse. When Nicholas was born, we had

241

moved to Oakwood Court, a block of mansion flats off Holland Park. Nicholas was upside-down and so Dinnie had to be rushed to a closer hospital off Cromwell Road for a caesarean delivery, which was performed by Mr. Lewis's Pakistani assistant, as Mr. Lewis was on the golf course. When I suggested a modest discount on his usual fee might be appropriate, he replied, "Nonsense! Ahmed delivered one of my own – he's probably better at obstetrics than me – and, by the way, you need have no concern over Dinnie's condition. She'll be able to have plenty more." I thought this little piece of marketing most inappropriate. In any case we were not to see Mr. Lewis again. Dinnie somehow found a lovely African woman from the Transkai, who had trained as a hospital nurse, to look after Tatyana. She called her charge "Cookie", for some reason. Our new nurse was named Beatrice and I used to walk her home before she lived in.

One evening she said, "Do you see, Master," pointing at all the parked cars. "The cars go to sleep at night just as we do."

Beatrice had a merchant seaman husband, who called every six months or so, when his ship was in port. He was over six feet tall and wore a broad brimmed fedora. Beatrice told Dinnie she loved her husband dearly, and saw him just about the right number of times a year. Her manner of addressing me was always a morale booster, and she would give my wife a hug when Dinnie felt low. When we went off to Bavaria with the von Clemms to visit his Uncle Carl, we left Tatyana with Beatrice with no qualms whatsoever. Beatrice had a part-time job cleaning a local pub. She used to take Tatyana with her and the publican's wife would look after her. At Oakwood Court, Michael von Clemm often called and, if the children answered the door, he would say "Hi!" – An Americanism they thought unique. They began calling him Uncle Hi, and so he remained for the family, until his untimely death a few years ago. One of our neighbours in Oakwood Court was a charming old Jewish lady called Mrs. Eberstadt, who used to say to Dinnie that she felt "squashed" in the very spacious flat which Oakwood Court specialised in. Clearly, like many widows living in that mansion block of flats, she had left some great house in the country and couldn't fit all her furniture. Her son Walter was a partner of Lazard in New York, and when he came to visit his mother, he would drop in on me to hear what was happening in the City.

"Surely Lazard in London keeps you in the picture?" I said.

"You are joking – they are useless. We hardly speak," replied Walter.

I did not quite believe this. It's true that Lazard Frères in New York and Lazard Brothers in London were only historically linked, and the Pearson Group was the controlling shareholder of London. There was surely correspondent contact. One day Lord Poole, Chairman of Lazard, London called me to complain at being left out of an underwriting syndicate we were leading – I think for an American corporate Eurobond issue. He claimed André Meyer in New York had phoned him to say that Lazard absolutely had to be represented. I was so taken aback at the time, that I did not immediately doubt this cock-and-bull story. In retrospect, however, why had Andre Meyer not simply called Alec White in New York? Or even more likely, asked his syndicate manager to call Charlie Lee at White, Weld, in New York. Furthermore, why would His Lordship ring a junior partner in London, rather than the boss in Europe, Bob Genillard? It's true, Poole did mention that Meyer knew DY, but I still don't see it. I did call Bob in Zurich, who I think took pleasure in telling me to suggest to Lord Poole that he get lost – or words to that effect, which I duly did, as politely as I could. Bob was not one to be impressed by a peer of the Realm, and Lazard, after a brief and hesitant start, no longer counted in the Eurobond world. Nevertheless, I was privileged to know Walter Eberstadt, a gentleman banker of the old school.

Another most amusing resident of Oakwood Court was Jack English and his family, CFO – U.K., of Phillips Petroleum, based in Bartlesville, Oklahoma. At European Banking Company, in the early '70s, we were active in project financing North Sea oil exploration and development, and Phillips was a target client. With Bill Slee, my number two, and our senior oil banker, we visited Bartlesville, a touristic excursion I recommend for its sheer oddity. Visitors lunched with the bosses in the staff canteen and were required to give a speech to the assembled employees. Back in London, Jack English was our point of contact and my North Carolina sojourn with the U.S. Marines was useful in understanding Jack who, despite his surname, tortured the language of Shakespeare with an accent you could hole with a drilling bit. The favourite tipple of the Phillips delegation in London was bourbon and Doctor Pepper, an indescribable soft drink prevalent in the Southwest. A German delicatessen in Notting Hill Gate stocked it especially for the British based Phillips team. On my visits to Jack English in Oakwood Court, I was forced to accept the offer of a bourbon and Doctor Pepper, with plenty of ice – fortunately. Once I was there, trying to discuss the finer points of the ABC project finance construct, and wishing Bill Slee was there to help me, when Jack's little daughter galloped in and started trying to play "horsey" with her father, who fended her off with a leg, whilst sipping his bourbon and Doctor Pepper. When he put his drink down, the little girl picked it up and slowly poured it over his head. English did not even pause as the liquid dripped down his face.

"Can I get you a towel?" I asked, rising.

"Don't need no towel – but that reminds me, one thing I larn'd from those towelheads in Araby is don't take no shit from the damn laryers."

Then to his daughter, still standing there with a smile:

"Now you rascally pickinin, you hurry and get your old man a fresh drink or I'll wup the hell outer you."

Perhaps it was all a family ritual. Oakwood Court was full of little surprises. A French family lived below us with two little boys we called *Les Fils Dumas* who never stopped making a racket and ringing our doorbell because we spoke to them in French. Our two boys set their room on fire, playing spaceships with a lighted candle under the bed, which duly ignited the mattress. I learned the truth of the matter using the old trick of telling each one

243

the other had confessed. The David Montagu's had two flats in Oakwood Court, facing each other across the lift vestibule – one for them and the other for the staff and the children. David would kindly give me a lift to the City in his Rolls-Royce, dropping off a daughter at the *Lycée Français.* David sat next to his chauffeur reading the *Racing Post*, and I sat in the back reading the *Financial Times*.

Anyone who has visited Africa will have experienced its unique atmosphere, which is not duplicated in any other part of the globe. The smells, sounds and sights, together with the graceful movements of the people, and the animals, are entirely distinct. When many Rhodesians immigrated to Australia, after the Mugabe land grab, they found a big sky, expansive space and a similar climate to their last home. But a vital ingredient was missing, and most noticed it right away – there were no Africans. In most countries the indigenous population represents a vital part of the national *ambiance*. But when Europeans, bought up in Africa, express a sentimental attachment to the Africans which surround them, it is considered patronising. Dinnie often describes herself as a *Shona*, after the tribe in Mashonaland, where she grew up. It is true that the Africans she grew up with, and is so fond of, were servants and farm workers. But to suggest that one cannot have the same affection for menials as for one's peers is a terrible example of lateral snobbism, as opposed to reverse. Ignorance about Africa is rife, particularly in America, where it is widely assumed that all Africans are the same because they are black, ignoring the obvious fact that, although they are white, all Europeans are hardly the same. The misconception is apparent in the fact that President Obama is universally described as African-American, thus placing him in that category of Americans descendent from slaves of West African origin. But his mother was a white Anglo-Saxon and his father of East African origin. East and West Africans are as different as Swedes and Portuguese. Presumably to describe him as simply being of mixed race would not be politically correct. When my sister-in-law was living in Omaha, Nebraska, she mentioned to an educated lady that her family lived and farmed in Africa. "I didn't know white people lived in Africa," remarked the lady. "I thought the only white people there were missionaries." She had not heard about Afrikaners in South Africa.

My first trip to Africa would have been Christmas 1961 as we went with Tatyana as a baby, for Christmas, and she was born on April 1st of that year – the only family birthday that I can remember. I had heard a great deal about it all from Dinnie, and so struggled to keep an open mind. Her family story is not untypical. In 1898, her grandfather Thomas Crofton Townsend spotted an announcement in a Dublin newspaper that a secretary was sought for a new club doing established in Salisbury, the new capital of Southern Rhodesia. This new colony was administered by the British South Africa Company, a royal charter having been obtained by Cecil Rhodes from Lord Salisbury by promising to name the capital after him, and this despite the fact that incursions into that part of southern Africa were against government policy. It is noticeable that whenever Englishmen begin to settle in a new, distant outpost, their first joint initiative is the foundation of a club. The next step is to find people to exclude – in the case of the new Salisbury Club, it would have been native Africans and prospectors. In those days the only acceptable occupation for gentlemen in Africa was farming, policing or big game hunting, yet they still wanted a gentleman as secretary of their new club. Thomas, or "T.C.", as he was universally known, was a landless Townsend, and so he jumped at the chance. He was engaged to Ethel Obré, one of two daughters of the last of the Obré male line. Having been quickly accepted for the post, T.C. persuaded her to go with him, and married her on arrival in Cape Town. In Salisbury, then virtually a tent village, T.C. discovered land was being almost given away by the British South Africa Company. The population in Mashonaland at the time would have been less than 100,000 and the land the BSA disposed of was not tribal land, as is now claimed. The Shona, an agrarian and pastoral tribe, had been virtually enslaved by the Ndebele, a warrior tribe and Zulu off shoot from the area around Bulawayo, and the BSA had fought two wars against them in the 1890s. The first war broke out because Lobengula, the N'bele chief was extracting tribute from a Shona chief. The second war is far more confused in terms of causes and effects, but the Shona generally regarded the BSA, i.e., the British, as their liberators. Relations between natives and settlers were now peaceful, and T.C. bought land in the Mazoe valley, not far from the source of the Mazoe River, which runs through the farm. Lowdale Farm is only 50 miles or so from what is now the centre of Harare. Early farming in Rhodesia was not an easy task, but I suspect T.C.'s duties as Club secretary were not onerous, and he began to build a typical, tin roofed farm house, plant an alley of Jacaranda trees and hire labour, mostly Nyasas, as Nyasaland, now Malawi, lived on exporting labour to the South African mines and the Rhodesian farms. When Mugabe was asked what would happen to all the farm workers on the expropriated commercial farms, he replied they were Malawians, and could simply go home – even though most were third and fourth generation settled in Zimbabwe. When I first visited Lowdale, there were forty or fifty families living in the compound, mostly from Malawi. T.C. took on an apprentice in 1912 named Arthur Harris, and made him farm manager when the Townsends went to England on leave. Harris was called to the colours in 1914 and eventually joined an air reconnaissance unit in East Africa. He ultimately became "Bomber" Harris, head of Bomber Command in WW2. In his biography, by Air Commodore Henry Probert, the story is told of how T.C. Townsend banged on his door on a Christmas morning, when Harris was hoping for a lie-in and shouted, "Get out! Get to work – there are fences to be mended." Another anecdote has Harris delivering a steam driven, maize sheller by ox cart to Ballaneety, a farm some thirty miles away – a two-day journey. On returning his boss T.C. was horrified to learn Harris had charged Mr. Glanfield for use of the sheller. In those days farmers lent each other rare pieces of equipment. When returning to Lowdale in 1945, Harris was delighted to see that same sheller, rusted and overgrown, in the corner of a field. T.C.'s grandson, Michael Townsend, married Cathy Glanfield of Balaneety, granddaughter of the unfairly charged farmer. Harris also recalls being taken by T.C. to meet the family of Judge Freddy Brooks, which included a small daughter named Patricia. He gave her a teddy bear. She later married T.C.'s son Raife, kept the present all her life, and finally gave it to a teddy bear museum in London. "Bomber" Harris's daughter Jaqueline married Nick Assheton, who was on the Council of the Stock Exchange during my deputy chairmanship. He then joined Coutts and ended up as comptroller of the Queen Mother's Household. We have remained great friends with the Asshetons.

In those days, first time visitors to Africa were subject to leg pulling, as so much rubbish was being written about the situation in Rhodesia, and other British colonies, where the Colonial Office was seeking to run down the Union Jack as quickly as possible, urged on by anti-colonial Washington. On almost the first night I was taken to a party in Salisbury, when a cat ran across the room. Jamie Guys, then working for Anglo-American in Rhodesia, turned to me and said, "Look! Big game!" A few days later my father in law took me racing at Borrowdale Race Course and spotted Ian Smith, not yet politically prominent, standing at the bar. I was introduced, and Smith asked

"How long are you staying?"

"Only a week, I have to get back to work," I replied.

"Oh! Going to write a book, are you?"

Instant experts on Africa were everywhere. Some years later, after Rhodesia's unilateral declaration of independence, we were amongst a few still visiting the country. Dinnie's cousin Jane Singleton served as PA to Prime Minister Ian Smith. Jane's father Sandy had been a well-known Worcestershire cricketer, capped for England, and later a master at Salisbury's leading public school. Jane insisted I call on the PM, who obviously received precious few visitors from England. Smith was hungry for political gossip from London, and I had to explain I didn't move in political circles – I could only report what people were saying in the City. Nevertheless, the PM chatted on, and when the subject of the Liberal Party came up, he said, "The Liberal Party reminds me of a dog at a rugger match – it gets in the way of both sides and does nothing for the game." It was the best description of the party I have ever heard. When explaining what I did as a job, I was able to remind him that Southern Rhodesia had been perhaps the only British Crown Colony to issue a foreign dollar bond in New York, through Dillon Read, in the 1950s. As I recalled it had been for $15m and secured by the Reserve Bank's gold bullion, as the country was, and still is, a not insignificant gold producer. Of course it had since been redeemed, and Smith wasn't aware of it. He was essentially a farmer, unsophisticated in the ways of the geo-politics, which was his undoing. Despite being described by the liberal media in London as a "white supremacist", Smith did believe that universal suffrage, and hence a native African dominated government, was both inevitable and desirable. It was a question of timing, and he pointed out that Britain had not achieved universal suffrage until women were granted the vote in 1928. Finally, as my meeting seemed to run over the usual appointed time, Smith would suddenly say "Doing anything for lunch?" Of course, I wasn't, and we would stroll down the street to the Salisbury Club. There were two BSA policeman standing outside his door, who saluted smartly as we passed out, and as we walked, people called out "Hi Smithy!"; there was no sign of any security. Now when Mugabe travels a block, half the town is cordoned off and police and military vehicles top and tail his cavalcade. Even three or four years ago, as Zimbabwe sank into the slough of inflationary despond, an aged Ian Smith would come to town, and Africans in the street would shout "Come back Smithy!" But the tragedy that is Rhodesia/Zimbabwe is to profound and complex for an in depth discussion in a lighthearted memoir, so I shall confine myself to an inadequate evocation of what the country was to me.

One awoke in the morning to the sound of the *shalili*, the summons to morning roll call of the farm workers, created by banging a hammer on an old section of iron rail, hanging from a tree. Then a house boy would appear with tea and biscuits which I don't normally enjoy, but I partook, as it was the tradition, and in any case we were riding before breakfast. On the way to the stables, Dinnie would give her breakfast order to Msimbe, the cook boy. Msimbe was a Nyasa who had been with the family since T.C. and Ethel Townsend had first established Lowdale. He had been supplied with an Edwardian cookbook which Ethel had brought from Ireland and helped him to decifer. The resulting meals were distinctly Edwardian, with roast fowl and beef, potatoes and rice, and at least five vegetables, for Sunday lunch. Msimbe carefully planned for his retirement, keeping back one of his daughters, Reneka, by placing such a high bride wealth value on her that no one could afford to marry her. She had several children, of course, but she was there to look after Msimbe when he retired to a tribal trust land at Umbashawa. When my father-in-law died, Msimbe walked for two days, back to Lowdale for the funeral. At the stables there was always a small fire of damp straw burning. The smoke was thought to ward off the fly that causes African horse sickness. We rode all over the farm, Dannie recalling her childhood rides, mostly on her father's uncontrollable polo ponies, and noting changes here and there. Work gangs would be repairing dykes and the dam, which provided for the dry season, de-tasselling the maize stalks, and in the barns, shelling seed maize. Lowdale was a mixed farm known for its seed maize, but also grew winter wheat, and kept some cattle and pigs. Tobacco was grown on a neighbouring farm called Thetford, which was supposed to go to the youngest son Andrew, but was sold before he could inherit. Tobacco was the big cash crop in Rhodesia, and still is in Zimbabwe, but is highly volatile, and climate sensitive, with extremes between good and bad years – rather like investment banking, when it was honest. Maize is the staple diet for the populations of central and southern Africa. Back in 1922, a strain of maize had been developed in the Salisbury Agricultural Research centre and named SR 22. It is the most popular strain used in the maize growing world. In America, maize is called corn; in England, corn is the generic term for all grain crops. Southern Rhodesia used to have the highest per capita production of maize, outside the U.S., exporting to Northern Rhodesia and South Africa. After the expropriation of the commercial farms, Zimbabwe was no longer able to grow enough to feed its own people and now has to import at least half of its needs. After riding, we breakfasted on home produced, egg, bacon and sausages with homemade toasted bread, and homemade marmalade. The coffee was from the Vumba region, and every bit as good as Kenyan. Lounging on the lawn in front of the veranda, where the young African girl assigned to Tatyana was pushing her back and forth in a stroller, we waited for morning tea or coffee. In effect, if you count early morning tea, there were five meals a day served – yet everyone was slim. My young sister-in-law, Linda, always known as Mattie, had a pony called Pumkin Joe, and would canter around the garden, popping over various obstacles, which included me lying on the lawn on my first morning. Below that lawn was a fairly primitive but entirely adequate swimming pool. The water was cold as it was constantly being emptied and refilled from a bore hole, as there was no filtration. After a copious lunch, washed down by the local Castle lager beer, it was siesta time for all – a sacred tradition which Dinnie has continued for the rest of her life, often in unusual venues. At Lowdale, bed rooms were always available for any lunch guest, who was expected to snooze and stay for tea. After tea, we would walk around the farm, with the ridgebacks, a laid back breed – rather like the Shona. Originally imported by Malay traders to the cape, Rhodesian Ridgebacks are now a Cruft's class, and were developed in Southern Africa to track, rather than confront lions – rather like pointers with game birds. There was a so-called police boy, who patrolled the farm, armed with an ancient Enfield rifle, which probably hadn't been loaded for years. He would snap to attention and salute as we passed. Those who thoroughly disapprove of such colonial fripperies would have been even more shocked to see elderly women from the compound, bearing huge stacks of fire wood on their heads, drop a curtsey as we passed. Their grace and style would have made an English debutante look awkward. In the evening, the distinctive tinkle of the drinks trolley being wheeled in would announce sundowners. Everyone tended to be early to bed after supper, as the day started at six for most, although we visitors from England had our morning tea at the late hour of seven. The days varied little and were perfection for me. At Christmas, on Boxing Day, the household gathered behind the kitchen for something which would have had the *bien pensant* throwing their hands up in despair at such a thoroughly colonial display. Most of the compound gathered before us, with drums, and the men wearing outlandish and fearful costumes, to ward off evils spirits. After my father-in-law's death, his widow Patsy presided, as she was called *Ambuya* by the Africans. The Shona are a matriarchal tribe and have priestesses to administer their religion. They also bear the title *Ambuya,* which means grandmother or matriarch of an extended family. The dances would become wilder and wilder, with a bogeyman character gesticulating fiercely and threateningly at *Ambuya* Townsend, only to be chased away by other costumed dancers, to cheers from the crowd. The sound of the drums and the singing would become louder and louder, until it stopped quite suddenly, and Patsy would rise and shake hands in the African manner with the leaders, a bit like the Queen, but without saying "Have you come far?" The finale consisted of the young Boss, Micky Townsend, throwing handfuls of "tickys", which were thru'pence coins, into the air whilst hordes of *pickinins* scrambled for them, egged on by their laughing mothers – rather like American soccer mums. The whole thing was a much appreciated and a highlight of the year for the compound. All this was in semi-tropical weather, although the country being on a high plateau never suffers great heat. Harare is at the same altitude as Zermatt.

When we visited in our summer, it was, of course winter, at Lowdale. The days were bright and sunny, and there might be a very light frost at night, so that a paper thin sheet of ice would form on the bird bath. A cosy fire was lit in the evening, and one still dressed warmly to ride before breakfast, shedding jumpers as the sun rose in the sky. Polo was played in the Rhodesian winter when the ground was dry and hard, preventing the very good players from playing in England in our season – except for the several polo playing Rhodesian students to be found at Cirencester Agricultural College. One morning, I watched my father-in-law's ponies being loaded on the lorry, by Dick, the lorry driver, who helped the stable boys groom. We went off to watch the match which consisted of a large cloud of dust moving rapidly up and down the field. Every once in a while, a player would emerge briefly and then re-join the dust cloud. The ball bounced erratically on the hard pitch and connecting with it was challenging. When I took up the game, I played on lush, carpet-like lawns, where the ball sat up and asked to be hit. Polo in Rhodesia was played almost exclusively by farmers and their horses were descended from the many which had been imported to South Africa from the Argentine, during the Boer War. My first mentor at Cirencester, when I started playing, was Jack Williams, who had been born in the Argentine, because his father had been in charge of the cavalry remount. The other equestrian sport which much occupied the farming community was paper chasing, a sort of combination of drag hunting and team chasing. Proper hunting with hounds, entered for wild pig, for example, was not possible because the lands were full of hidden holes. In paper chasing, a course of varied obstacles was laid over someone's farm and chasers competed against the clock. As with English country horse trials, it was a jolly, full bar in the car boot, heavy betting, and neighborly occasion. On one such ride, Dinnie was on her favourite horse Harry, given her by her father, as Harry was useless at polo. He was no better over jumps, it seems, and he topped one solid fence and dumped his rider onto the hard ground. My father-in-law, who was watching anxiously, rushed to her side, not so much to determine whether his beloved daughter was injured, but to make sure she remounted as quickly as possible, as he had backed her with serious money. Raife was not a cruel man – he was just horsey. It turned out Dinnie had concussion.

The life style of the Rhodesian farmer seems idyllic and reminiscent of the ante bellum American south – but without the pretentions to elegance, and certainly, with salaried staff and farm workers. Tobacco farmers could have an extremely prosperous year, followed by several loss-making seasons. Thetford, which was purely tobacco, would sometimes finance an extravagance, such as a new car, or a holiday hunting in Ireland but on the whole, farming in Rhodesia was not a route to a fortune, but it was something of an earthly paradise. Zanu-PF, the political freedom party headed by Robert Mugabe, was full of people who believed the white commercial farmers were enormously rich, and the commissars of the party, and generals of the new army, hastened to grab as many farms as they could, during the raids and sequestrations ordered by Mugabe. They have been seriously disappointed and most of the commercial farms now lie ruined and semi-abandoned. During the all too brief honeymoon period, after the Lancaster Agreements when HM Government handed power to Mugabe, life continued for the over-confident farmers who were greatly encouraged by the several speeches made by the new President praising their contribution, and insisting he wanted them to stay. He was married to a very clever Ghanaian lady called Sally who was well-educated and from a merchant family in Accra. She recognised Mugabe's volatile nature – he is undoubtedly bipolar, and kept him properly medicated – probably with lithium. Sadly, the First Lady died from cancer prematurely. When Sally was alive she used to buy the meat for the Presidential residence from my brother-in-law's butchery at Lowdale, renowned for its quality. Mick would get a call warning him, and saying the First Lady would appreciate tea on the veranda after completing her shopping. The whole of the compound would turn out to watch the First Lady sipping tea with the Boss. But even Sally believed the popular myth that the white farmers were all rich. When she mentioned this once, Mick excused himself, went and fetched his bank statement, and showed Sally the substantial overdraft.

"Are you sure you're not gambling at Borrowdale racecourse, Mr. Townsend?" said the first lady with a wry smile. So Mick took her through the whole statement, detailing the expenses and then showed her a schedule of estimated crop yields. There had been a drought for some time and Mick had been in the red for several years. She was convinced. What surprised her most was the banks' willingness to keep lending. Barclays and Standard Bank were the main ones then. We visited Lowdale almost every year with the children and I often arrived late, due to business commitments. One year I was met at the airport by Mick, Dinnie and the children, who were in a great state of excitement because a young African girl had been pushed down a mine shaft by two young men fighting over her favours. There was a family prospecting for gold on Lowdale, who actually managed to scratch a living doing so. For the children, Lowdale was a magical place where something extraordinary happened almost every day. For Mick, this particular happening simply meant he would have to arrange to have the girl pulled up. When the children had paused in their excited accounts of this event, Mick asked me if, by chance, I had bought a dinner jacket. Of course, I hadn't. But Mick said:

"Well, it's alright, as you are a guest – a blazer will do."

"Black tie dinners! – whatever next?" I remarked.

"It's my dining club that meets monthly at the Harare Club. A few farmers who have lost their farms, some businessmen, including several African, and a politician or two."

Mick's description was accurate. We were twenty or so, and the speaker was a former Cambridge oar who gave a fascinating and detailed description of how the University Boat Race is organised, and the tactical challenges involved for the competing crews. We could have been in any London club. I was seated next to Simba Makone, a Zanu-PF stalwart who had been with Mugabe in Mozambique, fought in the civil war and been a member of Mugabe's first cabinet. He was a great friend of Mick, who had fought against him as a member of PATU, the BSA Police anti-terrorist unit, which campaigned SAS style in the bush. As with other former adversaries, Mick and Simba Makone used to amuse themselves comparing battle notes to see if they had ever actually fired on each other. Relations between black and white in those days were truly remarkable, with no sign of bitterness, following a fierce and protracted war. Still optimistic in that honeymoon period, Mick used to say that Zimbabwe's was the only revolution in history where the losers had been allowed to keep their land and other assets. Alas, it was not to be. At the time of this dinner, things in the country were already sliding and Makone had resigned from the cabinet, in protest at Mugabe's increasingly unconstitutional behaviour. Makone and I chatted about the brain drain of young, educated Africans which was already beginning. Zimbabweans were getting good jobs in South Africa, as they were better educated. I asked how many might come back if things improved and he opined less than half. Makone made a very brave run against Mugabe in the next presidential elections, as an independent – but got wiped out by the Zanu PF political machine, whose election campaign slogan might have been "Vote for Zanu Pf and vote as often as possible – every vote counts!"

During dinner, I had an ear half-cocked to the conversation Mick, sitting on my left, was having with his neighbour David Hatendi, as they were certainly talking politics. Hatendi was a figure straight out of an Evelyn Waugh novel. Grandson of an African Anglican Bishop, descended from Shona chiefs, educated at Peterhouse, Rhodesia's top public school, and at the University of Rhodesia, he was Rhodesia's first African Rhodes Scholar. At Oxford, he played cricket for the "Authentics", participated in many activities and took a D.Phil. in Politics. David Suratgar, a Persian also up at Oxford, with whom Hatendi worked when he was at the World Bank, recalls him becoming so immersed in an Oxford life of the kind Waugh would describe, as to be almost a caricature. He adopted and retained all his life, an accent so theatrical and plummy, that P. G. Wodehouse would have considered it over the top. After Oxford, Hatendi was at Morgan Grenfell, then after spells in Washington with the IFC/World Bank, an executive director at N M Rothschild, returning to Rhodesia to run the Merchant Bank of Central Africa, in which Rothschild was the prime mover. David Hatendi was the only black member of White's and he much enjoyed the Osbert Lancaster cartoon which hangs in the bar. Two black gentlemen are propping up a club bar and one says to the other:

"Did you hear about poor Jones? He's been white balled from Black's."

I'll never forget Hatendi's remark to Mick, that evening, as they lamented the state of the country. "Do you know, Mick, the trouble with this bloody government is that none of them are gentlemen!" I believe one could have read a long analysis of Zimbabwe problems in *The Economist*, and not come away with a better summary than Hatendi's. He was also a great practical joker. Once, coming out of White's, David spotted Patrick Mavros in Jermyn Street. Mavros was a Greek who achieved great success in Rhodesia as a sculptor of African animals and other subjects, in legal ivory and various native materials and hardwoods. He eventually opened a shop in London. When Mavros failed to acknowledge him, Hatendi rang him up, and in the thickest Shona accent he could muster, represented himself as the London agent of Zimbabwe's fraud squad investigating Mavros's export of artefacts. Mavros panicked and began mumbling denials before Hatendi put him out of his misery. David Hatendi would have been a very successful actor. One day he said to me:

"Can you believe it? I sent my son to Stowe expecting he'd go up to University, my old Oxford College, and he tells me he wants to go to RADA and become an actor!"

"So what's wrong with that," I countered.

"But, I say – an actor! Is that a "pukka" thing to do?"

"My daughter is an actress."

"And that's all right with you?"

"Of course!"

David seemed relieved. I think his son would have done what he wanted anyway. He is Nyasha Hatendi and is pursuing a successful career as an actor and playwright. His father David ended up as CEO of NMB, formerly Nedbank, and helped stabilise it during the great banking crisis in Zimbabwe. Mindless africanisation of management had caused the collapse of several banks. The new management couldn't keep their hands out of the till. A Bank of England fraud investigation team, sent out to help restore order, reported that they had never seen banking fraud of such sophistication.

Our son photojournalist Michael, together with his then girlfriend, now wife, Krystal, sneaked into Zimbabwe for one of the elections. Journalist's had been barred for reporting on this to-be-rigged election – as a punishment for having reported that the previous election had been rigged. They were staying with some farming friends when the police swooped and arrested everyone, as they lounged by the pool one Sunday morning. Their host had been campaigning for the opposition, and the charge was that he was using walkie-talkies, licensed only for farm business, in helping organise the opposition. Michael and Krystal were deemed guilty by association, and jailed in Bindura. Friends brought them food and changes of clothes, but Dinnie had to call Krystal's parents to tell them. A friend gave me a telephone number at the State Department in Washington. A man's voice answered:

"Americans Abroad in Trouble – how can I help you?"

"I hate to trouble you," I began, "you must have more serious cases, but my son Michael Yassukovich is in jail in Zimbabwe; He's a journalist and isn't supposed to be there in the first place."

"That's amazing! I happen to have his file in front of me. We've already made an official complaint to their ambassador, as your son wasn't given consular access within the required 48 hours."

"How did you know about it?"

"A Mrs. Craig Dankwertz let us know – don't worry, we're on it."

What he didn't tell me was that the consular official in Harare who was assigned to the case had only just arrived in Zimbabwe, and didn't know where Bindura was. She was embarrassed to ask her boss the Consul General, and took two days to research the location. The Belgian Embassy got to Krystal almost immediately. They were released on bail, with the trial set for an a few weeks hence. When that day came they set off for Bindura and, leaving Harare, came across an African in a neat suit and tie, carrying a brief case, and thumbing a ride. They stopped:

"Excuse me," said the hitchhiker. "My car has broken down – can you give me a lift?"

"Where to?"

"Bindura, I need to get to the Court House. I'm the prosecuting attorney."

"Hop in – we're going there to. We're the defendants."

"Thank you – I thought I recognised you."

At the trial, the judge summed up.

"I hope you two understand the seriousness of your offence – or to put it another way, the seriousness of the offence your host has been charged with, but not yet convicted of. I fine you both 100 Zimbabwe dollars. Case dismissed." At the time, this was the equivalent of roughly ten U.S. cents. Let no one say Zimbabwe is a dysfunctional country. It functions, but not in a way we find familiar.

The Mrs. Craig Dankwertz referred to was Roxy, the daughter of Sally Carney, whose family farm almost marched with Lowdale. Sally had been an Olympic showjumper, competing in Mexico City, and eventually marrying Danny Carney. The son of a widower Irish born diplomat, Danny had suffered an unsettled life, and finally "got in with the wrong crowd", as apologists for juvenile delinquents like to say. A magistrate was about to send him to Borstal, when his father intervened, from some foreign posting, and the Foreign Office agreed to send him off to Rhodesia to join the BSA Police. Once there, he became a passionate fan of the novels of Wilbur Smith, and began to write. He was introduced to Euan Lloyd, a former Rank executive, who already had some film successes under his belt. One afternoon, Euan was sitting in Danny's little writing *rondavel*, when he noticed a typed manuscript, warped and yellowed from sitting in the sun on a window shelf.

"What's this?" asked Euan.

"It's a record breaking manuscript, as it's been rejected by more publishers than any work in recent history."

"Let me read it."

"Be my guest."

Two days later:

"I like it. I want to buy the film rights – who's your agent?"

"Haven't got one – talk to Sally. She'll negotiate."

The result of this badly scripted little scene was a film called *The Wild Geese,* starring Richard Burton, Roger Moore, Richard Harris and Hardy Kruger. Controversially filmed in South Africa, it was the highest grossing film of 1978. It was Euan Lloyd's most successful production but not his first hit. His filmographical details are as interesting as Danny Carney's early history. Encouraged by Allan Ladd, who was in England filming *The Green Berets,* and who recognised Lloyd's knowledge and enthusiasm for the film industry, he went on to become an assistant to Cubby Broccoli and producer of documentaries and feature films. Lloyd was an ardent admirer of the Western novels of Louis Lamour, an African-American writer who lived in New Orleans. When Lloyd finally met Lamour, introduced by Ladd, he so impressed the writer with his knowledge of his work – which he almost knew by heart, that Lamour offered Lloyd a free, six months option on the film rights of his latest book. Lloyd set out to raise the money and his first port of call was Henry Fonda.

"Young man," said the great star, "you've come to the wrong place. You won't raise a dime on my name. Due to the antics of my politically active daughter Jane, I am dead meat at the box office."

Jane Fonda was known as "Hanoi Jane", at this point, having given the wrong signals in speaking in the enemy camp during the Vietnam War.

"But, let me give you a tip," continued Fonda. "There are plenty of younger European film stars who grew up on American cowboy movies and would love to be in one. For example, why not give Sean Connery a call? He's an up-and-coming name and has just the he-man looks you need."

Lloyd did so.

"Will there be a scene where I can come in through the swinging saloon doors, draw a six-gun and shoot up the bar?" asked Connery, in his best Scottish accent.

"I'll see to it," replied Lloyd.

"Count me in," said Connery, "and following up on Mr. Fonda's idea, why not call Brigitte Bardot, she'll love it."

"Bardot! But I don't know Miss Bardot," protested Lloyd.

"Tell her I said to call."

Again, Lloyd had a favourable response.

"A Westairn! I love ze Westairn! All my life I want to be in ze Westairn!" cooed the French permanent starlet. So *Shalako* was cast, adding Jack Hawkins, Honour Blackman, Woody Strode and Eric Sykes, filmed in Spain, directed by veteran Edward Dimytrick – Euan Lloyd never looked back. If it didn't happen exactly this way, it should have. I got to know Euan Lloyd through the Carneys and, at European Banking Company, financed one of his films, *Who Dares Wins*, a thriller inspired by the SAS hostage rescue raid on the Iranian legation in London, and introducing a talented newcomer, the Australian Judy Davis, as a terrorist gang leader. It wasn't a great critical success, but Stanley Kubrick is reputed to have congratulated Lloyd on the film, and on finding Judy Davis. After some research I found film financing not as risky or complex as some would believe. In fact, it's as simple as ABC, meaning it follows classic project finance principles. Completion guarantees, distribution contracts, insurance policies of various kinds, and the intellectual property, serve as security, draw down is against tightly budgeted schedules, and the lender is the first paid out of the gross receipts. Where banks have gotten into trouble is because they rely on the fame and record of a producer, forgetting that even the best can lay an egg, from time to time. As in all banking transactions – best stick to the fundamentals. Euan Lloyd is known as the last of the "gentlemen producers". I cannot validate this view because he is the only producer I know – but he is certainly a great gentleman. I was once asked to chair a committee organising a charity auction, by Lady Howard de Walden. I cannot remember why, but the charity was the Injured Jockeys Fund, and we were collecting sporting and entertainment memorabilia to auction. I had asked Jarvis Astaire, a sports impresario and brother of Edgar, the stockbroker, to join the committee and also Euan Lloyd. We were nearing the auction day and still short of notable items, when Euan, who had already donated some Louis Lamour signed first editions, suddenly took off his watch and placed it on the table. It was platinum and engraved on the back "To Euan Lloyd from his friend Frank Sinatra".

"You can't donate that, Euan!" I exclaimed.

"Why not?" he replied. "Frank loves to play the horses and he would want to support the jockeys."

I had one disappointment. In his declining years, a widowed Fred Astaire had married a young lady jockey – the first to race at Santa Anita race track in

California. Astaire had since died, but I wrote his widow and asked if she might donate some article of Fred's elegant clothing. I had in mind the socks with horizontal stripes he wore in several films. I thought, surely, as a jockey herself, she will relate to the cause. I had no reply.

We went almost every year to Lowdale, and even once or twice after the farm was invaded by squatters and so-called war vets, many of whom would have been babes in arms during the war. Mick continued to serve in various capacities. He considered himself a Zimbabwean and was not prepared to "take the gap", as the expression went to describe the emigres. One year, when he was Deputy Chairman of the Harare Show, he had to step in for Dennis Norman, the Chairman who was hospitalised in London. Norman was the last European to serve in Mugabe's cabinet and at one point had two ministries, Agriculture and Transport. The Harare Show is a big annual event and Mugabe invites a fellow dictator from another African state as a guest of honour. Mick was summoned to the presidential presence to discuss arrangements for the grand opening. The guest was to be Kabila of Zaire. Mugabe began by enquiring
"Will we see the amusing competition for prize seed maize between Lowdale and your wife's farm Ballanetee?"
"I'm afraid not, Mr. President, both our farms are occupied."
"What! Seed maize producers are exempt from our land reform," then; picking up a phone, "Send Minister Madé in here!"
Madé was Minister of Agriculture; He soon appears;
"What's this? Mr. Townsend tells me Lowdale is occupied. It is supposed to be exempt."
"Mr. President, I don't understand why Mr. Townsend has gone over my head to you on this matter."
"He hasn't. I summoned him here to discuss the Show."
"Clearly there has been an administrative error. If Mr. Townsend will come and see me, I will look in to the matter immediately."
This was the first inkling Mick had that Mugabe had little idea of what was going on. Indeed, as Mick escorted him around the greatly diminished agricultural displays at the Show, Mugabe looked around and asked, "Where are all the white farmers?" The original land reform proposals were to take absentee owned farms – of which there were far too many, or one farm from a farmer who owned more than one. But the process was taken over from the Ministry of Agriculture by the Politbureau of the ruling party Zanu PF, and even it lost control, with thugs roaming around and attacking farms at random. But the underlying cause of the destruction of the white owned commercial farming sector was that Mugabe felt betrayed. He had begun by pledging a continuing welcome to white commercial farmers who were Zimbabwean citizens and would commit to serving the country. Mick was on the committee of the Commercial Farmers Union and pleaded with them to stay out of politics. He pointed out that trade associations, like the CBI, have to work

with whichever party is in power. Furthermore the African concept of democracy is different from ours. It is more a question of one man, one vote, once. The Chief remains in power for life. The British expression "Her Majesty's Loyal Opposition" is an oxymoron for the African politician. How can the opposition be loyal? Unfortunately Mick's colleagues wouldn't listen and, not only publically backed the opposition to Zanu PF, but encouraged their workers to do the same. With extreme naïvté, they thought they were merely exercising their rights under the new constitution, and – were they not responsible for guiding their poorly educated farm workers? There was a whiff of arrogance in this sort of paternalism. It might have been sincerely applied, but in today's politicised world, paternalism is viewed with suspicion. Mugabe, when he realised what was happening, considered he had been stabbed in the back. The whites were not loyal at all! He would extract his revenge. The rest is history.

During the honeymoon period, Mick had a visit to Lowdale from one of the new ministers. He gave him an extensive tour, the school, where the African teacher, seeing the Boss arrive with a Minister, led his class in a loyal party song, the medical and dental facility – a dentist came once a week, the farm store, the *rondavels* in the compound, where not only the working families lived, but also the old, retired people. The minister was impressed. Like most at Zanu PF, he was a London School of Economics Marxist. The party members called each other "Comrade".

"Mr Townsend," said the Minister, at tour's end. "You have a perfect Socialist state here. You look after your people from cradle to grave. You give them their work, educate their children and give them free health care. This is pure socialism!"

"Actually, Minister," replied Mick, unwilling to accept such a compliment, "I would call it feudalism."

After his meeting with Mugabe and , Mick did as instructed and followed strict procedure in trying to get his farm back, knowing full well that the system was now totally corrupted. Judges who ruled against illegal seizures were quickly replaced and their decisions overturned. Most of the farms seized were allocated to party apparatchiks, or allowed to go fallow, rather than being distributed to "landless peasants". One of Mick's friends, whose farm had been taken, was approached by a General, who was now its presumed owner.

"I know nothing about farming," said the General, "and in any case the farm is rather far away. Would you like to manage it for me? After all, you know it well."

"I'll have to get a crop loan from the bank."

"Go to it – and, of course, you can live in the house, while you are running the place."

The ex-farmer, bemused and sceptical, approached the bank – but they said they could not lend as the General had no title to the land.

"How do I tell him that!" he wondered. But summoning up his courage, he did.

"Hmm!" said the General, frowning only slightly. "I can fix that. Go back to them in a couple of days' time." He did, and the bank made the loan. As for Lowdale, no powerful figure had been given the farm – it was just squatted on by thugs, who chased the domestic staff out of their lodgings and generally abused the compound. Mick and his son Bryan would sneak on from time to time, fell some trees and sell the wood to pay the farm workers. For some, they found jobs at the University of Zimbabwe's experimental farm, which was fairly close by and still operating. One day a police chief with a squad of riot police turned up at Lowdale, summoned the squatters, and gave them 24 hours' notice to quit. He was accompanied by an unidentified official in a business suit. Of course the squatters protested vigorously, claiming they were war vets – and on whose authority were they being evicted? The police chief pointed to the man in the suit, who spoke two words: "The President". The squatters extinguished their fires on the front lawn and left. Mick was told he could return. The house had not been broken into, and Mick found his un-made bed, and other signs of his rapid departure, such as breakfast things on the table and dead rats in the toilet bowls. Cathy, his wife, never was able to regain Balaneetee, and the prize, pedigree herd of Sussex cattle, known worldwide, which her father had founded, and Cathy had maintained meticu-lously, was simple eaten by the squatters. Mick had had the good sense, some years previously, to donate a piece of land to the police for a training ground and target range. The police are jealous of the status quo and offer unofficial protection to Lowdale. Our nephew Bryan is still on the farm, has no idea how much of it he has, and is not inclined to enquire. He can no longer grow seed maize, as the distribution system has collapsed, so he market gardens, growing peas and things, which he can sell in Harare, and even export. When my brother-in-law Mick Townsend died prematurely of a heart attack, Mugabe went on the wireless and delivered a short eulogy. "Michael Town-send was a distinguished Zimbabwean, who served his country well, as a board member of the National Parks and Game Authority, Chairman of the Harare Show, and in other capacities. He understood and supported the need for land reform. I express my sympathies to his family". The speech was re-ported in the national press. There was a nice touch of African irony about it. On the National Parks and Game Authority, Mick had watched with dismay as ministers muscled in on the safari business, to get their hands on the for-eign exchange the sale of licences generated. He had also seen the best track-ers and guides poached by South African parks, able to pay higher salaries to the best trained men in all of Africa.

For Dinnie, Lowdale occupies a place in her heart almost in reverse pro-portion to the time she lived there. She was sent off to boarding school at eight years, travelling two and a half days on the train to attend Herschel School in Cape Town – only able to return home twice a year. After matriculation, she was soon sent to Lausanne, where the unlikely fate of meeting her future husband awaited her. After a brief return to Lowdale, she was off to London. From direct and vicarious experience, Lowdale entered my soul as well, and I make no apology for the fact that my impressions of Africa emanate from that unique vantage point. Whenever and where ever I land in Africa, the scent and sound that strike me are like the taste of Proust's *madeleine,* and I am back at Lowdale. When we settled in Gloucestershire, Dinnie suddenly found a host of Rhodesian friends in the immediate neighbourhood: Sandra Lamb, who sold us our first horse, Gladstone; Catherine Corbett, whose father Lord Acton farmed in the next valley to Lowdale; Michael and Helen Whitbread, who had lunched at Lowdale, whilst living in Northern Rhodesia; Jane Fearnley-Whittingstall, née Lascelles, whose son Hugo has become a celebrity chef; Nigel Gibbs, whose father Sir Humphrey was the last Governor of Southern Rhodesia, pre UDI; Peta Lodge, whose father Sir Albert Robinson was Chairman of Standard Bank in Salisbury, and High Commissioner of the Federation in London. Even here in France, Old Herschellians keep popping up, amongst the many South Africans, who spend their winters with us.

CHAPTER XVII

"England has saved herself by her exertions and will, as I trust, save Europe by her example"

-William Pitt, in a speech at the Mansion House, 1808-

I wonder if Pitt is really responsible for introducing that pernicious aberration in semantics which has England distinct from Europe, as opposed to the Continent, or is his meaning that England *within* Europe will accomplish the salvation? Judging from 19th century literature, the distinction between Europe as a whole, and the Continent as its largest part was widely understood. One spoke of the Continental ferry to Calais, not the European. Of course, Calais had been English for just as long as it's been French, but that fact was ignored with the popular expression "Wogs begin at Calais". I would submit that it is only in recent times, and with the political issue of European Union membership, that the British public, and media have begun to confuse the Continent with Europe. This is because the phrases "pro- Europe" and "anti-Europe" are thrown around with reckless abandon to denote a political view on the issue of EU membership. I am past bemoaning the rape of our beloved prefix "Euro" to name the object of a highly dubious monetary experiment. But to attach Euro to "sceptic" is ridiculous. One cannot be sceptical of one's geographical location. "EU sceptic" would be to the point – but clumsy for typesetters. But behind it all, is a propaganda campaign from Brussels which seeks to assign European legitimacy only to those who unreservedly support the European Union and its nefarious workings. This is dangerously close to the propaganda message of the National Socialists in 1930s Germany, which was that anyone who did not support the Party was not a good German.

We "Eurotrash" in the City in the early 1970s, wallowing in the extraordinary success of the Euromarkets, were not much fussed with such geopolitical issues as the relentless drive of the European Economic Community to be something more than most people wanted. We had long since overcome the regulatory inconvenience of operating in a multinational environment. We had Euro clear, and soon a competitor – Cedel. We had our increasingly influential trade association, the AIBD. The primary market operators were soon to set up their own, the International Primary Market Association – IPMA. There remained a social divide between secondary and primary market people, but this was fading. In essence we had our own culture, and although the epicentre was the City of London, the permanent market share of DM and Swiss Franc issues assured a continuing Continental flavour. There were attempts to use artificial currencies – the Unit of Account, even Special Drawing Rights, but these were no more than flashes in the pan. Eventually, a Euro sterling issue for an oil major was successful – even a euro-Canadian dollar issue appeared, according to Chris O'Malley – but I don't recall it. A further sign of the maturity of my heroine, the Eurobond, was the interest expressed by the U.S. rating agencies, Moody's and Standard & Poor. Retail investors, which predominated in the early period, were unconcerned with the absence of ratings – seen by some as an aid for lazy, box-ticking institutions, who couldn't be bothered to determine themselves whether an issue was investment grade. In the U.S. market the rating system was based on a feature which was to haunt it in the future: the rating agency was paid by the issuer. It was as if the Michelin guide was paid by restaurants to award stars – an obvious conflict. Faced with a lack of interest from Eurobond issuers and their bankers, the agencies decided to engage in loss leading, and began to provide unsolicited ratings. One of their first clumsy initiatives was for one of our issues at White, Weld. It was a five-year note issue for Barclays D.C. & O. failing to notice that the issue was *not* guaranteed by the parent Barclays Bank, Moody's happily rated it AAA. Most people assume that the rating is being assigned to the issuer, but it is not – it is assigned to the issue. It would be possible for a so-called, triple-A borrower to issue a double-B bond, by subordinating it, excluding a negative pledge clause, and loading it with other credit diluting conditions. In this case the issuer was a subsidiary of Barclays Bank, called Barclays District, Colonial and Overseas, a name which suggests much of its assets were in third world countries – and there was no parent guaranty. My boy hood faith in the god like attributes of the rating agencies was shaken. In modern times, they went on to assign investment grade ratings to packaged products of home mortgages and consumer credits, which, when taken apart, were clearly total rubbish.

A major shift in liquidity was looming on the horizon, which would institutionalise the Eurobond market further, but also boost the main alternative source of medium to long-term funding in the international market. This was the medium-term, syndicated bank loan market, which my friend Minos Zombanakis had feared would be snuffed out by FRN issues. Events were about to increase the price of oil, and the revenues of its producer countries. Armand Hammer, the maverick head of Occidental Petroleum, made a cut rate deal for concessions in Libya which undermined the pricing cartel of the "Seven Sisters", the major oil multinationals, and Egypt and Syria jointly attacked Israel, leading to the "Yom Kippur" war. OPEC became the determinant power in oil pricing, which hadn't moved much since 1947. Oil prices more than quadrupled and Saudi and Gulf State revenues ballooned. Thus was born the "petrodollar". The exporters were smart enough to avoid directly financing the corresponding deficits of second and third world country forced to import the new black gold. A candid Arab friend of mine once said to me "With all you dumb and greedy bankers around, why should we take the risk of sovereign defaults, when we can spread our money around the banks, and they can take the risk". As the business of recycling got under way, I was commissioned by The Banker Research Unit, to write a pamphlet entitled, grandly *Oil and Money, the Politics of Recycling.* I subsequently recommended it to friends suffering from insomnia as ideal bedtime reading. I dictated this tedious *oeuvre* into a recording machine and asked my long-suffering sister-in-law Mattie to type it. She reported that, after a while, my turgid prose seemed to flow directly from her earphones to her fingers. The banking world rushed to the Middle East to tap the new mega-wealth and hotel rooms in Jedda, Abu Dhabi and Kuwait City were fought for, with the most unlikely pairs of competing bankers having to share rooms. I made Beirut a first stop on my trips as the concierge at the St. George's Hotel was either related to, or the best friend of every concierge/hall porter in the Gulf. One would open one's heart and billfold to him, with pleas for help in finding a room. "*Mais Monsieur! Je téléphone à mon collègue à Abu Dhabi et on verra ce qui peut s'arranger*" » I could never prove it, but I believe all the hall porters kept a joint account at a bank in Beirut, where they pooled the bribes and shared them out according to a pre-agreed formula. On one of my first visits to the area, I flipped open the copy of the Koran, which one finds in the bedside table, where the Gideon Bible usually is in America. I came across a passage saying that not only lenders at interest would roast in Hell, but borrowers as well. This gave new meaning to Polonius's advice in *Hamlet* – neither lender nor borrower be. Of course, the nation's most in need of financing their hugely increased oil import bills were the ones with the weakest credit rating. It was during this period that commercial bankers began to shed their traditionally risk adverse habits. The old adage "never lend money to countries where they don't wear overcoats" was ignored. It had never been foolproof anyway, since they wear overcoats in Argentina, but the country defaults as easily as fashion changes skirt lengths. As the issue of sovereign risk began to be more openly discussed, Walter Wriston, Chairman of First National City Bank, by now known as FNCB, made one of those easily quotable, but essentially stupid remarks, celebrity bankers have become known for. "Countries can't go bankrupt," he intoned, "I consider our sovereign loan portfolio will have a lower rate of default than our automobile loans." Then, there was no Cassandra-like pundit to point out that automobiles can be easily seized in foreclosure, but modern sensitivities made gun boat collection more difficult. In the 19th century, the British had sent warships to make Venezuela pay up, and Napoleon III put an Austrian Arch Duke on the throne of Mexico, backed by French troops, to assure the repayment of Mexican bonds owned by

French *rentiers*. Poor, well meaning, Maximillian actually introduced more reforms to reduce the abject poverty of the peasants, than his predecessors or successors in power, and even adopted a Mexican lad to be Crown Prince – but they shot him anyway, and defaulted on the bonds. Even worse, Napoleon III abandoned his agent, and would not save him from the firing squad. "Put not they trust in princes" it says in the Book of Common Prayer, but then the Bonapartes were upstarts, not proper princes.

As the rush to recycle became all the rage, we at White, Weld were not in the game. Eurobond houses had little success selling bonds to the Sheiks. A number of private placements were arranged, but this was a hit-or-miss business. I cannot say I was then a doubter about the whole business of lending money to borrowers who could not qualify for the bond market. White, Weld was at the top of its game in the early '70s, always ranking in the top three of the lead management league tables, and maintaining its leading secondary market share. In the mid-'70s, securities markets suffered worldwide. Eurobond issue volume fell from over $5.3 billion in 1972 to $2 billion in 1974 – according to Chris O'Malley. Even more ominously, the U.S. Interest Equalisation Tax, which had been the main driver of the Eurobond phenomena, was first reduced to zero, and then repealed in 1974. My heroine, the Eurobond, was in tears. The New York market for dollar issues was open again, and for the next four years the volume of so-called Yankee bond issues exceeded the Eurobond issue volume. Some predicted the end of the City's revival as the premier international financial centre. But costs and clumsy regulation in the U.S. saved the day. The process of SEC registration, and the higher underwriting and selling costs in the U.S., made the Eurobond market more competitive, and its practitioners were more flexible and innovative than their brethren in New York.

In Europe, the syndicated loan market was growing apace, but the problem of liquidity limited the participation of smaller banks. In fact commercial bank balance sheets served as a cap on the total size of the market. An enterprising American named Joe Baird thought he had a solution. He ran an early consortium bank called Western American Bank in which Wells Fargo of California and Hambros in London were the main shareholders. His idea was to introduce liquidity into the syndicated loan market by making participations transferrable, capable in theory of being traded in a secondary market – a sort of halfway house to the Floating Rate Note market. Participations would not be bearer instruments, and it required somewhat complicated documentation to ensure transfer of the various covenants incorporated in a normal loan agreement. Nevertheless, Joe predicted great things for this concept and he approached me to join him. No one had ever tried to poach me before. Fortunately for my self-esteem, I had never bothered to wonder why. Baird came on strong: big increase in salary, bonuses galore, low interest home mortgage, insurance, pension, a limousine and driver – I wondered if he had researched the fact that none of these things were available at White, Weld. He wheeled me in to see Jocelyn Hambro, his chairman. Jocelyn was a charming, old school merchant banker, and I certainly did not begrudge him the fact that he employed the dreaded Robin Hutton. He could not have been more courteous. But my interview with him cost Joe Baird his recruit. It was clear to me that, although he gamely tried to support his CEO's recruiting effort, he did not quite share Baird's blind faith in the concept. I contrasted his presentation with the kind I had so often heard Bob Genillard make. When Bob laid out the prospects for White, Weld's European business model, you knew he *believed.* Jocelyn Hambro was just going through the motions. I said "thanks – but no" to Joe Baird, but my tiny mind started thinking. An expert fly fisherman would tell me if a trout which takes a first, but inconclusive nibble at the fly, is easier to catch the second time. Certainly I know that if one's horse refuses a fence, one becomes even more determined to get the brute over on the next attempt; the horse feels that determination, grows in confidence, and clears the fence with a foot or two to spare. I'm not sure the analogy works that well, but the fact remains – my feet had started to itch.

One day John Scott-Oldfield rang me up. John was at Spencer Stewart, the executive search consultants, but he was on his last assignment there, as he was about to set up his own consultancy. A Cambridge graduate, where he had been an Olympic standard runner, John had then been with Royal Dutch Shell, serving in Nigeria and the Philippines. John Loudon, head of Royal Dutch, was known for recruiting bright university graduates and putting them though the extensive Royal Dutch system, knowing full well he couldn't retain them all, as their experience would make them highly desirable executives to industry at large. This background makes me suspect that it was young John Loudon, then at Lazard, and a close friend of Scott-Oldfield, who gave the latter my name. John was married to Baroness Honora Furstenburg, who he had met in Manila, where her father was German Ambassador. I was invited to lunch at Le Caprice – in those days, one rarely lunched in the West End, and I reckoned John was not familiar with the ways of the City. After the usual small talk, John broached the subject.
"I need your help. I have a significant assignment from the EBIC group who are planning to open a new merchant bank in the City and they are looking for a chief executive. They have normally assigned on executive from one of the member banks to run their joint ventures, but for this important initiative, they are looking outside. I usually look after appointments in industry, and I don't have many contacts in the City."
EBIC was one of several associations of commercial banks, at this time. The trend was an early sign of a growing urge to consolidate in the banking sector. EBIC was the most prestigious example as it comprised Deutsche Bank in Germany, Midland Bank in the U.K., Société Genérale of France, Banca Commerciale Italiano in Milan, Générale de Banque in Belgium, Amsterdam-Rotterdam Bank in the Netherlands, and Creditanstalt in Austria. It

had already set up joint ventures: European-American Bank in New York, Banque Européène de Credit à Moyen Terme in Brussels and European- Asian Bank in Hamburg. The official line was that they were helping each other compete with the large U.S. banks – but had no intention to merge. Some wag had nicknamed them "the Batchelor's Club".

"How can I help?" was my naïve answer.

"If you could give me a few names you think might be suitable candidates."

"Well, can you describe what sort of profile you are looking for; The City's full of international bankers."

John took a deep breath.

"He should be of continental European background, but with Wall Street experience and connections. We want someone already prominent in the Euromarkets, particularly Eurobonds. He should speak at least one continental language, preferably French. We're looking for someone with a City profile, used to speaking at conferences, and skilled at building client relationships. Ideally he will have worked at a traditional merchant bank, but also with one of the American investment banks. I realise that's a tall order."

"I'm about to sound a bit immodest – but I can't help saying you have just described me."

"How extraordinary! You are right – it never occurred to me!" said John, lying through his teeth.

"But, I'm not the only fish in the pond that meets those specifications. I can probably think of one or two others," I was hedging now.

"But would you be interested?"

Scott-Oldfield had been employing the oldest trick in the head hunter's book. Always approach your target by claiming you want his help finding someone else. But I was flattered. With the second poaching attempt in a short while, I was beginning to think I had market value.

The approach came at a critical moment in my thinking with respect to both the situation at White, Weld, and the evolution of the international financial market. I had been uneasy about the growing gulf between our highly successful European operations under Genillard and the domestic franchise of White, Weld in New York. A corporate uncoupling had put our European businesses under the new holding company WW Trust A. G., in Zug, with Credit Suisse now a partner. In this construction, we had exploited and built on the base which had been created by DY and Jean Cattier, both essentially New York based, senior partners. They were now limited partners, Harold Mandelsohn had sadly died early and we no longer had a senior representative at head office. We were now the tail wagging the dog, as profitability of the domestic franchise was in decline. Emory Katzenbach was the senior partner in charge, and doing the best he could to cope with major change in the Wall Street scene. But there existed what might be termed a continuity vacuum, because, with Alec and Ogden White no longer active, their natural successors by blood and marriage, Sandy White, George Montgomery and Charlie Lee showed no inclination to lead the firm. A new partner Paul Hallingby, had been recruited from Middle South Utilities, where he had been a highly successful executive and also had developed a number of utility industry contacts. As a result he came with what is known as a "book of business" i.e. the potential for landing utility mandates, a sector where the firm was already fairly strong. Hallingby was not a White Weld "type", in my estimation, but he was certainly extremely ambitious and would work his way to the top of the firm in the next few years – and then sell it. I felt this transatlantic drifting apart very keenly, although Genillard and my other European partners did not. Even Johnny Cattier seemed relaxed about it. But I had been born and bred White Weld through DY, and I considered these people to be almost family. I felt the loss of a strong, working connection with New York would be damaging to our business. I was right in one sense but short-sighted in another, as the connection was eventually lost, but it was quickly replaced with another, and the European business prospered even more. Another issue was the strong emergence of the Eurodollar syndicated loan market, which was proving the principle recycling medium between oil producer surpluses and oil importer deficits. The Eurobond market could neither stretch its size, or its credit quality limits, to accommodate sovereign borrowers, such as Brazil, Argentina or the Philippines. I felt an international investment bank had to have this additional string to its bow. Investment banks like Kuhn, Loeb and Lehman had managed to earn arrangement fees on syndicated bank loans, but this was increasingly resented by the participating banks, who were taking the balance sheet risk, and was to be a short-lived phenomena. We had never sought such a role at White Weld. I saw the EBIC group as providing the lending credibility to an originating function. True, the group had already created a specialist medium-term lender in the clumsily named Banque Europeène du Credit à Moyen Terme, fortunately universally known as BEC, but it only participated in transactions originated and led by others. It was, in fact, a passive lender with a sole function. A London merchant bank could originate, structure and lead, whilst exploiting the balance sheet strength of its shareholders. Orion Bank, recently created by Chase Manhattan, Royal Bank of Canada, Mitsubishi Bank, Westdeutsche Landesbank and Credito Italiano, was the perfect example of the concept.

Perhaps the overwhelming consideration for me was the chance to create my "own" merchant bank in London. If I had a creative impulse in theatrical terms – and I did view investment banking as theatrical – it was to be a producer, rather than an actor, although I became both later on in my dotage. The business model outlined in very general terms by John Scott-Oldfield, and later in conversations with my Chairman to be, Fritz Karsten of AMRO, coincided with my own ideas. I don't think I was foolish enough to believe the concept of consortium banking was to be a permanent feature of the financial scene. I had already witnessed an aspect of corporate psyche, which I was to run across several times in my future associations. If the child fails, the parent abandons it or simply brings it home and eliminates its quasi-autonomy. If it succeeds, the parent becomes jealous, tries to undermine it, and also seeks to subjugate it and end its independence. In rare cases, the child wriggles out from parental control, and prospers as a free agent. This was to be the happy fate of White, Weld Europe – at least for a good period. Consortium banking was a fashion because financial markets were globalising so fast that few independent banks could remain competitive in terms of geographic reach and functional diversity without a collaborative association with others. The entities set up by these associations were designed to cover a geographic or a business void, or both. Once these spaces began to be filled by the joint subsidiary, the parents would gain the experience and confidence to enter them directly, thus making the entity, and the collaboration which created it, redundant. But even during its brief life as a fluttering butterfly, the consortium bank had to cope with permanent head office syndrome: jealousy and suspicion on the part of those within the parent who are not directly involved with the child. Much of this is a retrospective analysis. But I do think I accepted my new appointment, if not with my eyes wide open, at least with a steely eyed determination to make hay whilst the consortium sun shone.

I went to Geneva to meet Bob Genillard and Johnny Cattier for lunch and break the news. Bob was now mostly in Geneva as Clariden Bank, now back in the WW Trust fold, had opened a branch there, and he had acquired a chateau surrounded by vines, near Rolles, between Geneva and Lausanne. Johnny also now had a house overlooking the Lac Léman, as the Vaudois like to call it – as opposed to the Lac de Genève. In justifying my decision to jump ship, I focussed on my interest in the syndicated loan market and my belief it would become a major financing medium, alongside the Eurobond market. I did not focus on my concerns over the transatlantic strains within the White Weld group. I though this too sensitive, as many in New York were bitter over Bob Genillard's refusal to ride to the rescue of the domestic firm, by moving to New York and taking charge. To this day there are White Weld alumni who blame him for the firm's eventual demise as an independent investment bank. I found my two senior partners both sad and understanding. Perhaps I was a little disappointed they did not make a greater effort to retain me. I don't know what they could have done. Bob was in the process of setting up a unique Swiss form of share option, called a *schuldshein*, which would make the executives of WW, and eventually Credit Suisse White Weld, and even finally Credit Suisse First Boston, all millionaires. Neither Bob nor Johnny pointed out that this was what I was leaving behind, because neither was in the habit of making compensation promises to retain key people, a habit which was eventually led to a compensation explosion in the industry. I think John Stancliffe was sad to see me go.

In those days the concept of "gardening leave" between jobs had not been invented, but I nevertheless decide to take a break and checked in to a health clinic called Forest Mere. I cannot for the life of me recall why I did this – I was super slim, in those days. On arrival, the staff expressed surprise and probably thought I was hiding from a wife on the warpath over some infidelity. Not true. Within a few days I was feeling like death warmed over. Breakfast consisted of a glass of warm water, with a slice of lemon in it. Lunch was a half grapefruit and dinner was a half grapefruit with a maraschino cherry in the middle. The regime consisted of massages, saunas and Royal Canadian Air Force exercises. One day I ran into Michael Belmont, a partner of Cazenove, in the sauna.

"How would you like a weekend break?"

"I didn't know that was allowed," I said.

"Absolutely – but you have to promise to eat nothing but strawberries and only drink champagne while you are away."

"You're joking."

"Not a bit. I come here every year and I always do it. You live quite near me. Meet me Saturday morning in front of the house and I'll give you a lift."

It's true Michael had a house in Oxfordshire, very near ours in Bibury, which is close to the Gloucestershire/Oxfordshire border. As Forest Mere is in Hampshire, I visualised a longish drive, but I was becoming stir crazy in this so-called health resort, but I wouldn't contemplate sneaking out to a local pub, as many regulars did. I reported as requested, and, rather than a waiting motorcar, found a helicopter in the lawn, its rotor blades turning slowly, and Belmont beckoning me. I told the pilot there was a paddock in front of our house, slightly sloping, but large enough to land in. Dinnie and the children were having lunch in the breakfast room, which looked out on the paddock in question, as our helicopter dropped down and disgorged me. We had only recently arrived in Bibury, and helicopter visits were an infrequent event. Given my mysteriously exotic name, a rumour spread in the village that I was either a Soviet agent, or MI5 engaged in Cold War operations. On the Sunday evening, Dinnie drove me to the Belmont's house and the chopper took us back. Belmont's partiality for Forest Mere had an unfortunate consequence. He persuaded the Savoy Group, a major Cazenove client, to acquire Forest Mere, but the transaction was funded with equity and the resulting dilution just dropped the D'Oyley Carte Trust below the level of a controlling stake in the Savoy Group. The percentage change was so small that no one noticed it at the time. The sensitivity to dilution which this caused was to bring us a piece of business in future at European Banking Company – EBC, as we became known. One day I had a call from the finance director of the Savoy Group saying they were buying a hotel in Paris from owners with a Swiss holding company who wanted to be paid in Swiss francs. Had I any idea how the deal could be financed in "Swissie"? He didn't want to take the counterparty risk of currency hedging. I pointed out the risk could be spread, but an obvious solution was a Swiss Franc note placement. This was an active private placement market, with maturities usually five years. He liked it and mandated us to arrange it. We were well into the placing phase when I got another call;

"I've just discovered to my horror that these Swiss Franc notes we are issuing are in bearer form," said a panicky CFO.

"Of course." I replied. "All Swiss Franc note placements are bearer – just like Eurobonds."

"But that means we won't know who holds them!"

"That's right. It's a fundamental feature of the market."

"This could be a deal breaker. I'll have to get back to you. I'm not sure the Savoy Group can effectively do business with perfect strangers."

A nail-biting two days went by and he rang again.

"This has been a very difficult problem for us. But we are prepared to proceed on condition that EBC gives us an assurance that the people who will hold these notes are the sort of people we would be happy to see staying at the Savoy."

I paused.

"I can't put that in a legal agreement, but I can give you a personal assurance that that will be the case."

"That's enough for me. Let's go ahead."

But the CFO was hoist with his own petard. We had placed some of the notes with the Kuwait Investment Fund, and the expatriate Englishman who ran it telephoned me a year later, during Royal Ascot week.

"The Savoy tells me they are fully booked and can't give me a suite. I own a bunch of their notes. Do something."

I called the CFO.

"This is awkward. I suppose we shall have to accommodate him."

"Yes, please! He is certainly the sort of person you would like to see staying at your hotel. I'm sure you remember my assurance."

"We will – although I never promised to give every note holder a room at any time."

It had been a pleasure doing business with him.

But this was in the future. In the meantime, I was released from Forest Mere, no thinner, but decidedly weaker. I vowed not to try such a thing again. I went to Amsterdam for long session with my new Chairman. Fritz Karsten was a Rotterdam Bank man who had risen to the top of the merged bank. AMRO was an interesting example of the difficulty of combining corporate cultures, a problem which plagues most mergers – particularly in the banking sector. Several years after the merger of these two Dutch banks, from cities a stone's throw from each other each, the staff was not merged and people were still labelled as Amsterdam or Rotterdam. Karsten's Head of International was an Amsterdamer called Fop Hoogendijk. The two were very close and worked effectively together, particularly on EBIC related matters. And yet they were like chalk and cheese. Karsten was a bluff, no nonsense banker of modest background, and intensely reliable and loyal. Hoogendijk shared those qualities, but he was aristocratic, diplomatic, suave and cultured. Whilst Karsten went straight to the point, Fop negotiated his way around it, but often secured it where Fritz didn't. "Fop" was short for Fopbertus, a name sometimes written without the "p", and appropriately, Fop was somewhat foppish in his dress. Both stressed that AMRO's international strategy was entirely based on their EBIC membership and they would give full support to the new London merchant bank, which they saw as the most exiting of the EBIC joint venture affiliates. This sentiment was to be echoed, with varying degrees of sincerity, by each of my seven shareholders. It had been agreed that I could ask for seconded personnel to help staff the bank, but the choice of individuals was to be mine alone. AMRO had no one to send. But when Fritz Karsten retired, George Loudon, John Loudon's seriously intellectual younger brother, joined my board.

I welcomed with pleasure the French candidate Jean-Pierre Marchand, not only because he told me his grandparents had owned the largest department store in St. Petersburg, but because he was a typical product of the French *hautes ecoles,* and a typical French commercial banker. I looked forward to turning him into an investment banker. My French board members were to be Maurice Lauré, an *inspecteur de finances*, now running Société Générale, and Marc Viennot, head of international, who had done a tour with the International Monetary Fund in Washington and become Americanised. Lauré regularly fell asleep at board meetings, but had the uncanny ability of suddenly waking up and picking up the discussion as if he had been listening, rather than quietly snoring. He had been a senior Tax inspector, and claimed to have invented the *taxe sur la valeur ajoutée*, known as TVA in French and VAT in English, perhaps the most insidious of all indirect taxes, as when you buy an end product, you have no idea how many times it has been paid. Lauré had been at the "*fisc*" when the concept of charging income tax based on so-called external signs of wealth had been introduced. He loved to tell the story of how rich Parisian society ladies would approach him and plead.

"M. Lauré! I assure you this diamond necklace is a fake. Please don't count it – but please don't tell my husband that I sold the real one years ago to pay my *coutourier!*"

Générale de Banque in Brussels was traditionally the house bank within the huge Belgian conglomerate Société Générale de Belgique which had originally be founded by William Ist of the Netherlands to administer his ducal estate in the part of his kingdom which was to become independent Belgium in 1830. By now the bank was independent but still close to the many spin-offs from the original holding company which had financed Belgium's industrialisation. Paul-Emmanuel Janssen, of a leading Belgian financial and industrial family, was to be my main Belgian director. He eventually became chairman of Générale de Banque, and also my chairman, succeeding Fritz Karsten. There was something of a White, Weld link here. The EBIC joint venture in New York, European American Bank, had appointed my former partner Jean

Cattier as Chairman, probably at the suggestion of the Belgians. A forebear of Jean, Felicien Cattier, had once been the managing Director of Société Générale de Belgique. The "old boy network" in Belgium was small but tight. The problem is it was exclusively Wallonian, and the Flemish were getting restive. The Belgians had already helped staff BEC in Brussels, so they proposed no secondee for me. Neither did Banca Commerciale Italiano, but BCI appointed Enrico Braggiotti, its senior international director to my board. Braggiotti was, in fact, a Monegasque, and had close connections with Lehman Bros. in New York, probably due to Marcel Palmaro, another Monegasque and a partner of Lehman. It took a while to "click", but I suddenly realised why the two people staffing Lehman's small representative office in Paris Jean-Francois Malle and "Babu" Poniatowski, as he was known, had such an *entrée* with Italian borrowers. It was Enrico, of course, who was definitely an investment banker *manqué* and highly supportive of my projects, when the pure commercial bankers on my board sometimes greeted them with furrowed brows.

Creditanstalt in Vienna was the smallest of my shareholders and the neediest in terms of EBIC membership strategic aid, as it had no foreign branches or subsidiaries. Its speciality was Eastern Europe, as Vienna was a turntable for commercial and financial exchanges with the COMECON bloc. Austria was then run as a political duopoly with the Social Democrats on the left sharing patronage with the Peoples Party on the right, and alternating as the government, in what seemed to outsiders as a form of political Viennese waltz, so gracefully was it orchestrated. Creditanstalt, originally the Rothschild bank in Vienna, was on the right and Öesterreichische Länderbank on the left. To ensure total fairness, the number two in each bank was appointed by the opposing party, so that at Creditanstalt, Hannes Androsch, a socialist, was deputy chairman. He eventually became prime minister in a socialist government. Creditanstalt's chairman was Heinrich Treichl who presided over a very bright team who managed to ooze Viennese charm from every pore. Head of international was Otto-Karl Finsterwalder, who was not Viennese, or even Austrian, but from Northern Germany. Otto-Karl had gone native with vengeance and adopted a laid back, almost Mediterranean approach to life and banking, combining a charming vagueness with a razor sharp intellect. His PA was a long suffering Frau Fischer who became the best known PA throughout the international banking community, as she spent most of her time apologising for her boss's missed connections, late arrivals and forgotten appointments. In fact, just as Sigmund Warburg contrived to arrive precisely on the dot, Otto-Carl went through timing contortions to ensure he arrived late. Creditantstalt was determined to place two of its brightest with me in the new London bank, and I was delighted to have them. One was Marco Musulin, who went on to run a New York branch for Creditanstalt, and the other was Heronymous Spannochi, Otto Karl Finsterwalder's brother-in-law, who retired early to run his family estate. When Musulin was on the way to London, Treichl rang me and said:

"Not only do I want you to train Musulin in investment banking, I want you to find him a wife – a nice English girl from a good family."

"But I'm told he's one of the most eligible bachelors in Vienna," I reposted, hoping this was not a forerunner of shareholder requests.

"That's just it. I don't want him distracted when he comes back here. You must send him back married. You're supposed to be an investment banker. Consider it a merger assignment."

I did not lift a finger for this mandate, and Marco eventually found a wife in New York.

Deutsche Bank was at the other end of the scale in size and power. Even though EBIC had been the brain child of the legendary Herman Abs, now semi-retired but still chairing the supervisory board, one sensed that his successors were not so keen on the concept. In particular Wilfrid Guth, co-chairman of the *vorstandt*, the management board, had probably been cool on the idea of an EBIC merchant bank in London. Deutsche Bank took the view that it didn't need anyone to accomplish its international mission, and it shared the German market on sufferance, with Dresdner, Commerzbank, Westdeutsch Landesbank, and a few smaller fry – to accommodate anti-trust law. Although joining in the expression of general support, Guth made it clear that I had better stick to a narrow brief and keep out of Deutsche Bank's way. It became just as clear in future that Deutsche Bank was unconcerned with the interests of its fellow shareholders in Herman Abs's "Batchelor's Club". I was neither shocked nor surprised by this attitude. I knew perfectly well that Deutsche Bank played to win and that it played rough – as anyone who had competed in the Eurobond market had come to know. I first received a nice man as a secondee, but the poor chap's wife ran off with another London based German banker, and he became distracted by a messy divorce case. Michael von Brentano was the other board member with Wilfrid Guth, and he was generally sympathetic, although he had to toe the party line.

Midland Bank was effectively the host bank for this new venture, and took its position seriously. Len Mather, fresh from helping quell the secondary bank crisis, asked me to lunch and introduced me to Jack Hendley, the senior international officer who was to join my board. Jack was a clearing banker from central casting. Grammar school educated, sound as a bell, he had a manner which went down very well with Midland's overseas correspondents. Like most clearing banks, Midland had been formed through a series of acquisitions of country banks in the 19th century – in its case, mostly in the North. Midland's international franchise had been based largely on correspondent banking, a business model being overtaken by the surge of foreign banks opening branches in London. Midland had recently acquired control of Samuel Montagu, which Louis Franck, experiencing the typical sentiment

272

après moi le deluge, had first tried to sell to Pearl Assurance. Someone had the very good idea of placing Paul Jeanty on my board as the second Midland representative. Paul was a nephew of Louis Franck, his wife was a relation of Claude Cattier, Johnny's wife, and DY and I had known him for years. I felt I had someone I could relate to, and who would understand where I was coming from. We got on very well. I shared my innermost thinking and strategic plans with him and he gave me outstanding advice. Many years later, after events terminated our business collaboration, Paul suddenly cut me dead. He had retired to Soto Grande in Spain, and was often in London, but would turn away if he spied me in the street or at some gathering. I never found out why.

The most interesting thing about the launch of a new EBIC venture in London was the timing. 1973 is generally considered an *annus horribilus*, un-matched in recent British history, particularly financially. Everything was go-ing wrong. Despite a recent devaluation and IMF intervention, reserves con-tinued to bleed. Industrial strife was wide spread. In the City, the fringe bank crisis was in full cry – there were failures and rumours of failures. It was at this time that one began seeing bumper stickers bearing the legend: "Will The Last Person Leaving Britain Please Turn out the Lights". And yet what seemed to some a final melt down of Britain, was no deterrent to the EBIC Group's desire to open a merchant banking venture in the City of London fo-cussed entirely, however – and this is the crucial point – on Euromarkets activity. Although euro-business had paused somewhat in the wake of the oil price crisis, it was rebounding now as a result of the consequent liquidity shift. As Chris O'Malley points out, the retail investor dominance of the Eurobond market was fading fast in favour of new institutional interest. The syndicated loan market was assuming the major role in recycling oil producer liquidity to fund oil importer deficits. As had been the case from its outset, the Euromarkets in London was splendidly isolated from the host country's polit-ical and economic woes. Still, I had a curious combination of feelings about all this. There was the thrill of starting something new, which could be a very personal endeavour made even more challenging by the immediate environ-ment. And this was two rooms in the building next to Midland's headquarters in Poultry which one reached through a narrow passage and which was con-nected to the main building by a Venetian style arch. The drama of the setting was enhanced by the three storm lamps I was issued, as we were in the three day week period, which Edward Heath had decreed, and there were frequent blackouts. On my first day at work, a steward from the executive suite at Midland bought a tray of tea and biscuits to my PA, Sally Maple and me, but explained this was the one and only time, and we were advised to purchase an electric kettle. Sally had come with me from White Weld, and she seemed re-laxed at this rather inauspicious inauguration of a new merchant bank set up by seven of Europe's greatest commercial banks.

273

My change of career path excited press interest, but the focus was more on White, Weld's loss than on EBIC's gain. This was only natural as the former was now highly established and the latter an as yet unproven construction. Despite the rapid rise of the consortium bank phenomena, and the early success of Orion Bank, doubts about the long-term viability of the concept were already being expressed. The most insightful and prescient comments prompted by my move arose in an article by Chris Welles of the *Institutional Investor*, Gil Kaplan's rival publication to Patrick Sergeant's *Euromoney*, based on interviews held some three years after I had been up and running with the new bank. Welles includes a flattering thumbnail sketch "Though with his well-tailored wardrobe of double-breasted suits he is far better dressed, his large, squared head and thinning, slicked-back hair make him resemble a British version of actor Jack Nicholson. Like Nicholson, he emanates a distinct sense of presence and appears much taller than his 5 feet 10 inches" modesty prohibits further quotation from this aspect of the article. But Welles quotes me correctly as saying "the only thing that protects Wall Street from being swallowed up by the sheer size of the commercial banks is the protective wall of Glass-Steagall. If a really unified capital market emerges in Europe, there is no question in my mind who (sic) would control it. It would be the commercial banks". I went on to extoll the virtues of my new institutional model, which would have the "essential elements which merchant banks have, being small, mobile and free of the major structural problems of large organisations". In other words, I was suggesting I would have the best of both worlds – the flexibility of a small firm combined with the financial and geographic support of the large commercial banks, all in Europe and each the largest in their own country. Not content with blowing my own as yet unproven horn, I had the effrontery to mock my principle competitor, Orion Bank, whose shareholders were from the U.S., U.K., Canada, Japan, Italy and Germany, suggesting that "the only thing the members have in common is that they happened to be in the same corner at a cocktail party". Reading Welles's article today, some forty years later, and leaving aside my outrageously arrogant self-promotion, I cannot but observe I was right about the commercial banks. Glass-Steagall fell under the Clinton administration, and Wall Street is dominated by commercial banks, the only two important houses to have remained independent Morgan Stanley and Goldman Sachs, having acquired commercial bank status themselves, to ensure access to taxpayer funded depositor insurance. Still, Welles also ends his article by quoting an ex-White Weld colleague, who points out White Weld is now Credit Suisse White Weld, i.e., an investment bank with commercial bank backing. "Stani walked away from what he was hoping to find," perhaps a bit feebly, I counter with the fact that I have seven backers, not just one. Running through the interviews – Welles also interviewed my chairman Fritz Karsten – is the underlying suspicion on the interviewer's part, that conflict with shareholders would follow collaboration. The parents would become jealous of the child's success. Furthermore, whatever new beach head the child might secure, the parents would lumber in after to occupy the new territory. Perhaps in the back of my mind I suspected this might be the case, but I was a youth in a hurry, not a wise old man. With twenty/twenty hindsight, and for a variety of reasons, my anonymous ex-colleague was correct.

My final piece of parental blessing – one might say almost papal blessing, before the full launch of the new EBIC merchant bank in London, came from Herman Abs, the founder of EBIC, who invited me to lunch at the Savoy Grill. After the usual "I know and admire your father" pleasantries, Abs explained his original motivation for EBIC had been to try and defend European banking against being overwhelmed by the larger and more powerful American banks.

"In any field of international commercial and financial business, the size of a competitor's home market gives it the defining advantage," he said. "Europe must create banks or banking groups whose home market is the whole of Europe – as big as the home market of the American banks." We didn't touch on the obvious hitch to an eventual total merger of the EBIC parent banks. That is that two were state owned: Société Générale and Creditanstalt. But by then, I don't think Abs was assuming eventual merger into a megabank. He reminded me of the group's nick name the "Batchelor's Club". He considered that close co-operation between the parent banks, and their joint ventures, would help create a buffer against total domination by the Americans. He gave me one piece of fundamental advice: "Don't forget – we didn't choose you to administer some subsidiary in which we decide to place some business. We chose you because you have showed yourself to be innovative and creative. So do not worry about what the shareholders do or don't do for you – go and innovate and create". We then talked about current market conditions, the impact of the oil price increase, the emerging imbalances in global affairs, the potential excesses of medium term sovereign lending by the recycling banks, the increasingly speculative velocity of exchange and securities markets, and various associated issues – leaving me in little doubt that I was in the presence of a banker whose like we would not see again.

A first issue was the name of the bank. I favoured European Banking Company. I though it stuck a neutral note between traditional investment and commercial bank nomenclature. The Bank of England, which had to be consulted, was not keen – remarking that anything including the words "European" and "bank" needed to be reserved for an eventual EEC central bank. I replied, with some cheek, that there had never been a central bank employing the word "company" in its title. In the "dead" pages of the Banker's Almanac, I found a European Banking Company that had been established in London in the 1860s, and had failed or been wound up. There was no clue as to its ownership or business, but I suspect it was trade finance. In the end, the Bank agreed and we were named, and quite quickly, authorised. The process was far more streamlined at the time. Then came the business of determining a basic business plan. I was convinced the foundation had to be some daily, "bread and butter" business – mundane, perhaps, but there to pay the overheads whilst we laboured to produce major transactions. We could not rely solely on earnings on capital and on a basic loan portfolio, like ordinary commercial banks. Wall Street investment banks had stock exchange commissions, and London merchant banks had acceptance business, to provide this all important, regular revenue. I decided foreign exchange would be our staple. I discussed this with Paul Jeanty and with Chris Sheridan at Montagu, who had taken over from a now retired Julius Weinberg. Sheridan suggested we focus on the spot market, as forwards required greater balance sheet support. We could "day trade" the main spot markets – cable and $/DM, and limit overnight position risk to virtually nothing. Our main structural requirement was counterparty limits, and the nature of our shareholding would ensure these were significantly greater than our modest capital would justify, if we were a free standing independent. I liked it. My sharcholders shrugged their shoulders, but hardly objected due to the risk free nature of the activity. The culminating break was finding and engaging a young forex trader called David Mitchum , who had been making a name for himself at Bankers Trust. David saw the potential immediately and his enthusiasm for the opportunity made me think I was some sort of genius for having thought of it.

I now believe this decision, and the recruitment of David Mitchum, were the two best things I did at EBC. "Cable" is, of course, £/$ – so called from when everything was a telegraph market. But the £ sterling was, and still is, the only currency quoted *against* the dollar. All other currencies are so much to the dollar. Sterling is so many dollars to the pound. This proud tradition, a throw back to when sterling was the reserve currency, was in danger when the pound sank almost to parity. Mitchum built a high grade team at EBC, and we became kings of the cable market. Known from our "answerback" as EBCO in the forex market, we assumed an extraordinary share of the market and also were responsible for a major innovation. At the time the Reuters Monitor service was a pure data feed, used to track and record historic prices of currencies, commodities, bonds and equities. You switched to the right page and you saw a price at which the value you were interested in had *just* traded. The dealers registered prices once they had traded – and not always immediately. We decided to input *dealing* prices in cable and $/DM. The quote you saw on EBCO's page was the bid and offer you could deal on – and it changed as you watched – even as you were on the phone to our trader. This was revolutionary and even caused a Bank of England eyebrow to rise for a few moments, until it was understood we were enhancing liquidity. The eyebrow was to rise again when we started keeping an open line, during trading hours, to the forex broker Birbaum in Frankfort, for $/DM. The Bank was always sensitive to any hint of collusion between principals and intermediaries in the forex market. An official rang me and, very politely, asked if he could come and sit in our dealing room, to observe just how this open line worked. Of course, I welcomed him and he went away satisfied and complimentary. I was struck by the way the Bank always knew exactly what we were up to in the market. This finger on the pulse of the City was the key to the Bank's success as a financial supervisor. It was lost when Chancellor of the Exchequer Gordon Brown moved the supervisory role to a, new, distant agency. Paul Jeanty gave me a piece of advice when we were discussing our entry into the forex market, which I never forgot and tried hard to follow. "Always make it a point, when you are London, to walk into the dealing room at least twice a day. Just a short, casual stroll, enquire a quote, ask 'how's business?' You don't have to look over a shoulder. You may not have the slightest idea what they are doing – but they don't know that". It's called *acte de presence* and there isn't an equivalent expression in English. But it offers a protection against rogue dealers, and the fact that it has become impossible in today's extended, mega institutions is one of the reasons that particular breed of dealer has proliferated. Jeanty also explained why we were a greater risk from rogue dealers. "If a trader leaves Montagu, a well-established house, the rest of the market will wonder why. If a trader leaves EBC, a complete newcomer, the rest of the market will assume he hadn't found the opportunity he hoped for. So your trader is more inclined to take the risk of being fired than mine". Cynical perhaps, but true. We were making our mark in the forex in the forex market when Sterling was often in free fall. In a heated debate on the crisis in the House of Commons, a Labour MP made an impassioned intervention in which he virtually accused City forex traders of being traitors and "selling the pound down the drain". I wrote him angry letter pointing out that, quite the contrary, City dealers were highly patriotic and had an unreasonable bias in favour of Sterling, being inclined to be long, when market forces suggested they should be short. I invited him to spend a morning with our lads from East London and see for himself. He wrote me a curt letter saying he had no time for such visits.

Since John Scott-Oldfield had hunted my head, I decided to engage him to hunt the heads I would need to staff EBC. It was not just a question of identifying candidates. I considered it useful to have an intermediary in early discussions with a candidate. Normally, I subscribe to the well-known definition of a consultant as someone who borrows your watch to tell you what time it is. But John was very helpful in judging, not only the suitability of a candidate, but the true level of understanding and enthusiasm he displayed for the EBC concept. The most important, and often elusive, aspect of executive selection is the determination of whether a candidate is a "fit" within the corporate culture of the employing organisation. I believe John's period at Shell had taught him how important this is – and it cannot be judged from a candidate's CV. From the first, I realised I needed to secure a strong administrative presence. I had always been a hopeless manager in the traditional sense. The back office is a place of mystery to me, and for that reason I attach more than the usual importance to its functions. An ideal person emerged quickly to be chief administrative and compliance officer, as well as company secretary, in James Chandler, a long serving Morgan Guranty officer who had been Euroclear's first Secretary General. He was happy to move his family from Brussels and he gave maximum confidence to my board that the shop was running smoothly. At the cutting edge, my major find was William Slee, from First National City Bank. Bill's father was prominent in the Dutch publishing world, and his mother was American. FNCB was one of the great banking schools, but always had difficulty retaining people. It was said that if you wanted to organise a reunion of ex-FNCB people in London, you had to hire the Albert Hall. Sadly this great American bank went in to decline when it lost respect not only for the English language, by adopting a misspelt nickname as its corporate style, but also for the normal principles of risk management. Bill Slee left a brilliant career at FNCB to join me at EBC and he eventually became my second in command. He had a rare combination of originating and executing skills and inspired immediate confidence in clients. Sadly our relations deteriorated at the end of my tenure at EBC due to a misunderstanding. Recognising, as we all did, that consortium banking had had its day after a good ten-year run, Bill left to join Schroeders. When a journalist asked me whether I would be replacing my deputy chief executive, as he then was, I replied in the negative, suggesting I didn't think the function was necessary and had no one who could fill it. Of course, I meant I had no one of Bill's stature within the bank. Bill took it to mean I didn't think his role had been important. I assumed his role had been so widely recognised as critical to the bank's success, that I didn't need to stress it to a journalist. Bill had originated and handled some of EBC's greatest triumphs, and our reputation in the City was in no small part due to his efforts. We had an ongoing discussion about our leisure activity. Bill was a yachtsman, often engaging in ocean racing, and I was in to horses. The issue was – which of these pursuits was the greater drain on one's resources. Of course the major difference was the fact that Bill always replaced his boats at a profit. He sailed a series Finnish made racing sloops which always gained in value. My horses lost value as soon as I threw a leg over them. Amusingly, this had been a life time point of conflict between Louis Franck, also a sailor, and David Montagu, a keen racing man. This had been just one source of enmity between these two, which had greatly troubled the latter history of Samuel Montagu. On the other hand, I don't recall Bill and me ever disagreeing on a policy matter, and we worked hand in hand on EBC's business.

Another star followed Bill from FNCB. This was Roger Parsons, an Englishman who had handled FNCB's shipping business in London. His industry contacts were substantial, and we decided ship financing was a suitable strain of business as it is very much project related, with moveable security and predictable loan servicing revenue through long-term charters. Roger soon landed a piece of advisory business for a work out of a major shipping group bankruptcy, involving several of our shareholders as lenders. Roger convened and conducted meetings of the creditor banks and painstakingly negotiated complicated solutions to rescue as much value as possible. His performance earned plaudits from an important sector of the international banking community and helped to establish EBC as a serious player in international finance. It also led to a further series of ship loan work out assignments. As the team grew so did its variety. Neil Balfour had been at Barings since coming down from university. His branch of the Balfour clan had owned Balfour Williamson, a shipping and trading company, originally from Liverpool, but focussed on Chile and other Andean countries. Neil's mother was Chilean. Neil definitely bought in to the EBC concept and was excited by our potential. He was also interested in politics and asked if he could seek and accept nomination for a candidacy. I took the view, and still do, that the British tradition of amateur politicians, who had experience of ordinary life, was the greatest strength of its democracy. I thought it a duty of the City to encourage parliamentary involvement, if only to ensure government understanding of and sympathy for what we were up to. In the usual fashion, Neil was adopted as Conservative candidate for Hayes and Hartlington, a solid Labour constituency, which includes Heathrow Airport. One day, during the campaign, Neil came to me and said:

"Just want you to know, I'll be working late in the office this evening."

"I admire your zeal," I replied, "but I thought you might be out canvassing."

"No, and I have to wait and sneak out the back. You'll see what I mean when you leave yourself in a bit. The front entrance is crowded with *paparazzi.*"

"What on earth for?"

"I'm afraid Elizabeth has just run off to St. Moritz with Richard Burton. Rather an awkward time for one's wife to leave one."

Neil's then wife was Elizabeth of Yugoslavia, daughter of King Paul and sister of the present Crown Prince Alexander. The Princess had been previously married to a New York textile tycoon Howard Oxenburg. Neil's *sang froid* in the face of this marital upset was truly remarkable. He was never expected to wrest Hayes and Hartlington from a Labour grip, but went on to be elected MEP to Strasburg for a Yorkshire constituency. He set off bubbling with enthusiasm for the EEC, became *rapporteur* to an important committee, and came back totally disillusioned and convinced the project would eventually drown in a morass of beurocratic complacency and corruption. Neil tried again for Westminster in a safe Conservative constituency, Thirsk and Malton, in North Yorkshire but ran into difficulty. The fact that he had been educated at Ampleforth, the leading Roman Catholic public school did not help, despite its Yorkshire location. But his habit of calling on local farmers wearing Gucci shoes and a blue blazer was deemed by some to dilute his southern charm, and actually grate within that dour and severe community. Calling for help from Central Office was the final straw, and Neil lost the seat which was eventually reclaimed by Jonathan Aitken – of all people.

If Neil's political career was colourful but unsuccessful, his career as an investment banker at EBC was a triumph. He secured several mandates for capital market operations in Spain, including an FRN issue for the state oil company. He was a friend of King Juan Carlos and managed to secure a royal audience for the entire EBIC board. I remember observing my senior EBIC colleagues, standing somewhat awkwardly to converse on economic topics with the affable young King of Spain. I sensed they could not but be impressed that this honour had been secured by the most junior of their joint ventures. Here perhaps my latent, and suspicious, imagination is at work, for I also suspect Wilfred Guth of Deutsche Bank was thinking "What pretentiousness! Deutsche Bank does not need EBC to arrange an audience with the King of Spain. Deutsche Bank can gain entry anywhere it wishes". Indeed, we were soon to learn an early lesson with respect to our German shareholder. Neil, through persistent and painstaking solicitation of the officials involved at the Ministry of Finance, had obtained a mandate to lead a Eurodollar bond issue for the Kingdom of Spain. As soon as Deutsche Bank learned of this, they objected – taking the extraordinary line that EBC was not mature enough to lead manage a prestigious issue for a European sovereign state, and insisting we pass the mandate to Deutsche Bank for a DM issue. The fact that it was depriving its fellow EBIC partners of association with such a transaction, which none could have possibly landed on its own, did not trouble Deutsch Bank one whit. Fritz Karsten was particularly unhappy, but no one was going to rock the EBIC boat and we were told to grin and bear it. Neil bore the reverse with his usual fortitude and went on to handle diverse business, and to originate imaginative advisory and other investment banking assignments. By now Neil had married Serena, niece to the Duke of Marlborough, Her much married mother, who lived in Nassau, had befriended an inventor who had developed a means of fast drying building timber without risk of cellular distortion. After doing considerable due diligence on the technology, which involved a sort of microwave process from inside out, we decided to back the commercialisation of the process, which would have revolutionary benefits for the building trade. Sadly the patents were disputed by an estranged friend of the inventor's, and it ended up in court in a southern state where a red neck jury ruled against "those greedy bankers from London, England". We wrote off our investment. But Neil never tired of handling our most intricate and challenging transactions and, in many ways, he represented exactly the type of investment/merchant banking I had set out to undertake with the EBC venture.

A particularly colourful member of the team was Rainer Kharmann, a German who had migrated to Switzerland to work for Dow Banking Corporation, set up by the Dow Chemical Company at a time when American corporates were diversifying mindlessly. Dow Banking was based in Zurich and no one was ever exactly sure what it did, including the people back in

Midland, Michigan, Dow Chemical's home town. But Rainer joined us at EBC well trained, steeped in a north German work ethic and keen as mustard. He had some difficulty adjusting to our work habits. One day, he asked to see me. He had a complaint.

"My door is always open, as you know, Rainer." I wondered what his complaint could be. Salaries had just been revised upwards and it was not yet bonus time.

"My complaint is that you make jokes at the morning meeting."

It was true that I invariably started the meeting with a pleasantry or funny story of some kind.

"I like to lighten the atmosphere before we get down to serious business. I can't see why you object."

"In Germany, we do not joke in the office."

Poor Rainer was to suffer from English eccentricity on more than one occasion. During the famous miners' strike the National Union of Mineworkers had violated various labour laws and the Government had moved to sequester union funds. We received a visit from a senior NUM official asking if we could devise a means of placing the funds outside of the reach of the government appointed receiver. I asked Mark Sheldon of Linklaters, our solicitors to advise. We were assured that, as exchange control no longer existed, there was no legal impediment to the NUM placing their funds outside of UK jurisdiction. I put Rainer in charge of the case and he came up with a perfect solution. We had acquired, from White Weld, a closed- end Luxembourg based bond fund called the International Income Fund, which was invested entirely in Eurobonds, and provided bearer units to its subscribers. We simply put the NUM funds into bearer units of the IIF. But Rainer was in a permanent panic, fearing he would be subject to a dawn raid at his home by the authorities, despite assurances from our solicitors that our actions were entirely lawful. It so happened that the receiver appointed by HMG was an accountant who hunted with the VWH, my home pack. He had discovered the NUM was acting through EBC, and one Saturday morning our Master, Martin Scott, introduced him to me. During a pause, as hounds drew a covert, the accountant trotted over to me and we exchanged pleasantries.

"I don't suppose you are going to tell me where the money is?" he said, patting his horse's neck.

"I don't suppose you would expect me to," I replied, smiling.

"Of course not – but I'll find out eventually. Oh! I think they've found! We're off! Cheers." And we both galloped off.

On Monday morning, I started the morning meeting with this story. Rainer was outraged. "You English! You take nothing seriously!"

"Rainer, first of all, you know perfectly well I am not English. Secondly, although our interests are opposed, it does not mean I should not be friendly with this accountant, or he with me."

At this point I was still trying to train Rainer in the ways of the City. I gave up eventually, but Rainer was a big contributor to the success of EBC, and he must have eventually become accustomed to English ways, because he has remained in London ever since. He even adopted a degree of eccentricity in his manners. Recently, he asked to see me and so I asked him to lunch at White's. We were no sooner seated when he pulled out a bunch of papers about some property deal.

"Rainer, one cannot discuss business here," I pointed out.

"Then what is the point of this lunch?"

"All right, tell me about it, but without flashing papers."

Afterwards, I received a note of thanks: "Thank you for lunch. The food was terrible and I had serious indigestion. Your club illustrates everything that is wrong with this country. Yours, etc."

Here is a letter that could have been written by Evelyn Waugh.

One day, I received a call from Ann Money-Coutts, who I had met through Claude Hankes-Driclsma, a somewhat mysterious South African. She was divorced from her husband, who was to become the 8th Lord Latymer, and their son Crispin was just down from Oxford. Would I give him a job for a while? She didn't want him to go straight into the family bank before he had seen something of the City. I said yes without hesitation and put Crispin straight into the dealing room. The result was magical. The mostly Cockney lads in David Mitchum's department were amused and delighted to have a six foot plus, Old Etonian called Money-Coutts as a team member, and Crispin took to the business like a proverbial duck and was soon contributing to our substantial profits from exchange and money dealing. After a respectable interval, Crispin went off to Coutts where he was the last family member to work there, before leaving to join Cazenove's wealth management business. We ended up on a board together many years later. Variety continued to be the theme of team building at EBC. From Hambros, a Cambridge graduate called Tim Eggar arrived. A school master's son, Tim had earned an industrial scholarship from Enfield Rolling Mills. He also expressed an interest in standing for Parliament, and I agreed, telling him that, if he succeeded, his work load would be adjusted accordingly. He was adopted as Conservative candidate for Enfield North, again a solid Labour seat. Taking note of the large and prosperous Indian community in the constituency, Tim campaigned on an immigration control platform, appealing to the "there are enough of us here already" sentiment, widespread in immigrant circles. He won the seat on the first Thatcher landslide and went on to have a brilliant parliamentary career, ending as Minister for Energy in the Thatcher and Major governments. My senior executives always had both an assigned industry and a geographic speciality. I gave Tim energy and New Zealand, which he could visit during Parliamentary recesses and where the letters "MP" after his name did no harm. The industry assignment bore fruit for EBC, for his career in Government, and for Tim's subsequent highly successful career with a number of energy industry companies. We used the University Appointments Boards to recruit, like many in the City. One day a Cambridge graduate called Richard Wohanka turned up for an interview.

"There's been some mistake at the Appointments Board," he said. "I read musicology and have no interest whatsoever in finance. In fact, I've just been awarded a scholarship to Harvard for a two-year Master's degree in Musicology. I'm so sorry to waste your time."

"Not a bit. Your Eastern European name intrigues me. I have a suggestion. You'll have a long summer break at Harvard. Why not take an internship at our sister bank European American in New York? You'll meet young people and, who knows, you might develop a taste for banking."

Richard agreed, I rang my counterpart at EAB in New York, who readily accepted my suggestion – and I thought no more about it. Two years later, I suddenly had a call from Richard, still in the U.S.

"Remember me?" he asked. "I had a great time at EAB and came to a realisation, that even if I could land a position as a music critic – the only thing my education has qualified me for – I'll never earn as much money as in banking. Would you be willing to consider me again for a job?"

"You've got the job," I replied, and without hesitation. "When can you start?"

Richard turned out to be a star. From EBC, he went to Paribas and eventually ran Fortis Investment Management, an autonomous arm of the Fortis Bank Group. Richard asked me to join its board and I was able to directly witness his outstanding leadership of a large multinational fund manager. Unfortunately, the parent, which had been originally a Dutch farmers' co-operative, ruined itself with an orgy of mergers and acquisitions becoming yet another badly managed megabank. When it was finally broken up, the investment management business was sold to BNP Paribas – another badly managed megabank. Rather than keep Richard who had basically built the business, it put its own man in. Another import, this time from a consortium bank entirely working the oil patch, was Ian Logie, an excellent deal maker. He had an air of mystery about him, vaguely suggesting a former career in intelligence. It turned out that he had an unusual hobby collecting weaponry of various kinds. One day he was stopped at customs having a number of firearms in his luggage. After EBC he joined the leading firm of forensic investigators and security consultants – a most appropriate environment for Ian. My only American recruits were Frank Shields, a Princetonian I had known on Long Island, and Bill Blackwell, a Texan oil banker.

We moved three times in the decade of our existence at EBC. Each of our offices was decorated by the Charles Hammond partner and brother, Christopher, who specialised in what he liked to call the "rich" look. Actually it was simply the English country house style made fashionable by a score of London decorators. Christopher had been introduced by John Scott-Oldfield and was keen on well carved architraves and other architectural features which, if not quite the standard of Janssen's work at Samuel Montagu, satisfied my desire for premises of a suitable prestige to reflect the standing or our shareholders. The meeting rooms, which also served as luncheon rooms, were discreet and well used, as I was not going to tolerate leaving clients in a common waiting room, as had Jim Slater. Lunch was served properly, allowing guests to take as much or as little as they wished. I consider the "plated" service, now common in restaurants, to be an abomination and insisted on a service standard suitable to proper private houses. We served one course, followed by cheese and fruit, and only a choice of dry sherry or tomato juice before lunch, and a light white wine with. We did not aspire to the Warburgs tradition of two lunches – one early, one late. This required a rather larger stock of existing and potential clients than we could muster. It was known in the City that the late lunch at 1:30 at Warburgs was the prestigious lunch, and some were even prompted to decline an invitation to the 12:30 lunch as being beneath their standing. We had three stewards and Arthur Mattock, the senior steward eventually became office manager. He had started in private service, his father being butler in a grand establishment, and our Welsh cook at home remembered him as a young footman, in one of her households. Arthur had an extraordinary degree of natural taste and a flair for interior design, to the point that Christopher Hammond, quite tactlessly, tried to poach him to join his firm. Our other steward Lionel turned out to be a natural stand-up comic. For our Christmas party, the full team organised a review, as a surprise for me as I was kept entirely out of its preparations and rehearsals took place after I had left in the evening. There were various satirical skits, often gently mocking my management style and habits. It was then we discovered Lionel's hidden talent as a *raconteur*. He had us in stitches with a tale of his time as a steward on the Cunard line. Apparently, he was once assigned to the Captain's table and, two spoons in hand, was about to serve the vegetables when a lady at the table made a sudden gesture and one breast popped out of her poorly fitting *décoltage*. Quick as a flash, Lionel used a spoon to pop the exposed breast back into her corsage, only to notice that he had been observed doing so by the head waiter – whose frown of disapproval was alarming. "I'm for the sack" thought Lionel, as he sidled up to his boss. "You should have warmed the spoon first," admonished the head waiter.

We undertook a degree of corporate entertainment, but not on the scale which has since been established by the new City megabanks. I had business guests for the small but high quality shoot I ran for my neighbour Toby Clarke, but my only charge to the bank was the services of Arthur Mattock and one of the other stewards, Richard, who came to help with meals. We also took some grouse shooting and Neil Balfour was in charge. One year "Stoker" Hartington, then heir to and now Duke of Devonshire, suggested we be the first to take a few days at Abbey, which he had decided to let for the first time. He wanted some friends to act as guinea pigs and provide honest, critical comment on all the arrangements, and he offered us a cut price. We invited a Spanish client among several other client guests; he was head of one of the main electric utilities in Spain, and an accomplished performer on the famous Spanish partridge shoots of La Mancha. But an interesting example of European culture clash arose. When partridge shooting in Spain one's butt, or blind, is protected by sheets of lead on each flank. Spanish guns happily shoot up and down the line, and one often sees a bird drop in front of one's nose, from a neighbouring gun. The lead sheets protect against injury to both shooter and loader – also known in Spain as *secretarios*. In addition to loading, and some Spaniards shoot with three guns and two loaders, the *secretarios* rush to pick up after each drive, and since they are betting amongst themselves on their gun's bag, they engage in unseemly struggles as they seek to pick up each other's birds. Somehow, they always manage to return with more birds than one recalls having killed. In grouse shooting in England and Scotland, a simple stake is placed on the flank of each butt, indicating how far one can swing the gun without endangering the neighbouring butts. For some reason, the butt peppered, when this limit is breached in the heat of a drive, is always two down from the miscreant's. Already in the first drive of the day, our Spanish guest was shooting wildly, and my loader immediately noticed stray pellets hitting us. We were two down from the Spaniard. On the next drive, my loader's Labrador let out a yelp, and indeed, turned up the next day with one eye closed, as a pellet had, fortunately, stuck only the edge of the poor dog's eye. Still, my loader, a very correct and knowledgeable local man, quite rightly raised a complaint, and Stoker summoned Neil and myself and said, "I'm truly sorry, but I am going to have to ask your guest to stop shooting." We agreed entirely and our guest received the ban quite calmly and spent the rest of the time watching and enjoying the lunches and dinners. On another occasion, at a shoot we had taken in Scotland, a Swedish guest hauled out his portable telephone, announcing he had excellent reception up on the moor, and proceeded to chat to his office, even as the grouse were flying over his butt. I was disgusted, said nothing at the time, but vowed not to do further business with him.

We finally gave up taking shooting to entertain clients and fell back on my own shoot at Bibury. I frequently entertained my old friend Michael von Clemm, even, though he was strictly speaking now a competitor at Credit Suisse White Weld. It might have been otherwise. Soon after my decision to leave White Weld to set up EBC, it so happened Michael and I were both in Madrid, and there I broke the news to him. "I want to come with you" was his immediate reaction. Michael and I were extremely close. We shared a common European émigré background, had grown up as neighbours on the North Shore of Long Island, had been class and club mates at Harvard and worked closely together at White Weld. I was his wife Lisa's godfather, for the curious reason already explained; Dinnie is godmother to Charlotte, the younger von Clemm daughter, and Michael was godfather to our youngest son Nicholas. Stephanie von Clemm and our daughter Tatyana are exact contemporaries and the closest of friends. The two families could not be more tightly linked. Michael's reaction was based largely on this history, although he shared my concern about the growing gulf between Europe and New York with in the White Weld family. I would have loved to have Michael with me at EBC, but from the start a small voice inside told me it was not the best idea. Nevertheless, I arranged an interview for Michael with my chairman Fritz Karsten. It was a total disaster. Michael shared a quality with Marmite – you either love it or hate it. I call this a quality because it is a feature of a strong and well-defined character. Perhaps Michael was too Prussian for a Dutchman, who took exception to the fact that Michael had ordered a coffee from his PA before entering his office for the interview. When I heard this, I was reminded of my father's reaction to one of my sister Ariane's beaux asking our Swiss butler Francis for a whiskey and soda as soon as the door was opened to him, as he was calling to pick up Ariane. DY considered this the height of bad manners, and his annoyance was made worse as the hapless suitor was Peter, son of a close parental friend Henri Stehlie, from a prominent Swiss textile family. For more fundamental reasons than this lapse in good manners, I hope, Fritz Karsten pronounced himself opposed to Michael joining EBC, although he left the final decision to me, in accordance with the commitment that I should have an entirely free hand in staffing. I decided against, that small voice having grown louder. In the longer term, it was probably the best *non* career move for Michael, who went on to be a prime mover in the ensuing success of Credit Suisse White Weld and then Credit Suisse First Boston. He probably would have eventually leapfrogged me in the hierarchy anyway, but my removal from WW accelerated his promotion. We stayed in close touch throughout this period and had one, fortunately short-lived, falling out. EBC had secured a mandate to lead manage a floating rate note issue for the Republic of Costa Rica. I had no idea Credit Suisse White Weld were competing for this business until I had a call from Michael during a week end in the country. To my astonishment, he asked me to stand aside, allowing CSWW to lead manage the issue, implying that as the senior and more established house, it should take precedence over EBC. I was both flabbergasted and furious. Not only did I categorically reject his suggestion, but was so angered that I told him we would suspend our dealing relationship with CSWW. I did not carry out that threat, but Michael and I did not speak for a while, until our respective wives, who remained close, insisted we end our estrangement. Years later, we were together again at Merrill Lynch. Strangely enough, the Costa Rica issue became a subject of further controversy, when sovereign loan defaults began to accumulate in the late '70s and early '80s. Costa Rica joined a growing list of over borrowed developing countries forced to restructure their external debt. I had a call from a senior officer at FNCB, now the acknowledged doyen of the restructuring business. He wanted to include the Costa Rica FRN in a restructuring of the country's syndicated loans on the grounds that most FRNs were held by banks and, therefore, merely a variation of a typical syndicated loan. I argued there was no way of proving that, as the notes were bearer, whereas in a syndicated loan the participants were registered and their interests effectively nontransferable.

In any case it was the contractual expression of a loan that defined its character, not the nature of the lender. Our discussion became somewhat heated. He
needed EBC's co-operation, or at least he thought he did. In fact, a meeting of
note holders, with a proper notice period, would have been required and a
75% majority needed to alter the terms of the issue – probably impossible to
achieve within the timetable of FNCB's restructuring.

If our team at EBC had been eclectically assembled, by accident rather
than design, our business mix also became increasingly varied as EBC developed. This mix had never been clearly defined, although the mandate of
our sister bank BEC in Brussels, as a pure medium-term lender, suggested
that EBC would be focussed primarily on capital market transactions, i.e.
Eurobonds. But this principle was violated at the outset by our own chairman
Fritz Karsten. I was in Fritz's office in Amsterdam for a very early strategic
discussion, when he took a call from Sigmund Warburg. After listening for a
while, I heard my chairman say:
    "Of course, Sigmund – I am sure the EBIC group will come in for a ma-
jor share. I have Stani Yassukovich, the head of our new London bank EBC in
my office at the moment and he will participate, as will BEC." Fritz finished
with many 'thank yous' and greetings and turned to me to explain.
    "That was Sigmund. Warburgs are leading a syndicated loan for Venice.
This will be your first tombstone appearance."
    I pathetically demurred from pointing out that I was setting up a credit ap-
proval procedure which certainly did not authorise me, or any board member,
to agree a loan unilaterally, and that I was not intending to participate in medium-term syndicate credits, except where EBC was the originating and lead
bank. In his excitement Fritz had neglected to enquire as to the terms of the
loan. In fact the borrower turned out to be the Italian State Institute for Public
Works, and the declared use of proceeds was to be for various schemes for
barrages, and other means of stemming Venice's increasing deterioration from
tidal erosion. This avowed purpose, and the romance of Venice in general,
was extensively used in syndicating the transaction. In fact, in typical Italian
style, the proceeds were hijacked for some more politically useful project in
the Mezzogiorno. Later on, a mini scandal emerged briefly, when it was pointed out that this violation of the use of proceeds clause in the loan agreement
actually put the loan in default and would trigger cross default clauses in a
myriad of other Italian loans. But no one was going to pull this bit of carpet
from under the whole of Italy's external indebtedness. It is a good example of
a central fact of Italian life; the sheer enormity of the country's problems ensures they never actually come home to roost. But this first deal for EBC, executed by Bill Slee, whilst we were still in our temporary quarters at Midland
Bank, lighted by storm lamps, during the occasional black outs of the three
day week, somewhat soured our potential relationship with BEC. But worse
was to come in this respect.

I received a call from Marc Viennot at Société Générale in Paris, telling me the Republic of France had decided to go to the Eurodollar syndicated loan market for its first major postwar borrowing. Various State Agencies, such as Credit Foncier, had been frequent visitors to the Foreign Dollar bond market in New York, and subsequently the Eurobond market, but the Republic itself was virginal in this respect. Of course, there was no question that a French bank, most still nationalised, was to lead such a prestigious transaction, and competition between them was going to be fierce. Would I come to Paris to advice on Soc Gen's bid to the *Trésor*? On the face of it, this call should have gone to Hans Kippenberger, the highly competent Deutsch Bank seconded officer who ran BEC, very efficiently indeed. But BEC was an entirely passive lender and did not compete to originate transactions, on the very sound principle that their portfolio was built on securing the best lender's terms – not the best borrower's terms. Nevertheless, Kippenberger was understandably hurt that, as EBIC's prime medium-term loan provider, he was not consulted. Jean-Pierre Marchand, my seconded and very professional Soc Gen man, travelled with me to Paris and we met in Viennot's office. Jean-Pierre told me after he was shocked to see a senior officer shed his jacket and invite us to do the same. Viennot had returned from a stage at the IMF in Washington, and had become somewhat Americanised. The discussion centred on what terms should be offered to win the mandate but also to avoid getting stuck with the whole loan, if syndication proved impossible. I argued strongly that syndication would not be a problem, even on the tightest terms, as what major bank, hoping to do business in France, would turn down a participation in such a deal? The going "spread" for AAA borrowers at the time was ½ % over LIBOR. I suggested offering 3/8%.

"But we will be breaking the market!" countered Viennot. "Can we sell it, and what if the market then boycotts us in future deals?"

"Take that chance," I said, "and secure a partner right away. You will need a New York agent bank for a Eurodollar loan. Morgan Guaranty is the obvious choice. Morgan has been prime banker to France since the 19th century. With any luck, your competitors have not yet called. Get Morgan on board and the terms are legitimised."

Viennot picked up the phone right away. I learned later that he spoke to Fabian vom Hoffe, an Argentinian who was then running Morgan in Paris.

"Well?" I asked, as Viennot put the phone down, smiling.

"He's agreed – and he didn't even ask what terms we were bidding. We have our agent bank."

And Société Générale got the deal, which, over some grumbling, it syndicated with ease. Years later, I was on the Cragnotti board with Fabian years later, and he recalled the transaction vividly. When he had to disclose the terms of the loan he had committed to, New York was not best pleased – but everyone knew Morgan could not refuse to act for the Republic of France. J. P. would have turned over in his grave.

Our capital market activity focussed on the floating rate note market, where our correspondent relationships with banks, based on our prominent position in the forex market, gave us natural distribution, as banks found FRNs a useful, liquid asset. We handled FRN issues for a variety of borrowers such as Empresa, the Spanish state oil company, and Adela, the Latin American development company. We also led issues for shareholders, Midland, BCI and Creditanstalt. But when Société Générale decided to float an FRN issue, they gave the mandate to Morgan Stanley, cheerfully ignoring the help we had given them to win the Republic of France loan. But then gratitude is a filial, rather than a parental, virtue. Somewhat ironically, I congratulated M. Lauré, our Soc Gen board member, on thus demonstrating of EBC's autonomy – showing the market that it was not just a tied vehicle of the parents. Equally ironically, he congratulated me on having won the other shareholder's FRN mandates. In diversifying our business model, we had early on identified project financing as an area in which our shareholders were entirely inactive. Our skills in this area were supplemented by the recruitment of Michael Woolgar, who had long oil industry experience. This was a sector in which creativity and industry knowledge were essential features. Woolgar recalled in a later interview that I had been a tough task master at morning meetings, always pushing for new business acquisition. I have no such recollection, of course, but our entry into the project finance business set a certain tone at EBC, which affected the whole team, and I believe it to have been a first rate business choice – on a par with the forex business.

In addition to working for Phillips Petroleum and others, in the North Sea, we worked on an interesting deal for DuPont, introduced by our sister bank European American in New York. The project was a joint venture with Persian interests to build a large acrylic fibre facility at Isfahan. Of interest to me was the fact that, when excavations began for the factory foundations, an ancient polo field was discovered, with the foundations of the small stone towers which served as goal posts at either end, and total dimensions almost exactly those of a modern polo ground. Work had to halt briefly whilst archaeologists poured over the find. Bill Slee was in charge of the project, and he witnessed one of those slightly surreal events which often occur in exotic parts. He was being driven along a country road in one of the motor cars of Iranian manufacture which entirely dominated the domestic market. A puncture required a tyre change, which Bill's driver executed perfectly, but then, inadvertently, locked the ignition keys in the boot.

"What do we do now?" enquired Bill of the driver.

"Oh, we wait – another of these cars will be along soon."

"But his keys won't fit our car."

"There's a good chance it will – that's one of the advantages of this fine Iranian motorcar," said the driver, proudly.

Sure enough, another of the same model appeared and was flagged down. The driver happily lent his keys to Bill's driver, who opened the boot with no difficulty, recovered his keys, suggested Bill offer a gratuity to their rescuer, and all carried on, in total satisfaction with this most practical features of Iranian motorcars. Bill Slee also handled a major project financing for an oil transhipment facility in Bonnaire, a lonely island in the Dutch Antilles, now a major tourist destination for snorkelling and diving enthusiasts, but then rather barren. The East Coast ports of the United States were not then in a position to handle the new generation of super tankers and the facility at Bonnaire would reload oil cargoes from these on to smaller tankers to serve the East Coast ports. The only risk in the project was that the U.S. would stop importing oil – a far off prospect at the time. At about this time, the BBC was running a series on the City and focussed an episode on the Euromarkets in their various forms. The programme devoted a large section to EBC, including an embarrassingly self-serving interview with its managing director. With its traditional disregard for economy with licence payers' money, the BBC sent a camera team all the way to Bonnaire to accompany Bill Slee, who can be viewed, his blonde hair flapping in the Caribbean breeze, expounding on the benefits of oil transhipment terminals – a super tanker lurking in the background. Although it had nothing to do with our Bonnaire mandate, I had become exposed to the new world of super tankers through an acquaintance with Ravi Tikkoo, who I first met when still at White Weld. The son of a senior naval officer in the Indian Navy, Tikkoo ran a one man ship, and ship finance, broking business out of a little office near the Baltic Exchange. I use the term "one man" loosely, as his main asset at the time was a tall, beautiful, "drop dead" gorgeous Norwegian PA who ensured a continuous flow of visitors from the shipping and banking world. Tikoo was an early proponent of giant bulk carriers, and his dream was to build the world's largest oil tanker. Whilst securing a number of long-term charters from the oil majors, he founded Globtik Tankers in the late 1960s and finally launched the "Globtik Tokyo" in 1973, built in a Japanese yard, and then the world's largest tanker at 483,000 dwt. Tikoo became an extraordinary ship owner, eventually a race horse owner, and a sponsor of university polo at Cambridge, where his son played. I used to lunch with him when he was still dreaming, and he would describe a vision he had of himself on the bridge of his largest tanker in the world, cruising slowly into the harbour at Le Havre, with his guest of honour, General de Gaulle standing beside him. I don't believe this scene came to past, but he did get to meet HM the Queen, as his horse won the Gold Cup at the Ascot Royal meeting. History does not relate whether the Globtic Tokyo called at the Bonnaire transhipment terminal, but I like to think it did. It was scrapped in 1986.

One of the characteristics of the City's traditional merchant banks, the practitioners I revered the most, was their ability to live on "walk in" business – or so it seemed to me. I recall reading a memoire by a former Rothschild partner about an unsolicited visit by the Premier of Nova Scotia. He had a major piece of financing to propose. "After luncheon and farewells to our distinguished guest" runs the narrative "we all gathered around the globe in the partners' room to see exactly where Nova Scotia was located". The charming insouciance of this anecdote captured my imagination. I had further confirmation of the absence of active solicitation by established merchant banks when I was at Merrill Lynch and the head of investment banking in New York, Barry Friedberg, asked me to recruit a former Warburg executive to run investment banking in London. Illness cut short the individual's career at Merrill, but, during the short time he was with us, it became evident that he was a highly accomplished executer of transactions, but he was not comfortable with the business of going out to find them. He rather expected that they would come to Merrill Lynch because it was Merrill Lynch. Of course, Warburgs was only recently established and Sigmund and his initial team of Roll, Grierson, Korner and Whitman had certainly gone out to beat the bushes for business at the outset. But by the time I knew the house in the '60s, it had clients queuing. It was this capacity to attract business through reputation built, in most cases, over generations, which justified the premium over book value for "good will", the commercial banks paid in their acquisition orgy post "Big Bang". Driven by that well-known strategic principle known as "herd instinct", the acquiring banks proceeded to destroy the franchises they had paid so dearly for – but that is another story. We had two cases of "walk in" business at EBC, but they were entirely prompted by the distinction of our shareholding, rather than a reputation built over generations. One day I had a call from John Nash, a partner of Samuel Montagu I had known during my internship there. He was a particularly cosmopolitan Australian, with strong Swiss connections. He was now seconded as the senior official of the Finance Directorate of the Commission of the European Economic Community. In those days the Commission engaged experienced practitioners from the private sector, as opposed to political placemen – as is now its custom. John conveyed the rather surprising news that the EEC itself was going to the market for a major syndicated medium-term Euro-loan. The European Coal & Steel Community, the first treaty organisation and predecessor of the EEC, had been a frequent borrower in New York and then in the Eurobond market, and another Euro-agency, the European Investment Bank in Luxembourg also was a frequent international borrower. But this was the first time that the parent entity would borrow publically and the transaction was to attract great attention. Given its prestige, Nash explained, the completion to lead it was going to be intense. "Frankly," said Nash, "I don't want a competitive frenzy to turn this thing into a circus, and so I am going to simply award the mandate to you and David at Orion, as joint lead managers. Your consortia cover a reasonable selection of European, American and Japanese banks and that will be the end of it." The David in question was, of course, David Montagu, Nash's old partner, who had succeeded Ronnie Grierson as head of Orion Bank, widely seen as a similar, if senior, animal to EBC. Nash's decision was eminently reasonable, but events were to prove it somewhat idealistic. I had a call almost immediately afterward from David Montagu who pronounced himself delighted to be working with EBC and with me, personally, on this most prestigious of trans-actions. David seemed to have no doubt in his mind that his shareholders would easily accept the logic of John Nash's decision, but a little voice inside of me was whispering "Deutsche Bank". And so we set to work. I assigned Neil Balfour, with his Euro parliamentary experience, to be our main execut-ive officer for the deal. A first decision was the choice of a New York agent bank and David, surprisingly, backed my choice of Morgan Guaranty, rather than pushing forward his shareholder Chase. My reasoning was that Morgan Guaranty had a very strong presence in Brussels, effectively the headquarters of our client borrower, whereas Chase had none. Nash agreed entirely, and Neil set off to start work on the documentation with senior Morgan man John Evans in Brussels. The whole thing was far from straight forward. Despite its overweening pretentions as such – flag, anthem, several presidents, accredited ambassadors, etc. – the EEC, and its successor the EU, is not a sovereign state. It is a treaty organisation, like NATO, or the OECD. Ensuring the loan would represent a joint and several obligation of the member states, posed significant legal problems, and, consequently, disclosure issues. We had both New York and London lawyers to wrestle with the problem. In London, we struggled with the politics of syndication and allocation. One incident during the process remains seared in my memory. It must be recalled that at this time in the early 1970s, there were no ladies in executive positions in the City. My friend Emoeka Kiss might have temporarily broken the glass ceiling in a City dealing room, but the many dress shops in the City catered for personal assist-ants – secretaries, as they were still called – and other female support staff. However, a "first" suddenly burst on the scene, at Morgan Guaranty, of all places, in the shape of a highly competent lady from New York who arrived to take charge of Morgan's syndicate department. In fact, within a very few years after this bit of pioneering, syndicate departments became almost a pre-serve of the distaff portion of the bank's executive, presumably because the ladies were more adept at persuading other banks to join less than over-whelmingly attractive transactions. I had called a meeting of the management group at our then offices in Basinghall Street, to discuss aspects of the deal, and, of course Morgan Guaranty was there represented by their newly arrived head of syndicate. At one point, it became clear that a telex had to be sent to John Nash in Brussels seeking clarification of a particular point. As it im-pacted on the agent bank, the lady from Morgan was the obvious person to draft it. My PA was away, so I left the meeting to call in Bill Slee's PA to take down the telex. She was a well-educated, public schoolgirl who could easily have held an executive position at EBC. As she entered the room, dictation pad in hand, she realised that there was one other lady, sitting at the board-room table, surrounded by men, and that this lady was about to dictate to her. I was riveted by the change of expression on my colleague's face, which I can only describe as one of mortification. But, the worst of it is, that I hesitated to rise immediately and offer her my seat, as there was no seat free at the table. When I realised my *faux pas,* I hesitated further, thinking I would merely underscore the awkwardness of the situation by getting up late. So I remained frozen myself as the dictation continued, with the poor girl standing and the Morgan girl seated, and interspersing her dictation with the occasional, rather abrupt "got that?" When it was finished, I excused myself and rushed out after my colleague.

"I'm so sorry. I should have asked you to sit down – I don't know what I was thinking."

"Oh, it's no problem. I could see there wasn't any room. I'll just get this off right away."

She was a good sport. I knew she had been offended, and I worry about it even now – although sadly I don't remember her name. I think she was called Sue.

The explosion which rocked the managing boardroom of the Deutsche Bank in Frankfort, when news of the EEC loan reached it, registered on the Richter scale and could be heard as far as Dusseldorf. This last amplification is not as unreasonable as it seems because, at the time, there were two, joint spokesmen of the managing board: Wilfred Guth, for International, based in Frankfurt, and Wilhelm Christians, for domestic business, who made his office in Dusseldorf. No doubt the shock was almost as great there. Deutsche Bank calls the chairman of the *vorstand,* or managing board, a spokesman, and for many years his role was to say as little as possible. This sound tradition was still in force during my time of association with Germany's premier bank, but successors have taken to speaking out at the slightest provocation, often placing their foot firmly in their mouth. The immediate and privately expressed reaction of Guth and his colleagues could be paraphrased as follows: 'how can this little upstart, so-called merchant bank in London, which we allow to exist only out of respect for Dr. Abs's pet project EBIC – which we secretly think is a nonsense, anyway – aspire to lead manage the most important European transaction since the reopening of Europe's capital markets? How can this muelling infant have the outrageous pretention to aspire to such a role? Has Brussels taken leave of its senses?'

Of course, this was hardly the sentiment expressed directly to John Nash. Very cleverly, Deutsche began a lobbying campaign on a different tack. The Bank was not a believer in the medium-term syndicated loan market, participating only indirectly through BEC. There were several reasons. Deutsche believed medium and long-term capital should be raised through bond issues placed with final investors. The syndicated loan market was dominated by American banks, with Minos Zombanakis' Manufacturers Hanover Limited, the clear leader. Worse was the fact that the market was the principle vehicle for recycling the oil producing countries' surpluses to fund the balance of payments deficits of the oil importing countries – and these were largely in the developing world, i.e., borrowers who had no access to the bond market. For the EEC to associate itself with this category of borrower was invidious. This last bit of reasoning failed to take account of such borrowers as the Republic of France, a host of Italian State Agencies and a number of other investment grade entities. Another strongly felt objection to the proposed transaction was that, by mandating two London based banks as lead managers, the EEC appeared to be confirming the City's position as the leading financial centre of Europe – an absolute anathema to Frankfurt.

Deutsche Bank pulled out all stops, even at the diplomatic level. John Nash was disgusted but could do nothing about it. In the end a compromise was reached. The total amount to be raised was to be divided between a DM bond issues, led by Deutsche Bank, with the balance through the original Eurodollar syndicated loan, led by Orion/EBC. Work continued. The lawyers and Orion/EBC had worked hard to devise a language in the loan documentation for participating banks, which correctly pointed out the risk factors inherent in the borrower's status as a treaty organisation. No one doubted we were dealing with an AAA credit, but proper disclosure was deemed appropriate in such a transaction, as it was not a standard sovereign loan. Treaties have been known to be abrogated. When it came to incorporating the language in the DM issue prospectus, Deutsche Bank categorically refused. I remember a fraught meeting in Brussels when this was discussed. The Deutsche Bank representative said, "All any investor needs to see is the name 'Deutsche Bank' on the front page of the prospectus. Any other information is superfluous." The extraordinary arrogance of this statement silenced the room. When it came to the closing ceremony in Brussels, Wilfrid Guth turned up with a phalanx and proceeded to hog the limelight in a way which nullified some of the credit he hoped to gain. The presentation to the press was that the EEC had gone to market for the first time through a highly successful DM issue by Deutsche Bank, confirming that the DM was the premier European currency and Frankfurt the centre of the financial world. Some subsidiary transaction had been carried out amongst banks in London. David Montagu and I agreed we couldn't care less. Guth had the applause of his little community in Frankfurt – we had the applause of all the world's banks in London. Not that their German partner cared one whit, but our other EBC shareholders were proud, and had the courtesy to tell me so.

For me, the pleasure of the deal had been working with David Montagu and his people at Orion. I considered David the epitome of all I admired in traditional London merchant bankers. Louis Franck considered his partner to be a gambler because of David's keen interest in racing. Of course, Louis didn't have to gamble as he was one of a small coterie in Europe who received stock market tips from André Meyer at Lazard in New York. That the tips often involved companies about to merge or be taken over through Lazard, was purely coincidental. When Louis finally sold out Samuel Montagu to Midland, David was not going to be comfortable at the family bank, and I believe it was David Rockefeller at Chase who recruited him to run Orion, succeeding Ronnie Grierson, who had not found consortium banking very agreeable. David inherited and built on an all-star team including such as Christopher Arnander, Andrew Large, William de Gelsey and even celebrities like Christopher Chataway. William de Gelsey was a Hungarian émigré, who had decamped from a visiting junior golf team, working first for Shell and then for Dickie Bearsted at M. Samuel. He escorted my wife Dinnie a few times, when she was newly arrived in London, and used to give cocktail parties so packed, one had difficulty sipping the White Lady cocktails he served. William has the distinction of being the oldest City practitioner still working at over 90. Orion was a larger and more ambitious consortium project than EBC, perhaps because it was the sole joint venture of its shareholder group, whereas we were one of several. In his article for *Institutional Investor*, entitled, ominously, "What Makes Stani Run", Chris Welles summarised the differences in scale, pointing out that, in 1975, Orion managed or co-managed $1.8 billion worth of financings whereas EBC handled only $700 million. He also noted that Orion was three years older than EBC, had three times EBC's assets of £227 million, and three and a half times EBC' pre-tax profits of £2.1 million. A difference in our styles was relations with the shareholders. I tried as best I could to leave them alone, and roll with the occasional punches I received, especially from Frankfort. David Montagu seemed to be permanently at odds with his shareholders. Indeed, he finally presented them with some ultimatum, and they called his bluff. David then spent a most unhappy year, together with John Craven, trying to make sense of Merrill Lynch's ambitions in London, which, in their joint view, required an acquisition – and they had Hill Samuel in mind. But the culture clash between Montagu and Craven, and the retail brokers, who still ran Merrill in New York, was too great, and it ended in tears. I had no idea at that stage that I was to experience somewhat similar problems, occupying the same chair a few years later.

I was never unhappy at being number two in the consortium bank pecking order to Orion, and we collaborated more than once after the EEC affair. Most of the others were regional in nature and almost entirely dependent on shareholder referred business. Stephan Gadd's Scandinavian Bank and John Sclater's Nordic Bank were the best examples of this genre. For this reason EBC had declined to join the Consortium Banker's Association, because we were in no way dependent on shareholder referred business. Orion did join and, many years later I was invited to join the annual reunion luncheon given to commemorate that brief but invigorating era which was consortium banking. Stephan Gadd was finally recruited to run Samuel Montagu for Midland Bank. One day, out of the blue, he called me and suggested we meet to discuss an idea he had. This turned out to be a proposal that Samuel Montagu and EBC merge.

"Midland might find that a rather sweet idea," I commented, "but why would my other shareholders buy it?"

"Oh, they are all going to set up their own shops in London in the long run. Face it, consortium banking has no future."

This, of course, from an ex-consortium banker, was no doubt highly prescient, but I was not quite ready to acknowledge the future. Still, Bill Slee and I met at Stephan's Eaton Square house to explore the idea. Stephan generously proposed that I would be his number two in the merged bank, taking a position then occupied by David Stevens.

"What about him?" was my natural question.

"He'll go."

"What about Bill?"

"Number three, of course."

"What about David Mitchum and the forex business?

"Shouldn't be a problem. EBC is strong in spot, we are strong in forwards. David will be number two to Chris Sheridan."

As in so many cases, when the term "merger" is bandied about, this was clearly a takeover proposition. This was entirely justified as Montagu was bigger, more profitable and highly established. It was also clear that David Stevens was not party to this brain wave of Stephan's. Stevens went on to become a great press baron at the *Mirror* and a peer of the realm. I had a further brush with David. With his wife, a friend of Dinnie's, who had written a book entitled *How to Be a Perfect Wife*, the Stevens lived just opposite us in South Eaton Place. One evening, they had returned from a dinner, and David was already abed, when Lady Stevens stood gazing out of the window.

"Look, somebody's climbing into a window in the Yassukovich's flat!" she exclaimed. We were away.

"Oh, it's probably one of the children who has forgotten their key," said David from the bed.

"It doesn't look like one of the children – it looks like a burglar."

"Nonsense – I should forget about it. Come to bed."

Well, of course, we were being burgled. I cannot attest as to whether Lady Stevens was indeed a "perfect wife", but I can say she was a perfect neighbour. I rather lost touch with Lord Stevens and never had a chance to chide him over this. Nor was he aware of his possible fate if the Montagu/EBC deal had gone ahead. Bill Slee was highly sceptical of the whole thing, and rightly told me we might lose many of our key people. On the other hand, and looking back, I don't think it was such a stupid idea, and we might have built something permanent, although Stephan eventually fell out with Midland, and, at the time, their junior shareholder Aetna Insurance, over policy issues, and was succeeded by Michael Palliser, a born diplomat, who could not save it from its ultimate destruction through Midland's bungling ownership – the fate of all merchant/investment banks acquired by commercial banks.

Soon after my departure from White, Weld, I had been elected to succeed Rolf Hallberg of Stockholm's Enskilda Bank, as Chairman of the International Association of Bond Dealers. The IADB was acquiring increasing status, not just as a trade association, but as a quazi-self regulator. Despite constant harping about an unregulated Euromarkets, the fact remains that all the participants were authorised and regulated persons in their respective jurisdictions. But the market itself was not a stock exchange, where formal rules apply to dealings and each transaction is recorded with the result that volumes are known. No one had the slightest idea of the volumes in the Eurobond market, as there was no trade reporting on a consolidated basis. Officialdom abhors unmeasurable activity. The most important initiative which catapulted the AIBD to a more significant standing was Walter Koller's idea to set up an annual training symposium, which gathered dealers and back office personnel from the member firms, to spend a week at lectures and workshops in the Palace Hotel at Montreux, culminating in professionally designed examinations which, if passed, produced a qualification. Eventually, as Walter Koller's famous link phrase would put it, such qualification became a CV necessity for those seeking employment in the industry. Walter masterminded the construction and execution of this event, and turned out to have both inspirational and organisational qualities previously unsuspected. I would open and close the symposium and once stayed long enough to watch Michael von Clemm at work as a guest lecturer. It was an inspiration. Michael was back at the Harvard Business School, as, microphone in hand, he roved up and down the aisles of the auditorium, challenging, questioning, berating, and generally sowing seeds of knowledge and experience to a fascinated audience. As the AIBD found itself at the centre of a market exploding in volume and variety, the divide between the primary market and the secondary marked became more troublesome. There was a social divide, as primary market operators tended to be university graduates and secondary market dealers were not. In British terms: public school vs grammar school. There was the professional conflict, or perception of conflict, as primary market people represented the borrower, and the bond traders in the secondary market saw themselves as on the side of the investors. This all came to head in the so-called "grey market" controversy. The AIBD sought to enforce a rule that dealings in an issue began only after launch date, when the final terms were announced and allocations to the underwriting and selling group had been made. Stanley Ross, now at Kidder Peabody, could be described as a co-doyen, with Walter Koller, of the secondary market traders. He was certainly the most vocal. He felt, with some justification, that issuing houses were increasingly overpricing issues, as they competed for mandates, leaving the secondary market to clean up the distorted after-market. He began quoting a bid and asked price for an issue in course, but not yet launched, on terms he believed reflected the proper price level, given outstanding yields on issues of similar quality. He took little risk, as Kidder Peabody always received a generous allocation, so he knew any short was covered, but he put pressure on the investment bankers in negotiation with the borrower to fix final terms. As always with mavericks who chafe at regulation and seek to work outside, his was a legitimate free market position, but strongly objected to by the primary market community. According to Chris O'Malley's definitive work on the history of the Eurobond market, Stanley Ross had been the major supporter of my election as

AIBD Chairman. Perhaps he thought I would halt the primary market's increasing tendency to over price issues. I'm not sure what Stanley thought but he certainly gave me a hard time at our Annual General meeting, held in London, for the first time, with Gordon Richardson, then Governor of the Bank, as our honoured guest speaker. Anthony Loehnis, a former Chief Clerk at the Foreign Office and a friend of Michael von Clemm, and, thus, mine as well, had worked with Richardson at Schroeder's and was now with him at the Bank. I suspect Anthony wrote the Governor's speech, which included the statement "Your chairman can often be seen, the tails of his red coat flying, leaping over the stone walls of the Cotswolds, riding to hounds in pursuit of the fox". The allusion rang few bells with the Continental contingent. The grey market issue dominated the proceedings, after the key note speech by the Governor, which was full of praise for a market that had so quickly achieved maturity and stability. He did not stay for the grey market resolution debate. Stanley was up and down like a jack-in-the-box; "M m m ister Chairman! A p p point of order!" Stanley has a pronounced stammer, which many in the market thought gave him an advantage when trading on the phone, as he could change his quote in the course of a sentence punctuated by stammers. It was an equivalent to Walter Koller's link phrase "eventually" – as in "Eventually... I can make you 98 to 3/8ths". I found myself defending the status quo, as chairman do, but unsure as to how many on my board supported me. Stanley castigated me as a tool of the primary market and a champion of restrictive practices. It was all a bit academic as the AIBD had no authority whatsoever to ban grey market activity, short of expelling an offending member, which we were hardly likely to do, and Stanley knew it, and I knew it. Of course the grey market continued, but evolution made it redundant as well, as the era of the "bought deal" was soon upon us. As technology shortened the period of distribution, it became possible for investment bankers to quote fixed terms to a borrower with limited risk of major market movement before the issue was placed. In fact the history of distribution times for international bond issues provides a clear measurement of the impact of communications technology. In the 19th century, it took months to arrange, underwrite and distribute an international loan. Now it takes hours.

My term of office as chairman of the AIBD represented the end of my day-to-day affair with the heroine of my story – the Eurobond. I had seen her born, danced at her coming out party, attended her wedding and watched her mature into an attractive and increasingly matronly lady. Her adventures had attracted increasing attention from the media and from officialdom. Competition for her favours had intensified. Those of us who had escorted her to her early balls, now saw others filling her dance card. Although at the many conferences I spoke at, I was still introduced as one of the "fathers of the Eurobond market", at EBC, I had become a generalist, and certainly could no longer claim to be a Eurobond specialist. As the City of London developed as the world's premier financial centre, the specialist was to become king, and the generalist a dying breed. In a vastly expanded market place, my market value was on the way down. But I welcomed this as I had become exposed to a far wider range of interests and activities. Worker at many trades, but master of none, perhaps, but at EBC I had the satisfaction of having created a bank from scratch, leaving aside the fact that I had not experienced the toughest challenge for any creative entrepreneur, which is to find the start-up capital. But one does not chooses one's parents and it is churlish to underestimate their contribution to whatever success one has in life. My shareholders really made EBC, simply by being there.

Our second piece of "walk-in" business at EBC proved unusually exciting. A man called Peter Detweiler, who I hardly knew, and who was with E. F. Hutton in New York, called at our offices. E. F. Hutton was a pure retail brokerage firm founded by a San Franciscan, who eventually married Margery Merriweather Post, the breakfast cereal and General Foods heiress. They had a huge estate on the North Shore of Long Island and owned the mega yacht *Sea Cloud*, which I almost bumped in my little Lightning class centre board sloop sailing out of Seawanaka Yacht Club. They had one daughter, the actress Dina Merrill, married to the actor Cliff Robertson. E. F. Hutton was number two to Merrill Lynch as a nationwide retail brokerage firm, but came to a sticky end due to various scandals, and was eventually absorbed, through several mergers, by Citibank. Hutton had no investment banking arm and so I was a bit surprised when Detweiler told me he had a mandate from Allan Paulsen, the CEO of Gulfstream, the business jet maker, to do a management buyout. Gulfstream had been a division of the Grumman Aircraft Corporation, of Bethpage, Long Island, celebrated as the makers of the Hellcat and Wildcat carrier based aircraft, which helped win the war in the Pacific. David Grumman was a school mate and contemporary of my sister at Green Vale School. I suspect the photograph of my father in the cockpit of a fighter plane, referred to in my introduction, and was taken at Grumman's base at Bethpage. Paulsen, a former aircraftman in the U.S. Air Force, had gained a pilot's licence on demobilisation and built an extraordinary career as a TWA pilot, second hand aircraft salesman, Lockheed agent, designer of planes and racing pilot. Under contract to Grumman's Gulfstream division, he had designed an aircraft which was propeller driven for short take-offs and landings, but with a jet engine added in the tail for long range flights. It never went into production but Paulsen seems to have ended up running the Gulfstream division, which Grumman was intending to sell. Detweiler told me a colourful tale about an eccentric millionaire who was so convinced of a forthcoming nuclear holocaust; he lived in an underground mansion near Reno, Nevada. Somehow, according to Detweiler, this recluse had acquired control of the Gulfstream division, and was now prepared to grant Paulsen an option to buy the company, if he could raise the money within six months. I have never been able to corroborate this part of the story. All the histories simply say Paulsen bought the company. But, at the time, I was able to confirm

Paulsen had the option to buy Gulfstream, by making discreet enquiries through Shearman & Sterling, our New York lawyers. Detweiler went on to explain that Paulsen, who had no capital of his own, was stymied in raising the money by new Federal Reserve restrictions on U.S. banks, which the Fed considered overexposed to the management and leveraged buyout business, which had been booming in the early '70s. And so Detweiler had suggested coming to Europe, and hence to European Banking Company, owned by seven of the largest banks in Europe. So far the MBO/LBO business had been easily funded by deal-hungry U.S. banks and little, if any, of these deals had been offered to European banks. It soon became clear that my shareholders had hardly heard about such business. I told Detweiler I would consult with my colleagues and get back to him. I sat down with Slee, Parsons and Balfour and we discussed how we might sell the deal to our shareholders. We were immediately agreed that it was "our kind of deal".

There was no question that Gulfstream was the premier manufacturer of long range executive jets in the world, the only competitor being Canadair. Gulfstream was about to "roll out" the G III, and its order book had recently been swelled by a new tax exemption for the benefit of the oil industry, always adept at swinging fiscal legislation in its favour. The purchase and maintenance of corporate aircraft was to be considered an expense of exploration, and thus deductible. Exxon had three G IIIs on order, Mobil two, and so on, and so forth. A glance down the order book, which Detweiler had given me, showed an astonishing list of America's blue chip corporates, with some government agencies, the odd African dictator, and, amusingly, Tiny Rowland of Lonrho, as the only European customer. The surge in executive aircraft use was to a large extent the consequence of American companies moving away from the major conurbations to campus like corporate headquarters, near local airports which did not serve many intercity flights. Of course, this justification is somewhat stretched by the many large corporates who moved from central Manhattan to corporate campuses in Greenwich, Connecticut and now have their Gulfstream and Lear jets with General Aviation at Westchester County Airport, when LaGuardia and JFK are only a taxi ride away. I soon learned that a major qualification for an executive jet pilot was a low golf handicap, as he is often called upon to make up a foursome for a game at Palm Springs or Pebble Beach, where the greats of the corporate world gather for relaxation, and an occasional bit of price fixing. But, in considering our shareholder's view of this opportunity, we still had to overcome a European feeling that corporate jets were an executive toy, characteristic of the American corporate abuse of management perquisites. The credit quality of management buy-out loans was not so difficult to sell. They are an extension of the basic principle of cash flow lending, the issue being the quality of the borrower's assets and revenue. We were confident that Gulfstream's world renown in its field and the AAA quality of the order book would be convincing selling points, and I went back to Detweiler to accept the mandate. We pulled out all stops. I immediately contacted Shearman & Sterling and they assigned John Eaton, younger son of senior partner Fred Eaton, to handle the deal, which would be documented under New York State law. John described it as "the deal of the decade" and threw himself into it with extraordinary enthusiasm. I knew him slightly on a social level at that time, but we became great friends as a result of Gulfstream. He came to a sad end. Years of servicing the Taiwanese Government account for Shearman & Sterling, which involved weekly commutes from New York to Taiwan, brought on a mental strain which led to a complete breakdown and ultimate death. Unusually, my most difficult shareholder sale was to Midland Bank, normally amongst the first on our board to approve, and participate in our major credits. Flying back from an EBIC quarterly meeting, I sat next to Jack Hendley and said, "Look at this list of orders for the G III? Can you imagine companies of this quality reneging? And in any case there are progress payments and big cancellation fees. Furthermore, can you imagine that a company that has developed the world renowned G I and G II aircraft would fail to roll out the G III?"

"Well, OK – but Midland is not too keen on leveraged buyouts and we don't take equity as a matter of principle."

"But the equity kicker is a "freebie"! The terms of the loan are entirely commercial. The equity costs you nothing."

There were free shares to be allocated to the lenders, saleable on a planned initial public offering, which Paulsen was already discussing with Goldman Sachs.

"Alright," said Jack, grudgingly. "We'll participate in the loan, but we won't take the equity."

I was relieved, but thought to myself that Midland was acting like a child that goes to a birthday party but refuses to take home the small present traditionally handed out to the little guests.

At the closing at Shearman & Sterling's New York office, we met Allen Paulson's lawyer, a colourful partner in a Los Angeles firm, who wore heavy, Navajo Indian jewellery and a pigtail. Watching him and John Eaton – who was totally "preppy" – conduct the meeting over a huge board room table groaning with documents, was a joy in itself. Afterwards, we had a meeting of the new board of the newly constituted company Detweiler and I had been invited by Paulsen to join the board and we seemed to be the only members who did not possess a pilot's licence. Others, like Newall Bohnett, who lived on a large ranch in Hawaii, and David Nancarrow, who owned a restaurant chain and lived in Santa Barbara, had been Naval and Marine pilots. We were each asked to introduce ourselves and our backgrounds, and the only thing that made an impression on my new colleagues was that I had served in the U.S. Marine Corps. Newall Bohnett soon suggested we meet as a board at his ranch in Hawaii, and I decided to take Dinnie for a short holiday there, at a posh beach hotel on the Big Island. The breakers reminded Dinnie of the Cape and the sand was black volcanic. I decided I preferred the amicable Atlantic waves to the nonpacific Pacific surf, and the black sand burnt the soles of my feet. Newall gave us horses to ride and Brahman calves to watch being branded. On the way back Allen Paulson decided to try for a distance record in the G III, and we flew direct from Honolulu to Washington DC's national airport, watching a video of *Gone With The Wind*, on the way, and landing with just the statutory half hour's flying time of fuel. We made the record in under ten hours. David Nancarrow had his own Lear jet and complained that Santa Barbara airport was often closed down as President Reagan had a ranch nearby, and traffic was cleared whenever Air Force One came in. David Nancarrow was a charming and, it turned out, extremely correct client. He wanted to sell his chain of family restaurants, known as "Carrow's", which operated throughout the South West, and asked EBC to find a buyer in Europe. I contacted Rank Organisation, which was making similar acquisitions, and they expressed strong interest. I set up a meeting for David with Rank's CEO, a typical Establishment figure, and witnessed one of those Anglo-American culture clashes, which have been the subject of more than one novel. "I'm not selling my company to that f...ing stuffed shirt!" was Nancarrow's comment after the meeting. "Your client is rather an ill-mannered boor" was the Rank executive's somewhat more quiet comment. In any case – no deal. David had asked Alex Brown, in Baltimore, to find a U.S. buyer and it soon identified and closed with W. R. Grace. Shortly after, I received a cheque from David Nancarrow, for $100,000, with a note explaining that he, with Alex Brown, had upped the price W. R Grace was offering by constant references to the Rank Organisation interest, and the price that had then been bandied about. David felt EBC was owed a fee, as it had greatly facilitated the negotiation with the ultimate buyer by producing a competitor – even though we had zero contractual rights to one. That is what I call a highly correct – and rare –client.

The board of Gulfstream, which normally met quarterly in Savannah, provided much amusement for me. Allen Paulson was a super salesman and dealt directly with the CEOs of customer companies. Their aircraft were fitted and serviced at Savannah and one G II, belonging to an African dictator, and in for service, was parked at a far end of the runway area, fumigated by safety overall clad technicians, and left for several days, whilst various "skellums" crawled out and died, forming a circle of corpses around the plane. At one meeting Allen took me aside and asked me if I knew Kenneth Keith, then chairman of Rolls-Royce. Of course, I did – from the Beecham issue we had done at White Weld, when Keith was chairman of both Beecham and our co-manager Hill Samuel. "See if you can get him to join the board. Maybe he'll give us a discount on our engines." Gulfstream had switched from Pratt & Whitney to Rolls-Royce engines with the G I.

"I'll try," I said, "but I wouldn't count on the discount."

"Well, get him on the board, and we'll charm it out of him."

Kenneth Keith guessed the agenda immediately.

"I suppose Paulsen's looking for discounts?" he said when I reached him.

"Yes – but I told him not to hold his breath, and it's not a condition. But he is planning to use his 'southern charm' on you."

"I accept, and he can charm away – he won't get a discount."

Kenneth never offered a discount on his engines, and Paulsen stopped asking after a while. But an immediate difficulty arose at the first meeting.

"What the hell was Lord Keith saying?" whispered Paulsen to me at lunch, after the meeting. Kenneth not only spoke with a particularly "plummy" accent, but tended to swallow his words.

At the same lunch, Kenneth took me aside and said, "I can't understand a word that man is saying."

Although he was from California, Paulsen had adopted a very Dixie drawl. As the only board member who could understand both, I found myself acting as an interpreter, delivering summarised translations to each after the meetings. Yet another example of how Britain and America are separated by a common language. Kenneth was disappointed that Paulsen did not send a G III to London to pick us up for Savannah board meetings. We had to fly commercial as far as Washington where a company G III picked us up for the Savannah leg. On one occasion Kenneth and I were catching the hourly shuttle from LaGuardia to Washington National, and arrived at the last minute at the check-in desk. Suddenly, a very flustered Jessica Douglas-Home, then wife of the editor of the *Times,* rushed up and, in anguished tones, said to the check-in clerk, "I've had my passport, money and credit cards stolen, but I must get to Washington. Can I pay for a ticket with an English cheque?" She held a Coutts cheque book in a trembling hand.

"We can't take British pounds, lady," said the clerk, shaking his head.

At that point Kenneth intervened.

"You can write the cheque in dollars. Just put a dollar sign in front of the amount. Coutts will debit your account at the exchange rate prevailing on the date of the cheque."

"Wow!" said the clerk.

"Really?" said Jessica.

"Absolutely," said Kenneth, an old established Coutts client.

On the flight, Kenneth and I were up front when a note was passed up to us from Jessica, sitting further back. Could we land her some cash for the taxi on arrival? Kenneth sent $200 back. I don't know if he was repaid. Jessica was sadly widowed later, but went on to marry Rodney Leach, and lived in a neighbouring village to ours, at Quenington. She hunted with the VWH and kept her horse at livery with Jilly Scott, wife of our Master, Martin Scott, who was almost next door. The drill was Jilly would tack up the horse on hunting mornings, blanket it and put it in the trailer. Jessica would arrive, hitch up the trailer and drive to the unboxing area – only having to remember to remove the tail bandage before hacking off to the meet. One day, Jessica set out early, thinking she would read her book quietly before mounting up. I would guess the book was probably an obscure work on the use of rare woods in the manufacture of 17th century harpsichords. Jessica, amongst many other intellectual accomplishments, is an expert on harpsichords. With eleven o'clock approaching she got out, only to discover he had forgotten to pick up the trailer, and had to rush back to find Jilly Scott scratching her head, looking at the trailer, horse within, still sitting there.

Gulfstream duly went public and progressed from strength to strength. Allen Paulsen, suffered a tragic consequence of his new wealth, when a son was kidnapped – but thankfully was recovered unharmed. One day Allen told us he had decided to sell Gulfstream to Chrysler, having struck the deal with Lee Iacocca over the garden fence in Palm Springs. Paulsen still owned 70% of the company, as the IPO had offered only a third to the public. Goldman Sachs was brought in to negotiate the deal. During some intense sessions, I suffered a serious sense of humour failure. The partner of Goldman Sachs who turned up, seemed totally oblivious to the necessity of protecting the interests of the minority shareholders, and was quite happily crafting a "sweetheart" deal, as struck over the garden fence between Paulsen and Iacocca, on terms below those indicated by the market price of Gulfstream shares, and certainly not including a control premium. The great Iacocca's justification for the acquisition, on behalf of a troubled Chrysler Corporation, was his notion that the lightweight composite materials used in aircraft manufacture might be suitably adapted for motorcars – a notion which must have had his engineers laughing up their sleeves. I somewhat stunned the board by pointing out, that as far as I knew, Goldman Sachs was retained to advise the board, not just Allen Paulsen personally, and the board had a responsibility to all the shareholders – particularly the minority. Paulsen was furious. His decisions had never been questioned by the board, and with the exception of Kenneth Keith, who was completely with me, the others considered me out of order for daring to question our great leader. In the end, Paulsen had to go back to his Palm Springs chum Iacocca, and jack up the price. For me, it was a revelation. I had been brought up to believe Goldman Sachs was as pure as the driven snow. Its performance on this occasion was lamentable, to say the least.

At EBC, we had a happier experience with Chrysler. Rainer Kahrmann used his contacts with his former colleagues at Dow Chemical to gain access to Chrysler, which was being brought back from near death by some U.S. Government guaranties, which Congress had voted, representing something of a first in Federal rescues of private sector companies. Kahrmann suggested that the newly restored Chrysler credit be re-introduced to the European market through a placement of medium-term notes. The Chrysler rescue package had been put together by Salomon Brothers, and Jim Wolfenson, ex-Schroeders, was the partner in charge of the business – and the main architect of the rescue. I rang Jim, expecting to be ticked off for effrontery and told to leave such matters to Salomon Brothers. Not a bit of it – Jim was courtesy itself, totally supportive and helpful. He congratulated me on the idea, considered it timely, and offered a few insights. In fact, he behaved like the gentleman investment banker he was – amongst the last of a breed. He became an excellent President of the World Bank. The deal was a success and a triumph for Rainer Kharmann, who had developed his skill in dealing with American corporates through his association with Dow Chemical, and handled this deal superbly. Rainer was back and forth several times to Detroit, and I went with him once, for the usual senior courtesy visit. I was spared contact with Iacocca, but saw Bob Lutz, son of DY's old Credit Suisse friend Robert Lutz, who could claim some paternity for the Credit Suisse/White Weld relationship, which was to mature under Genillard and Guth. Bob had been born and brought up in Switzerland but shunned banking there to go to America, where, after a career as a Marine Corps pilot, Bob had been first at Ford, and then gone on to Chrysler with Iacocca. But, he fell out with the latter and missed succeeding him. He went on to continue a brilliant career at General Motors.

Deals we never did are as much a memory of my time at EBC. ITT had been binging on acquisitions in the '60s and '70s and had used a convertible preference share as currency, saving the vendors of private companies from immediate capital gains tax, by exchanging their shares for the ITT paper. As a result a good deal of these convertible preference shares was held around Europe, and it occurred to me that one might create liquidity by making a secondary market. My childhood friend Brewster Righter, always called Bruce, had worked for ITT for many years and he introduced me to its corporate counsel who was called Billyou. I considered this a perfect name for a lawyer and worked with him happily to see whether my concept could be facilitated. In the end there were insurmountable legal difficulties. But we were able to do something else with Bruce Righter. He had gone to work for the Bacardi Group, now headquartered in a Frank Lloyd Wright designed building in Hamilton, Bermuda, having fled Cuba, first for Puerto Rico and then Mexico. Still family owned, the Bacardi company's light rum was, and I believe still is, the largest selling spirit in the world. The company suddenly decided that its world-wide trade in a basic commodity – sugar, and its fleet of tankers transporting rum, justified a diversification into financial services. After all, many great banking dynasties had begun in commodities. Bruce was engaged to set up a dealing facility in Bermuda and suggested to me that we form a joint venture bank in Zurich, which would look after the extended Bacardi family resident in Spain, Mexico and other venues. The idea appealed and I put Rainer Kharmann on to it. After all, he had experience of a Swiss bank owned by corporate interests, with Dow Banking Corp. Rainer found a credible manager and Bacardi EBC AG was soon in place. Unfortunately, Bruce's team in back in Hamilton contained a rogue dealer who took advantage of his boss's absence to go haywire, and promptly lost millions. Bacardi decided that sticking to strong spirits might be safer than the financial services venture which had produced such a serious hangover. Bruce, as the man on the watch, lost his job, and the dealing room was closed. The bank in Zurich carried on for a while but was eventually sold. A more successful joint venture arose from a friend called Robert Lyle. Together with Control Risks, a kidnap and ransom insurance adjuster, we founded a new Lloyds broker called Berry, Palmer & Lyle, which was originally to specialise in placing K & R insurance, but has evolved as one of the leading insurance brokers in the field of emerging country credit risk. It's now called BPL Holdings, and whenever I see Robby Lyle, he hails me as one of BPL's founders.

We maintained two overseas representatives at EBC, on a fairly informal basis. Their main role was introductions and advice on their jurisdictions, but they also had great entertainment value and became fast friends. I had met Don Ignacio Gomez-Acebo y Duque de Estrada during my White, Weld days. Ignacio, born on St. Patrick's Day was called "Paddy" by his Irish nanny, and the name stuck. Paddy was incredibly well-connected. His father had been chairman of Banesto, Spain's largest bank, his mother the 9th Marchioness of Deleitosa, his brother Luis was married to the Infanta Pilar, sister to King Juan Carlos, and Paddy had married Isabel de Carvajal y Urquijo, sister to Jaime Urquijo of the banking family. Paddy was a co-founder of the leading law firm Gomez-Acebo y Pombo, the leading Spanish language patent registration firm Clarke y Modet, and chairman of the Spanish subsidiaries of Firestone, Chrysler Financial, AXA and Nokia. There was no one in Madrid he didn't know. Driving with him down one of Madrid's wide boulevard, when one stopped at a traffic light, the driver in the car in the next door lane would be friend, and traffic held up, as he chatted with Paddy. At our usual 3:30 lunch at the Jockey Club, almost every other table seemed to include a friend – it was like going to the Brown Derby with Clarke Gable in the old Hollywood. Paddy was a great bear of a man, whilst Isabel, his wife, was a waif. She had shocked Madrid society by becoming a lecturer in applied physics at the University. There was a squash court in his house where we played and one had to be very careful not to get in between Paddy on the move and a wall. Shortly after the restoration of the monarchy, some die hard Franco supporters tried to stage a *coup d'etat* and an army officer entered parliament and waved a pistol about. Paddy was driving when his care telephone rang. It was the King, and would he come to the palace where a telephone bank had been set up for friends to call around and rally support? Paddy drove straight to the palace with his fat phone number book in hand. The *coup* and Juan Carlos's popularity was confirmed. Paddy gave us myriad introductions and endless assistance in Spain.

Patricio Gordon Whitney was married to a cousin of Lisa von Clemm, and I met him when he came to play polo in England one summer. His father had gone out to Uruguay for the Swift Company of Chicago in the 1920s and married a girl with the typical Argentinian name of Jamieson. This Scottish

306

family had gone first to the Falklands in the 19th century, and then ended up owning a good piece of Patagonia, when a supply ship passed only once a year to pick up the wool clip. A Germany family were "neighbours" owning another chunk of Patagonia, and they intermarried and were on the best of terms before, and after, the First World War, when each had gone off to fight for their respective sides. "Gordo", as Whitney was known, owned Sudatlantica, a major agency for several European insurers, farmed south of Buenos Aires and had an estate in Bariloche, stuffed with red deer and other game. We appointed him our representative for Argentina, where he knew everyone there was to know and was on particularly good terms with Francisco Soldati, who was Undersecretary of Finance and the principal source of mandates for Argentina's extensive foreign borrowing. Francisco himself was a colourful figure, highly prominent at World Bank/IMF meetings and at Davos, where he would "look in" on his way to play polo on the snow at St. Moritz. The Soldati family were from the Ticino in Switzerland, and certainly fitted the description of a typical Argentinian, which I first heard from Gordo Whitney: an Italian who speaks Spanish and thinks he is English. Visits to Gordo were leisurely and only tangentially concerned with business. First off was a visit to 'il Turco", as he was known, actually a Lebanese who was the best maker of polo sticks. There I would order my own sticks, viewing with awe bundles made up for some of the ten goal greats of the country. On arrival at Sudatlantica, I would note Gordo's completely empty desk, and coffee would be served. Then weekend plans would be discussed and a call made to ensure Gordo's Piper Cub plane was prepared. Actually Gordo's brother, who had been at FNCB, ran the business. Just before the outbreak of the Falklands War, direct dialling between London and Buenos Aires had been introduced and I was able to chat quite easily with Whitney, even at the height of hostilities; At the time, Gordon was divorcing his wife and living at the Hurlingham Club just outside of town – an establishment so anglicised that convention required that luncheon, from a menu in English, be ordered in English from the Argentine waiters. Gordo remarked on the fact that no one had thought to take down a large portrait of the Queen which graced the Club entrance hall, and copies of *The Field* and *Horse & Hound* still cluttered the reading room table. On the subject of the Falklands War, I am not inclined to credit the story, much circulated in Argentine circles, that Lord Carrington cut short his fateful Washington meeting with the Argentine Foreign Secretary, because his hostess, the wife of the British Ambassador, had told him there was a soufflé for dinner and he couldn't be late. Although Lord Carrington resigned when the war started, it had nothing to do with a soufflé. For one thing, I know for a fact that the British Embassy in Washington never serves a cheese soufflé as a starter, but only sweet soufflés for desert, which can be started during the meal. One of Gordo's introductions was Cellulosa Argentina, a forestry products company, founded by Italians in the 19th century, then the leading blue chip. I went to see their trees growing in Missiones Province, and, although it was an optical illusion, you could almost see them grow, if you stood still for a half an hour. "Here's a company that couldn't possible go bust," said Gordo. We ended having to re-structure its loan. In the 1930s Argentina had the second largest per capita ownership of motorcars, after the U.S. On paper it is potentially the richest country in the world, but, since the Peronista era of the '40s, it has been a semi-permanent basket case, and certainly defies the old saying of only lending to countries where they wear overcoats. They wear very smart, English tailored overcoats in Argentina and they default as often as most people sneeze.

The binge of international bank lending in the 1970s produced a major hangover in the 1980s, the era of sovereign defaults. Mexico was the first to go in 1982, but Argentina was not far behind. The EBIC Group had remained largely aloof from the syndicated loan market, which was dominated by American banks, except through their joint venture BEC, whose *metier* was medium-term lending. Soundly managed by Hans Kippenburger, BEC found itself only on the fringes of the storm of defaults which began to rage in the mid-'80s. Nevertheless, loan loss reserves and work outs had both grown in its balance sheet and portfolio, and the shareholders began to grumble. We served on each other's boards, and I could see Hans had a greater difficulty defending BEC's casualties than I had EBC's – although these were smaller and confined to transactions where front end fees had been earned. The shareholders conceived the extraordinarily unfair means of stopping BEC's growth, by sending poor Hans back to manage Deutsche Bank, Hamburg and making me chief executive of both banks which would now be coupled, although not actually merged, as European Banking Group. Perhaps realising I had been handed a can of worms, I was consoled by being named Deputy Chairman of the new Group, within which the two banks would have one common board. Chairman of the Group was Paul-Emmanuel Jansen, who had succeeded Fritz Karston as my chairman and was already chairman of BEC. The only explanation of this strange reshuffle I can think of is that Deutsche Bank took the view that Kippenburger, as a career Deutsche Bank man, would do as he was told. It would have been difficult to recruit a new managing director for a bank going nowhere and so Yassukovich might as well be given the caretaker job, as he could easily be sacked when it all went pear-shaped. I tried to integrate the teams and held several meetings to that end. But there was a philosophical divide. Our team at EBC thought like investment bankers; the BEC team were commercial bankers through and through. For us, a borrower was a client, and if difficulties arose, we tried to find ways to ease the debt burden. For BEC, the borrower was a potential adversary, and if a loan condition was missed, it sought quickly to improve its security and even tighten the terms. I recall only one case when we almost did the same. We had project financed the Orient Express for Jim Sherwood's Sea Containers company. Sherwood had spent years locating, reconditioning and restoring old Pullman cars to achieve his dream of reviving luxury train travel. As in most project financing structures, there were thresholds to be met on the way to becoming cash flow positive, and, as in most project financings, Orient Express was running late. We met with the finance director, and were having a constructive meeting, when suddenly Jim Sherwood burst into the room and started to berate us.

"How dare you people come in here and beat on my finance director! You're lucky to have got this deal, and you have a letter of comfort from Sea Containers, signed by me – and I am Sea Containers!"

I rose from the table and adopted my most imperious tone.

"Mr. Chairman! We have come to this meeting to discuss ways of easing terms with your finance director, to accommodate an understandable delay in revenue generation. But if you are going to adopt that tone, we will be minded to alter course, and increase the level and frequency of stress testing the progress, and if you don't like it, we will call an event of default, which if you reread the loan agreement, you will see we are entitled to do. It will be no skin off our nose, because, as you say – we have your letter of comfort."

"Harrumph!" said Sherwood, and stalked out of the room.

"Did you mean that?" said the finance director.

"Of course not – but your boss is a big bully."

"He certainly is!" was a relieved reply.

Naturally, it all worked out. We got our money back and the Orient Express was a great success. I don't recall having received free tickets. Jim Sherwood went on to create a luxury hotel empire, having conveniently allowed Sea Containers to go bust. I had great respect for his entrepreneurship as an hotelier – but not for his taste. One of the jewels of the hotel group is the Villa San Michele, in Fiesole, with a magnificent view of Florence below. It was originally a nunnery designed by Michelangelo, and an oversized, late 18th century crystal chandelier has been hung in the entrance hall – a bit like hanging Impressionist paintings in the Sistine Chapel.

My real challenge was finding something original for the Brussels' team to do, apart from managing the existing portfolio. I felt this would motivate them. But it was impossible to identify a field in which the shareholders were not already engaged. By this time we were seeking diversification and had moved into trading blue chip European equities over-the-counter. We found two ex-jobbers to handle this, and I received an anonymous letter claiming the two had a poor reputation on the Stock Exchange. Of course we had taken references, but already then, no one dared give an honest reference for fear of defamation actions – so references had become useless. At one point Nicholas Goodison, unaware – as was I – which he would eventually have me as a deputy chairman of the Stock Exchange, called me in and asked if EBC intended to join the Exchange. His concerns were justified as there were already some alternative trading facilities popping up, and the Exchange's monopoly was on borrowed time – something Mrs. Thatcher failed to grasp. We also set up a private client investment management service, under Rainer Kharmann, with limited success. For me the worst aspect of my expanded role was that I had to spend one day a week in Brussels and, unwisely, chose Friday as the day. Getting home, in order not to miss a Saturday meet of the VWH hounds, a was a nightmare, as Brussels/Heathrow flights were notoriously overbooked with the British beaurocrats from the EEC Commission, also struggling to get home for the weekend. In Paul Emmanuel Jansen, I had a charming, knowledgeable and supportive chairman. His principle concerns at the time were an alcoholic wife and the necessity to learn Flemish as the chairman of Générale de Banque, where the switchboard was now answering in both French and Flemish. Strangely, Kredietbank N.V., the largest Flemish bank did not reciprocate and used English as its second language. The Jansen family had the shooting at Waterloo, and my chairman kindly invited me. My loader gave me a detailed description of the battle, as we waited in between drives. The pheasants flew remarkably well from coverts set at great distances apart.

The City was soon rumbling with pre-Big Bang tremors, focussed on the Stock Exchange, which had attracted the attention of the Office for Fair Trading as early as 1978. In the early '80s an interminable debate began over the issue of minimum commissions and single capacity, i.e., the separation of function between jobbers and brokers. Lloyds had suffered scandals and fresh regulatory legislation, the discount market was struggling to survive a dynamic evolution of the money markets, the rise to prominence of the Eurobond market had opened a discussion on capital adequacy in the merchant banking sector, the creation of the London International Financial Futures Market – LIFFE, bringing an influx of Chicago commodity traders – all had increased the Americanisation of the City and led to a growing sentiment that City could not survive in a global market without imitating Wall Street. No one stopped to consider that the elimination of fixed commissions there had dramatically altered the economics of the investment banking business. Naturally, this new focus on opening the City to new competitive forces did not go unnoticed in the EBIC group. It was becoming clear that universal banks, in particular, would require their own multi- function presence in London, if they were to term themselves "international". I suppose the gothic script on the wall came with the Deutsche Bank's acquisition of a 5% stake in Morgan Grenfell. I had never really believed Deutsche would be satisfied with a one-seventh stake in a City presence – and, of course, it needed a "name". It acquired the balance of Morgan Grenfell at the end of the turbulent decade. My right arm, Bill Slee, as a sailor, had seen the way the wind was blowing and taken off for Schroeder's. I could hardly blame him.

A number of events occurred in quick succession, altering my life significantly. EBIC decided to put EBC up for sale, and to put BEC into portfolio "run off" mode. It had not been booking new business for a while, anyway. I suggested Barings be engaged to find a buyer. This was agreed and I went to see Andrew Tuckey, Dinnie's childhood Rhodesian playmate, now running Baring's international division. Since he didn't ask me what my own future plans were, I assumed this was not an issue. Soon after I had a call from Giovanni Franzi, a fiercely intelligent MIT graduate who had worked with me at White, Weld and gone on to Merrill Lynch, where he was head of capital markets in London. "We are looking for a high profile chairman for Merrill Lynch Europe & Middle East."

"You've got a chairman – Donald Roth," I said.

"He's a low profile American."

"I'm an American."

"Come on, Stani, you are cosmopolitan, multilingual, a big deal in the City, and a Roman Catholic ex-Marine. You are perfect for the job," replied Franzi, who had honed his sales techniques at White, Weld.

"I'm no manager. How many thousands do you have in Europe? I can barely manage a hundred or so at EBC."

"You won't have to manage. You can appoint your own CEO and COO. It's a leadership and external figurehead position."

Franzi's reference to my religion and military service was appropriate as Merrill Lynch was traditionally a Roman Catholic firm, well outnumbered by the Jewish and WASP houses of Wall Street, and was regarded as run by ex-marines, with a former Commandant of the U.S. Marine Corps as a non- executive board member. I did not appreciate at the time that Franzi was seeking to "land" me, in the hopes I would ultimately appoint him as my CEO. I told him I would give the approach serious consideration. I'm afraid I had already decided this might be a suitable haven, following the inevitable demise of EBC as an independent entity – soon to be under single ownership. The third event was not itself a life changer but it occurred almost simultaneously with the others and serves to seer the period in my memory. I suffered a painful neck injury and spent the next several weeks wearing a neck brace. I played at number one on my polo team, and when the team is on the attack, number one is of necessity up front and looking over his shoulder to see what is happening behind. – Or hers, I should say *pace* Claire Tomlinson. This is an awkward posture in the saddle, and an unexpected jolt can do damage to the neck. I felt a twinge one Saturday morning during a friendly match, thought little of it, felt it again when dismounting to change horses between chukkas, and expected I might have a stiff neck on the morrow. It seemed all right on Sunday, but on Monday, back in town, I awoke in absolute agony. Our GP Dr. Richard Rossdale knew every top specialist in town, having played hospital league rugby with most. On this occasion he sent me to an osteopath lady, whose daughter was engaged to his son. I was near fainting when my driver Dennis Davies took me to her surgery. She was of the gentle, rather than the quick yank, school of treatment, relieved my immediate pain, said I would need a long course of treatment for the slipped vertebrae disc, and put me in the brace. I was to wear this for the next several weeks of traumatic career change.

In my new brace, I paid a call on Giovanni Franzi and Don Roth, his low profile American chairman, who was preparing to go back to New York to head up a new, ultra-high net worth private client unit, which eventually came to grief, providing margin facilities to speculators who often went spectacularly bust. When I pointed out the awkwardness of my situation, given EBC was up for sale, Don said, "We'll buy it, if that's what it takes to get you. We'd love to have the forex business." I replied that it might be easier to pick up the forex team after EBC had been sold – depending on who the buyer was. But there were too many personnel conflicts with the rest of the team, and I didn't think many of them would stick. Merrill Lynch itself was still in the throes of an identity crisis following its acquisition of White, Weld in 1979. My old firm had seen its domestic business decline even as its international franchise was in dramatic ascendency. Paul Hallingby, the former utilities executive, who had taken over as head of the firm from Emory Katzenbach, admitted in a *Euromoney* interview that the firm had failed to exploit the reopening of the foreign dollar bond market, after the suspension of the Interest Equalisation Tax, even though Credit Suisse White Weld was topping the league tables in the Eurobond market. Of course, there was a simple explanation for this. CSWW was primarily concerned with generating its own lead management mandates in the Euromarkets, and was not much concerned with pushing business to its New York majority owner. The transatlantic split I had feared after the Credit Suisse deal with WW Trust had become all too real. I knew Hallingby was hawking the firm around the Street because, whilst at EBC, I had received a call from my brother in law Keith Wellin, formerly at E. F. Hutton, but then with Reynolds Securities. He told me his chairman Tom Stacy was thinking of bidding for White, Weld but couldn't understand the CSWW situation – its background and future. Would I come to New York at their expense on a confidential mission to explain it? Reynolds was what was known in the trade as a "linoleum on the floor" firm – in other words, it ran a pure brokerage operation on a low cost base. Stacy had built up the franchise and then handed day-to-day management to Robert "Stretch" Gardiner, but he still determined strategy. At my meeting with Stacy and Keith, the former said that, the more he looked at White, Weld's very high cost base, the more doubtful he became, but he still wanted to understand what might be the real strategic value of CSWW, still some 70% owned by White, Weld. I narrated the history of White, Weld in Europe, but explained that there existed a strategic and, almost cultural, separation between Europe and New York, which would make any integration difficult. Even though it held a minority stake, the influence of Credit Suisse was now paramount and I saw disaffection amongst the key people, should the majority change hands. Reynolds lost interest immediately and Hallingby sold White, Weld to Merrill Lynch at a knock down price, which only just reflected the value of its leasehold in the Liberty Plaza building. The only word I can think of to describe this deal is "scandalous". Hallingby was named chief executive of a new investment banking division – Merrill Lynch White Weld. Merrill's interest was

312

obvious. Its vast distribution power had gone unexploited for years due to its inability to develop any investment banking origination capability. White Weld was to provide this. Of course, inevitably, most of its key people drifted away, with the notable exception of the very productive Chicago office. CSWW was seen as in conflict with Merrill Lynch's growing European activity, where it was beginning to make its mark as a Eurobond house. Michael von Clemm and John Craven, then the "movers and shakers" at CSWW, immediately set about looking for another New York partner, and found it in First Boston Corporation, who took the 70% stake, and the pure American brokerage business in London, Paris and Zurich went to Paine Webber. So CSFB was born.

But Merrill Lynch was still failing to exploit the strength of its traditional brokerage business, and was frustrated at its inability to position itself more broadly in the London market. And so it decided on high profile leadership in London, and engaged David Montagu as chairman and John Craven as chief executive. David had left Orion, having fought with his shareholders, and Craven had left CSWW, having fought with Michael von Clemm. I suspect personality conflicts emerged quickly. David was the quintessential British merchant banker, and Craven did not suffer fools. Dan Tully, number two at Merrill in New York, was an Irishman and no anglophile. Others in the top echelon took exception to Craven's analysis of the firm's weaknesses. The problem was that the two realised quickly that Merrill might have all the money in the world, but it did not have the executive strength needed to build the sort of City franchise it aspired to. It might have had through White, Weld, but the likes of Michael Dobbs-Higginson, David Reid Scott, Philip Seers, Dick Bristow, David Potter, Michel de Carhalho, Andrew Korner, etc., etc., were all at CSFB, with Michael von Clemm. Furthermore, Merrill's image was so strongly that of a retail brokerage house, that attracting investment banking talent in London was more than usually challenging. So Montagu and Craven pushed for an acquisition as the fast route, and identified Hill Samuel as a likely candidate – a very suitable target at the time. Amongst Merrill's many qualities was one that can impede bold strategic thinking. The firm had a high degree of self-esteem, and it did not take kindly to having its shortcomings pointed out by newcomers who, no matter how distinguished, did not fit with the firm's very distinctive culture. And so ended, after little more than a year, Merrill Lynch's first experience in high profile leadership – parachuted in from above.

I was quite aware of these problems, but felt that my Wall Street background, and American upbringing and education, would help me overcome any cultural divide. Moreover, my father was, in a sense, already with Merrill Lynch. As part of the deal, Merrill had agreed to give the limited partners of White Weld, permanent office facilities in New York, and had assigned some semi-honorary positions around the firm. DY had been put on the board of

Merrill Lynch (Suisse) – its private bank in Geneva. I thought it would be rather amusing to be back in the same firm as my father. Having pretty well made up my mind, I then took an action which, later on, friends described as the most stupid and naïve action they had ever come across in their long years in the City. I went off to Barings and told Andrew Tuckey that I was minded to accept a position with Merrill Lynch, and felt he should know that – in the interest of full disclosure. The next morning I was kneeling by the side of my bed. I was not in prayer – I had discovered that it was the most painless position I could assume with my injured neck. The telephone rang and it was Nico Schmidt-Chiari of Credietanstalt in Vienna, who had recently succeeded Paul Emmanuel Jansen as my chairman.

'You're fired," he said.

"May I ask why?" I said, once I had recovered my breath.

"Tuckey has told us you are going to Merrill Lynch, and that he considers EBC virtually unsaleable without you."

"That's nonsense."

"You have undermined our ability to sell the bank – and you must go."

"Can I say goodbye to my colleagues?"

"No – your things will be sent to you."

Needless to say, the pain in my neck subsided, and I suffered a panic attack instead. I had not yet received a firm offer from Merrill Lynch. I was still due to meet Bill Schreyer, the group chairman, in New York, but all I had in hand was Franzi's enthusiasm and casual remarks of the low profile American chairman Don Roth in London. I was just over 50 and unemployed for the first time in my life. I thought about what Paul Jeanty had said, and supposed no one would give me a job when it became known I had been sacked by the EBIC Group. But the more I thought about it, the more depressed I became, because what was being more than implied by Tuckey, was that the ten years plus I had spent building EBC had produced a franchise that was worthless on its own. It was a blow to my self-esteem from which I have never wholly recovered. Of course, my cynical friends were to say later "You big dummy! You should have never gone to Tuckey until you had the Merrill Lynch job sewn up". At the time, my immediate thought was that Dinnie and I would be homeless in London, because our Eaton Place maisonette was owned by EBC, this having been part of the package originally negotiated by John Scott-Oldfield with Fritz Karsten. I felt sick. I called Giovanni Franzi, and abandoning my full disclosure policy, merely said I was free to go and see Bill Schreyer in New York. Could that be arranged?

"Of course, we'll send you the first class ticket."

"Send it to Eaton Place, please," I said, light appearing at the end of the tunnel.

When I got to Merrill, now at Liberty Plaza, I was shown straight into Schreyer's office, and told he was stuck in traffic in the Holland Tunnel, but would be there shortly. I looked out at the view on Hudson River, pondering my fate. Schreyer walked in, looked at my neck brace and said:

"Good Lord! I told them to pull out all stops to recruit you, but I didn't tell them to beat you up!"

I could have hugged him.

In the end AMRO bought EBC, and hired my old friend Tony Lund as managing director. Tony had long represented Kuhn Loeb in London, with his office at S. G. Warburg. I'm sure he did his best, but AMRO did not survive to enjoy any role in London. After merging with rival ABN, it was the subject of a hugely overpriced takeover by Royal Bank of Scotland, together with Fortis and Banco Santander; which resulted in taxpayer rescues of RBS and most of Fortis, leaving the latter an empty shell with only some part of its original insurance business. In 1997, Fortis was the 20th largest company in the world in terms of revenue. From its origins as an obscure farmers' insurance co-operative, Fortis embarked on an orgy of ill-advised acquisitions, including of Générale de Banque in Belgium, and through appallingly bad management, vandalised most of the traditional banking industry of Benelux, destroying the great names of Pierson, Mees, Hope, AMRO, ABN, Générale de Banque, and others. Never in the history of banking has one group done so much damage in so short a period. Deutsche Bank finally acquired all of Morgan Grenfell and despite putting John Craven in charge, could make nothing of it and has never earned a place at the top table of international investment banking. John became the first foreigner to be named to the *Vorstadt* – the management board, but struggled to make Deutsche understand the potential of the asset it had acquired. He soon returned to the boutique, Phoenix Securities, he had founded, and a career in industry. Société Générale of Paris acquired the asset management side of Hambros, after it split following a family split, but has no meaningful presence in London, and suffered a rogue trader and other scandals – again a failed contender for international prominence. Banca Commerciale Italiano, once one of Italy's largest banks, and certainly once its most international, with branches and affiliates all over the world, was swallowed up in a series of mergers and is now Intesa Sanpaolo, a purely domestic bank. Creditanstalt, the most famous name in Austrian banking, suffered both a deterioration in the quality of its loan portfolio, and of its political influence. After passing through German ownership, it is now a subsidiary of UniCredit, an Italian holding company, now suffering acquisition indigestion. The name Creditanstalt disappeared a few years ago. Midland Bank was acquired by HSBC, which first incorporated Samuel Montagu into its private banking division, then abandoned the name, reducing the franchise to a private equity business, which was then spun off and continues the name as Montagu Private Equity. Not one of the EBIC banks is today a leader in global universal banking, except HSBC, as successor to Midland, and only two survive as independent banks – Deutsche and Société Générale. None has a meaningful investment banking presence in the City of London.

I learned a great deal during my time at EBC. But I also found confirmation of a lingering suspicion: full European Union at all levels is a hopeless dream. It is also a dangerous dream, for in a desperate search for its fulfilment, it has spawned a huge and semi-corrupt bureaucracy sewing discord and disaffection, through policy initiatives affecting all, and for which it cannot be held democratically accountable. Instead of a secure Union, we have a chimera. If a series of sophisticated and worldly banks, from seven European countries, each plying the same trade, cannot find any form of union, one has to question the whole concept. What distinguished my shareholders, more than anything else, was how entirely different were their practices, attitudes, cultures and reactions to external events. Hermann Abs's concept of a European banking entity to challenge the international ascendency of the American Banks was entirely unrealistic. Despite all the single market hype, there exists no retail or wholesale European bank today, and no prospect of one. In fact the only retail business serving the whole of Europe, through branches in every country, with a single brand and a single product range, is MacDonald's.

CHAPTER XVIII

"And now I dream of Bybury-in-the-Wold
And pray age's pain its memories will enfold,
My reveries contain no hurt or strife,
But joy and comfort full in this, my life.
Life's chase has killed the fear that death might hold,
And now I dream of Bybury-in-the-Wold"

-Anon-

During my brief, but traumatic, period of unemployment, a bolt hole in the back of my mind was our house at Bibury, often spelt with a "y" in more ancient texts and maps. I thought we might run chickens on our three acres and I could provide liveries in the nearby stable yard, which my neighbour Toby Clarke had placed at our disposal. The Malt House, situated at a corner of this iconic Cotswold village, was the best investment I ever made. We had developed a taste for weekends in the country at a charming cottage on the Bramshill Estate, in Hampshire, site of the famous police college, which we rented from Jan and Sarah Baily. Jan was one of a coterie of friends, including Edward Cazelet, Jacob Rothschild and Anthony Loehnes, which Michael von Clemm had made whilst up at Corpus Christi, Oxford. Jan formed a partnership with Frank "Butch" Hunnewell, Lisa von Clemm's brother, looking to do deals in the Middle East, and, for some entirely unaccountable reason, fixed their office in Paris. Butch Hunnewell was a somewhat eccentric entrepreneur, whose prospective deals were always imaginative, if not always successful. He often parked himself at our White, Weld offices in London, where I would shut him in a room to concentrate on calculating the huge returns he always expected on his next deal. After taking his MBA at Harvard Business School, his first venture had been chicken farming in Venezuela, where he conceived the notion of feeding his flock on the ground up feathers of the slaughtered birds – a sort of poultry perpetual machine. When chicks failed to grow to full size, Butch was undeterred, and, having called in a U.S. Food Inspector, who pronounced the stunted birds entirely safe to consume, they were marketed as Cornish game hens. On leaving for Paris, the Bailys had first let Arletts, their Bramshill cottage, to Johnny and Claude Cattier, who were spending time in England. When the Cattiers headed back to Geneva, they passed Arletts on to us. The cottage came complete with a cleaning lady, a black Labrador named "Pint", after his purchase price at a local pub, and a gardener – who fed Pint during the week. The rambling cottage was at the end of a lane, topped by an old church where Charles Kingsley, of *The Water Babies* fame, had been rector, and past a turkey farm which supplied us with our Christmas bird. David Mann, my old Montagu colleague, and son of Francis Mann, was a permanent weekend guest, and we spent long hours dissecting the financial world. Finally, the Bailys were due back from Paris, and our tenancy ended. But our country weekends were now an entrenched habit, and we began looking around for a house, casting in a westerly direction, as it was the route I knew best – past Heathrow. Having seen several which were either to large or to small, I spotted an advertisement in *Country Life* for a house in Bibury, just as we were planning a visit with the von Clemms to Michael's uncle at Broadwell, near Stow-in-the-Wold. Having ascertained that Bibury was on the way, I suggested we all have a look at this new prospect. At this time there was neither M4 nor M40, and one accessed the Cotswolds via Oxford. On the way, we dropped in on Michael's Aunt Clare, Lady Freake, at Childrey – she of the Coutts account and the Singapore Bar investment. Lady Freake was always hugely entertaining. A lady known to pull the emergency cord on a train if she saw a sheep cast in a field, her anecdotes, mostly involving animals, were legendary. For Bibury, we passed through Fairford, then Quenington/Coln St. Aldwyn, with Hatherup, adjoining villages in the Coln Valley. The road from Coln St. Aldwyn to Bibury brings you to the crest of a hill, and we stopped and looked down on the sleepy village, nestled in a valley, with the River Coln snakeing through. It had a definite feel of Brigadoon, the disappearing village created by Lerner and Loewe. I immediately spotted The Malt House, our destination, on the corner of the village nearest our vantage point, and said, "That's it! Bingo! We hardly need visit. We have found our house." Wisely, Dinnie suggested I might be premature. Who knows what drawbacks might emerge during a proper visit. We drove down the hill and were kindly received by Mr. Senior, who told me they were selling because Mrs. Senior had developed a passion for sailing, and they were moving to the Solent. "But, I must tell you that there has been so much interest that we have been advised to go to auction," he explained. "By all means get your surveyor in, but at this point, I hardly know how the bidding will go."

The guide price was £35,000. The house was perfect in every way. We asked the estate agent brother of a friend from Arletts days, Noel Thistlethwaite, to attend the auction and bid.

"If you really want it, you must give him a generous limit," said Dinnie. I did so.

After the auction, Thistlethwaite rang me and said. "Good news, and bad news. You've got the house, but the under-bidder was a Burmah Oil executive from Swindon. I had to go to your limit to win."

Some weeks later, the purchase was front page news in the Wilts & Glos local newspaper "City Man Pays £65,000 for Village House!" screamed the headline. Such a price had not been seen before. It must be remembered, the Cotswolds region had not yet been "discovered", as it would be when the Royals arrived – first the Princess Royal, then the Michaels of Kent, and finally the Prince of Wales. Now there are Hollywood style, bus tours that will take you on a visit of the "homes" of TV and pop stars, football players and sundry celebrities, who now crowd the roads and frighten the horses. As a result, it has become far less country, and much more Wimbledon.

When we arrived to take possession, we had my parents with me, and we stayed at "The Swan", a comfortable hotel, near the famous cottages of Arlington Row. We had no furniture yet. I had picked up the keys at the closing from the senior partner of Sewell & Logie in Cirencester, whose son Simon Logie, was to become a great friend. His father, clad in nubby tweed, with a roaring fire his office, was a country solicitor out of central casting. Swinging my large ring or old, rusted keys, I walked straight into an antique shop, immediately opposite the solicitor's chambers, spotted a so-called cricket table, and told the astonished gentleman in the shop, "I'll have that table, please."

"Oh!" said he, "I'm standing in for my wife who has gone to an auction. I can't tell you much about it. Don't you want to know the price? I suppose I can find that."

"Do, please, so I can write you a cheque, but, you see, we have just bought a house in Bibury, and its good luck to immediately buy a piece of furniture."

I can't remember what I paid, but it is now my bedside table. On the Saturday morning, the four of us went to our new, empty house, to deposit our new table, and found a note under the door knob. "We heard you were staying at 'The Swan', and wondered if you might like to drop around for a drink at sixish" signed Mrs. Ramus at Glebe House. I called from the hotel, and said we were four.

"I know," said Mrs Ramus, providing an early example of village bush telegraph. Glebe House, a Victorian Mansion, had been the Vicarage in the palmy days of the Established Church's prestige and wealth. Mr. Ramus was a Swiss. After a drink and a refill, and the usual exchange of pleasantries, Mrs. Ramus said, "Oh! I have an idea. We are due at some friends for a drink, just on the other side of the village. Why don't you come along with us? They would love to meet you – you are rather famous, you know."

This was an obvious reference to the news item in the local rag. I was at pains to entertain my parents, so I accepted with alacrity – certain they would find it amusing. Bibury is in two parts, with the north side of the Coln actually called Arlington, and it was to this side we now repaired. On arrival, we found the entire village assembled, or, to be clear, the "gentry" section of the population. It was evident the Ramus's, as our near neighbours, had been commissioned to "check us out", this being seen as a necessity, given our peculiar name. If they deemed us to be socially acceptable, we were to be brought along to meet the village. Presumably, if we had not passed muster, we would have made our adieus, and slunk back to our hotel. In those days, it was becoming insufficient to be "something in the City" to gain social acceptance in the country. As we settled in to country life, I sensed quickly that our warm reception was largely due to the fact that Dinnie, even though a colonial, was deemed "one of us". Some might have considered it a bit odd that she had married a WOG, which, as we know, begin at Calais, but, of course, eventually the horse blended me in. A short while after our arrival, we had a visit from Donald Taffinder, the Rector, who lived in the new, more modest vicarage, almost exactly opposite us. Dinnie was out. I gave him a gin and tonic and we talked dogs and shooting, which was his passion – or rather, picking up was his passion. His holidays were spent, with his two spaniels, picking up on smart grouse shoots in Scotland. After his second gin and tonic, Donald began to squirm in his chair, and finally said "Er.., ahem… do you belong to any church?"

"My wife is C of E," I replied, "but I am Roman Catholic."

I knew exactly what he was going to say next, and he duly said it.

"Oh! Some of my best friends are Roman Catholic!"

In fact, Donald was highly ecumenical, and always invited ministers of different denominations to preach at Lenten services. His daughter married Dominic Martelli, a Catholic educated at Ampleforth. One year he asked his son in law to invite Basil Hume to preach one of the services, Hume being then Abbot of Ampleforth, and happy to accept. A few weeks later, Donald read in the press that Basil Hume, to the surprise of all, had been elevated by the Pope to be Cardinal Archbishop of Westminster. "That's torn it" thought Donald. Not at all – he soon received a note from the new Cardinal, saying his diary was yet to fill up, and would he still be welcome in his new, and quite unexpected, dignity? Of course, he was, and I was deputed to play squash with him, in a court in the stable yard that Toby Clarke's father had built. I pointed out to His Eminence, that I understood Italian prisoners of war had been billeted there during the war.

"Really?" he said, "I wonder if I can work that in to my sermon."

It had been agreed with our Rector that the Cardinal should appear "in full fig".

I heard a lady, seated in the pew behind me, whisper to another, "How nice to see some red other than in the hunting field." Donald Taffinder had been left the shooting in the Glebe land, now owned by Gregory Phillips, and he used to invite me to walk up a few pheasants and hares with him. I hate shooting hares, but didn't like to disappoint Donald, so I was careful to miss the hares, but hit the pheasants. Phillips's grandfather had been a farm worker in the West Country who had migrated to the Coln Valley with his family to find work. He had eventually become a farm manager and then started buying land. When we arrived, the Phillips family owned well over 20,000 acres around Bibury and Aldsworth, as well as near Kemble. Gregory had lost an arm, going through a tunnel in a horsebox, with his elbow sticking out. But he shot with one arm, his gamekeeper stuffing the shells in, and hunted with a leather device that held the reins together to be manipulated with one hand.

I had an alarming experience concerning Donald Taffinder. Our village could have been the venue for a typical Agatha Christie murder story – we had all the usual characters. There was a retired Brigadier, two elderly maiden ladies à la Miss Marple, a retired doctor and other population staples. The Brigadier was chairman of the hunt, and of the parish council. One day he summoned me.

"I understand you have been giving some financial assistance to Donald?" I had indeed helped out poor Donald with a bit of petrol money. As was increasingly the case with a Church short of priests, he had three parishes to look after, Barnsley, Winson and Bibury.

"Yes," I replied, "but, with respect, I don't see how it is anyone else's business."

"But, you don't belong to our Church," said the Brigadier, disapprovingly.

"Correct – but I attend there, thanks to Donald's ecumenical liberality, and he is a near neighbour who kindly keeps an eye on our house during the week."

This was the first and last time that my "left footedness" was thrown in my face, so to speak. Actually Brigadier Mitchell and his wife Mary became the greatest of friends. Mary had a voice out hunting that could carry at least three fields. Alistair, as so he was named, passed me a beat on the river, which he had taken from Toby, and I spent a season or two flogging this excellent chalk stream, changing flies, getting my line caught in trees, and producing trout for lunch on only three occasions.

I had been introduced to Toby Clarke by Howard Cushing, a Deerfield and Harvard class mate, who was briefly with White, Weld in New York, and whose brother Freddy had bought our old house "Bittersweet", at Piping Rock. Toby was working at Bankers Trust in the City and we met for lunch. Shortly after arriving in Bibury, I had a call from Toby. "You've bought the Malt House!"

"How on earth do you know that?"

"Because Bibury belongs to my family and my grandparents lived in the Malt House when central heating was being installed at the Court."

I was astounded. Strangely enough I knew Sir Humphrey Clarke, who lived in Paris with a mistress called Arlette, and could often be found propping up one end of the bar at The Travellers, wearing an orchid in his buttonhole. I also knew the Clarke's were squires of Bibury, having purchased the estate only in 1910. The baronetcy had been created by William IV for his Court surgeon, who was from a Norfolk family of Clarkes. But I had not con-

321

nected Sir Humphrey in Paris with my new friend Toby in London. It turned out Sir Humphrey had been much married, and Toby was the son of an American wife. He had been born and brought up in California, after the parents divorced, and shipped from there straight to Eton, together with one of David Niven's sons. From there, he passed his holidays with his grandmother, née Elfrida Roosevelt, a cousin of President Teddy Roosevelt. She lived alone through the war, and after, at Bibury Court, an impressive, much restored, Elizabethan manor house. Toby's father in Paris had been more than neglectful, particularly in respect of estate planning. The Court was sold for a hotel after Elfrida's death, and Sir Humphrey kept Church House, just behind, as a shooting lodge, and ran a small stud in the magnificent stable yard, which had been kept back from the sale of the Court. One day, after shooting, Sir Humphrey shot himself, in front of the gamekeeper, Billy Brockbank, who had come to pick up the gun for cleaning. Theories abounded – the most common being that the unfortunate squire had learned he had incurable cancer. In fact, he had learned that Arlette was thus afflicted, and had been incapable of telling her. The upshot of all this, to use a most inappropriate phrase, was that Toby inherited a huge estate duty liability, together with the traditional overdraft at Coutts, which had to be greatly increased in favour of HM Inland Revenue. The estate never achieved sufficient revenue to clear the debt, and had to be ultimately sold. But for most of our time at Bibury, Sir Toby Clarke, 6th Baronet, was our much loved squire, living at Church House, which Arlette had decorated in a distinctly French style. I was a tenant, as Toby let me the shooting, and the stable yard. He had one gun reserved for the four shooting days we had each season, and I looked after Billy, the gamekeeper for half the year. And I kept his horse at livery in the yard – so no cash changed hands for these arrangements. Early on, Dinnie and I were delighted to be invited to Toby's tenants' Christmas party. There I chatted to one old boy who told me he had ridden second horse to Paul Mellon. In 1936, Paul Mellon, and his friend James Brady, had rented Bibury Court from Sir Orme, Toby's grandfather, who was spending the winter in Italy, recovering from a hunting accident. Mellon and Brady had shipped horses from America to hunt with the VWH, the Heythrop, the Beaufort, and the Cotswold – all easily reachable from Bibury. After a busy Christmas season, their idyll was interrupted by the untimely death of George V in late January. Hunting ceased in England as part of national mourning. Paul Mellon and his party shipped all the horses to Ireland, and carried on hunting there.

I make no apology for my love affair with horses, which started in earnest at Bibury. DY had put Ariane and me astride early on, and we used to hack out from the stables at Piping Rock, along the same bridle path where Cole Porter had suffered a terrible accident in the 1920s, his horse having thrown and rolled on him, crushing his legs and leading to lifelong agonies – and amputation of one. Our father made no mention of this unfortunate occurrence, as we rode past the spot. And, of course, I rode again at Lowdale, Dinnie's family farm in Rhodesia. But, on arrival in the Cotswolds, one sensed that the word "horse" was whispered from every nook and cranny, and, as one became acclimatized, the whisper became a shout. Again, I make no apology for my love affair with these cash guzzling quadrupeds, but the fact that I have made the statement twice in a few lines may make you doubt its sincerity. In retrospect, if, each time I bought a hunter, or a polo pony, I had invested the amount involved in Microsoft shares instead, I would today be in a position to call Bill Gates on the phone – and have him take my call. But I probably would have sold to early. Still, it is largely due to horses that I have ended up, like the girl in the old music hall song –"poor but rotten honest". I waited a season at least before beginning my headlong flight into horsiness. We first acquired a pleasant bay gelding called Gladstone, from Sandra Lamb, an old Rhodesian friend of Dinnie's, who made and sold horses in our area. My sister-in-law Linda, always known as "Mattie", for reasons lost in the mists of time, came to Bibury with her then husband, an engineer working on North Sea oil rigs. They took one of Toby's cottages, almost next door to the Malt House, and Mattie hunted Gladstone with the VWH, our local pack. At that point Toby had let the yard at the Court to Mark Palmer, for two years before I took over – Sir Mark, in fact, as he had inherited the baronetcy from his father, killed in the war. Mark had served as a page at the Queen's coronation, but was now going through a hippie phase. His widowed mother married Alex Abel-Smith, a Schroeder's partner, and served several terms as lady-in-waiting to the Queen. Mark was an extraordinary horseman, and an amateur jockey of distinction, but the yard under his management looked like a hippy commune, and one often saw caravans, and an open cart with a goat tethered on it, all drawn by coloured, gypsy ponies, on their way to some pop festival. I once went down to look in on Gladstone and found Bianca Jagger, leaning over the door of his box, with a piece of straw in her mouth. "Nice horse!" was her only comment. There was a very small and slight girl groom working for Mark, whose size made her perfect for "backing" young, unschooled horses. We discovered her previous career, as she published a memoir called *Groupie*, which caused something of a sensation, particularly in the village, as she described her sex life with various pop groups in graphic detail. She told me horses had helped her break her drug habit.

I had no drug habit needing a cure, but horses were a huge antidote to City stress for me. As soon as I was mounted on Saturday morning, to hunt, or play polo in the summer, or just go hacking, the stresses and strains of my week in the City melted away. On my first day out cub hunting with the VWH, then then joint Master,   , of a local family of brewers, greeted me warmly and asked, "Does your wife hunt?"

"She did as a girl, as her father would come from Rhodesia to hunt in England and Ireland."

"I would discourage her from starting again," said the master. "You want tea, and then whiskey and a hot bath, all ready for you after hunting – not to speak of a good dinner. If the wife has been out as well, the household arrangements always suffer."

I did no such thing and found a lovely mare, named just "Mare", an ex-master's horse, which turned out to be perfect for Dinnie. The chunky grey could jump anything from a standstill, had little pace, but would slowly make her way to the front, when the field was waiting at covert-side, to be well placed for the next run. Dinnie hunted Mondays, claiming I would make her nervous if she was out with me on Saturday. I had reports of her prowess with Mare. Sometimes the field, including the field master, would get stuck in a field as the jump out at the forward end was so tricky, horses were refusing. Mare would walk up to it and just pop over. Mare had one drawback – horses always do – she was extremely sensitive behind – probably as a result of a bad foaling experience. One had to be very careful backing her out of the trailer, and the blacksmith was forewarned when shoeing her. One hapless blacksmith was not, I learned later. We used to lend Mare to the kennels in July and August for early hound exercise. The blacksmith who served the VWH kennels also went to John P. Smail's polo yard, where I kept my string.

"Wasn't that your grey mare at the VWH kennels which almost killed me?" he asked me one day. "No one had warned me and when I went to shoe her behind, she kicked me all over the box before kicking me out, and I lay there, with my face in a puddle of horse pee, thinking my last hour had come. I was in hospital for a week."

When I took over the yard, I was fortunate to find a young girl groom called Debbie Strange, a graduate of the Talland Equestrian School in Cirencester. Most people seemed to change grooms as one changes socks, but Debbie stayed with me for almost 20 years and was the cornerstone of our life with horses. She found and schooled all our hunters, turned them out to show standards, kept the yard impeccable, and was loyal, almost to a fault. It may seem an odd observation, but her strengths and weaknesses reminded me of Margret Thatcher. Debbie did not suffer fools and you were either in her good books or bad. She was hugely disciplined and expected the same of others. There were "do's" and don'ts". One did not go out on exercise in the afternoon, one loosened the saddle girth immediately on dismounting, one was always exactly on time in the yard, etc., etc. Her dogs were always perfectly schooled. She was in fact a perfectionist, and my family sometimes complained. Our daughter Tatyana jokingly complained she had needed therapy later, having suffered psychological damage after being ticked off at summer pony camp for having turned her pony Circus Girl, who was shod, into a field with unshod ponies. I explained that, as Debbie was in charge of that summer pony club camp, she had not wished to be seen favouring her boss's daughter. Debbie suffered one mishap, which greatly troubled her. I had purchased the old walled garden, which had been part of the Court complex. A lame polo pony was put there to graze and some stupid tourists at the Court hotel fed it green apples through the iron gate, and we lost the horse to severe cholic, despite all the efforts of our Irish vet Charlie MacCarten to save it by piercing the stomach to let the gas out. "Shall I tell Debbie, or will you?" he said, when he informed me the horse would have to be put down. I'm afraid I shirked the duty, and Charlie gently took her aside. She broke down in tears – the only time I saw a crack in her sometimes icy reserve. Charlie was our vet for years and his stall side manner was unique. It was a fact of country life that you could not get a doctor to make a house call for a sick child, but a vet would come out for a sick horse at any time, day or night.

When Toby Clarke decided to take up hunting, we thought it would be both amusing and useful to attend Annie Backhouse's pre-hunting course in horsemanship. Annie is a former Olympic showjumper, whose family farmed near Fairford, and she would engage a horse master who had coached the Olympic team to put us through our paces. He watched me put Gladstone over some painted poles in the indoor riding school, then gave me two carriage whips to hold in each hand.

"When I say so, give him a wack with both – just twist your wrists." As I approached the fence, he shouted "Now!" – I wacked and Gladstone almost hit the roof of the riding school. Our coach had no luck with Michael Nightingale, who had rowed at Oxford and so had athletic prowess only from the waist up. It seems it is a well-known fact, or so the horse master told us, that "oars" can't ride, as that pursuit is all in the legs. Michael had made a name for himself in the City, as he had taken to heart a conclusion of the Harold Wilson Committee on the Functioning of Financial Institutions, which identified a gap in the availability of capital for start-up enterprises. Years before AIM and EASDAQ, Michael had tried to create an over-the-counter market for smaller company shares. He was obsessively driven, something I was much aware of when playing squash with him in the stable yard squash court. One evening, after a very late party, Dinnie found him in the kitchen explaining the finer points of the Wilson Report to our nanny. I can't believe Michael Nightingale enjoyed his hunting much, as he was usually thrown at the first fence, but he had decided to hunt and so hunt he would, regardless of his aptitude for the sport. Sadly, he died prematurely. Toby Clarke had a horse called Henry, and when he had the odd tumble, as one does in early days, he would shout for his horse, not having yet appreciated that horses do not answer to their names, like dogs. It happened that our Saturday field master Lord Bathurst was also called Henry, so some confusion ensued from time to time.

We much enjoyed those early hunting days, as every day out was different – one of the great features of hunting. It is said that hunting people fall into two categories; those who ride to hunt, and those who hunt to ride. I was very much in the first group, as my main joy was watching hounds work. For this reason I ended up hunting a good deal with the Cotswold, even though we were in VWH country. The Cotswold Saturday country is roughly between the Coln Valley and Cheltenham and so easily accessible from Bibury. It is on higher, hilly ground and so the field is in a position to observe coverts being drawn, and, often, the fox on the move. Tim Unwin had been master for several years when I started hunting with the Cotswold, and I much enjoyed watching him cast the pack and admired his style as a huntsman. Some said he was a bit slow, but the pace suited me, and the country, being very hilly, did not lend itself to the sort of pace one might find with the Leicestershire hunts. At the VWH, we were fortunate to have Martin Scott as master between 1977 and 1983. His father was Major Bill Scott, a celebrated MFH who had the North Cotswold, the Old Berks, and the Portman – twice. We knew his widow, a great lady of the old school, who looked after the family butler when he became infirm, even bringing him breakfast in bed. Martin's military career was punctuated, if I may use that expression, by his running off with a brother officer's wife, who had exercised his polo ponies when he was serving with the BAOR. Horses are often the cause of both broken, and made in heaven, marriages. After the Army, Martin was apprenticed to the famous Captain Ronnie Wallace, whipping in at the Heythrop, before taking on the Tiverton in deepest Devon. Wallace was a legendary figure at the Heythrop, and subsequently the Exmoor, and was known in hunting circles as "God". There is the story that a hunting man dies and goes to heaven, naturally, and wakes up on his first morning to the unmistakable sound of a meet. Peeping out of the window in his cloud, he sees hounds, the field gathering, and the master and hunt staff in green coats – as they wear at the Heythrop.

"Good Heavens!" he says to an angel standing nearby. "It's Ronnie Wallace and the Heythrop!"

"No," replies the angel, "Captain Wallace is not with us yet. Actually, it's God, pretending to be Ronnie Wallace."

We used to go down to the Exmoor for a few days of spring hunting after we had finished, as they carried on through April. A good many professional huntsmen went as well, not just for a busman's holiday, but because Captain Wallace presided at tea in a local inn after hunting, and huntsmen could voice their complaints to him, about un-cooperative landowners, or any difficulties they were experiencing in their countries. Wallace was the "Mr. Fix-it" of hunting, but also its most effective lobbiest. He used to attend both the Conservative and Labour Party conferences. Once when I was on the board of South West Water, I had a call from "God". Foxes were finding sanctuary in our reservoirs, where the gates were kept locked. Might keys be provided to the Exmoor hunt staff, so that hounds could get in and carry out their civic duty of protecting lambs from vulpine predation? I raised the issue under "any other business" at our next board meeting and found most of my colleagues somewhat non plussed. But I had an ally in Simon Day, not a hunting man, but a keen shooting man, supporter of field sports and a true countryman. He knew all about Ronnie Wallace. "You must understand," he told the board, "this is not a request, it's an order." We complied.

When Martin Scott arrived at the VWH, with his lovely wife Jilly, a suitably horsey ex-Sloane Ranger, a rumour spread that he could not jump. This because the Tiverton was a non-jumping country, fields being separated by huge, six foot plus hedges which even a puissance showjumper would have shunned. Would this have been true, it would have been like taking on a golf professional who could not drive off the tee. The arrangement the Committee had negotiated with Martin, had him sharing the hunting of the hounds with our celebrated professional huntsman Sidney Bailey, with Martin hunting the bitches and Sidney the mixed pack. Of course Martin could jump perfectly well and watching him I conceived the theory that huntsmen, whether professional or amateur, jump so effortlessly because, whereas we approach a fence with concentration, apprehension, and even fear, the huntsman is concentrating entirely on his hounds and hardly notices the obstacle, except as one he must cross to avoid being separated from his charges. If anyone doubts the degree to which the rider's mindset is communicated to his mount, let him try the following experiment. Get down on all fours, blindfolded, and have someone place a child astride on your back. Not only will you sense the slightest motion of the child's head, but you will also feel the child's mood, whether it be elation, fear, grumpiness – or whatever. Perhaps prompted by the baseless rumour of Martin's jumping skills, our group of friends took to jumping the sofa as an after dinner entertainment, first at the Scotts and then wherever we dined together – which was often. It is more likely, however, that we were inspired by the fact that our dinners were liberally lubricated by lashings of claret, port and kummel. When dinners were at the Malt House, we assumed our children were asleep in their beds. In fact they were wide awake, as our antics were accompanied by loud gramophone music by the then fashionable Bee Gees, and they told us later, they thoroughly disapproved of our raucous sofa jumping. Our children are our severest critics. My sister often came to stay, to witness, as she put it, "the uninhibited life style of the Gloucestershire hunting set". Of course, Americans shouldn't throw stones when it comes to heavy drinking, but it amuses them to think of the English gentry as permanently in their cups. Sexual promiscuity is also associated with the horsey crowd, and the novelist Jilly Cooper has not helped to dispel this entrenched myth. When she was preparing her novel about polo, I was chairman of Cirencester Park Polo Club, and she called me to ask if she could attend our AGM as part of her research. I assured her she would find it as tedious as a vicarage tea party and if she was expecting to meet randy Argentine ten goal players, and hear accounts of *assados* turning into orgies, she would be disappointed, as they were usually in bed by nine when they had next day matches. My friend Eva Lewis, who took over from the celebrated *Tattler* gossip columnist "Jennifer", was so convinced of the libidinous nature of hunting people that she believed they would sneak off to the woods between runs and engage in a "quickie". I tried to point out to her the sheer impracticability of such, given the difficulty inherent in adjusting breeches and boots sufficiently to allow for such activity, not to mention the risk of losing the next run. My sister Ariane certainly remembers a dinner party at the Scotts, when Martin picked up one of Jilly's Pekinese dogs and threw it across the length of the table, well over the candles, to be caught neatly by his best friend Ian Farquhar, Master of the Beaufort, seated at the far end. This has remained her enduring vision of those heady days. Martin Scott enjoyed a highly successful career post mastership – a rare event for MFHs... Not only is he a world renowned judge and breeder of foxhounds, he is a private client banker of distinction. Mark Weinberg was one of a group of Jewish South African entrepreneurs who, since emigrating, have made a significant contribution to British finance and commerce. He persuaded Hambro's to back him in a new venture selling unit linked life assurance to a British public starved of equity based, savings products. Weinberg engaged as chief executive one Mike Wilson , the most outstanding sales manager I have ever met – and I knew quite a few at Merrill Lynch. Mike had the bright idea of hiring Martin Scott as a salesman. After all, he reasoned, not only was an MFH the second most important person in the county, after the Lord Lieutenant, but he spent time visiting prosperous farmers, to arrange a day's hunting, and then again to apologise for the damage done to fences and crops. At first Martin's sales technique was a bit primitive, reflecting his straight forward, "in your face" style as a Master of Hounds. He would open by saying "Have you thought about what happens after you fall off your perch?" But after training, Martin became, and remains, with the successor company, a top provider of advice and product to private clients.

A new chapter opened with racing – inevitably. I met Jeremy Norman at Harvard, but he was entirely English, belonging to the Norman clan – heirs to the Boots fortune, a Norman having married Jesse Boot's only daughter. I also knew Jeremy's cousin Torkwell, who made a fortune in toys. One of Jeremy's uncles owned most of the Antibes peninsular, with one of the largest estates on the Riviera. Jeremy had been an amateur jockey and was very much in the racing world. He decided to keep a hunter with us, or rather with Debbie, in the Court yard – now very full with my horses, Toby's Henry, and one or two other friends' hunters. Jeremy suggested we share a steeplechaser, and put it in training with Jenny Pitman, wife of well-known National Hunt jockey Richard Pitman, who had recently won the Grand National. Jenny had been training point-to-point horses but was now about to embark on a new career as a trainer of horses racing under rules – the first lady to invade this previously all male preserve. The horse in question was sired by Spartan General, a well-known stallion standing in Ireland, whose progeny had already had considerable success. Ireland is to steeplechasers as Bordeaux is to red wine. Our horse was called Gyllipus, and indeed such had been named one of Sparta's greatest generals in antiquity. This adventure was irresistible to me. I had never had a horse in training, and Dinnie sensibly pointed out that racehorses who earn their training fees in prize money are as rare as honest politicians. But Jeremy pointed out that, if the horse was not a success on the racecourse, I could always hunt it – which I eventually did. Gyllipus was at preschool with a friend of Jeremy's, who had an equine prep school near us, where horses go before they go to a proper trainer – rather as boys do before going to public school. We went to see him. He was beautiful. So are potential race horse owners seduced. At Jenny's training yard, he began to shine. After a few warm up races, Gyllipus was entered in the Welsh Grand National at Chepstow, where he was to run in Dinnie's newly registered colours of red and black, with red cap – almost the Royal colours, but without the frogging in gold braid. Before this auspicious event, Dinnie began to suffer from owner's nerves. Richard Pitman offered to pick her up and escort her to Chepstow, but moments before the start of the race, Dinnie disappeared to the Ladies, and Richard could be seen by racegoers, standing outside the Ladies, shouting "Dinnie! Come out! They're about to start!" Actually Gyllipus ran a great race, but had an apprentice jockey up, who was so surprised to find himself in front approaching the last fence, that he looked over his shoulder, and promptly made a mistake at the last – allowing Rag Trade, owned by Raymond Bessone, the hairdresser known as "Teezie Weazie", to coast by for a win. Rag Trade eventually won the famous Grand National. Gyllipus went on to win the Kim Muir Challenge at the Cheltenham Festival, sweeping up the hill in the final furlongs, as if he were just out hacking. But after two seasons, it became clear that Gyllipus's legs were not up to big time National Hunt racing. All agreed he was a "National" quality horse, and might well have gone on to win that classic – but for the legs. I'm sure there is many a ballet premier dancer who thinks he could have been Nureyev – "but for the legs". And so we retired him to the hunting field. I had never even sat on a thoroughbred horse. It is rather like going straight from a Land Rover to a Lamborghini. There is an unmistakable bounce in the step as one sets out at the walk, and the trot and canter are smooth and rangy. But most striking of all is the stamina. No matter how long the day, or how sticky the plough, Gyllipus would jog me home tirelessly – as seemingly fresh as if out for morning exercise. But most unusual was his perfect comportment. Few steeplechasers make good hunters. They are accustomed to going fast without stopping and taking off well back from the neat, stick fences placed, with or without a ditch, fairly evenly on the course. Hunters have to stop frequently, at a check, or to queue for a jump. And the obstacles are often trappy, uneven and ill shaped, with room for only a few short strides before take-off – an anathema to the 'chaser. But Gyllipus was not fazed by such unfamiliarity and took to crossing any bit of country faultlessly. So sure was I that he was an entirely safe ride, that I put my daughter Tatyana on him for a day's hunting, when she was home from school. I had a memorable run on Gyllipus. Latish in the afternoon, we found in the Bratch, a covert near Bibury, and our field master Derek Arkle, from a local brewing family, told us to go on, as he had no second horse. Hounds got away so quickly that I soon found myself alone with Milly Scott, the fearless and hard riding daughter of Martin and Jilly, together with our huntsman Sidney Bailey, who was himself having difficulty keeping in touch. Milly might have been twelve at the time. We ran past Aldsworth and the old Bibury race-course, which was a few miles from Bibury, through the valleys and Wolds below Eastleach, with Milly popping off and on from time to time, when a gate needed opening, where there was no other way through. But we had plenty of stone walls and wooden fences to leap. Hounds finally caught their fox a field away from the football pitch at Southrop, where a match was in progress. The distance and time of runs out hunting are always inflated by those fortunate enough to participate from start to kill. So you may deduct ten per cent from my estimate of 40 minutes and eight miles, for this run. Gyllipus jogged me home, fresh as if he was out on morning exercise.

Gyllipus had two further sorties as a race horse, which caused me considerable embarrassment. We decided to enter him in the member's race at the VWH point-to-point, with our friend Mark Palmer on bord – a very experienced amateur jockey. Gyllipus won handily, but that evening I had a call from Maurice Lait, chairman of the VWH, to say Christine Mason, a neighbour and hunting friend, who was riding the horse which came second, had lodged an objection, as insufficient time had elapsed since Gyllipus's last win under rules. The rules of the member's race stipulated three months, and although Mark and I had read them, we had miscalculated. I was mortified and, still insecure as to my place in this new world, wondered if I should resign from the hunt and immigrate to Siberia. Our difficulties were compounded by the fact that we had entered Gyllipus in the Cotswold point-to-point, in the right race this time, but somehow our horse's name had appeared misspelt on the race board. These infractions were subject to disciplinary action by the Jockey Club, which regulated all racing, including point-to-points. Naturally, Dinnie, as the registered owner, would be in the dock. I had a call from Sam Vestey, who found he was to be in the chair of the disciplinary committee on the day of Dinnie's appearance, and would I like him to recuse himself, as we were friends? I rather thought that was his decision, but he is a courteous man. I told him I was entirely happy and had asked Simon Logie, our friend and solicitor to accompany Dinnie.

"It's just a formality, you know," said my Lord Vestey, thinking I must be confusing the Jockey Club with the Old Bailey. Bravely appearing without me, but flanked by Simon, Dinnie explained she had left it all to me, and I had miscalculated.

"Perfectly understandable" said Sam, from the chair. "Everyone knows bankers can't count. But do learn to spell the name of your horse. £20 fine. Case closed."

Simon had agreed that we stand him lunch after the "trial", in lieu of a fee. We had one more racehorse – a hurdler, this time. I named it Norman Bank, after Jeremy and my trade. It had little success and eventually broke down, and couldn't even be hunted. Our brief racing career ended.

As night follows day, so began my next equestrian extravaganza. I became increasingly troubled by stiffness, when the cub hunting season began in late August, and one found oneself mounted again. The riding muscles, after being rested all summer, take longer and longer to return to normal strength, as the ageing process begins in earnest – around 40, in my experience. How to keep the riding muscles in trim in the summer, when the hunters are at grass, and there is nothing to ride? Polo! How devastatingly simple is the answer – particularly when one lives eight miles away from one of the oldest polo clubs in England. My old friend and colleague Douglas MacMillannow lived near us. He had managed Sumitomo White Weld, the joint venture, and then Sumitomo Finance in London, when Sumitomo Bank bought out White, Weld. All this was very fresh in my mind, as I had shocked Takahashi-san at Sumitomo, when I had to tell him I was leaving White, Weld. I was its representative on the board of the joint venture. The Japanese never moved firms in those days. The clan system which underpins the economy was so strong. For a Sumitomo man to move to Nikko, or Daiwa, was like a Campbell joining the MacDonald's. Douglas McMillan, avoiding any clan unpleasantness, had simply retired from the City, and was taking up the life of a country gentleman, with a French wife, one of two identical twins – so identical, in fact, I once spent an hour with one, thinking it was the other. Douglas introduced me to polo and I introduced him to hunting. It was during Badminton week that I stopped off at Claire Tomlinson's, where Douglas was trying some horses. He put me on one, gave me a stick and said, "Walk on, tap the ball, then trot on, and swing the stick a bit, then canter and give it a full swing." I did exactly as instructed and managed to connect with the ball, even at the canter. If one has played any stick and ball game, and knows how to ride, that is not the difficult part of the game. Unfortunately, many now take up the game without knowing how to ride – often with disastrous results. Claire Tomlinson is the great lady of polo. She is to the game as Margaret Thatcher was to the Conservative party, or Margot Fonteyn to English Ballet. Claire has the toughness of the former when organising, and the grace of the latter when playing. She spotted me that day as a potential low goal patron, and didn't give up on me until I was a low goal patron. I bought my first horses from Jack Williams who had been born and brought up in Argentina, where his father had gone to buy horses for the British Cavalry remounts in the Boer War. Eventually John P. Smail became my polo manager and main supplier. And in fact, one of my first ponies, called Samantha, had been bought by John P.'s mother for a load of firewood. This easy mare, taught me how to play, then my son Michael, and ended up semi-retired, playing pony club polo at the age of 25. She was so into the game that she anticipated. If she saw the player in front about to take a backhand, she would stop and turn, which was fine – unless the player missed his stroke, in which case we were facing the wrong way.

Polo is played at three basic levels. Players are handicapped individually, starting at minus two and working up to ten. The team handicap is an aggregate. Low goal tournaments are played by teams with an aggregate handicap between four and eight, medium goal from eight to sixteen, and high goal up to 24 in England, but up to 40 in Argentina. The difference in aggregate handicap between the teams provides goal advantages on the score board, at the start, to the team with the lower number. Thus teams are fairly evenly matched even if comprised of players of differing skill levels. Teams at all levels tend to have a patron, pronounced in the French manner for some reason. I suppose one could compare low goal polo to country house tennis, medium goal to club or county tournament tennis, and high goal to Wimbledon. The Cirencester Park Polo Club was founded over a hundred years ago, and is situated on the Bathurst estate, given to her Chancellor by Queen Anne. It encompasses probably the most beautifully sited set of polo grounds in England, surrounded by a landscape even more striking than that of Windsor Great Park, where Guards Polo Club is located. When I joined, the Club consisted almost entirely of retired British army officers, now farming in the region. Lord Bathurst was President, but didn't play. His younger brother George was a well rated player. The only "tycoons", and high goal patrons, were the Vestey brothers, Sam, with an estate at Stowell Park, and his younger brother Mark, with an estate at Foxcote. Each had their own ground at home. I was one of only two or three "City types" – one being Nigel a Brassard, from Kleinwort Benson, who had a cottage at Bibury. Exotica was provided by a charming Egyptian called Alex Abeid, soon to be joined by an equally engaging, turban-less Sihk, called Dhillon, whose father had been an Indian Army cavalry officer. I was proud to join this small, exotic element. Dhillon was universally known as "Sooty", a nickname he not only tolerated, but rather revered. This earned the Club a splash of negative publicity, when the Prince of Wales was overheard addressing him as such. Sooty wisely let the story run for a few days, before stating that he would have been offended if his good friend HRH had *not* addressed him in the same manner as all his other friends and polo colleagues. There were hardly any professionals then. Jack Williams, and his son Nick, were essentially professionals, and made, and sold horses. John P. Smail did the same, and ran a large yard, eventually providing practice and tournament play, on his three pitches. Simon and Claire Tomlinson were not yet professionals, but were increasingly treating the game as a business, and eventually left to found their own club on their property at Badminton. Claire had made headlines by threatening to sue the Hurlingham Polo Association, the game's governing body, if they didn't drop the ban on ladies playing at the high goal level. There were a number of polo playing South Africans, Rhodesians and Australians, who were studying at Cirencester Agricultural College, and were given membership privileges at student rates. The Vesteys had the only high goal team, at that time, and they imported two leading Argentine professionals each season for several years. They were Hector Barrantes, at nine goals and Eduardo Moore, at ten. They were like Mutt and

Jeff – Hector, a great bear of a man, and Eduardo very diminutive. We had practice chukkas every Saturday morning on Sweethills, a ground somewhat away from the others. One turned up and looked at the chukka list, compiled by Major Ronnie Scott, our polo manager, an ex-artillery officer – often accused of being inflexible, as most "gunners" are said to be. There one saw if one was in blue or white, and in which of the dozen or so chukka's one would be playing. They were entirely mixed and open, i.e.; un-handicapped. One day I found I was playing in the same team as Hector Barrantes. He and Eduardo often played their young horses at practice chukkas. As we were lining up for the throw in, Hector, who was at back, said to me, playing number one, "On the throw in, I want you to gallop as fast as you can to the goal When you are 20 yards or so away, look over your right shoulder."

I did as commanded, and found the ball sailing in and dropping just off my horse's off side fore, allowing me a gentle stroke to score a goal. To accomplish this trick, Hector would have had to capture the ball almost immediately, and then time his striking to place the ball as he did. It is a feature of the game, often forgotten, that a well struck ball travels faster that a pony can gallop. I was dumbstruck, but after, a wag said, "Hector does that to all new players. It's his way of introducing himself – he has horses for sale."

I decided to justify my increasing investment by taking some lessons, and went to spend a week at a polo school near Waterford in Ireland run by Major Hugh Dawney, whose mother was a Beresford, and therefore part of the great polo playing family of the Marquess of Waterford. Hugh had coached polo in the Army and helped to found the civilian polo clubs in Germany. Hugh's focus was on the oft neglected fact that polo is a team game, and ball chasing is a sin. He also taught polo riding, which differs from every other equestrian style. The essence is to be "outside your pony". A well-schooled pony is led by how and where the rider throws his weight, not by the mouth. Hugh used to illustrate this by galloping past his students and having one shout "turn!" He would immediately turn in the saddle, facing back, having given just a tug on the neck strap, but without touching the horse's mouth. His mount would stop, turn and gallop off in the opposite direction. For the rest, it was all team tactics. Thus I learned that if, on the attack and in front as number one, the ball was between me and the goal, the right move was to ignore the ball and ride off the defending back, allowing my number two, or three, behind me to shoot for goal, unhindered by the defending player. When, later on, I would successfully carry out this manoeuvre, my team captain John P. Smail would say "That was your goal".

During the best years of my polo career, I sponsored a low goal team consisting of John P. Smail at number two, a New Zealand professional from a polo playing family, called Simon Kyte, at three, and a promising youngster at back – a different one each season. We entered low goal tournaments at Cirencester, sometimes played away at Cowdray, Ham, or Cheshire, and occasionally strengthened our team with another professional and entered a medium goal tournament. We won the Apsley Cup, in this manner. In the photo I have, Lord Apsley – now Earl Bathurst - is with us, having presented the cup, wearing his habitual gumboots. It was all made very easy for me. I would call John P. on a Friday, and he would tell me where and when to turn up. He looked after my horses, schooled them, hired and fired girl grooms, and de-livered my string of four to the ground in my horse box, which stayed at his yard. Our colours were green and white horizontal stripes, laundered and looked after by Mrs. Smail. Simon Kyte was that rare professional who did not hog the ball, but contrived to have his patron share as much in the game as possible, and still win. John P., as he was always known, was a superb horseman, a quiet and steady player and a true sportsman. I was soon on the Club committee, members assuming, quite erroneously, that my City back-ground justified this. Then I was asked to take the chair, but it was not deemed necessary to warn me that the Club would be celebrating its one hun-dredth anniversary during my term of office. I suppose I should have checked. There were also some political issues, as is common to all organisations – es-pecially those devoted to leisure pursuits – which are taken more seriously than anything else in England. Henry Bathurst was not on good terms with the Vesteys, and Sam and Mark were the Club's principal patrons. One would have hoped the two Peers would be at one on most things, but the difficulty, no doubt, arose from the fact that the Henry's first Lady Bathurst, called Judy, had left him for a Vestey cousin. Lord Bathurst was not only our President, he was also our landlord – but even that was not entirely straight forward. The estate was owned by a mosaic of family trusts, and the Club grounds occu-pied some land directly under Henry's control and some under the control of his heir, Allan Apsley. The complication was that the two did not get on. In fact, My Lord Bathurst was hardly on speaking terms with My Lord Apsley. I must admit I found a neat way of getting around this. If I had a controversial proposal affecting the land, I would first go to Henry, and, while he was stroking his chin, I would say, "I'm afraid Allan is not too keen."

"Is that so! Well you have my approval," Henry would reply. I would then go to Allan.

"I think your father is rather against this."

"Then I'm for it!" would say Viscount Apsley, stamping a gumboot for emphasis.

This little bit of chicanery apart, I must say that both father and son were extremely kind to me, as well as helpful in every regard. I had hardly the typ-ical background of a chairman of a major English polo club. As we had one high goal tournament, the Warwickshire Club, we were classed as a high goal club, and allocated two places amongst the Stewards of the Hurlingham Polo Association, which had governed the game since the Hurlingham Club, where the game was first brought from India by the Army, drew up the rules of the game in 1875. Henry considered me thoroughly American, a country he greatly admired, and called me "Stan" throughout our friendship. His second wife Gloria, first married to a property tycoon, was my lifesaver. Dinnie, having been brought up in a polo household, had hoped to escape her horsey past by marrying a City type. Not for her the boring prize giving and stilted social events surrounding the game. She asked to be excused. Our daughter Tatyana, loved it, and often acted as proxy. Gloria, now the Dowager Countess Bathurst, was entirely understanding, and stepped into the breech to chair the committee organising the great ball we were to have for our centenary. This, as with all other social events, Gloria handled brilliantly. Despite her somewhat café society background, which *les mauvaise langues* liked to refer to, Gloria was, and is, a great lady, who did justice to her husband's rank and position in life – and to the Cirencester Park Polo Club.

By the time of my chairmanship, we had acquired a new and powerful patron in Urs Schwarzenbach, a Swiss – cousin to Inez, who had married my old friend Eric Franck. Urs made his fortune in foreign exchange trading. He ran two high goal teams, the Black Bears, and was a generous sponsor and patron of the Club, laying on splendid fireworks for our centenary ball. Even more useful to our greatly expanded franchise, was our member Major Christopher Hanbury, who at the end of a distinguished Army career, became ADC to the Sultan of Brunei, with special responsibilities for the Sultan's expenditures – by far the best role to have in the Sultan's extensive household. The Sultan and his brother Jeffrey were polo mad, and in fact, our own Jack Williams had been commissioned to go to Brunei to set up the Sultan's polo establishment, fields, stables, vets, farriers, and saddlers – the lot. Christopher arranged various sponsorships from the Sultan's interests, including the Dorchester Hotel. More importantly he convinced the Sultan to base his English polo at Cirencester, and several memberships were taken out to accommodate the Sultan, Prince Jeffrey and various high goal professionals. So began the "helicopter age" of polo at Cirencester, and, in my opinion, its eventual degradation. Charity matches began to dominate our programme. They raised a good deal of money for charities, and for the Club. HRH the Prince of Wales, risked his neck all season long, playing charity matches, raising considerable sums – much of it through charity days at Cirencester, where he enjoyed playing, as we were close to Highgrove, and had better control of the *paparazzi* than the Guard's Club. At one Dorchester Day, a culinary delight, as well a social must, the Sultan, Prince Jeffrey and the Prince of Wales were all playing. At the marquee before luncheon, I couldn't help noticing the Sultan's boots. He and the other players had changed into shirts, ties and blazers, but still had on their white britches and boots. The Sultan's were the oldest, most worn out, patched up boots I had ever seen on a polo field. In fact, they were held together by the patches. I quickly realised that they were the good luck pair, as the Sultan, considered the richest man in the world, was hardly likely to have spared his boot maker for want of ready cash. Christopher had told me that the Sultan did not consider it proper to be looked in the eye by women, and would I please warn Gloria. Well, I had plenty to do as the chairman/host, and I forgot. I had placed Gloria on the Sultan's left. I was at the same head table, sitting next to the King of Greece. We were just both agreeing that polo was a boring sport to watch, when I looked over and, to my horror, saw Gloria enthusiastically conversing with the Sultan, at a deb's mother's pace, looking him straight in the eye. The Sultan showed no sign of annoyance. On the contrary, he was entranced. Only Gloria could have pulled that off. Christopher Hanbury made a huge contribution to the Club, and should have been chairman – rather than me.

As part of my duties, I had to be over by the lines to greet him when the Prince of Wales came to play. In fact I had been introduced by Ronnie Scott who, early in the season, would ring me in the evening to whisper on the telephone that the Prince was minded to play a practice match at Aston Down, where we had a supplementary ground, few were aware of. The Prince was plagued by press photographers whose sole aim was to catch him in a spectacular fall. We were able to guarantee him privacy at Aston Down. Ronnie would arrange the teams, of course, including myself as chairman, according to our discretion, rather that our goal ratings. Since I played at one and Prince Charles at back, we were supposed to mark each other. Once on the ground, the Prince would lose me by keeping up a conversation.

"Expecting a good season, Chairman?" he would say. As I hesitated slightly with my answer, he would spur his horse and be off. Later in the season, I would wonder over to the lines early when I saw his then polo manager Major Ronnie Ferguson, had arrived with the horses. I did not have a good relationship with Ronnie Ferguson. He made it abundantly clear that he did not consider me a suitable person to be chairman at Cirencester. Not only was I not a former British Army officer, but I was in the City, and my "Who's Who" listing had me down as a former NCO in the U.S. Marines! But a worse problem was that my President, Earl Bathurst, could not stand Ronnie Ferguson, and more than once, told me he would like to ban him from the Club. I could see the headline "Earl Bans Prince's Aide from Club". Once at a prize giving, in front of HRH, Henry thought Ronnie Ferguson was standing in the way.

"Get out of the way, Ronnie!" he shouted. Poor Ronnie Scott, our long suffering polo manager, was there in charge of the prize giving, and, thinking Henry was addressing him, jumped like a scalded rabbit. "Not you, Ronnie!" shouted Henry. "That idiot Ferguson!"

If the Prince overheard all this, he showed no sign. After the match, I would go back to the lines, where the Prince was often lying flat on his back, as he suffered greatly from a back condition – which polo does nothing to alleviate. We would walk back to the club house for the prize giving and, sometimes, the Prince would say, "Remind which charity I was playing for today?" They were always on his extensive, approved list.

Once, I hesitatingly replied, "It's the rebuilding of Tetbury Church Steeple, sir"

"Oh, oh," he said, with a start, "I suppose the Rector is there, and I have to hand him the cheque?"

336

"I'm afraid so, sir."

"I do not like that man."

I half expected him to say "who will rid me of that troublesome priest?" The rector of Tetbury had preached a sermon, widely reported in the press, in which he had made less that positive references to the Prince's marital situation. Usually, our little chats were a treat and the Prince was courtesy itself. Ronnie Ferguson was eventually replaced as his polo manager by a charming ADC, with whom I got on splendidly and we used to chat about many things, waiting for HRH to drive up in his Aston Martin, dogs in front and security guard in the back. Once, on the way over to the club house, HRH said, "You live at Bibury, don't you? I suppose you know your neighbour Charlie Farringdon? I have never visited Barnsley House."

Now the Prince of Wales loves visiting houses. Barnsley House is a very pure 18th century house in the next village to Bibury, and was one of Lord Farringdon's properties. He is head of the Henderson family and we were on the board of Henderson Administration together. The next time I saw him, I reported what seemed to me a heavy hint.

"Good Lord," said Charlie. "We must put that right!"

When I retired as chairman, the committee asked the Prince of Wales to present me with my goodbye memento.

"I hope you won't stop playing," he said. "We must both go on as long as we can." In fact, I played my last chukka in France, at the age of 68, having taken a couple of horses down to play with Guy Marchand, a French actor/singer, who had laid out a ground near Lacoste.

My chairmanship at Cirencester was a mixed experience for me. I didn't mind the almost impossible decisions when Ronnie Scott would ring me up first thing, after appalling weather, and ask, "Do we play today? We have some key tournament rounds to play" or "it's our most important charity day."

"What's the state of the ground?"

"Slippery but not dangerous" or "we'll cut it up completely."

"What would you do?"

"It's your decision, Chairman."

I did not mind Sooty Dhillon giving me hell for exercising my prerogative, together with Ronnie Scott, to waive or reduce fees to promising youngsters who couldn't afford them, but whose participation was critical to the Club. I didn't mind coping with reports of drug abuse, or unruly young. I put young Stuart Lodge on the committee to supervise his generation. I didn't mind the tedious charity luncheons when I had to give a speech about polo. I finally got my predecessor Doug Brown, a retired RAF officer, to give his very amusing description of the game, which would have everyone in stitches. I would start by saying "The one thing you need to know about polo is, if you have to work in order to afford to play it – you will have little time to play it". I made a great many friends playing polo, and I have mentioned a few of them. What I minded was seeing the sport deteriorate from a game played by gentleman, to a commercial business catering to vulgarians. The rot started with an explosion of high goal patrons drawn from the world's newly rich tycoons, who saw polo as a route to social prestige, culminating with a chance to meet the Queen, if they could win the Gold Cup, and whose attitude of "win at any cost" corrupted overpaid Argentine professionals, whose skill at engineering fouls became their hallmark. If you know you never miss a sixty yard penalty, the easiest way of winning a match is to trap less skilled players into fouling. Kerry Packer, an Australian press baron who had invented "pyjama cricket" was something of a case in point. One weekend, I had a call from Mark Vestey, then chairman of the HPA Stewards, saying we had to meet immediately to adjudicate an appeal to an umpire/referee's decision, lodged by Kerry Packer, following a Gold Cup round match. The threat was he would pull his team from the most prestigious tournament of the season, if he didn't get satisfaction. This was not the first time Packer had acted like a spoilt child. There are two mounted umpires in tournament matches, and a referee seated on the side-lines who makes a final determination, when the umpires cannot agree. Before the likes of Packer turned up, one accepted the referee's decision and moved on. Packer would turn up in front of the Stewards, with top City solicitors and QCs in tow, to argue against a decision. I felt like shouting, "It's a game, you idiot! Not a takeover battle". These new attitudes trickled down and began to infect the game at all levels. I had to chastise the Earl of Tyrone, of all people, the heir to the Marquess of Waterford, for shaking his fist in the air, having won a match, like a Black Panther demonstrator, even before trotting around to shake hands with the losers, as is the convention. Triumphalism does not belong in a gentleman's game – I thought. Courtesy and manners began to go out the window. I threatened to throw Claire Tomlinson's brother out of a match. A medium goal professional, he somehow found himself in a low goal match, and kept complaining to the umpires that play was not fast enough for his taste. He was taken aback by my intervention. He thought the Lucas family owned the game and he could behave as he liked. The worst offence, unforgivable for me, was committed by his sister Clare Tomlinson – that great lady of polo. A rather strange Persian had acquired Thomas Goode & Co., the famous china ware shop and Royal Warrant holder. Perhaps his antecedents prompted him to become a polo sponsor. We gave him a major day at Cirencester and he had made up extraordinary prizes to be handed to the winning team. These consisted of full size, silver replicas of polo sticks – the heads in solid silver, and the shafts in hollow silver, carved to imitate bamboo, with handles in silver, including the wrist straps. I cannot imagine what these might have cost. Claire Tomlinson, who together with her husband Simon, now had their own club, was playing on the winning team. The event was well attended, the match a good one, and our Persian was delighted. There were, as usual by now, several helicopters in the field behind the club house. As the prize giving was being organised, Claire rushed up to me and said she couldn't stay for the prize giving, there was a helicopter waiting to take her to Cowdray, where she was running late to play in another match and – "Sorry". I couldn't believe it. The sponsor was to be deprived of the photograph of the prize giving, with the silver sticks. The photographs of this occasion were to be his principle mementos of the whole event, on which he had spent a fortune. On Claire's part, it was an act of ill-mannered selfishness, for which I have never forgiven her – not to this day. But this was what polo was becoming. Arrogance, bad manners, money grubbing, unsportsmanlike behaviour, rule bending – all this was ruining the atmosphere. Of course I had fun playing polo. I didn't really like anything else about it – and I hated it as my, perhaps unrealistic, ideal was destroyed. Clubs incorporated, even the Guards Club at Windsor, claiming this provided greater protection against litigation risk in a dangerous game. This was flawed legal thinking. Company directors are just as liable to accident claims as club committee members, where wilful neglect can be proved. The real reason was to facilitate various moneymaking schemes. Finally, a Chairman of Cirencester Park Polo Club, now an incorporated business, relegated our President from the top table at the AGM, and then, after Earl Bathurst's death, had the discourtesy to tell the press that his widow was being difficult over the lease, because she wanted to increase the rent – assuming, presumably, that the Dowager Countess Bathurst shared his own crass, commercial instincts. I resigned my life honorary vice-presidency in protest.

We had a life at Bibury unconnected with horses, although somehow they tended to be omnipresent. The Malt House was where we brought up the children, whose schools we had chosen with distance in mind. Tatyana was at Hatherop Castle School as a weekly boarder, a short hack from Bibury. I would pick her up on Saturday morning in the season, with her pony and my horse in the trailer, and drive straight to the meet. Hatherop was not a school which would ever produce another Madame Curie, and few of its old girls went on to university. Years later, when Tayana was a sometimes working actress in New York, there was a rumour the school would close. That distinguished journalist Quentin Letts, was then writing the "Peterborough" gossip column in the *Telegraph*. One day I saw a startling reference. "Rumours abound that exclusive Hatherup Castle School for young ladies, is too close" wrote Quentin. "I spoke to Tatyana Yassukovich, daughter of well-known City banker Stanislas. 'We were all beautiful and married well' – she told me. 'My father has a weakness for Hatherup girls. We wore red bloomers at games'". Before my own phone hotted up with sarcastic calls from friends, I called Quentin; "How can you do this! You have virtually suggested I am a dirty old man, peering at schoolgirls through the fence. I can't believe Tatyana said that!"

"Well," replied Quentin, languidly, "I guess I must have spoken to her for a good fifteen minutes. She did say all that, but, I must admit, not quite in that order."

So are the journalistic techniques of our press men honed early in their careers. Quentin is now the leading Parliamentary sketch writer and a top theatre critic. His father Richard Letts was headmaster of Oakley Hall, the prep school in Cirencester both Michael and Nicholas attended. The greatest compliment I can pay Dick Letts and his school is that both boys adored it, were successful within their own limits, and yet are totally different in character and skill sets. Few schools could achieve this. Actually the reason, the boys were admitted, virtually sight unseen, is that Dinnie happened to mention she was related to Sandy Singleton, a well-known cricketer, once capped for England. I became chairman of governors of this family school, which ran at a permanent loss, bankrolled through the accreting development value of its land. Dick Letts was an old fashioned schoolmaster whose philosophy was based on the three "Cs" – classics, chapel and cricket. He saw no reason to roam much further than this with the school programme. As chairman of governors, I made a suggestion. "Why not add another 'C', Dick? Teach the little horrors how to work a computer, and you'll impress parents and enhance admission prospects to public school. At Merrill Lynch we are always disposing of one generation of computer to make way for the next, and I can put one on every boy's desk for free."

"Computers!" said Dick, with horror. "I won't have one of those nasty things in my office!" Dick handed out bursaries like confetti. He also insisted on keeping boys whose fees went unpaid, term after term. "But we can't lose Fotheringdale major!" he would protest at a governor's meeting "He's my best spin bowler! And so we must keep his younger brother as well. Actually, Fotheringdale minor's shaping up as quite a decent batsman."

A good many fees were paid by grandparents, on behalf of impecunious or divorced parents. Our Nicholas, who became classical scholar, before becoming a tax accountant, started Greek and Latin at Oakley Hall, and at Cheltenham, he was one of only a handful of boys doing A level Greek – before the recent revival of interest in Classics. To encourage him, I sent him a quote from Shaw's *Major Barbara*, where the heroine's fiancé is explaining his profession to the munitions tycoon – his father-in-law to be. "Greek scholars are privileged men. Few of them know Greek and none of them know anything else; but their position is unchallengeable. Other languages are the qualifications of waiters and commercial travellers: Greek is to a man of position what the hallmark is to silver". Shaw might have added "international investment bankers" to "waiters and commercial travellers".

Our shooting days were cosmopolitan, as I had Scandinavian, Austrian and Belgian guests – clients and colleagues. Paul Emmanuel Jansen came, as did Otto-Karl Finsterwalder – usually late, after several panicky calls from Frau Fischer. We also had the de Pontalba's, my parents friends and neighbours in Senlis, and the Baroness, conscious that few English ladies shot, was extremely nervous, poking away at our very high pheasants – with a surprising degree of success. Once they brought their son, who was being force-fed an education in preparation for one of the *grandes écoles*. The poor lad was made to go straight to his room after shooting, to do homework. The Pontalbas would kindly invite me to shoot at their chateau near Senlis, where eleven guns lined up to deal with a certain paucity of low flying pheasants, sent over by beaters shouting at the top of their lungs. Henri was French president of the *Federation Internationale de la* Chasse, or some such body, and the younger brother of the Shah of Iran, who had chaired the Persian chapter, was often a guest. Henri fawned on *Son Altesse Imperial*, in the most exaggerated fashion, ignoring the fact that this charming prince's grandfather had been a sergeant in the real Shah's guards, and had staged a *coup d'état*. In all other respects, I believe Henri was *ligitimiste*. But he had a white stake in the middle of the line, on each drive, reserved for the prince, claiming this had been the practice when a member of the French royal family was invited to a *battue*. I was fond of the Pontalba's, and I think it snobbish to mock other people's snobbishness.

Mostly through hunting contacts, I ended up on the board of the British Field Sports Society, chaired then by the Member for Wimbledon, Dr. Charles Goodson-Wickes. Our other parliamentarian on the board was the Earl of Stockton, Harold MacMillan's heir, and between them, they plotted ingenious parliamentary tactics to frustrate the growing attempts to legislate against hunting. Through mergers and amalgamations, the BFSS, ended up representing all fields sports, from wildfowling, through game fishing to stalking, shooting, of course, and hunting with hounds. The board contained representatives of each, although shooting had its own body, chaired by the Duke of Westminster, and all attempts to merge with it failed, leaving a harmful split, when the crunch came with anti-hunting legislation. Many shooting people felt hunting should be thrown to the wolves, thus saving shooting from the animal rights lobby. Of course, anti-hunting sentiment had nothing whatever to do with animal rights, but was an entirely political movement, based on the false premise that hunting was elitist, whereas shooting was "popular" and practised by ordinary folk. Actually the exact opposite is the case. Try turning up at someone's shoot, with your gumboots and gun, and ask "May I join your shooting today?" On the other hand, you can trot up to any hunt meet in the country, neatly dressed, and you will be welcome to hunt, on payment of a few pounds to the "wire fund". A City based American, no doubt a keen hunting man, decided to set up his own pro-field sports group, seeking support from the large community of businesses serving sportsmen, such as saddlers, cartridge makers, fishing equipment suppliers etc., etc. – not a bad idea, but it diluted the work of existing lobby groups. He found funding from the Fleming family, who were already major benefactors of the BFSS. The new group embarked on a huge advertising campaign and quickly ran out of money. At the BFSS, we were told we had to rescue this entity, as its threatened bankruptcy would be terrible publicity for our common cause. In fact, pressure for a rescue came largely from the Fleming family. It was clear the association had been wastefully managed. It had appointed Lord Steele as chairman, the retired head of the Liberal Party, who has publicly stated he is anti-hunting –

as is his party. It was further revealed, that his lordship was drawing a six fig-ure salary. We were told he would have to join our board, without pay, of course. Our chairman Goodson-Wickes was unpaid, like the rest of us. I was not going to sit on the board of a field sports association with someone who was anti-hunting. I resigned. After a great deal of politicking by those who enjoy that kind of thing, the BFSS was succeeded by the Countryside Alli-ance, to form the most broadly based grouping to fight the anti-hunting bill. Some of the largest and most peaceful demonstration ever held in England were organised by the Countryside Alliance – to no avail. Prime Minister Blair pushed the bill through to placate some critics in his own party, who were threatening to derail some other, totally unrelated, pet project of his. The bill banning the hunting of mammals with dogs is one of the worst examples of the latent hypocrisy which characterises much of British politics. The Burns Inquiry, commissioned by a Labour, produced an anodyne conclusion that hunting with dogs "compromised the welfare of the quarry species" but did not opine as to whether hunting should be banned or not. In the Lord's de-bate following, Lord Burns said, "Naturally, people ask whether we are im-plying hunting is cruel. The short answer is no." The Inquiry's conclusion, from an animal welfare point of view, was wrong. No one disagreed the fox population had to be controlled to protect sheep and flocks of fowl from de-predation, and to avoid disease from overpopulation. Hunting with hounds has ensured the survival of this revered genus of British wildlife, because, in general, the weak are caught and the strong get away – as in nature for most mammals. In fact, hunting duplicates a law of nature, but in a more controlled and benign manner. The first hound that lays a tooth on a fox kills it instantly, snapping its neck, whereas, trapping, poisoning, and shooting foxes leads to a lingering and painful death – and is non-selective. In Scotland, a different ver-sion of the law permitted the use of a few hounds to flush a fox, which could then be shot. To kill outright a bolting fox with a rifle or shotgun is almost impossible. The English law had to be drafted in a convoluted fashion to avoid criminalising the person walking their Labrador, which suddenly comes across a rabbit, or a farmer whose terrier catches a rat in the barn. The Gov-ernment had the further hypocrisy to suggest to chief constables not to devote to many resources to enforcing the bill, effectively admitting it was unen-forceable. More people are now hunting than before the passage of the bill and there have been no more than a half a dozen prosecutions. Unenforceable laws bring the justice system into disrepute.

Our "vacations" from Bibury followed something of a set pattern. The children, Dinnie and nanny spent some time with the DYs at Senlis, and I joined when I could. My father still went to the Paris office of White, Weld, until his health began to fail bit. After becoming a limited partner, he had signed up with a senior executive group which providing consulting assign-ments to retirees of distinction. He spent some time in Morocco for the World Bank, sorting out their affiliate there – without much success as the problem was a chairman related to the King, and untouchable. Before he left, he had been briefed by David Suratgar, then general counsel at the World Bank, who went on to become a confidante and advisor to Othman Benjalloun, who created Banque Maroccaine du Commerce Exterior, from the privatisation of that affiliate. David recalled all this when he asked me to join the board of BMCE's London subsidiary. DY also carried out two assignments for Bankers Trust, one in the Philippines and one in London – which led to the famous Rodochnachi name change incident. At Christmas, we alternated for some time between Dinnie's Lowdale, and "Courandair" our family house on Jupiter Island, Hobe Sound, Florida. It was there the children learned to play tennis. When Rhodesia blew up, we were more often in Florida. With our friends John and Honora Scott-Oldfield, we also began going to Tuscany, at the end of the polo season. Honora lectured in fine art at the V & A, and we did all the churches and museums in that almost culturally over-favoured part of the world. It was like having Kenneth Clarke along as our personal guide. Sometimes Honora's exhaustive knowledge of the *rinascimento* would get the better of her, and I would catch her "schmoozing" a bit. As an investment banker, I can always spot a piece of schmoozing, which prattle is leading usually to embellishment of pure fact with some improvisation.

"Did that really happen?" the schmooze catcher enquires.

"Well, maybe not exactly," says the schmoozer – "but it certainly could have."

Some of you will have spotted a possible sub-title for this book. Honora admitted she also "coloured" her lectures with some relevant invention. But this helped her students to understand the soul of western art – which a cold and unembroidered presentation of pure fact could not. We rented a house belonging to Bona Frescobaldi, near Pontesieve outside Florence for some years, until Bona's children wanted it in August. As many advertising signs along Tuscan roads point out, the Frescobaldi's have been wine makers since 1308, and we drank a good deal of their wine Pomino, whilst there. Bona allowed us to park in the courtyard of the family palace in Florence, just off the Piazza de Frescobaldi, which was very convenient in a city then rapidly pedestrianising, and fearing we might be bored, would arrange dinner parties for us, turning up suddenly and giving appropriate orders to her staff.

But the break from Bibury, which became the most entrenched, was our annual visit to Hobe Sound. For various reasons, the role played in my life by this particular destination is far greater than might be suggested by the amount of time I have spent there. This is to a large extent due to the connection with the Reed family, my parent's first and oldest American friends. We grew up with the Reed children, my sister Ariane married the eldest son Adrian, and had four children with him. I was at Deerfield Academy with the Reed boys, was particularly close to the two youngest, Samuel and Joseph, and was in trouble with the latter, once or twice. I introduced Samuel to his wife Annette Englehardt, latterly de la Renta, and am godfather to their daughter Beatrice. My godfather Jack Barrett's family was, and still is, closely connected to the Reeds. Jupiter Island, in reality a long sand bar, politely called a "barrier island", off the so-called Treasure Coast of Florida – on the Atlantic side, separated from the mainland by the intercoastal waterway, and reached by bridges at each end. The St. Lucie area, of which it forms part, was occupied by English owned pineapple plantations in the late 19th century. These failed after two severe winters in succession, and the island then hosted deep sea fisherman at a small inn, and had few residents. Joseph and Permelia Reed discovered it in the early 1930s, when Florida was just recovering from the busted real estate boom of the 1920s. They decided it could be developed as an alternative to Palm Beach, twenty miles to the south, which was becoming, by contemporary standards, over developed, and, in the Reeds' estimation – rather stuffy. Early on, Joseph Reed liked to boast that, whereas in Palm Beach, stiff fronted evening shirts and starched wing collars were *de rigeur* with evening dress, a soft shirt and collar would be acceptable on Jupiter Island. Nowadays, a neck tie at dinner is a rarity. The Reeds began buying up the island, building their own house, and encouraging friends to do the same, having founded the Hobe Sound Company as landowner/agent, bought the small inn, and expanded it into a proper club, with golf course, tennis courts, and beach club – in a superbly landscaped environment. Over the ensuing years, the Reeds created probably the most beautiful and exclusive winter resort in all America. Greenwich, Connecticut based friends and neighbours were amongst the first to settle, but the population expanded quickly to include a greater mid-western contingent, than usual in high society circles, and finally, contained representatives of many of the great American industrial and commercial fortunes – Fords, Harrimans, Mercks, Colgates, Doubledays, Dillons, Fields, Hamms, Johnsons, Meads, Strawbridges, Whitneys, Whites, and a heavy sprinkling of North Eastern Yankee families – including a great many from my childhood stamping ground on Long Island. The Jupiter Island Club was proprietary, and admission rigorously controlled by Permelia Reed, and there was no point in buying land and building a Jupiter Island residence if one could not gain admission to the Club. The Club was the Island, and the Island was the Club. Jupiter Island was a benevolent dictatorship and Permelia was eminently qualified as the dictator, being a born organiser, administrator and, above all, possessing impeccable taste, strongly supported in this by Joseph, a polymath patron of the arts... An example of the celebrity she achieved in her role is Douglas Dillon's *faux pas* in extending an invitation without prior consultation. When Dillon was Secretary of the Treasury in the Kennedy Administration, a weekend arose when the President was on his own, and disinclined to go to Camp David. Dillon suggested he spend the weekend at his house on Jupiter Island, an invitation gladly accepted. At the last minute, Secretary Dillon thought "I'd better have a word with Permelia".

"You've done what, Douglas?" barked Permelia over the phone.

"I've invited the President for the weekend," repeated Dillon.

"Well, you can tell him it's off! I'm not having secret service men, and helicopters, and all the rest, all over the Island."

When Dillon made an embarrassed call to the White House, President Kennedy said:

"It's Permelia, isn't it? Don't worry, I'll stay with my mother in Palm Beach."

Later, Permelia had to bear such an invasion, when the son of the Reed's close friends, and early Jupiter Island residents, Senator and Mrs. Prescott Bush, became President. She could hardly stop President Bush from visiting his mother, who lived, as a widow, quite close to Courandair, our house.

Permelia struck a unique combination of fear, respect and affection in the hearts of most. She often arrived for lunch at the Beach Club, and would sit knitting for a while, greeting all and sundry in a monarchical fashion. Legend had it she was knitting sweaters, rather like Madame Desfarge, in *Tale of Two Cities* – and a black one was reserved for a transgressor who, on banishment from the Island, would need it to face the cold of the North. My first visit was with schoolmates from Deerfield for our Spring break, or Easter vacation, as it was known then, and the privilege was really reserved for friends of the Reed boys, in my case that meant my classmate Samuel. We stayed in comfortable, barracks style quarters reserved for the young – known as "the Brig". Of course, due to my parent's friendship with the Reeds, I would have been welcome anyway, and I was given the severest parental warning to be on my best behaviour. I was – with the notable exception of one, off-site, louche excursion organised by one of our little band. A poor memory, and discretion, prevents me from identifying the individuals involved, but someone had discovered the existence of a brothel in West Palm Beach, and it was decided a surreptitious visit was in order. If this was to constitute a loss of virginity for some, it was not admitted by any. Our main concern was that we were probably underage. Why this risked being a concern of the professional ladies staffing the establishment, I cannot imagine – but we went through the trouble of checking the dates of Spring breaks at Princeton, as we had decided to pose as college students. On arrival we found the ladies attired in evening dresses – mostly taffeta and strapless. Already attuned to ladies fashion, I could not help noticing that many gowns were better cut and more elegant than those worn by the pre-debs of my acquaintance. At any rate, all passed off to the satisfaction, and, if I may use the expression, relief of our party. However, some years later, I came within a few stitches of receiving a black sweater. It was a time when young Joseph Reed and I were drinking heavily and behaving lightly. A Long Island based incident has already been referred to. Again during an Easter holiday, we had both been late to several parties, and teamed up to have a midnight spin on some golf carts, newly purchased by the Club which were, as we said to ourselves, "just sitting there". We raced around the first fareway, as if in dodgem carts, mindless of the sprinklers, which operate at night. The next morning, the damage was all too evident, due to the moist ground, and somehow word got around that the culprits were young Joseph and Stani. At the Beach Club before lunch, all were abuzz – waiting for Permelia's arrival. "When I find out who is responsible, he, or they, will never set foot on this Island again!" was her declaration, the knitting needles flashing in the sun. It seemed, to the astonishment of all, that she was the only person on the Island ignorant of the identity of the malefactors. Sometimes, when I wake up, after a recurring nightmare of this incident, I wonder. Permelia, like many matriarchs, was often in denial when negativity struck, particularly involving the family. She had a Panglossian streak and saw everything in life as bordering on perfection. Perhaps she knew at once who the culprits were, but she was not going to admit it, and she could not very well single me out. In any case, I think she was rather fond of me.

Family relations were rather strained when Ariane divorced Adrian, but Joseph *père* was saintly in his continued affection and support for his ex-daughter-in-law, and helped with the children's school fees and Ariane's expenses. His generosity knew no bounds. About the time the DYs were planning to build a house, Joseph had acquired a huge and extremely valuable carpet, but had failed to identify a place for it, and now found it did not fit in any of the several Reed residences. One day, he dropped into "Pieces of Eight", the Club cottage we were staying in. My father was scribbling the plans for the new house on the back of an envelope.

"Dimitri! You must have the carpet," Joseph said, dropping off a small present, or box of chocolates – he was never without, when visiting.

"How much?" asked my father, inwardly wondering which securities he would have to sell.

"Don't be silly, Dimitri! It's a present. You must ask Kemp Caler to measure it and be sure the drawing room in your new house is designed to fit."

Caler was our architect, and the architect of choice for many Island residents. He did so, and Courandair may be the only house on the Island built to fit a carpet. When my father became increasingly unwell, my mother felt the house in Senlis was too much, and transatlantic travel would have to be curbed anyway. Unfortunately, Senlis was sold at the bottom of the French property market – soon after Mitterrand was elected president with a Socialist agenda. Afterwards, my parents divided the year between Jupiter Island, and a small house near Locust Valley. In between they often spent a week or two at my mother's club in New York, the Colony. This is an exclusively ladies' club, but my father used to enjoy telling people – putting on a very straight face, "Yes, the rules of my wife's club very specifically state that members may stay with their husband, or with the husband of another member." DY did not enjoy Jupiter Island that much, particularly when he became wheelchair bound and unable to play golf. He missed Europe, quite simply. In Florida, he belonged to a luncheon club called the "Whizz Kids" made up of retired corporate executives and Wall Street law and banking partners. They discussed serious topics and had guest speakers – including me, recently. General McChristian, a soldier with a distinguished record in military intelligence and diplomacy, from an old Southern family long resident on the Island, used to fetch DY in his wheelchair and take him to Whizz Kid meetings. Their shared military back ground made them fast friends, and these moments eased my father's rather sad decline in physical and mental health. Towards the end he began confusing his daughter Ariane, his granddaughter Tatyana, and his lost sister Marie – understandably, as they each had rather Slavic looks. My mother, on the other hand, absolutely loved Jupiter Island, and most of the people on it. They represented everything she most admired about Americans – especially the Reeds, particularly as they had absorbed a good deal of French culture. I often pointed out to her that the residents of this little paradise on earth, with the second highest income per capita of any American community, could hardly be said to be representative of the nation as a whole. In fact, being relative paupers in a community of extremely rich people, would have posed difficulties for our family in many other such places – where the residents might not have been so gracious and cultured, as on Jupiter Island. But at the time of my parent's *séjour*, from the '50s to the '80s – such was largely the case. My father never wondered at the ease with which he was welcomed in such circles. My mother did, and feigned surprise at any gesture of acceptance. When Permelia invited her to join the Garden Club, she replied. "But I know very little about gardens here in Florida!"

"Mummy," I had to say. "The Garden Club has nothing to do with gardening – or at least only tangentially. It's a social thing, for goodness sake!"

"Oh," said my mother, still puzzled.

If I were to launch into a description of Jupiter Island in its glory days, my prose would soon creep over the top – which is exactly what the Island was not. The houses were architecturally varied, but strikingly pleasant and well-proportioned – sited with a maximum of surrounding garden. Although their density was suburban, somehow they seemed well-distributed through the lush vegetation. The Island had been extensively landscaped by Richard Webel, a garden service entrepreneur from Long Island, who rose to be one on the country's top landscape architects, with an uncanny skill at combining native flora with harmonious imports. The necessity for this is quickly confirmed by a trip to Florida's interior scrub land. The Club buildings were tastefully furnished and decorated in a subtle mix of Caribbean rattan, French provincial and New England colonial. Pictures of every description, from Audubon prints to French *belle époque* posters adorned the walls, together with nostalgic black and white photos of old members from the age of elegance. Club service was near perfect, the staff well trained, the *cuisine* excellent without being tortured. But, I suppose when heights are reached, the only way forward is down. All this began to erode, perhaps influenced mysteriously by the beach erosion on the ocean which has plagued the Island – but

347

without the remedial action, which cost dear, but generally worked. First Joseph Verner Reed died, then after a short few years, Permelia. The boys quarrelled, as is often the case with the rich. Family quarrels are a luxury the poor cannot afford. The Hobe Sound Company decided to sell the Club, first seeking third party buyers at excessive prices, and then to the members. Where Permelia ran the Club perfectly as a committee of one, now eighteen different committees run the Club badly, and cannot keep a manager, as conflicting instructions cause managerial havoc. The service level and value for money have declined, as fees have risen inexorably. As the committees seek to justify their existence, wasteful projects produce annual assessments. The latest is the destruction of the iconic Beach Club, which had survived multiple hurricanes since its inauguration in 1936, and is now to be replaced by a cross between the Taj Mahol and Penn Station. How ironic that Joseph Reed's dream to counter the excesses of Palm Beach, should end with an attempt to outdo the oversized Bath & Tennis Club. Worse than all this, a new generation of newly rich hedge fund managers, joined by some legacies, but with similar tastes, it would seem, has arrived to build huge, vulgar houses, the architects mixing styles to meet uncultured client fancies. Oversized for their plots, as well as in general, these "McMansions" now scar the Island, and disgorge a new population of loud, ill-mannered and badly dressed folk who clamour for more opportunities to eat with their fingers. The island is now seriously overcrowded, and the roads clogged with garden service trucks tending gardens, which *sans* Webel, look increasingly municipal. In fact, one should bear in mind the Club is no longer the Island, nor vice-versa. An increasing proportion of residents are not, and do not seek, to be members. This includes a number of celebrities, such as Tiger Woods and Celine Dionne. Because, my recent visits have been an exercise in nostalgia, I feel the ravages of time and an unwelcome social tide more strongly than my essentially philosophical nature should permit. Nostalgia is a bitter sweet condition, and with its indulgence comes indigestion and a cantankerous temperament. I plead guilty to suffering from the condition. But I deeply regret that a much adored country – it was almost a separate country, whose overwhelming characteristic was understated, good taste, is now replaced by one of over-stated, bad taste. Equally troublesome to me is that its current population shows little sense of gratitude for the extraordinary contribution the Reed family made to the haven they now wallow in. On the contrary, some are disdainful of the Reed legacy. Leave aside the fact that the family covered the Club's significant deficits, year after year. It might be said this was used to justify a dictatorship, which however benign, some objected to. But the indefinable atmosphere that one feels, on any walk, in any part of the Island, seated in any part of the Club, looking over any part of the landscape, is a creation of the Reeds – whether one admits it or not. Nathaniel and Alita Reed, and their children, are the last of the Reeds resident on the Island. A noted environmentalist, conservationist and sportsman, Nathaniel served as an Under Secretary of the Interior, and has been highly active on the Florida environmental scene. Adrian and Samuel have both died. Joseph, and his wife Mimi, left Jupiter Island some time ago. Joseph has had a distinguished career as a banker and diplomat – most recently as a Deputy Secretary General of the United Nations.

At least two or three annual family trips abroad notwithstanding, Bibury remained my emotional home, even if I was technically a weekender. Dinnie would normally stay over Monday, particularly when she was hunting, and come up to town on Tuesday. Being much attached to a nest, Dinnie did not enjoy this bi-residential life. No sooner was she settled in the country, it was back to town, and then vice-versa. Perhaps for this reason, but more probably from deep-seated causes, she fell ill with a full-fledged, clinical depression. Our GP, Dr. Richard Rossdale, from a family of GPs, was stumped. Having played in the hospital rugby league, he knew every prominent specialist, and sent Dinnie off to the best. But the best in any field is always overloaded with patients, and Dinnie received only fleeting attention and was overdosed with pills. She ended up at the Priory clinic in Roehampton, known for treating celebrities for the "Ds' – drugs, drink and depression. The more friends told me it couldn't be my fault, the more I suspected it was. I read every work on the subject I could find, becoming quite conversant with the world of seraton-in-norepinephrine reuptake inhibitors, and the like. In the end, she was packed off to the family farm in Zimbabwe, still as yet unsequestered by Mugabe's thugs. My beloved mother-in-law and sister-in-law looked after her, and the cure turned out to be simply a long spell in her original home environment – one she had sorely missed by being sent far away to boarding school at too young an age. Dinnie is definitely not the corporate wife, a source of relief to me as I have known many an American corporate wife, and they scare me to death. And she is not overly fond of large gatherings. In private life we tend to the quiet. The world is divided between those who are hopelessly social, and those who are socially hopeless – we fall more neatly in this latter category. We once forgot to go to a luncheon given by the Lord Lieutenant of Gloucestershire. The Bathursts were there, and Gloria never stopped pulling my leg about it. We are still known to be somewhat casual about social engagements.

CHAPTER XIX

"Change is not made without inconvenience, even from worse to better "

-Richard Hooker, quoted by Johnson-

On arrival at Merrill Lynch, after getting used to being called "chairman" by everyone down to the messengers, a first challenge was to discover exactly what my job description might be. My immediate boss became Jerry Kenney, then head of investment banking. A brief interregnum had me reporting to a head of international, but he had to retire due to illness, and the position was effectively passed to Jerry. He told me my role should be one of non-executive leadership, coupled with senior relationship development. My position was hence different from that of my predecessor, as Don Roth had been an Executive Chairman. I was to select a chief executive officer, from a list Jerry would provide. He did not believe a candidate existed in London, and from what I could see, I agreed – to the great disappointment of Giovanni Franzi, who had fully expected I would choose him in recognition of his having proposed me as the new chairman. It was also clear to me that New York would be more comfortable with a home trained American. Head office was still smarting from the Montagu/Craven experience. Like many of the emerging megabanks, Merrill was still searching for a methodology of management able to cope with a multi-discipline and multi-location empire. It had already divided the empire into dominions: Europe, Middle East & Africa, the largest; Pacific Region, headquartered in Hong Kong; Japan; Canada, and eventually Latin America, headquartered in Miami. Each dominion had a governor general, called a chairman, but his executive responsibility varied from region to region. These chairmen sat on the global executive committee, together with product heads, under Kenny's chairmanship. The firm alternated between phases of centralisation and de-centralisation – as each proved less than satisfactory. The compromise was supposed to be "matrix management", no doubt the invention of some McKinsey guru. Under matrix management, client relationships and compliance were devolved entirely to the regions, whereas product heads in each region had a dual reporting line – to the head office product head, and to the regional executive. The regional chairman was responsible for adjudicating the inevitable conflicts. Like so many management consultant ideas, it was beautiful on paper, and hopeless in practice. The ironic thing about Merrill Lynch's new, international ambition was that, in its earliest times, the firm had been an investment bank/private equity house, making such headline investments in the 1920s, such as the Pathé Group, which became RKO, and a small grocery business, Safeway, which became one of the nation's leading grocery chains. In 1930 it had sold off its brokerage business to E. A. Pierce, to concentrate on investment banking, Charles Merrill retaining a minority interest. Later, when Pierce ran short of capital in 1940, it was Winthrop Smith, a co-founder with Charles Merrill and Edmund Lynch, who engineered the re-merger with Pierce. Then Fenner & Beane was acquired to create the nation's largest "wire house". Investment banking had gone by the boards until the 1979 acquisition of White, Weld. Being then already interested in Wall Street history, I was intrigued when I saw the name Win Smith on the list of CEO candidates for London. Win Smith, a direct descendent and name sake of a co-founder of the firm, had been running a domestic retail division. I told Jerry, I would plump for him.

"Wrong choice," said Jerry. "He's a retail man. He has no international investment banking experience."

"Neither does anyone else in this shop," I replied. "We've got plenty of investment bankers in London. I need someone who can manage people in a large organisation. And his name will go down well in the City. We love founding family names."

Jerry would not be moved and strongly recommended Jean Rousseau, who was running the municipal bond department, on the grounds that fixed income, i.e., the Eurobond business was our biggest. I should have insisted. Despite his outstanding qualities, Rousseau was the wrong choice, but I wasn't going to pick a fight in these early days. Win Smith ended up in charge of China, years later – after my time.

Early in my tenure, I had a call from Cob Stenham, who, having failed to land the top job at Unilever, had accepted the chairmanship of a fast expanding Bankers Trust in London. Cob had been finance director of Unilever for a number of years – and a tough nut to crack from an investment banker's point of view. He was so wedded to Lazard that, if he reluctantly accepted an invitation to lunch with a competitor house, he would put on dark glasses and a slouch hat to go there, fearful someone from Lazard might spot him. Now he said, "Come to lunch and we can exchange ideas as to how to cope with those idiots at head office in New York." I wondered how long he would last. I did not anticipate great difficulty, despite my early disagreement with Kenny. This was because I found everybody so nice and supporting – from Bill Schreyer on down. Perhaps Dan Tully was not so warm, but he was an Irishman, and not that partial to things English. I think he thought I had gone a bit too native in London. On the other hand, his wife Grace was truly gracious. I had an early lesson in Merrill Lynch culture. On my accession, Merrill was mostly lodged in a lugubrious building off City Road, which had been decorated under David Montagu, in a style which would have made his old partner Louis Franck turn in his Gstaad chalet. Various parts of the firm were scattered in other buildings and so a consolidation was imperative. Several new locations were being canvassed, but, if Michael von Clemm had already decamped from CSFB to join us, the choice would have been Canary Wharf, even before a yellow bird could tweet. My old friend is known for many things, but one is his passionate belief in the "new City on the Thames" for which his First Boston colleague G. Ware Travelstead had conceived the notion, and gone bust as its first developer. I recall Michael calling me at EBC to ask about the City Clearing. "Does an authorised bank have to have a physical presence within the clearing zone?" was his question. This was a theoretical zone in the City within which interbank transactions were cleared, which had originally involved bills as collateral. I doubted it still existed, but I suggested he ask the Bank. He was asking me because I had obtained the banking licence for White, Weld & Co., Limited which CSFB had inherited. This was my first inkling Michael was aiming to move CSFB to Canary Wharf. At Merrill, two locations had been short listed. One was certainly Canary Wharf, as Olympia & York, its current developers, was a major Merrill Lynch client. Paul Reichmann, the senior of the three orthodox Jewish brothers who had founded O & Y, had been on too me like a shot, and had taken me in his motor yacht to visit Canary Wharf – then only about a quarter finished. What struck me was the architecture, by Skidmore, Owens & Merrill – no relation. It was neoclassical, but very Mussolini style – in fact, rather fascist. Canada Square, with several finished buildings, featured skyscrapers in heavy concrete, with imposing architraves and other imperialistic features. Apparently, the Reichmann's were not architecturally sensitive and had not noticed. The other alternative was a new complex at Ropemaker Place, near the Barbican development. I was persuaded that, whereas investment banking clients of a now, well-established house like CSFB might hack all the way out to Canary Wharf, Merrill should not carry any handicap weight. I also felt that I was there as a City personality, and, therefore, we should stay in the Square Mile. But the fact is that tearing me way from the City would have been like tearing Jeffrey Barnard away from Soho. Came the big moment to make the presentation of my choice to the global executive committee in New York, and I had my first lesson in Merrill Lynch culture. Ropemaker Place was a skyscraper with an interesting feature. It could easily be divided vertically, with two banks of lifts serving each side. I kept to last the culminating, and, I thought, devastatingly convincing argument. "And if we ever have to retrench," I intoned, "the building allows for easy sub-letting." A gasp of inward breathtaking, was followed by a stony silence, and people in the audience suddenly staring at their shoes. I had clearly made what is known in New York vernacular as a major "boo boo". Merrill Lynch does not "retrench" it was explained to me afterwards. Merrill Lynch does not go backwards. Merrill Lynch only goes forward, etc., etc. What had sunk Montagu/Craven in the eyes of New York was their correct observation that Merrill Lynch did not have the resources on its own to fulfil their London ambitions. Nevertheless, we did go to Ropemaker Place, and Merrill did sublet some years later. I don't doubt Canary Wharf has been a success, but I still think it's an awful place. Padraic Fallon, much lamented editor of *Euromoney*, sponsored a bust of Michael von Clemm, to mark his championship of Canary Wharf, and I attended its unveiling in Canada Square. I looked around, at the forest of pedestrian skyscrapers, the airport-style shopping malls, and thought to myself "this is dreadful – a poor man's Wall Street. Give me the real City, any day".

My remit importantly included providing strategic advice to Merrill Lynch, to help guide it through the smoke and craters caused by Big Bang. It must be remembered that, although the focus was overwhelmingly on London, what was laughingly referred to as "deregulation" was also happening on the Continent. Various restrictive practices which had protected indigenous institutions from foreign competition were being removed, allowing the likes of Merrill Lynch to participate directly in domestic capital markets. In fact, not only was there little interest in doing so, other than in London, but both Frankfort and Paris maintained protectionist equivalents of non-tariff barriers – and have continued to do so ever since. If the jury is out on the true consequences of Big Bang, it will probably stay retired because, the world has changed so dramatically in other respects, that it is impossible to isolate Big Bang causes from others. David Kynaston quotes a reflection on Big Bang by Nicholas Goodison, which I consider so apt that I will repeat it here. "The real cause I think was the abolition of exchange controls in 1979, because that completely freed international capital markets as far as London was concerned. It made it possible for far more attention to be paid to overseas markets by domestic investors. It forced members firms of the Stock Exchange to think more constructively about overseas markets than they had before. It freed capital movement, and it really was not possible, after 1979 for the Stock Exchange restrictions to remain in force if you think about it historically. Other markets abroad, other practitioners, were going to operate under freer rules, different rules. So change was inevitable from 1979 onwards ..." The trigger point for Big Bang was the Office of Fair Trading threat against the Stock Exchange, as fixed commissions, dual capacity, and the prohibition of foreign controlled members was deemed monopolistic. No one really considered that a monopolistic, members co-operative might well be the best formula for the maintenance of liquidity in a securities market – as long as unfettered competition exists between members. Was it all necessary? Fixed commissions would have gone anyway, as they had done in New York. Dual capacity would have ended as jobbers were unable to raise sufficient capital. Single capacity members would then have sought outside investors and probably incorporated, again as they had in New York. The City, as a whole, had already shown a capacity to evolve, with the development of Euromarkets, and the Stock Exchange, perhaps a bit slow at the start, would have done so the real consequence of Big Bang was an abrupt and catastrophic change in ethos. As foreign banks began to buy up Stock Exchange member firms, and merchant banks, in a lemming like fashion, not really with any fixed objective in view, the partners took the money and ran. Overnight the City was denuded of people with experience, ethics and a commitment to the reputation of both firm, and City as a whole. The retiring guard was replaced by a combination of foreign and domestic practitioners out for a quick kill, and entirely disinterested in the reputation and strategic future of whatever franchise they might be temporarily be hosted by.

As preparation for the enabling legislation, and the alphabet soup of self-regulating bodies to be created, gathered momentum, the question of the Eurobond market soon arose. Its participants did not belong to any existing body, Stock Exchange, Accepting Houses Committee, Issuing Houses Association – or whatever. It was a big, noisy, fast growing, homeless orphan. Whilst still at EBC, I had been contacted by Whitehall and invited to join the board of the Securities and Investments Board – SIB, which was to be the overreaching, statutory authority to regulate the self-regulators. Rather strangely, the invitation was withdrawn as soon as I told them I was joining Merrill Lynch. I had assumed I was to represent the Eurobond market, not the consortium banks, which were falling like ninepins. A committee of Euro-wise men was formed under the able chairmanship of Ian Steers of Wood Gundy. We assumed we might be the board in waiting for a Euro SRO, a self-regulating organisation. It was presumed, correctly, there would be one for the domestic securities market, one for the investment managers, one for futures dealers, and one for the amusingly entitled "independent financial advisors", as unit trust mongers liked to call themselves. No one seemed to reflect, least of all members of the Thatcher Government, that this community represented the weakest link in the chain that was to bind the process of capital formation to the public – creating Margaret Thatcher's dream of a share-owning democracy. Untrained and poorly qualified, IFAs were hardly independent, as they were paid by the unit trust industry. The public liked the idea that their "advice" was free, not appreciating that free advice is worth exactly what you pay for it. On the Steers committee we struggled to lobby for inclusion, or exclusion, of clauses, in the new Bill which would accommodate the particular features of the Eurobond market. It was then we had the all-night session with Michael Howard on the vexed issue of market stabilisation, through the "green shoe" over-allotment process. Ian Steers, and many on the committee were in favour of an SRO specifically for the Euromarkets, and discussions between the AIBD and the International Primary Market Association – IPMA, to this end, promised to end the tense relations between the two sides of the market. Ian Steers, according to David Kynaston, was quoted as saying "we want to manufacture our own set of clothes". Steers was not the only Euro-practitioner to be highly suspicious of a solution joining the Euro-securities world with the Stock Exchange. And on his side, Nicholas Goodison, the

Stock Exchange chairman was not keen on a combined solution. It was not so much Eurobonds which troubled him, but the prospect of an emerging euro-equity market challenging the Stock Exchange's dominant position in equities. Finally both sides backed down from earlier positions, and it was decided to merge the domestic and international securities markets in London, from a regulatory point of view. A single SRO was to be established covering members of the Stock Exchange and of the AIBD/IPMA, although there was hardly an existing regulatory parity between the agencies. AIBD/IPMA were more trade associations than regulators, whereas the Stock Exchange wielded serious disciplinary powers. So Stock Exchange members ended up being regulated twice – rather unfair.

Governance arrangements for the new SRO – to be dubbed The Securities Association, were soon agreed. The chairman of TSA was to be a deputy chairman of the Stock Exchange and vice-versa. As it happens, Nicholas Goodison, chairman of the Stock Exchange, declined the honour, but his co-deputy Graham Ross-Russell, assumed the position. Nicholas was not very comfortable with the "euro trash", although we were certainly not even a majority of foreigners and the new TSA chairman, Andrew Large, was a proper "Brit". All this was momentous, in a way, as the separation between foreign and domestic securities activity was now ended, and the internationalisation of the City was virtually complete. The creation of the London International Financial Futures Exchange – LIFFE, was to be a culminating event. The public knew little of financial futures and Michael Jenkins, the first CEO, and its PR consultant Christopher Morgan embarked on an education programme. Some in the City didn't know much either and traditionalists were alarmed by the multi-coloured blazers worn by the floor traders. LIFFE was the last building block to slip into place and confirm the City's unchallenged ascendancy. Soon after all this hectic banging, I was still in my dingy office at Merrill's old building, when Andrew Large, the first chairman of TSA, came to see me to tell me Swiss Bank Corporation, where he was the major player in London, had asked him to move to Basle and join the managing board – an unprecedented appointment in Switzerland. Andrew felt, rightly, that this was an irresistible opportunity. But he would have to relinquish the chairmanship of the TSA, and the other senior members there considered that I should replace him. I said I was flattered and would have to check with New York. Of course, it meant I would also become a co-deputy chairman, with Ross-Russell, of the Stock Exchange. Although it was to be held against me later on, New York, from Schreyer through Kenny, was enthusiastic, considering these appointments as confirmation of the wisdom of their choice of London chairman. Indeed, Schreyer served on the board of the New York Stock Exchange. I expect poor Nicholas Goodison was less impressed. A proper English public school boy like Andrew Large, even though engaged in this funny business of Eurobonds, was one thing, but somebody with the extraordinary name of Stanislas Yassukovich as a deputy chairman of The Stock Exchange, London?

How he must have cursed Big Bang and all its workings. On top of it all, it was decided to abandon that simple, world renowned name, in favour of a new appellation: "The International Stock Exchange of the United Kingdom and the Republic of Ireland". Yes – the Republic of Ireland! My American friends marvelled at the fact that the two parts of the Emerald Isle were at violent loggerheads, but shared a common stock exchange. In fact it was to be some years before Dublin decided to have their own. Nicholas was to suffer another, heart stopping shock – lasting only moments fortunately. Still in my dingy office, I had a call from Steve Hamermann, Merrill's general counsel in New York. We knew each other well, having been partners at White, Weld. Steve had spent a few years at the New York office of the SEC, before assuming at Merrill Lynch the same position he had held at White, Weld. He had some bad news. Our head of Mergers & Acquisitions in London, an Israeli called Nahum Vaskevitch, had been caught insider dealing. Nahum came from a well-known Israeli family and was heir to a tobacco fortune. He had served in Mossad, the Israeli Intelligence Service. He was a skilled M & A practitioner. The M & A departments in head office and London participated in a daily conference call in which they exchanged information on deals in progress, and transactions being solicited. With a non-Merrill Lynch partner-in-crime in New York, Nahum was trading on the confidential information.

"What do I do?" I asked.

"Fire him. Seal his office. Inform the Fraud Squad. I'm sending a team, including NYSE people, to handle the investigation. It's an open and shut case," said Steve. His assistant for International, Don Gurshuny was already on his way.

The NYSE had insisted an immediate announcement be made, and so the story duly appeared on the Reuters screen. Jeffrey Knight, the Stock Exchange's chief executive, read the text at speed, almost fainted, but rushed into Nicholas Goodison's office, and gasped out, "Our new deputy chairman has been arrested for insider dealing!"

Nicholas turned to the screen, read it more carefully and said, "Vaskevitch! Jeffrey, Vaskevitch! – Not Yassukovich! It's the head of M & A at Merrill, not the chairman."

Sighs of relief. But not a happy start for my tenure. I had reached Vaskevitch on his car telephone to fire him, and he had said, rather lamely, "There is an explanation." At his trial, he claimed he was funding a highly secret operation for Mossad.

I passed the first protocol test. Andrew Large had decided the TSA board should conduct itself in a less formal way than the Council of the Stock Exchange, which met in a sort of amphitheatre, whilst the TSA board just met around a table in large room. Both bodies were housed in the Stock Exchange building. At my first meeting, I could sense most were wondering if I would rise to my feet on speaking, which the custom was. I duly did. It must be admitted, the custom tended to make council meetings a bit ponderous. But I was privileged to be sitting, or standing, amongst the last and distinguished representatives of the traditional Stock Exchange: Andrew Hugh Smith, Nick Assheton, George Nissan, Peter Stevens, Richard Lawson, Peter Stanley, Peter Wills, Ian Salter and my co-deputy chairman Graham Ross Russell. The firm of each and every one was soon to be swallowed up, merged or just gone, within a short period. Big Bang came into force in waves. The first major event, known as "Little Bang" was the admission of foreign firms, and the first two were Merrill Lynch and Nomura Securities of Japan. Nicholas had arranged a major press conference, with television cameras, in the gallery overlooking the floor, which was enjoying its last moments before its desertion in favour of electronic trading. Takahashi-san, Nomura's man in London was given first voice and he proceeded to recite a paean in honour of Merrill Lynch, expressing appreciation at the joy of joining the London Stock Exchange on the same day as Merrill Lynch, the firm Nomura admired most in the world, the firm on which it had modelled itself, and so on and so forth. Of course, I felt I had to return the compliment and so threw bouquets at Takahashi-san. Nicholas became rather annoyed.

"I was rather hoping you would both talk about the International Stock Exchange," he said, gagging somewhat on the new name. We proceeded on a ceremonial visit to the floor – cameras following.

The jobbers and brokers all began executing mock Japanese bows, chanting, "Ah so! Ah so!" Nicholas was embarrassed. It was to be a last opportunity for the traditional horse play on the floor of the exchange. The burning issue, as the new world began to dawn on the council of the International Stock Exchange, was how to defend its traditional equity business, and incorporate non U.K. equity trading through the new electronic trading system known as SEAQ for Stock Exchange Automatic Quotations. An international version was to be introduced which could be accessed by nonmember firms, but only those with a presence in London. Much of the paranoia exhibited by the old guard was due to fear of the rise of a euro-equity market, which, as David Kynaston reports, seemed imminent after a successful euro-equity issue for Nestlé, by CSFB. But the reports of the birth of a euro-equity market, like the reports of Mark Twain's death, were greatly exaggerated. In 1979, in a speech at a conference, I had predicted that such a market would soon develop, but I believe I also invented a phrase to describe the major impediment to this happy event - "flow back". This was the tendency of any block of equities placed outside its home market to gradually revert to its natural centre of liquidity. Morgan Stanley had attempted a euro placing of a large block of General Motors shares at one point, and these had almost immediately flowed back to New York, leaving the Euro underwriters with their commissions as a profit, but frustrating the attempt to create a stable base of shareholders outside the U.S. If truth be told, exactly the same thing happened with the Nestlé issue. Flow back did not occur with Eurobond issues because these had no national liquidity pool to act as the magnet. So a true euro-equity new issue market ever really took off, not even later when mega privatizations were underwritten with national blocks separately managed. The stock always came home. My 1979 prediction was wrong, but, ironically, included the explanation of why it would be wrong.

Through all this orgy of change and reform, the Stock Exchange missed a huge, financial world changing opportunity for the second time in modern history – the first having been its failure to recognise and incorporate the Eurobond market back in the '60s. As the representative of the foreign interest, I pleaded with my colleagues on the council to allow foreign brokers and banks without a London presence to join the new exchange, pointing out that it would be the simplest thing in the world to place a SEAQ terminal on the desk of any securities dealer on the Continent. The old guard was horrified. How would we be able to monitor the financial condition and compliance of foreign houses except through a physical presence in London? I pointed out the existence of international accounting firms, with offices in every major Continental centre, which we could mandate to provide financial oversight, and the fact that the Eurobond market relied successfully on authorisation procedures in all EU countries, plus Switzerland. I was butting my head against a stone wall. I argued that we could scoop the pool in Europe. Everyone would have to join. London would become the preferred place of listing for European companies. We would become to Europe what the NYSE was to America. The national stock exchanges would scream blue murder, but would have no recourse in view of Single Market legislation in Europe. Just as regional exchanges had slowly disappeared in the U.S., so would they in Europe. None of my arguments prevailed. One lovely old boy said to me, "You know, we like to have the top chaps in a member firm into lunch from time to time. Helps us to get a feel of the firm. How could we do that with member firms in Paris, Frankfurt or Rome?" It seemed the concern was whether a partner in a Continental firm would know which fork to pick up. The other bone of contention within the council was the vexed question of the degree of transparency which was needed to protect market makers on SEAQ, who would be largely the ex-jobbers. In the old floor based system, broker's order books were not disclosed and volumes of trades not visible. The difference between jobbing as it was, and market making, as it was to be, is extremely subtle. The difference between proprietary trading and market making is a bit more straightforward. I was guided for my input to council debates on these issues, by advice from my senior equity trader at Merrill in London, and colleagues in New York, throughout various reforms on the NYSE, including the end of fixed commissions, the floor had been maintained as the trading centre, with specialist performing roughly the same function as jobbers in London. But so called "upstairs trading" had grown in importance and large block trades were handled partially on the floor and partially on dealing desks in members firms. At Merrill we practised what was known as facilitation trading, in other words we took positions to facilitate the execution of a large trade, rather than primarily to make a turn for our own account. Order flow was the watch word at Merrill Lynch. How the world was to change, as own account trading came to dominate, clients became counterparties, and the distinction between agency and principal functions became blurred – and eventually redundant. The problem of transparency in the cash market had haunted the traded options market for years. In fact, it never took off and the poor chap who represented it on the council was an object of derision whenever he rose to complain about the fact that you cannot trade options successfully if the cash market is not transparent. But now there was LIFFE, and an obvious solution was to take traded options away from the Stock Exchange, give it to LIFFE, and hope the new trading system at the Stock Exchange would increase transparency. LIFFE had been quickly populated by traders from Chicago, where all the American futures markets are based. In fact LIFFE provoked a second American invasion of the City. A committee was set up under the Bank of England, who very much favoured this move, to negotiate the merger of the traded options market with LIFFE. "You represent us, Stani," said Nicholas to me. "You'll know how to deal with those cowboys from Chicago." Nicholas shared a general disdain amongst traditional stockbrokers for people who dealt in "those funny derivatives".

Back at Merrill Lynch, the move to Ropmaker Place was handled smoothly as I had a large specialist group, supplemented by people from New York. Schreyer had suggested the formation of an International Advisory Board, a fashionable concept pioneered by David Rockefeller at Chase. The ability of modern corporate management to invent excuses for travel and well catered meetings is rivalled only by that of the political class. Schreyer and I were to be the only internal members, but there would be one or two of our main board, non-executive directors, including a retired Commandant of the U.S. Marine Corps. As a retired corporal, I looked forward to his company. I suggested Michel François-Poncet of Paribas, and Arnold Weinstock . This last was a cheeky suggestion as Weinstock was known to be extremely close to Warburgs and to never accept invitations to join external boards – whether advisory or no. Schreyer said "give it a try". Michel François-Poncet was no problem and said he was delighted. "*J'adore Wall Street*", he told me. To my utter amazement, Weinstock accepted, and he turned out to be the most useful member. I wish I had been able to record his summaries of the political and economic situation in the U.K., which was his star turn. He could have been a stand-up comic, and would have the board in stitches. But, as Rope maker preparations were in course, I had a call from Arnold in my old office. "Which telephone exchange system have you selected for Ropemaker Place?" he asked. I was taken aback.

"I'll have to ask – I haven't the foggiest," I replied – possibly less flippantly than I recall.

"Well, you had better and it had better be GEC equipment, or I shall be greatly embarrassed as a member of your Advisory Board."

Fortunately, it was, and I was truly impressed that the Managing Director of GEC, perhaps the most celebrated industrialist of the land, should be personally concerned over a relatively minor order. I didn't believe the bit about embarrassment, as no one would have known. I got on very well with Bill Schreyer. On one of his early visits to my office, he handed me a small envelope and said, "This is a little welcome note I like to give new people. Put it in a drawer and read it when I'm gone." I did so and when I opened the envelope, it contained a printed message: "No one said it was going to be easy". Soon after my appointment it was decided to hold a main board meeting of Merrill Lynch, Inc. in London. This was another fashion amongst U.S. Banks, before the lawyers told them to be concerned about "mind and matter" implications in which corporate domicile can be determined for tax purposes by the location of board meetings. Not only the whole board, but their wives and other hangers on, such as Schreyer's personal physician, arrived in the firm's corporate jets, a Gulfstream IV and a Canadair. I lent my driver Dennis, an ex-soldier, to one of the wives.

"Oh, I just loved your bodyguard," she gushed to me at dinner that evening. "You were so kind to lend him." Merrill in New York was terrified of kidnapping at the time, as there had been incidents in the Street. We were supposed to share this concern. We had one ex-Metropolitan senior policeman as our "security consultant". Dennis had found a licence number "MLE-1" and wanted to put it on our Daimler.

Our security man got wind and said, "Absolutely not! New York will have a fit."

Dennis Davis had been my driver at EBC. A boy soldier who later served in the Transport Corps, he had driven General Montgomery when the great man was at SHAEF in Paris. When he had a major conference and AGM of the AIBD in Paris, Dennis insisted on taking the Daimler over by ferry so that he could drive me around, claiming he knew the town like the back of his hand. He did, but he drove with English courtesy, stopping at the pedestrian crossings, much to the astonishment of the Parisians. My PA Joyce Anderson, who was pure Morningside Edinburgh, had worked for Jack Hennessey at CSFB. When she left to join me, Hennessey convened an emergency meeting of his executive committee, to discuss the risks of information leakage – of which, of course, there was none whatsoever, Joyce being the soul of probity. His sensitivity was understandable, as CSFB had just suffered a major loss of key people to Merrill Lynch, just before my arrival.

The security concern in New York was very real. I was just settling in when I had a panicky call from Schreyer. Beirut was suffering one of its regular blow ups, with all hell breaking loose in every direction. "You've got to close Beirut, Stani! Right now! Get them all out! Charter a private jet! Move them to Athens!"

Rising to attention at my desk and saluting, I shouted "Yes, sir!" down the phone, thinking for a moment I was back in the Marine Corps. It wasn't their safety, he was worried about – it was kidnapping. I called my head of private clients Macram Zaccour, as it happens a Christian Lebanese, and long term Merrill Lyncher. Macram was in charge of all our retail branches, two in London, and one in Paris, Amsterdam, Brussels, Frankfurt, Geneva, Monte Carlo, Madrid, Milan, Rome, Athens, Beirut, Kuwait City and Abu Dhabi. I relayed the order. "But we can't do that! They're making money hand over fist. They will refuse to go." Naturally, the Lebanese were queuing up to open accounts with gold, cash, and jewellery – anything to get their money out of a fast deteriorating situation. As we talked, Macram suggested we might force the non-Lebanese account executives to go, but we certainly couldn't force Lebanese citizens to leave their country. Macram was a very close personal friend of Bill Schreyer's. I persuaded him to go over my head – which he was always inclined to do anyway. He was able to placate Bill to some extent. We moved the non-Lebanese to Athens – the rest continued to coin it in Beirut, ducking gun fire where necessary. The other New York invasion was annually for Wimbledon. Bill Schreyer was tennis mad and two executive jets, filled with corporate heads, would arrive for the corporate entertainment event of the year. Our public affairs lady was forced into the black market to pay outrageous prices for centre court tickets for the final, as we had never ordered enough in the normal fashion. I was expected to attend at our hospitality tent, when I would have been happier in the office, calling those clients who were not at Wimbledon. The worse aspect was that, for the final, after the slap-up lunch in our tent, the guests sat and drank on, watching the tennis on the large television screen we had installed, leaving their expensive seats empty.

Soon after my arrival I was informed that I was entitled to an ADC – just like a colonial governor general. A short list, with photographs, of eligible young men, lurking within the bowels of my vast dominion, was produced. Without hesitation, I chose Oliver Stanley, an ex-guards officer who was in one of the West End private client offices. Often treated with contempt by investment bankers, the best place to learn the investment business is as a private client stock broker. If nothing else, you learn to deal with the eccentricities of clients. Of course, I speak of the time when clients were important. I also reckoned that if I was to have an ADC, he should be soldier. This turned out to be one of the best appointments I ever made. Oliver was of extraordinary assistance in all matters, and had the ability to get on with everyone, both in house and with clients. I am sure he became more popular than his boss. I didn't let him linger in this subservient position any longer than necessary and sent him off into the mainstream of a Merrill Lynch career. Oliver succeeded in everything he turned his hand to, eventually going on to found one of the top executive search firms in the City. Meanwhile Jean Rousseau and I struggled to make matrix management work. I had assumed that Jean's long held relationships with his peer group in New York would facilitate matters. After all, he was a Merrill Lynch man through and through. This turned out not to be the case and relations with the product heads were unfortunately even more strained. It could be that a certain jealousy existed, and envy – over the fact that Jean had landed this plum job in International, the division where the glamour and limelight were now focussed. The Merrill Lynch bull, having galloped down Wall Street in a famous TV commercial, was now off to enjoy the pastures, and cows, of the wider world. I was less vulnerable in this respect, because I was seen as a temporary ornament that could be discarded once the firm was solidly placed in the City establishment. I did not represent a threat to the upper tier management, whereas Jean did, and, in retrospect, I think some of these product heads were out to sabotage him. But for now, we were like a producer/director team staging an opera with a cast full of prima donnas. Amongst these were two star dealers that had been part of a recent semi-mass exit from CSFB in favour of Merrill. Steven Licht and Caleb Watts were highly productive highflyers who resisted any attempt at discipline, whether imposed locally or from New York. The firm had resisted joining the vogue for acquiring London stock broking houses and merchant banks, but had bought a small gilt edge jobbing firm. The former partner/chief dealer there, having been a minnow in the gilts market, had now decided to become a whale. He spent his time going over our heads to have his limit excesses sanctioned by the product head in New York. It would have been easier if he had been busting his limits profitably, but he managed to run up persistent losses. Investment banking, under Franzi, was making good progress and diversifying rapidly, but overall we were loss making, as the large establishment investment which had been made quickly, was unable to produce a positive return as quickly.

The private client division was ably managed by Zaccour and the head of retail in New York, who was entirely benign. On the whole the branch managers were experienced and loyal. I was sent on several grand tours of the branches with Zaccour, who appreciated the fact that I was sympathetic and supportive of this business, whereas I suspect Montagu/Craven had not been. Where I failed was to persuade Merrill Lynch to enter the retail business in the U.K. and eventually on the continent. The franchise was strictly concerned with American securities, for which there has always been a huge appetite in Europe. Merrill had launched a brilliant retail product in the U.S. Called a CMA account: a single statement showed your securities portfolio, your credit card and chequing account, and your small business loan, which the firm offered to self-employed clients. A Canadian $ version had been launched but I was unable to persuade the firm to lunch a £ Sterling version. After all Merrill Lynch Limited had a banking license, there were credit card processing suppliers we could use, we were members of the London Stock Exchange, and we had a highly recognisable trademark. Actually Mark Weinburg of Hambro Life once told me he had been so interested in this product that he had opened a CMA account in New York to see just how it worked.

I had a generous sponsorship budget, and when I learned that the Olympic gold medal winner, three-day event champion, Mark Todd had lost his sponsor after the Los Angeles Olympics. I wrote to Todd, a New Zealander, and offered to step into the breach. He replied that he was very grateful but could not promise that the horse Charisma, on which he had won his gold medal, would still be fit for the Tokyo Olympics in four years' time. Charisma was an extraordinary horse, at 15.3 hands so small a half-sister was a polo pony. He carried long-legged Mark Todd, his feet almost scraping the ground, over Olympic cross country courses as though he had been 16 hands. I told him we would be sponsoring him, not his horse. Although it was my call, New York expressed concern. I had not known it was policy not to sponsor individual athletes, as they were more likely to be involved in scandalous behaviour that a whole team. Todd turned out to be an excellent sponsoree, carrying the Merrill logo all over the equestrian world. He would send me handwritten, detailed accounts, after an event, apologising for having made a mistake at the sixth fence, or whatever. Of course the sponsorship return value would have been greater if we had gone retail in England.

I found myself both a beneficiary and amused spectator, as the leakage at CSFB continued, with the most senior defection to date being my old friend Michael Dobbs-Higginson, who had joined Merrill Lynch and be made chairman of Asia Pacific, based in Hong Kong, and so become a fellow governor general. We were in touch daily, as he would call me from his car going home at the end of the Hong Kong day and I was in my car heading for the start of my London day – which was unconscionably early due to the Merrill Lynch breakfast meeting habit. Michael was a great producer at CSFB and he and Michael von Clemm had reinvented the business of client stalking at the annual IMF/World Bank meetings, where finance ministers gathered to attend lavish receptions, with groaning buffet tables and ice sculptured centre pieces – whilst the third world starved. Von Clemm and Dobbs-Higginson, and their acolytes, would communicate by walkie-talkie, tracking their hapless prey, and their crackling messages could be heard by those nearby, "The minister is approaching the far corner of the room. Move in quickly and one of the Michaels will be there in a minute."

A young associate would rush to confront the victim, as he struggled with a cream cheese and caviar sandwich, and glass of bubbly.

"Oh, Minister! It's Jones of CSFB. My chairman would like a word – and here he is, just arriving."

Many a nation found itself issuing a new kind of Eurobond, after such a contrived encounter. I was never a wholehearted participant in this annual gig, even in my White Weld days when our star performer was Ogden White. When George Moore retired from First National City, he joined White, Weld as a limited partner and I was assigned to carry his bag. He once produced a great throwaway line at the IMF/World Bank meetings in Washington. A Latin American finance minister was approaching down the corridor and an em-

bracao was clearly immanent. George began madly leafing through his little black book. "His name! What's his name? I saved his currency once – I know him well!" George Moore was a force of nature. He invited me to his house in Soto Grande once. He must have been 80. I was kept awake by a baby crying next door. It was no grandchild – it was George's latest. But I never enjoyed these networking meetings. They made me feel like a lady in fishnet stockings, twirling a little bag on a finger, standing under a street lamp with a cigarette dangling from carmine lips. The only similar occasion I enjoyed at Merrill Lynch was due to Dobbs-Higginson's showmanship and was a meeting of the African Development Bank in Harare. Regional development banks aped the World Bank event and investment bankers turned up to do some finance minister hunting at the regional level. Dobbs-Higginson was a close friend of Babacar Ndiaye, the Senegalese president of the ADB, and we decided to stage a Merrill Lynch reception with a difference. Most banks just gave boring old cocktail parties at the main hotel, in the case of Harare being Miekles. "Why don't we do the reception as a lunch at Lowdale, Dinnie's family farm? It's only 45 minutes from the centre of town, we can lay on a bus – although they've all got limmos," suggested Dobbs-Higginson.

We were both actually staying a Lowdale, and Michael was billeted in the now preserved rondavel in the garden where Bomber Harris had lived during his apprenticeship with Dinnie's grandfather. My brother-in-law Mickey thought it a splendid idea and could he invite a few chums? Well, a great lunch was laid on, with tables on the veranda and on the lawn, and a solid selection of African finance ministers and central bankers turned up, curious to have a look at a typical, European owned, commercial farm. Babacar came himself, which was a great compliment to Michael, as the President clearly had to strictly ration his attendance at such events. Most of the compound turned out to gawk. We reckoned we'd wiped the eye of the competition – hospitality wise. I can't remember whether Merrill ever led managed an issue for the African Development Bank – but I jolly well hope so.

The IMF/World Bank jamboree is held every fifth year away from Washington in an alternating region and it was in Seoul, soon after my arrival at ML. Jerry Kenney led the usual large delegation. At one point, he took me to a bench in the middle of a park, and glancing around to ensure no Korean correspondent of the *Financial Times* or *Euromoney* was lurking, whispered to me, "This is top secret. No one knows except Schreyer, me, and now you. We're talking to Michael von Clemm." Kenney glanced around again, to see if a passing jogger might have heard. "But it's up to you. If you are against – it's off. You are our number one international star and if you think Michael might be a problem for you, we won't go ahead."

"Jerry! How could it possibly be a problem?" I said, thinking it well might be. "Michael is my oldest friend. We grew up together. We were in the same club at Harvard. I recruited him to White, Weld where we were colleagues for years. He is godfather to our youngest son. Dinnie is godmother to his youngest daughter. I would have to put my hand in the fire to go against him." I was referring to a club custom, Jerry would know nothing about.

"He would be New York based as chairman of International," Jerry said, showing relief.

"A sort of *capo di capos,*" I said, thinking of the *mafia.*

"No! No!" protested Jerry; "Equal level as the other chairmen. Everyone reports to me."

I was not all that surprised. CSFB was haemorrhaging. Michael had brought in Hans Georg Rudloff from Kidder Peabody where he had become a great mover and shaker in the Eurobond market. But the addition of this strong personality exacerbated tensions already existing between Craven, Hennessy and von Clemm. The stars were departing from a franchise which had been the MGM of the business. Genillard was retired, Mulford was gone, and Craven was to leave with Phillip Sears, to create a very well-timed boutique, Phoenix Securities which arranged most of the City marriages, and then advised on the subsequent divorces. David Reid Scott, Claus Labes from syndicate, soon David Potter, head of trading – the list went on. And so I was to be together again with my old friend. Lisa and the girls stayed in London, and Michael began to intensify his lifelong addiction to long distance travel. He was truly based in New York, but usually in the air. Jerry Kenney had told me he would be under strict instructions to ask for my permission to set foot in my territory; "I hereby give him blanket permission to visit his family in London," I said, humorously, but Jerry didn't see the joke. Merrill Lynch, like so many mega organisations, was hung up on elaborate protocols, and Jerry had difficulty understanding the working habits of people like Michael and me – brought up in a partnership environment, where we were not concerned with stepping on one another's toes. In fact, although I told Michael I would give him a nice office with all the trimmings at Ropemaker Place, he insisted on finding himself a West End office for his London visits, which, by a curious coincidence, was just around the corner from Le Gavroche, in Park Street.

When we were still in the old firm, Michael had put together a little group of backers for the two Roux brothers, Albert and Michel, who were leaving private service to set up a restaurant. Albert had been with the French Ambassador and Michel with Peter Cazalet, trainer to the Queen Mother's National Hunt horses. The two brothers cooked a pre-opening dinner for our little group, which included Edward Cazalet, Peter's son, Jan Bailey, Michael, me and one or two others. The Rouxs had bought a former spaghetti house in Lower Sloan Street, which was to be renamed *Le Gavroche,* and the place had not yet been redecorated by David Hicks. I remember the menu: *Soufflés Suissesses, Emincés de Veaux à L'Annnas, Bombe au Framboise avec Sucre Cheveux d'Ange*
. Le Gavroche became an iconic representative of a new wave of culinary awareness, first in London, and then throughout the land. A Thames-side restaurant, The Waterside Inn, with Michel in charge was opened in Bray. The

Roux Brothers were much acclaimed, had their own TV show, were amongst the first in England to be starred by Michelin, and had sons, each named after their uncle, who now preside in the two establishments. Michael became chairman of the group, its main promoter and a regular customer. Spin-offs, by former under chefs, which the brothers backed, were financed by syndicates put together by Michael – the most celebrated being *La Tante Claire* for ex Roux chef Pierre Koffman, where Dinnie was induced to be an investor. Unfortunately, Dinnie is not into *la haute cuisine*, being a roast, potato and two veg girl, so we rarely enjoy our life time discount. The Roux brothers and their enterprise became very much a part of Michael's life, and at his memorial service in London, Albert rendered an homage in which he suggested that on entering the Pearly Gates, Michael would probably ask to see the kitchens. One of Michael's many "bright young man" recruits, which by some strange chance were invariably Porcellian Club members, was Ian Molson, of the Canadian brewing dynasty. Molson remembers being summoned to the presence at CSFB, but kept outside to receive instructions from Michael's PA, Sue Teff. These were for him to remain in the office late, until Australia opened, as an important telex was due to arrive from Sidney which was to be hand delivered by Molson to the Chairman, who was dining at *Le Gavroche.* "Where's *Le Gavroche*?" asked Molson, newly arrived from New York. The door to Michael's office was open, and he had heard this exchange.

"Where's *Le Gavroche!*" shouted Michael. *"You don't know where the* best restaurant in London is located?"

"I'm hardly likely to be able to afford to dine there on what you pay me," Molson shouted back.

Ian was never one to be intimidated. Michael certainly made a splash at Merrill Lynch, and his marketing budget enjoyed highly elastic limits. In fact, I don't think the firm had ever seen a programme of corporate entertainments quite like the one Michael showered on potential and existing clients. They were dominated by events one might describe as being in the realm of wildlife management. Grouse in Scotland, of course, but also partridge in Spain, quail in Georgia, wild turkey in Oklahoma, sand grouse in the Kalahari, duck in the Punjab, salmon in Scotland and in Iceland, black bear in Alaska. The more exotic the quarry and location, the better. Michael insisted I attend a good many of these expeditions. As he put it, Merrill's "Mr. Europe" has to be there. I must admit I didn't resist, as it was all coming out of his budget, rather than mine. On one week of quail shooting, I counted three Gulfstream 1Vs parked at the airport at Albany, Georgia, or "Albinny" as the locals call it. The only guest I knew was Fred Smith of Federal Express. Michael had a special PA, who had been with him at CSFB, just to organise corporate entertainment. Michael competed with Schreyer to rack up hours in the corporate jet and helicopter. But he brought in all manner of profitable clients. One of these, Massachusetts Mutual, one of America's largest insurers, topped the list of fees paid, one year. Kenny had told me that a few corporate clients in the U.S. were the wrong side of the Marmite divide, as far as von Clemm was concerned, and so I was to be the senior calling officer. Michael was not at all fussed about this, just as he had some very senior connections in Europe which I didn't know, and I was delighted to have him calling on these.

I had a memorable visit to one client on the "no von Clemm" list, and that was MacDonald's, and I was asked to pay a high level visit to its HQ in Oak Brook, just outside Chicago. I was delighted to pay calls with the Chicago office as it was the last resting place, one might say, of ex-White, Weld investment bankers, headed by the indomitable Brick Meers, who was still milking his extensive Chicago contacts well into his seventies. Off I went with a small delegation, but without Brick. "I don't want to cramp your style," he said.

The senior relationship officer had warned me that MacDonald's adopted a much laid back and informal style, and everyone was on a Christian name basis. On arrival we were given our name badges at security – mine with STAN, written in large letters. In the executive suite was the chairman and CEO, the CFO, the COO, the head of communications and one or two others. They also wore name badges with JOE, BILL, JACK, SAM, etc. and no hint as to their title. The conversation was made a bit difficult because I couldn't figure out who was who. Finally Joe, or maybe it was Bill, or Jack said, "OK, Stan, tell us how we are doing over there in Europe."

I had still not set foot in a MacDonald's, but I replied, "Brilliantly! Your locations are very well chosen, you seem to have maintained franchise discipline and quality. Even your French franchise is highly popular. Who would have guessed that?"

"Come on, Stan, there must be something you can criticize!" said one of the lads.

"Well, I think your sign in your main Vienna branch sticks out like a sore thumb. You are located in between the Schwarzenberg Place and the Imperial Hotel, the heart of classic Vienna – and I have heard a lot of negative comment."

"What! Hey! Bill, what's the name of our Austrian franchisee, Fritz? – Or Hans? – Something like that. Get him on the line, pronto!"

"But, Jack, its three o'clock in the morning in Vienna."

"Doesn't matter – phone him. Stan says we've got a signage problem."

Frantic action ensues. No one knows the country code for Austria. Whilst this is happening, I explain that highly decorated signs in wrought iron are a feature in that part of the world, and that an artisan could easily be found who would design a typical, hanging sign in wrought iron, incorporating the MacDonald's "M", perhaps in blue rather than red. By this time the hapless Hans has been woken up.

"Hans, we've got Stan here, who runs Merrill in Europe, and he says your sign is all wrong. It's gotta be in iron, or something... yes! That sounds good. Fix it, Hans. You can charge it to head office, not the franchise account."

The next time I was in Vienna, I saw a very elegant, wrought iron sign, with the "M" in the appropriate type style, neatly incorporated.

Dealing with New York provided endless challenges, but never more than with new initiatives, where the "not invented here" syndrome was prevalent. I was introduced to the most successful mutual fund sales company in Italy, which enjoys the highest personal savings rates in Europe. They were looking for a partner. I thought this could be of interest to Merrill Lynch Asset Management, which was highly autonomous and located in Princeton, New Jersey, next to the firm's training academy. Its most celebrated product was Merrill lynch Ready Asset Trust, the largest money market fund in the country. A public affairs lady in New York got wind of this and raised a fuss, claiming that anything in Italy was *mafia* connected – a strange position as we had two highly successful branches in Italy – in Milan and Rome. Fiat was a shareholder in the mutual funds company, and von Clemm, who knew Gianni Agnelli, threatened to have him call Schreyer. We did the deal. I hired an Italian called Adriano Dispenza from Northern Trust, a commercial banker, who became immediately an effective investment banker, stealing the Benneton account from Morgan Stanley, which had done the first equity initial public offering – we did the next. On my visit to its headquarters in Treviso, our Milan branch manager, a former racing driver, drove me from Malpensa airport with my eyes shut tight. Adriano also landed the Luxotica account, the premier maker of spectacle frames and one of Italy's great growth companies.

The principle event of historical importance during my period at ML – apart from Big Bang, that is – was privatisation, and Margaret Thatcher's dream of turning Great Britain into a share owning democracy. She succeeded in creating a home owning democracy by forcing council house sales, but I fear her next great initiative failed. I would cite three principle reasons: a public which had not been educated in the risk/reward aspects of equity investment, a City which had no experience in large scale distribution of common shares, and, in any case favoured the collective investment scheme alternative, and a government which had no idea of either of these realities. The prime minister's principle advisor on the methodology of executing her privatisation dream was Michael Richardson, a grammar schoolboy who had joined the Establishment, first at Cazenove and then at Rothschild, a fact which endeared him to Mrs Thatcher. In general the City insisted on using the "offer for sale" technique which almost always results in miss-pricing on an offering. Raising equity in the U.K. bore little resemblance to the process of equity capital formation in the U.S. The deeply discounted rights issue was the favourite technique for capitalising British business, due largely to an institutional obsession with dilution. I used to argue the point with institutional investors, and my favourite example was an imaginary tennis club. "Say a tennis club has five courts and one hundred members," I would predicate. "So that's a court for very twenty members – who don't all play at once. Say the club decides to build a sixth court and invites twenty new members to join; is that dilutive?"

"Yes!" says my institutional friend;

"But there are still twenty members per court," I plead.

"It's still dilution, unless the existing members are first offered a double membership to finance the new court. They should have the benefit of a larger number of courts for the same number of members."

I thought – no wonder there are so few growth companies in Britain. In fact, the first privatisation was for a growth company Amersham International, a small issue which Rothschild grossly underpriced, producing an immediate premium in the aftermarket and red faces in the cabinet – the reddest being that of Nick Ridley, who I first met at dinner in his Cotswold constituency. It was just before an election. "I suppose the City will vote Labour as usual," he said.

"I thought the City was Conservative." I was a neophyte in such matters. "No, it votes Labour, because Labour always uses taxpayer's money to clean up the City's messes."

No doubt this attitude explains the reception we received when invited to dinner by Nicholas Ridley, together with Tom Manners of Lazard. I had decided to try and persuade HMG to use a different method of marketing the soon to be launched British Airways privatisation, namely the so-called "book building" offering, where pricing is based on indications of interest by the underwriting and selling group, in turn based on their canvassing prospective investors, à la Eurobond issue. I found an unusual ally in Tom Manners, an intellectual, and somewhat shy, managing director at Lazard. We were going to lobby Nick Ridley. On arrival in the corridor where the private dining rooms in the House of Commons are located, Tom hung his umbrella on a hook. At dinner we hardly had a chance to state our case as Nick launched into a bitter attack on the City, characterising its practitioners as a "bunch of bandits" who had robbed the public by miss-pricing the Amersham issue, etc., etc. Tom was shocked by the violence of the minister's tirade. As we emerged after dinner, Tom's umbrella was missing from the hook; "OH, my," said Nick Ridley, "how very strange. I can't believe someone has taken it."

"I'm not at all surprised," said Tom. "After all – we are in the House of Commons."

I had been interviewed at one point and mentioned to the press that I thought the offer for sale system inappropriate for large scale privatisation issues, and that the book building approach might be better. This drew a phone call from David Scholey of Warburgs. "Stani, you may be head of Merrill lynch in London, but you are also deputy chairman of the Stock Exchange and chairman of TSA, and you should not speak against established City procedures publicly. You're letting the side down. If you want to push American systems to tout for Merrill, you should get someone else to do it, not a City personality like yourself."

I had not expected to be ticked off by David Scholey and was a bit nonplussed. In retrospect, it is interesting how quickly Warburgs had joined the

Establishment, having been pioneering, and even revolutionary, not that long ago.

The most iconic of the privatisation issues was for British Gas, as it was the largest and the most publicised. The Government had engaged Roddy Dewe, of Dewe, Rogerson, the City PR moguls. He mounted a huge marketing campaign including the invention of a fictional character named "Sid" which was to represent the fictional member of the public being solicited to invest. I found the whole thing alarming. Not only was Sid a patronising contrivance, but the shares of British Gas were being marketed as a "punt" like a Derby favourite, or a new chocolate breakfast cereal. There was no hint of investor suitability, and the implication was that the investment was as suitable for a maiden aunt on a pension as for a betting shop regular one meets in the local pub. The clear message was that a quick turn might well be available, and that the issue would be priced accordingly. The result was highly predictable. The public sold as soon as they could and the shares ended up almost entirely in institutional hands, where that community believed they should have been all along. The investment management industry firmly believes that the unwashed public is better served by entrusting their savings to those collective investment schemes managed by its good self.

I had an interesting insight into the ignorance about investment and City matters which prevailed at the highest level of government on visit to Number 10 Downing Street, with my global chairman Bill Schreyer. The visit had been easy to arrange, as the Consul General in New York had given a luncheon for Mrs. Thatcher on a recent visit to New York, when she had met the heads of all the main Wall Street houses. As we settled into a comfortable drawing room at Number 10, the Prime Minister, surprisingly on her own, opened with, "How nice to see you again, Mr. Schreyer, and you, Stani." It is a consequence of my difficult name that I am invariably addressed by my Christian name by the great and the good. I can hear an aide saying, as the PM gagged on my name "Just call him Stani, Prime Minister". She then continued, "Now, Mr. Schreyer, I want to hear all about the American economy and where you think it's going."

Bill Schreyer opened his mouth, but before he could utter a squeak, Maggie was off. There followed a concise, accurate, insightful and eloquent description of the current state of the American economy and where it might be heading.

Later, once outside, Bill said to me, "Gee, but wouldn't I like to have her as our chief economist!" But we were not let off so quickly, as the PM turned to me in my Stock Exchange capacity and, bluntly, asked me why we were making a dog's breakfast of our overhaul of the settlements system. She feared for the consequences on the mass privatisation issues. We were, of course, being plagued by incompetent systems consultants, probably badly briefed, and with a difficult mandate. I did not mention the total lack of co-operation of the clearing banks who were seeking to protect their highly remunerative custody franchises.

But I chanced my arm and said, "Prime Minister, the right solution would be to move immediately to an entirely paperless system as in New York, where transfers and ownership are registered electronically." Schreyer was nodding vigorously next to me.

"Oh, no!" said the PM. "Dennis says people like to have their own share certificates."

"But, when people see on their bank statement a balance of a hundred pounds, they don't insist on seeing the bank notes. If they had a statement from a reputable agency showing that they owned a hundred shares of ICI, surely they would be satisfied?" I was risking opprobrium for gainsaying Dennis.

"No, no. Dennis says it is not the same thing."

It was then I realised that the Prime Minister's principle advisor on all matters relating to the Stock Exchange was her husband Dennis. We moved on to another subject – the chances of truly broadening private share ownership. A new national curriculum for schools was being introduced.

"Prime Minister," I started again. "Is this not an opportunity to include a mandatory course in personal financial management? A good many of the fraudulent investment product scams might have been avoided if the public was savvier on money and investment matters. Many don't know the difference between stocks and shares, or unit trusts and investment trusts, and the so-called IFAs are just product pushers." I was guessing Mrs. Thatcher knew what an IFA was, and wouldn't mind my insulting them;

"Oh! I'm afraid not. You see, the teachers unions would never accept that. The NUT is very socialist, you know. They would accuse the Government of brainwashing children with capitalist dogma."

I couldn't believe it. The Iron Lady, who had faced down the country's most militant and aggressive union – that of the miners – was afraid of the teachers! We left Number 10, Bill Schreyer dreaming of a retired Mrs. Thatcher as Merrill's chief economist, and me thinking of the British investor, with share certificates in a biscuit tin in the kitchen.

Merrill Lynch had no chance of securing a primary role in a privatisation issue, but for the largest of these, a concept of regional distributions on the Continent, and particularly in America, had been introduced. We presented for the role of manager for any U.S. tranche. We had been fortunate to engage a young Englishman called Kevin Watts, who the Treasury had sent off for a spell on Wall Street, with the wise objective of gaining knowledge from a financial centre with far more diverse and profound knowledge of equity issuance than could be found in the City of London. Unfortunately, the knowledge he had gained was not to be transferred to his erstwhile employers, as Kevin quickly determined that a career as an investment banker was likely to be far more remunerative than one as civil servant. He joined Merrill Lynch in London and was quickly assigned to the management of our solicitation efforts vis a vis various ministries, depending on the privatisation in question. We fielded teams of experts from New York, in the relevant fields – utilities, rails, energy, etc. The advice of these teams was not only ignored, but largely resented. One official, John Guinness, Permanent Secretary at the Department of Energy, did not trouble to hide his disdain for Americans, and American investment banks, in particular. I think Sir John, as he is now, considered poor Kevin Watts as a traitor for having sought employment with the likes of Merrill Lynch – Morgan Stanley, perhaps, but "The Thundering Herd"? Horrors! We had better receptions at the Treasury, where Kevin had been a highly promising young official. Moreover, Kevin knew his way around the building, where one might be lost for days. For this and other reasons we thought we had more than a fighting chance for a lead management role of the U.S. tranche of the British Petroleum issue. BP was already partially privatised and quoted. But Mrs. Thatcher wished to reduce the Government's holding further, so this was to be a secondary offering. As Government held industrial positions fell under the purview of HM Treasury, it was responsible, rather than the Department of Energy, and so the dreaded John Guinness, might be powerless to blackball us. Our presentation had all the advantages of simplicity, but unanticipated dangers as well. BP was already widely held by U.S. institutions, as one of the old "seven sisters" and a diversification from domestic oil companies. Our case was that distribution amongst a wide range of private investors would provide a valuable counterweight to the already very dominant institutional bias in the company's share register. It would also provide a degree of political protection to the company's extensive investment in U.S. production and refining – particularly in the Gulf of Mexico. If one accepted the validity of this argument, there was only one house which had the retail distribution to realise this objective – the firm "that brought Wall Street to Main Street". Almost imperceptible, up and down motions of the heads of those officials listening to us in a dingy Treasury meeting room, gave us hope that our argument was finding favour. Kevin Watt's network of discreet former colleagues seem to confirm that we were leading the field. Bottles of champagne were being put on ice. It was late 1987. And then I had the call from Peter Middleton, Permanent Secretary of the Treasury. "Stani." I knew from the tone of his voice what was coming. "Stani" he repeated "I have in front of me a research report on BP from your highly esteemed oil analyst Gus Vlachos. He rates BP a 'sale' – at best, a 'hold'." And highly esteemed he certainly was – a member of *Institutional Investor's* A Team. A recent photograph of the A Team, a mock up, with the analyst's heads superimposed on football players, showed Mr. Vlachos over the heading "oils". Peter Middleton continued. "You will understand that it's quite impossible....."

I interrupted. "I understand completely, Peter It's the 'old Chinese wall' – no need to explain."

"I must complement Merrill Lynch on maintaining its integrity," said Peter. I wonder if he would have liked to say "free of chinks".

"Who is it to be?" I asked.

"Goldman Sachs," replied Peter

Kevin and his privatisation team were devastated, but hardly blamed Gus Vlachos. This story may seem quaint and old-fashioned to contemporary investment bankers, but there really was a Chinese wall then, without complicated regulatory oversight, and no respectable securities analyst would have dreamed of overtly supporting an investment banking solicitation by colouring his opinion. His fiduciary duty was to the investment client – not the investment banking client.

As with other memorable events, I remember where I was for the great crash of October 1987. More precisely, I remember where I was on the Friday, October the 16th – which is more significant as I might have had a hand in this event. I was flying back from New York on the "red eye" flight, when the pilot announced, shortly before landing, that the terminals were unusually crowded for that time of day, but he had no idea why. This was a bit odd, as an unexpected hurricane had devastated southern England during the night. An unfortunate BBC weather man called Michael Fish, had happily announced the night before that the great storm was veering south over the Azores and England could sleep soundly. This prediction haunted him for the rest of his life. The reason the terminals were crowded was that transport to London was seriously disrupted, as there were trees down everywhere and widespread power cuts. I found that not only Dennis had managed to get to Heathrow, but there was a Stock Exchange driver waiting for me as well. Nicholas Goodison was in Japan, and Graham Ross-Russell was also away, and Jeffrey Knight had sent a message saying I should come to the Exchange immediately. So I took the Stock Exchange car, and we wended our way through back streets as the M4 was completely clogged. On arrival I found a very concerned Jeffrey and his team. The burning issue was "do we try to open?" Few City workers had managed to get in and there were widespread power cuts affecting various sectors, so a good many SEAQ terminals would be out of action. I remember Nichols saying we should adopt the motto of the Windmill Burlesque Theatre during the war "we never close". Just as the girls kept stripping as bombs fell, we all decided we should attempt to open for trading, so as to at least avoid a formal closure. But of course, it was a token opening, as I would guess trading was perhaps 10% of normal. A good many programme trades, initiated in Tokyo, with the expectation they would be closed out in London, could not be – and these caused New York to suffer a major fall at its opening. By Monday, the backlog of open positions had reached even greater volumes, and external geopolitical events, pronounced weakness in world markets during the previous week, as well as the semi-shut down of London on the Friday, culminated in "Black Monday" on October 19th when the market fell by almost 20%.

The British Petroleum issue coincided with these unusual events, as even though the market situation had been showing distinct signs of weakness, it had been decided not to postpone. The result was Goldman Sachs was left holding the largest share of the 22% of the entire issue allocated to the U.S. underwriters – which included Salomon, Morgan Stanley and Shearson Lehman – no Merrill Lynch. Wood Gundy was stuck with the Canadian tranche, and that revered old Canadian house, one of the pioneers of the Eurobond market, went bust as a result. The underwriters made a brief attempt to invoke a "force majeur" clause in the underwriting agreements, and the senior Goldman partner flew to London to plead at Whitehall. But it was a non-starter, and Goldman and the others did themselves no service in trying it on. The risk of sudden changes in market conditions are the reason issues are underwritten and the underwriters paid fees for taking that risk. Gus Valchos at Merrill probably got a mega bonus for saving the firm millions.

I suppose I was too busy at Merrill and with my other activities, to suffer immediate anguish on the frittering away of the City Financial, which was taking place all around me. I use the term "City Financial" which is Corporation of London speak for that aspect of the City the public is familiar with. In fact, the City's physical infrastructure was changing as well, and development was eliminating those little passages and courts our old Sergeant at White, Weld had guided me through. Stock exchange firms were being gobbled up. The merchant banks disappeared slowly through merger and acquisition – mostly by foreign banks. First the small fry: William Brandt, Leopold Joseph, and Singer & Frielander. Then Hill Samuel, Kleinwort Benson, Barings, Hambros, Mogan Grenfell – not necessarily in that order, but with devastating predictability. Those with strong family control held out longer. Fleming's, Schroeder's – but they all fell. Schroeder's managed to keep the asset management business under family control. Finally, only Lazard and Rothschild are left. But it was the exodus of the people, more than the institutions, which was to devastate the City I had known. A generation of practitioners, who held their own personal reputation, that of their firm, and that of the City as a whole, at the heart of their career persona, was slowly replaced by overseas adventurers, out for a quick kill, mindless of the standing of their often temporary employer, and entirely disinterested in the reputation of the City. I will be accused of an excess of class consciousness. "Oh yes!" I hear you saying. "What he means is that the City was better, and more honest, when populated by 'toffs', than it is now, when populated by 'yobs'". Well.... yes. *Mea culpa*. But, my Cockney dealer from the East End at EBC, had a greater ethical instinct in his little finger, than the head of Goldman Sachs in London today – whoever he, or she, may be – has in his, or her, entire body. And so did the Frankfurt Jews, who had crowded to the City in the 1930s. They had not only merged with the City standards of the time, they had strengthened them.

374

At Merrill Lynch, I felt the change in attitudes and motivations two examples stand out. Barry Friedberg headed Investment Banking in New York, now that Jerry Kenney ran International as a whole. Barry was an A. G. Becker import. Merrill had bought Becker for its corporate client list, the Chicago based house being the biggest player in the commercial paper market by a considerable margin. Funnily enough, Sigmund Warburg had made a similar mistake, not realising that Becker's franchise was highly specific, and whilst a blue chip corporate might give its commercial paper business to Becker – as most did – it didn't necessarily give any other business to the same firm. Warburg has set up a three way joint venture with Becker and Paribas, hoping to break into the U.S. corporate market – with little success. I had a call from Barry telling me to turn out my top investment banking troops for a major client who was on his way to London with a hostile takeover planned of a major U.K. company. Whilst a London merchant bank had been retained, there was the chance of a joint advisory assignment. I did so and received the client in the main boardroom, surrounded by salivating colleagues. He laid out the deal. It was rubbish. The target company had a little known control position which would require a substantial premium to unlock and it had been losing market share in its field for several years. I said, "I wouldn't go for it if I were you."

A sharp intake of breath from my colleagues. "The client, on the other hand, perked up and said, "Thank you! We need to take another look. Our advisors haven't mentioned this. I am beginning to wonder now."

I walked him to the lift and went back. Consternation and anger greeted me. "You have lost us a major fee! How could you do that."

"Friedberg told me he was an important client. We owe him best advice. Does anybody disagree with what I told him?" I pleaded.

"No – but if he wants to do the deal, we shouldn't discourage him. We've lost a fee!"

The following week, Friedberg called me. "The client is delighted! He's dropped it. He says your advice was correct. He's giving us another big piece of business."

"Barry, my people are furious. Can you carve out a piece of your bonus pool and reserve it for them?"

"Done," said Friedberg.

My people were placated. But I had learned a fresh lesson about the new world of investment banking. Apparently, one didn't say "no – don't do it" to a client if a fee was in sight. But it was also an example of that major cancer which has infected mega-banking with disastrous consequences. I am not sure who started it, but the concept of individual bonus pools for individual disciplines within a diversified banking establishment, spread like wildfire. The theory was that it would be impossible to recruit the specialist talent which firms increasingly relied on, if its productive efforts were not remunerated, regardless of the overall results of the employer. If the bond dealers made a big profit, but the equity dealers lost it – why should the bond dealers suffer? The next obvious question, which no one posed, was: if the firm lost money and the shareholders had no dividend, why should the employees have a bonus? The concept of individual bonus pools broke for ever the link between owners and employees, and is one of the things which threatens capitalism as a whole.

I witnessed the degradation of employee motivation, when I was asked to be part of the recruiting frenzy which accompanied the annual University Employments bureau list of City candidates. Hot prospects quickly emerged and, although I had said I wanted no part of the process, colleagues pleaded with me to "close" on one. "Everybody's after him" I was told "Morgan, Goldman, Warburg, the lot. Being interviewed by our high profile chairman might just clinch it for us." Apparently, it was as if a hot European star like Bergman was about to sign with RKO, and I had to save her for MGM. Reluctantly, I saw the young man – a callow youth with an arrogant smirk.

"The great thing about Merrill Lynch," I began, "is that we are in so many different businesses, and we will put you through a training period which familiarises you with them all."

"No good," he replied, "I want an assurance that I will go straight on to the Turkish Lira swap desk. I understand that's where the big money is being made now."

"Well, a few months from now it may be the Chinese Renmimbi – but let's leave that for the moment. Tell me – what are your ambitions? I imagine you would like to work your way up the ladder and eventually sit where I'm sitting?"

"You must be joking! I know there are at least a dozen people in your outfit making more money than you are. The last thing I would want to be is Chairman of Merrill Lynch Europe. I want to make as much money as quickly as possible and after that – I'm off. I have my eye on a farm in Hampshire."

I walked the candidate politely back to the lift. My colleagues crowded in to my office.

"As long as I'm chairman, that man will never work here, even as a janitor. And if you don't like it, you can complain to New York."

I wouldn't be surprised if someone did. The candidate was absolutely right about the people making more money than me – except that it was closer to twenty.

My time at Merrill Lynch was nearing its end. An old friend, Peter Spira, enlightened me eloquently about the pitfalls inherent in being parachuted in at the top of large organisations populated by hungry sharks. Peter had been one of the stars at S. G. Warburg, much involved in that firm's dynamic entry into the Eurobond market. A deal maker and executer *par excellence,* he had complemented the stature of Sigmund, and his main collaborators, Eric Roll, Henry Grunfeld, Ronnie Grierson and Gert Whitman. As Warburg unravelled with Sigmund's retirement, Spira joined Christie's as finance director, and, I suspect, quickly became aware of the shenanigans the main auction houses were engaged in. He was then recruited to a senior position at Goldman Sachs. But no matter how much he insisted he was there to bring his contacts and experience to bear, and not to compete with Goldman executives for promotion, and gallons from the bonus pool – he was treated with suspicion and a marked lack of co-operation. I suffered less from this syndrome because I treaded water in a far less ruthless body of water, with porpoises rather than sharks nipping at my heels. But even at Merrill, I never managed to convince everyone that I would claim no share whatsoever of their bonus pool if I assisted in landing a piece of business. And I believe Michael Dobbs-Higginson, Michael von Clemm and myself were seen by many as blocking their promotion. But my failure was that I never "covered my ass" at head office, was an infrequent visitor there, and displayed a marked lack of understanding of Merrill Lynch politics – which sometimes made Washington seem simplistic. And, although my Stock Exchange and self-regulator positions had been welcomed at first, they generated bitterness in some influential quarters later on. One of these influential quarters resulted from Merrill Lynch's acquisition of A. G. Becker in Chicago. Becker introduced a different culture. It was not only essentially a Jewish firm, but its unique franchise engendered a different approach to client and colleague relationships. Merrill's culture emanated from its private client and retail history, and produced a softer sales approach. Becker's client base consisted of sophisticated, take no quarter, corporate chief financial officers and required a tougher service approach. The two main Becker movers and shakers gained in the acquisition were Barry Friedberg and John Heimann. Friedberg was a highly accomplished investment banker, but he did not go down with some clients. I was in Bill Schreyer's office when he received a call from Peter Grace. W. R. Grace was not only a major corporate client, but Merrill handled the family's

investments as well. I watched Schreyer's face turn pale as he stammered, "Yes, Peter. I'm so sorry, Peter. Yes, I understand, Of course, I'll see to it, etc., etc."

"Oh, boy! Oh, boy!" said Bill, as he put down the phone. "That was Peter Grace. He's in a rage after a visit from Barry Friedberg. I don't understand quite what happened but he told me 'If that little blankety blank sets foot in my office again, I'm closing our accounts at Merrill!' What the hell I am going to do? I've got to take the head of investment banking off one of our biggest accounts!" Schreyer was distraught.

The 'blankety blank' was an insulting reference to poor Barry Friedberg's religious persuasion. I have no idea if Peter Grace was already a known anti-Semite. John Heimann was a different type – a political animal to his fingertips. He had been Comptroller of the Currency in the Carter administration. This is a far more important position than even most Americans realise, as this official has a large oversight on the banking system. Heimann was rightly proud of having held this post and his office, wherever located, always displayed the twin American and Departmental flags behind his desk, which such officials retain for life. With New York unhappy with results of the European operations, and Jean Rousseau having been sent home in undeserved disgrace, Heimann was suddenly asked to go to London and assume chief executive responsibilities. Michael von Clemm was bitterly opposed to this decision, but it was a sign of his slowly declining political influence, that his objections were overruled. I was philosophical. In any case, we were building a remunerative financial institutions advisory business in London, and Heimann's commercial bank contacts were outstanding, as he had also been New York State Supervisor of Banking, at one point. Soon after Heimann's arrival, the annual Lord Mayor's banquet at the Mansion House was to be held – then still white tie and decorations. I arranged for Heimann to be invited. On arrival, John was horrified to find he was seated well "below the salt", but worse still, well below me, in terms of distance from the top table. I sometimes wonder whether Heimann suspected I had engineered this humiliation. He never forgot it and returned to New York determined to take me down a peg, or two.

My TSA chairmanship was smooth and uneventful due to an outstanding CEO, John Young – a diminutive but solid individual who had played rugby for London Scottish. I had only twice to pronounce sentence, so to speak. The Guinness affair has been so well documented that I won't cover it again. It rolled on and on, due to succeeding investigations. At Merrill, I knew Jimmy Gulliver, and during one of the several cliff-hanging moments in this most hostile of takeovers, I was having dinner with Dinnie and eldest son Michael in an Italian restaurant in Chelsea, when Gulliver spotted me. He was dining with an attractive lady who turned out to be his PA. He waved and suddenly the lady got up and came over to our table. Would I change places as Jimmy wanted a quick word? So she sat down with my wife and son and I went over to Gulliver. It transpired he wanted Merrill to intervene in the market on his behalf in a struggle which already had myriad interventions on behalf of the Guinness camp, which did, or did not – depending on your view of the war – constitute an undisclosed concert party. I told him Merrill was disinclined to join in this increasingly bitter affray, wished him luck and went back to my table. But the legal and regulatory roof fell in on Morgan Grenfell and Cazenove, acting for Guinness, then led by a buccaneer called Saunders. Eventually it fell to me to inform Cazenove that David Mayhew, the corporate broker involved, had to be relieved of any management position whilst the case was pending. But highly embarrassing for me was that I was forced to summon to my office in the Stock Exchange building, Anthony Forbes and John Kemp-Welch, the senior partners of Cazenove, to inform them that the disciplinary procedures of the TSA required that I exact from them a commitment that David Mayhew would not be involved in the management of the firm whilst his case was pending. I will never forget the courtesy, understanding, and what I can only describe as good sportsmanship, displayed by these two im-

378

mensely senior City figures, confronted as they were by a foreign representative of a foreign house, exercising regulatory dominion over them. If I was asked to cite one outstanding example of the conduct "befitting an officer and a gentleman" that then graced the City I knew and loved – that episode would be it. The principle behind all this was ridiculous. The suspension of presumption of innocence in our new regulatory world was justified by citing the examples of policemen and doctors. But the idea that David Mayhew would constitute a danger to the public, even if he were found to have transgressed the Takeover Code or Stock Exchange rules, or that, by participating in management, he could somehow divert Cazenove from its honourable tactical or strategic course, was laughable. But, although TSA was a so-called self-regulatory body, our disciplinary procedures were pretty well imposed by SIB, the statutory body. And the justification for self-regulation was that we practitioners would be more severe on ourselves. I had to do the same thing to a County Bank investment banker over the Blue Arrow affair.

I served on the Takeover Panel as one of the Stock Exchange representatives. The Panel met infrequently, as the Director General had wide decision-making powers, but we heard appeals to his decisions and met at the request of parties in contention. One appeal from a highly dubious property developer, who had made a bid for a small mining company, violating a number of Code principles, illustrated an enforcement difficulty. The Panel is not a statutory body and relies on the various self-regulating agencies to enforce its decisions – including the Bar Council, The Solicitors Regulatory Authority and the Institute of Chartered Accountants. The individual in question had employed a small firm of accountants in Brighton to handle his irregular bid, but when we informed the Institute of our disciplinary decision, it replied it was too busy to pursue small firms. The lesson appeared to be: if you want to ignore the Takeover Code, use a small firm of accountants. A more serious lapse, to my way of thinking, involved the famous Mohammed Fayed bid for Harrods, which, after winding its way through the courts, landed with the Panel. The document produced for the bid would certainly have been expensive in terms of fees paid to Klienwort Benson, the name on the front page, and various lawyers, but it was highly economical with the truth – in the famous words of Robert Armstrong. In fact, the document contained a series of "whoppers" with regard to Mr. Fayed's background and the sources of his funding. But Kleinwort Benson, a director of which sat on the Panel, escaped censure on the grounds that it was entitled to accept the declarations made by its client. Apparently the expression "due diligence" had not reached the marbled halls of this merchant bank – which ended up in the hands of Dresdner Bank. My most amusing case was undoubtedly the hostile bid for British American Tobacco, launched by a jolly triumvirate of Jacob Rothschild, Kerry Packer and Jimmy Goldsmith. Robert Alexander, a highly distinguished barrister, had assumed the chairmanship of the Panel and told us he knew nothing of high finance and would rely entirely on us, the members of the Panel, his only contribution being judicial wisdom. For the hearing we had to hire a livery hall, so great was the horde of lawyers. BATS, as it was universally known, had diversified into insurance and made a major U.S. acquisition in Farmers Insurance. The insurance business is state regulated in America, and so we had lawyers in attendance from every state in which Farmers was registered. The triumvirate was represented by an impressive phalanx of City law firms, as well as a barrister or two. But at one point, Jimmy Goldsmith became so frustrated by the ponderous nature of his advisors presentations that he rose to his feet, cut them off, and took over the pleading himself. I scribbled a note "if you keep a dog, don't bark yourself", and asked someone to pass it to Jimmy – but he never did. We on the Panel had a sandwich lunch break at one point in a side room, and Bob Alexander said of Goldsmith's intervention, "What a brilliant advocate that man would make! – it's too bad he's a crook." This last was untrue, unfair, libellous, and a far cry from the judicial wisdom Lord Alexander, as he became, was supposed to bring.

My days at Merrill Lynch wound to a close. Michael von Clemm warned me there were rumblings in New York against me, instigated I now believe by John Heimann and Barry Friedberg. Michael was unable to intervene on my behalf, or perhaps reluctant to, as his own star was dimming. He had acquired the nickname "Michael von Overhead" from those jealous of his success. His main supporter was Dan Tulley who appreciated in Michael a *bonhomie* which I was incapable of. Jerry Kenney came to London to give me the good bye kiss, traditional, I believe, in certain organisations. I don't suppose I was actually sacked, as I received no severance pay of any kind. I was simply made to understand I was no longer needed, rather as one tells Nanny, when the children are off to boarding school – although we kept our nanny as a cook, for a while. Actually Michael von Clemm and I had assured my succession because we had offered Christopher Reeves sanctuary at Merrill Lynch, after he had resigned from Morgan Grenfell over the Guinness affair. Like David Mayhew, he had his licence as an authorised person endorsed and could only join us as a consultant whilst in purdah. His time served, he became chairman Merrill Lynch Europe, Middle East and Africa, and, keeping a lower profile than I had, as well as possessing greater political skills, lasted quite a few years. I think I had served my purpose as Merrill was certainly better anchored in the City, and in Europe, than it had been pre Big Bang. I had even increased the territory. One day Michael Dobbs-Higginson had called me from his car in Hong Kong. "It's your birthday next week so I have decided to give you Pakistan," he said.

"Is there any business in Pakistan? I'd rather have India," I replied.

"There's a great deal of business in India. That's why I'm giving you Pakistan."

"Thanks, Michael."

Bill Schreyer came to London to host a farewell dinner for me at Brooks' Club. In my thank you speech, I had the temerity to proffer some advice to Merrill Lynch. "To Thine Own Self Be True!" was my parting thought. By this I meant "don't try to be Goldman Sachs". Well, the firm did exactly that, binged on proprietary trading, gorged itself with toxic assets, went bust and was bought by Bank of America.

CHAPTER XX

Variety's the very spice of life
That gives it all its flavour

-William Cowper-

My time at Merrill afforded me extra-curricular activities, which came to me, not because of my bright brown eyes, but because of my charitable budget, which was deemed greater by the outside world than it was in reality. One of these was the Development Committee of the Save the Children Fund, chaired by HRH the Princess Royal – who might have graced the chair of any major corporation with considerable competence. Fellow members were Lord Boardman of Nat West, Mike Angus of Unilever, Ian Maclaurin of Tesco, Tim Bell, the public relations guru, and one or two others. We met in the Chinese Room at Buckingham Palace, and Tim Bell had been given special permission to smoke. The Princess Royal opened the first meeting saying "I hope you are all happy to meet here. It's easy to find and there's plenty of parking." I expect she had used that phrase before. Finding no one brave enough to speak up at first, she asked us each to introduce ourselves in turn and say briefly what Save the Children meant to us. We were there to dream up new ways of raising money. For some reason, HRH picked a bit on Tom Board-man. I think they had dealt over a horse, with dissatisfaction on the part of one or the other. We were discussing encouraging companies to covenant con-tributions. "I think seven years would be an appropriate term," said HRH.

"Oh, ma'am," intervened Lord Boardman, "I think companies will find that too long a covenant. I believe three years would be more acceptable."

"Is that what they mean by 'short termism' in the City, Lord Boardman?" said HRH, quick as a flash.

Angus and MacLaurin offered special promotions on products, which when purchased provided pennies from the price to the Fund. My main con-tribution was an idea from the United States – just as our "innovations" in the Eurobond market had usually been. An American environmental charity had introduced the first "affinity credit card", and I suggested such might be launched for the Fund. The concept is simple. The card issuer benefits from the data base of the charity, which receives pennies from each card use.

"I think that's a most important and innovative idea," said Lord Boardman. "We should pass it by the Charities Commission."

"Are you mad, Lord Boardman?" HRH almost shouted. "Do we want this idea hawked around, so that my aunt and my father pick it up, and maybe even be first?"

It was then I realised how intense was the competition between Royal patrons of our main charities. The Princess Royal's concern was that the National Society for the Prevention of Cruelty to Children, of which her aunt, the late Princess Margaret was patron, might steal a march on a funding idea. I think I only heard HRH pronounce the name of this rival once, and then I think stressing the word "National", as if to underscore a difference which always puzzles foreign observers of our customs. Whereas animals benefit from protection under a Royal charter specified in the title of the RSPCA, children have to make do with a mundane "National" status, even though the NSPCC is also incorporated under Royal charter... The Princess Royal also regarded the World Wildlife Fund, of which her father was patron, as a potential competitor for those elusive donations. In any case, I had a target in mind for the first affinity card. My Stock Exchange chairman Sir Nicholas Goodison had stepped down, being replaced by Andrew Hugh-Smith, my last co-deputy chairman. Nicholas had gone on to chair the Trustee Savings Bank, which had recently suffered some traumas. I went off to see him and impressed him with the size of the SCF database, which contained the names and addresses of any one who had ever contributed to the Fund. "Your credit card will be an instant success – no need for a marketing budget," I cooed. Nicholas looked at me with that bemused expression I knew so well.

"But we haven't decided to issue a credit card," he said.

"Well, here's a chance to put TSB back on the retail map – after your recent difficulties. I'm giving you first crack at this concept."

It was the first and only time I ever sold anything to Nicholas. When the card appeared, it had a distinctive background showing a group of little, multi-coloured children's heads – smiling engagingly. I think it made a tidy sum for the Fund. Infinity cards are now a shilling a dozen.

My next charitable involvement put me back in contact with Nicholas. This was the National Arts Collection Fund of which he was chairman. And what a chairman. Nicholas was in his true element. The museum and art world lost a significant player when Nicholas decided to join the family stock broking firm. His addresses to the annual fund raising dinner should have been published. His knowledge of the art world was not only encyclopaedic, it was beautifully presented. He was acknowledged as a leading expert on clocks, and published a coffee table book on this antique sector. The NACF had as its mission to assist in the purchase by domestic museums of works of art being offered, and liable to leave the country for lack of domestic funding. It also topped up museum funds for restoration and other expensive maintenance projects. Nicholas's taste was often offended by public pressure to save works he though unworthy of saving. A case in point was Canova's *Three Graces* which the Duke of Bedford was selling. A national press campaign erupted with "Save the Three Graces for the Nation!" – And that sort of headline.

"Kitsch! Pure kitsch!" exclaimed Nicholas. "It would be better off in California – preferably in the lobby of some nightclub." But the NACF couldn't ignore the public clamour, as its funding came from the public, and so a contribution was made, and the work is now shared between the V & A and the National Gallery of Scotland. I didn't do much as a member of the fundraising committee, other than take a table at the annual banquet – but I enjoyed every minute of my association with the NACF.

Whilst still in Ropemaker Place, I had a call from Peter Parker. Would I join the development committee of the National Theatre? Peter had wanted to become an actor whilst still up at Oxford, where he had been regarded as a star in the Dramatic Society. His son Nathaniel has fulfilled his father's ambition, becoming a highly successful actor. Peter had been chairman of British Rail, but now chaired the National Theatre main board. Of course, I said yes and attended regularly at the dreadful block house by Denys Lasdun, which the National got stuck with early on. Some of the block houses the Germans built along the Normandy coast have greater architectural merit than the monstrosity on the South Bank. I kept this opinion to myself, because in due course I received a letter from the Minister of Arts inviting me to join the main board, which was now to be chaired by Lady Soames. Winston Churchill's youngest daughter threw herself into this role with great enthusiasm and before long knew the names of every stage hand, their wives and latest baby. At sponsor's evenings she shone like a leading lady, puffing on a small cigar, and entertaining all with anecdotes heard on her father's knee. If she had a weakness, it was with the technique of chairing the meetings. She was determined that all should have their say, and after an interminable discussion of an agenda point, she would look around and say "Can anyone tell me what we have decided?" We quickly found Rhodesia as a mutual interest as, of course, Sir Christopher Soames had been the last Governor General before the Lancaster House Agreements, and we had common friends in April and Ian Piercy. But I made a hit with Lady Soames in another way. After an early meeting she took me aside and said, "I can't tell you how much I appreciate your calling me chairman. I cannot abide being called after a piece of furniture. We now have a few female Lord Lieutenants, and they are still called Lord Lieutenant!"

"Yes, Chairman," I replied, "and we have plenty of lady Masters of Foxhounds!"

A politically correct lady from the North was seated next to me on the board, and she persisted in calling Lady Soames "chair". Michael Palliser was one of the members I knew already, as was Stuart Lipton, plus one or two others. As ministerial appointments, care had been taken to represent what is

384

sometimes referred to as "society as a whole". The attempt always fails and it is a sort of contemporary elite which ends up sitting on such bodies. A seat was reserved for a representative of the Arts Council, which provided more than half the budget, but it was invariably empty. The two representatives of the "talent" were Judy Dench and Tom Stoppard. Judy never attended, but Stoppard was an active participant. Surprisingly, for someone who writes like an angel, he was ineloquent to an extreme. "I think... that is to say... I'm not sure but, maybe... no... let me put it this way... couldn't we... you know ... perhaps try... well, you see... I just think..." is a fairly faithful rendition of one of his interventions. Once he got it out, what he was suggesting was always eminently sensible, to the point, relevant – spot on, in fact. Getting it out took a bit of time. But it was our director Richard Eyre who made the running. He had without doubt the toughest job in British theatre. He had to plan and execute a repertoire which kept three theatres of different capacity busy and full, whilst satisfying public taste, dealing with critical and peer group pressures, ensuring a dose of experimental theatre from new playwrights, drawing on a wide casting and director pool, charming corporate sponsors and keeping the main board happy – all without bankrupting the theatre, and having constantly to convince HMG the taxpayer was getting value for money. As a happy board member, I can attest Richard pulled all this off, without visible signs of strain. He was assiduous in keeping the board informed. If a production ran over budget, he would explain exactly why and how he might improve the process. He shared his artistic thinking with us generously, even though artistic matters were no part of our brief. He arranged tours for us of the whole theatre complex, and those who paid attention, as I did, learned a great deal about theatrical production. I made two memorable interventions. One was totally wrong and the other prescient. A production of that old war horse *An Inspector Calls* by J. B. Priestly, went way over budget and I told Richard I thought it had been way over-produced. "A sledgehammer to crack a nut", I think I said. There was a collapsing set, presumably to symbolise the oncoming war, as the play is set in 1913. For me the play was a light piece much favoured by "am-dram" and high school theatre groups, which had been well filmed with Alistair Sims as the Inspector. Our production and direction treated it as an iconic piece of serious theatre. Richard said, "Wait and see." It was a great success at the National and was then sold to Cameron Macintosh for the West End, where it ran, and ran, and ran – producing more royalty income for the National than we could count. As chairman of the content TV Company Flextech, I became convinced that people loved watching rehearsals. A cameraman friend had worked with Sony to produce a digital camera which was totally silent and with a tape which could run for hours, allowing for unobtrusive filming of stage productions. I suggested to Richard he might allow rehearsals to be filmed and sell the product as TV content. Now Richard has worked extensively in TV and film, as well as theatre, but he made it clear he would tolerate no crossover between these art forms.

"If I catch a camera on this side of the river," he said, "I'll chuck it in the Thames." That was that. Nowadays, actual performances at the Opera, and at the National, are regularly filmed and distributed on TV.

Donny Gordon, a South African shopping mall developer was making quite a splash in England, and Dinnie and I were invited to a dinner he gave at the St. George's Hotel. Dinnie was a hit as a Rhodesian, and all the South African accents there present made her feel at home. Donny invited her on his private jet, saying he would drop her off in Harare, on his way to Jo'burg – so that she could visit her family. I wondered whether he might not forget. At the dinner we met Max Ulfane and his charming wife Joy, heiress to a South African shoe fortune. The Ulfanes had taken a lease from the National Trust on Ashdown House, on the Berkshire Downs – a bijou, 17th century, Dutch style house built by the Earl of Craven for Elizabeth Stuart, Electress Palatine and briefly Queen of Bohemia. They kept it beautifully and even searched out and purchased paintings which had hung there in its glory days. William II, nephew of the "Winter Queen", used it as a hunting lodge, when he hunted in Ashdown Forest. The Ulfanes gave lovely luncheon parties where one met everyone from Jim Sherwood to Terry Wogan.

One day Max came to see me and asked if I might be willing to be non-executive chairman of a small oil field services company called Flextech, which Cazenove had floated, with a view to increasing British investor participation in the North Sea Oil bonanza, which risked becoming an American sea in exploration, production and rig servicing. The shares were selling for a few pence. I looked at the shareholder register and it was the Cazenove client list. The chief executive was Roger Luard, a very bright and hugely entrepreneurial accountant. I said "yes" to Max, and as usual, omitted to buy any shares. Although we had small, off shore oil field support operations in West Coast Africa, and Hong Kong, as well as the North Sea, out of Aberdeen, it soon became evident that, as a "mom and pop" operation, we could not hope to compete in the long-term with the likes of Schlumberger, Brown & Root or Halliburton. So Roger Luard set about seeking a new business model. Almost as an afterthought, Roger suggested buying 20% of HIT Communications, a programming company started by his friend PeterOrton, who eventually made a fortune with a cartoon character called *Bob the Builder.* This led us next to acquire from BT an interest in the Children's Channel, then the only one of its kind. I heartily approved these moves as I have always been addicted to cartoons – my favourite being *Tom & Jerry.* We were now launched in a new strategic direction and there followed an absolute whirlwind of transactions initiated and executed by Roger Luard, with my full support. These included interests in the Family Channel and a momentous deal with John Malone's TCI, the largest cable company in the U.S. Through a share exchange with TCI, we acquired interests in Bravo, UK Gold, UK Living and the balance of the Children's Channel. The acquisition of United Artists European Holdings extended our media interests, including Maidstone Studios. We bought 27% of HTV and then swapped it for a stake in Scottish Television. We raised money by selling stakes to U.S. West, a cable operator and Hallmark, the greeting cards company, which had started an entertainment division by buying the Robert Halmi production company, and Robert Halmi, Jr. joined our board. We set up an independent sales company which managed the air time of 14 channels, including Discovery.

But our epoch making deal was the joint venture with the BBC. The rise of cable and satellite carriers ushered in the age of multi-channel TV, and the grand old lady of broadcast, the BBC, began to wonder whether they could ignore this phenomena. Our interest in UK Gold was the attraction for the BBC, and we saw access to the BBC extensive library of programming as the basis for a whole new generation of channels to be carried by cable and Sky, Rupert Murdoch's dominant satellite provider. As part of our deal with TCI we had acquired a brilliant media executive in Adam Singer, who had cut his teeth working for John Malone, the leading cable and programming tycoon in the U.S. Adam was the son of Aubrey Singer, a legendary BBC producer, who had often interviewed me when he presented the *Today in the City* programme. Adam knew his way around the labyrinth which is the BBC, but even with his special insights, the bureaucratic nature of the beast made the negotiations complicated and protracted. I tried to establish a "back channel" with my friend David Scholey who was on the board of Governors. I met with David in my Berkeley Square office but he said, "Stani, I have to tell you that we Governors haven't the slightest idea what the management is up to – they give us a lot of superficial overviews when we meet, and we usually find out what's going on by reading the newspapers."

Roger and Adam thought it was all wrapped up, when one of their BBC counterparts said, "Oh, we still have to run this past our other legal department."

"You have more than one legal department?" asked an astonished Roger.

"Yes, one for domestic and one for international."

And so is the licence payers' money spent – and the governance of the BBC assured. But finally the deal was done and an elaborate press conference was staged at the BBC's Shepard's Bush studios. Roger and I were standing there as we watched stage hands putting up two huge banners, with the well-known BBC logo on one and Flextech on the other. Roger turned to me and said, "Did you ever dream that you would see those two names side by side in equal size?" The end result of this venture is the vast range of UK Living channels you see on the Sky package and on cable.

At a press conference once, a reporter asked Roger, "What does your non-executive chairman do?"

Roger turned to me to answer, so I said, "I follow Roger about with a bucket of cold water, and every once in a while, I pour it over him."

This was an apt job description. Roger was an inveterate and passionate deal maker, and, sometimes, I had to restrain him I believe ours was a perfect relationship between a hyperactive CEO and a non-executive chairman. He consulted me on every move. We were near neighbours in the country and our consultations were often on the platform at Kemble RR station on Monday morning, as we waited for the 07:40. The shares of Flextech rose from 40p to five pounds during my chairmanship, and were about there when we merged with Telewest. But I never owned a share. The frenzy of deal making meant we were almost always in a closed period for dealing by insiders. The board was always able to grant Roger options, but non-executive directors do not get options. If there was the occasional window when I was free to deal, I always felt the price was rather high, and perhaps I should wait.

Our relationship with John Malone of TCI blew hot and cold. Malone had a major programming company in the U.S. called Liberty Media, but he seemed unable to decide whether programming and carrier interests should be separate or together. I think he used his U.K. interests to experiment, because he eventually had effective control of Telewest, one of two major U.K. cable operators, and of Flextech, the leading programmer. When he withdrew his two directors from our board, I suspected he was planning to provoke a merger with Telewest, where the same two were also directors, and he wanted to avoid being an insider in both quoted companies. In the end, we did merge, and our world changed. I stayed on the Telewest board, now chaired by my old friend Cob Stenham. Roger Luard fell ill with a mystery illness, and the multiple attempts to find a cure destroyed his immune system and he died. Adam Singer became CEO of Telewest. The cable industry was going through a similar phase of heavy investment financed by huge borrowings, and near bankruptcy as funding sources dry up, as railways did in the nineteenth century. By now the build out was virtually completed and it was a question of fashioning an appropriate product offering to compete with Sky satellite. Cob was a patient and hardworking chairman, as the company began to suffer the usual growing pains. At one point he told me he felt we should have a lady on the board. Cob was a politically correct Labour supporter. I interviewed his candidate. She had all the right credentials and business experience, and she proved a disaster. She seemed to be under the impression that all male boards converse in language heavily sprinkled with profanities – isn't that how boys talk? And so to be one of the boys, she used four letter words as often as possible. Her main interest was in the female to male ratios in each category of employee. They were always too low on the distaff side. The moment came, as our fortunes declined, to change CEO's, replacing Adam Singer with the finance director Charles Burdick and I, as chairman of the remuneration committee, had to negotiate Adam's severance package, which I considered should be generous. My lady director colleague had taken an immediate dislike to Adam and wanted him unceremoniously sacked. When I insisted otherwise, she called me "a stuffed shirt and an ass hole". I went to Cob and said, "It's her or me."

"Please, please, hang on, Stani," Cob said, "She's just insecure."

She may have been, but she is now a Life Peeress of the Realm. Our fate was to be sealed, however, by a drying up of the junk bond market, which had funded the build out of the cable system for both Telewest and NTL, our only competitor. We had no choice but to seek a restructuring of our debt, which was likely to wipe out the equity. A committee of the bond holders was formed in New York, where most were located. But a vulture fund from New Jersey, the vehicle of a father/son team called Huff, had smelt blood and bought bonds heavily. They refused to join the committee so as to avoid being insiders, and therefore able to short the shares at will. The Huffs were insisting on much tougher terms, including switching the listing of the shares to NASDAQ from the London Stock Exchange, in order to escape the U.K. regulatory regime, which is far less tolerant of the sort of market manipulations employed by vulture funds. A deal was stuck with the committee, the Huffs refused to accept it, and Cob and the board caved in. I resigned – in a huff, you might say. I received plaudits from the financial journalist Anthony Hilton, who found it refreshing to see a non-executive director resign on a matter of principle. Telewest merged with NTL and eventually became Virgin Media, when Richard Branson took a small stake. Poor Cob Stenham died in his hotel room on a visit to New York. The Flextech division was first renamed Virgin Media Television, then bought by BSkyB and renamed Living TV. Flextech represented as exciting a non-executive directorship as one would hope to find. If the *dénouement* was less satisfying than the build-up, all one can say is – that's life.

I was still in smaller office at Ropemaker Place when I had a visit from Ben Wray and Jeremy Edwards from Henderson Administration. Jerry Kenney had said I could be housed there as long as I liked and given me some anodyne title, like Senior Advisor. In City terms, a visit from Henderson was like a visit by Royalty. It was to the Establishment as the Enclosure is to Ascot. Almost joined at the hip with Cazenove, Henderson had been founded to administer the estate of a railway engineer turned financier, the first Lord Farringdon. The firm now managed a string of investment and unit trusts, the premier trust being Witan, chaired by the present Lord Farringdon, also a partner of "Caz". Its board of directors was entirely internal and having an international outsider join was thought to be "a good idea". Of course, I jumped at the chance, and unfamiliar with usual non-executive compensation, asked for rather more than I should, and also for an office, which, being equally unfamiliar with the usual arrangements, I suppose – they accepted without question. Years later, I am still embarrassed about this. Ben said, "Just one thing – our chairman Johnny Henderson would like to meet you." I must say, I thought this a rather fundamental condition to be put forward in such a casual way. The meeting took place at the bar at White's, where I was not yet a member. We talked horses. Johnny Henderson was a keen racing man and had several horses in training. He mentioned Gyllipus, and Jenny and Richard Pitman. We discussed the different challenges and satisfactions of the flat and national hunt racing. He never mentioned Henderson Administration once. After about twenty minutes he said, "You know, I told my colleagues they had no chance of landing you and they should try for a smaller fish." That was it. Soon after, it was decided an outside chairman should be appointed. Henderson was in the process of acquiring Touche Remnant, and a friend and neighbour David Backhouse, was appointed to the board. For some reason he came to see me in the country and asked if I would prefer to be chairman.

"Of course not," I replied, and David was appointed. He was hardly in his new office before IMRO, the self-regulating agency for the investment management industry, decided to re-open an old case involving a company where David had been a director. The company, chaired by a Labour peer married to a Lebanese millionaire, had suffered some irregularities in a Venezuelan operation. The timing of this was extraordinary, as Henderson was engaged in merging with another company, and anything of this kind was price sensitive. Exploiting my background as an ex-SRO chairman, I went to see the chairman of IMRO and told him I thought his action might well have the result of creating a false market in Henderson shares. An incredibly stuffy patriarch, he looked down his nose at me, and told me to mind my own business. I went to see David Walker at SIB. He was loathe to interfere in the disciplinary process of an SRO. Although he was the regulatory supremo, the system was based on maximum autonomy of the SRO's, and SIB only intervened if an SRO was clearly failing in its mandate. David had to step down and Ben Wray took his place as chairman. Of course David was entirely exonerated, and this was the most insensitive regulatory intervention I ever witnessed. Once ensconced at Henderson, I felt I was in the heart of the City establishment, even more than at the Stock Exchange. Everything about the house, the people, the culture, the fiduciary ethos, its approach to business – represented for me all I admired about the old City. There was some joshing about a Cotswold mafia, as Charles Farringdon was in the next door village of Barnsley, Backhouse was near Fairford, Charles's daughter Susan was a friend and classmate of Tatyana's at Hatherop Castle School. Her eventual husband proposed to her whilst they were sitting on the fireplace fender in our drawing room. I was keen to find a U.S. partner to attack that market. Seligman Brothers seemed ideal, as it had been a railroad finance house in the 19th century, but was now a pure investment manager, with Tricontinental, the nation's largest closed end fund, as its flagship client – almost a twin of Henderson's Witan. But Seligman was now in the hands of some ex-Kuhn Loeb partners who had staged a management buyout, and, after a few meetings, it was clear the chemistry wasn't right.

Whilst I was sitting at Henderson, trying to make myself useful, I had a call from an official at the Department of Trade & Industry. Would I accept an honour, if one was proposed? Since it was after lunch, and I was a bit sleepy. I said, "Of course!"

"It will be an honorary honour, you appreciate, as you are not a British subject." I enjoyed the juxtaposition of the two words.

"As an honorary honour, it will be presented by a Minister, rather than Her Majesty," the official continued, "and you can invite family and friends to the ceremony."

I thanked him, and he said he would get back with a date. When it came, I thought I would invite a U.S. Treasury representative, as I reckoned I was a first American to be honoured for what I assumed were services to the City. In the early euromarket days, I had been asked to brief the U.S. Treasury representative in Grosvenor Square, as they were very curious about all these dollars washing about. I had no reply to my invitation. Perhaps the Marine Corps mascot ate it. On the big day, a master of ceremonies addressed the thirty odd in attendance – including wife and children. "As the Minister making the presentation is representing Her Majesty the Queen, you will kindly rise on his entrance," he intoned. A suppressed titter was audible, when the Rt. Hon. Peter Lilley MP walked in, as he looked like a youthful, sixth form public school boy – and still does. He gave a most gracious little speech and handed me the insignia of a CBE. Lisa von Clemm was annoyed that he mispronounced my name, but the poor man had probably not been briefed to just call me Stani, or perhaps thought it inappropriate, as we had never met. I gave a little speech thanking the Minster, my heroine, the Eurobond market, and my first boss John Stancliffe, who was grinning at me in the audience. There was a "photo op", and then Michael von Clemm, muttering "it should have been a 'K'", took me and family to dinner at the Michelin building restaurant. Sitting at a table close by was Tony Bennett, a hero of mine. In her usual, easygoing fashion, Tatyana got up, went over to his table and said, "My father's just been given a medal. Will you autograph a menu for him? – he's called Stani."

A menu came back autographed. "Congrats on the medal, Stani! Tony Bennett."

I often wonder what sort of medal Tony Bennett thought it was. When I became a British subject, a few years later, I received a very formal letter from the Order telling me my honour as a Commander had been declared "substantive" – an English word I was unaware of.

A far less wonderful, and rather dubious honour, was next sent my way. I had a call from David Mulford, under Secretary of the Treasury, under Secretary Nick Brady. David was no doubt busy inventing Brady bonds, for which his boss got the credit, but he had a request for me. "You know we get to nominate the number two at the EBRD?" I did. This was part of a deal struck by Prime Minister Thatcher with President Mitterrand, and Brady, when the feudal lords in Brussels decided to create yet another institution to provide yet another batch of placemen with yet another series of fat appointments. The European Bank for Reconstruction and Development was a sort of poor man's

World Bank, aimed at weaning the former Comecon countries away from Moscow. Jacques Attali always claimed it was his idea. Maggie Thatcher had been determined to snatch the location from Paris, which the French had made every effort to engineer. But she had to agree to a French President, and the U.S. as the biggest bank roller, insisted on naming the Deputy President.

"Jacques Attali, the President, has been driving us crazy," said Mulford "– You are perfect for the job – by the way, are you a Republican?"

"I've never voted. How much does it pay?" I was instantly wary.

"As long as you don't vote Democrat... peanuts, I'm afraid – but you don't need the money."

"Of course I do! Can I keep my non-executive directorships?"

"Probably not – but think of the prestige!"

"David, you can't feed horses on prestige, and let me tell you, after Merrill Lynch, I know I'm not a big organisation type."

"Think about it," said David. "You'll be getting us out of a jam." This appeal to my patriotism left me cool.

Only a few days later, my PA Joyce Anderson, who had accompanied me to Henderson, came to me while I was in a meeting and said, "There are two very strange men outside who insist on handing you an envelope in person."

"Who are they? Can't you just take it?" I was in a meeting, and embarrassed by this.

"No, they are from the EBRD, and they say they have instructions from the President to hand it only to you. They look like bodyguards, if you ask me."

I went out, and sure enough, I thought they might be nightclub bouncers. I took the envelope, opened it and found it contained an employment contract with everything filled in, signed by Attali, and with a covering note telling me to sign it and send it back by the same messengers. I sent it back unsigned, but thought I had better make a courtesy visit.

"Mon cher ami – quelle joie! Je vais avoir un Français comme adjoint!" My dear friend, what joy. I will have a Frenchman as my Deputy!

"Monsieur le President, je m'excuse, mais je suis la parce que je suis American." Mr. President, I'm sorry, but I am here because I am American.

The conversation continued in this vein. He refused to consider me as anything other than a native born Frenchman. "Those stupid Americans! Can you imagine me working with one? At least your Monsieur Mulford is clever enough to send me you to satisfy their stupid condition." I sent back a polite refusal. A First Boston man took the job. Interestingly, his mother was French. Mulford forgave me for turning it down. Attali got the sack eventually.

Life at Henderson was smooth and cosy but merger and acquisition fever was permanently in the air in the City, and no one had devised an equivalent of a flu shot to contain it. The largest mutual assurer in Australia decided to demutualise and float under the name of AMP Limited, and needed to show an investment management presence in London to add credibility to the offer document. It had hired an American to manage the process of becoming a quoted company. Coincidentally, he was an old boy of my school Deerfield. He hit on Henderson as an ideal candidate and an offer was made which could not be refused. Absolute autonomy and no change in branding was guaranteed, and, most unusually with such commitments, AMP were true to their word. AMP had built a presence "up over" with Pearl Assurance and National Provident and all this was thrown together. The board of Henderson changed to accommodate the new owners and so ended my membership. But Henderson had launched a new investment trust to add to their extensive stable, and I was asked to chair this. Henderson Euro Trust was to concentrate on identifying undervalued medium and large capitalisation Continental companies, so as not to conflict with an existing trust which had been successful with the small cap growth sector across the whole of Europe. My already well-known Euro-scepticism was not seen as a barrier to my chairmanship – on the contrary, I think our highly competent and successful investment manager, Tim Stevenson, considered it useful contrariness. A German board member we added, Robert Bischoff, thought it most amusing. We struggled, together with our brokers Cazenove, to limit persistent discounts from NAV, which is the bane of the investment trust sector, but which is ruthlessly exploited by vulture type speculators, who happily sell in to the share repurchase programmes naïve investment trust boards engage in, as a discount defence mechanism. Of course such repurchase programmes are a form of slow suicide, as the dilution obsessed investment *mafia* refuses to permit resale of shares purchased – even at a profit to the trust. In fact the whole thing is what Americans call "a bit of a racket". But I enjoyed the continued connection with Henderson.

When one is no longer in a permanent job, word gets around, and odd opportunities arise. My old partner Johnny Cattier called me and said an Italian entrepreneur called Sergio Cragnotti was intending to set up a London subsidiary of his new "merchant bank" and was looking for a high profile chairman. I put merchant bank in inverted commas, because the term has become so abused. Cragnotti & Partners was in Italy a *banca d'affari,* which, I suppose is like a *banque d'affaires* in France, but, in my view both are fancy terms for a private equity business. I was getting a bit fed up with the term "high profile" which reminded me of silent movie stars famous for their profile – like John Barrymore. Apparently, Cragnotti had first thought of Michael von Clemm, and then John Craven, but neither spoke Italian or French, the only languages, besides Brazilian Portuguese, Cragnotti was comfortable conversing in. Johnny didn't know much about Cragnotti, but was friendly with one of his senior people in Geneva, who was the soul of financial respectability. I said I would take a reference or two. When you ask an Italian for a reference on another Italian, he tells you what city the subject is from and leaves it at that – particular if your reference provider is Roman "Oh! He's a Turinese!" or "Ah ha! What can I tell you? A Milanese!" This is supposed to be all you need to know. Italy is still a collection of City states which hate each other. Now I learned Cragnotti was a Roman, but closely connected with Ravenna, because he had been mentored by Raul Gardini, who in turn had been mentored by Serafina Feruzzi, and had married his daughter – and that lot were all Ravenna. But Cragnotti was not yet well known in Italy as he had built his career managing the Brazilian interests of the Feruzzi Group, originally grain traders in Ravenna, but now an international conglomerate due to the swashbuckling entrepreneurship of Raul Gardini. Unfortunately Gardini, who I met only once, had swash buckled his way into the Montedison/Enimont scandal in which he had relied on political favours gained through bribery, only to be stabbed in the back by the same politicians he had helped to corrupt. I would need the skill of those who write the plot summaries in Covent Garden programmes to describe briefly this particular *opera bouffe,* but the end result was poor Gardini's suicide. After Brazil, where Unicem, a major cement business was Feruzzi's main interest, Cragnotti had headed the sugerbeet company Eridania Behgin Say in Paris, one of Gardini's signature acquisitions for Feruzzi. With encouragement from Gardini, Cragnotti raised capital from Banca di Roma, Société Générale and Swiss Bank Corp, who were the partners in Cragnotti & Partners. At the time these were all successful and highly reputable banks, and so I told Cattier I would be happy to meet Sergio. In fact, I learned eventually just how close Cragnotti was to Banca di Roma. They soared to the private equity sun together, and like a double Icarus, fell together – but that comes later. Cragnotti had taken a floor in the Economist building in St. James's, where I went to see him, noticing how ugly and inefficient that edifice is. Set back from the street, with a plaza in front, on which eccentric sculptures are displayed, the building consists of a huge lift, stair and service bloc in the middle around which is strung narrow office space, so that the usable square footage is considerably less than one pays for. Sergio laid out his business plan which was to acquire controlling stakes in major companies in traditional, consumer related sectors, add value through disposals, acquisitions and balance sheet restructuring and sell them on – private equity 101, in fact. He also said he expected me to move into the Economist building, and that he was planning a major launch of Cragnotti & Partners Limited, at the Savoy, to which he would like me to invite the entire City – cost no object. Although architecturally not to my taste, I needed a new office, and thought it might be time to try working in the West End. I found this a most difficult adjustment, because for me, the City was work and the West End was play. Somehow, I acquired a marvellous new PA, as Joyce had decided to retire to look after her ailing mother in Edinburgh. Marisa Alcock was a Gibraltarian, an intelligence officer in the Royal Navy Reserve, a musician and choir leader, with talented children, married to a Royal Navy Reserve officer. She was fully trilingual in English, Spanish and Italian and spoke passable French. Like many Gibraltarians, she was of Italian origin, as the Rock belonged to the Kingdom of Naples for a time, and she was fiercely British. Marisa paved my way on entry into the very Italian world of Cragnotti & Partners.

Sergio Cragnotti was keen to enter that rarefied world of Italian entrepreneurs, and, therefore had acquired football team, a *sine qua non* if one craves acceptance in that club; Gianni Agnelli of Fiat, Tanzi of Parmalat, Berlusconi of Media – all owned football clubs. Not just expensive toys as in America, football franchises in Italy provide a degree of political protection, where the mosaic of public and private sector relationships is unique – and generally corrupt. I was no sooner settled in when Sergio called from his Milan office. We always communicated in French, but I translate.

"Yassukovich – do you know the Chairman of Midland Bank?"

"Yes, of course – it's Kit MacMahon."

"Call him, please. Midland are bankers to Tottenham Hotspur, and I want to buy one of their players. They are refusing to sell, but they are bust and need the money. Midland must put pressure on them to sell Gascoigne to me. I offer a fair price."

Cragnotti always called me Yassukovich and I called him Président. I reckoned this was an unusual but amusing assignment. I called.

"Kit, you don't know it, but I'm chairman of Cragnotti & Partners Limited in London. My boss owns Lazio, the second club in Rome and he's trying to buy a player called Gascoigne from Tottenham Hotspurs. He says you're the bankers, the team's finances are weak, it needs the money, and please will you put some pressure on. How's that for request?"

"I must say I never thought you and I would be talking about a football player, Stani. I'll have the right man call you." Kit was nothing if not broad minded.

I received a call from someone speaking in whispers.

"Do you know what a price sensitive conversation is?" he whispered.

"I'm a deputy chairman of the Stock Exchange, so I believe I do," I whispered back.

"So you appreciate Tottenham Hotspur is a quoted company. The discussions between M. Cragnotti of Lazio and our customer are highly confidential."

"Yes – will you help?"

They did and the deal was done. Then came the problem of insurance, which was played out in my office. Through Robbie Lyle I got the name of Lloyd's broker who specialised in sports insurance. The problem was Gascoigne had already broken a leg – an X ray lay on the desk in the Economist building of a lawyer working on the contracts. We managed to get a policy written but it only covered injuries on the pitch. Gascoigne proceeded to break his leg in a Roman nightclub brawl – not covered by the policy. Although Gacoigne turned out to be a bad investment, when he was in hospital with another injury, Cragnotti flew to London in his private jet, having arranged through me a visit out of normal hours, for fear of *paparazzi*. He sat for an hour at Gascoigne's bedside, unable to exchange a word. *Paparazzi* were Sergio's bugbear, and he was plagued through his association with

Gardini. In Italy, tycoons excite the same hysteria as pop stars and TV personalities do in England. Cragnotti was revered by his Lazio players. We took the whole team to China where we went looking to buy a dairy company. I realised the whole team were university graduates. Poor Gascoigne must have felt like a fish out of water. Sergio had arranged for the team to play an exhibition match against the Chinese national team. At halftime it was Lazio- six, China-nil. I know nothing about football, but the Chinese seemed to have only one play, and they were half the size of the Lazio players but no faster. Sergio called his manager up for a whispered conversation. The Chinese scored three goals in the second half. At a banquet that evening I was seated next to a French speaking lady who was a senior official at CITIC, the largest holding company. Her son was football mad and could I arrange to have a menu autographed by one of the players? I went over to the two round tables where the team were seated, all perfectly turned out in team blazers and ties. They took the menu and passed it around the two tables, so I returned with it signed by the whole team. The lady was almost in tears. We never bought a dairy company. Sergio had me making all the speeches. This turned out to be my principle function at Cragnotti & Partners as, beside the language problem, Sergio didn't like speaking in public.

A star member of the team at Cragnotti & Partners was a Bocconi University graduate called Angelo Cattapano. Bocconi's MBA degree is an equivalent of Harvard's – and nowadays better. Cattapano was to company valuations what von Karajan is to Beethoven symphonies. I have never seen anyone work the variations on the standard triangulation valuation formula like Angelo. For the uninitiated, this basic formula consists of averaging values arising from price/earnings ratios of comparable companies, recent sales or mergers of such, and discounted cash flow – the sensitivity there being the discount rate. But Angelo built on this the way Oscar Peterson improvises on an American song book standard. He could strip down a company, like a Formula One racing car, and put it back together, having spotted the weaknesses in the business model. Sergio was keen to acquire the U.S. Del Monte interest which had been spun out of the Kohlberg, Kravis and Robert's leveraged buyout and breakup of RJR Nabisco, a mega deal which produced an iconic business book, *Barbarians at the Gate*. Del Monte, the famous Hawaiian pineapple grower, had been split between international and U.S. brands and businesses. The California based, U.S. business had ended in the hands of an ad hoc private equity consortium, first led by Citibank, but then by Merrill Lynch, when the Fed clamped down on commercial bank private equity transactions. Also in the group was a vulture fund holding a particularly nasty form of cumulative convertible preferred stock, where not only the unpaid interest grew, but the conversion terms provided more and more shares as time passed. After an unproductive funding meeting with the cowboys that now ran Chemical Bank in New York, we flew on to San Francisco to start the due diligence. Cattapano, one or two others and myself commuted to San Francisco over several weeks, and after a while, the management said they would love to have Angelo Cattapano run the company, as not only had he understood every aspect of the business, his suggestions for improvements were brilliant. I negotiated at length with Merrill, on behalf of Sergio, who was determined not to overpay. I think Merrill would have dealt, but the vulture fund would not give on price. After all, time was on its side with its lethal convertible preference share. Sometime after I had left him, Sergio bought Del Monte Europe.

A somewhat more controversial deal not done was for Bertolli Olive Oil. This had been part of the SME group of food and agricultural interests controlled by IRI, the Italian State Holding Company. The famous Italian, archetypal politician/ businessman/ financier/ consultant/ EU mandarin/ Goldman Sachs banker, and just about everything else you can think of, Romano Prodi, was running IRI and in charge of the privatisation programme. SME was being auctioned in parts and Bertolli excited Sergo Cragnotti's interest, but the auction turned out to be not really an auction, but a sort of indication of interest, and lo and behold, Unilever turned out to be in somewhat privileged discussions with IRI. I was literally getting on a polo pony at Cirencester Park when a groom handed me a portable phone. It was Sergio asking me to find out what was happening. We were both under the impression that John Thornton at Goldman Sachs was advising Prodi at IRI. I wonder. Sergio asked me to call Thornton to establish the seriousness of our interest and the credentials of our group. I did so. Thornton was evasive, unhelpful and generally scornful. In retrospect, I have no doubt Prodi did not want to sell Bertolli to Cragnotti & Partners, but to Unilever, for which his consulting company had done business in the past. To complicate matters further, Cragnotti had helped form an agricultural consortium called Viz.Fi which had successfully bid for the part of SME which contained Cirio, and Cragnotti had a secret deal with Viz.Fito pass him Cirio. The spin out of Bertolli was part of the IRI/Viz.Fi. Deal. That was done before I became involved. Unilever was actually being advised by Goldman Sachs. So, in the end, Unilever got Bertolli and Cragnotti got Cirio. Prodi ended up as a highly paid advisor to Goldman Sachs. This was corporate finance business *à l'Italienne*. The whole web of IRI transactions under Prodi came under critical scrutiny at a later stage.

Another project of an unusual nature was the *portage* of the foreign partners interest in a joint venture called Jamont, created by the James River Corporation to enter the European market for paper products mainly that termed discreetly "bathroom tissue". If someone had told me I would end up in the toilet roll business, I would have been taken aback, but so would Fabian vom Hofe have been, and he was on the board of Jamont as well. In fact Fabian was a main board director of Cragnotti & Partners with me, and that's how I found out he was the Morgan Guaranty Paris head who had taken the call from Marc Viennot at Société Générale, inviting Morgan as agent bank for the French Republic syndicated credit. The concept of *portage* is very continental and is a device for having a third party hold an investment for a shareholder wishing to remain anonymous. It arises out of the fact that the Napoleonic Code, on which most Continental European law is based, does not recognise the concept of trusts, or indeed the general principle of fiduciary ownership on behalf of ultimate beneficiaries. Even today, histories of James River Corporation speak of Jamont as a joint venture with "European partners" not specifying who they were. I never knew myself but suspected it was Banca di Roma, or one of its clients – perhaps Montedison. In any case, Cragnotti & Partners exercised the rights of ownership against an agreement to resell to the ultimate beneficiary, guaranteed against loss, and splitting any profit on resale. Based in Brussels with 23 plants in 10 European countries, Jamont was the third largest paper towel and tissue manufacturer in Europe and produced 30% of James River's profits at one point. Dick Comfort, the founder of CVCC, Citicorp's venture capital division, and a Jupiter Island and Locust Valley neighbour, was on the James River and the Jamont boards, and we met once a year at James River, when early morning duck flighting was laid on – a speciality of the Chesapeake Bay area. Michael von Clemm was rather jealous of this perk. James River finally bought out the minority interest paying over $200 million.

The deal which portended trouble for Sergio was Lawson Mardon, a major Canadian packaging group. Cragnotti liked consumer products, and therefore he also liked packaging, and so we bought a minority stake in Lawson Marden. As I worked with Sergio, I became satisfied that he was basically an honest and moral individual. But I also began to notice that he had a streak of amorality with respect to rules and regulations, considering those he felt to be unreasonable to be not worth complying with. Sitting through various audit meetings, it was clear he considered certain standard accounting principles to be both illogical and unreasonable. We all know the accounting profession grows standard accounting principles the way gardeners grow bushes. After all, how can audit fees be increased if chargeable hours are not increased? And how can chargeable hours be increased if the number and complexity of standard accounting practices are not increased? I did point out once or twice to Sergio, that SAP's were a fact of life like occasional bouts of indigestion, and one just had to live with them. Lawson Mardon was a perfect example of the dangers of Sergio's simplistic view of the rules of the game. A rights issue was planned to raise needed capital for the Canadian company. Discounted rights issues are the standard capital raising methods in Canada, as in the Mother country. But, standard operating procedure was for the broker handling the issue to quietly tip off the major institutional shareholders of its imminence, allowing these to lighten up their holding, which they would restore on the issue, thus neatly reduced the average cost of their holding. Of course, this led to a fall in the price of the shares, even before the issue was announced. If Sergio had asked me, I would have explained this to him. But I was in London and Sergio was always jetting all over the place. As he saw the price of Lawson Mardon falling, he thought "This means our rights issue will have to be priced lower, raising the cost of the new capital, to the detriment of all shareholders". And so he began buying Lawson Marden shares, through the Geneva office. Of course, he was had up for insider dealing, and I had to fly to Ottawa to plead for leniency. With our Canadian lawyers, the case we put was that, since Sergio would have had dozens of ways to disguise his purchases, but didn't bother, and was caught immediately, this suggested at best ignorance and at worst naïveté. We all know ignorance of the law is never an excuse – but we tend to try it on anyway. I think Sergio knew perfectly well he was sinning, but he also felt he was sinning on behalf of the shareholders – so didn't that make it all right? *Basta!* Sergio as an individual, but not Cragnotti & Partners, was banned from dealing in Canada. I suppose this was just, as none of us knew what he was up to.

But the jewel in the crown, the love of Sergio's life was Cirio. But how often is the love of one's life one's undoing? Not too often – fortunately, but it was to be for Sergio. Francesco Ciro was a Turinese business man and delicatessen owner who developed the process of appertization, the use of heating to sterilise food, to allow packing in tins. He started exporting tinned tomatoes in the 19th century and then founded a company which was to become a leading European brand for all manner of things in tins and jars. My mother remembered Cirio jams as a child in Paris. Cirio was a much reduced and essentially domestic company when it ended up in IRI's portfolio, and Cragnotti dreamed of restoring it to its former glories. I much enjoyed board meetings in Naples, where Cirio was head quartered, because of a lovely collection of old posters and photographs of Cirio products in the company's palmy days. But Sergio always had trouble deciding whether he was a financier or an industrialist. The two disciplines do not sit well together. Several board members, as well as myself urged the appointment of a CEO with experience in managing an international food company. But Sergio was too busy trying to see how Cirio, a quoted company, could be used as a platform for further acquisitions. He was keen to get into the fresh milk business to compete with Parmalat, which was mostly in long-life milk. He wanted to re-establish himself in Brazil and began looking up his old interests there. One day he decided we should all meet in Sao Paulo. I told him I had only a day free. "Here's a first-class return Air France ticket – please be there," he said. I arrived at eight in the morning and a suite had been reserved for me to shower and change. But I had a message that Sergio couldn't be there until the next day; I had lunch with some of the Feruzzi people and took the Air France "red eye" back. I was the sole passenger in first class. Sergio didn't think it strange at all that I had gone to Sao Paulo for the day. Cragnotti's partners, the three banks, were getting restive. They had expected quick and dramatic returns, and did not like the idea that they were turning into long-term investors. Sergio was still thick as thieves with Banco di Roma, an expression I feel justified in using in the light of subsequent events. I was sent off to pacify Société Générale and Swiss Bank Corporation. Some ill-mannered minions at my former EBC French shareholder made me lose my temper, but Marcel Ospell, head of SBC, heard me out courteously, merely remarking that this type of investment was no longer in fashion at Swiss Bank Corp. The problem was the non-Italian shareholders couldn't see an exit.

I was sitting in my office at the Economist building, brooding over the problem of my own exit, when Robert Pasley-Tyler, an ex-Kleinwort Benson director came to see me. He told me his colleagues had sent him off to the U.S. to research the potential for establishing a private banking franchise aimed at that huge market. He had returned to report that that huge market was already over private banked and there was little prospect of a London merchant bank gaining a foot hold. But many people amongst an extensive contact list had told him what they would really like to see in London was an office facility, organised as club, but where business could be done and discussed, unlike in the usual social clubs – and where full office facilities were available on an hourly, daily, weekly, monthly, or even, semi-permanent basis. Temporary office facilities in London abounded, but most required medium-term leases and had no supporting facilities – as well as being extremely depressing. So Robert had acquired the old Polly Peck headquarters town house on the corner of Berkeley Square and Hill Street, re-decorated it completely, found a number of shareholders and potential clients and was now "off to the races". He wanted a high profile board. Would I agree to be chairman? I must say, my profile was becoming a bit broad rather than high, as my tailor would attest. But when Robert said, "There's no fee, but I'll give you an office," I accepted. Sergio was not particularly unhappy to see me go, and Marisa was delighted to escape the somewhat chaotic office atmosphere in the Economist building, and the difficulty of managing my diary with last minute demands to attend meetings here and there. She moved with me to 42 Berkeley Square. I kept a link with Giuseppe Ciardi, a cracker jack hedge fund manager we had hired to run a proprietary trading fund. Giuseppe had been the head "prop" trader at Lazard and then at BNP. He eventually started his own hedge fund management company Park Place Capital, and I served on a couple of his fund boards. I did not follow Sergio Cragnotti's subsequent career very closely as he dropped out of the international news, but stayed more than prominent in Italy. Cragnotti & Partners became Cominvest, a subsidiary of Cirio, which in turn began to stagger from one crisis to another, ending in a major and controversial default. The circumstances surrounding the default eventually provoked judicial action, involving Sergio's great Banco di Roma partner Cesare Geronzi. But convictions and appeals carry on at the traditional snail's pace of Italian justice.

I soon had another office in the City. Whilst still at Merrill Lynch, I had been sitting at a World Bank/IMF annual Washington meeting, bored to tears at a plenary session, when Abdullah Saudi came up and whispered to me, "I want to talk to you about something. I'll call you when we are back in London." Despite his name, Abdullah Amar al Saudi, to give him his full moniker, is a Libyan, founder of Libyan Arab Foreign Bank, and Arab Banking Corporation of Bahrain. He had a long history of working with the Central Bank of Libya, but is in essence an exile, originally a loyal subject of King Idris and not one of Gaddafi's henchmen. He had engineered several notable transactions on behalf of the central bank and Libyan government investment companies, in particular the purchase of 10% of Fiat in 1976. I did not know him well at this time, but had spoken to him about David Mitchum, who at Bankers Trust had done considerable business with the Central Bank of Libya. Abdullah's enthusiastic reference had been a factor in my hiring David for EBC. I didn't hear from Saudi for some time after that brief encounter in Washington, but suddenly he called me and said he wanted me to be Deputy Chairman of ABCIB, the London subsidiary of Arab Banking Corporation of Bahrain, which one might describe as a governmental consortium bank, as the shareholders were the Central Bank of Libya, the Abu Dhabi Investment Authority, the Kuwait Investment Authority, the Central Bank of Bahrain, and a group of Saudi Arabian investors. The Libyans had the largest stake. At this time, Saudi was CEO of the Group and chairman of ABCIB in London. He and the Group in general were under mounting political pressure: Saudi because he was a Libyan and the ABC because of the large Libyan interest. After the Lockerbie disaster, widely presumed to be a Libyan planned outrage, relations between the U.S. And Libya, already badly strained, had worsened. A very effective pressure group comprised of the victims' families worked in Washington to promote sanctions against Libya, and the agency in charge was, and is, OFAC, the Office of Foreign Assets Control, created in World War II, to locate and sequester enemy assets. I called David Mulford in Washington to try and understand what OFAC's position really was. David and I shared the same tailor, and so I thought I'd start with a pleasantry.

"David, should I be ordering a prison stripe suit from Anderson & Shepard?"

"What's up?" he replied.

"I have become Abdullah Saudi's deputy chairman of the Arab Banking Corporation subsidiary in London, and I'm told OFAC is out to get him and ABC."

"OFAC may claim to be part of the Treasury," said David, "and its office is in our building. But we have no idea what those people are up, as they don't report to us. We don't know who they report to – maybe to the White House. Their financial sanctions programmes often conflict with our policy to keep world financial markets as open as possible, and they don't consult us on anything."

This was an interesting take on the situation, but no help. However, he assured me he would log my enquiry and didn't think I was in any way vulnerable. In fact it turned out Abdullah Saudi had recruited me to give the Bank of England some comfort if he was forced to resign. Within a short few months Abdullah was gone from the ABC Group altogether, and OFAC seemed satisfied. I think his role in arranging the Libyan purchase of the stake in Fiat, had convinced OFAC that Abdullah Saudi was an agent of Gadhafi, which he was not. But the persecution continued and Abdullah's daughter was denied a visa to take up an American university scholarship.

ABCIB's main business was trade finance, and my long connection with the bank was the closest I ever came to what I would term pure commercial banking – and I enjoyed every moment. The Bank's selling point was its intimate knowledge of the banking community in the MENA region – Middle East & North Africa. European, American and Japanese exporters to that area preferred to have letters of credit, drawn on little known local banks by importers, accepted by ABCIB, a London authorised bank owned by the major Arab states. Exports to Libya were a major source of business, and ABCIB was assiduous in complying with sanctions imposed on that country. In fact I chaired the sanctions committee, and we set out to be more catholic than the Pope, if I may use a completely inappropriate metaphor. However, we were aware that more than one American bank was happily ignoring sanctions and seeking to eat into our major Libyan market share. I immediately encountered the typical head office/subsidiary tensions that I had known so well at Merrill Lynch. The Bank of England was increasingly urging foreign banks to operate in London through subsidiaries rather than branches. This was a direct result of The BCCI collapse where a bank registered in Luxembourg had centred the bulk of its nefarious activities in a London branch. But as Luxembourg was the primary regulator, the Bank of England had been seriously hampered in exercising its supervisory role. The Bank required letters of comfort from the parents, but the London subsidiary was expected to be properly capitalised, with independent board ensuring that "mind and matter" of management was truly sited in London. This policy was transferred to the SFA when Gordon Brown took bank supervision away from the Bank of England. Once a year, a so called "high level control" visit took place, and executive and non-executive members of the board were interviewed by a pimply youth with a clipboard holding a printed checklist. The questions were simplistic and often inane, and the FSA official read them out and then ticked a box when they were answered. It was obvious the official had little understanding of the questions and even less of the answers. I decided to put this to the test.

"Are you satisfied that you have a good understanding of the products dealt in by your dealers and their compliance with limits and other risk control measures?" was the question, with pencil poised to tick the box.

"Actually, I find the cricket scores easier to understand," I replied.

"Thank you," said my interviewer, ticking the box, and moving on to the next question. By this time my chairman was a 34-year-old Deputy Governor of the Central Bank of Libya called Farhat Ekdara, a charming and well-educated man with wisdom that belied his youth. He enjoyed the fact that his deputy chairman was almost twice his age. I asked our senior contact at the FSA whether he considered it tactful and appropriate to subject a deputy governor of a central bank to this type of interview, but he said he had no choice. Actually Ekdara frequently had to cancel visits to London for our meetings as either he, together with all senior officials, was summoned to the presence of the "Brotherly Leader", or he had stomach problems that prevented him flying. As a result I chaired a good many board meetings.

Our board consisted mainly of shareholder representatives who also sat on the main board, and my sole non-Arab colleague was Terry Stone, recently retired senior partner of Ernst & Young, auditors to the ABC Group. Terry chaired the audit committee and was genuinely taken aback by a marked decline in the quality of the people and the work done by his old firm. It was also Terry who constantly reminded the board of the insistence of our regulator that "mind and matter" be sited with the London board on matters regarding ABCIB. All would nod their heads in enthusiastic agreement. Once back in Bahrain, these same gentleman would alter course and support the Bahrain based Group CEO's efforts to wrest control of our affairs back to head office. We had an outstanding CEO in London in Abdulmagid Breish, from an old Libyan family whose members had been prominent in the court of King Idris. Educated in Italy, as many prominent Libyans, Magid was a true gentleman, generous to a fault, efficient and hardworking, and a highly competent banker. I benefited from executive perks as Abdullah Saudi, in engaging me, had not quite grasped the different compensation arrangements between executive and non-executive directors, so, in addition to my office, I had health insurance, also covering my family and was in the pension plan. When my wife suffered a clinical depression and had to be confined to a clinic in Roehampton, the insurance picked up the entire cost and Magid told me that if policy limits were exceeded, the bank would cover the rest. Magid also was the source of my knowledge of the Muslim faith. I have no idea whether he was Sunni or Shiite and never enquired. He told me the Faith had been hijacked by Mullahs, as its most distinguishing feature, in his view, was the lack of institutional intermediation between the faithful and the Almighty, unlike my religion with its priests and bishops. Magid liked to point out that the only two women mentioned in the Koran were the mother of the Prophet (Peace be upon Him) and the Virgin Mary. He also told me that a main reason for the contempt held by so many Muslims for Christians, as opposed to the other "People of the Book" the Jews, was that Christians not only failed to defend their own religion but actively allowed it to be mocked and blasphemed. I liked to point out to Magid and the board that the earliest bankers were Arabs, even more than the Jews, as they sat on the spice trade routes, as important a commodity for

403

the West as oil today. It took me some time to persuade the board to appoint Magid a member. They were reluctant because the CEO in Bahrain was not a main board member, but I pointed out that a fault in governance arrangements at head office was no excuse for repeating them in London, where CEOs are always board members. Terry Stone and I always prevailed in our proposals by falling back on the simple argument "that's how it's done in London". We incorporated the other European branches of Bahrain in Paris, Milan and Frankfurt into branches of ABCIB. I had to fire an uncooperative manager in Paris, who had all the arrogance of French bankers, without the charm. We closed down a Monte Carlo office which was up to no good. I like to think that ABCIB incorporated all the best features of foreign commercial banks operating in London – and this was due to the inspired leadership of Magid Breish. We stuck to our last and focussed on solving the problems and challenges faced by clients seeking to export to, and do business in the MENA region. Our strategic problem was multiple ownership by governmental entities directed by civil servants. Despite all being Arab, they could never agree on a fixed strategic direction, and wasted money on consultants who could find no consensus for their recommendations. I tried to get my chairman Farhat Ekdara to persuade the Central Bank of Libya to buy out the others. This was before Libya blew up, of course. In retrospect, it's a good thing I was unsuccessful, as the ABC Group, and ABCIB survives.

Non-executive directorships began to sprout like crocusi in spring, or, in my case, like apples falling in autumn. I had a call from my friend John Scott-Oldfield asking if I might be interested to join the board of Bristol & West Building Society. I thought here was a chance to complete my commercial banking education on the retail side of the business. Although always a corporate finance banker by trade, I have never looked down my nose at retail banking, as so many of my peers do. When I met with Sir John Wills he was exactly as I would have expected a former Master of the Merchant Venturers of Bristol, Lord Lieutenant of Avon, heir to the Wills tobacco fortune, cattle breeder and pillar of Bristol society, to be. He told me he felt City experience on the board was now necessary as the building society movement was under pressure to demutualise. In fact it turned out his life was being made miserable by a Bristol solicitor who had appointed himself chief gadfly at the Annual General meeting of members, and who kept loudly complaining that the board of the Society consisted mainly of relatives of Sir John, fellow members of the Merchant Venturers, or both. At the first AGM when I appeared sitting on the dais as a new director, this solicitor rose and said, "I would like to congratulate the Chairman on finally appointing a director who cannot by any stretch of the imagination, be a relation of his." Both Sir John and I took this in good heart. I enjoyed everything about Bristol & West. The product development on the liability side and the residential mortgage business on the other side was of great interest to me. We also had a small but prosperous commercial lending business where we followed a strict policy of only lending to property companies owned by ethnic families, either Jewish or Indian. I introduced my polo friend "Sooty" Dilhon, who had a neat little commercial property empire started by his Sikh father. There is no question that these communities, where family and family ties are paramount, represent the highest credit quality. We pursued a conservative residential mortgage lending policy, with loans rarely exceeding 75% of net asset value, and insisting on comfortable income/interest and repayment ratios. All around us competition was driving a deterioration of loan/NAV ratios, culminating in the 100% plus ratios offered by Northern Rock. My only waywardness as a director was my refusal to be interviewed by an American lady our trendy CEO had dug up. Sir John, fearful that his background and position would cause him to reject modernity, was keen to accept every bit of contemporary corporate jargon and gimmick. The lady was keen on "mentoring" and felt the need to "mentor" the non-executive directors, including the chairman. I refused point-blank. My attitude did not prevent me from being appointed vice-chairman. All too soon Sir John felt it appropriate to retire from the chairmanship to be replaced by Sir Robert Armstrong, who had pursued a distinguished civil service career, ending as cabinet secretary to Margaret Thatcher's government – perhaps the most challenging cabinet secretary ship in the history of that office. Robert Armstrong made more than one contribution to history, but the inclusion of his phrase "economical with the truth" in the Oxford Dictionary of Quotations will be amongst the most lasting. He grasped the essence of our business almost immediately and was an excellent chairman. Perhaps to create a familiar comfort zone, we were soon joined by two of Lady Thatcher's former ministers, John Wakeham and William Waldegrave. Once when I gave a dinner at 42 Berkeley Square to raise funds for Lady Thatcher's Summerville College, I had the great lady on my right of course and struggled to make conversation, so I mentioned our colleagues in common.

"John Wakeham was an excellent chief whip," she announced. "He did exactly what I told him to do." I had the feeling she considered William Waldegrave "a very nice man" but on the humid side – in other words, his Conservatism was probably slightly to the left of her's. At that same dinner, I had placed Sir Dennis Thatcher next to Robin Hambro, Rupert's wife, and an old friend of my "deb's delight" days. From one leg of our U-shaped table, I spotted Sir Dennis trying to catch his wife's eye and surreptitiously waving his cigarette case.

"I think Sir Dennis would like to smoke, Lady Thatcher. I'll just see glasses are filled and propose the Loyal Toast." I looked around for the head waiter.

"Mr Chairman!" said Lady T, severely, "Dennis can wait! You just take your time and propose the Loyal Toast whenever you like." I nevertheless moved on quickly and afterwards, she gave the best speech I ever heard her make – on how a scientific education had prepared her for both politics and life in general.

The board under Robert Armstrong was effective and stimulating. John Wakeham sat next to me, and I could sense he was in permanent pain – which is not surprising as he had suffered severe injuries in the Brighton Bombing, in which he had lost his wife. Having chaired a U.K. energy company acquired by the American conglomerate Enron, he now sat on that board. I asked him if he enjoyed his quarterly visits to Houston. "Two days of endless power point presentations, and the board hardly has a chance to ask questions," he complained. This set me thinking about a very nefarious trend, I was increasingly observing at the boards where I sat. Modern management has developed techniques for evading proper scrutiny of its activities by overloading meetings with power point presentations. These are prepared to waste a maximum of time, with title and subtitle pages and endless graphic illustrations of the same trend, with bar, pie and linear charts – as thought the board members are incapable of grasping the point without a variety of diagrams. Management argues that its morale is enhanced by giving as many officials as possible an opportunity of presenting their accomplishments to the board, and if some restraint is not applied, one ends up with twenty minutes being devoted to the head of security on car park arrangements. Poor John Wakeham was to be caught up in the collapse of Enron, one of the most resounding bankruptcies of modern times, and one in which criminal fraud was found to have been perpetrated by that same management which had pulled the wool over the eyes of the board of directors quarterly, with two days of power point presentations. I resolved to curtail this presentational tendency at Bristol & West, interrupting management as often as possible, and forcing it to exchange Q & A sessions for slide shows. My interventions, which always began with "Excuse me, chairman, but...." became notorious. Another eye-opener was when the necessity arose to dismiss the trendy CEO. Sir Robert asked me to sit in on this difficult interview with an entirely unsuspecting chief executive. To my amazement, the chairman began to read prepared remarks from a paper on his desk, and became so nervous that I gently took over. Here was someone who had held one of the most senior positions in the land, who had headed the entire Civil Service, whose experience and wisdom had tempered many a domestic and international crisis – and who had never had to fire someone. The building society world was soon in the throes of a major change, with its traditional mutual status being abandoned in favour of incorporation, quotation and consolidation through mergers. Members began to seek out the profits to be earned on post quotation sales of their shares, heedless of the instability which would follow in that previously most stable of retail financial services sector. Access to fresh capital was the standard justification. Bristol & West was no exception and soon fell to the blandishments of the Bank of Ireland, whose successful overtures caused Aer Lingus to increase its Dublin-Bristol service. This bank, headed by Pat Mulloy, and a paragon of sound banking at the time, impressed Robert Armstrong by having a Court and a Governor, rather than a mere board and chairman, as it gloried in a Royal Charter, despite its republican domicile. We fell to a combination of Irish charm and industry wide inevitability.

My patronage of the Great Western Railroad – also known as 'God's Wonderful Railroad" – increased when I joined the board of South West Water, although Dennis Davies often insisted on driving me to Bristol, and then Exeter. South West Water Authority had been the victim of the nation's worst poisoning incident pre-privatisation, when a lorry driver dumped aluminium sulphate into the wrong tank at the Lowermoor treatment works. As recently as three years ago, a coroner blamed the incident, the Authority, as it was then known, and its chairman Keith Court, during the inquest of an unfortunate lady who had been a resident in the Camelford area affected. For some unaccountable reason, Keith Court blamed the forthcoming privatisation of the water industry as responsible in part for the tragedy. Equally unaccountable, is the fact that Keith remained chairman of the new corporate entity post-privatisation. What is true is that South West Water was a victim of an ill thought out denationalisation project, as it was left with a disproportionate infrastructure deficit to be remedied at the cost of its hapless customers. The region, essentially Devon and Cornwall, contained some 70% of the nation's most popular bathing beaches, but only 3% of its population. The condition of the pipe and treatment network was lamentable, hardly any investment having been made since installation in Edwardian times. We set up a mini-museum at head office showing cutaway pipes so clogged with sediment that only a tiny hole in the middle allowed water to pass, and other examples of totally exhausted infrastructure. A pressure group called Surfers against Sewage, or SAS, attended our AGM in wet suits. Ineffective sewage outfalls of insufficient length polluted bathing beaches and the company struggled to meet urgently EEC directives on bathing water quality, which were studiously ignored by Mediterranean member's states. It is a known fact that water bills always arrive on a rainy day, and the customer looks angrily out of the window as the heavens open and wonders why he is being charged. No amount of customer education on the realities of drinking water treatment and sewage disposal imperatives, reconciled our customers to the fact that ours were the highest charges in the industry. Too late it was recognised that project financing of our huge capital investment programme might have taken part off balance sheet and extended repayment times, alleviating the immediate impact on our charges.

Despite the fact that the few friends we had living in the Devon and Cornwell area considered that I had joined a coven of the Evil One, I appreciated my experience on the board of South West Water, eventually Pennon Group. It was there I discovered that the Devonians hate the Cornish and vice versa. We had to alternate AGMs between the counties. Cornwall was more than amply represented by Lady Mary Holborow, a daughter of the 8th Earl of Courtown. She was an early Lord Lieutenant of the female sex. She told us that, after her appointment, she rang Downing Street to ask if she got a dress allowance. After all, the 'gents' had a uniform allowance. She was told "no" – all she got was a chain of office, and the only one suitable for ladies was with the Dowager Duchess of Westminster, who hadn't yet returned it. Lady Mary was deeply shocked at my first AGM. Rather like AGMs at Bristol & West, these were essentially customer complaint sessions, those in attendance ignoring the fact that they owned the business. But one lady got up and asked, "Mr. Chairman, I see that our new director Mr. ya... Sorry, can't pronounce it – doesn't own any shares in the company. Why is that?"

"I'll ask Mr. Ya-su-ko-vich, to answer that," said Keith Court, helpfully.

"Rhymes with 'Shostakovich' Madame' I started. "The reason is, I am on a host of boards now that I am no longer full time in the City, and I simply can't afford to own shares in them all. I am no less committed to the company."

"Oh! I can't believe that," said the Lady, wisely not trying my name again. "All you Jewish gentlemen in the City are very rich."

"Very sadly, madame, I am not Jewish," I replied. "How I wish I were! Perhaps then I would be rich – as you say."

This elicited an embarrassed rustle of laughter from the hall, but Lady Mary was outraged. She actually got up from the table on the dais and said, "I think your remarks are entirely inappropriate, Mrs. Whoever you are!"

Actually, I felt rather sorry for the lady who was, no doubt, the wife of a Cornish farmer and would have strongly denied harbouring anti-Semitic sentiments. At luncheon after, we always entertained the chairman of a customer representative group, who tuned out to be author Jessica Mann, sister of my friend David, with whom she was on bad terms, and daughter of Francis Mann, senior partner of Herbert Smith. Keith Court was replaced as chairman by Ken Harvey, who had a distinguished record in the energy business, and was identified by John Scott-Oldfield. Keith had done his best but suffered from his association with the preceding Authority and the poisoning scandal, and also had a difficult relationship with the then head of the regulator OFWAT. I never attended a meeting between them, but I believe it was a question of personal chemistry. Our waste management business had grown from being a sideline of the basic waste disposal activity, to a full scale franchise on its own, with land fill development and management and industrial scale treatment centres. We decided to and rename the group, and operate through two divisions – utility and waste management. We hit on Pennon, after a thirty minute discussion and had no need to engage expensive branding discussions. A name search cost and a few hundred pounds. A pennon is the military version of the naval pennant, and is the triangular flag flown at the end of a cavalry lance. Our excellent finance director struggled to cope with the funding of our huge capital programme. As a result he made extensive use of the City and liked to include me in beauty contests when an investment bank was being selected. I enjoyed sitting on the other side of the table for once but had to restrain myself. Not only did I know what was coming next in the pitch, but I thought I could have done it better – of course. Once Merrill Lynch was a candidate for selection and, probably improperly, I rang my old colleague Kevin Watts, now a senior figure at Merrill, to "prep" him for the forthcoming interview.

"I would stress Merrill's long experience in the water utility business in the States," I suggested. "You are the only U.S. House we are interviewing." Although water utilities are largely state or municipal owned in America, they make extensive use of various, project type, financing techniques for their capital expenditures. Merrill had inherited White, Weld's utility franchise.

"Yes, of course," said Kevin. "We have a new, very successful ex-Morgan Grenfell man, I'll put him in charge of the team. Maybe we'll get someone over from New York."

I attended the presentation and it was a disaster. The ex-Morgan Grenfell man exhibited all the worst tendencies of merchant bankers brought up on walk-in business, talking down to our finance director in a known-it-all fashion, and almost suggesting the only reason someone of his seniority was present was as a courtesy to me as a former Merrill chairman. There was no reference whatsoever to American experience. I was embarrassed and annoyed. I apologised to my colleague, but never admitted I had contacted Watts in advance. In general, my "career" as a non-executive director afforded me several amusing opportunities to play client, after a lifetime of pitching. I found glaring examples of failure to carry out even the most basic research on the prospective client, before soliciting his business. But the worst was the bald face lying. "What you see is what you will get" would intone the senior man, with one or two senior colleagues and one note-taking junior. Rubbish – once the mandate awarded, one never saw the same team again.

My non-executive list diversified further. I was asked to chair a quoted property company called Hemingway, run by Michael Goldhill, son of a celebrated North London estate agent, and Andrew Browne, an accountant. Ours was an archetypal portfolio of office, retail and industrial properties sited throughout England, selected on location and tenant quality – the two linked principles of property investment. As with closed end funds investment funds, we sold at a permanent discount from even a conservatively calculated net asset value – rendering expansion virtually impossible. We were eventually acquired by Prudential of America. I also joined the board of Union America Insurance Ltd, run by Ian Sinclair. We were a speciality casualty and property reinsurer and insurer operating in the Lloyd's of London reinsurance and insurance markets. Our speciality of interest was the medical malpractice market in the U.S., where we reinsured the self- insurance pools maintained by groups of doctors and other healthcare providers. Despite constant cries for "tort reform" in the U.S., the lawyer dominated State assemblies are slow to take steps to rectify the scandal of extreme malpractice litigation awards which are an important contributor to the high cost of health care in the U.S.

Our medical malpractice reinsurance business was highly profitable due to the skills of our underwriter, who knew how to select amongst the medical practice groups, based on their varied experience in malpractice suits. One of our main shareholders was a U.S. Private Equity fund focussing on bottom fishing in the Lloyd's market, recently decimated by scandal and huge losses by names. It eventually took over Union America.

My experience of City based, non-executive activity can be best described as a series of well-meaning failures. Perhaps "failure" is too strong a word for one of these. "Waste of time" might be more generous. I had conceived the notion of commissioning a major study of the competitive advantages of the City of London as a global financial centre. I sought support from the Department of Trade & Industry and received the reply from Lord Young referred to in my introduction to this light hearted ramble through my life. I have not kept the copy of his letter but the message was quite clear. "A thoroughly bad idea" would be a fair summary. I should have taken notice and spent more time playing polo. But I persisted and found support from the Bank of England, through Alastair Clark an advisor to the Governor, and, crucially, from the Corporation of the City of London, our much esteemed local authority. The Lord Mayor, Sir Hugh Bidwell, a Grocer, saw the idea as marking his term. Michael Cassidy, chairman of the all-important Policy & Resources Committee was enthusiastic. I was invited to breakfast at the Mansion House by Sir Hugh, a Lord Mayor in the great tradition, who happily strolled around the Square Mile in fairly full regalia. At breakfast he complained about over starched and tight stiff collars, causing me to ruminate on Mansion House housekeeping arrangements. I put together a committee of so called "City Grandees" one of which was Peter Baring, who was to tell the Bank that his house had created a highly profitable and risk-free business in Singapore – perhaps one of the greatest *non sequiturs* of modern City history. We produced a raft of individual studies on all aspects of the City's pre-eminence, but pointing out important failings which needed attention. The greatest was transport, and if we had any tiny influence of future actions, it would have been the strong recommendation for the Cross Rail project. Michael Cassidy decided we should "travel" the final report, roughly the size of the "yellow pages" and only slightly more interesting. Off we went to New York, Tokyo and Washington, where we were received, for some reason, by a Mormon Senator for Utah. The Japanese took copious notes. The City Research Project Report has now descended into such obscurity that it cannot even be found on Wikipedia. However, I became *persona grata* at the Mansion House for a while. This was relatively short-lived. When Lord Levene, after distinguished service as Chief of Defence Procurement, and many other posts, became Lord Mayor, the debate over membership of the Euro Zone was raging. Rodney Leach had set up a pressure group called "Business for Sterling" with lovely "£" lapel pins for adherents. He had asked me to head the City chapter. Rodney was an early hero of the Eurobond market, having, with Jacob Rothschild, devised the Transalpine Pipeline issue "take or pay" project style financing in the Eurobond market – a deal White Weld should have won with its American pipeline finance experience. Tony Blair, an avowed Europhile, was clearly in favour of adopting the Euro, but some of his party was not – just as the Conservative opposition was split. I believe it was Tony Blair, together with other Europhiles, who sent the Lord Mayor on a tour of the Continent, during which he gave a series of speeches declaring the City would wither on the vine if the United Kingdom did not join the Eurozone – but I could be wrong about that. But several speeches to that effect he did make. I was amazed that the Lord Mayor should defy tradition and involve his office in a burning political issue of the moment. The Corporation of London is strictly nonpolitical. But I was also amazed that he should be as ignorant of City affairs as not to realise its unique experience as a guest currency centre. It was as if a Lord Mayor had said, in the early '60s, that London could not maintain a Eurodollar market unless it applied for statehood in the U.S. and adopted the $ as its currency. I wrote him a letter. I did not mark it "Private & Confidential" or even "Private" and I sent a few copies to interested people – such as Rodney Leach. Lord Levene hit the very high Mansion House ceiling and wrote me a terrifying letter, castigating me for circulating a copy of my letter, and implying I should be grateful for having some position in the City but which did not entitled me to criticise the Lord Mayor. I was promptly black balled from the Mansion House, and have never received an invitation to any City Corporation function since. My only regret is this incident has probably robbed me of any chance of receiving the Freedom of the City – the only honour I have ever really coveted.

Lord Levene went on to many important positions, becoming a very successful Chairman of Lloyd's of London – something it badly needed. As far as I know, not a murmur of regret over his erroneous prediction has passed My Lord's lips – but I am sure we will find him on many a platform when the referendum debate on continuing British membership of the EU begins in earnest – together with many others who predicted disaster for the City, if Britain did not join the Euro.

I had remained friends with Michael Cassidy after the City research Project, and he supported my next failed project. Richard Freeman, a lawyer of considerable City experience, had served on an arbitration panel at the SFA. The Securities and Futures Authority had been the culmination of my TSA tenure when, with SIB's encouragement, we merged with the SRO dealing with futures, headed by Nick Durlacher. Richard came to me with an idea. ADR was becoming all the rage in legal circles. For those who choke on acronyms, I should make clear that this one does not refer to American Depository Receipts, used to facilitate trading in foreign equities in New York. No, this ADR refers to Alternative Dispute Resolution. That, in turn, means that instead of going to court to settle an argument, you rely on arbitration, mediation and conciliation. The result is a substantial reduction in cost and a substantial increase in speed. Richard considered rightly that the speed factor would very much favour the application of ADR to financial disputes, where the uncertainty generated can create false markets, if allowed to fester. His idea was to set up a City Disputes Panel with a group of leading lights from the judicial and financial worlds. Richard had already lined up two Law Lords in support, Lords Ackner and Templeton, as well as Silks David Calcutt and John Hall. He asked me to be chairman. Once again, I was able, with Richard Freeman, to get backing from both the Bank of England and the City Corporation, but also from the CBI and Lloyd's of London. We traipsed around to all the main City law firms and, in almost every case, got the warmest reception from the senior partners. I remember the words of one: "We are here to solve clients' problems and we can't do this in a timely fashion if we have resources tied up in lengthy litigation. If CDP can resolve cases rapidly, it will bring economic benefits to the partnership. Of course, we will refer cases whenever appropriate and in our power to do so." What encouraging words! Unfortunately the litigation partners in the same firms didn't see it that way at all. For them, we were taking food out of their children's mouths by seeking to limit their billable hours through speedy case resolution. For others, we were East End barrow boys trying to break in to the business of Fortnum & Mason. Most City grandees were enthusiastic, however. I went to see Bob Alexander, Q. C., now Lord Alexander and chairman of Nat-West. "A brilliant and timely idea! Congratulations!" How delightful this was – and would we be able to handle the flood of cases which would pile up at the doors of our modest little cubbyhole office? Our panel of Law Lords, leading Q. C.s and various financial wizards stood by, waiting to be assigned to cases. We waited, and we waited. An early success boosted morale. Lloyd's was in the throes of a plan called *Restructuring and Renewal* after the huge losses on American asbestos liabilities and the Ian Postgate scandal. An entity called Equitas had been created to absorb all disputed pre-1993 claims, amounting to close to $21 billion. But claims had to be settled by a deadline to be accepted by Equitas. The City Disputes Panel set up an assembly line operation under Desmond Ackner and Sidney Templeman, using a new ADR technique called "case review". Under this system, counsel acting for each disputant presented the case for rapid, but nonbinding, adjudication by one of the Law Lords. As their judgements were nonbinding, litigants could refuse to accept them and go on to an ordinary court procedure. But they then risked missing the Equitas deadline, and the judgements were so well presented by the Law Lord presiding, that parties could not but agree that the same judgement would likely emerge from a lengthy and expensive trial. The acceptance rate was almost 100%

This early success was misleading, as the circumstances surrounding the Lloyd's restructuring and Equitas were uniquely suited to the CDP approach. When we were landed with Barings post collapse bevy of lawsuits and asked to produce an ADR solution, we were in a different world. Everyone was suing everyone – two audit firms, the liquidator, bond holders – all heavily represented. The sound of meters running in the City was deafening. KPMG, the liquidator had referred the case. Richard asked Sidney Templeman to chair the panel which was to include David Calcutt QC, one of our staunch supporters, Michael von Clemm and Richard. But Michael's health was failing and Richard asked me to stand in. Even with my aptitude for speed reading, the volume of documents to digest was formidable. Lord Templeton set to work with impressive application. I won't go into the details of the case as they are too obtuse and, frankly, boring. But we were met with a quite extraordinary lack of cooperation by the distinguished firms of City solicitors representing the various parties, who refused to answer letters, or did so in a curt fashion, telling us they would entertain no intercession by the CDP. One firm, which condescended to attend at Lord Templeman's behest, treated him with such discourtesy that I was truly shocked. Here was a senior Law Lord with a long record of public service to the judiciary, a former Lord of Appeal in Ordinary, and some junior City lawyers were treating him with disrespect – and this in the presence of David Calcutt, a leading Silk and former chairman of the Bar Council – who was as shocked as I. This was the new City of London. A major key to a settlement proposal was the extent of insurance available to the two firms of auditors involved. Understandably, they, and their Big Four colleagues, were loath to have this sensitive information in the public domain. It took all the skills of Lord Templeman to wheedle it out, on an understanding of the strictest confidentiality. I will not reveal it, even now – nor will Richard Freeman, and poor Lord Templeton took the knowledge to his grave. In the end, all was in vain. American vulture funds had bought large positions at bottom prices in the outstanding Baring bonds and were in a position to frustrate the 75% bond holder vote which would have been necessary to accept a proposal. They would not accept our proposal in the belief that, ultimately, sufficient insurance moneys would be available to ensure higher values. With this failure, we received no further referrals, and ran out of money to keep the CDP going as an independent ADR facility. Judith Mayhew had represented the Corporation on our board, but she didn't much like us, as she was a member of Chartered Institute of Arbitrators, and considered us an annoying competitor. After Richard and I decamped, she must have managed to incorporate the name under the Institute, where it still languishes – unused and forgotten.

My last and greatest failure in the realm of financial services initiatives was undoubtedly EASDAQ. Again a chorus of approval and admiration created the announcement of this project, and lip service began to flow from all quarters. If only lip service could be monetised we would have had the funding to carry on the project as an independent entity. I was not the originator. Paternity was shared between Ronald Cohen of Apax, then chairman of the British Venture Capital Association and Jos Peeters, chairman of the European Venture Capital Association. Apax was historically associated with

Alan Patricoff, a grandfather of the venture capital industry in the U.S. Ronald Cohen, now Sir Ronald, as a co-founder of Apax, and former Patricoff colleague, has become as legendary a figure in British venture capital. I came into the EASDAQ project when my former Stock Exchange colleagues Graham Ross-Russell and Andrew Beeson, came to see me in the Economist Building offices of Cragnotti. A European Association of Securities Dealers was being formed to imitate to some extent the American NASD, which represented the entire community of equity traders, not just NYSE members, this reflecting the fact that an over the counter market in unlisted shares had existed nationally for years in the U.S., and had provided the breeding ground for a whole generation of entrepreneurial start-up companies. Many would reflect that that community represents a defining aspect of American capitalism. It was the NASD which had fostered the creation of NASDAQ, the last two letters in the acronym signifying "automatic quotation". Before NASDAQ was the "pink sheets" market, quotations mimeographed daily on pink paper and circulated to over-the-counter dealers in all the major cities. It was the national, coast to coast nature of this market which provided a capital formation facility to the small, start-up venture. NASDAQ's publicity used to refer to a trading floor so many thousands of miles wide, i.e., the distance from the Atlantic to the Pacific. This recognised the obvious fact that the smaller and the more unknown a company, the broader the audience needed to raise capital. In Europe some members of the traditionally myopic political class were beginning to realise that small and medium-sized enterprises, particularly those engaged in the new technologies, represented the economic future – as traditional, big industry moved east. A nascent venture capital industry was seeking to duplicate the American experience. Venture capitalists require an exit for their investments, in order to recycle and attract funds to invest with. The traditional exits are trade sales or flotations. There is a third exit; they prefer not to mention – bankruptcy and liquidation. In America, an initial public offering with quotation on NASDAQ, is the classic exit. Why can't we copy this in Europe? Was not the question in many minds? The population of prospective investors is roughly the same in numbers. Unfortunately, their investment habits are not.

Quite a bit of discussion took place between the promoters of the EASD, and Ronnie Cohen and Jos Peeters representing the venture capital industry, before all decided to go the whole way and set up EASDAQ. Ronnie favoured a European statesman/political figure as first chairman. In retrospect, he was right. If such a person could have been identified and attracted, the project might have received the political support it needed – and never received. Names like Ted Heath and Willy Brandt were bandied about, but this route seemed increasingly unlikely to supporters like Ross-Russell and Beeson. Finally eyes at the endless meetings began to focus on me – and, like the slow-witted, ageing trout that I was – I took the fly. A good deal of favourable publicity ensued. I have a cartoon by the *Guardian's* Chris Riddell on my wall, showing a goose named "Goose Tech, Ltd. being spoon fed a laxative called "EASDAQ", and a venture capitalist at the nether end, hands cupped. Many thought a golden age of European high tech entrepreneurship had finally arrived. A totally mistaken decision was made to locate in Brussels, to avoid annoying The Stock Exchange – and to be in the "capital" of Europe. We might just as well have been in Timbuctoo. I ran into Jeffrey Knight in the street. He looked at me and said, "How could you?" For him, I was like a heavily tattooed English football player going off to play for a team in Los Angeles. We had a mole/supporter at the European Commission in the person of Paul Goldschmidt, of the great banking family, a former Goldman Sachs partner, who now held a senior position in a key directorate in Brussels. As chairman of EASDAQ, my contacts with the Commission were enlightening and depressing. Edith Cresson, Commissioner for the appropriate directorate, convened a meeting of heads of all the European exchanges, including new-boy EASDAQ, to discuss the challenge of creating a single European equity market. The lady – she of the Christopher Fildes quotation of my remark on rewards for ex-mistresses – was indeed a former mistress of President Mitterrand, but she had also been briefly his Prime Minister. She made history by appointing her dentist as her chief of staff. He kept his surgery in Lille, and continued filling the teeth of its citizens, whilst drawing his salary and benefits from Brussels. This scandal was a factor in the decision of the European Parliament to sack the entire Commission of President Jacques Santerre, universally known as Jacques "Sancerre" – the sacking of a single commissioner being beyond its powers. Madame le Commissionaire was late arriving, and one of her lackeys – not the *dentiste* – opened the meeting with a round of self-introductions. Discussions began quite happily in English, in which all were fluent – even the head of the Paris *bourse*. After a while, Madame floated in, with a train of additional lackeys *"Ou sont les interprètes?* She queried, looking at the empty translators' glass fronted booths; *"J'ai commander des interprètes! Ou sont ils?"* The crestfallen man who had opened the meeting tried to explain that everyone was happy speaking in English. Madame Cresson wouldn't have it. We all waited twenty minutes whilst interpreters were dug up from somewhere. The meeting was a waste of time, with each simply extolling the virtues of their own exchange. But the luncheon afterwards was truly memorable – four courses, including cheese, and two wines.

EASDAQ was not seeking to compete with the main list on national exchanges, but they, on the other hand, were determined not only to compete with EASDAQ, but to crush it completely. Each opened its own sub-exchange for smaller growth companies: London with AIM, Paris *Le Nouveau Marché*, ditto in Brussels and Amsterdam and the *Neue Markt* in Frankfort. This proliferation, and national segmentation, was a complete denial of the necessity to construct the widest possible market, reaching the broadest investor audience, to serve the needs of smaller growth companies. It was proof positive that the people who ran Europe's stock exchanges, London included, I fear, had little notion of how securities markets should work, and simply used existing exchanges as instruments of protectionism, and furtherance of their own careers. Paul Goldschmidt kept reporting the encouraging whispers he would pick up in the corridors of Brussels from a few who wished us to succeed. But he would elicit a shrugging of shoulders when he tried to promote action to help pave the way to a truly European exchange for smaller companies – which would help reproduce the American entrepreneurial experience, and drag the EEC kicking and screaming from its post-industrial lethargy. A fundamental reform would have been to force national financial regulators to lift language and other restrictive features from new issue prospectus requirements, making investor protection regulation uniform, and suited to higher risk equity investment. But the protectionist tradition of each national exchange was far too embedded. Our first major listing was an excellent example, on the face of it, of just the sort of company EASDAQ targeted. Lernout & Hauspie was a hi-tech, voice recognition company from so- called Flanders Language Valley, where linguistic skills are so prevalent. It went public simultaneously on NASDAQ and EASDAQ, a very suitable construction, which accessed both investor time zones. Indeed, NASDAQ had taken a small share in our new exchange and promised technical assistance, with a view to encouraging such dual listings. Kredietbank were the sponsors and lead managers and its chief dealer Marcel Stappers was on our board. On impact day, a technical hitch delayed the start of dealing by about fifteen minutes, after announcement of the issue price. But it turned out Kredietbank had engaged in preferential allocation and other practices which, in the U.S., would have had them up before the SEC in two shakes. The issue was vastly oversubscribed and grossly under-priced by Kredietbank, which had encouraged its branches to take subscriptions coupled with immediate sale orders. In other words, the investment banker to the issuer had conspired in a huge "stagging" operation. Stagging is the practice of subscribing to an issue solely for the purpose of immediate resale at a profit. The president of Kredietbank had the nerve to complain to me about the short delay in the commencement of trading, which had slightly reduced the immediate post issue premium. At a meeting, he displayed not only arrogance, but a total lack of understanding of new issue procedures. I wanted to dismiss Kredietbank from the membership of EASDAQ but was not going to hurt Marcel Stappers, who had been a keen supporter and had lobbied his investment banking colleagues to choose EASDAQ for the European listing of L & H. He had not been responsible for his bank's outrageous behaviour as investment bankers – which of course they were not, no more than I am a ballet dancer. As for Lernout & Hauspie, with a market capitalisation of $10 billion at its peak – worse was to follow. With far superior analytical and research resources at its disposal, NASDAQ discovered that the company was cooking its books. Revenue recognition is always a sticky issue with new, high growth companies – particularly those with foreign franchise arrangements. But Lernout & Hauspie was engaging in blatantly fraudulent accounting. Its founders ended up with jail terms – but served with ankle bracelets. I should have resigned right away after this lamentable performance by Kredietbank, which I recall with disgust. I should have resigned after the failure of our own due diligence in not recognising the true nature of the founders of Lernout & Hauspie – but I soldiered on.

The struggle and decline of EASDAQ illustrated graphically the inherent weaknesses in the European capital market for equity financing. In the first place, we never had the flow of listings anticipated by our venture capital fathers. Many were skimmed off by the national rival small company exchanges. Their sponsors had no understanding of the broader market concept. Low deal flow meant low levels of interest by dealers and investment bankers. Failure breeds failure. At conference after conference, the European entrepreneurial gap was discussed, with much analysis and little solution. The problem was, and still is, cultural and social. In the U.S., bankruptcies by entrepreneurs are worn like campaign ribbons, and venture capitalists look with disfavour on applicants for funding who haven't fallen on their face once or twice. In Europe, bankruptcy is a disgrace, causing a hapless entrepreneur to remove his children from school and move to another city. There are few serial entrepreneurs. Those few who "make it big" retire to a country estate or buy a yacht in Monte Carlo. Specialist financial intermediation is lacking. The large banks, who happily take risks with their own balance sheet, have no idea how to deal with risk-taking entrepreneurs. In Germany, they just take a mortgage on the entrepreneur's home as security. Boutique investment banks specialising in the sector a few and far between. But EASDAQ's fundamental miscalculation was to believe that Europe's drive for unification at the political, monetary and fiscal level would overcome the dogged protectionism which plagues its financial community. Even today, the champions of monetary union seem oblivious to the fact that the lack of a unified equity capital market within the Eurozone makes that monetary experiment even more ridiculous than it is already, on the economic and political level. In the end, after three CEOs, false trails with possible outside investors, further capital calls on our shareholders, and all the familiar thrashings of a venture in death throes, we were bought out by NASDAQ, whose ambitious president Frank Zarb enjoyed trips to Europe. He did nothing with it, and I suspect EASDAQ still exists somewhere, in a filing cabinet at NASDAQ. Apart from the eye-opening experience, I relished the opportunity of mixing with such highly personable and stimulating venture capitalists as Ronnie Cohen and Jos Peeters. They were kind and generous with me, but they no doubt thought I didn't quite have the "clout" to turn their dream into a reality.

This "pick and mix" part of my non-working life certainly lived up to the spice of variety evoked in my chapter heading, but I don't think a notional biographer would deem it a success, and this auto biographer calls it a bit of a damp squib. I believe I provided a change from the bog standard type of non-executive director on the boards I served on. Colleagues would describe my attitude as frequently provocative, and, hopefully, sometimes constructive. Management was usually glad to see the back of me. A very brief interlude in my non-executive life was BMCE International, the London subsidiary of the privatised Banque Marocaine du Commerce Exterieur, now known as BMCE Bank, a fiefdom of Moroccan entrepreneur Othman Benjelloun, of an insurance based fortune. David Suratgar, ex Morgan Grenfell, was Benjelloun's man in London and persuaded him to open a London subsidiary. By a strange coincidence, David had briefed my father, as a young general counsel at the World Bank, when DY was engaged as a consultant to sort out problems at the World Bank's affiliate in Morocco – the pre-privatisation BMCE. David made a couple of mistakes in setting up the London venture. He complicated matters by having two separate boards, one for the holding company and one for the bank itself. But more seriously, he filled the boards with City grandees, such as Peter Cook, Sir David Walker, Ian Plenderleith, Christopher Reeves, and even me – but without any directors from head office, except Chairman Benjelloun, who never turned up. Not to put too fine a point on it, the head office management, considering they had no "ownership", of this toy of their boss Benjelloun, proceeded to undermine BMCE International in London at every turn, taking the art of non-co-operation to new heights. I did tell David Suratgar, that I was witnessing a degree of parent/subsidiary tension which made the same condition I had witnessed at Arab Banking Corporation pale into insignificance. Worst of all, the attitude of head office executives in Casablanca was driving a coach and horses through the London supervisor's rules governing subsidiaries of overseas banks, and this under the very noses of two ex-Bank of England officials sitting on the board. I was sorely tempted to blow a whistle, but I couldn't do this to David Suratgar, an extremely nice and well-meaning Persian exile, and it would have been totally incorrect board procedure. In the end, it was all wound down, and I was invited to resign, along with a couple of other vocal directors – and I imagine David Suratgar regretted he had miss judged me as a docile City "grandee".

As for the charitable positions I held on the expectation I would bring lots of money, the score is more difficult to calculate. I think my idea of the affinity card for Save the Children, might well have saved one or two. I hope HRH the Princess Royal thinks so. At the National Theatre, I served as chairman of the Development Committee as well as the board, but my puny efforts to round up sponsors were eclipsed by the deputy chairman, the marvellous Lois Sieff, an American lady married to a Marks & Spenser scion, and a fund raiser *extraordinaire*. But her reports to the committee were sometimes alarming. "I've been calling on our suppliers" she would say – meaning M & S's suppliers, not the National. "I tell them 'I guess you value your contract with M & S? Yes? …well, a cheque made out to the National Theatre will certainly help renew it!'"

"Lois! You can't do that," I would say.

"Why the hell not? What's the point of being called Seiff, if I can't do that?"

"The board of the company will go ballistic – if they hear about it."

"Let them! We'll have the money!" Lois was a treasure, and knew perfectly well she had absolutely no say on M & S suppliers.

I had some success in another place. I was asked to join a centenary committee for Westminster Cathedral, chaired by Pat Sheehy of BATS, and including our old auditor at White, Weld, Brandon Gough, who had become senior partner of Coopers & Lybrands. I was not a parishioner, but someone must have tipped I was "left-footed". Few realise the Cathedral is only a century old and I much enjoyed becoming acquainted with it. I was intrigued to find the memorial to Aleksander Contsantinovich Benckendorf, Russian Ambassador to the Court of St. James during the First War, who died in London in 1917. He was of the Baltic nobility, born a Lutheran and converted to Roman Catholicism. One of my first fund raising calls was on Stuart Hampson, chairman of the John Lewis Partnership. "What a lovely view you have of the Cathedral," I commented, looking out from his Victoria offices.

"I know what you're after," he said. "Let me call my Public Affairs officer. It's our employee's money, you know."

This gentleman arrived and opined that there were a sufficient number of employees/partners who were Catholic to justify a contribution. My next was a real coup. On the pretext of discussing British Field Sports Society business, I called on Gerald Westminster at the Grosvenor Estate offices. A possible merger was under discussion, between the BFSS and the shooting organisation the Duke chaired – this to strengthen our hand for the forthcoming anti-hunting bill debate. After exchanging views on the problem of the wild fowling set, who wanted nothing to do with fox-hunting, I ventured, "I know you have been a great supporter of the Abbey, but I imagine you know the Cathedral is celebrating a centenary – and, of course, it is on your patch."

"Leave it with me," said the Duke. Shortly after, a letter arrived from a Grosvenor Estate official saying: "His Grace thanks you for your recent visit and has asked me to pass you the enclosed cheque, with best wishes for the Cathedral's centenary celebrations."

Enclosed was a cheque for six figures. Pat Sheehy thought I was a magician and said it would have never occurred to him to approach a worthy stalwart of the Church of England. A truly "lump in the throat" event occurred at that time. HM The Queen agreed to grace the Cathedral with her presence – not at a Mass, that would have been too controversial, but to a specially arranged Evening Service. On the evening in question, the Cathedral was packed, and there were demonstrators outside with placards with "Shame on you, Your Majesty", "Down with Popery!", "No Whore of Rome here!" and the like – presumably carried by Northern Irishmen, but more probably by professional agitators, always happy to have an outing. HRH the Duchess of Kent, a convert, was already seated when the Queen arrived. On HM's entrance, the congregation rose as one and burst into applause. I am rather against applause in church, but I grant this was a justifiable exception. After, the committee members and Cathedral staff lined up in a circle in the refectory and Basil Hume, Cardinal Archbishop, took HM around on the usual Royal walk about. Two nuns standing next to me were jumping up and down with excitement. I was able to remind the Cardinal Archbishop of our squash game at Bibury.

Finally, I come to two non-executive positions which have languished in my portfolio until recently. My old EBC colleague Crispin Money-Coutts, still then at the family bank contacted me and said:

"This will blow your mind. A client of ours, Jhitesh Ghadia, is one of the Ugandan Asian community expelled by Idi Amin. He works at Barings. He has two fellow exile brothers called Manek as friends. They are pharmacists and have some chemist shops in the Harrow area. But one, Jaycsh Manek has won the *Sunday Times* Fantasy Fund Manager contest twice in a row, beating some professionals who compete. This has attracted the attention of no less that Sir John Templeton, who has given them his own money to invest, and now suggests the Maneks turn professional and launch a unit trust. Ghadia has explained they need a properly governed management company to gain authorisation, and they need a chairman. Any interest?"

"Yes!" I replied, "and I'll tell you why. I have a great sympathy for people chucked out of their country by nasty dictators, as my father was chucked out of his country by a nasty dictator called Lenin."

I have a sneaking suspicion Crispin knew this before he called me. I met the two brothers, Jayesh and Hasu, and was impressed by their correctness, their seriousness and their general character. I had already decided to accept when I had Sir John Templeton on the phone from Nassau. I had met Sir John once at lunch at Merrill Lynch in New York, because at one time the Templeton Funds owned over 5% of Merrill.

"You would be doing me a personal favour if you agreed to chair the Manek company," he said. "I have always favoured new entrants to the fund management business which needs shaking up with new blood. I have told them to roll the £2 million of mine they are managing into a new unit trust."

"I was hesitating," I fibbed – "but your call has persuaded me, Sir John." Old schmoozers never die.

Sir John flew to London, for the launch, Crispin agreed to come on the board with me, and the financial press greeted the new arrival with disdain, "What does a chemist know about fund management?" The Manek Growth Fund topped performance against the relative benchmark for a while, and then Jayesh lost his way. He has always been a keen Elliot Wave theorist and that promotes bearishness, a handicap in growth fund management. But I have enjoyed every moment of my association with the Maneks and their little team. Breaking into the unit trust market is challenging. One needs a large marketing budget and IFAs, the main distribution channel prefer easy sales of well-known brands. The Maneks have a private Indian equity fund which has done very well, but its distribution in the U.K. would also be difficult. Still, I would not have missed this connection for the world.

My old friend and colleague John Craven provided me with another twilight position. John was advising the dissident Cayzer family members, led by Sir James Cayzer and his heir Nigel, who had all grown impatient with their lock up in a Cayzer family trust, and its semi-control position in the quoted investment trust Caledonia. In effect, they suffered a double discount on their holdings, no liquidity and no ability to pursue a different investment strategy than that determined by Caledonia, chaired by Peter Buckley. His mother was a member of this great Scottish shipping family, and he also chaired the family trust company – which the dissidents considered a conflict. The battle had simmered for some time, flared up, then simmered, and then flared up. Fairly recent proposals for a restructuring put to the AGM of Caledonia by Sir James had been seen off by Peter Buckley, and some changes made, but not enough to satisfy the dissidents, which included Ian Molson, married to a Cayzer, and Robin Rotherwick, holder of the Cayzer family's peerage title. John was cooking up a new solution involving splitting Caledonia into two parts, and wanted my view. Although complicated, what John had devised made perfect sense and should have suited both camps. He had informally canvassed one or two institutional shareholders such as Hermes and Schroeder's, and they liked it. But when he said he intended an informal approach to Peter Buckley, I was alarmed.

"But, John, it will leak," I said.

"Oh, no," replied John, "Peter Buckley is a proper gent. He will respect confidentiality."

"But, he's just hired a new CEO and he'll be out of a job, or in a greatly diminished one, under these proposals. Turkeys don't vote for Christmas."

"He certainly won't have a job if he blabs," remarked John.

Oh John! How could one of the City's greatest investment bankers be so naïve! Of course, the fellow blabbed, the word was out, and the Takeover Panel immediately issued a "put up or shut up" order as Caledonia, a quoted company, was now in play. The new scheme could not be ready in time and so that was that. But Mr. Buckley, who I am sure had not been the source of the leak himself, was not only a proper gentleman but a smart one. He realised that the dissidents and their advisor John Craven, would not go away. So he decided to simply buy them off with the declaration of a special dividend to be paid solely to them. Dividends paid to only one shareholder or group of shareholders are extremely rare and require approval of 75% of shareholders at an Extraordinary General Meeting, convened for the purpose. His case to shareholders was in the manner of "will no one rid me of this troublesome shareholder?" but Peter Buckley did not have the murder of Sir James in mind. He argued that Caledonia had carried the distracting burden of the dissidents to long, and it was time to separate. His proposal was accepted and Sir

James's party was able to gain approval from the Inland Revenue for roll over relief from immediate capital gains tax, using the proceeds of the special dividend to subscribe to ordinary and preference shares in a new protected cell company being establish in Guernsey, to be called Cayzer Continuation PCC Ltd. The protected cell company is a construction initially devised for corporate owners of captive insurance companies, which allows them to ring fence each company within an overall corporate entity, without mutual contagion risk – and the ability to pursue differing investment strategies suitable to each insurer's risk profile. The structure has been adapted for use by family offices, or family groups, where, again, each member has his or her own cell, chooses their own individual investment manager and strategy, but benefit from the governance and administrative services of a single umbrella entity. The tax position is exactly the same as in an investment or unit trust. Distributions are taxed as income, but capital gains tax only arises on sale or liquidation of the cell itself. As the board needed to be nonresident in majority, and I was now resident in France, I was asked to be chairman. The controlling family opened the company to approved preference shareholders from other groups in similar circumstances, and so has grown as the leading, quoted protected cell company in Guernsey. We meet in Paris and in Guernsey. All in all, a happy swan song to the non-executive phase of my life's work.

These extra-corricular activities deadened the pain I felt witnessing the degradation of the City. Most observers still regard Big Bang as a defining moment in the positive sense. I do not. For me it was a turning point in the wrong direction. Of course, the problem is trans-atlantic and now global. Writing in 1863, Jules Michelet, the great French historian, said "*Dans la finance, comme partout, il faut une âme, et, pardessus, un principe pour la guider*" (In finance, as in everything, there must be a soul, and, above, a principle to guide it). Well finance has lost its soul, and its guiding principle used to be service to the client/customer. Now it just serves itself.

CHAPTER XXI

"Why didn't anyone see it coming?"

-Attributed to Her Majesty the Queen-

If I had been at the London School of Economics, when Her Majesty is re-puted to have posed the question above, referring to the Great Financial Crisis of 2008, I would have answered "A great many did, Your Majesty, but they were too busy making money in the short-term, to worry about the longer term". Perhaps, given the venue which inspired her query, HM was address-ing her question to economists, rather that the practitioners. But they were too busy devising complex algebraic formulae to give much attention to the com-ing storm. Economists have always regarded financial services the way mech-anics regard motor oil – as long as you change it from time to time, there is no problem, and you can't make the engine work without it. It would not have occurred to them that drivers would be stupid enough to flood the engine with motor oil. As for those directly involved, their attitude was well summed up by the head of one of the major money centre banks who said, "As long as the music keeps playing, we have to keep dancing."

I wrote an article for *The Financial World* in which I likened the blame game being played out, as the crisis deepened, to Hercule Poirot's investiga-tion in Agatha Christie's masterpiece *Murder on the Orient Express*. An American tycoon has been found murdered in his compartment on the Orient Express by multiple stab wounds. Each of the passengers in the carriage is a suspect, and it turns out each had a motive. Poirot solves the case by proving that every suspect had a hand in the crime, taking turns to stab the victim, out of revenge for the wrong he had done each. And so, I argued, the crisis had a series of perpetrators, and there was no point in trying to assign the blame to anyone. A politician picked up my simile in a House of Commons debate on the crisis, and I was annoyed not to be credited. Perhaps it was all too obvi-ous. A better way of illustrating this historic financial crisis would be to ima-gine a series of relatively minor streams, growing slowly in volume of water, as one or two small dams burst along the way, and which all flow into one single river, which soon becomes a torrent – sweeping away towns and villages, as it heads for the sea. Perhaps the most important stream was the heady expansion throughout the early '80s of Fannie Mae and Freddy Mac, two so-called Government Sponsored Enterprises, "GSEs", which, began to exploit their privileged funding access to the market by gorging on residential mortgages in the secondary market, thus allowing the primary lenders, small regional banks, to lower their credit criteria and increase their volumes, secure in the knowledge they could pass the mortgages on to the GSEs. Congressional oversight of these agencies lapsed, in the light of booming house prices, and the affordable housing political imperative. Wall Street was not going to allow the GSEs a monopoly of fishing this fast-growing stream, and so began to enter the secondary mortgage market with a new generation of securitised instruments, such as collateralised mortgage obligations, CMOs, spawning an even more lethal concoction, collateralised debt obligations, CDOs, which represented pools of a variety of consumer loans. CDOs, in particular gave rise to extreme financial engineering, involving tranches and tiers of varying loan quality, interest paying characteristics, and maturities. Individual tiers were often internally leveraged and linked to credit protection derivative products. As the housing boom began to subside, the so-called subprime element in these securitised pools began to grow exponentially. A most popular risk hedging instrument was the credit default swap, CDSs, essentially a bet between two parties, one believing a high level of default will occur, and the other believing it won't – rather akin to betting on whether it will rain in Ireland in the next week. Soon there was a two-way traffic between the GSEs and Wall Street – bankers as well as product. Never had the relationship between the Street and Washington been so symbiotic.

Wall Street had taken to heart the great circus man P. T. Barnum's adage – "there's a sucker born every minute", and began to distribute this new alphabet soup, like confetti at a mafia wedding. In this new profitable trade, it had an invaluable co-conspirator. The rating agencies Standard & Poor's and Moody's, traditionally pristine in their integrity and independence, finally became corrupted by the inherent conflict in their remuneration arrangements. They had always been paid by the issuer in rating a security – not by the investment banker underwriting and distributing it. But the CMOs and CDOs, and their endless permutations, were issued by "special purpose vehicles" – in essence, shell companies created by the distributing investment bankers. It was as if the Roux Brothers had bought the British edition of the Michelin guide and were awarding stars to themselves. Tiered CDOs were structured to put the investment grade underlying obligations on top with the quality declining as one worked ones way through the complex tranches. These were like layer cakes with the icing on top and subprime dough and marzipan on the bottom. The rating agencies were prepared to give investment grade ratings on the basis of the icing. And so, what eventually became termed "toxic assets", were sold worldwide to yield hungry buyers, and the distributors carried larger and larger inventories themselves. Needless to say, each piece of structuring carried fees. It was rather like VAT applied throughout the manufacturing, assembly and distribution phases. No one seems to have thought of inventing the acronym VAF – value added fees.

In the war on drugs, the dealers are usually lumped together with the addicts, and so I consider that both the sellers of toxic assets and the buyers were white water rafting down the same stream. Both sectors were acting out this high risk adventure due to profound changes in their business models, and the nature of their managers and employees.

Technology and accompanying globalisation has changed the economics of both investment banking and commercial banking. The bread and butter revenue from commissions on executing stock exchange transactions for one group, and commercial lending of customer's deposits for the other, no longer covered rising costs. For the investment industry, fixed commissions ended first in New York and then in London and this also ended the essentially agency nature of the business. In a famous communication, Morgan Stanley wrote to all its institutional clients, thanking them warmly for their past business, but informing them that they would no longer be regarded as clients, but as counterparties. Just as they were increasingly dealing with Morgan Stanley only when it suited them, Morgan Stanley would deal with them only when it suited Morgan Stanley. The loss of profitability from pure agency functions, forced a move to proprietary functions. This in turn increased capital requirements and partnerships began to incorporate and seek outside capital, particularly since younger partners were no longer happy to leave part of their annual gain in the firm. The move to incorporation fundamentally changed the culture and the ethos of the Wall Street community, and would eventually do the same in the City of London, as all things American, such as Starbucks and MacDonald's, eventually cross the Atlantic. The simplest way to summarise what has happened in the world of high finance is to point out that in both Wall Street and the City, the major firms were once owned and operated by people who were already rich, mostly from inherited wealth. Their life style was not dependent on any individual year's profit. They easily survived the volatility inherent in the business of finance. Their overriding concern was reputation – their own, their firms, and their community's. In New York, the religious divide between Jewish and Episcopalian, "white shoe" firms, supported this ethos – as a rogue let down not just his firm, but his "side". In the City, the segmentation of functions – the Stock Exchange, the Accepting Houses, the Discount Market, etc., did the same. In addition, people were bound by their common educations and backgrounds. To make an elitist but obvious point, when it was all in the hands of public schoolboys in London, and their equivalents in New York, the intellectual average may well have been lower, but the ethics were certainly higher. Ask the average client or customer – would he prefer a clever banker, or an honest one?

In commercial banking, the traditional business model was also under threat, particularly for the money centre banks. Both working capital and medium-term lending was being disintermediated by the commercial paper market and the emergence of a subprime bond market. Margins were squeezed throughout the range of traditional businesses. Commercial banks looked enviously at the higher returns apparently achieved by investment banks, and used their increasing lobbying power in Washington to urge a suspension of Glass Steagal, which had separated the functions after the excesses of the 1920s. They succeeded under President Clinton. Meanwhile, investment bankers were trying to be commercial banks – illustrated by my Merrill Lynch colleague's suggestion that I offer an "unlimited" commercial paper facility to a corporate client, as an inducement to a merger & acquisition mandate. In fact, the two disciplines are profoundly different and, with obvious exceptions, investment bankers make bad commercial bankers and vice versa. Consolidation was touted as the answer to the new competitive pressures facing the commercial banks, and merger mania, fuelled by deal hungry investment bankers, took hold. U.S. anti-trust regulators looked at narrow market share definitions and decided the shrinking, but still quite healthy, regional bank sector would contain monopolistic tendencies in the new mega-bank world. And in Europe, they considered global competition would offset the dangers of national consolidation. They did not feel called upon to judge whether these new bloated entities could be prudently managed. In fact, much touted economies of scale seemed to evaporate post-merger. What came to be known as "too big to fail" banks, were, in fact "too big to manage" banks. The wise men of Basle recognised the new proliferation of risks inherent in globalisation, but focussed on increased capital requirements as the prophylactic. Some product regulation was inherent in the concept of tiered capital but by and large little attention was paid to asset quality. I would argue that increased capital requirements were self-defeating, as banks found it increasingly difficult to earn a competitive return on the larger capital through traditional, lower risk activity, and were driven to higher risk business, such as proprietary trading, and increased portfolios of CDOs and other high yielding derivatives. No one has bothered to calculate the amount of shareholder value destroyed by post acquisition fair value adjustments and further write-offs of good will due to the prices paid by merger happy bank boards, but it would go a long way to reducing U.S. and U.K. national debts.

As the old guard retired, a new generation with totally different ideas and motivations took its place, and changed the ethos of the financial world almost beyond recognition. This new ethos spread like a virus from bottom to top. Short-term gain in the maximum amount possible was its creed. My interviewee at Merrill Lynch personified this new breed. Interested only in how much and how quickly they will be compensated, their loyalty to the firm of the moment is nil, as they move immediately on a better offer. Their interest in the reputation of the City of London is also nil, as they plan to retire as soon as they had made their pile. In fact reputation, personal, firm or community, is no longer in the vocabulary. Rogue traders, like Nick Leeson, who bankrupted Barings, are celebrities on the well remunerated speaker's circuit. And since references must be entirely anodyne, those sacked for misdemeanours are employed immediately elsewhere. When a Merrill Lynch trader in New York lost almost the whole of the firm's earnings for the quarter, trading stripped mortgage bonds, it was front page news. He was fired and almost immediately hired by Drexel Burnham. The instrument he was trading is a good example of the new generation of financial products which has led to the great crisis. Pooled residential mortgages, with the interest stripped out and packaged in a separate pool, are rather like zero coupon bonds with no fixed maturity. Their value fluctuates with the level of early redemptions of the mortgages, in turn influenced by economic circumstances affecting the mortgagees, in particular the level of interest rates prevailing, allowing attractive refinancing. You may well question what possible contribution such activity makes to the wellbeing of the economy as a whole. If you think it creates liquidity that increases the availability of mortgage finance to those starting on the housing ladder, you would be hard pressed to find evidence to support your claim. The dealer in question was hedging his position with interest rate futures. He had busted his limits on both position and hedge and was trying to recover losses, "hiding tickets in the drawer" – the classic rogue trader ruse. This new class of financial practitioner is encouraged in its new ethos by the introduction of a terrible poison in the compensation system – the unit bonus pool. The logic behind this remuneration approach is that a participant in a profitable unit – say, merger & acquisitions – should not lose his variable compensation, i.e., bonus, just because some idiot in another department – say, the stripped mortgage dealing desk – has lost a bundle. Therefore, instead of basing variable compensation on the results of the firm as a whole, individual bonus pools are created for each unit, discipline, department, region, etc., etc. Of course the result is a total disconnect between the interests of shareholders, and those of their employees. Once entrenched, the poison cannot be eradicated, as a firm which does will lose star players to a firm still infected. And were national regulators to try and contain it, firms would move to another centre. A major side effect of this poison is the destruction of firm wide loyalties and the cross referencing of business, or even collaboration between units in executing a transaction. Every man or woman becomes an island in a bonus pool. Soon after Michael von Clemm joined me at Merrill Lynch, he was invited to give a pep talk at a major internal conference of all the key people on the investment banking side of the firm. His theme was "super-conductivity", a scientific concept which was all the rage at the time, based on the development of materials which allow energy to be transmitted with minimum loss from friction. "Super-conductivity!" bellowed Michael, in his best professorial style. He meant that co-operation between regions and functions were critical to realising Merrill's potential. He could have been talking to himself. Every year the global executive committee, with hangers on, would spend a week in New York haggling over bonus awards, creating complicated fee splitting and transfer arrangements, like a pack of wild dogs around a kill.

A determining feature of the new ethos is the absence of what was once the most powerful of regulators – shame. In the City I first knew, if you put a foot wrong, you were not invited to lunch. You were expected to hang your head in shame for a decent period, and if the transgression was serious, you slipped out of view. And the American concept of "the buck stops here" was in force. Of course, this was before the emergence of the "to big to manage" mega-bank. Now, it is an accepted excuse that the man at the top "couldn't possibly have known". When a London based trader, known affectionately in the market as "the London Whale", lost $2 billion trading credit default swaps, Jamie Dimon, executive chairman, murmured some apologies, but there was no question of his resigning, and he remains a paragon of the New York banking establishment, nor was his compensation meaningfully affected. The fraying of an ethical culture in the financial services industry did not go unnoticed. Even the Church of England commented on it, although their massive property losses in the American shopping mall boom had been the result of incompetence by the Church Commissioners – not loss of moral fibre. The Archbishop of Canterbury appointed a South African director of Lazard's to look into the problem of ethics, or lack thereof, in the City. He was never heard of again. With rather unfortunate timing, a Guild of International Bankers was founded at the beginning of the decade which culminated in the great crisis of 2008. This was the newest aspirant to seek membership of the great tradition of City Guilds, and has now gained a Royal Charter to become the Worshipful Company of International Bankers, a suitable title for a community given to self-worship. After some ex-Lord Mayors, and Willy Purvis of "Honkers and Shankers", as HSBC was known, as Masters – Eddie George became Master on his retirement as Governor of the Bank. Some of us were hanging around the bar at an early Guild dinner, and I told the story of Julius Weinberg at Samuel Montagu, ticking off a young Cockney dealer for "picking up" a counterparty who had quoted him the wrong big figure. We all agreed that nowadays, the dealer in question would have laughed all the way to his bonus pool, and no one would have dreamt of criticising his sharpness. Someone suggested the Guild produce a Code of Conduct to try and reinstate the sort of ethical code the City was once world famous for. Off we trooped to Eddie George's new office at Rothschild, suggested the idea – and he loved it. In fact, he decided to make it the main theme of his Mastership. At the next big annual bash of the Guild at the Guild Hall, the Master actually sang two bars of an American standard "Santa Claus Is Coming to Town". His phrasing might not have been up to Tony Bennet's, but his tone was as sincere – and the key line in the lyric was "be good, for goodness sake". This exhortation to children to qualify for Santa's bounty by good behaviour left many of us with a lump in our throats. A committee was duly set up, including myself, to draft a set of principles, which would eventually be known as Lord George's Rules, as Eddie was awarded a peerage before his sad, early death. The ink was no sooner dry on our code, than the lawyers informed us that, of course, they were unenforceable. Lawyers always say "of course", before delivering a devastating opinion. Our only means of enforcement was dismissal from the Guild. But if the breach was not also a breach of statutory rules of the FSA, our dismissal of a member would be subject to judicial review, and almost certainly reversed as prejudicial to the individual's career. A Guild is not a statutory body, and although it is entitled to ask members to acknowledge and sign rules, it cannot dismiss a member for noncompliance, if such would be prejudicial to his employment. This was a very important opinion, because it confirmed once and for all that the City could no longer be governed by the "spirit" of a code of conduct, but only by statutory rules of such volume and complexity that they provided a huge opportunity for "loophole" hunting. But the death of shame, even at the top, was also soon to be confirmed. Citicorp government bond dealers executed a vast manipulation in the market, netting huge profits but violating even the loosest interpretation of "trust, honesty and integrity" which represented the core of the Guild's new code.... In fact it was a massive "pickup", and several European governments complained at this abuse of the market in their bonds. The chairman of Citibank's corporate finance division in London at the time was Mr. Michael Kirkwood, and he quite happily assumed the position of Master of the Guild, succeeding Eddie George. I resigned in protest.

"Ou sont les neiges d'antant?" One might well ask "where are the regulators of yesteryear?" George Brown made a terrible mistake in stripping the Bank of England of its supervisory role in banking. In doing so, he illustrated the lamentable ignorance which exists in the political class on most matters financial. Ronnie Cohen was an advisor to George Brown, and I imagine he tried hard to educate him in matters relating to entrepreneurship. I attended a conference on that very subject, chaired by George Brown, but I fear Ronnie's lessons had yet to make a mark, because the Chancellor, as he then was, looked totally blank throughout. But he clearly failed to appreciate the tragic degradation of supervisory skills he was perpetrating. The Bank supervised the banking market with great skill because it was in the market itself – with both feet. It had its ear to the ground. It knew everything that was happening, good and bad, before anyone else. It was not just the question of "the Governor's eyebrows", it was its networking skills, its information harvesting, and its "feel" of markets. It was also incorruptible because of its sheer grandeur, its marbled halls, liveried messengers, traditions, style, "above it all" atmosphere. Inevitably, its skilled and experienced supervisory staff decamped, took early retirement, joined boards, etc. The FSA in Canary Wharf, in its concrete box, with transparent, glass-fronted interview rooms, had to content itself with those incapable of securing positions as practitioners. The result was the box ticking youth that came to ABC International Bank to con-

duct a "high level control" visit. It was also the failure to realise that, whilst the Northern Rock Building Society might be engaged in the low risk business of residential mortgage lending, its liability profile was extremely risky as it relied almost entirely on the interbank market, rather than customer deposits, to fund its 100%+ loan to NAV mortgages.

In Washington, hardly an SEC official had not been, or was not to be, general counsel in a Wall Street investment banking house or partner in a law firm. The traffic between the Street and the Beltway certainly helped Amtrack and the LaGuardia-National airport shuttle, but it did not ensure healthy independence in the regulatory community. It must be remembered that Glass Steagal was not a law, but a clause in the Banking Act of 1934. It could therefore be rescinded by executive action and President Clinton did just that. What followed was overlap and confusion between agencies regulating securities, derivatives, which were with the commodities regulator, the Federal Reserve Bank in New York, the Federal Housing Finance Agency, which regulated the GSEs, the State Insurance regulator which was responsible for AIG, and other various odds and sods. Add to this a steady rise in the lobbying power of Wall Street, due to an exponential increase in its campaign contributions, and it is not impossible to conclude that the regulatory community suffered a decline in both competence and ethics, perhaps subconsciously, to match that of Wall Street – so that the Street wouldn't be made to feel inadequate. What to make of the fact that a responsible Boston based analyst blew the whistle on Madoff, with documented proof that he was operating a Ponzi scheme, and the SEC studiously ignored him? But the underlying seismic flaw in the whole regulatory and supervisory system was the fatal blurring of the distinction between agency and proprietary functions – which had always been the bedrock of financial regulation. And how to stop the banks from rushing lemming like over the toxic asset cliff? Nothing stops the lemmings because the dead one's pile up at the bottom, not at cliff edge. Failed banks might have acted like dead lemmings, but banks were now "to big to fail" and contagion panic set in. The taxpayer still does not know the full cost of the bail outs, and is too ignorant to insist the mega banks be broken up. The banking lobby insistence that mega banking is an efficient answer to globalisation, suggests that finance directors of large corporations are incapable of multi-sourcing commercial and investment banking services. The fact that these corporations multi-source insurance, executive search and recruitment services, software and communications consultants, security services, catering, building works, industrial cleaners, transport and travel, etc., etc., suggests that, what finance directors are incapable of, is resisting the blandishments of bankers.

But now, I hear you ask, what about the shareholders? Why did they tolerate an outrageous destruction of value through ill-judged and overpriced mergers and acquisitions in the banking sector? Why have they tolerated en-

430

tirely unjustified levels of compensation granted to managers by docile directors? Why have they accepted that management be paid bonuses when they, the shareholders, suffer losses? Why have they retained incompetent executive management even after it has made huge mistakes and refused to resign? Why have they swallowed hook line and sinker the tall tales they are told at AGMs, and in annual reports, where the horrors are in the fifty pages of notes at the back? A tiny few so called activist fund managers do ask these questions loudly and frequently, but they are drowned in the silence and lethargy that now characterises the shareholder community. I believe there is a breakdown in ownership duty, and this is because the nature of that community has changed profoundly. Not only is it institutionalised though collective investment schemes, pension funds, insurance companies, large charities, foundations, and so forth, but a growing portion of its funds under management is either formally passive, i.e. indexed, or informally passive – managed by sector allocations. A significant amount of total equity in the large cap, global corporate sector is managed by people who do not need to, or wish to, exercise the rights of ownership, except through sale, but not even then – as sector allocation is distorted.

Reviewing the multiple causes of the as yet unresolved great financial crisis, the decline in the exercise of ownership rights is the most dangerous, as it carries within it the seeds of the destruction of capitalism, a system which has produced the greatest prosperity for the greatest number. Like most things in nature, capitalism in its pure form depends on a balance of power between those who own the means of production, those who manage it, and those who purchase its output. Each is in a position to sanction the other if a power is abused. The owner can sack the manager, and the manager can leave the owner. The customer can refuse to buy the product, and the producer can withhold it from the customer. If any one of the three abdicates its power, the system ultimately collapses into monopoly, whether state owned or private, corrupt management and product quality decline. We are now witnessing an abdication of power by the owners. The passive sector is the leader of this abdication, and one wonders how it has the nerve to charge a management fee, as a chimp could be trained to sell an overweight position and buy an underweight one. But even the large, active managers regularly buy new entrants to the main index, regardless of a governance deficit, simple because "it's there". And, lemming like, they rush into the fashionable, fearful of being caught in a miniskirt when calf length is back. Pension fund consultants recommend trustees to sack the manager who is under performing, usually just as he is about to over perform, and to retain the over performing manager, just as he is about to lose his way – because the consultants depend on turnover. Short-termism is the inevitable consequence of complex performance fee structures and herd instinct is a major market driver. And who bothers with proxy forms for AGMs? Many of the negative evolutions in corporate structure, ill-conceived business models, management deficiencies, poor and conflicted regulation can be ascribed to a failure by shareholders to behave responsibly, and exercise the rights of ownership.

"Your Majesty, I must apologise for this long-winded answer to the question you so rightly posed. I also realise I have failed to document my assertion that a great many people did know, but were too busy exploiting the short-term, moneymaking opportunities to worry about the long-term consequences. All I have done is offer a highly personal view of how and why it all went wrong. If Your Majesty were to ask a follow up question, such as 'will everyone learn from this experience?' I would answer with a resounding 'No Ma'am!'."

EPILOGOUE

"So we beat on, boats against the current,
borne back ceaselessly
into the past"

-F. Scott Fitzgerald – *The Great Gatsby*-

An epilogue suggests a conclusion, a *dénouement* of some sort. I have none. My two lives, social and financial, have not provided any. In any case, I am still living. My father is dead, but he would have resented any attempt to fix a conclusion to his existence. Since I have spent my whole life wallowing in nostalgia, I don't know how to look forward to a conclusion. It would be useless and boring to list the things I regret not having done. They are too numerous. I have never been back to Texas to see the waving wheat, and I don't know why that song fragment still haunts me. "And they lived happily ever after" is what we read as children – but who lives happily ever after? Old age is not for sissies, they say. My father's was not a success. Wheelchair bound in his last years, he was not particularly happy either in Florida, where he wintered, or on Long Island, where he summered. He missed Europe and *les vielles pierres*. Whilst still active, he was never happier than when motoring on the small roads in France, or as a *flaneur* on the Left Bank in Paris. In London, he relished the elegance of the City and the West End, and fortunately was no longer there to see its disappearance. He was always dressed to the nines, stiff collar, bowler hat and tightly furled umbrella, and his military bearing often caused him to be mistaken for a senior Guards officer, providing him the pleasure of doffing his bowler to a saluting sentry outside St. James's Palace. Once no longer able to travel to France, Switzerland and England, he felt he had nothing to look forward to, and he didn't suffer from my obsession with the past, and so was not able to amuse himself recalling it. He missed the office and surrounded himself with its paraphernalia, filing cabinets, paperclip removers, every size of envelope, and a permanent selection of postage stamps. He kept his little black books with redundant addresses in the capitals of Europe. He valued most his few remaining White Russian friends or those from his earliest time in America, but was not able to make new friends, as I have done. He became hugely pessimistic about the economic

433

and political outlook for the Western powers, including the United States. He was convinced excessive indebtedness could only be cured by default or hyperinflation. He had little exposure to Asian markets and didn't really think about globalisation. He took a Russian view that China was not actually a single nation, never had been, and so was not a threat. His favourite reading became the Russian classics, and I began to realise that his view of the world was regressing to that which one finds expressed in Russian literature. I never ceased to enjoy my conversations with him, even when his mind began to wander, as it always wandered in unexpected directions. He would never have considered his life interesting enough to justify a memoir of any kind, which is why I have felt prompted to write one for him. Although not a church goer, he had requested an Orthodox funeral, and so, to make arrangements, I visited the small wooden Russian Orthodox chapel his friend Serge Belosselski – Beloserski had built in Glen Cove, Long Island. As I approached a Russian Orthodox priest emerged from a small house, bearded, and wearing the traditional conical hat and vestment. "G'day!" he said. He was Australian, the grandson of White Russian emigres. He, his wife and three children sang the lengthy Orthodox funeral service in Church Slavonic, with the congregation standing around a coffin with three candles on it. Bob Genillard and François Champion had travelled from Europe to attend, and there were many Long Island friends. I cannot help suspecting he died unhappy, as my mother refused to contemplate the internment of his ashes at a family vault near the wooden chapel on the Chodow estate in Poland, where my grandfather is buried, thanks to great efforts made by DY to arrange this through a Vatican intervention, when Poland was still behind the Iron Curtain. But she wanted him near her, and so they both rest in a rather twee "garden of remembrance" near the Christ Chapel, on Jupiter Island, Hobe Sound, Florida – about as inappropriate a location as one could imagine.

I am always intrigued by a phrase that occurs frequently in obituaries – my favourite reading. "In retirement, he lived quietly in..." Does that mean the subject led a noisy life previously? I suppose it means he, or she, became socially less active. We live now in a very quiet place – the Luberon Valley of the Vaucluse region of Provence in the South of France. If I must criticise, I would say it is a bit too social as a large, and very cosmopolitan, community maintain holiday or retirement residences here. But we have found many old friends: Old Herschellians from the Cape who summer here, friends of my early days, such as Inez Franck, now divorced and with City grandee Nick Villiers, Michael Butt, Mike Chapman, ex Wood Gundy, Mike Pochna, the Dobbs-Higginsons, Joan de Mouchy, *née* Dillon, and sundry other past connections. Of course we have made a host of new friends, too numerous to mention even in a shameless, name-dropping tome as this.

Amongst the various veterans here of business, financial, diplomatic or just "coupon clipping" previous existences, are several from the performing arts.

This has prompted me to turn my theatrical bent, lived vicariously through my daughter's professional career in the "business", into actual experience. I began with a production of two one act plays by Chekhov, *The Bear* and *The Proposal,* the first being in Tatyana's repertoire. She has actually done a command performance of the piece for former Mayor Gullianno, having met his second wife at the Actor's Studio. I found collaboration from neighbours Mike Messenger, Ridley Scott's former cameraman, and a maker of commercials for Pearl & Deane, and his wife Caroline, with a distinguished past career in costuming for opera, ballet and theatre. I brought a former Bibury neighbour, Jackie Smith-Wood down to direct. She had starred in West End productions of *Pygmallion* and *Macbeth* with Peter O' Toole, as well as in film and TV, before marrying a Gloucestershire farmer and retiring from the stage to bring up her children. But they are grown up, and she now directs and coaches. I found local scene builders, lighting technicians and a stage manager. I played Luca, the serf servant in *The Bear,* and the father of the bride in *The Proposal.* My next venture was more ambitious – a production of Noel Coward's *Blithe Spirit*, again directed by Jackie Smith-Wood. I asked Jackie to audition and cast in England, and she found Annabel Leventen, a very experienced actress to play Madame Arcati, Sarah Finch, well-known for her one woman Jane Austen show, to play Elvira, and Paul Ansdell to play Charles Condamine. When the latter was told I was the producer, he said, "But he is a friend of my father-in-law!" Indeed, I was, as Paul is married to the daughter of Joanna Trollope, first wife of my old White, Weld colleague David Potter. Tatyana played Ruth, and I took the small part of Dr. Bradman. For Mrs. Bradman, we cast Frances Goodwin, a singer, who, with her ex-solicitor, now pianist, husband Duncan have a successful musical act in the region. One of our neighbours, Clive Robey is the ex-senior British Airways Concorde captain, and we wonder together how many times I flew with him, when, at Merrill, I "concorded" monthly to New York executive committee meetings. Clive and his wife Janet have a stage struck daughter Catherine, who we cast as Edith, the maid, and she also served as assistant director to Jackie. I believe we put her on the road to a real career in the theatre, as soon after Cat was accepted at the Guildhall drama school and began as a director, having had several out -of-town production successes. The Messenger's close friend Mike Fox, a distinguished BBC cameraman came down, and with Mike Messenger, shot and edited a "making of" documentary film called *A Spirit in Provence*, which has still to find a TV buyer. Whilst we were in rehearsal, another neighbour and City friend, Christopher Morgan, who had been public relations officer for the LIFFE market, told me there was someone who was interested in what we were doing. Lunch was arranged with a charming man called Christopher Neame, whose name meant nothing to me at first.

"How much do you know about *Blithe Spirit?*" I said to get the conversation rolling.

"Well..." he replied, putting in a nice theatrical pause, "my godfather wrote it and my father produced the film version." It turned out his father was Ronald Neame who was Noel Coward's principle film collaborator, on such iconic films as *In Which We Serve, Brief Encounter* and, of course, *Blithe Spirit* with Rex Harrison as Charles Condamine and Margaret Rutherford as Madame Arcati. It seems Ronald Neame had asked for a day off shooting *In Which We Serve* for the birth of his son, and Coward had let him go on condition he be godfather. Christopher had a long career himself in film and TV, responsible for such productions as *Flame Trees of Thika, Memoirs of an Irish RM* and the film of Graham Greene's *Monsignor Quixote* with Alec Guinness. Christopher had retired to write in Bedoin, near the Mt Ventoux, our highest peak. He had also started a theatre company with Veronica Grange, a former singer and now director of opera and theatre. Veronica turned out to be a close cousin of my fellow Porcellians John and Jonathan Winthrop, direct descendants of the first Governor of Massachusetts.

Christopher Neame and I decided to merge our theatrical companies, now known as "What Larks", and I met another neighbour, our artistic director and frequent star Catriona MacColl, who had been married to actor Jon Finch, famous for his Macbeth in Polanski's film version, for Hitchcock's *Frensy*, and also for having turned down the role of James Bond, when it was first offered by Ian Fleming. Catriona's film and TV career is impressive. Jacques Demy's historical film *Lady Oscar* was her first notable success. She then starred in the Italian director Lucio Fulci's trilogy of films *The Gates of Hell.* Fulci was inspired by James Carreras's Hammer Productions, and specialised in the horror film *genre.* When I first met Catriona, I glanced at her neck to see if there were two puncture marks left over from her vampire movie era. She has many other film, stage and TV credits, and is entirely bilingual. Another collaborator is Tracy Seacombe, also bilingual, who turned out to be a former Gloucestershire neighbour. For an amateur, in any sport or occupation, it is a unique thrill to play with professionals. In a way, I experienced this thrill in my business life, because I never saw myself as a real banker, but I worked surrounded by so many. Most golfers know that playing with the club pro raises one's game. Playing polo with professionals was a thrill. I have now found that acting with professionals produces the same emotion. But I also discovered something when I first appeared on stage with my daughter Tatyana. I experience no nerves at all on stage. On the contrary, I am more comfortable than in many other places. The professionals are nervous. Tatyana was shaking a bit in the wings before we went on, in quick succession, in the Chekhov, and Catriona is nervous in the dressing room. The reason is simple. For the professional, every performance, whether in the West End, Broadway, or an out of the way, small provincial town, represents the same test of their craft. Their fear of a mistake is the same, regardless of the relative importance of the performance. I couldn't care less if I dry up, fluff or forget a line, or a piece of business. My career is not at stake – hence, I am not nervous. I have been thrilled to appear on stage with Catriona, and other professionals, in Patrick Hamilton's *Gaslight,* and Ira Levin's incredibly dark piece *Veronica's Room,* directed by another neighbour and friend, the supremely professional David Ambrose, a screen writer, playwright, and general author who has worked in Hollywood and the West End. What Larks is even presenting a light, frothy comedy of mine – *Who's Afraid of Peter Mayle.* Just as Edward Albee's piece has nothing to do with Virginia Wolfe, mine has nothing to do with Peter Mayle.

And so my declining years have not been altogether quiet, in the way obituary writers may mean. I also think suffering from nostalgia, a most pernicious condition, has its compensations. Like an archaeologist, one scrapes away with one's trowel, looking for signs of civilised moments in one's past. Following the current meltdown in the world's geopolitical and financial fabric, merely reminds one how lucky one was to have lived out its last moments of sanity. As I read of continuing City scandals: LIBOR rigging, foreign exchange market skulduggery, mis-selling of dicey products, stock exchange listings of dubious mining companies from the Caucasus, rogue dealers abounding, corporate directors dissembling, auditors being sued for certifying cooked accounts, regulatory fines growing faster than the national debt, and bankers dropping below estate agents in the occupational popularity stakes, I cannot help but wonder at how lucky I was to have seen so much in the City, when it still basked in its twilight of greatness. Living in France, a country in terminal decline from the lingering and apparently incurable disease of socialism, I am sometimes asked, why? My answer is that life in countries in decline is far more pleasant than life in countries in ascendency – particularly when one reaches a certain age. Who would want to live in Beijing when one can live in Paris? Life throughout the Roman Empire was far more pleasant in 300 AD than it was in 300 BC. As the sun sets on Western civilisation, I am sorry for the grandchildren and their grandchildren, but my *pastisse* before lunch, and my rosé with, will see me out. As to a conclusion, anyone who has struggled with Proust's *A La Recherché du Temps Perdu,* knows that it's the interminable expedition which is the point – not the end.

-FINIS-

DY, 1st Imperial Cadet Corps, Petrograd, 1915

DY, New York, 1920

DY & Jack Barrett, Greenwich, Conn. 1970

DY & Denise, New York, 1970

The General, Central Park, New York 1924

SY & DY Senlis, France, 1980

Ariane as a Debutante, 1951

Dinnie & Ariane, France, 1990

Dinnie with cat Bibury, Gloucester, 1994
Courtesy Jackie Nickerson

Ariane & SY with Denise, Westbury L.I. 1941

SY, 2nd Marine Division, Camp Lejeune, North Carolina, 1957

Stanislas Yassukovich
Courtesy Jackie Nickerson

SY, European Banking Company, 1969

Tatyana, Michael & Nicholas, Lowdale Farm, Southern Rhodesia, 1975

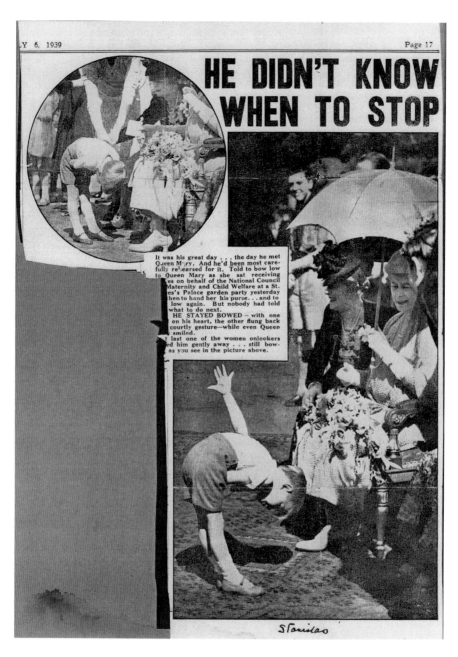

HE DIDN'T KNOW WHEN TO STOP

It was his great day . . . the day he met Queen Mary. And he'd been most carefully rehearsed for it. Told to bow low to Queen Mary as she sat receiving ...es on behalf of the National Council ... Maternity and Child Welfare at a St. ...es's Palace garden party yesterday ... hen to hand her his purse . . . and to ... low again. But nobody had told ... what to do next.

HE STAYED BOWED — with one ... on his heart, the other flung back ... courtly gesture—while even Queen ... smiled.

... last one of the women onlookers ...ed him gently away . . . still bow- ... as you see in the picture above.

SY, London, 1939
Courtesy The Daily Mirror

Index